Welcome to
McGraw-Hill Education
SAT

Congratulations! You've chosen the SAT guide from America's leading educational publisher. You probably know us from many of the textbooks you used in school. Now we're ready to help you take the next step—and get into the college or university of your choice.

This book gives you everything you need to succeed on the test. You'll get in-depth instruction and review of every topic tested, tips and strategies for every question type, and practice exams to boost your test-taking confidence. To get started, go to the following pages where you'll find:

▸ How to Use This Book: Step-by-step instructions to help you get the most out of your test-prep program.

▸ Your SAT Action Plan: Learn how to make the best use of your preparation time.

▸ SAT Format Table: This handy chart shows the test structure at a glance: question types, time limits, and number of questions per section.

▸ The 40 Top Strategies for Test Day: Use this list to check your knowledge, or as a last-minute refresher before the exam.

▸ The 5 Top SAT Calculator Tips: Learn some smart ways that your calculator can help you.

▸ Getting the Most from the Free Online Practice Tests: Log on to the companion website for more test-taking practice.

ABOUT McGRAW-HILL EDUCATION

This book has been created by McGraw-Hill Education. McGraw-Hill Education is a leading global provider of instructional, assessment, and reference materials in both print and digital form. McGraw-Hill Education has offices in 33 countries and publishes in more than 65 languages. With a broad range of products and services—from traditional textbooks to the latest in online and multimedia learning—we engage, stimulate, and empower students and professionals of all ages, helping them meet the increasing challenges of the 21st century knowledge economy.

Learn more. **Do more.**

How to Use This Book

This book is designed for students who want an effective program for the most dramatic SAT score improvements. It is based on the College Hill Method™, the elite training system used by the tutors of College Hill Coaching since 1990. It focuses on what works best in SAT prep: mindful training in the reasoning skills at the core of the SAT, and not just test-taking tricks or mindless drills.

This book provides all the material you need to score well on the SAT. It will teach you the knowledge that is required for this exam, including information about each type of question on the test. It also provides ample practice for you to refine the skills you are learning and then test yourself with full-length practice tests. For best results as you work your way through the book and the accompanying online tests, use this four-step program that follows:

1 Learn About the SAT

Don't skip Chapter 1. In it you'll meet the SAT and learn exactly what academic skills it tests. You'll also find valuable test-taking strategies and information about how the test is scored.

2 Take a Realistic Practice SAT

Take the SAT diagnostic test in Chapter 2 of this book. Take the test strictly timed, in one sitting, and proctored if possible. Then use the answer key to evaluate your results so you can learn your strengths and weaknesses.

3 Study What You Need to Learn with the Lessons and Exercises

If you miss a question on your practice SAT, read its answer explanation at the end of the test. If it refers to a lesson in Chapters 4–10, make that lesson part of your weekly review.

▶ First read each **Lesson** carefully, underlining important ideas or writing notes in the margins.

▶ Check your understanding of the concepts and skills in these lessons by working through the questions and answers in each Exercise Set.

▶ When you're done, read all of the explanations in the **Answer Key**, even for questions that you got right. Why? Because very often, there are many ways to get a question right, and some may be much more efficient than the one you used!

4 Repeat the Cycle Until You've Surpassed Your SAT Score Goal

Take the practice tests in this book and on the companion website, trying each time to simulate actual testing conditions. Then correct your test with the detailed answer key, and review the relevant lessons in Chapters 4–10 that will help you to improve your skills for the next test.

Your SAT Action Plan

To make the best use of your SAT preparation time, you'll need a personalized action plan that's based on your needs and the time you have available. This book has been designed for flexibility; you can work through it from cover to cover or you can move around from one chapter to another in the order you want based on your own priorities and needs. However, before you jump in, maximize the effectiveness of your preparation time by spending a few minutes to develop a realistic action plan. Use the tools provided in these pages to help you focus on the areas where you are weakest, plan your study program, and gain the discipline you need to pace yourself and achieve your goals.

The College Hill SAT Study Plan

Each time you take a practice SAT in this book or online, take a few minutes to review your performance and make a plan for improving your scores on the next test.

Questions About Your Performance

1 **What were your test conditions?** Did you take your practice SAT as you would take a real SAT? Were you sitting at a desk and at a neutral site? Did you time yourself strictly? Did you take the test all at one sitting? If your conditions were not realistic, make sure that they are more realistic next time. Also, note any conditions that may have affected your performance, like "broken clock," "noisy radiator," "freezing room," or "phone interruption." Learning to deal with distractions and with the length and time limits of the SAT is very important to peak performance.

2 **What was your pre-test routine?** What you do just before the test can be very important to your performance. Having a raging argument with someone, for instance, probably won't help. To perform your best, get at least 8 hours of sleep the night before, get 30 minutes of exercise prior to the SAT, and have a good breakfast. Write down anything significant that you did just prior to the test, like "ran 4 miles," "had oatmeal and orange juice," "was yelled at by Dad," or "did 15 minutes of yoga."

3 **Did you attack the questions you need to attack?** The score conversion tables at the end of each practice test (for instance, those on pages 68–69), show you how many questions you need to answer correctly on each section to make your score goals. After each test, ask yourself, "How many more points do I need, and how can I get them?" Try to find patterns among the questions you missed, so you know which sections in this book to review before the next test.

4 **Did you rush to complete any section?** Rushing is never a good strategy on the SAT. You must learn to work briskly, but attentively. After you complete a practice SAT, ask yourself: did I make any careless errors because I was rushing?

5 Study Plan. This is the real key to improving your SAT score. Go to the answer explanations and carefully read the explanations for the questions you missed. Then notice the types of questions you missed, and make a plan to review the corresponding lessons in this book. For instance, you might write down in your notebook that you need to "Learn about dangling participles," or "Review how to simplify polynomials."

Your Weekly SAT Study Schedule

A complete SAT preparation program usually requires between 8 and 12 weeks, depending on your skill and comfort level with the test. Be diligent, but don't overwhelm yourself. Your schoolwork should take priority over SAT prep—colleges care a lot about those grades, and for good reason! But if you make a manageable plan to work for at least 30 minutes every weeknight on your SAT review, you will see great results in just a matter of weeks.

Remember that it is more productive to do some work every day rather than a lot of work just one day a week.

Your daily SAT work should include learning 5–10 new vocabulary words and roots from Chapter 3 and, if you are taking the Essay component, reading and analyzing at least one Op-Ed from the *New York Times*. (Chapter 6 will explain how to do this.) Analytical reading is more important than ever on the SAT, so practice it every day! Also, set aside 20–30 minutes each day to work through the lessons and worksheets in this book.

How to Stick to Your Study Plan

- Twenty minutes of cardiovascular exercise is a great warm-up before you start your homework. Exercise doesn't help just your muscles; it also helps your brain. When your brain is well oxygenated, it works more efficiently, so you do your work better and faster. If you don't already have an exercise routine, try to build up to a good 20- to 45-minute aerobic workout—running, rowing, swimming, biking—every day. Your routine will also help you enormously on test day; exercising on the morning of the SAT will help you to relax, focus, and perform!

- If you get nervous when you think about the SAT, try learning "mindfulness" exercises, like deep breathing, meditation, or yoga. Such exercises will also help enormously on test day.

- Prepare your space. Many students waste a lot of study time because they don't prepare their work space properly. Find a quiet, clean place where you can stay focused for a good stretch of time, away from the TV and troublesome siblings. Sit in an upright chair at a table or desk with good lighting. Also, make sure that all the tools you will need are within easy reach: a dictionary, note cards, calculator, and pencils with erasers. Turn off your cell phone and close the door!

- Sit up straight when you work. Don't work on your bed, on the floor, or in a reclining chair. When your body tilts, your brain goes into "sleep mode" and has to work harder to focus.

- Whenever you feel fatigued from studying, take a 10-minute break. Get a quick snack or listen to a couple of your favorite songs. But stay focused. Don't get sucked into returning twenty text messages.

40 Top Strategies for Test Day

Here are 40 key reminders for success on test day. Take a quick glance through this list on the morning of the test to make sure you can put all of your preparation to use and get your best score.

General Strategies

1 **Take control.** Not every student will ace the SAT, but any student can *take charge of it.* Go into the test with confidence and the game plan that you've put together.

2 **Lay everything out the night before.** You'll sleep easier the night before the SAT knowing that you're ready to go. Lay out three #2 pencils *with good erasers,* your calculator *with fresh batteries,* your admission ticket, your photo ID, and a snack.

3 **Have a good breakfast.** Your brain can't work well without fuel. Have a good breakfast including fruit, complex carbohydrates, and protein. You'll be glad you ate a good breakfast when you're entering hour 3 of the SAT!

4 **Know where you're going.** If you're taking the SAT at an unfamiliar school, acquaint yourself with it before test day. Take a trip there in a few days before the test so you don't worry about getting lost on test day.

5 **Dress properly.** Dress in light layers so you'll be comfortable whether the testing room is sweltering or frigid. An uncomfortable body makes for a distracted brain.

6 **Get a good two nights' sleep.** A rested brain is a smarter brain. The nights before the SAT are for sleeping, not for all-nighters. Get a good eight hours each of the two nights before your SAT.

7 **Get some exercise.** The SAT is given in the morning, when most of us are a bit foggy, so get a leg up on the competition by waking your brain with exercise. Twenty minutes of cardio will keep you alert.

8 **Bring a snack.** Your brain burns calories when it's thinking hard. Bring a granola bar, banana, or energy bar to the SAT to refuel during the break.

9 **Know what to attack.** As you begin each section of your SAT, know how many points you need to make your score goal on that section, and focus on hitting that goal. Even if you have to guess on all the rest of the questions for that section, you won't feel discouraged if you've hit your goal.

10 **Take a "two-pass" approach.** If you've built a smart game plan and practiced with it, you should have enough time to tackle all of your "must answer" questions, then take one more pass through them, checking for common mistakes. Once all of your "must answer" questions have been double-checked, you can approach the hardest questions carefully.

11 **Shut out distractions.** If you have a game plan and have practiced it, you should feel confident enough to shut out everyone else during the test. Don't speed up just because the girl next to you is racing through her test. Ignore her: she's probably rushing because she's nervous. Stick to your game plan. Also, if you are easily distracted by noises around you like tapping pencils, sniffling testers, or clanking radiators, bring a pair of wax earplugs.

12 **Watch the clock—but not too much.** If you have taken enough practice SATs, you should go into the test with confidence in your ability to pace yourself through each section. But, for insurance, you might want to bring a silent stopwatch (not a cell phone timer) and check it occasionally to make sure you're on pace.

13 **Work briskly, but not carelessly.** Don't get bogged down on tough questions: if you get stuck on a question, just make a guess, circle the question in your test booklet (in case you have time to come back to it later), and move on. Remember, rushing is never a good strategy. Optimize your score by working briskly enough to attack all of the questions you need to, but not so quickly that you make careless errors.

14 Don't worry about answer patterns. Some SAT takers refuse to make certain patterns on their answer sheet. For instance, they won't mark (C)—even if it's clearly the best answer—if they already have three (C)s in a row. Bad idea: pick what you think is the best answer, regardless of any answer patterns.

Reading Test

15 Don't psych yourself out on the reading sections. On the Reading Test, don't psych yourself out with negative self-talk. Instead, take a positive attitude, remind yourself of the key strategies from Chapter 5, and tell yourself that you're going to learn something interesting.

16 Focus on the 3 key questions. The key to good reading comprehension is answering three key questions discussed in Chapter 5: What is the purpose? What is the main idea? And what is the overall structure of the passage?

17 Get your own answer first. On the Reading Test, don't jump to the choices too quickly. Instead, read each question carefully and think of your own answer first, then find the choice that best matches it. This will help you avoid the "traps."

18 Deal with your "space outs." Many students "space out" on the Reading Test because they get overwhelmed or disoriented when reading about topics like paleontology or primitivism. If it happens to you, don't panic and don't rush. Just continue from where you left off.

19 Be selective on the reading questions. Unlike the other SAT sections, the reading questions don't get progressively harder. If you get to a tough reading question, make a guess and move on; the next one might be easier.

20 Don't fall for the traps. Always read critical reading questions very carefully. Many choices are "traps:" they make true statements about the passage, but they are not "correct" because they do not answer the question asked. You won't fall for them if you get your own answer first.

21 Know how to attack the "paired passages." On the "paired" passages (Passage 1 vs. Passage 2), it is generally best to read Passage 1 and then go right to the questions that pertain to Passage 1 before moving on to Passage 2. If you try to read the passages back-to-back, it may be harder to recall and distinguish the key information from the two passages. Don't let them run together.

Writing and Language Test

22 Know the key grammar rules. Go into the SAT writing with a solid understanding of the key grammar rules. If you can't explain parallelism, dangling participles, or pronoun case errors, make sure you study Chapter 4 carefully!

23 Trust your ear (at least at first). If you've read a lot of good prose in your life, you have probably developed a good ear for the rules of grammar and usage grammar. On the easy and medium writing questions, then, your ear will be your best guide: bad phrases will "sound" wrong. On harder questions, however, your skill in analyzing sentences will come into play.

24 Know how to analyze the tricky sentences. Chapter 4 provides lots of exercises to help you to recognize the most relevant grammar mistakes and to analyze sentences like a pro. You'll need to know how to do things like "trim" sentences to catch the trickiest errors.

25 Don't fear perfection. On SAT Writing and Language Test questions, the NO CHANGE choice should be correct roughly 1/4 of the time over the long term. Bottom line: don't shy away from NO CHANGE but choose it only after careful analysis.

26 Make sure it's a real mistake. On SAT Writing and Language Test questions, a word or phrase isn't necessarily wrong just because you might say it differently. For instance, if the word *since* is underlined, don't assume it's incorrect just because you prefer to say *because*—the words are interchangeable. Make sure that you know how to fix the mistake—and that it's a *real* grammatical or semantic mistake—before choosing it.

27 Keep the overall purpose and tone in mind. Many Writing and Language Test questions require you to understand the overall purpose and tone of particular paragraphs or the passage as a whole. Don't lose the overall picture by focusing too narrowly on the details.

28 Read it again to check. Before choosing an answer on a Writing and Language Test question, always re-read the entire sentence, including the correction, to make sure the sentence flows smoothly and logically. If the whole *sentence* doesn't sound better, it's wrong.

Math Test

29 Mark up the test. The best SAT takers do lots of scratch work, particularly on the math section. Don't be afraid to write on your test booklet. The SAT doesn't award points for neatness! Write down what you know and show your steps. Mark up diagrams, write equations, and show your work so that you can check it when you come back later.

30 Look for patterns and use them. One important skill the SAT Math Test is "pattern finding." Always pay special attention to simple patterns or repetitions in a problem, because exploiting them is usually the key to the solution.

31 Keep it simple. If you're doing lots of calculations to solve an SAT math problem, you might be overlooking a key fact that simplifies the problem. Always look for the easy way.

32 Know the basic formulas. Many formulas you will need for the SAT Math Test are given to you in the "Reference Information" at the beginning of each Math Test section. Even so, get fluent in them so you can easily recognize when to use them. Also, use flash cards to review the key formulas from algebra, geometry, trigonometry, and statistics from Chapters 7–10.

33 Check your work. There are many ways to make careless mistakes on the SAT math. Give yourself time to go back and check over your arithmetic and algebra, and make sure everything's okay.

34 Consider different approaches. If you're stuck on a math question, try working backwards from the choices, or plugging in numbers for the unknowns.

35 Watch out for key words. Pay special attention to words like *integer, even, odd,* and *consecutive* when they show up, because students commonly overlook them. And make sure you don't confuse *area* with *perimeter*!

36 Don't overuse your calculator. Your calculator can be handy on the the Math with Calculator section, but don't overuse it. If you're doing a lot of calculator work for a problem, you're probably making it too hard. Keep it simple.

37 Re-read the question. Before finalizing your answer, re-read the question to be sure you've answered the right question. If it asks for $5x$, don't give the value for x!

Essay

38 Be ready for the essay. If you are taking the Essay component of the SAT, you will need to go in to the test with a clear understanding of what SAT essay readers are looking for: an essay that shows good reading comprehenison, thorough rhetorical analysis, logical organization, and strong writing skills.

39 Put aside 20 minutes. When the essay section starts, take at least 20 minutes to read the target essay carefully, analyze it, and plan your response, as discussed in Chapter 6. You should still have plenty of time to write a solid essay, and it will flow much more easily.

40 Write at least 5 paragraphs. According to The College Board, a good SAT essay "is well organized and clearly focused, demonstrating clear coherence and smooth progression of ideas." This means that you must use paragraphs effectively. Think of your paragraphs as the "stepping stones" of your essay. Three or four stepping stones don't make for much of a journey, do they?

The 5 Top SAT Calculator Tips

1. Don't Overuse the Calculator

Even though a calculator is permitted on one of the SAT Math sections, don't let your calculator think for you. The SAT Math Test is more of a reasoning test than a calculation test. If you find yourself depending on your calculator for every question, you need to wean yourself off of it and start working on your thinking skills!

Of course, smart calculator use is occasionally helpful, as the following examples show.

2. Know How to MATH▶FRAC

Let's say you're solving an SAT math problem about probabilities and you get 34/85 as an answer, but the choices are

A. 4/17
B. 2/7
C. 2/5
D. 3/7
E. 7/17

Did you mess up? No—you just have to simplify. Here, a TI-83 or similar calculator with ▶FRAC might save you time. Type "34/85" and enter, then press the MATH button and then ▶FRAC. Like magic, it will convert the fraction to lowest terms: 2/5. Sweet!

On "grid in" questions, it's also a good idea to MATH▶FRAC any decimal answer you get to make sure that it gives a fraction that can fit into the grid. If not, you've probably done something wrong!

3. Know How to Get a Remainder

Consider this math question: The tables at a wedding reception are set up to accommodate 212 people. There are 24 tables, some seating 8 people and the rest seating 9 people. How many 9-seat tables are there?

Without getting into the details, the answer is simply the remainder when 212 is divided by 24. You could do this by long division, but you can probably do it faster with a calculator:

Enter the division problem and enter:	$212 \div 24 = 8.833333\ldots$
Subtract the integer part:	$ANS - 8 = 0.833333\ldots$
Multiply by the original divisor:	$ANS \times 24 = 20$

So the answer is 20! Memorize this handy procedure to streamline "remainder" problems.

4. Beware of "Killer Program" Gimmicks

Don't believe your friends who tell you they have a killer "SAT-busting" calculator program. They don't. These are usually gimmicks that waste time rather than save it. Again, if you're depending on your calculator to do anything but check basic calculations, you're thinking about the SAT in the wrong way.

5. Get Fresh Batteries

Even if you don't use your calculator much, you won't be happy if it dies halfway through the SAT. Put in a set of fresh batteries the night before!

McGRAW-HILL EDUCATION

SAT
2016

McGRAW-HILL EDUCATION

SAT
2016

CHRISTOPHER BLACK, MA

MARK ANESTIS, MA

and the TUTORS of
COLLEGE HILL COACHING™

New York | Chicago | San Francisco | Athens | London | Madrid | Mexico City
Milan | New Delhi | Singapore | Sydney | Toronto

1 2 3 4 5 6 7 8 9 0   RHR/RHR   1 2 1 0 9 8 7 6 5 (book for cross-platform edition)
1 2 3 4 5 6 7 8 9 0   RHR/RHR   1 2 1 0 9 8 7 6 5 (book alone)

ISBN   978-1-2595-8589-0   (cross-platform edition)
MHID   1-2595-8589-1

e-ISBN   978-1-2595-8590-6   (e-book cross-platform edition)
e-MHID   1-2595-8590-5

ISBN   978-0-07-184344-7   (book alone)
MHID   0-07-184344-2

e-ISBN   978-0-07-184345-4   (e-book alone)
e-MHID   0-07-184345-0

SAT is a registered trademark of the College Entrance Examination Board, which was not involved in the production of, and does not endorse, this product.

McGraw-Hill Education books are available at special quantity discounts to use as premiums and sales promotions or for use in corporate training programs. To contact a representative, please visit the Contact Us pages at www.mhprofessional.com.

College Hill Coaching® is a registered trademark under the control of Christopher F. Black.

Visit the College Hill Coaching website at www.collegehillcoaching.com.

ACKNOWLEDGMENTS
We would like to acknowledge the help of those who have contributed to this project: Elizabeth, Sarah, and Anna Black for their patience and support; Stephanie Anestis for her invaluable efforts in reading and editing the text and for her incredible love and support; and Robert, Janice, Michael, and Matthew Anestis, who also gave their insight on the work in progress. We appreciate the hard work of those at McGraw-Hill Education who made this project work and the thoughtful help of our agent, Grace Freedson. Finally, we would like to thank all the students of College Hill Coaching who have contributed to the growth of these materials over the years.

CONTENTS

McGRAW-HILL EDUCATION

SAT
2016

CHAPTER 1

ATTACKING THE NEW SAT: TWELVE FAQs

1 WHAT'S NEW IN THE REDESIGNED SAT?

Beginning in spring 2016, the redesigned SAT features ten major changes.

1. More time per question

The redesigned SAT gives you more time per question, making it less likely that you will underperform due to time restrictions.

Section	Old SAT Time Per Question	New SAT Time Per Question
Writing and Language	43 seconds (49 questions, 35 mins)	48 seconds (44 questions, 35 mins)
Mathematics	78 seconds (54 questions, 70 mins)	84 seconds (57 questions, 80 mins)
Reading	63 seconds (67 questions in 70 mins)	75 seconds (52 questions, 65 mins)

Bottom Line: The new SAT should give you a bit more time to breathe.

2. "Rights-only" scoring

The redesigned SAT no longer penalizes you 0.25 point for getting a multiple-choice question wrong. Now your raw score on each section is simply the total number of correct answers on that section. The College Board claims that this will encourage you to make educated guesses, and discourage you from "thinking strategically" about whether to guess on a question, since that is not central to the reasoning skills the SAT is designed to assess.

Bottom line: *On the new SAT, answer every question.* On the toughest questions, just pick an answer and move on rather than leaving it unanswered. You can't hurt your score, and you may help it.

3. Four choices instead of five

All multiple-choice questions now have four choices instead of five. This makes guessing on tough questions even more beneficial, since the chances of getting the question right by luck alone have now increased from 20% to 25%.

Bottom Line: All the more reason to guess rather than leaving a question unanswered.

4. Academic vocabulary in context

The SAT no longer includes "sentence completion questions" or any other specifically vocabulary-focused questions. Rather, it tests your knowledge of vocabulary by challenging you to read and analyze college-level prose in the liberal arts and sciences, and to answer questions about how vocabulary is used to clarify ideas, establish tone, and indicate point of view.

Bottom Line: Chapter 3 discusses how SAT vocabulary is changing and provides comprehensive "new SAT" vocabulary and root lists.

5. Return to the 400-to-1600 point scale

The redesigned SAT scores return to the 400-to-1600 point scale, based on the sum of the Reading and Writing test score (from 200 to 800) and the Mathematics test score (from 200 to 800). The Essay component is no longer mandatory.

Bottom Line: Now you can compare your SAT scores with your parents' SAT scores!

6. Essay optional, and a new essay task

On the new SAT, you have the option of taking the Essay component, in which you are given 50 minutes to read and analyze an argumentative essay that examines an idea, debate, or trend in the arts, sciences, culture, or politics. You are then expected to "produce a clear and cogent written analysis in which [you] explain how the author . . . builds an argument to persuade an audience through the use of evidence, reasoning, [and] stylistic and persuasive elements."

Many competitive colleges will require you to submit the SAT Essay score with the rest of your SAT scores. If you are considering applying to any of these schools, you should choose the Essay option when you register to take the SAT. Check the college websites for their policies on the SAT Essay.

Bottom Line: Chapter 6 gives you complete review and practice in the new SAT essay, together with sample essays with complete grading explanations.

7. More advanced math questions

The redesigned SAT Math test includes questions on topics from trigonometry and second-year algebra, such as complex numbers, trigonometric identities, and analysis of polynomials.

Bottom Line: Chapters 9 and 10 provide comprehensive review of these new more advanced math concepts, as well as lots of practice problems and answer explanations.

8. Calculator and no-calculator math questions

The redesigned SAT Math test is composed of two sections: a calculator section and a no-calculator section. The no-calculator section is designed to assess your arithmetic and algebraic fluency, which are essential to mathematical problem solving.

Bottom Line: The practice problems in the math review chapters (7 through 10) will give you plenty of practice in both calculator and no-calculator problem types, so you can hone the particular skills you need for every possible SAT math question.

9. **Graphical analysis required in some reading and writing questions**

Some of the passages in the redesigned SAT Reading and Writing tests include information in the form of graphs, diagrams, or tables that you may be expected to interpret and synthesize with the content of the passages.

Bottom Line: SAT Reading isn't just about textual analysis anymore, it also includes a bit of graphical analysis.

10. **Lots more data**

As explained in Question 5 below, in addition to the basic Math and Reading/Writing scores, the new SAT will also supply you (and colleges) with up to *sixteen* (yes, you heard right) other "Test Scores," "Cross-Test Scores," and "Subscores."

Bottom Line: Don't worry for a second about all these extra scores. They're just the College Board's way of showing you that it's really good at statistics. The only scores that really count are the Math score and the Reading and Writing score.

2 | WHAT ARE THE PRIMARY SKILLS ASSESSED BY THE REDESIGNED SAT?

SAT Reading

- Interpreting, analyzing, and drawing inferences from college-level texts across the liberal arts and sciences such as arguments, narratives, and personal or expository essays
- Interpreting and drawing inferences from data in the form of graphs, tables, and diagrams that accompany reading passages

SAT Writing and Language

- Analyzing sentences and paragraphs in terms of their grammatical correctness and semantic coherence
- Analyzing essays in terms of their overall development, tone, and effectiveness

SAT Math

- Solving algebraic problems involving equations, inequalities, systems, formulas, and functions
- Solving data-analysis problems involving concepts such as ratios, proportions, percentages, units, and numerical relationships
- Solving problems in advanced mathematics involving concepts such as quadratics, polynomials, angles, polygons, areas, volumes, exponentials, complex numbers, and trigonometry

SAT Essay (Optional)

- Writing an effective essay that analyzes and critiques a given argumentative passage

3 | WHAT IS THE FORMAT OF THE REDESIGNED SAT?

The redesigned SAT is a 3-hour test (3 hours 50 minutes with Essay) consisting of four mandatory sections and an optional Essay.

Total Time: 3 hours (3 hours 50 minutes including Essay)

1. **Reading Test**	52 questions	65 minutes
2. **Writing and Language Test**	44 questions	35 minutes
3. **Mathematics Test (No calculator)**	20 questions	25 minutes
4. **Mathematics Test (Calculator)**	38 questions	55 minutes
5. **Essay (optional)**	1 question	50 minutes

4   WHAT KINDS OF SCORES ARE REPORTED BY THE SAT?

The new SAT returns to the classic 1600-point, "Math + Verbal" format (although now the sections are called "Math" and "Reading and Writing"), but these scores are enhanced with what the College Board calls "Insight Scores," which include three or four "Test Scores," two "Cross-Test Scores," and seven to ten "Subscores."

SAT Insight Scores

	Composite Score (400–1600)			Optional
Sections (200–800)	**Math**	**Reading and Writing**		
Test Scores (10–40)	**Math**	**Writing and Language**	**Reading**	**Essay** (6–24)
Cross-Test Scores (10–40)	**Analysis in History/Social Studies**			
	Analysis in Science			
Subscores (1–15)	**Heart of Algebra**	**Relevant Words in Context**		**Reading** (2–8)
	Problem Solving and Data Analysis	**Command of Evidence**		**Analysis** (2–8)
	Passport to	**Expression of Ideas**		**Writing** (2–8)
	Advanced Math	**Standard English Conventions**		

5   WHAT WILL COLLEGES DO WITH MY SAT SCORES?

Your SAT scores show colleges how ready you are to do college-level work. Students with high SAT scores are more likely to succeed with the challenging college-level math, writing, and reading assignments. Recent studies have also shown that SAT scores correlate strongly with post-college success, particularly in professions like medicine, law, the humanities, the sciences, and engineering. Students with high SAT scores are more likely to graduate from college and to have successful careers after college.

But let's face it: one reason colleges want you to send them SAT scores is that high scores make them look good. The higher the average SAT score of their applicants, the better their rankings and prestige. This is why most colleges cherry-pick your top subscores if you submit multiple SAT results. (It's also why some colleges have adopted "SAT-optional" policies: only the high-scoring students are likely to submit them, and so the college's average scores automatically increase, thereby improving its national rankings.) In addition to your SAT scores, most good colleges are interested in your grades, your curriculum, your recommendations, your leadership skills, your extracurricular activities, and your essay. But standardized test scores are becoming more important as colleges become more selective. Without exception, high SAT scores will provide you with an admission advantage, even if the college does not require them. Some large or specialized schools will weigh test scores heavily. If you have any questions about how heavily a certain college weighs your SAT scores, call the admissions office and ask.

The majority of colleges "superscore" your SAT, which means that they cherry-pick your top SAT Reading and Writing score and your top SAT Math score from all of the SATs you submit. So, for instance, if you submit your March SAT scores of 520R 610M (1130 composite) and your June SAT scores of 550R 580M (1130 composite), the college will consider your SAT score to be 550R 610M (1160 composite). Nice of them, huh?

6   WHAT CONTROL DO I HAVE OVER MY SAT SCORES?

No college will see any of your SAT or Subject Test scores until you choose to release them to that particular school. So you never have to worry about a college seeing a score you don't want to release. Most colleges also allow you to use Score Choice to select which particular SAT and SAT Subject Test scores are submitted to the colleges among all that you've taken. Some colleges, however, may request that you not use Score Choice, and instead submit all scores of all SATs you've taken. Typically, colleges do this for two reasons: (1) to give you the maximum possible SAT "superscore," and (2) to identify students who are inappropriately test-obsessed (for instance, those who have taken the SAT six or more times).

So don't worry about taking the SAT two or three times, if you need to. In fact, most colleges encourage students to take multiple tests, since one data point isn't as trustworthy as multiple data points. But don't go overboard. If you take it more than four times, a college might think you're test-obsessed.

7 SHOULD I TAKE THE ACT AS WELL?

The ACT is a college admissions test—administered independently of the SAT by a completely different company—that you may submit to colleges in lieu of your SAT and Subject Tests. It is roughly the same length as the SAT and tests roughly the same topics: grammar, math, reading, and science, as well as an optional rhetorical essay.

Many students take the ACT in addition to the SAT and Subject Tests in order to have as many possible options as possible when submitting their applications.

Some students prefer the ACT to the SAT, and some do not. You owe it to yourself to check it out and consider it as an option. You can find out more about the ACT at ACT.org.

8 WHAT IS THE BEST WAY TO PREPARE FOR THE REDESIGNED SAT?

"Start where you are. Use what you have. Do what you can."
    –Arthur Ashe

Step 1: Make a testing schedule

First, decide when you will take your first SAT. Sit down with your guidance counselor early in your junior year and work out a full testing schedule for the year, taking into account the SAT, SAT Subject Tests, AP tests, and possible the ACT. Once you have decided on your schedule, commit yourself to beginning your SAT preparation at least 3 months prior to your first SAT. Commit to setting aside 30–40 minutes per night for review work and practice, and to taking at least two or three full-scale practice tests on the weekends.

Step 2: Take a diagnostic SAT or two

When you're ready to begin your SAT preparation (ideally 3 months before your SAT), you'll first need to assess your readiness. Chapter 2 contains a full-scale practice SAT. It requires 3 hours (or 3 hours and 50 minutes if you include the essay). Take it on a Saturday morning, if possible, at roughly the time you will start the real SAT (around 8:00 a.m.), and make sure that you have a quiet place, a stopwatch, a calculator, and a few #2 pencils. This will give you a solid idea of what the experience of taking the new SAT is like.

Step 3: Use the lessons in this book

The detailed answer keys after each practice test will give you plenty of feedback about the topics that you may need to review in order to prepare for your SAT. If you set aside about 30 minutes per night to work through the chapters, review the lessons, and complete the exercises in this book, you can make substantial progress and see big SAT score improvements in just a few weeks. But to get the full benefit of this book, you should start at least three months before your SAT.

Step 4: Take practice tests regularly and diagnose your performance

Practice is the key to success. This book includes three full-scale practice SATs. Use them. Take one every week or two to assess your progress as you work through the chapters in this book.

Step 5: Use online tutorials

You can find a lot of SAT advice and review material online, some of it good, most of it mediocre, some of it horrible. For the redesigned SAT, the College Board has partnered with Khan Academy to offer online video tutorials on many of the key topics for the SAT.

The best review, of course, comes from actually tackling the test yourself and getting direct feedback on your performance and specific advice on how to improve. Nevertheless, it can still be helpful to watch someone else working through tough problems and explaining strategies in a lecture format. Many of the Khan Academy lessons also include linked discussions where you can ask questions about the lectures.

Throughout this book, we will provide you with links to some of the more helpful Khan Academy videos that may help you to boost your preparation, as well as links to other online resources from McGraw-Hill.

Step 6: Read as often as you can from the College Hill Coaching Power Reading List

Engaging big ideas and honing your analytical reading skills are keys to success in college and on the SAT. Make a point of working your way though these books and checking these periodicals regularly.

Online/Periodical

The New York Times (Op-Ed, Science Times, Front Page)
BBC News (Views, Analysis, Background)
The Atlantic (Feature Articles)
Slate (Voices, Innovation)
Scientific American (Feature Articles)
The Economist (Debate, Science & Technology)
TED Talks (Innovation, Culture, Politics, Inspiration)
The New Yorker (Talk of the Town, Feature Articles)
ProPublica (Feature Articles)
Edge (Essays)
Radiolab (Weekly Podcast)

Books

To Kill a Mockingbird, Harper Lee
Macbeth, William Shakespeare
Frankenstein, Mary Shelley
The Color Purple, Alice Walker
Pride and Prejudice, Jane Austen
Jane Eyre, Charlotte Bronte
Heart of Darkness, Joseph Conrad
Narrative of the Life of Frederick Douglass, Frederick
     Douglass
The Great Gatsby, F. Scott Fitzgerald
Walden, Henry David Thoreau
The American Language, H. L. Mencken
Notes of a Native Son, James Baldwin
The Stranger, Albert Camus
Night, Elie Wiesel
Animal Farm, George Orwell
Things Fall Apart, Chinua Achebe
The Language Instinct, Steven Pinker
The Mismeasure of Man, Stephen J. Gould

The Republic, Plato
A People's History of the United States, Howard Zinn
Guns, Germs, and Steel, Jared Diamond
A Short History of Nearly Everything, Bill Bryson

Step 7: Take strong math courses

Challenge yourself with strong math courses that introduce you to the ideas, skills, and methods or advanced mathematics, such as trigonometry, analysis of polynomials, statistical reasoning, plane geometry, and even complex numbers. These advanced topics have become a greater focus for both the SAT and ACT.

Step 8: Take strong writing courses

Take courses from teachers who emphasize strong writing skills, particularly by giving challenging writing assignments and providing timely and detailed feedback. Reading and writing skills are at the core of both the SAT and the ACT, so working with strong reading and writing teachers is invaluable.

9 | HOW CAN I GET THE MOST OUT OF MY STUDY SESSIONS?

1. **Create a schedule, a study log, and place to study.** Stick to a firm schedule of 30–40 minutes a day for SAT preparation. Write it down in your daily planner and commit to it like you would to a daily class. Also, keep a log of notes for each study session, including key strategies, important formulas, vocabulary words, and advice for your next test. Then make an effective study space: a well-lit desk with a straight-back chair, plenty of pencils, a timer for practice tests, flashcards, your study log, and even a stash of brain-healthy snacks.

2. **Eliminate distractions.** Turn off all alerts on your phone and laptop, and tell everyone in the house that this is your study time. Make sure everyone is in on the plan. Even kick the dog out of the room.

3. **Stick to focused 30 to 40-minute sessions.** Set a very clear agenda for each study session, such as "Master six new roots and complete the first half of Algebra Practice 4 in Chapter 7" or "Read and annotate one complete New York Times Op-Ed and read Lesson 2 in Chapter 9." Then find your study spot, shut out all distractions, and set to work. Try not to go beyond 40 minutes for each session: stay focused and engaged, and keep it brisk.

4. **Do 30-second checks.** Once you've completed your session, take out your study log. Give yourself 30 seconds to write down the most important idea(s) that helped you through that study session. Reread your notes just before you begin your next session.

5. **Learn it like you have to teach it.** Now step away from your log and imagine you have to run into a class of eighth graders and teach them what you just learned. How would you communicate these ideas clearly? What examples would you use to illustrate them? What tough questions might the students ask, and how would you answer them? How can you explain the concepts and strategies in different ways? How can you help the students to manage potential difficulties they might have in a testing environment?

6. **Sleep on it.** A good night's sleep is essential to a good study program. You need at least eight hours of sleep per night. To make your sleep as effective as possible, try to fall asleep while thinking about a challenging problem or strategy you're trying to perfect. As you sleep, your brain will continue to work on the problem by a process called consolidation. When you awake, you'll have a better grasp on the problem or skill whether you realize it or not.

7. **Make creative mnemonics.** Whenever you're challenged by a tough vocabulary word, grammar rule, or mathematical concept, try to visualize the new idea or word as a crazy, colorful picture or story. The memory tricks are called mnemonics, and the best ones use patterns, rhymes, or vivid and bizarre visual images. For instance, if you struggle to remember what a "polemic" is, just turn the word into a picture based on its sound, for instance a "pole" with a "mike" (microphone) on the end of it. Then incorporate the meaning into the picture. Since a polemic is a "strong verbal attack, usually regarding a political or philosophical issue," picture someone having a vehement political argument with someone else and

hitting him over the head with the "pole-mike." The crazier the picture, the better. Also, feel free to scribble notes as you study, complete with helpful drawings. Write silly songs, create acronyms—be creative.

8. **Consider different angles.** Remember that many math problems can be solved in different ways: algebraically, geometrically, with tables, through guess-and-check, by testing the choices, etc. Try to find elegant, simple solutions. If you struggled with a problem, even if you got it right, come back to it later and try to find the more elegant solution. Also, consider experimenting with pre-test rituals until you find one that helps you the most.

9. **Maintain constructive inner dialogue.** Constantly ask yourself, What do I need to do to get better? Do I need to focus more on my relaxation exercises? Should I try to improve my reading speed? Should I ask different questions as I read? Should I refresh myself on my trigonometry? Having a clear set of positive goals that you reinforce with inner dialogue helps you to succeed. Banish the negative self-talk. Don't sabotage your work by saying, "This is impossible," or "I stink at this."

10. **Make a plan to work through the struggles.** Before you take each practice test, have a clear agenda. Remind yourself of the key ideas and strategies for the week. But remember that there will always be challenges. Just meet them head on and don't let them get you down.

10 WHEN AND HOW OFTEN SHOULD I TAKE THE SATs AND SUBJECT TESTS?

Most competitive colleges require either SAT or ACT scores from all of their applicants, although some schools are "test-optional," allowing you to choose whether or not to submit your standardized test scores with your application. Many competitive colleges also require two or three Subject Test scores. The Subject Tests are hour-long tests in specific subjects like mathematics, physics, chemistry, foreign languages, U.S. history, world history, and literature.

If you want to be able to apply to any competitive college in the country, plan to take the SAT at least twice, as well two to four SAT Subject Tests, by the end of spring semester of junior year, and retake any of those tests, if necessary, in the fall of your senior year. This way, you will have a full testing profile by the end of your junior year, and you'll have a much clearer picture of where you stand before you start your college applications. Also, if you plan well, you will have some choices about which scores to submit.

Even if your favorite colleges don't require standardized tests, you may be able to submit them anyway to boost your application. The Subject Tests, specifically, can provide a strong counterbalance to any weaknesses in your grades. For instance, a strong chemistry Subject Test score can offset a poor grade in chemistry class.

Take your Subject Test when the subject material is fresh in your mind. For most students, this is in June, just as you are preparing to take your final exams. However, if you are taking AP exams in May, you might prefer to take the SAT Subject Tests in May, also. Learn which SAT Subject Tests your colleges require, and try to complete them by June of your junior year. You can take up to three SAT Subject Tests on any test date.

11 WHAT SHOULD I DO THE WEEK BEFORE MY SAT?

1. **Get plenty of sleep.** Don't underestimate the power of a good night's sleep. During sleep, not only do you restore balance and energy to your body, but you also consolidate what you've learned that day, and even become more efficient at tasks you've been practicing.

2. **Eat healthy.** Don't skip meals because you're studying. Eat regular, well-balanced meals.

3. **Exercise.** Stick to your regular exercise program the weeks before the SAT. A strong body helps make a strong mind.

4. **Visualize success.** In the days before your SAT, envision yourself in the test room, relaxed and confident, working through even the toughest parts of the test without stress or panic.

5. **Don't cram, but stay sharp.** In the days before the SAT, resist the urge to cram. Your best results will come if you focus on getting plenty of sleep and staying positive and relaxed. If you're feeling anxious, take out your flashcards for a few minutes at a time, or review your old tests just to remind yourself of basic strategies, but don't cram.

6. **Keep perspective.** Remember that you can take the SAT multiple times, and that colleges will almost certainly "superscore" the results, so don't get down about any single set of test results. Also, keep in mind that colleges don't base their acceptance decisions on SAT scores alone.

7. **Lay everything out.** The night before your SAT, lay out your admission ticket, your photo ID, your #2 pencils, your calculator (with fresh batteries), your snack, and directions to the test site (if necessary). Having these all ready will let you sleep better.

12 WHAT SHOULD I DO ON TEST DAY?

1. **Wake up early and get some cardiovascular exercise.** A good 20-minute cardiovascular workout will get your blood flowing, wake up your brain, and release stress.

2. **Eat a good breakfast.** Don't skip breakfast. Your brain needs energy for a three- to four-hour workout!

3. **Bring a snack.** You'll have a couple of short breaks, during which you can have a quick snack. Bring a granola bar or some other quick burst of energy. You'll need it!

4. **Take slow, deep breaths—often.** Most test takers feel some anxiety before and during the test. Don't worry—it's a normal physiological response to keep you on your toes. If this anxiety begins to overwhelm you, just take three long, deep breaths and remind yourself that you are prepared, and you will perform better if you are relaxed rather than tense. It works wonders.

5. **Dress in layers.** Since you won't know whether your test room will be hot or cold, dress in layers so you'll be ready for anything.

6. **Don't worry about what anyone else is doing.** If you've been practicing as this book recommends, you will have a good sense of your own pacing and game plan. Trust your preparation, and resist any temptation to take your cues from what anyone around you is doing.

7. **Don't panic when things get tough.** Don't psych yourself out every time you get to a hard question or even a hard section. That might be an experimental section! Just stay positive and keep going.

CHAPTER 2

DIAGNOSTIC SAT

ANSWER SHEET

Start with number 1 for each new section. If a section has fewer questions than answer spaces, leave the extra answer spaces blank. Be sure to erase any errors or stray marks completely.

SECTION 1

1 Ⓐ Ⓑ Ⓒ Ⓓ	13 Ⓐ Ⓑ Ⓒ Ⓓ	25 Ⓐ Ⓑ Ⓒ Ⓓ	37 Ⓐ Ⓑ Ⓒ Ⓓ	49 Ⓐ Ⓑ Ⓒ Ⓓ
2 Ⓐ Ⓑ Ⓒ Ⓓ	14 Ⓐ Ⓑ Ⓒ Ⓓ	26 Ⓐ Ⓑ Ⓒ Ⓓ	38 Ⓐ Ⓑ Ⓒ Ⓓ	50 Ⓐ Ⓑ Ⓒ Ⓓ
3 Ⓐ Ⓑ Ⓒ Ⓓ	15 Ⓐ Ⓑ Ⓒ Ⓓ	27 Ⓐ Ⓑ Ⓒ Ⓓ	39 Ⓐ Ⓑ Ⓒ Ⓓ	51 Ⓐ Ⓑ Ⓒ Ⓓ
4 Ⓐ Ⓑ Ⓒ Ⓓ	16 Ⓐ Ⓑ Ⓒ Ⓓ	28 Ⓐ Ⓑ Ⓒ Ⓓ	40 Ⓐ Ⓑ Ⓒ Ⓓ	52 Ⓐ Ⓑ Ⓒ Ⓓ
5 Ⓐ Ⓑ Ⓒ Ⓓ	17 Ⓐ Ⓑ Ⓒ Ⓓ	29 Ⓐ Ⓑ Ⓒ Ⓓ	41 Ⓐ Ⓑ Ⓒ Ⓓ	
6 Ⓐ Ⓑ Ⓒ Ⓓ	18 Ⓐ Ⓑ Ⓒ Ⓓ	30 Ⓐ Ⓑ Ⓒ Ⓓ	42 Ⓐ Ⓑ Ⓒ Ⓓ	
7 Ⓐ Ⓑ Ⓒ Ⓓ	19 Ⓐ Ⓑ Ⓒ Ⓓ	31 Ⓐ Ⓑ Ⓒ Ⓓ	43 Ⓐ Ⓑ Ⓒ Ⓓ	
8 Ⓐ Ⓑ Ⓒ Ⓓ	20 Ⓐ Ⓑ Ⓒ Ⓓ	32 Ⓐ Ⓑ Ⓒ Ⓓ	44 Ⓐ Ⓑ Ⓒ Ⓓ	
9 Ⓐ Ⓑ Ⓒ Ⓓ	21 Ⓐ Ⓑ Ⓒ Ⓓ	33 Ⓐ Ⓑ Ⓒ Ⓓ	45 Ⓐ Ⓑ Ⓒ Ⓓ	
10 Ⓐ Ⓑ Ⓒ Ⓓ	22 Ⓐ Ⓑ Ⓒ Ⓓ	34 Ⓐ Ⓑ Ⓒ Ⓓ	46 Ⓐ Ⓑ Ⓒ Ⓓ	
11 Ⓐ Ⓑ Ⓒ Ⓓ	23 Ⓐ Ⓑ Ⓒ Ⓓ	35 Ⓐ Ⓑ Ⓒ Ⓓ	47 Ⓐ Ⓑ Ⓒ Ⓓ	
12 Ⓐ Ⓑ Ⓒ Ⓓ	24 Ⓐ Ⓑ Ⓒ Ⓓ	36 Ⓐ Ⓑ Ⓒ Ⓓ	48 Ⓐ Ⓑ Ⓒ Ⓓ	

SECTION 2

1 Ⓐ Ⓑ Ⓒ Ⓓ	11 Ⓐ Ⓑ Ⓒ Ⓓ	21 Ⓐ Ⓑ Ⓒ Ⓓ	31 Ⓐ Ⓑ Ⓒ Ⓓ	41 Ⓐ Ⓑ Ⓒ Ⓓ
2 Ⓐ Ⓑ Ⓒ Ⓓ	12 Ⓐ Ⓑ Ⓒ Ⓓ	22 Ⓐ Ⓑ Ⓒ Ⓓ	32 Ⓐ Ⓑ Ⓒ Ⓓ	42 Ⓐ Ⓑ Ⓒ Ⓓ
3 Ⓐ Ⓑ Ⓒ Ⓓ	13 Ⓐ Ⓑ Ⓒ Ⓓ	23 Ⓐ Ⓑ Ⓒ Ⓓ	33 Ⓐ Ⓑ Ⓒ Ⓓ	43 Ⓐ Ⓑ Ⓒ Ⓓ
4 Ⓐ Ⓑ Ⓒ Ⓓ	14 Ⓐ Ⓑ Ⓒ Ⓓ	24 Ⓐ Ⓑ Ⓒ Ⓓ	34 Ⓐ Ⓑ Ⓒ Ⓓ	44 Ⓐ Ⓑ Ⓒ Ⓓ
5 Ⓐ Ⓑ Ⓒ Ⓓ	15 Ⓐ Ⓑ Ⓒ Ⓓ	25 Ⓐ Ⓑ Ⓒ Ⓓ	35 Ⓐ Ⓑ Ⓒ Ⓓ	
6 Ⓐ Ⓑ Ⓒ Ⓓ	16 Ⓐ Ⓑ Ⓒ Ⓓ	26 Ⓐ Ⓑ Ⓒ Ⓓ	36 Ⓐ Ⓑ Ⓒ Ⓓ	
7 Ⓐ Ⓑ Ⓒ Ⓓ	17 Ⓐ Ⓑ Ⓒ Ⓓ	27 Ⓐ Ⓑ Ⓒ Ⓓ	37 Ⓐ Ⓑ Ⓒ Ⓓ	
8 Ⓐ Ⓑ Ⓒ Ⓓ	18 Ⓐ Ⓑ Ⓒ Ⓓ	28 Ⓐ Ⓑ Ⓒ Ⓓ	38 Ⓐ Ⓑ Ⓒ Ⓓ	
9 Ⓐ Ⓑ Ⓒ Ⓓ	19 Ⓐ Ⓑ Ⓒ Ⓓ	29 Ⓐ Ⓑ Ⓒ Ⓓ	39 Ⓐ Ⓑ Ⓒ Ⓓ	
10 Ⓐ Ⓑ Ⓒ Ⓓ	20 Ⓐ Ⓑ Ⓒ Ⓓ	30 Ⓐ Ⓑ Ⓒ Ⓓ	40 Ⓐ Ⓑ Ⓒ Ⓓ	

Start with number 1 for each new section. If a section has fewer questions than answer spaces, leave the extra answer spaces blank. Be sure to erase any errors or stray marks completely.

SECTION 3

1 Ⓐ Ⓑ Ⓒ Ⓓ
2 Ⓐ Ⓑ Ⓒ Ⓓ
3 Ⓐ Ⓑ Ⓒ Ⓓ
4 Ⓐ Ⓑ Ⓒ Ⓓ
5 Ⓐ Ⓑ Ⓒ Ⓓ
6 Ⓐ Ⓑ Ⓒ Ⓓ
7 Ⓐ Ⓑ Ⓒ Ⓓ
8 Ⓐ Ⓑ Ⓒ Ⓓ
9 Ⓐ Ⓑ Ⓒ Ⓓ
10 Ⓐ Ⓑ Ⓒ Ⓓ
11 Ⓐ Ⓑ Ⓒ Ⓓ
12 Ⓐ Ⓑ Ⓒ Ⓓ
13 Ⓐ Ⓑ Ⓒ Ⓓ
14 Ⓐ Ⓑ Ⓒ Ⓓ
15 Ⓐ Ⓑ Ⓒ Ⓓ

CAUTION **Use the answer spaces in the grids below for Section 3 only if you are told to do so in your test book.**

Student-Produced Responses

ONLY ANSWERS ENTERED IN THE CIRCLES IN EACH GRID WILL BE SCORED. YOU WILL NOT RECEIVE CREDIT FOR ANYTHING WRITTEN IN THE BOXES ABOVE THE CIRCLES.

16 17 18 19 20

	⊘	⊘	
○	○	○	○
	⓪	⓪	⓪
①	①	①	①
②	②	②	②
③	③	③	③
④	④	④	④
⑤	⑤	⑤	⑤
⑥	⑥	⑥	⑥
⑦	⑦	⑦	⑦
⑧	⑧	⑧	⑧
⑨	⑨	⑨	⑨

Start with number 1 for each new section. If a section has fewer questions than answer spaces, leave the extra answer spaces blank. Be sure to erase any errors or stray marks completely.

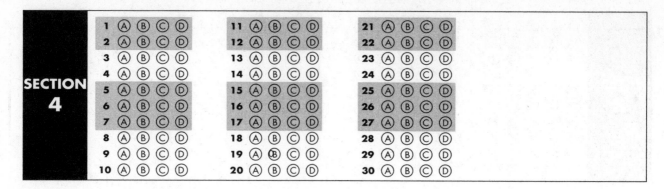

CAUTION Use the answer spaces in the grids below for Section 4 only if you are told to do so in your test book.

Student-Produced Responses ONLY ANSWERS ENTERED IN THE CIRCLES IN EACH GRID WILL BE SCORED. YOU WILL NOT RECEIVE CREDIT FOR ANYTHING WRITTEN IN THE BOXES ABOVE THE CIRCLES.

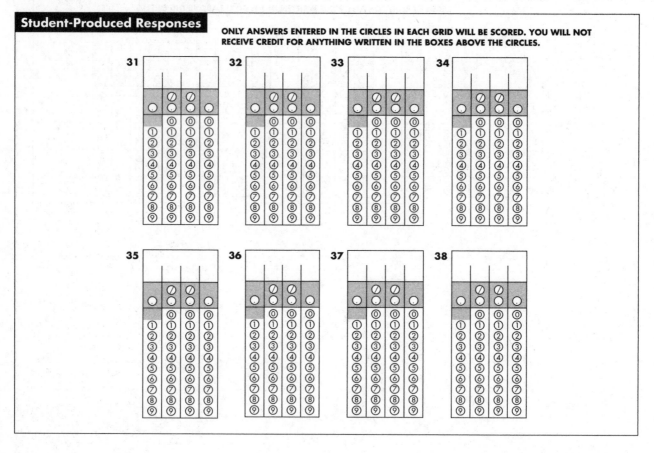

SECTION 5: ESSAY

You may wish to remove these sample answer document pages to respond to the practice SAT Essay Test.

Begin WRITING TEST here.

_____

_____

_____

_____

_____

_____

_____

_____

_____

_____

_____

_____

_____

_____

_____

_____

_____

_____

_____

_____

_____

_____

_____

If you need more space, please continue on the next page.

1

SECTION 5: ESSAY

You may wish to remove these sample answer document pages to respond to the practice SAT Essay Test.

WRITING TEST

_____

_____

_____

_____

_____

_____

_____

_____

_____

_____

_____

_____

_____

_____

_____

_____

_____

_____

_____

_____

_____

_____

_____

_____

_____

If you need more space, please continue on the next page.

Cut Here

SECTION 5: ESSAY

You may wish to remove these sample answer document pages to respond to the practice SAT Essay Test.

WRITING TEST

_____
_____
_____
_____
_____
_____
_____
_____
_____
_____
_____
_____
_____
_____
_____
_____
_____
_____
_____
_____
_____
_____
_____
_____
_____
_____
_____

If you need more space, please continue on the next page.

Cut Here

SECTION 5: ESSAY

You may wish to remove these sample answer document pages to respond to the practice SAT Essay Test.

WRITING TEST

STOP here with the Writing Test.

1   **1**

Reading Test

65 MINUTES, 52 QUESTIONS

Turn to Section 1 of your answer sheet to answer the questions in this section.

DIRECTIONS

Each passage or pair of passages below is followed by a number of questions. After reading each passage or pair, choose the best answer to each question based on what is stated or implied in the passage or passages and in any accompanying graphics.

Questions 1–10 are based on the following passage and supplementary material.

This passage is adapted from Kevin Drum, *"America's Real Criminal Element: Lead"* ©2013 Mother Jones.

Experts often suggest that crime resembles an epidemic. But what kind? Economics professor
Line Karl Smith has a good rule of thumb for cat-
egorizing epidemics: If it spreads along lines of
5 communication, he says, the cause is informa-
tion. Think Bieber Fever.[1] If it travels along major transportation routes, the cause is microbial. Think influenza. If it spreads out like a fan, the cause is an insect. Think malaria. But if it's every-
10 where, all at once—as both the rise of crime in the '60s and '70s and the fall of crime in the '90s seemed to be—the cause is a molecule.
A molecule? That sounds crazy. What mol-
ecule could be responsible for a steep and sudden
15 decline in violent crime?
Well, here's one possibility: $Pb(CH_2CH_3)_4$.
In 1994, Rick Nevin was a consultant work-
ing for the US Department of Housing and Urban Development on the costs and benefits of remov-
20 ing lead paint from old houses. A growing body of research had linked lead exposure in small children with a whole raft of complications later in life, including lower IQ, hyperactivity, behavioral problems, and learning disabilities. A recent
25 study had also suggested a link between childhood lead exposure and juvenile delinquency

later on. Maybe reducing lead exposure had an effect on violent crime too?
That tip took Nevin in a different direction.
30 The biggest source of lead in the postwar era, it turns out, wasn't paint, but leaded gasoline. If you chart the rise and fall of atmospheric lead caused by the rise and fall of leaded gasoline consumption, you get an upside-down U. Lead emissions
35 from tailpipes rose steadily from the early '40s through the early '70s, nearly quadrupling over that period. Then, as unleaded gasoline began to replace leaded gasoline, emissions plummeted.
Intriguingly, violent crime rates followed the
40 same upside-down U pattern (see the graph). The only thing different was the time period. Crime rates rose dramatically in the '60s through the '80s, and then began dropping steadily starting in the early '90s. The two curves looked eerily iden-
45 tical, but were offset by about 20 years.
So Nevin dug up detailed data on lead emis-
sions and crime rates to see if the similarity of the curves was as good as it seemed. It turned out to be even better. In a 2000 paper he concluded that
50 if you add a lag time of 23 years, lead emissions from automobiles explain 90 percent of the varia-
tion in violent crime in America. Toddlers who ingested high levels of lead in the '40s and '50s really were more likely to become violent crimi-
55 nals in the '60s, '70s, and '80s.

[1] Enthusiasm for the music and person of Justin Bieber.

And with that we have our molecule: tetra-ethyl lead, the gasoline additive invented by General Motors in the 1920s to prevent knocking and pinging in high-performance engines. As auto sales boomed after World War II, and drivers in powerful new cars increasingly asked service station attendants to "fill 'er up with ethyl," they were unwittingly creating a crime wave two decades later.

It was an exciting conjecture, and it prompted an immediate wave of . . . nothing. Nevin's paper was almost completely ignored, and in one sense it's easy to see why—Nevin is an economist, not a criminologist, and his paper was published in *Environmental Research*, not a journal with a big readership in the criminology community. What's more, a single correlation between two curves isn't all that impressive, econometrically speaking. Sales of vinyl LPs rose in the postwar period too, and then declined in the '80s and '90s. No matter how good the fit, if you only have a single correlation it might just be

a coincidence. You need to do something more to establish causality.

So in 2007, Nevin collected lead data and crime data for Australia, Canada, Great Britain, Finland, France, Italy, New Zealand and West Germany. Every time, the two curves fit each other astonishingly well.

The gasoline lead hypothesis helps explain some things we might not have realized even needed explaining. For example, murder rates have always been higher in big cities than in towns and small cities. Nevin suggests that, because big cities have lots of cars in a small area, they also had high densities of atmospheric lead during the postwar era. But as lead levels in gasoline decreased, the differences between big and small cities largely went away. And guess what? The difference in murder rates went away too. Today, homicide rates are similar in cities of all sizes. It may be that violent crime isn't an inevitable consequence of being a big city after all.

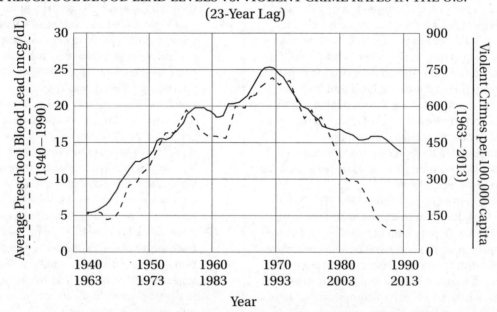

PRESCHOOL BLOOD LEAD LEVELS VS. VIOLENT CRIME RATES IN THE U.S.
(23-Year Lag)

Source: Rick Nevin, *Lead Poisoning and The Bell Curve*, 2012

CONTINUE →

1

1

1

In the first paragraph, Karl Smith's work is presented primarily as

A) a controversial sociological hypothesis.

B) a warning about potentially dangerous economic trends.

C) a useful model for conceptualizing a variety of phenomena.

D) a potential medical solution to a persistent social problem.

2

The author suggests that promising research in the social sciences is sometimes ignored because it

A) is not presented by authorities with the proper credentials.

B) is not supported by controlled scientific experiments.

C) relies on complex mathematical calculations that are not easily understood.

D) uses historical data that are not necessarily valid in the modern era.

3

Which of the following provides the strongest evidence for the answer to the previous question?

A) Lines 24–27 ("A recent study . . . later on")

B) Lines 49–52 ("In a 2000 paper . . . America")

C) Lines 68–72 ("Nevin is . . . community")

D) Lines 72–74 ("What's more . . . speaking")

4

According to the graph, which of the following is closest to the percent increase in violent crime in America from 1963 to 1993?

A) 600%

B) 400%

C) 75%

D) 20%

5

According to the graph, which decade of violent crime statistics provides the LEAST support to Rick Nevin's hypothesis?

A) 1963–1973

B) 1980–1990

C) 1983–1993

D) 2003–2013

6

The author mentions "sales of vinyl LPs" (line 74) primarily as an example of

A) another economic factor that may explain a social trend.

B) how harmful chemicals can be spread via consumer products.

C) a statistic that may be more coincidental than explanatory.

D) a counterintuitive trend in consumer behavior.

CONTINUE ➔

7

The "complications" in line 22 are

A) obstacles to gathering relevant data.

B) controversies about theoretical models.

C) challenges to the implementation of social policies.

D) psychological problems.

8

The author characterizes the "drivers" in line 60 primarily as

A) inadvertent abettors.

B) unintentional heroes.

C) greedy consumers.

D) devious conspirators.

9

In line 49, "even better" most nearly means

A) less controversial.

B) more correlative.

C) easier to calculate.

D) more aesthetically engaging.

10

The final paragraph (lines 85–98) serves primarily to

A) suggest topics for future research.

B) concede a theoretical drawback.

C) propose a novel alternative.

D) describe a supportive implication.

CONTINUE ➞

1   **1**

Questions 11–21 are based on the following passages.

Passage 1 is adapted from an essay written by John Aldridge in 1951. ©1951 by John Aldridge. Passage 2 is adapted from Brom Weber, *"Ernest Hemingway's Genteel Bullfight,"* published in The American Novel and the Nineteen Twenties. ©1971 by Hodder Education.

Passage 1

By the time we were old enough to read
Hemingway, he had become legendary. Like
Lord Byron a century earlier, he had learned
to play himself, his own best hero, with superb
5   conviction. He was Hemingway of the rugged
outdoor grin and the hairy chest posing beside a
lion he had just shot. He was Tarzan Hemingway,
crouching in the African bush with elephant gun
at ready. He was War Correspondent Hemingway
10 writing a play in the Hotel Florida in Madrid
while thirty fascist shells crashed through
the roof. Later, he was Task Force Hemingway
swathed in ammunition belts and defending
his post singlehandedly against fierce German
15 attacks.
   But even without the legend, the chest-
beating, wisecracking pose that was later to
seem so incredibly absurd, his impact upon us
was tremendous. The feeling he gave us was one
20 of immense expansiveness, freedom and, at the
same time, absolute stability and control. We
could follow him, imitate his cold detachment,
through all the doubts and fears of adolescence
and come out pure and untouched. The words
25 he put down seemed to us to have been carved
from the living stone of life. They conveyed
exactly the taste, smell and feel of experience as
it was, as it might possibly be. And so we began
unconsciously to translate our own sensations
30 into their terms and to impose on everything
we did and felt the particular emotions they
aroused in us.
   The Hemingway time was a good time to
be young. We had much then that the war later
35 forced out of us, something far greater than
Hemingway's strong formative influence.

Later writers who lost or got rid of Hemingway
have been able to find nothing to put in his
place. They have rejected his time as untrue
40 for them only to fail at finding themselves in their
own time. Others, in their embarrassment at the
hold he once had over them, have not profited
by the lessons he had to teach, and still others
were never touched by him at all. These last are
45 perhaps the real unfortunates, for they have been
denied access to a powerful tradition.

Passage 2

One wonders why Hemingway's greatest
works now seem unable to evoke the same sense
of a tottering world that in the 1920s established
50 Ernest Hemingway's reputation. These novels
should be speaking to us. Our social structure
is as shaken, our philosophical despair as great,
our everyday experience as unsatisfying. We have
had more war than Hemingway ever dreamed of.
55 Our violence—physical, emotional, and intellectual—is not inferior to that of the 1920s. Yet
Hemingway's great novels no longer seem to
penetrate deeply the surface of existence. One
begins to doubt that they ever did so significantly
60 in the 1920s.
   Hemingway's novels indulged the dominant genteel tradition in American culture while
seeming to repudiate it. They yielded to the functionalist, technological aesthetic of the culture
65 instead of resisting in the manner of Frank Lloyd
Wright. Hemingway, in effect, became a dupe of his
culture rather than its moral-aesthetic conscience.
As a consequence, the import of his work
has diminished. There is some evidence from
70 his stylistic evolution that Hemingway himself
must have felt as much, for Hemingway's famous
stylistic economy frequently seems to conceal
another kind of writer, with much richer rhetorical resources to hand. So, *Death in the Afternoon*
75 (1932), Hemingway's bullfighting opus and his
first book after *A Farewell to Arms* (1929), reveals
great uneasiness over his earlier accomplishment. In it, he defends his literary method with a
doctrine of ambiguity: "If a writer of prose knows
80 enough about what he is writing about he may

CONTINUE ➡

omit things that he knows and the reader, if the writer is writing truly enough, will have a feeling of those things as strongly as though the writer had stated them."

85   Hemingway made much the same theoretical point in another way in *Death in the Afternoon* apparently believing that a formal reduction of aesthetic complexity was the only kind of design that had value.

90   Perhaps the greatest irony of *Death in the Afternoon* is its unmistakably baroque prose, which Hemingway himself embarrassedly admitted was "flowery." Reviewers, unable to challenge Hemingway's expertise in the art of
95 bullfighting, noted that its style was "awkward, tortuous, [and] belligerently clumsy."

Death in the Afternoon is an extraordinarily self-indulgent, unruly, clownish, garrulous, and satiric book, with scrambled chronologies,
100 willful digressions, mock-scholarly apparatuses, fictional interludes, and scathing allusions. Its inflated style can hardly penetrate the façade, let alone deflate humanity.

CONTINUE ➡

1

1

11

On which topic do the authors of the two passages most strongly DISAGREE?

A) The economy of Hemingway's writing

B) The incisiveness of Hemingway's prose

C) The sincerity of Hemingway's portrayals

D) The extent of Hemingway's reputation

12

Which pair of sentences provides the strongest evidence for the answer to the previous question?

A) Lines 5–7 ("He was . . . just shot") and lines 85–89 ("Hemingway . . . had value")

B) Lines 37–39 ("Later writers . . . his place") and lines 55–56 ("Our violence . . . the 1920s")

C) Lines 24–26 ("The words . . . stone of life") and lines 56–58 ("Yet . . . existence")

D) Lines 34–36 ("We had much . . . influence") and lines 90–93 ("Perhaps the greatest . . . was 'flowery'")

13

Which of the following best describes how each passage characterizes Hemingway?

A) Passage 1 portrays him as a tortured poet, but Passage 2 portrays him as a crass amateur.

B) Passage 1 portrays him as a master of refinement, but Passage 2 portrays him as a literary revolutionary.

C) Passage 1 portrays him as a hero, but Passage 2 portrays him as a cultural conformist.

D) Passage 1 portrays him as an absurd warmonger, but Passage 2 portrays him as an undisciplined artist.

14

Which statement about Hemingway is supported by both passages?

A) He was an artistic pioneer, although he was underappreciated in his time.

B) He was a consistent practitioner of spare and evocative prose.

C) His characters serve as archetypes for masculine adventure.

D) His wartime narratives do not fully capture the horrors of war.

15

In line 26, the phrase "living stone" most nearly means

A) salient experience.

B) inevitable regret.

C) stubborn resistance.

D) durable memorial.

16

Lines 28–32 ("And so we . . . aroused in us") suggests that many of Hemingway's readers were inclined to

A) emulate his adventures.

B) resent his glorification of war.

C) imitate his literary style.

D) identify with his language.

17

The "lessons" mentioned in line 43 most likely include stories of

A) transformative romantic love.

B) confidence in the face of danger.

C) indulgent self-examination.

D) corporate or political ambition.

CONTINUE

18

In line 49, the word "tottering" is intended to evoke a sense of

A) infantile frailty.

B) economic instability.

C) artistic immaturity.

D) societal upheaval.

19

The author of Passage 1 would most likely regard the statement in lines 66–67 ("Hemingway, in effect . . . conscience"), with

A) journalistic detachment.

B) grudging acquiescence.

C) vehement disagreement.

D) good-natured amusement.

20

Which statement provides the best evidence for the answer to the previous question?

A) Lines 2–5 ("Like Lord . . . superb conviction")

B) Lines 28–32 ("And so . . . aroused in us")

C) Lines 34–36 ("We had much . . . formative influence")

D) Lines 39–41 ("They have rejected . . . own time")

21

The author of Passage 2 suggests that, in comparison to Hemingway, Frank Lloyd Wright was relatively

A) minimalist.

B) iconoclastic.

C) volatile.

D) traditional.

1   **1**

Questions 22–32 are based on the following passage.

This passage is from Christopher F. Black, *"The Mystery of the Strong Nuclear Force."* ©2015 by Christopher F. Black and College Hill Coaching.

    As any good contractor will tell you, a sound structure requires stable materials. But atoms, the building blocks of everything we know and love—bunnies, brownies, and best friends—
5 don't appear to be models of stability. Why are some atoms, like sodium, so hyperactive while others, like helium, are so aloof? Why do the electrons that inhabit atoms jump around so strangely, from one bizarrely shaped orbital to
10 another? And why do protons, the bits that give atoms their heft and personality, stick together at all?
    We are told that every atom has a tiny nucleus containing positively charged protons
15 and uncharged neutrons, swarmed by a cloud of speedy electrons. We are also told that like charges, such as protons, repel each other with a force that shoots up to infinity as they get closer. Even worse, you can't get much closer
20 than two protons in the nucleus of an atom. So what's keeping atomic nuclei from flying apart? Obviously, some other force must be at work inside the atom, something that we can't detect at our human scale. Physicists call this the
25 "strong nuclear force." But where does it come from?
    In order for this force to account for the binding of protons in the nucleus, it must have certain interesting features. First, it can't have any size-
30 able effect beyond the radius of the atom itself, or it would play havoc with the nuclei of adjacent atoms, destroying matter as we know it. Second, it must perfectly balance the repulsive force of electricity at an "equilibrium point" of about

35 0.7×10^{-15} meters, the average distance between bound protons, in order to create a stable nucleus. Third, it must *repel* at even shorter distances, or else neutrons (which don't have any electrostatic repulsion to balance the strong nuclear force)
40 would collapse into each other. The graph shows the behavior of such a force relative to the repulsive electrostatic force.
    In 1935, Japanese physicist Hideki Yukawa proposed that the nuclear force was conveyed by
45 a then-undiscovered heavy subatomic particle he called the pi meson (or "pion"), which (unlike the photon, which conveys the electrostatic force) decays very quickly and therefore conveys a powerful force only over a very short distance.
50 Professor Yukawa's theory, however, was dealt a mortal blow by a series of experiments conducted at Los Alamos National Laboratory in the early 1990s that demonstrated that pions carry force only over distances greater than the distance
55 between bound protons. The pion was a plumber's wrench trying to do a tweezer's job.
    Current atomic theory suggests that the strong nuclear force is most likely conveyed by massless particles called "gluons" according to
60 the theory of quantum chromodynamics, or QCD for short. According to QCD, protons and neutrons are composed of smaller particles called quarks, which are held together by the aptly named gluons. This quark-binding force has a
65 "residue" that extends beyond the protons and neutrons themselves to provide just enough force to bind the protons and neutrons together.
    If you're hoping that QCD ties up atomic behavior with a tidy little bow, you may be just a
70 bit disappointed. As a quantum theory, it conceives of space and time as tiny chunks that occasionally misbehave, rather than smooth predictable quantities, and its mathematical formulas are perhaps as hard to penetrate as the
75 nucleus itself.

CONTINUE ▶

1

1

ELECTROSTATIC AND STRONG NUCLEAR FORCES BETWEEN PROTONS

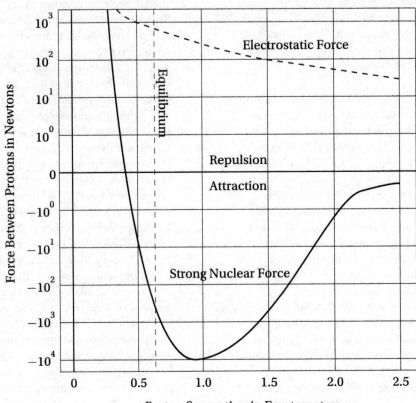

1

22

The primary purpose of the first paragraph (lines 1-12) is to

A) describe a popular misconception.

B) introduce a physical theory.

C) suggest a scientific conundrum.

D) present a personal account.

23

In line 7, "aloof" most nearly means

A) impenetrable.

B) formal.

C) retracted.

D) nonreactive.

24

The question in lines 10–12 ("And why . . . at all?") indicates

A) a minor curiosity to scientists exploring deeper questions.

B) a socially significant puzzle that is unfortunately ignored in scientific circles.

C) a humorous irony in an otherwise serious field of investigation.

D) a central conundrum at the heart of an important scientific field.

25

Which sentence provides the best evidence for the answer to the previous question?

A) Lines 2–5 ("But atoms . . . stability")

B) Lines 19–20 ("Even worse . . . an atom")

C) Lines 55–56 ("The pion . . . tweezer's job")

D) Lines 68–70 ("If you're . . . disappointed")

26

In lines 13-16, the repetition of the phrase "We are" serves primarily to emphasize

A) the predominance of certain conceptions.

B) the personal nature of scientific research.

C) the effectiveness of a particular analogy.

D) the deficiencies in public education.

27

Which of the following best describes the relationship between the electrostatic force and the strong nuclear force between protons at the equilibrium point as shown in the graph?

A) The strong nuclear force is at its maximum, but the electrostatic force is not.

B) The strong nuclear force is at its minimum, but the electrostatic force is near its maximum.

C) The sum of the two forces is zero.

D) The strong nuclear force is zero and the electrostatic force is greater than 100 Newtons.

28

According to the graph, the electrostatic repulsion between two protons separated by 1.5 femtometers is closest to

A) 2 Newtons.

B) 20 Newtons.

C) 100 Newtons.

D) 1,000 Newtons.

CONTINUE ▶

29

The "mortal blow" (line 51) to Hideki Yukawa's theory was the fact that

A) the existence of pions was not confirmed by experimental evidence.

B) pions were discovered to be massless, thereby refuting his theory that they were heavy.

C) experiments showed pions to be ineffective in the range required by atomic theory.

D) pions had a destabilizing effect on atomic nuclei, rather than a stabilizing one.

30

Which of the following best describes the structure of the passage as a whole?

A) a series of intuitive illustrations of a complex physical theory

B) a description of a technical puzzle and the attempts to solve it

C) an account of an experimental finding and its surprising implications

D) a historical overview of a heated scientific controversy

31

The author's writing style is particularly notable for its use of all of the following EXCEPT

A) rhetorical questions.

B) illustrative metaphors.

C) technical specifications.

D) appeals to common intuition.

32

In line 68, "ties up" most nearly means

A) constrains restrictively.

B) resolves neatly.

C) obstructs completely.

D) fastens securely.

1   **1**

Questions 33–42 are based on the following passage.

This passage is adapted from Jean-Jaques Rousseau, *"Discourse on Inequality and Social Contract."* Originally published in 1762.

Just as, before putting up a large building, the architect surveys and sounds the site to see if it will bear the weight, the wise legislator does not begin by laying down laws good in themselves,
5 but by investigating the fitness of the people, for which they are destined, to receive them. Plato refused to legislate for the Arcadians and the Cyrenæans,[1] because he knew that both peoples were rich and could not tolerate equality. Also,
10 good laws and bad men were found together in Crete, because Minos had inflicted discipline on a people already burdened with vice.

A thousand nations that have achieved earthly greatness could never have endured good
15 laws. Even those nations that could have endured good laws could have done so only for a very brief period of their long history. Most peoples, like most men, are docile only in youth. As they grow old they become incorrigible. Once customs have
20 become established and prejudices inveterate, it is dangerous and useless to attempt their reformation. The people, like the foolish and cowardly patients who rave at sight of the doctor, can no longer bear that any one should lay hands on its
25 faults to remedy them.

There are indeed times in the history of States when, just as some kinds of illness turn men's heads and make them forget the past, periods of violence and revolution do to peoples what
30 these crises do to individuals. Horror of the past takes the place of forgetfulness, and the state, set on fire by civil wars, is born again, so to speak, from its ashes, and takes on anew, fresh from the jaws of death, the vigor of youth. Such was
35 Sparta at the time of Lycurgus.

But such events are rare exceptions, the cause of which is always to be found in the particular constitution of the state concerned. Such renewals cannot even happen twice to the same nation,
40 for it can make itself free as long as it remains barbarous, but not when the civic impulse has lost its vigor. Then disturbances may destroy it, but revolutions cannot mend it: it needs a master, and not a liberator. Free peoples, be mindful of this
45 maxim: "Liberty may be gained, but can never be recovered."

There is for nations, as for men, a threshold of maturity before which they should not be made subject to laws. But the maturity of a people is not
50 always easily recognizable, and, if it is anticipated, the work is spoiled. One people is amenable to discipline from the beginning; another, not after ten centuries. Russia will never be really civilized, because it was civilized too soon.
55 Peter the Great had a genius for imitation, but he lacked true genius, which is creative and makes all from nothing. He did some good things, but most of what he did was out of place. He saw that his nation was barbarous, but did not see that it
60 was not ripe for civilization: he wanted to civilize it when it needed only hardening. His first wish was to make Germans or Englishmen, when he ought to have been making Russians; and he prevented his subjects from ever becoming what
65 they might have been by persuading them that they were what they are not. In this fashion too a French teacher turns out his pupil to be an infant prodigy, and for the rest of his life to be nothing whatsoever. The empire of Russia will aspire to
70 conquer Europe, but will itself be conquered. The Tartars,[2] its subjects or neighbors, will become its masters and ours, by a revolution that I regard as inevitable.

[1] the peoples of two regions of ancient Greece
[2] a Mongol-Turkic tribe of Eurasia

CONTINUE ➡

33

This passage is primarily concerned with

A) restoring the reputation of some widely maligned leaders of the past.

B) comparing the merits of various ancient systems of government.

C) examining the social conditions that foster effective legal systems.

D) establishing the philosophical basis for universal democracy.

34

In line 2, the word "sounds" most nearly means

A) resonates.

B) enunciates.

C) probes.

D) appears.

35

In the first paragraph, the author discusses the activities of an architect in order to make the point that

A) the success of a nation's civil code depends on the nature of its people.

B) good laws must be based on sound philosophical principles.

C) nations that lack good laws cannot support a professional class.

D) effective government requires experts to design civic infrastructure.

36

The author suggests that long-established societies are characterized primarily by

A) stubborn resistance to political change.

B) an honorable respect for good laws.

C) periodic but predictable social renewal.

D) a tendency toward imperialist expansion.

37

Which sentence provides the best evidence for the answer to the previous question?

A) Lines 9–12 ("Also, good laws . . . vice")

B) Lines 19–21 ("Once customs . . . reformation")

C) Lines 30–34 ("Horror . . . vigor of youth")

D) Lines 71–73 ("The Tartars . . . as inevitable")

38

In lines 17–18, the distinction between "peoples" and "men" is essentially one between

A) barbarism and civilization.

B) societies and individuals.

C) youth and maturity.

D) rebellion and obedience.

39

The author mentions "Sparta at the time of Lycurgus" (line 35) primarily as an example of a place where

A) the citizens were paralyzed with fear in the face of invasion.

B) the society was rejuvenated through conflict.

C) the people lost sight of their own sacred traditions.

D) the leaders had become foolish and cowardly.

40

In lines 37–38, the phrase "particular constitution of the state" refers most specifically to

A) the documented rules by which a nation defines its governmental institutions.

B) the social composition and cultural habits of a population.

C) the enumeration of popular rights in a democratic society.

D) a manifesto about the philosophical motivations for political change.

1   **1**

41

In lines 51–52, the phrase "amenable to discipline" most nearly means

A) ready to be governed by the rule of law.

B) susceptible to exploitation by neighboring countries.

C) prepared to accept an oppressive ruler.

D) trained for offensive or defensive military activity.

42

The author suggests that Peter the Great's main flaw was

A) military ruthlessness.

B) undue reverence for custom.

C) excessive political guile.

D) irresolution in exerting control.

CONTINUE

Questions 43–52 are based on the following passage.

This passage is adapted from Bertrand Russell, *A History of Western Philosophy*. ©1945 by Bertrand Russell, renewed by Edith Russell. Reprinted with permission of Simon & Schuster.

To understand the views of Aristotle, as of most Greeks, on physics, it is necessary to apprehend
Line his imaginative background. Every philosopher, in addition to the formal system that he offers to
5 the world, has another much simpler system of which he may be quite unaware. If he is aware of it, he probably realizes that it won't quite do; he therefore conceals it, and sets forth something more sophisticated, which he believes because it
10 is like his crude system, but which he asks others to accept because he thinks he has made it such as cannot be disproved. The sophistication comes in by way of refutation of refutations, but this alone will never give a positive result. It shows, at best,
15 that a theory may be true, not that it must be. The positive result, however little the philosopher may realize it, is due to his imaginative preconceptions, or to what Santayana calls "animal faith."
In relation to physics, Aristotle's imagina-
20 tive background was very different from that of a modern student. Nowadays, students begin with mechanics, which, by its very name, suggests machines. They are accustomed to automobiles and airplanes; they do not, even in the dimmest
25 recesses of their subconscious imagination, think that an automobile contains some sort of horse inside, or that an airplane flies because its wings are those of a bird possessing magical powers. Animals have lost their importance in
30 our imaginative pictures of the world, in which humans stand comparatively alone as masters of a mainly lifeless and largely subservient material environment.
To the ancient Greek, attempting to give a
35 scientific account of motion, the purely mechanical view hardly suggested itself, except in the case of a few men of genius such as Democritus and Archimedes. Two sets of phenomena seemed important: the movements of animals, and
40 the movements of the heavenly bodies. To the modern man of science, the body of an animal is a very elaborate machine, with an enormously complex physical and chemical structure. Every new discovery consists in diminishing the appar-
45 ent gulf between animals and machines. To the Greek, it seemed more natural to assimilate apparently lifeless motions to those of animals. A child still distinguishes live animals from other things by the fact that animals can move
50 themselves. To many Greeks, and especially to Aristotle, this peculiarity suggested itself as the basis of a general theory of physics.
But how about the heavenly bodies? They differ from animals by the regularity of their
55 movements, but this may be only due to their superior perfection. Every Greek philosopher, whatever he may have come to think in adult life, had been taught in childhood to regard the sun and moon as gods. Anaxagoras was pros-
60 ecuted for impiety because he thought that they were not alive. It was natural that a philosopher who could no longer regard the heavenly bodies themselves as divine should think of them as moved by the will of a Divine Being who had a
65 Hellenic love of order and geometric simplicity. Thus the ultimate source of all movement is Will: on earth the capricious Will of human beings, but in heaven the unchanging Will of the Supreme Artificer.

1   **1**

43

The passage as a whole primarily serves to

A) contrast the ideas of several ancient Greek philosophers.

B) examine the means by which philosophical ideas become popular.

C) describe the conceptions that inform a particular mindset.

D) discuss the debt that modern physics owes to ancient thinkers.

44

The statement that "animals have lost their importance" (line 29) means that

A) humans no longer treat other species with appropriate respect.

B) animistic beliefs no longer inform our physical theories.

C) scientists no longer regard animal behavior as a productive topic of study.

D) humans do not use animals for transportation to the extent that they once did.

45

The "simpler system" in line 5 is a

A) method for translating complex writings of ancient thinkers.

B) streamlined system for reaching logically valid conclusions.

C) formal theory based on a very small number of assumptions.

D) relatively unrefined way of thinking.

46

Which of the following statements about ancient Greek philosophers is best supported by the passage?

A) Their astronomical theories were closely associated with their religious ideas.

B) Their ideas about mechanics inspired many important technological innovations.

C) They regarded human intellect as a divine gift, rather than a cultivated skill.

D) They valued imagination and creativity even more than reason and logic.

47

Which sentence provides the best evidence for the answer to the previous question?

A) lines 61–65 ("It was natural . . . simplicity")

B) lines 45–47 ("To the Greek . . . of animals")

C) lines 40–45 ("To the modern . . . animals and machines")

D) lines 3–6 ("Every philosopher . . . quite unaware")

48

In line 46, "assimilate" most nearly means

A) incorporate.

B) comprehend.

C) embrace.

D) liken.

CONTINUE ➡

49

The passage suggests that the "men of genius" (line 37) are noteworthy for their

A) creative metaphors for the laws of motion.

B) ability to integrate many different fields of study.

C) effectiveness in articulating their ideas to others.

D) willingness to disregard conventional wisdom.

50

Which of the following would best bridge the "gulf" in line 45?

A) creating a system of gestures to help humans better communicate with dolphins

B) writing a computer program that analyzes and categorizes mockingbird calls

C) discovering the mechanical laws that describe bumblebee flight

D) teaching modern students more about ancient Greek philosophy

51

The passage suggests that the "views of Aristotle" (line 1) are characterized primarily by their

A) logical rigor.

B) animistic tendencies.

C) reliance on refutation.

D) unwavering skepticism.

52

Which sentence provides the best evidence for the answer to the previous question?

A) lines 3–6 ("Every philosopher . . . quite unaware")

B) lines 12–14 ("The sophistication . . . positive result")

C) lines 19–21 ("In relation . . . modern student")

D) lines 45–47 ("To the Greek . . . animals")

STOP

If you finish before time is called, you may check your work on this section only.
Do not turn to any other section of the test.

2   **2**

Writing and Language Test
35 MINUTES, 44 QUESTIONS

Turn to Section 2 of your answer sheet to answer the questions in this section.

DIRECTIONS

Each passage below is accompanied by a number of questions. For some questions, you will consider how the passage might be revised to improve the expression of ideas. For other questions, you will consider how the passage might be edited to correct errors in sentence structure, usage, or punctuation. A passage or a question may be accompanied by one or more graphics (such as a table or graph) that you will consider as you make revising and editing decisions.

Some questions will direct you to an underlined portion of a passage. Other questions will direct you to a location in a passage or ask you to think about the passage as a whole.

After reading each passage, choose the answer to each question that most effectively improves the quality of writing in the passage or that makes the passage conform to the conventions of Standard Written English. Many questions include a "NO CHANGE" option. Choose that option if you think the best choice is to leave the relevant portion of the passage as it is.

CONTINUE ▶

2   **2**

Questions 1–11 are based on the following passage and supplementary material.

Physician Assistants

As the American population grows, ages, and gains better access to affordable health insurance, the demand for primary medical services **1** are expected to skyrocket. As a result, the United States Department of Health and Human Services projects a shortage of about 20,000 primary care physicians by 2020. Therefore, an important challenge facing the healthcare industry is how to address this shortfall without sacrificing quality of care. One possible solution is to **2** elevate more medical school graduates to choose primary care as their field instead of **3** their choosing the more lucrative specialties like surgery and dermatology.

1
A) NO CHANGE
B) is
C) has been
D) would be

2
A) NO CHANGE
B) interest
C) incentivize
D) expect

3
A) NO CHANGE
B) to choose the more lucrative specialties
C) the more lucrative specialties
D) the more lucrative specialties they might choose

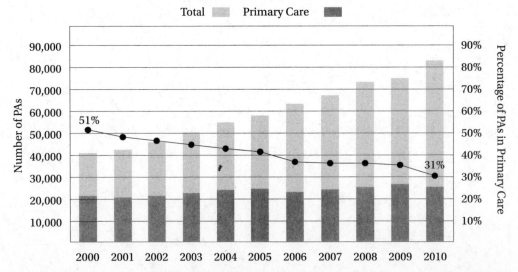

PHYSICIAN ASSISTANTS IN THE U.S.

Source: American Academy of Physician Assistants, *American Medical News*, September 27, 2011

2   2

[1] Another option is to incorporate more medical professionals like physician assistants (PAs) and nurse practitioners (NPs) into primary care teams. [2] They can talk with patients about treatment options, prescribe medications, and even **4** perform technical procedures like bone marrow aspirations. [3] Many healthcare providers are moving toward this "team-based" model, **5** where physicians can better focus on their specialties while relying on trained professionals to provide other necessary services. [4] Team-based medicine allows medical practitioners to best utilize their particular skills, **6** still sharing the successes and struggles of the team. [5] If organized around the principles of professionalism, trust, communication, and accountability, these teams may be able to provide better care to patients at less cost. **7**

For all the promise of team-based primary medicine, it cannot work without an adequate supply of well-trained health professionals. Although the total number of PAs in the United States more than doubled between 2000 and 2010, **8** the number of PAs going into primary care has decreased by 20% over that same time period. In the years ahead, we must encourage more of these new PAs to choose careers in primary care.

4

A) NO CHANGE
B) performing technical procedures
C) technical procedures
D) to perform technical procedures

5

A) NO CHANGE
B) whereby
C) by this
D) when

6

A) NO CHANGE
B) while at the same time
C) while
D) although

7

The author is considering inserting the following sentence into this paragraph.

> Although they receive less training than physicians do, these professionals have advanced degrees and can provide direct treatment to patients.

Where should it be placed?

A) After sentence 1
B) After sentence 3
C) After sentence 4
D) After sentence 5

8

Which choice is best supported by the data in the graph?

A) NO CHANGE
B) the number of PAs going into primary care has increased by only 50%
C) more PAs have gone into dermatology than into primary care
D) the fraction of those PAs going into primary care has declined from over one-half to under one-third

CONTINUE ▶

2   **2**

Undergraduate students considering a career in medicine have many more options **9** than they did just a generation ago. Graduate PA and NP programs, which take about three years, are becoming increasingly attractive, especially **10** being that MD programs, including residency, lasting seven to ten years and often leave students saddled with tens of thousands of dollars in debt.

Anyone thinking about pursuing a PA or NP degree should keep in mind that these programs aren't cheap, either, and that most states impose strict limits on the kinds of treatment **11** they can provide.

9

A) NO CHANGE
B) than
C) than it was
D) to choose from than

10

A) NO CHANGE
B) when MD programs, including residence, are lasting
C) being that MD programs last, including residency,
D) because MD programs, including residency, can last

11

A) NO CHANGE
B) he or she
C) these professions
D) these professionals

2   2

CONTINUE ➤

Questions 12–22 are based on the following passage.

Maria Montessori

What is education? Is it a program of institutionally approved performances, or a collection of self-directed experiences? Such questions absorbed Maria Montessori throughout her life. Born in 1870 in **12** Chiaravalle Italy, Montessori showed a strong independent will even as a child. As a teenager, she told her parents that she wanted to study engineering, **13** a position that was widely thought unladylike. By the age of 20, she had changed her mind and decided to pursue an even less traditional path: medicine. Despite suffering ridicule and isolation, **14** Montessori's medical studies at the University of Rome were completed and she became one of the first female physicians in Italy.

Although Montessori's practice focused on psychiatry, her interests gravitated toward education. In 1900, she was appointed co-director of the *Scuola Magistrale Ortofrenica*, a training institute for special education teachers. Montessori believed that, in order for so-called "deficient" children to thrive, they needed respect and stimulation rather than **15** the regimentation they were receiving in institutions.

12
- A) NO CHANGE
- B) Chiaraville, Italy. Montessori showed a strong independent will, even
- C) Chiaraville, Italy, Montessori showed a strong, independent will, even
- D) Chiaraville, Italy; Montessori showed a strong, independent will even

13
- A) NO CHANGE
- B) despite its reputation for being unladylike
- C) although widely considered unladylike
- D) which was unladylike in reputation

14
- A) NO CHANGE
- B) Montessori completed her medical studies at the University of Rome by becoming
- C) Montessori's medical studies were completed, at the University of Rome, and thus she became
- D) Montessori completed her medical studies at the University of Rome and became

15
- A) NO CHANGE
- B) receiving regimentation in institutions
- C) the regimented institutions they were receiving
- D) the regimentation of the institutions they were receiving

2

2

In 1907 Maria opened the Casa dei Bambini, or "Children's House," a daycare center for impoverished children in which she could test her theory that **16** children's minds each learn according to they're own schedule. She personalized a curriculum for each child rather than providing a standardized course of study. While learning important academic and life skills, many formerly aggressive and unmanageable children became more emotionally balanced and self-directed. Word of her success with the Casa dei Bambini soon began to **17** distribute internationally, and her methods for child-centered education became widely adopted across Europe.

18 In the 25 years after their founding, Montessori schools were regarded as a remedy to the educational problems associated with rapid urban population growth throughout Europe.

16

A) NO CHANGE
B) each child's mind learns according to its own schedule
C) childrens' minds learn according to its own schedule
D) children's minds each learn according to their own schedule

17

A) NO CHANGE
B) increase
C) spread
D) exhibit

18

Which choice provides the most effective introduction to this paragraph?

A) Montessori dedicated herself to travelling the world and preaching the benefits of child-centered education.
B) Montessori's first school enrolled 50 students from poor working families.
C) Montessori did not have a particularly nurturing relationship with her own son, Mario, who was raised by another family.
D) As the Montessori method was gaining a foothold, Europe was undergoing dramatic social and political change.

CONTINUE ➡

2

2

19 <u>So as</u> fascism began to proliferate in the 1930s throughout Spain, Italy, and Germany, child-centered education came to be seen as a threat to the power of the state. In 1933, the totalitarian regimes in Italy and Germany closed all Montessori schools and declared **20** <u>them subversive and that they were undermining their power</u>.

Even outside of Europe, **21** <u>the response to Montessori's ideas were</u> divided. Many eminent scholars, inventors, and politicians—among them Alexander Graham Bell, Helen Keller, Thomas Edison, Mahatma Gandhi, and Woodrow Wilson— greeted her ideas with enthusiasm. But her theories were challenged by William H. Kirkpatrick, a leading educational reformer and professor at Teachers College, Columbia University. His 1914 book, *The Montessori System Examined*, declared Montessori's psychological theories wildly out-of-date. **22**

It was not until 1958 that a new generation of Montessorians revived and updated her methods in the United States. In 1958, the first American Montessori school, the Whitby School, was founded in Greenwich, Connecticut, where it thrives today.

19
A) NO CHANGE
B) When
C) However, as
D) Furthermore, as

20
A) NO CHANGE
B) that they were subversive in undermining their power
C) them subversive in undermining power
D) them subversive

21
A) NO CHANGE
B) the response to Montessori's ideas was
C) Montessori's ideas had a response that was
D) Montessori's ideas response was

22

At this point, the paragraph would benefit most from a discussion of

A) how Kirkpatrick's book was received among American educators
B) why totalitarian governments regarded Montessori's methods as a threat
C) those American educators whose influence was comparable to Montessori's
D) how other reform movements of the era contrasted with Montessori's

CONTINUE ➤

2   2

Questions 23–33 are based on the following passage.

Platonic Forms

When we look at the moon, we see a spherical object, but do "spheres" really exist? This may seem to be a silly question, because it's not hard to understand the definition of a sphere: "the set of all points in space that are a fixed distance (called the radius) from a fixed point (called the center)." We see examples of "spherical" objects all the time, don't we?

23 First, nothing that we can observe in our physical world **24** complies perfectly to this mathematical definition of a sphere. The moon, a beach ball, and even water droplets are all "bumpy," at least at the atomic level. So can we say that the concept of "sphere" is real **25** if there is no such thing as a real sphere?

Pondering this question as so many ancient Greek philosophers did, **26** the argument Plato made was that the sphere is an "ideal form," inaccessible to our physical senses yet **27** the mind can apprehend it through pure reason.

23
- A) NO CHANGE
- B) So
- C) While
- D) In fact,

24
- A) NO CHANGE
- B) overlaps
- C) corresponds
- D) concurs

25
- A) NO CHANGE
- B) where no such thing exists
- C) as if nothing is
- D) if there were nothing

26
- A) NO CHANGE
- B) it was Plato who argued
- C) Plato had argued
- D) Plato argued

27
- A) NO CHANGE
- B) it can be apprehended by the mind
- C) apprehensible to the mind
- D) it is apprehensible to the mind

2   2

He also reasoned that, since our senses can be fooled, logic provides a much more reliable path to the truth. Therefore, a Platonic idealist believes that these abstract forms are **28** as effective, if not more so, than sensory experience at revealing the nature of reality. **29**

Modern scientists and philosophers are unlikely to be Platonic idealists. Today, we can understand the origin of abstract concepts **30** and not having to believe that they come from a higher, physically inaccessible reality. We simply need to understand **31** the process by which our brains make inferences.

Take an abstract idea like "orangeness." Most of us would say that orangeness "exists" because we see examples of it every day, such as carrots, traffic cones, and pumpkins. But what if, by some magic, we could remove all orange-colored objects from the universe? In other words, what if, as with "sphereness," no real examples of "orangeness" **32** would exist? Would "orangeness" still exist?

28

A) NO CHANGE

B) as effective as, if not more effective than,

C) as effective, if not more effective, than

D) equally as effective, if not more effective than,

29

At this point, the author is considering adding the following true statement:

> The sphere is just one of many ideal forms, like lines and tetrahedrons, that are studied in geometry.

Should the author make this addition here?

A) Yes, because it indicates a particular application of ideal forms.

B) Yes, because explains a claim made in the previous sentence.

C) No, because it detracts from this paragraph's discussion of philosophy.

D) No, because it undermines the Platonists' point of view.

30

A) NO CHANGE

B) in not having to believe

C) and not be believing

D) without having to believe

31

A) NO CHANGE

B) our brain's process by which they

C) the process by which our brain's

D) the process by which our brain

32

A) NO CHANGE

B) would have existed

C) existed

D) had an existence

CONTINUE ➡

2   2

In an important sense, the answer is yes. We can demonstrate the existence of "orangeness" without appealing to any higher reality. We could measure the wavelength of red light (about 650 nm), and yellow light (about 570 nm) and make the reasonable inference, because wavelengths fall on a continuum, that a color exists with an intermediate wavelength, of 610 nm, even if we have never directly measured such light.

Our brains do not contain sophisticated instruments for measuring wavelengths of light, but they do make similar inferences constantly. **33** For instance, when you drive, you unconsciously make inferences about quantities like the speeds of surrounding cars and qualities like dangerous driving conditions. Our brains are continually making inferences based on the limited information from our senses, and these inferences are the substance of abstract thought.

33

Which of the following changes would best improve this sentence's cohesiveness with the rest of the paragraph?

A) Change "For instance" to "Nevertheless."

B) Change both instances of "you" to "we."

C) Change "you unconsciously make changes" to "changes are unconsciously made"

D) Delete the phrase "like dangerous driving conditions."

CONTINUE →

2

Questions 34–44 are based on the following passage and supplementary material.

The Eureka Effect

You've probably had the experience. After racking your brain for hours to solve a problem, you finally put it aside and move on to other things. Then, much later, seemingly out of **34** nowhere, perhaps while showering or driving—the answer suddenly strikes you. Psychologists call this the "Eureka effect," from the ancient Greek word meaning "I have found it," **35** which Archimides is said to have shouted as he ran naked from his bathtub through the streets of Syracuse upon suddenly solving a vexing physics problem.

Does this feeling arise from our emotional centers or our cognitive centers? In other words, is it simply an emotional response to finding a solution, or does it **36** foretell a fundamentally different way of thinking? Psychologists have tried to answer this question by looking inside subjects' brains as they solve problems, using electroencephalograms (EEGs) and other tools.

34
A) NO CHANGE
B) nowhere—perhaps
C) nowhere: perhaps
D) nowhere; perhaps

35
A) NO CHANGE
B) what Archmides is said to shout
C) that Archimedes shouted, it is said
D) which Archimedes it is said had shouted

36
A) NO CHANGE
B) indicate
C) provide
D) generate

GAMMA-BAND INTENSITY IN RIGHT ANTERIOR TEMPORAL REGION
DURING VERBAL ASSOCIATION TASK

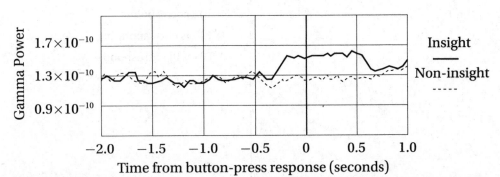

Source: Adapted from Beeman, Bowden et al., "Neural Activity When People Solve Problems with Insight," *PLOS*, 2004

CONTINUE ▶

In one **37** experiment, subjects performed a word association task, scientists measured the activity in the region of the brain called the right hemisphere anterior superior temporal gyrus (RH aSTG). This region is known to be active in tasks, such as finding a theme in a story, **38** that requires integrating and bringing together information from many distant parts of the brain, but is not particularly active in emotional responses.

The subjects were asked to perform a challenging verbal association task, press a button as soon as **39** solving it, and report whether or not they felt the "Aha!" feeling. If they did, the response was classified as an "insight" solution. If they did not, it was classified as a "non-insight" solution.

40 What was interesting, experimenters found that the insight solutions were accompanied by an elevated level of "gamma band" activity in the RH aSTG, supporting the theory that the feeling **41** had corresponded

37

A) NO CHANGE
B) experiment by which subjects
C) experiment where subjects
D) experiment, in which subjects

38

A) NO CHANGE
B) that require integrating and bringing together
C) that require integrating
D) that requires integrating

39

A) NO CHANGE
B) it was being solved
C) they solved it
D) it's solution

40

A) NO CHANGE
B) The interesting thing was that
C) It was interesting that
D) Interestingly,

41

A) NO CHANGE
B) corresponds
C) is corresponding
D) will correspond

CONTINUE ➔

2   **2**

to a cognitive process rather than purely an emotional one. **42**

Interpreting **43** this data is not a very simple matter, however. Many questions remain to be answered. For instance, does the increased gamma-band activity represent a transition of cognitive processing from an unconscious state to a conscious one? **44** If that is true, a question would be what are the unconscious processes that are working? Also, in what way do those processes become conscious all of a sudden?

42

At this point in the passage, the author wants to mention specific evidence indicated by the graph. Which statement is most justified by the data in this graph?

A) The gamma power in the RH aSTG for the insight solution is more than double that for the non-insight solution.

B) This increase in activity seems to begin about 0.3 seconds prior to the button-press response, and to lasts about 1 second.

C) The gamma activity for the insight solution appears to be roughly equivalent to that for the non-insight solution until the instant the button is pushed.

D) This increase in activity seems to begin about 0.3 seconds after the button-press response, and to last about 0.5 second.

43

A) NO CHANGE

B) this data are

C) these data are

D) these data is

44

Which of the following best combines the last two sentences into one?

A) If so, what are the unconscious processes that are working, suddenly becoming conscious?

B) If so, what unconscious processes are at work, and how do they suddenly become conscious?

C) If so, what would be the unconscious processes working, and how would they suddenly become conscious?

D) If so, what are both the unconscious process at work, and how do they suddenly become conscious?

STOP

**If you finish before time is called, you may check your work on this section only.
Do not turn to any other section of the test.**

3   **3**

Math Test – No Calculator

25 MINUTES, 20 QUESTIONS

Turn to Section 3 of your answer sheet to answer the questions in this section.

DIRECTIONS

For questions 1–15, solve each problem, choose the best answer from the choices provided, and fill in the corresponding circle on your answer sheet. **For questions 16–20,** solve the problem and enter your answer in the grid on the answer sheet. Please refer to the directions before question 16 on how to enter you answers in the grid. You may use any available space in your test booklet for scratch work.

NOTES

1. The use of a calculator is NOT permitted.
2. All variables and expressions used represent real numbers unless otherwise indicated.
3. Figures provided in this test are drawn to scale unless otherwise indicated.
4. All figures lie in a plane unless otherwise indicated.
5. Unless otherwise indicated, the domain of a given function f is the set of all real numbers for which $f(x)$ is a real number.

REFERENCE

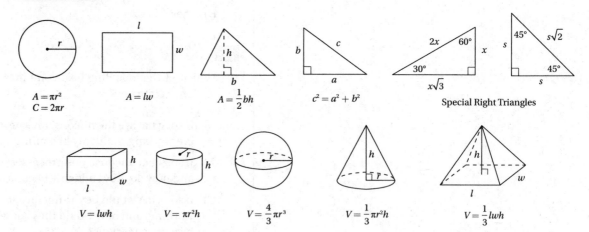

$A = \pi r^2$
$C = 2\pi r$

$A = lw$

$A = \frac{1}{2}bh$

$c^2 = a^2 + b^2$

Special Right Triangles

$V = lwh$

$V = \pi r^2 h$

$V = \frac{4}{3}\pi r^3$

$V = \frac{1}{3}\pi r^2 h$

$V = \frac{1}{3}lwh$

The number of degrees of arc in a circle is 360.
The number of radians of arc in a circle is 2π.
The sum of the measures in degrees of the angles of a triangle is 180.

CONTINUE ➡

3 **3**

1

If $6x + 9 = 30$, what is the value of $2x + 3$?

A) 5

B) 10

C) 15

D) 20

2

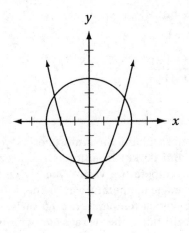

$$x^2 + y^2 = 9$$
$$y = x^2 - 4$$

A system of two equations and their graphs in the *xy*-plane are shown above. How many solutions does the system have?

A) One

B) Two

C) Three

D) Four

3

A total of 300 tickets were sold for a performance of a school play. The ticket prices were $5 for each adult and $3 for each child, and the total revenue from tickets was $1,400. Solving which of the following systems of equations would yield the number of adult tickets sold, *a*, and the number of children's tickets sold, *c*?

A) $a + c = 1,400$

  $5a + 3c = 300$

B) $a + c = 300$

  $5a + 3c = 1,400$

C) $a + c = 300$

  $3a + 5c = 1,400$

D) $a + c = 300$

  $3a + 5c = 1,400 \times 2$

4

Which of the following expressions is equivalent to $2(x - 4)^2 - 5x$?

A) $2x^2 - 21x + 32$

B) $2x^2 - 21x - 32$

C) $2x^2 - 13x + 32$

D) $2x^2 - 16x - 21$

5

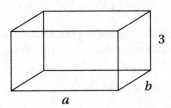

Note: Figure not drawn to scale

A rectangular solid above has dimensions 3, *a*, and *b*, where *a* and *b* are integers. Which of the following CANNOT be the areas of three different faces of this solid?

A) 15, 18, and 30

B) 18, 24, and 48

C) 12, 15, and 24

D) 15, 24, and 40

CONTINUE ➔

6

The cost in dollars, C, to manufacture n necklaces is given by the equation $C(n) = an + b$, where a and b are positive constants. In this equation, what does a represent?

A) the fixed costs, in dollars, independent of any necklaces being manufactured

B) the total cost, in dollars, to produce n necklaces, not including fixed costs

C) the total cost, in dollars, to produce one necklace, including fixed costs

D) the cost, in dollars, to produce one necklace, not including any fixed costs

7

Line l intersects the graph of the function $f(x) = 2x^2 - 4x + 1$ at two points where $x = -1$ and $x = 2$, respectively. What is the slope of line l?

A) -2

B) $-\dfrac{2}{3}$

C) $\dfrac{3}{2}$

D) 2

8

Which of the following equations represents a parabola in the xy-plane with a vertex that lies on the x-axis?

A) $y = (x-3)^2 + 2$

B) $y = 2(x-3)^2$

C) $y = 2x^2 - 3$

D) $y = 3x^2 + 2$

9

If the function $m(x)$ satisfies the equation $\dfrac{m(x)}{x+3} - \dfrac{x+1}{x-1} = 1$ for all values of x greater than 1, then $m(x) =$

A) $\dfrac{2(x+3)}{x-1}$

B) $\dfrac{2(x^2+3x+3)}{x-1}$

C) $\dfrac{2(x+6)}{x-1}$

D) $\dfrac{2x(x+3)}{x-1}$

10

In the mesosphere, the atmospheric layer between 50 km and 80 km in altitude, the average atmospheric temperature varies linearly with altitude. If the average temperature at 50 km altitude is 10°C and the average temperature at 80 km is −80°C, then at what altitude is the average temperature −50°C?

A) 60 km

B) 65 km

C) 70 km

D) 75 km

11

The graph of the equation $y = 2x^2 - 16x + 14$ intersects the y-axis at point A and the x-axis at points B and C. What is the area of triangle ABC?

A) 42

B) 48

C) 54

D) 56

CONTINUE

3   **3**

12

What is the total number of x- and y-intercepts in the graph of the equation $y = (x + 2)^2(x - 3)^2$?

A) Two

B) Three

C) Four

D) Five

13

If the complex number A satisfies the equation

$A(2 - i) = 2 + i$, where $i = \sqrt{-1}$, what is the value of A?

A) $5 - i$

B) $5 + i$

C) $\dfrac{3}{5} + \dfrac{4}{5}i$

D) $\dfrac{3}{4} + \dfrac{5}{4}i$

14

If $k > 2$, which of the following could be the graph of $y + x = k(x - 1)$ in the xy-plane?

A)

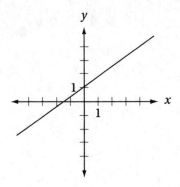

B)

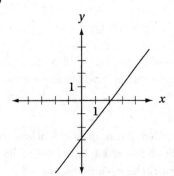

C)

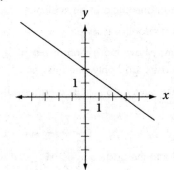

D)

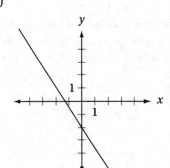

15

The function $g(x) = ax^3 + bx^2 + cx + d$ has zeroes at $x = -2$, $x = 3$, and $x = 6$. If $g(0) < 0$, which of the following must also be negative?

A) $g(-3)$

B) $g(-1)$

C) $g(4)$

D) $g(5)$

CONTINUE ➡

3   **3**

For questions 16–20, solve the problem and enter your answer in the grid, as described below, on the answer sheet.

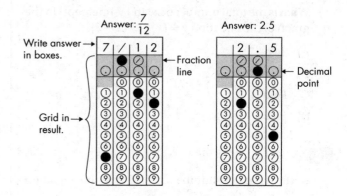

1. Although not required, it is suggested that you write your answer in the boxes at the top of the columns to help you fill in the circles accurately. You will receive credit only if the circles are filled in correctly.

2. Mark no more than one circle in any column.

3. No question has a negative answer.

4. Some problems may have more than one correct answer. In such cases, grid only one answer.

5. **Mixed numbers** such as $3\frac{1}{2}$ must be gridded as 3.5 or $\frac{7}{2}$.

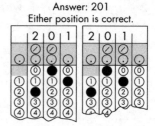

(If $3\frac{1}{2}$ is entered into the grid as [grid], it will be interpreted as $\frac{31}{2}$, not $3\frac{1}{2}$).

6. **Decimal answers:** If you obtain a decimal answer with more digits than the grid can accommodate, it may be either rounded or truncated, but it must fill the entire grid.

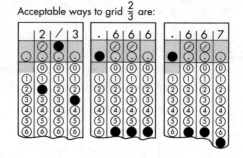

Acceptable ways to grid $\frac{2}{3}$ are:

CONTINUE ▶

3 **3**

16

If $\dfrac{2}{3}x + \dfrac{1}{2}y = 5$, what is the value of $4x + 3y$?

17

If $\dfrac{5}{x} - \dfrac{2}{5} = 1$, what is the value of x?

18

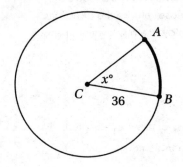

Note: Figure not drawn to scale.

In the circle above, arc AB has a measure of 7π. What is the value of x?

19

$$\frac{1}{2}x = \frac{1}{3}y + \frac{1}{10}$$
$$6x - 4y = k$$

For what value of k will the system of equations above have at least one solution?

20

If x represents the radian measure of an angle, where $0 \le x \le \dfrac{\pi}{2}$, and $\sin x = \dfrac{5}{13}$, then what is the value of $\tan\left(\dfrac{\pi}{2} - x\right)$?

STOP

**If you finish before time is called, you may check your work on this section only.
Do not turn to any other section of the test.**

4 4

Math Test – Calculator

55 MINUTES, 38 QUESTIONS

Turn to Section 4 of your answer sheet to answer the questions in this section.

DIRECTIONS

For questions 1–30, solve each problem, choose the best answer from the choices provided, and fill in the corresponding circle on your answer sheet. **For questions 31–38,** solve the problem and enter your answer in the grid on the answer sheet. Please refer to the directions before question 31 on how to enter your answers in the grid. You may use any available space in your test booklet for scratch work.

NOTES

1. The use of a calculator **is permitted.**

2. All variables and expressions used represent real numbers unless otherwise indicated.

3. Figures provided in this test are drawn to scale unless otherwise indicated.

4. All figures lie in a plane unless otherwise indicated.

5. Unless otherwise indicated, the domain of a given function f is the set of all real numbers for which $f(x)$ is a real number.

REFERENCE

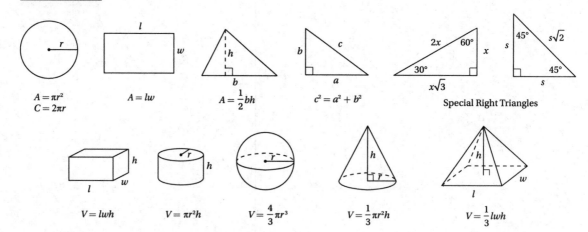

$A = \pi r^2$
$C = 2\pi r$

$A = lw$

$A = \frac{1}{2}bh$

$c^2 = a^2 + b^2$

Special Right Triangles

$V = lwh$

$V = \pi r^2 h$

$V = \frac{4}{3}\pi r^3$

$V = \frac{1}{3}\pi r^2 h$

$V = \frac{1}{3}lwh$

The number of degrees of arc in a circle is 360.
The number of radians of arc in a circle is 2π.
The sum of the measures in degrees of the angles of a triangle is 180.

CONTINUE

4

4

1

$$a - b = 10$$
$$a - 2b = 8$$

Based on the system of equations above, what is the value of b?

A) −2

B) −1

C) 1

D) 2

2

The average (arithmetic mean) of three numbers is 50. If two of the numbers have a sum of 85, what is the third number?

A) 75

B) 70

C) 65

D) 55

3

What number is the same percent of 225 as 9 is of 25?

A) 27

B) 54

C) 64

D) 81

4

RESULTS OF FAVORABILITY POLL

	Favorable	Unfavorable	No Opinion	Total
Men	26		12	
Women			13	89
Total	59			162

The table above shows the partial results of a favorability poll for a local politician. If the data shown are correct, how many of the women who were polled viewed the politician unfavorably?

A) 33

B) 43

C) 61

D) It cannot be determined by the information given.

5

If $2^{2n-2} = 32$, what is the value of n?

A) 2.0

B) 2.5

C) 3.0

D) 3.5

6

A bag of Nellie's Nut Mix contains x ounces of walnuts, 15 ounces of peanuts, and 20 ounces of pecans. Which of the following expresses the fraction of the mix, by weight, that is walnuts?

A) $\dfrac{x}{35}$

B) $\dfrac{x}{35-x}$

C) $\dfrac{x}{35+x}$

D) $\dfrac{35-x}{35+x}$

CONTINUE

4 **4**

7

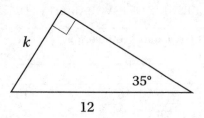

In the triangle above, what is the value of k? ($\sin 35° = 0.574$, $\cos 35° = 0.819$, $\tan 35° = 0.700$)

A) 6.00

B) 6.88

C) 8.40

D) 9.83

8

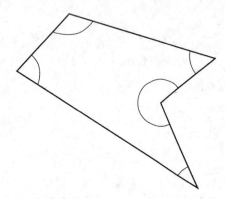

The figure above shows a polygon with five sides. What is the average (arithmetic mean) of the measures, in degrees, of the five angles shown?

A) 108°

B) 110°

C) 112°

D) 114°

Questions 9 and 10 are based on the graph below.

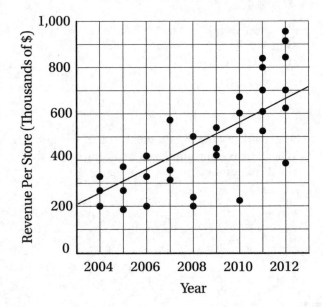

ANNUAL REVENUE PER STORE

9

The scatterplot above shows the annual revenue for each of the individual retail stores operated by a clothing company for each year from 2004 through 2012. Based on the line of best fit to the data shown, which of the following is closest to the average annual increase in revenue per store?

A) $5,000

B) $50,000

C) $100,000

D) $500,000

4   **4**

10

Which of the following statements is most directly justified by the data shown in the scatterplot above?

A) The average revenue per store increased by over 100% from 2005 to 2009.

B) The total number of retail stores increased by 50% from 2005 to 2012.

C) The total revenue from all stores in 2012 was more than three times the total revenue from all stores in 2004.

D) The total revenue from all stores in 2008 was over $1 million.

▲

11

Which of the following statements expresses the fact that the product of two numbers, a and b, is 6 greater than their sum?

A) $ab + 6 > a + b$

B) $ab = a + b + 6$

C) $ab + 6 = a + b$

D) $ab > a + b + 6$

12

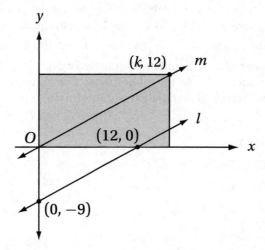

Note: Figure not drawn to scale.

In the figure above, if $m \parallel l$, what is the area, in square units, of the shaded rectangle?

A) 156

B) 168

C) 180

D) 192

13

The Glenville Giants have played a total of 120 games and have a win-to-loss ratio of 2 to 3. How many more games have they lost than won?

A) 24

B) 30

C) 40

D) 48

CONTINUE ▶

14

A culture of bacteria initially contained p cells, where $p > 100$. After one hour, this population decreased by $\frac{1}{3}$. In the second and third hours, however, the population increased by 40% and 50%, respectively. At the end of those first three hours, what was the population of the culture?

A) $1.3p$

B) $1.4p$

C) $1.5p$

D) $1.6p$

15

If $(6^{-2})(m^{-2}) = \frac{1}{16}$, what is the value of m^2?

A) $\frac{1}{9}$

B) $\frac{4}{9}$

C) $\frac{9}{16}$

D) $\frac{9}{4}$

16

A jar contains only red, white, and blue marbles. It contains twice as many red marbles as white marbles and three times as many white marbles as blue marbles. If a marble is chosen at random, what is the probability that it is <u>not</u> red?

A) $\frac{1}{5}$

B) $\frac{2}{5}$

C) $\frac{3}{5}$

D) $\frac{4}{5}$

17

$$y = -3(x - 2)^2 + 2$$

In the xy-plane, line l passes through the point $(-1, 3)$ and the vertex of the parabola with equation above. What is the slope of line l?

A) $-\frac{2}{3}$

B) $-\frac{1}{2}$

C) $-\frac{1}{3}$

D) $\frac{1}{3}$

18

A certain function takes an input value and transforms it into an output value according to the following three-step procedure:

Step 1: Multiply the input value by 6.

Step 2: Add x to this result.

Step 3: Divide this result by 4.

If an input of 7 to this function yields an output of 15, what is the value of x?

A) 12

B) 16

C) 18

D) 24

CONTINUE

4 **4**

19

The variables x and y are believed to correlate according to the equation $y = ax^2 + bx + c$, where a, b, and c are constants. Which of the following scatterplots would provide the strongest evidence in support of the hypothesis that $a < 0$?

A)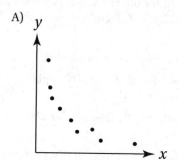

B)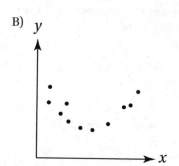

C)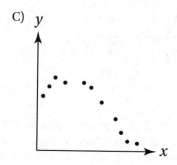

D)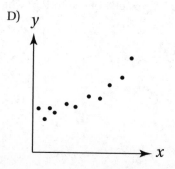

20

On a number line, the coordinates of points P and R are p and r, respectively, and $p < r$. If the point with coordinate x is closer to p than to r, then which of the following statements must be true?

A) $x < \dfrac{p-r}{2}$

B) $x < \dfrac{p+r}{2}$

C) $|x-p| < r$

D) $|x+p| < r-p$

21

Let function $f(x)$ be defined by the equation $f(x) = \dfrac{1}{2-x}$. If m is a positive integer, then $f\left(\dfrac{1}{m}\right) =$

A) $\dfrac{m}{2m-1}$

B) $\dfrac{m}{m^2-1}$

C) $\dfrac{1}{2-m}$

D) $2 - m$

22

The value of y varies with x according to the equation $y = a(x - 2)(x + 1)$, where $a < 0$. As the value of x increases from 0 to 5, which of the following best describes the behavior of y?

A) It increases and then decreases.

B) It decreases and then increases.

C) It increases only.

D) It decreases only.

CONTINUE ▶

23

If the expression $\dfrac{n^2-9}{n^2+3}$ is equivalent to the expression $1-\dfrac{k}{n^2+3}$ for all values of n, what is the value of k?

A) −12

B) −6

C)   6

D)   12

24

An online trading company charges a 3% commission for all stock purchases. If a trader purchases 200 shares of a stock through this company and is charged $3,399 including commission, what is the cost per share for this stock?

A) $16.45

B) $16.48

C) $16.50

D) $16.52

25

For nonzero numbers w and y, if w is 50% greater than y, then what is the ratio of w^{-2} to y^{-2}?

A)   4 to 9

B)   2 to 3

C)   9 to 4

D)   4 to 1

26

Every athlete in a group of 60 female varsity athletes at Greenwich High School either runs track, plays soccer, or does both. If one-third of the athletes in this group who play on the soccer team also run on the track team, and one-half of the athletes in this group who run on the track team also play on the soccer team, which of the following statements must be true?

A) This group contains 40 soccer players.

B) This group contains 20 athletes who play soccer but do not run track.

C) This group contains 20 athletes who play both track and soccer.

D) The number of soccer players in this group is 15 greater than the number of track team members in this group.

27

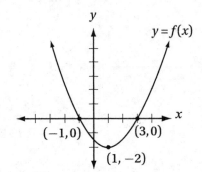

A portion of the graph of the quadratic function $y=f(x)$ is shown in the xy-plane above. The function g is defined by the equation $g(x) = f(x) + b$. If the equation $g(x) = 0$ has exactly one solution, what is the value of b?

A) −2

B) −1

C)   1

D)   2

4 **4**

28

If $\cos x = a$, where $\dfrac{\pi}{2} < x < \pi$, and $\cos y = -a$, then which of the following could be the value of y?

A) $x + 2\pi$

B) $x + \pi$

C) $x + \dfrac{\pi}{2}$

D) $-x + 2\pi$

Questions 29 and 30 refer to the following table.

OPINION POLL ON PROPOSAL 81A

Age of Voter	Approve	Disapprove	No Opinion	Total
18 to 39	918	204	502	1,624
40 to 64	1,040	502	102	1,644
65 and older	604	420	115	1,139
Total	2,562	1,126	719	4,407

29

Of those surveyed who expressed an opinion on Proposal 81a, approximately what percentage are under 40 years of age?

A) 30%

B) 38%

C) 68%

D) 72%

30

If the data in the table above are assumed to be representative of the general voting population, which of the following statements is most directly justified by these data?

A) The approval rate for Proposal 81a generally decreases with the age of the voter.

B) The disapproval rate for Proposal 81a generally increases with the age of the voter.

C) Those who express an opinion on Proposal 81a are more likely to be over 64 than they are to be under 40.

D) In all three age categories, voters are more than twice as likely to approve of Proposal 18a than to have no opinion about it.

CONTINUE

4 **4**

Student-Produced Response Questions

DIRECTIONS

For questions 31–38, solve the problem and enter your answer in the grid, as described below, on the answer sheet.

1. Although not required, it is suggested that you write your answer in the boxes at the top of the columns to help you fill in the circles accurately. You will receive credit only if the circles are filled in correctly.

2. Mark no more than one circle in any column.

3. No question has a negative answer.

4. Some problems may have more than one correct answer. In such cases, grid only one answer.

5. **Mixed numbers** such as $3\frac{1}{2}$ must be gridded as 3.5 or $\frac{7}{2}$.

   (If $3\frac{1}{2}$ is entered into the grid as [3 1 / 2], it will be interpreted as $\frac{31}{2}$, not $3\frac{1}{2}$.)

6. **Decimal answers:** If you obtain a decimal answer with more digits than the grid can accommodate, it may be either rounded or truncated, but it must fill the entire grid.

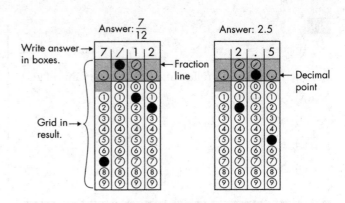

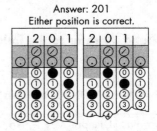

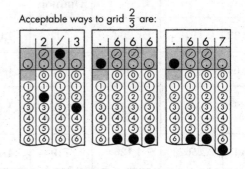

CONTINUE →

4 **4**

31

If y varies inversely as x, and $y = \frac{1}{2}$ when $x = 10$, then for what value of x does $y = 25$?

32

If $x^2 + 12x = 13$, and $x < 0$, what is the value of x^2?

33

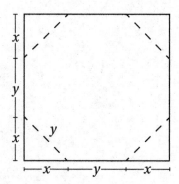

Four triangles are to be cut and removed from a square piece of sheet metal to create an octagonal sign with eight equal sides, as shown in the figure above. If the total area of the removed material is 196 square centimeters, what is the perimeter, in centimeters, of the octagon?

34

If m and n are integers such that $m^2 + n^2 = 40$ and $m < 0 < n$, what is the value of $(m + n)^2$?

35

If $(\cos x)(\sin x) = 0.2$, what is the value of $(\cos x + \sin x)^2$?

36

MONTHLY SALES (FEBRUARY)

Item	Price Per Item	Number Sold
Model AT350	$120	20
Model U32	$98	80
Model GY53	$140	62
Model CDP3	$162	38
Model AP14	$110	40

The table above shows information about the February sales for five different cell phone models at a local store. What was the median price, to the nearest dollar, of the 240 phones sold in February?

CONTINUE

Questions 37 and 38 are based on the scenario described below. Enter your responses on the corresponding grids on your answer sheet.

Performance Banner Company creates promotional banners that include company logos. The Zypz Running Shoe Company would like a 4-foot high and 20-foot long banner that includes its logo, which has a height-to-length ratio of 5:8.

37

If the logo were scaled so that its height matched the height of the banner and then were placed in the center of the banner, then what would be the width, in feet, of each margin on either side of the logo?

38

Performance Banner Company charges its customers $1.20 per square foot for the banner material, $2.50 per square foot of any printed logo, and $32 in fixed costs per banner. The Zypz Running Shoe Company is considering two options for the banner: one with a single logo, and another with two logos. If these logos are all to be the same size as described in Part 1, what percent of the banner costs would the company save by choosing the single-logo option instead of the two-logo option? (Ignore the % symbol when entering into the grid. For example, enter 27% as 27.)

STOP

If you finish before time is called, you may check your work on this section only.
Do not turn to any other section of the test.

5   **5**

Essay

50 MINUTES, 1 QUESTION

DIRECTIONS

As you read the passage below, consider how Steven Pinker uses

- evidence, such as facts or examples, to support his claims
- reasoning to develop ideas and connect claims and evidence
- stylistic or persuasive elements, such as word choice or appeals to emotion, to add power to the ideas expressed

---

Adapted from Steven Pinker, "Mind Over Mass Media." ©2010 by The New York Times. Originally published June 10, 2010.

1 New forms of media have always caused moral panics: the printing press, newspapers, paperbacks and television were all once denounced as threats to their consumers' brainpower and moral fiber.

2 So too with electronic technologies. PowerPoint, we're told, is reducing discourse to bullet points. Search engines lower our intelligence, encouraging us to skim on the surface of knowledge rather than dive to its depths. Twitter is shrinking our attention spans.

3 But such panics often fail reality checks. When comic books were accused of turning juveniles into delinquents in the 1950s, crime was falling to record lows, just as the denunciations of video games in the 1990s coincided with the great American crime decline. The decades of television, transistor radios and rock videos were also decades in which I.Q. scores rose continuously.

4 For a reality check today, take the state of science, which demands high levels of brainwork and is measured by clear benchmarks of discovery. Today, scientists are never far from their e-mail and cannot lecture without PowerPoint. If electronic media were hazardous to intelligence, the quality of science would be plummeting. Yet discoveries are multiplying like fruit flies, and progress is dizzying. Other activities in the life of the mind, like philosophy, history and cultural criticism, are likewise flourishing.

5 Critics of new media sometimes use science itself to press their case, citing research that shows how "experience can change the brain." But cognitive neuroscientists roll their eyes at such talk. Yes, every time we learn a fact or skill the wiring of the brain changes; it's not as if the information is stored in the pancreas. But the existence of neural plasticity does not mean the brain is a blob of clay pounded into shape by experience.

6 Experience does not revamp the basic information-processing capacities of the brain. Speed-reading programs have long claimed to do just that, but the verdict was rendered by Woody Allen after he read War and Peace in one sitting: "It was about Russia." Genuine multitasking, too, has been exposed as a myth, not just by laboratory studies but by the familiar sight of an SUV undulating between lanes as the driver cuts deals on his cellphone.

7   Moreover, the evidence indicates that the effects of experience are highly specific to the experiences themselves. If you train people to do one thing, they get better at doing that thing, but almost nothing else. Music doesn't make you better at math; conjugating Latin doesn't make you more logical; brain-training games don't make you smarter. Accomplished people don't bulk up their brains with intellectual calisthenics; they immerse themselves in their fields. Novelists read lots of novels; scientists read lots of science.

8   The effects of consuming electronic media are also likely to be far more limited than the panic implies. Media critics write as if the brain takes on the qualities of whatever it consumes, the informational equivalent of "you are what you eat." As with primitive peoples who believe that eating fierce animals will make them fierce, they assume that watching quick cuts in rock videos turns your mental life into quick cuts or that reading bullet points and Twitter postings turns your thoughts into bullet points and Twitter postings.

9   Yes, the constant arrival of information packets can be distracting or addictive, especially to people with attention deficit disorder. But distraction is not a new phenomenon. The solution is not to bemoan technology but to develop strategies of self-control, as we do with every other temptation in life. Turn off e-mail or Twitter when you work, put away your BlackBerry at dinner time, ask your spouse to call you to bed at a designated hour.

10 And to encourage intellectual depth, don't rail at PowerPoint or Google. It's not as if habits of deep reflection, thorough research and rigorous reasoning ever came naturally to people. They must be acquired in special institutions, which we call universities, and maintained with constant upkeep, which we call analysis, criticism and debate. They are not granted by propping a heavy encyclopedia on your lap, nor are they taken away by efficient access to information on the Internet.

11 The new media have caught on for a reason. Knowledge is increasing exponentially; human brainpower and waking hours are not. Fortunately, the Internet and information technologies are helping us manage, search, and retrieve our collective intellectual output at different scales, from Twitter and previews to e-books and online encyclopedias. Far from making us stupid, these technologies are the only things that will keep us smart.

Write an essay in which you explain how Steven Pinker builds an argument to persuade his audience that new media are not destroying our moral and intellectual abilities. In your essay, analyze how Pinker uses one or more of the features listed in the box above (or features of your own choice) to strengthen the logic and persuasiveness of his argument. Be sure that your analysis focuses on the most relevant features of the passage.

Your essay should NOT explain whether you agree with Pinker's claims, but rather explain how Pinker builds an argument to persuade his audience.

DIAGNOSTIC SAT ANSWER KEY

Section 1: Reading	Section 2: Writing and Language	Section 3: Math (No Calculator)	Section 4: Math (Calculator)
1. C	1. B	1. B	1. D
2. A	2. C	2. D	2. C
3. C	3. C	3. B	3. D
4. B	4. A	4. A	4. B
5. D	5. B	5. C	5. D
6. C	6. C	6. D	6. C
7. D	7. A	7. A	7. B
8. A	8. D	8. B	8. A
9. B	9. A	9. D	9. B
10. D	10. D	10. C	10. C
11. B	11. D	11. A	11. B
12. C	12. C	12. B	12. D
13. C	13. B	13. C	13. A
14. D	14. D	14. B	14. B
15. A	15. A	15. B	15. B
16. D	16. B	-------	16. B
17. B	17. C	16. 30	17. C
18. D	18. D	17. 25/7 or 3.57	18. C
19. C	19. C	18. 35	19. C
20. B	20. D	19. 1.2	20. B
21. B	21. B	20. 2.4	21. A
22. C	22. A		22. A
23. D	23. D		23. D
24. D	24. C		24. C
25. A	25. A		25. A
26. A	26. D		26. D
27. C	27. C		27. D
28. C	28. B		28. B
29. C	29. C		29. A
30. B	30. D		30. B
31. A	31. A		-------
32. B	32. C		31. 1/5 or 0.2
33. C	33. B		32. 169
34. C	34. B		33. 112
35. A	35. A		34. 16
36. A	36. B		35. 1.4
37. B	37. D		36. 115
38. B	38. C		37. 6.8
39. B	39. C		38. 25
40. B	40. D		
41. A	41. B		
42. D	42. B		
43. C	43. D		
44. B	44. B		
45. D			
46. A			
47. A			
48. D			
49. D			
50. C			
51. B			
52. D			

Total Reading Points (Section 1)	Total Writing and Language Points (Section 2)	Total Math Points (Section 3)	Total Math Points (Section 4)

SCORE CONVERSION TABLE

Scoring Your Test

1. Use the answer key to mark your responses on each section.

2. Total the number of correct responses for each section:

    1. Reading Test   Number correct: _____ **(Reading Raw Score)**

    2. Writing and Language Test   Number correct: _____ **(Writing and Language Raw Score)**

    3. Mathematics Test – No Calculator   Number correct: _____

    4. Mathematics Test – Calculator   Number correct: _____

3. Add the raw scores for sections 3 and 4. This is your **Math Raw Score**: _____

4. Use the Table 1 to calculate your **Scaled Test and Section Scores (10–40)**.

    Math Section Score (200–800):   _____

    Reading Test Score (10–40):   _____

    Writing and Language Test Score (10–40):   _____

5. Add the **Reading Test Scaled Score** and the **Writing and Language Test Scaled Score** and multiply this sum by 10 to get your **Reading and Writing Test Section Score (20–80)**.

    Sum of Reading + Writing and Language Scores: _____ × 10 =

    Reading and Writing Section Score: _____

Table 1: Scaled Section and Test Scores (10–40)

Raw Score	Math Section Score	Reading Test Score	Writing/ Language Test Score	Raw Score	Math Section Score	Reading Test Score	Writing/ Language Test Score
58	800			29	520	27	28
57	790			28	520	26	28
56	780			27	510	26	27
55	760			26	500	25	26
54	750			25	490	25	26
53	740			24	480	24	25
52	730	40		23	480	24	25
51	710	40		22	470	23	24
50	700	39		21	460	23	23
49	690	38		20	450	22	23
48	680	38		19	440	22	22
47	670	37		18	430	21	21
46	670	37		17	420	21	21
45	660	36		16	410	20	20
44	650	35	40	15	390	20	19
43	640	35	39	14	380	19	19
42	630	34	38	13	370	19	18
41	620	33	37	12	360	18	17
40	610	33	36	11	340	17	16
39	600	32	35	10	330	17	16
38	600	32	34	9	320	16	15
37	590	31	34	8	310	15	14
36	580	31	33	7	290	15	13
35	570	30	32	6	280	14	13
34	560	30	32	5	260	13	12
33	560	29	31	4	240	12	11
32	550	29	30	3	230	11	10
31	540	28	30	2	210	10	10
30	530	28	29	1	200	10	10

DIAGNOSTIC SAT DETAILED ANSWER KEY

Section 1: Reading

1. C   **Specific Purpose**

Let's translate this question into a "stand-alone" question: "How is Smith's work presented in the first paragraph?" The passage states (line 3) that *Karl Smith has a good rule of thumb for* **categorizing** *epidemics*, then goes on to describe various types of epidemics in an effort to help visualize the types of spread. In other words, he is proposing a model for *conceptualizing phenomena*. (Note that the word *phenomena* refers simply to common occurrences. It has a neutral tone, not a positive one.)

2. A   **Inference**

The passage states in lines 67–72 that *Nevin's paper was almost completely ignored* because *Nevin was an economist, not a criminologist, and his paper was published in* Environmental Research, *not a journal with a big readership in the criminology community.* In other words, Nevin's paper was ignored because it *was not presented by authorities with the proper credentials.*

3. C   **Textual Evidence**

As the explanation to question 2 indicates, the evidence for this answer is lines 67–72, which includes the statement in (C).

4. B   **Inference from Data**

According to the graph, in 1963 there were 150 violent crimes per 100,000 capita, and in 1993 there were 750 violent crimes per 100,000 capita. This is an increase of 600 crimes per 100,000, and 600 is 400% of 150.

5. D   **Inference from Data**

Nevin's hypothesis is phrased in the form of a question in lines 27–28: *Maybe reducing lead exposure had an effect on violent crime too?* Therefore, the portion of the graph that would *least* support his hypothesis is the portion that shows the *least* correlation between lead exposure and crime. The biggest gap in the two graphs (and hence the portion that provides the least support for his thesis) corresponds to the set of violent crime statistics from 2003 to 2013.

6. C   **Specific Purpose**

The *sales of vinyl LPs* are mentioned to describe a statistic that also happens to correlate with preschool blood lead levels, thereby making the point that *a single correlation between two curves isn't all that impressive, econometrically speaking . . . No matter how good the fit, if you*

only have a single correlation it might just be coincidence. Hence, it is a statistic that may be more coincidental than explanatory.

7. D   **Interpretation**

The sentence in lines 21–24 indicates that *lead exposure in small children [had been linked] with a whole raft of complications later in life, including lower IQ, hyperactivity, behavioral problems, and learning disabilities.* These *complications* are *psychological problems* for those exposed to lead at a young age.

8. A   **Interpretation**

When the passage states that the *drivers* were *unwittingly creating a crime wave two decades later* (lines 63–64), it indicates that they were *inadvertent abettors.*

9. B   **Word in Context**

The phrase *even better* (line 49) refers to the finding mentioned in the previous sentence that *the similarity of the curves was as good as it seemed*, suggesting that the data showed an even stronger correlation than Nevin had hoped.

10. D   **Specific Purpose**

The final paragraph discusses the fact that the *gasoline lead hypothesis* explains many additional phenomena, such as the difference between the murder rates in large cities (where there are lots of cars) and small cities (where there are fewer cars and therefore less lead exhaust exposure). These implications further support the hypothesis.

11. B   **Cross-Textual Inference**

The author of Passage 1 indicates that Hemingway was a legendary figure whose work *seemed . . . to have been carved from the living stone of life* (lines 25–26) and therefore had a great impact on the author and his friends. Passage 2, however, suggests that Hemingway's works don't have the impact they once did, saying that they *now seem unable to evoke the same sense of a tottering world that in the 1920s established Ernest Hemingway's reputation* (lines 48–50) and *no longer seem to penetrate deeply the surface of existence* (lines 57–58). Therefore, the two passages disagree most strongly on the *incisiveness* (deep analytical quality) of Hemingway's work.

12. C   **Textual Evidence**

As the answer to the previous question indicates, the best evidence for this answer is found in lines 24–26 and lines 56–58.

---

13. C **Cross-Textual Interpretation**

The author of Passage 1 regards Hemingway as a *legend* (line 16) whose *impact upon us was tremendous* (lines 18–19), but the author of Passage 2 calls Hemingway a *dupe of his culture rather than its moral-aesthetic conscience* (lines 66–67).

---

14. D **Cross-Textual Inference**

The author of Passage 1 indicates that, although Hemingway's work had a strong formative impact on him, it ultimately could not capture the true horrors of war that he and his friends were later to encounter:

The Hemingway time was a good time to be young. We had much then that the war later forced out of us, something far greater than Hemingway's strong formative influence (lines 33–36).

Likewise, the author of Passage 2 indicates that Hemingway's work did not fully capture the horrors of war: *We have had more war than Hemingway ever dreamed of* (lines 53–54) . . . *yet Hemingway's great novels no longer seem to penetrate deeply the surface of existence* (lines 56–58).

---

15. A **Word in Context, Purpose**

In saying that *the words he put down seemed to us to have been carved from the living stone of life* (lines 24–26), the author of Passage 1 means that Hemingway's words represent living truths that have the weight and permanence of stone carvings. In other words, his words represent the *salient* (prominent and important) *experience* of life.

---

16. D **Interpretation**

In saying that *we began unconsciously to translate our own sensations into their terms and to impose on everything we did and felt the particular emotions they aroused in us* (lines 28–32) the author is saying that he and his friends *identified* with Hemingway's language.

---

17. B **Inference**

According to Passage 1, the *lessons that [Hemingway] had to teach* (line 43) included the example he set as a war correspondent *writing a play in the Hotel Florida in Madrid while thirty fascist shells crashed through the roof* (lines 10–12) and as a soldier *defending his post single-handedly against fierce German attacks* (lines 13–15), both of which exemplify *confidence in the face of danger*.

---

18. D **Specific Purpose**

The phrase *a tottering world* (line 49) is used to describe the Europe of the 1920s that Ernest Hemingway depicts in his novels. The author compares this world to one whose *social structure is . . . shaken* (lines 51–52) and which had *more war than Hemingway ever dreamed*

of (line 54). In other words, a world filled with *societal upheaval*.

---

19. C **Cross-Textual Inference**

The author of Passage 1 clearly views Hemingway as a personal and literary hero. Hence, a withering accusation such as the one in Passage 2 that *Hemingway, in effect, became a dupe of his culture rather than its moral-aesthetic conscience* (lines 66–67) would almost certainly be met with *vehement disagreement*.

Tip: Questions about how the author of one passage might *most likely* respond to some statement in another passage require us to focus on the *thesis and tone* of that author. Before attempting to answer such questions, remind yourself of the central theses of the passages.

---

20. B **Textual Evidence**

The best evidence for this answer comes from lines 28–32, where the author of Passage 1 says that *we began to unconsciously translate our own sensations into their terms and to impose on everything we did and felt the particular emotions they aroused in us*. In other words, Hemingway was in fact a kind of *moral-aesthetic conscience* for the author of Passage 1 and his friends.

---

21. B **Interpretation**

Passage 2 states that Hemingway's novels *yielded to the functionalist, technological aesthetic of the culture instead of resisting in the manner of Frank Lloyd Wright* (lines 63–66). In other words, Frank Lloyd Wright was more *iconoclastic* (culturally rebellious) than Hemingway.

---

22. C **Specific Purpose**

The first paragraph establishes the idea that *atoms, the building blocks of everything we know and love . . . don't appear to be models of stability*, a fact that represents a *scientific conundrum* (riddle), because instability is not a quality that we expect of *building blocks*.

---

23. D **Word in Context**

By asking *[w]hy are some atoms, like sodium, so hyperactive while others, like helium, are so aloof?* the author is drawing a direct contrast between chemical reactivity and relative *nonreactivity*.

---

24. D **Inference**

This question, about why protons stick together in atomic nuclei, is the guiding question for the passage as a whole. The next paragraph analyzes this question in more detail, explaining why this well-known fact is actually so puzzling. The remainder of the passages discusses attempts to resolve this puzzle, which remains at the heart of quantum physics.

25. A **Textual Evidence**

The evidence that this question represents a *central conundrum* is found in lines 1–5, where the author makes the uncontroversial claim that *a sound structure requires stable materials*, but then makes the paradoxical claim that *atoms, the building blocks of everything we know and love . . . don't appear to be models of stability.*

26. A **Specific Purpose**

The two sentences in lines 13–19 (*We are told . . . electrons. We are also told . . . closer*) indicate that we, the educated public, have been taught two seemingly contradictory facts about atoms. In other words, these are *predominant conceptions.*

27. C **Inference from Data**

In the graph, the equilibrium point is indicated by a dashed vertical line labeled *Equilibrium*. If we notice where this line intersects the two curves, we can see that the corresponding electrostatic force is precisely opposite to the corresponding strong nuclear force. That is, the equilibrium point is where the two forces "cancel out" and have a sum of 0.

28. C **Inference from Data**

Tip: When a question asks about a graph or table, it helps to circle the words or phrases in the question that correspond to the words or phrases in the graph or table. In this case, circle the key phrases *electrostatic repulsion* and *separated by 1.5 femtometers* in both the question and the graph.

Now, if we go to the graph and find the vertical line that corresponds to a *separation of 1.5 femtometers*, we can see that it intersects the curve for *electrostatic force* at the horizontal line representing 10^2, or 100, Newtons.

29. C **Interpretation**

In the fourth paragraph, we are told that Hideki Yukawa *proposed that the nuclear force was conveyed by a then-undiscovered heavy subatomic particle he called the pi meson (or "pion"), which (unlike the photon) decays very quickly and therefore conveys a powerful force only over a very short distance* (lines 44–49). However, his theory *was dealt a mortal blow by a series of experiments . . . that demonstrated that pions carry force only over distances greater than the distance between bound protons* (lines 50–55). In other words, pions are *ineffective in the range required by atomic theory*, so they cannot be the carriers of the strong nuclear force.

30. B **General Structure**

The first paragraph of this passage introduces the *scientific conundrum* of how protons adhere in atomic nuclei. The second paragraph analyzes this strange situation.

The third paragraph describes a force, the strong nuclear force, that could solve the conundrum. The fourth paragraph describes a particular theory, now refuted, about what might convey this strong nuclear force. The fifth and sixth paragraphs indicate that the problem has yet to be satisfactorily resolved. Thus, the passage as a whole is *a description of a technical puzzle and the attempts to solve it.*

31. A **Literary Devices**

A **rhetorical question** is a question intended to convey a point of view, rather than suggest a point of inquiry. Although the first and second paragraphs include five questions, they are all inquisitive, not rhetorical.

The passage includes **illustrative metaphors** in lines 15–16 (*a cloud of speedy electrons*) and lines 55–56 (*a plumber's wrench trying to do a tweezer's job*), **technical specifications** in lines 29–40 (*First, it can't have . . . each other*), and **appeals to common intuition** in lines 1–2 (*a sound structure . . . materials*) and lines 13–16 (*We are . . . electrons*).

32. B **Word in Context**

The hope that *QCD ties up atomic behavior with a tidy little bow* is the hope that the QCD theory *resolves* the problem in a tidy way.

33. C **General Purpose**

The passage as a whole develops the thesis that *the wise legislator does not begin by laying down laws good in themselves, but by investigating the fitness of the people, for which they are destined, to receive them* (lines 3–6). In other words, the passage is concerned with *examining the social conditions that foster effective legal systems.*

34. C **Word in Context**

In saying that *the architect sounds the site to see if it will bear the weight*, the author means that the architect *probes* the proposed location for a building to make sure that it is safe to build upon.

35. A **Specific Purpose**

The analogy of the architect in the first paragraph illustrates the thesis of the passage that *the wise legislator does not begin by laying down laws good in themselves, but by investigating the fitness of the people, for which they are destined, to receive them* (lines 3–6). That is, that a *nation's civil code depends on the nature of its people.* Choice (B) is incorrect because the analogy is not about the *foundational principles* of laws, but rather the *fitness of the people* for whom they are intended.

36. A **Inference**

The author states that as a nation grows older, its citizens *become incorrigible* (unable to be improved). *Once customs have become established and prejudices inveterate* (deep-seated), *it is dangerous and useless to attempt their reformation* (lines 19–21). That is, the people become stubbornly resistant to political change.

---

37. B   **Textual Evidence**

As the explanation to the previous question indicates, the relevant evidence is found in lines 20–21.

---

38. B   **Interpretation**

When the author says that *[m]ost peoples, like most men, are docile only in youth* (lines 17–18), he is saying that societies (the *peoples*) as well as individuals (*men*) become less manageable as they age.

---

39. B   **Specific Purpose**

The author refers to *Sparta at the time of Lycurgus* (line 35) as an example of *a state, set on fire by civil wars, [which] is born again* (lines 31–32). That is, a *society rejuvenated by conflict*. Choice (A) may seem tempting, because the beginning of the paragraph mentions the fact that *periods of violence* (lines 28–29) can make people *forget the past*, but the paragraph explains that this forgetting has the effect of renewal, not paralysis.

---

40. B   **Interpretation**

Although the word *constitution* can be used to mean *the documented rules by which a nation defines its governmental institutions* (as in the *Constitution of the United States of America*), the phrase *the constitution of the state*, as it is used in this passage, clearly refers to the *composition* of the state, that is, the people who constitute the nation.

---

41. A   **Interpretation**

In saying that *[o]ne people is amenable to discipline from the beginning; another, not even after ten centuries* (lines 51–53), the author means that some nations are *ready to be governed by the rule of law* as soon as they are founded, but others require much more time.

---

42. D   **Inference**

The passage states that *Peter the Great . . . lacked true genius [because he] did not see that [his nation] was not ripe for civilization: he wanted to civilize it when it needed only hardening* (lines 55–61). In other words, he did not give his nation the *hardening* it needed: his flaw was his *irresolution* (hesitancy due to a lack of conviction) *in exerting control*.

---

43. C   **General Purpose**

The first sentence of the passage establishes its central purpose: *to understand the views of Aristotle*, and asserts that to do this *it is necessary to apprehend his imaginative background* (lines 1–3). In other words, the purpose of this passage is to *describe the conceptions that inform a particular mindset*.

---

44. B   **Interpretation**

When the author states that *Animals have lost their importance in our imaginative pictures of the world* (lines 29–30), he is reinforcing his point that modern students *are accustomed to automobiles and airplanes; they do not, even in the dimmest recesses of their subconscious imagination, think that an automobile contains some sort of horse inside, or that an airplane flies because its wings are those of a bird possessing magical powers* (lines 23–29). In other words, *animistic beliefs no longer inform our physical theories.*

---

45. D   **Interpretation**

When the author states that every *philosopher, in addition to the formal system that he offers to the world, has another much simpler system of which he may be quite unaware* (lines 3–6), the *simpler system* refers to the *imaginative background* (line 3) that informs a scientist's formal theories. However, if a scientist is aware of this simpler system, *he probably recognizes that it won't do* (line 7). Therefore, this system is a *relatively unrefined way of thinking*.

---

46. A   **Inference**

In lines 61–65, the author states that *It was natural that a philosopher who could no longer regard the heavenly bodies themselves as divine should think of them as moved by the will of a Divine Being who had a Hellenic love of order and geometric simplicity*. In other words, the astronomical theories of some ancient Greek philosophers were closely associated with their religious ideas.

---

47. A   **Textual Evidence**

As the explanation to the previous question indicates, the evidence for this answer is in lines 61–65.

---

48. D   **Word in Context**

When the author states that, to the Greek, *it seemed more natural to assimilate apparently lifeless motions to those of animals* (lines 46–47), he means that the ancient Greeks found it easy to *liken* the motion of machines to the motion of animals.

---

49. D   **Inference**

The passage states that *To the ancient Greek, attempting to give a scientific account of motion, the purely mechanical view hardly suggested itself, except in the case of a few men of genius such as Democritus and Archimedes*. In other words, most Greeks were not inclined toward the mechanical view, except for the men of genius, who had more accurate *metaphors for the laws of motion, and therefore were "willing to disregard conventional wisdom."*

50. C   **Inference**

As it is discussed in the passage, the *apparent gulf between animals and machines* (lines 44–45) is the ever-shrinking gap between the animistic and the mechanistic view of animal physiology. To the modern scientist, each piece of evidence that demonstrates how *the body of an animal is a very elaborate machine, with an enormously complex physical and chemical structure* (lines 41–43) serves to bridge this gulf. One example of such evidence might be *the mechanical laws that describe bumblebee flight*.

51. B   **Inference**

The first paragraph discusses the fact that *the views of Aristotle* (line 1) are *due to his imaginative preconceptions, or to what Santayana calls "animal faith"* (lines 17–18), which the author goes on to explain include *animistic tendencies*, that is, tendencies toward seeing living spirits in all physical phenomena.

52. D   **Textual Evidence**

Lines 45–47 also reinforce the author's point that Aristotle, like other ancient Greeks, was inclined toward an animistic view of the world: *To the Greek, it seemed more natural to assimilate apparently lifeless motions to those of animals.*

Section 2: Writing and Language

1. B   **Subject-Verb Agreement**

The subject of this verb is *demand*, which is singular. Therefore, *are* must be changed to *is*.

2. C   **Diction**

This question asks you to choose the word that best fits the semantic context of the sentence, that is, the word that helps the sentence to convey a logical idea in the context of the paragraph.

This previous sentence states that *an important challenge facing the healthcare industry is how to address this shortfall without sacrificing quality of care.* Among our options, the only one that suggests a *possible solution* to this problem is *to incentivize more medical school graduates to choose primary care.*

Although it may seem that *interest* is a reasonable choice, notice that its use would violate idiom in this sentence: the correct idiom is not *interest someone to do something*, but rather *interest someone in doing something*.

3. C   **Logical Comparisons**

This portion of the sentence is part of a parallel construction in the form *A instead of B*. In such constructions, the

words or phrases in *A* and *B* must have the same grammatical form and describe logically comparable (or contrastable) things. Since in this case *A* is *primary care* (a noun phrase indicating a medical specialty), the most logical choice for *B* is *the more lucrative specialties* (a noun phrase indicating medical specialties). The original phrasing is incorrect because *their choosing* does not indicate a medical specialty, (B) is incorrect because *to choose* does not indicate a medical specialty, and choice (D) is incorrect because it is redundant.

4. A   **Parallelism**

Words or phrases in a list should have the same grammatical form. In the original phrasing, the three items in the list are all present tense verbs: *talk . . . prescribe . . . perform.*

5. B   **Diction**

Because a *"team-based" model* is not a location, the use of the pronoun *where* is incorrect. Likewise, choice (D) *when* is incorrect because a *"team-based" model* is not a time. Choice (C) is incorrect because it produces a comma splice. The correct answer is (B) *whereby*, which means *by which*.

6. C   **Diction**

The adverb *still* means *even now* or *nevertheless*, neither of which fit the logical context of this sentence. Only choice (C) *while*, meaning *at the same time*, fits logically. Choice (B) *while at the same time* is redundant, and choice (D) *although* implies a contrast, which is illogical.

7. A   **Coordination of Ideas, Cross-References**

The subject of the inserted sentence is *these professionals*. The pronoun *these* requires an antecedent, which is best provided if the sentence is placed after sentence 1, which specifies *medical professionals like physician assistants (PAs) and nurse practitioners (NPs).*

8. D   **Data Analysis**

The descending line in the graph shows clearly that the percentage of PAs in primary care has declined from 51% in 2000 (over one-half) to 31% in 2010 (under one-third).

9. A   **Logical Comparisons, Pronoun-Antecedent Agreement**

This sentence is correct as written. The pronoun *they* agrees in number and kind with its antecedent *students*, and the comparison is logical. Choice (D) is redundant.

10. D   **Idiom, Pronoun-Antecedent Agreement**

Using the phrase *being that* to mean *because* is colloquial and nonstandard for written American English, therefore choices (A) and (C) are incorrect. Choice (B) is incorrect because *when* should only be used to refer to a time.

11. D — Pronoun-Antecedent Agreement, Cross-References

The definite pronoun *they* must refer to some plural noun, but the only possible plural antecedent in this sentence is *programs*, which would be illogical. Choice (D) clarifies the reference.

12. C — Punctuation

The four choices differ only in their punctuation. Any reference to a city-and-country or city-and-state must separate the two with commas: e.g. *London, England* or *Providence, Rhode Island.* Therefore the original punctuation in (A) is incorrect. Choice (B) is incorrect because it produces a sentence fragment. Choice (D) is incorrect because it misuses the semicolon: the two phrases on either side of the semicolon should be independent clauses.

13. B — Logic, Dangling Participles

Since *engineering* is a class of profession and not a *position*, the original phrasing is illogical. Choice (C) is incorrect because it is a dangling participial phrase: the past participle *considered* does not share a subject with the main clause. Choice (D) is incorrect because the phrase *in reputation* is not idiomatic.

14. D — Dangling Participles

The sentence begins with the participial phrase *suffering ridicule and isolation.* Any participial phrase must have the same subject as the main clause. In the original phrasing, the subject of the main clause is *Montessori's medical studies,* but this cannot be the subject of *suffering ridicule and isolation.* Therefore, choices (A) and (C) are both incorrect. Choices (B) and (D) both correct this problem by changing the subject of the main clause to *Montessori,* but (B) is incorrect because the phrase *by becoming* is illogical.

15. A — Parallelism

This sentence contains the parallel construction *A rather than B.* The original phrasing provides parallel phrasing: *respect and stimulation* shares the same grammatical form and semantic category as *the regimentation.* Choice (D) provides a parallel phrasing but illogically implies that the students *were receiving* institutions.

16. B — Diction, Agreement

The original phrasing is incorrect because *they're* is a contraction of *they are,* which is illogical in this context. Choice (C) is incorrect because *childrens'* is not a word at all. *Children* is the plural form of *child,* and the possessive form of *children* is *children's.* Choice (D) is incorrect because *their* disagrees in number with the antecedent *each.*

17. C — Diction

This sentence discusses how word of Montessori's success with her school began to *spread* of its own merit

and accord. Choices (A) and (D) are incorrect because both *distribute* and *exhibit* imply intentional action. Choice (B) is illogical: *word* of someone's success cannot *increase.*

18. D — Logical Cohesiveness

To understand which sentence most effectively introduces this paragraph, we must first understand what the paragraph is about. As a whole, the paragraph discusses how *Montessori schools were regarded as a remedy to the educational programs associated with rapid urban population growth in Europe . . .* but then *came to be seen as a threat to the power of the state.* Choice (D) encapsulates this idea the best.

19. C — Logical Transitions

Choice (C) provides the most logical transition between ideas in the paragraph: the shift from a positive view of Montessori's work to a negative view requires a contrasting transition like *however.*

20. D — Redundancy

The original phrasing is redundant: being *subversive* is the same as *undermining power.* The most concise correct phrasing is that in (D).

21. B — Subject-Verb Agreement

In the original phrasing, the subject *response* (singular) disagrees with the verb *were* (plural) *divided.* Choice (B) provides the most effective correction.

22. A — Logical Cohesiveness

The remarkable thing about this paragraph is its introduction of dissenting views on Montessori's work from within the field of education, rather than merely from political opponents. Any additional discussion in this paragraph should elaborate on the nature of that dissent in the educational community. Only choice (A) extends the discussion in a relevant way.

23. D — Redundancy

This sentence is asserting a claim that directly contrasts the point of view presented in the previous paragraph. Choice (D) *In fact,* introduces just such an assertion. Choice (A) *First* is incorrect because this claim is not part of an enumerated list. Choice (B) *So* is incorrect, because this sentence is not asserting a logical consequence of the previous claim. Choice (C) *While* is incorrect because it produces a sentence fragment.

24. C — Diction, Idiom

The original phrasing is incorrect because the phrase *complies [to]* is not idiomatic. The same is true of (B) *overlaps [to]* and (D) *concurs [to].* Choice (C) *corresponds [to],* however, is idiomatic and logical.

25. A   **Coordination of Ideas**

This phrase is correct as written. It is expressing a condition, and so the use of the conjunction *if* is correct.

26. D   **Dangling Participles**

The participle *pondering* and the main clause must share the same subject, or else the participle "dangles." Who was *pondering*? Plato. Therefore *Plato* must be the subject of the main clause. Choice (C) is incorrect, however, because there is no need for the past participle form *had argued*.

27. C   **Parallelism**

The sentence contains the parallel construction *A yet B*. The phrasing *inaccessible . . . yet apprehensible* provides a parallel form, since both *inaccessible* and *apprehensible* are adjectives.

28. B   **Modifier Usage**

The phrase between the commas is an interrupting modifier. Any sentence should remain grammatically complete even when any interrupting modifier is removed. Notice that if we did this with the original sentence, it would read *as effective . . . than sensory experience*, which is clearly unidiomatic. (The correct comparative idiom is *as effective as*.) The only choice that corrects this problem is (B).

29. C   **Logical Cohesiveness**

The information the author is proposing does not fit with the discussion about the philosophy of Platonic idealism.

30. D   **Modifier Form**

In the original phrasing, the conjunction *and* is incorrect because it does not conjoin comparable words or phrases; therefore, choices (A) and (C) are incorrect. In choice (B) the prepositional phrase *in not having to believe* is illogical. Choice (D) is correct because the prepositional phrase *without having to believe* logically modifies the verb *understand*.

31. A   **Possessives**

This sentence is correct as written. Choice (B) is incorrect because the pronoun *they* has no clear antecedent. Choice (C) misuses the possessive *brain's*, and choice (D) yields the subject-verb disagreement *brain make*.

32. C   **Verb Mood**

This clause is part of a counterfactual hypothesis. As we discuss in Chapter 4, Lesson 30, a present counterfactual hypothesis takes the form of the present subjunctive mood, which is usually the same form as the simple past tense: *existed*.

33. B   **Pronoun Consistency**

Since the previous sentence refers to *our brains*, pronoun consistency requires that this sentence continue to use the first-person plural pronoun *we*.

34. B   **Coordination of Clauses**

The interrupting modifier (*perhaps while showering or driving*) must be "bracketed" on either end by commas, em dashes, or parentheses. Since it clearly ends with an em dash, it must start with an em dash as well.

35. A   **Pronoun Form**

This sentence is correct as written. Choice (B) uses the wrong pronoun form *what* and incorrectly implies that Archimedes is shouting in the present. Choice (C) uses the wrong pronoun form *that* and misplaces the modifying clause *it is said*. Choice (D) misuses the past perfect form *had shouted*.

36. B   **Diction**

The sentence discusses the relationship between the *feeling* of the Eureka effect and *a fundamentally different way of thinking*. In the context of the discussion, the only choice that indicates a logical relationship is (B): this feeling *indicates* a different way of thinking.

37. D   **Coordination of Clauses**

The original phrasing is incorrect because it includes a comma splice. Choice (B) is incorrect because the prepositional phrase *by which* is illogical. In choice (C), the use of the pronoun *where* is incorrect because an experiment is not a place.

38. C   **Subject-Verb Agreement, Redundancy**

The verb *requires* (singular) disagrees with the subject *tasks* (plural), therefore choices (A) and (D) are incorrect. Choice (B) is redundant.

39. C   **Subject-Verb Agreement**

The modifying phrase *as soon as solving it* is vague and awkward. Choice (C) clarifies the modifier by indicating that the *subjects* are solving the task.

40. D   **Awkwardness, Logical Transitions**

The underlined phrase is a sentence modifier, that is, a phrase that modifies the statement in the main clause *experimenters found*. Choices (A), (B), and (C) are needlessly awkward and wordy, but choice (D) provides a concise and clear modifier.

41. B   **Verb Tense**

This clause is describing a general fact (*the theory that . . .*), not an event. To express general facts, we use the simple present tense: *corresponds*.

42. B Data Analysis

According to the graph, the line indicating the Insight condition separates from the line representing the Non-insight condition approximately 0.3 seconds prior to the button being pushed, and remains elevated until about 0.7 seconds after the button is pushed, for a duration of approximately 1 second.

43. D Pronoun-Antecedent Agreement, Subject-Verb Agreement

The verb *is* agrees with the subject *interpreting* (both are singular), but the pronoun *this* disagrees with its antecedent *data* (*this* is singular, but *data* is plural).

44. B Coordinating Clauses

The correct choice should combine the two questions into a single sentence. Choice (A) misstates the second question. Choice (C) inappropriately uses the subjunctive mood. Choice (D) misuses the parallel construction *both A and B*.

Section 3: Math (No Calculator)

1. B Algebra (solving equations) EASY

$$6x + 9 = 30$$

To solve in one step, just divide
both sides by 3: $\qquad 2x + 3 = 10$
Most students waste time solving for x,
which will work, but takes longer: $\qquad 6x + 9 = 30$
Subtract 9: $\qquad 6x = 21$
Divide by 6: $\qquad x = 3.5$
Evaluate $2x + 3$ by
substituting $x = 3.5$: $\quad 2x + 3 = 2(3.5) + 3 = 7 + 3 = 10$

2. D Advanced Mathematics (nonlinear systems) EASY

The solutions to the system correspond to the points of intersection of the two graphs. The figure shows four such intersection points.

3. B Algebra (algebraic expressions) EASY

Let a = # of adult tickets sold, and c = # of child tickets sold. If 300 tickets were sold altogether: $\quad c + a = 300$

The revenue for a adult tickets sold at \$5 each is \$5a, and the revenue for c child tickets sold at \$3 each is \$3c. Since the total revenue is \$1,400: $\quad 5a + 3c = 1,400$

4. A Advanced Mathematics (polynomials) EASY

$$2(x - 4)^2 - 5x$$

Factor: $\qquad 2[(x - 4)(x - 4)] - 5x$
FOIL: $\qquad 2[x^2 - 4x - 4x + 16] - 5x$
Simplify: $\qquad 2[x^2 - 8x + 16] - 5x$
Distribute: $\qquad 2x^2 - 16x + 32 - 5x$
Combine like terms: $\qquad 2x^2 - 21x + 32$

5. C Special Topics (three-dimensional geometry) MEDIUM

On the drawing, we should first mark the areas of the three faces. The front and back faces both have an area of 3a. The left and right faces both have an area of 3b. The top and bottom faces both have an area of ab. We should now try to find integer values for a and b so that these areas match those given in the choices.

(A) 15, 18, and 30   This is possible if $a = 5$ and $b = 6$.
(B) 18, 24, and 48   This is possible if $a = 6$ and $b = 8$.
(C) 12, 15, and 24   This cannot work for any integer values of a and b.
(D) 15, 24, and 40   This is possible if $a = 5$ and $b = 8$.

6. D Algebra (linear equations) MEDIUM

$$C(n) = an + b$$

Since this expression is linear in n (the input variable, which represents the number of necklaces produced), the constant a represents the slope of this line, which in turn represents the "unit rate of increase," in other words, the increase in total cost for each individual necklace produced.

The constant b represents the "y-intercept" of this line, which in this case means the costs when $n = 0$ (that is, the fixed costs before any necklaces are produced).

7. A Algebra (lines) MEDIUM

To find the slope of line l, we can find two points on l and then use the slope formula.

$$f(x) = 2x^2 - 4x + 1$$

Plug in -1 for x: $\qquad f(-1) = 2(-1)^2 - 4(-1) + 1$
Simplify: $\qquad f(-1) = 2(1) + 4 + 1 = 2 + 4 + 1 = 7$
Therefore line l intersects the function at $(-1, 7)$.
Plug in 2 for x: $\qquad f(2) = 2(2)^2 - 4(2) + 1$
Simplify: $\qquad f(2) = 2(4) - (8) + 1 = 8 - 8 + 1 = 1$
Therefore line l intersects the function at $(2, 1)$. Now we find the slope of the line containing these two points.

$$\text{slope} = \frac{y_2 - y_1}{x_2 - x_1} = \frac{7 - 1}{-1 - 2} = \frac{6}{-3} = -2$$

8. B Advanced Mathematics (parabolas) MEDIUM

The general equation of a parabola in the xy-plane is $y = a(x - h)^2 + k$, in which (h, k) is the vertex. Now let's express each choice in precisely this form.

(A) $y = (x - 3)^2 + 2$ $y = 1(x - 3)^2 + 2$ $a = 1, h = 3, k = 2$
(B) $y = 2(x - 3)^2$ $y = 2(x - 3)^2 + 0$ $a = 2, h = 3, k = 0$
(C) $y = 2x^2 - 3$ $y = 2(x - 0)^2 - 3$ $a = 2, h = 0, k = -3$
(D) $y = 3x^2 + 2$ $y = 3(x - 0)^2 + 2$ $a = 3, h = 0, k = 2$
If this vertex is on the x-axis, then $k = 0$. The only equation in which $k = 0$ is (B).

9. **D**   **Advanced Mathematics (rational equations)**
MEDIUM

$$\frac{m(x)}{x+3} - \frac{x+1}{x-1} = 1$$

Add $\frac{x+1}{x-1}$:

Express right side in terms
of a common denominator:

$$\frac{m(x)}{x+3} = \frac{x+1}{x-1} + 1$$

$$\frac{m(x)}{x+3} = \frac{x+1}{x-1} + \frac{x-1}{x-1}$$

Combine terms on right
into one fraction:

$$\frac{m(x)}{x+3} = \frac{x+1+x-1}{x-1}$$

Combine terms:

$$\frac{m(x)}{x+3} = \frac{2x}{x-1}$$

Multiple by $x+3$:

$$m(x) = \frac{2x(x+3)}{x-1}$$

---

10. **C**   **Algebra (linear relationships) MEDIUM**

We are told that the temperature varies linearly with
altitude, so if y represents the temperature (in °C) and x
represents altitude (in km), these variables are related by
the equation $y = mx + b$, where m (the slope) and b (the
y-intercept) are constants.

We are given two points on this line: (50 km, 10°) and
(80 km, −80°). We can use these points to find the slope, m:

$$\text{slope} = \frac{y_2 - y_1}{x_2 - x_1} = \frac{10 - (-80)}{50 - (80)} = \frac{90}{-30} = -3$$

Recall that the slope of a linear relationship is the
"unit rate of change." In other words, the slope of −3
means that the temperature declines by 3° for every 1 km
of additional altitude. Since we want the altitude at which
the temperature is −50°, we want the value of x such that
$(x, -50°)$ is on this line. To find x, we can simply use the
slope formula again, using either of the other two points:
Slope formula using (50, 10) and $(x, -50)$:

$$\text{slope} = \frac{y_2 - y_1}{x_2 - x_1} = \frac{10 - (-50)}{50 - x} = \frac{60}{50 - x} = -3$$

Multiply by $50 - x$: $60 = -3(50 - x)$
Distribute: $60 = -150 + 3x$
Add 150: $210 = 3x$
Divide by 3: $70 = x$

---

11. **A** **Advanced Mathematics (triangles/quadratics)**
MEDIUM-HARD

Any point that intersects the y-axis has an x-value of 0.
So, to find point A, plug in 0 for x and solve for y:

$$y = 2x^2 - 16x + 14$$

Plug in 0 for x: $y = 2(0)^2 - 16(0) + 14 = 14$

Any point that intersects the x-axis has a y-value of 0. So,
to find points B and C, plug in 0 for y and solve for x:

$$y = 2x^2 - 16x + 14$$

Substitute 0 for y: $0 = 2x^2 - 16x + 14$
Divide by 2: $0 = x^2 - 8x + 7$

Factor: $0 = (x - 7)(x - 1)$
Use the Zero Product Property: $x = 7$ and $x = 1$
If we connect these three points, we get a triangle with
a height of 14 (from $y = 0$ to $y = 14$) and a base of 6 (from
$x = 1$ to $x = 7$).
Use the triangle area formula $A = \frac{1}{2}bh$:

$$A = \frac{1}{2}bh = \frac{1}{2}(14)(6) = 42$$

---

12. **B**   **Advanced Mathematics (polynomials)**
MEDIUM-HARD

Given equation: $y = (x + 2)^2(x - 3)^2$
To find the y-intercept, set $x = 0$: $y = (0 + 2)^2(0 - 3)^2$
Simplify: $y = (2)^2(-3)^2 = (4)(9) = 36$
Therefore the y-intercept is at (0, 36).
To find the x-intercepts, set $y = 0$: $0 = (x + 2)^2(x - 3)^2$
By the Zero Product Property, the only solutions to this
equation are $x = -2$ and $x = 3$, so there are two x-intercepts
and a total of three x- and y-intercepts.

---

13. **C**   **Special Topics (complex numbers) HARD**

$$A(2 - i) = 2 + i$$

Divide by $(2 - i)$: $A = \dfrac{2 + i}{2 - i}$

Multiply numerator and denominator by the conjugate
$(2 + i)$: $A = \dfrac{(2 + i)(2 + i)}{(2 - i)(2 + i)}$

FOIL: $A = \dfrac{4 + 2i + 2i + i^2}{4 - i^2}$

Combine terms: $A = \dfrac{4 + 4i + i^2}{4 - i^2}$

Substitute $i^2 = -1$: $A = \dfrac{4 + 4i + (-1)}{4 - (-1)}$

Simplify: $A = \dfrac{4 + 4i - 1}{4 + 1}$

Combine terms: $A = \dfrac{3 + 4i}{5}$

Distribute to express in
standard $a + bi$ form: $A = \dfrac{3}{5} + \dfrac{4}{5}i$

---

14. **B**   **Algebra (graphs of linear equations) HARD**

Given equation: $y + x = k(x - 1)$
Subtract x: $y = k(x - 1) - x$
Distribute: $y = kx - k - x$
Collect like terms: $y = (k - 1)x - k$
The slope of this line is $k - 1$ and its y-intercept is $-k$. If
$k > 2$, then $k - 1 > 1$, and $-k < -2$. In other words, the
slope of the line is greater than 1 and the y-intercept is
less than −2. The only graph with these features is the
one in choice (B).

15. **B**   **Advanced Mathematics (analyzing polynomial functions) HARD**

Because this polynomial has a degree of 3 (which is the highest power of any of its terms), it cannot have more than 3 zeros. These three zeros are given as −2, 3, and 6. We also know that $g(0)$, the y-intercept of the graph, is negative. This gives us enough information to make a rough sketch of the graph.

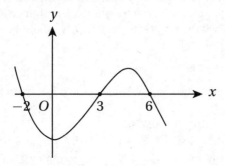

This shows that the only values of x for which the function is negative are $-2 < x < 3$ and $x > 6$. Therefore the only negative value among the choices is (B) $g(-1)$.

---

16. **30**   **Algebra (linear equations) EASY**

$$\frac{2}{3}x + \frac{1}{2}y = 5$$

Multiply by 6 (the common denominator):

$$6\left(\frac{2}{3}x + \frac{1}{2}y = 5\right)$$

Distribute:

$$\frac{12}{3}x + \frac{6}{2}y = 30$$

Simplify:

$$4x + 3y = 30$$

---

17. **25/7 or 3.57**   **Advanced Mathematics (rational equations) EASY**

$$\frac{5}{x} - \frac{2}{5} = 1$$

Add $\frac{2}{5}$:

$$\frac{5}{x} = 1 + \frac{2}{5}$$

Simplify:

$$\frac{5}{x} = \frac{7}{5}$$

Cross multiply:

$$25 = 7x$$

Divide by 7:

$$\frac{25}{7} = x$$

---

18. **35**   **Special Topics (radians and arcs) MEDIUM-HARD**

Since an arc is simply a portion of a circumference, let's first calculate the circumference of the circle:

$$C = 2\pi r = 2\pi(36) = 72\pi$$

Because arc AB has a measure of 7π, it is $\dfrac{7\pi}{72\pi} = \dfrac{7}{72}$ of the entire circumference. Since $x°$ is the measure of the central angle that corresponds to this arc, it must be the same fraction of the whole:

$$\frac{x°}{360°} = \frac{7}{72}$$

Cross multiply:

$$72x = 7(360)$$

Divide by 72:

$$x = 7(5)$$

Simplify:

$$x = 35$$

---

19. **1.2**   **Algebra (linear systems) MEDIUM-HARD**

First, we should simplify the first equation:

$$\frac{1}{2}x = \frac{1}{3}y + \frac{1}{10}$$

Subtract $\frac{1}{3}y$:

$$\frac{1}{2}x - \frac{1}{3}y = \frac{1}{10}$$

Multiply by 12:

$$6x - 4y = 1.2$$

This equation represents a line with slope of $\dfrac{6}{4} = \dfrac{3}{2}$. The second equation, $6x - 4y = k$, also represents a line with slope $\dfrac{6}{4} = \dfrac{3}{2}$. In order for this system of equations to have at least one solution, these two lines must have an intersection. How can two lines with the same slope intersect? They must be identical lines, and therefore intersect in all of their points. If this is the case, then k must equal 1.2.

---

20. **2.4**   **Special Topics (trigonometry) HARD**

Since x represents the radian measure of an acute angle, and $\sin x = \dfrac{5}{13}$, we can use the definition of sine $\left(= \dfrac{O}{H}\right)$ to draw a right triangle:

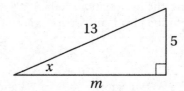

We might notice that this is a 5-12-13 special right triangle, or simply use the Pythagorean Theorem to show that $m = 12$. We can also show that the other acute angle in the triangle must be complementary to x (that is, together they form a right angle), and so must have a measure of $\dfrac{\pi}{2} - x$.

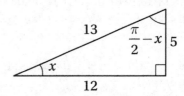

To find $\tan\left(\dfrac{\pi}{2} - x\right)$, we simply have to use the angle with measure $\dfrac{\pi}{2} - x$ as our new reference angle, and use TOA:

$$\tan\left(\frac{\pi}{2} - x\right) = \frac{12}{5} = 2.4$$

Section 4: Math (Calculator)

1. D   Algebra (systems) EASY

When faced with a system of equations, notice whether the two equations can be combined in a simple way—either by subtracting or adding the corresponding sides—to get the expression the question is asking for.

$$a - b = 10$$
$$a - 2b = 8$$

Subtract corresponding sides: $b = 2$

2. C   Data Analysis (central tendency) EASY

The average of three numbers is 50: $50 = \dfrac{a+b+c}{3}$

Multiply by 3: $150 = a + b + c$
Two of the numbers have a sum of 85: $85 = a + b$
Substitute into the previous equation: $150 = 85 + c$
Subtract 85 to find c: $65 = c$

3. D   Problem Solving/Data Analysis (proportions) EASY

Set up a proportion: $\dfrac{9}{25} = \dfrac{x}{225}$

Cross multiply: $2{,}025 = 25x$
Divide by 25: $81 = x$

4. B   Data Analysis (tables) EASY

Let's fill in the table with the information we're given and work our way to the value the question asks us to find. First, use the information in the FAVORABLE column to determine how many women viewed the politician favorably:

$$26 + w = 59$$
Subtract 26: $w = 33$
Next, go to the WOMEN row: $33 + x + 13 = 89$
Combine terms: $46 + x = 89$
Subtract 46: $x = 43$

5. D   Algebra (exponentials) EASY

$$2^{2n-2} = 32$$

When dealing with exponential equations, it helps to see if we can express the two sides of the equation in terms of the same base. Since $32 = 2^5$, we can express both sides in base 2:

$$2^{2n-2} = 2^5$$

If $x^a = x^b$ and $x > 1$, then $a = b$ (if the bases are equal, the exponents are equal): $2n - 2 = 5$
Add 2: $2n = 7$
Divide by 2: $n = \dfrac{7}{2} = 3.5$

6. C   Algebra (representing quantities) EASY

The question asks us to find the "part-to-whole" ratio of walnuts: walnut fraction $= \dfrac{\text{ounces of walnuts}}{\text{ounces of nuts}}$.

Since the walnuts weigh x ounces, and the total weight of all the nuts is $x + 15 + 20 = x + 35$ ounces,

$$\text{walnut fraction} = \dfrac{x}{x+35}$$

7. B   Advanced Mathematics (triangle trigonometry) EASY

Remember the definitions of the basic trigonometric functions: SOH CAH TOA. Since the "side of interest" (k) is the OPPOSITE side to the given angle (35°), and since we know the length of the HYPOTENUSE (12), we should use SOH.

$$\sin x = \dfrac{\text{opp}}{\text{hyp}}$$

Plug in the values: $\sin 35° = \dfrac{k}{12}$

Substitute $\sin 35° = 0.574$: $0.574 = \dfrac{k}{12}$

Multiply by 12: $(12)(0.574) = 6.88 = k$

8. A   Special Topics (polygons) EASY

The sum of the measures if the interior angles of any polygon is $(n - 2)180°$, where n is the number of sides in the polygon. Since this is a 5-sided polygon, the sum of its interior angles is $(5 - 2)(180°) = 3(180°) = 540°$. Therefore the average of these measures is $540°/5 = 108°$.

9. B   Data Analysis (scatterplot) MEDIUM

We want to find the slope of the line of best fit because it represents the average annual increase in revenue per store. Although the question asks about the years 2004 and 2012, we can choose ANY two points on this line to find its slope. We should choose points on the line of best fit that are easy to calculate with, such as (2005, $300,000) and (2011, $600,000).

$$\text{slope} = \dfrac{\text{rise}}{\text{run}} = \dfrac{y_2 - y_1}{x_2 - x_1} = \dfrac{600{,}000 - 300{,}000}{2011 - 2005}$$
$$= \dfrac{300{,}000}{6} = 50{,}000$$

10. C   Data Analysis (scatterplot) MEDIUM-HARD

When faced with a question like this, we must analyze each statement individually.

(A) *The average revenue per store increased by over 100% from 2005 to 2009.* True or false? In 2005, according to the line of best fit, the average revenue per store was approximately $300,000. In 2009, the average revenue per store was approximately $500,000. This is a percent increase of

$$\dfrac{500{,}000 - 300{,}000}{300{,}000} \times 100\% = \dfrac{2}{3} \times 100\% = 67\%$$

FALSE

(B) *The total number of retail stores increased by 50% from 2005 to 2012.* True or false? According to the scatter-plot, in 2005 there were 3 stores corresponding to the three dots above 2005. In 2012 there were 6 stores corresponding to the 6 dots above 2012. This is a percent increase of

$$\frac{6-3}{3} \times 100\% = 100\%$$

FALSE

(C) *The total revenue for all stores in 2012 is more than three times the total revenue from all stores in 2004.* True or false? In 2004, there were 3 stores with an average revenue per store of approximately $250,000. Therefore the total revenue in 2004 was approximately 3 × $250,000 = $750,000. In 2012, there were 6 stores with an average revenue per store of approximately $650,000. Therefore the total revenue in 2012 was approximately 6 × $650,000 = $3,900,000. Since $3,900,000 is more than three time $750,000, this statement is TRUE.

---

11. B   **Algebra (translating quantitative information) MEDIUM**

This question tests your ability to translate words into algebraic expressions. Systematically translate the sentence phrase by phrase.

The product of two numbers, a and b is 6 greater than their sum.
Translation: ab $=$ $6+$ $a+b$
Use commutative law of equality
on right side: $ab = a+b+6$

---

12. D Special Topics (coordinate geometry) MEDIUM

First, find the slope of *l* using the points $(0, -9)$ and $(12, 0)$:

$$\text{slope} = \frac{y_2 - y_1}{x_2 - x_1} = \frac{0-(-9)}{12-0} = \frac{9}{12} = \frac{3}{4}$$

Since the two lines are parallel, line *m* must also have a slope of $\frac{3}{4}$. Now we can solve for *k* using the slope equation and the two points on line *m*, $(0, 0)$ and $(k, 12)$:

$$\text{slope} = \frac{y_2 - y_1}{x_2 - x_1} = \frac{12-(0)}{k-0} = \frac{12}{k} = \frac{3}{4}$$

Cross multiply: $4(12) = 3(k)$
Simplify: $48 = 3k$
Divide by 3: $16 = k$
Notice that the coordinates of the point $(16, 12)$ correspond to the *width* and the *length* of the rectangle, respectively. Therefore, the area of the rectangle is $16 \times 12 = 192$ square units.

---

13. A   **Problem Solving/Data Analysis (ratios) MEDIUM**

If the Giants' win-loss is 2:3, then they won $2n$ games and lost $3n$ games, where *n* is some unknown integer. (For instance, perhaps they won 2 games and lost 3, in which case $n = 1$, or perhaps they won 20 games and lost 30, in which case $n = 10$, etc.) This means that the total number of games they played is $2n + 3n = 5n$. Since they won 120 games,

$$5n = 120$$

Divide by 5: $n = 24$
Therefore they won $2n = (2)(24) = 48$ games and lost $3n = (3)(24) = 72$ games, and so they lost $72 - 48 = 24$ more games than they won.

---

14. B Advanced Mathematics (exponential growth) MEDIUM

We might begin by plugging in a number for *p*. Let's say $p = 120$ cells to start. We are told that after one hour the population decreased by $\frac{1}{3}$. Since $\frac{1}{3}$ of 120 is 40, the population decreased by 40 and the population was then $120 - 40 = 80$ cells. In the second hour, the population *increased* by 40%. Increasing a number by 40% is equivalent to it by 1.40 (because it becomes 140% of what it was), so the population was then $80(1.40) = 112$ cells. In the third hour, the population *increased* by 50%, so it became $112(1.50) = 168$ cells.

Substituting $p = 120$ into each of the answer choices yields (A) $1.3p = 1.3(120) = 156$, (B) $1.4p = 1.4(120) = 168$, (C) $1.5p = 1.5(120) = 180$, and (D) $1.6p = 1.6(120) = 192$. Therefore the answer is (B).

Alternately, you can solve this problem algebraically: $p(2/3)(1.40)(1.50) = 1.40p$.

---

15. B   **Advanced Mathematics (exponentials) MEDIUM**

For this one, we'll need the Laws of Exponentials from Chapter 9, Lesson 9. $(6^{-2})(m^{-2}) = \frac{1}{16}$

Translate by using Exponential Law #3: $\frac{1}{6^2} \times \frac{1}{m^2} = \frac{1}{16}$

Multiply by m^2: $\frac{1}{6^2} = \frac{1}{16}m^2$

Multiply by 16: $\frac{16}{6^2} = m^2$

Simplify: $\frac{16}{6^2} = \frac{16}{36} = \frac{4}{9} = m^2$

---

16. B   **Data Analysis (probability) MEDIUM**

Let R = the number of red marbles, W = the number of white marbles, and B = the number of blue marbles. If the jar contains twice as many red marbles as white marbles, then $R = 2W$. If the jar contains three times as many white marbles as blue marbles, then $W = 3B$. We can substitute numbers to these equations to solve the problem. Let's say $B = 10$. This means there are $3(10) = 30$ white marbles and $2(30) = 60$ red marbles. The total number of marbles is therefore $10 + 30 + 60 = 100$, and the number of non-red marbles is therefore $10 + 30 = 40$ marbles, so the probability that the marble is *not* red is $\dfrac{40}{100} = \dfrac{2}{5}$.

---

17. C   **Advanced Mathematics (parabolas)**
MEDIUM

The vertex of a parabola with the equation $y = A(x - h)^2 + k$ is (h, k). For this parabola, $h = 2$ and $k = 2$. So, the vertex is $(2, 2)$. The slope of the line that passes through $(1, -3)$ and $(2, 2)$ is

$$\text{slope} = \frac{y_2 - y_1}{x_2 - x_1} = \frac{3 - 2}{-1 - 2} = \frac{1}{-3} = -\frac{1}{3}$$

---

18. C   **Advanced Mathematics (functions)**
MEDIUM-HARD

Let the input number be 7.
Step 1: Multiply the input value by 6:   42
Step 2: Add x to that result: $42 + x$

Step 3: Divide this result by 4: $\dfrac{42 + x}{4}$

This must yield an output of 15: $15 = \dfrac{42 + x}{4}$

Multiply by 4: $60 = 42 + x$
Subtract 42: $18 = x$

---

19. C   **Data Analysis (graphing data) MEDIUM-HARD**

The graph of the quadratic $y = ax^2 + bx + c$ is a parabola. If $a < 0$, the parabola is "open-down" like a frowny-face. The only graph with this feature is (C).

---

20. B   **Algebra (expressing relationships)**
MEDIUM-HARD

Draw a number line, and to show that $p < r$, place p to the left of r on the number line. The points that are closer to p than to r are all the points to the left of their midpoint. The midpoint is the average of the endpoints: $\dfrac{p + r}{2}$, so if the point with coordinate x is closer to p than to r, then $x < \dfrac{p + r}{2}$.

---

21. A   **Algebra (simplifying expressions)**
MEDIUM-HARD

$$f(x) = \frac{1}{2 - x}$$

Substitute $\dfrac{1}{m}$ for x: $f\left(\dfrac{1}{m}\right) = \dfrac{1}{2 - \left(\dfrac{1}{m}\right)}$

Simplify the denominator:

$$f\left(\frac{1}{m}\right) = \frac{1}{2 - \left(\dfrac{1}{m}\right)} = \frac{1}{\dfrac{2m}{m} - \dfrac{1}{m}} = \frac{1}{\dfrac{2m - 1}{m}}$$

Divide by multiplying by the reciprocal:

$$1 \div \frac{2m - 1}{m} = 1 \times \frac{m}{2m - 1} = \frac{m}{2m - 1}$$

---

22. A   **Advanced Mathematics (quadratics)**
MEDIUM-HARD

The graph of $y = a(x - 2)(x + 1)$ is a quadratic with zeros (x-intercepts) at $x = 2$ and $x = -1$. The axis of symmetry of this parabola is halfway between the zeros, at $x = (2 + -1)/2 = 1/2$. Since $a < 0$, the parabola is "open down," and so we have a general picture like this:

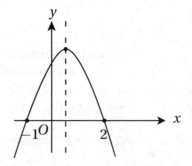

If you trace the curve from $x = 0$ to $x = 5$, that is, from the y-intercept and then to the right, you can see that the graph goes up a bit (until $x = 1/2$), and then goes down again.

Alternately, you can pick a negative value for a (like -2) and graph the equation on your calculator.

---

23. D   **Advanced Mathematics (rational equations)**
HARD

Given equation: $\dfrac{n^2 - 9}{n^2 + 3} = 1 - \dfrac{k}{n^2 + 3}$

Add $\dfrac{k}{n^2 + 3}$: $\dfrac{n^2 - 9}{n^2 + 3} + \dfrac{k}{n^2 + 3} = 1$

Combine the fractions into one: $\dfrac{n^2 - 9 + k}{n^2 + 3} = 1$

Multiply by $n^2 + 3$: $n^2 - 9 + k = n^2 + 3$
Subtract n^2: $-9 + k = 3$
Add 9: $k = 12$

---

24. C   **Problem Solving (percentages) MEDIUM-HARD**

Let $p =$ the price per share of the stock. The cost of 200 of these shares (before commission) is therefore $200p$. With a 3% commission, the cost becomes $(1.03)(200p)$
$$(1.03)(200p) = \$3,399$$

Divide by 1.03: $\qquad$ $200p = \$3,300$
Divide by 200: $\qquad$ $p = \$16.50$ per share

---

25. A $\qquad$ **Algebra (expressing quantities) MEDIUM-HARD**

It may be easiest to choose number for w and y. Assume $y = 4$. If w is 50% greater than y, then $w = 1.5(4) = 6$. Therefore $w^{-2} = 6^{-2} = 1/36$, and $y^{-2} = 4^{-2} = 1/16$. Therefore the ratio of w^{-2} to y^{-2} is

$$\frac{\dfrac{1}{36}}{\dfrac{1}{16}} = \frac{1}{36} \times \frac{16}{1} = \frac{16}{36} = \frac{8}{18} = \frac{4}{9}$$

---

26. D $\qquad$ **Data Analysis (set relations) HARD**

Let's let $s =$ the total number of athletes in the group who play soccer, and $t =$ the number of athletes in the group who run track. We can set up a Venn diagram to show the relationship between these two overlapping sets.

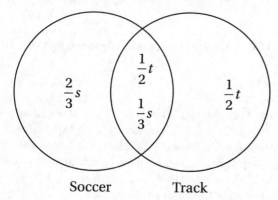

Soccer $\qquad$ Track

Since one-third of the soccer players also run track, we must put $\frac{1}{3}s$ in the overlapping region between soccer and track, and therefore the number who play only soccer is $\frac{2}{3}s$. Likewise, since one-half of the athletes who run track also play soccer, we must put $\frac{1}{2}t$ in the overlapping region, and therefore the number of athletes who only run track is $\frac{1}{2}t$.

Sincer there are 60 athletes in total: $\qquad$ $\frac{2}{3}s + \frac{1}{2}t + \frac{1}{2}t = 60$

Simplify: $\qquad$ $\frac{2}{3}s + t = 60$

Multiply by 3 to simplify: $\qquad$ $2s + 3t = 180$

The number of soccer players who run track must equal the number of track athletes who play soccer: $\qquad$ $\frac{1}{3}s = \frac{1}{2}t$

Multiply by 6 (the common denominator): $\qquad$ $2s = 3t$

Substitute $2s = 3t$ into the previous equation: $\qquad$ $3t + 3t = 180$

Simplify: $\qquad$ $6t = 180$
Divide by 6: $\qquad$ $t = 30$
Substitute $t = 30$ into the other equation to solve for s: $\qquad$ $2s = 3(30)$
Simplify: $\qquad$ $2s = 90$
Divide by 2: $\qquad$ $s = 45$

Now we can use these values to complete the Venn diagram:

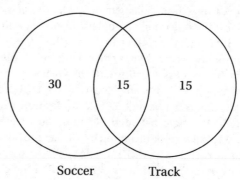

Soccer $\qquad$ Track

From this diagram, we can see that the only true statement among the choices is (D).

---

27. D $\qquad$ **Advanced Mathematics (transformations) HARD**

The graph of $y = g(x) = f(x) + b$ is the graph of f vertically shifted up by b units. If $g(x) = 0$ has exactly one solution, the graph of $y = g(x)$ can touch the x-axis at only one point: the vertex. Since the vertex of f has a y-coordinate of -2, this can only happen if f is shifted up 2 units, so $b = 2$.

---

28. B $\qquad$ **Special Topics (trigonometry) HARD**

The statement $\frac{\pi}{2} < x < \pi$ indicates that x is an angle in quadrant II, where the cosine is negative. Let's draw this situation on the unit circle so we can visualize it. (We don't want to confuse the *angles* called x and y in the problem with the x-coordinates and y-coordinates in the xy-plane. For this reason, let's label the terminal rays for the angles "angle x" and "angle y.") Recall that the cosine of any angle is the x-coordinate of the point on the unit circle that corresponds to that angle. If $\cos x = a$, then a is the x-coordinate of the point on the unit circle that corresponds to "angle x," as shown in the diagram.

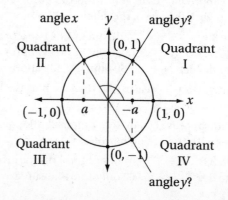

Now notice that, since a is a negative number, $-a$ (that, is, the *opposite* of a), is a *positive* number. More specifically, it is the reflection of the point labeled a over the x-axis, as shown in the diagram. Now, if $\cos y = -a$, then "angle y" corresponds to a point on the unit circle with an x-coordinate of $-a$. There are two possible locations for this point on the circle, and both are shown in the diagram above. Notice that one of these angles is the reflection of "angle x" over the y-axis. This is the supplement of "angle x," that is, $\pi - x$. The other is the reflection of "angle x" over the origin, that is $x + \pi$. Therefore, the correct answer is (B).

Alternately, we could use the calculator to solve this problem by process of elimination. We can choose a value of "angle x" between $\pi/2$ and π. (In radian mode this is an angle between 1.57 and 3.14, and in degree mode it is an angle between 90° and 180°.) Let's pick "angle x" to be 2 radians (about 115°). According to the calculator, $\cos(2) = -.416$. Therefore, $\cos y$ must equal .416. Now we can substitute $x = 2$ into all of the choices and see which angle has a cosine of .416.

(A) $\cos(2 + 2\pi) = -.416$

(B) $\cos(2 + \pi) = .416$

(C) $\cos(2 + \pi/2) = -.909$

(D) $\cos(-2 + 2\pi) = -.416$ Therefore the correct answer is (B).

---

29. **A**   **Data Analysis (table) HARD**

Since the question asks about those "who expressed an opinion on Proposal 81a," we must *ignore* those who are listed as having No Opinion.

The number at the bottom right of the table indicated that there were 4,407 total people surveyed. But 719 of those had No Opinion, so $4,407 - 719 = 3,688$ *did* have an opinion. What percentage of *those* are under 40? The answer is in the first row of the table (18 to 39): 917 of these Approve and 204 of these Disapprove. Therefore $917 + 204 = 1,121$ of those showing an opinion are under 40 years of age.

Therefore the percentage of those showing an opinion who are under 40 is $\left(\dfrac{1,121}{3,688}\right)100 = 30.4\%$

---

30. **B**   **Data Analysis (table) HARD**

(A) The approval rate for Proposal 81a generally decreases with the age of the voter.

Age 18 to 39:   918 out of 1,624 approve (56%)
Age 40 to 64:   1,040 out of 1,644 approve (64%)
Age 65 and older: 604 out of 1,139 approve (53%)

The approval rate increases and then decreases with age, so (A) is not correct.

(B) The disapproval rate for Proposal 81a generally increases with the age of the voter:

Age 18 to 39:   204 out of 1,624 disapprove (13%)
Age 40 to 64:   502 out of 1,644 disapprove (31%)

Age 65 and older: 420 out of 1,139 disapprove (37%)

The disapproval rate INCREASES as age increases, therefore (B) is correct.

---

31. **1/5 or 0.2**   **Data Analysis (variation) MEDIUM**

If y varies inversely as x: $y = \dfrac{k}{x}$

Substitute $\frac{1}{2} = y$ and $10 = x$: $\dfrac{1}{2} = \dfrac{k}{10}$

Cross multiply: $10 = 2k$
Divide by 2: $5 = k$

Therefore the general equation is: $y = \dfrac{5}{x}$

Substitute $25 = y$: $25 = \dfrac{5}{x}$

Multiply by x: $25x = 5$

Divide by 25: $x = \dfrac{5}{25} = \dfrac{1}{5}$

---

32. **169** **Advance Mathematics (quadratics) MEDIUM**

$$x^2 = 12x = 13$$
Subtract 13: $x^2 + 12x - 13 = 0$
Factor: $(x + 13)(x - 1) = 0$
Use the Zero Product Property: $x = -13 \text{ or } x = 1$
If $x < 0$, x must be -13. Therefore $x^2 = (-13)^2 = 169$.

Alternately, if you have QUADFORM (a quadratic formula program) programmed into your calculator, select PROGRAM, QUADFORM, and input $a = 1$, $b = 12$ and $c = -13$ to find the zeros (-13 and 1).

---

33. **112**   **Special Topics (polygons) MEDIUM-HARD**

Notice that the "cutouts" can be reassembled to form two squares with side x and diagonal y, leaving an octagon with perimeter $8y$.

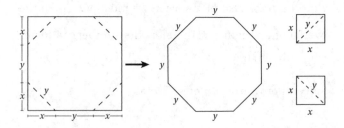

Since each of the cutout triangles is a
right triangle: $x^2 + x^2 = y^2$
Simplify: $2x^2 = y^2$
If the total area of the "cutouts"
is 196 square centimeters: $2x^2 = 196$
Substitute $2x^2 = y^2$: $y^2 = 196$
Take square root: $y = 14$
Therefore the perimeter of the octagon is $8 \times 14 = 112$.

34. 16   **Algebra (solving equations) HARD**

Because $m^2 + n^2 = 40$, where m and n are both integers, we must look for two perfect squares that have a sum of 40. The perfect squares are 1, 4, 9, 16, 25, 36, 49, 64, 81, 100 . . . and the only two of these with a sum of 40 are 4 and 36. So either $m^2 = 4$ and $n^2 = 36$ or $m^2 = 36$ and $n^2 = 4$.

CASE 1:	$m^2 = 4$ and $n^2 = 36$
Take square root:	$m = \pm 2$ and $n = \pm 6$
Since $m < 0 < n$:	$m = -2$ and $n = 6$
Evaluate $(m + n)^2$:	$(m + n)^2 = (-2 + 6)^2 = 4^2 = 16$
CASE 2:	$m^2 = 36$ and $n^2 = 4$
Take square root:	$m = \pm 6$ and $n = \pm 2$
Since $m < 0 < n$:	$m = -6$ and $n = 2$
Evaluate $(m + n)^2$:	$(m + n)^2 = (-6 + 2)^2 = (-4)^2 = 16$

---

35. 1.4   **Advanced Mathematics (trigonometry) MEDIUM-HARD**

Recall the Pythagorean Trigonometric Identity, which is true for all x:	$\sin^2 x + \cos^2 x = 1$
Expression to be evaluated:	$(\sin x + \cos x)^2$
FOIL:	$(\sin x + \cos x)(\sin x + \cos x) = \sin^2 x + 2(\sin x)(\cos x) + \cos^2 x$
Rearrange with Commutative and Associative Laws of Addition:	$2(\sin x)(\cos x) + (\sin^2 x + \cos^2 x)$
Substitute $\sin^2 x + \cos^2 x = 1$:	$2(\sin x)(\cos x) + 1$
Substitute $(\sin x)(\cos x) = 0.2$:	$2(0.2) + 1 = 1.4$

---

36. 115   **Data Analysis (central tendency) MEDIUM**

Begin by putting the data in order from least expensive to most expensive:

80 phones sold for $98
40 phones sold for $110
20 phones sold for $120
62 phones sold for $140
38 phones sold for $162

We don't have to actually write out the prices of all 240 phones to find the median price. We can divide any set of 240 numbers, in ascending order, into two sets of 120 numbers. The median is in the middle of these, so it is the average of the 120th and 121st numbers. Since the first two categories account for $40 + 80 = 120$ of these numbers, the 120th number in the set is $110, and the 121st number in the set is in the next higher category, $120. The median price is therefore $(\$110 + \$120)/2 = \$115$.

---

37. 6.8   **Problem Solving (extended thinking) HARD**

If the height of the logo is to match the height of the banner, it must have a height of 4 feet. Let x be the corresponding length of the logo.

Since the logo has a height-to-length ratio of 5:8:	$\dfrac{5}{8} = \dfrac{4}{x}$
Cross multiply:	$5x = 32$
Divide by 5:	$x = 6.4$

Since the banner is 20 feet long, there are $20 - 6.4 = 13.6$ feet in total for the side margins. If the logo is centered, then each margin is half this length, $13.6 \div 2 = 6.8$ feet.

---

38. 25   **Problem Solving (extended thinking) HARD**

The banner has dimensions of 20 feet by 4 feet, so its area is $20 \times 4 = 80$ square feet. If the company charges $1.20 per square foot for the banner material, this cost is $80 \times \$1.20 = \$96$. Based on the logo dimensions we determined in the previous problem, the area of the logo is $4 \times 6.4 = 25.6$ square feet. If the company charges $2.50 per square foot for the logo, the cost per printed logo is $25.6 \times \$2.50 = \$64$.

If the company charges a fixed cost of $32 per banner, then the total cost of a banner with ONE logo would be $\$96 + \$64 + \$32 = \$192$. The total cost of a banner with TWO logos would be $\$96 + \$64 + \$64 + \$32 = \$256$.

We can calculate the percent savings with the "percent change" formula, since we are considering a "change" from the more expensive banner to the less expensive banner.

$$\frac{192 - 256}{256} \times 100\% = \frac{-64}{256} \times 100\% = -25\%$$

Therefore the percent savings is 25(%).

Section 5: Essay

Sample Response

Reading Score: 8 out of 8
Analysis Score: 8 out of 8
Writing Score: 8 out of 8

In this essay, Steven Pinker examines the "moral panics" surrounding new forms of media and the supposed cognitive and moral decline they cause. His essay provides a measure of balance to our modern discussions of social media and instantaneous digital information. He supports his thesis, that "such panics often fail reality checks," with examples dating back as far as the 1950s, logical analysis, vibrant illustrative images, and touches of humor. He provides historical and scientific context for his claims and effectively encapsulates the broad misconceptions that cultural critics have about the relationship between modern media and the human brain. Although his argument could have been bolstered with more specific scientific support, his essay as a whole effectively argues for a reprieve from the hysteria about intellectual and moral decline allegedly caused by Twitter and Facebook.

Pinker makes use of "reductio ad absurdum," or indirect proof, to make his case. This technique proceeds by arguing that if the point to be refuted were true, it would lead necessarily to a contradiction, and therefore it cannot be true. For instance, Pinker hints at this logical technique in the second paragraph: "When comic books were accused of turning juveniles into delinquents in the 1950s, crime was falling to record lows, just as the denunciations of video games in the 1990s coincided with the great American crime decline." Here, Pinker is suggesting that sociological and psychological evidence refutes claims of social decline.

He uses reductio ad absurdum even more explicitly in the third paragraph: "If electronic media were hazardous to intelligence, the quality of science would be plummeting. Yet discoveries are multiplying like fruit flies, and progress is dizzying. Other activities in the life of the mind, like philosophy, history and cultural criticism, are likewise flourishing." Unfortunately, Pinker does not provide substantial evidence to bolster these claims. He fails to address the common counterclaim that much of the "science" published on the Internet is flimsy, and the "cultural criticism" lazy.

Pinker then goes on to outline a basic lesson in human information processing, in an attempt to ground his argument in science. To Pinker, the claim that "information can change the brain" is facile ("it's not as if the information is stored in the pancreas") and misleading ("the existence of neural plasticity does not mean the brain is a blob of clay pounded into shape by experience"). Rather, Pinker suggests, "the effects of experience are highly specific to the experiences themselves. . . . Music doesn't make you better at math; conjugating Latin doesn't make you more logical; brain-training games don't make you smarter." Unfortunately, Pinker here seems to mistake assertion for argumentation. He is directly contradicting the claims of thousands of music and Latin teachers, as well as dozens of Lumosity commercials. But he is only gainsaying. Here again, we might expect some data to support his points.

Next, Pinker attempts to refute cultural critics by drawing analogies between their reasoning and the faulty reasoning of "primitive peoples" who believe that "eating fierce animals will make them fierce." He likens this to the thinking of modern observers who believe that "reading bullet points and Twitter postings turns your thoughts into bullet points and Twitter postings." But of course just because one line of reasoning parallels another does not mean that both are equally incorrect. Here again, Pinker's argument would benefit from information about the actual cognitive effects of reading Twitter feeds.

Next, Pinker provides a qualification: "Yes, the constant arrival of information packets can be distracting or addictive, especially to people with attention deficit disorder." But here again, even in conceding a point, Pinker doesn't quite offer the information a reader might want: How significant is this distraction or addiction, and does it have any harmful long-term effects? We don't get this information from Pinker, but we do get some practical advice: "Turn off e-mail or Twitter when you work . . ." We get even more substantial advice in the next paragraph: to cultivate "intellectual depth," we must avail ourselves of "special institutions, which we call universities" and engage in "analysis, criticism, and debate." But why, a reader might wonder, should we moderate our use of electronic media if it doesn't have any real harmful effects?

Finally, Pinker ends with a broader perspective and a note of hope: "the Internet and information technologies are helping us manage, search, and retrieve our collective intellectual output. . . . Far from making us stupid, these technologies are the only things that will keep us smart." Perhaps Pinker is right, but his argument would be stronger with more substantial quantitative evidence and more direct refutation of our real concerns about how the Internet might be changing our brains.

Scoring

Reading—8 (both readers gave it a score of 4)

This response demonstrates extremely thorough comprehension of Pinker's essay through skillful use of summary, paraphrase, and direct quotations. The author summarizes Pinker's central thesis and modes of persuasion (*His thesis, that "such panics often fail reality checks," is supported with examples dating back as far as the 1950s, careful logical analysis, vibrant illustrative images, and touches of humor*) and shows a clear understanding of Pinker's supporting ideas and overall tone (*He provides historical and scientific context for his claims and effectively encapsulates the broad misconceptions that cultural critics have about the relationship between modern media and the human brain. . . . Pinker ends with a broader perspective and a note of hope*). Each quotation is accompanied by insightful commentary that demonstrates that this author thoroughly understands Pinker's central and secondary ideas, and even recognizes when Pinker seems occasionally to fall short of his own purpose.

Analysis—8 (both readers gave it a score of 4)

This response provides a thoughtful and critical analysis of Pinker's essay and demonstrates a sophisticated understanding of the analytical task. The author has identified Butler's primary modes of expression (*logical analysis, vibrant illustrative images, and touches of humor*) and has even provided a detailed examination of Pinker's preferred logical method, reductio ad absurdum, with a discussion of several examples. Perhaps even more impressively, the author indicates where Pinker's evidence falls short, providing critical analysis and suggesting alternatives (*Unfortunately, Pinker does not provide substantial evidence to bolster these claims. He doesn't address the common counterclaim that much* of the "science" published on the Internet is flimsy, and the "cultural criticism" lazy. . . . Pinker here seems to mistake assertion for argumentation. . . . Here again, Pinker's argument would benefit from information about the actual cognitive effects of reading Twitter feeds). Overall, the author's analysis of Pinker's essays demonstrates a thorough understanding not only of the rhetorical task that Pinker has set for himself, but also the means by which it is best accomplished.

Writing—8 (both readers gave it a score of 4)

This response shows a masterful use of language, sentence structure to establish a clear and insightful central claim (*Although his argument could have been bolstered with more specific scientific support, his essay as a whole effectively argues for a reprieve from the hysteria about intellectual and moral decline allegedly caused by Twitter and Facebook*). The response maintains a consistent focus on this central claim and supports it with a well-developed and cohesive analysis of Pinker's essay. The author demonstrates effective verb choice (*effectively encapsulates the broad misconceptions. . . . He likens this to the thinking of modern observers*), strong grasp of relevant analytical terms, like *reduction ad absurdum, facile, sociological and psychological evidence, counterclaim, assertion, argumentation,* and *gainsaying*. The response is well-developed, progressing from general claim to specific analysis to considered evaluation. Largely free from grammatical error, this response demonstrates strong command of language and proficiency in writing.

CHAPTER 3

THE LANGUAGE OF IDEAS: VOCABULARY FOR SAT EVIDENCE-BASED READING

The SAT Reading Test: Vocabulary

Why is vocabulary important on the SAT Reading, Writing, and Essay tests?

Although the SAT no longer includes strictly vocabulary-focused questions—such as antonym, analogy, or sentence completion questions—vocabulary-building is still an essential component of improving your SAT Reading, SAT Writing, and SAT Essay scores. The new SAT assesses your *effective* vocabulary by asking you to comprehend, analyze, and write about extended college-level passages that may include vocabulary from the humanities, like *iconoclast*, *aesthetic*, and *colloquial*; vocabulary from the physical and human sciences, like *catalyst*, *catharsis*, and *anomaly*; and vocabulary from rhetoric, like *apologist*, *polemic*, and *advocate*.

According to the College Board, numerous SAT Reading and Writing questions will assess

> *whether students are able to interpret the meanings of relevant words and phrases in context and/or analyze how word choice influences meaning, shapes mood and tone, reflects point of view, or lends precision or interest.*

Sound intimidating? It's not. Here's how to build an effective vocabulary for the SAT:

- Spend one hour per week making 30 flashcards of new words and/or roots from this chapter, using the formats described below.
- Spend 10 minutes per night, at least three nights per week reviewing the flashcards.

Vocabulary Flashcards

> Although some people appreciate obedience in others, I find OB-<u>SEQUI-OUS</u> behavior revolting.

Front: Since the SAT tests your vocabulary in context, **write each new word in a meaningful sentence** on the front of the card. Also, **capitalize** the new word and **underline the important roots and affixes**.

> Excessively obedient or servile
> (to + follow + (adj))
> *servile, sycophantic, deferential, fawning, ingratiating*
>
>   O

Back: On the back, **write the definition** of the word, as well as the **meanings of the roots and affixes** below it. Also **include the synonyms** from the synonym entry for each word, and the **first letter of the word** in the lower right-hand corner. (This is for the **crossword method** of vocabulary review described below.)

Root Flashcards

> mag, maj, max
> *magnus* (L)

Front: Write the **different forms of the root or prefix** as it commonly appears in English words. You may also want to include the original Latin or Greek word.

> great
> *magnificent* (impressively elaborate)
> *magnanimous, maxim, majesty, magnitude*

Back: Write the **definition of the root or affix** on the back of the flashcard, followed by the **anchor word** (that is, the word with the clearest and most meaningful connection to the root or affix). Below that, write the **root family**, that is, those words (especially the SAT "challenge" words) that also contain the root.

Daily Flashcard Study Methods

Sentence Method: Your friend reads you the word, and you give its definition and use it in a sentence different from the one on the front of the card. Try to come up with a different sentence each time.

Root Method: Your friend reads you the word, and you identify and define its roots and affixes and give examples of other words that share the root or affixes.

Crossword Method: Your friend reads you the definition and first letter of the word, and you give the word.

Mnemonic Method: For obscure words, teach your friend a clever mnemonic trick—like a crazy picture or sound association—for remembering its meaning.

1   THE LANGUAGE OF IDEAS AND LEARNING

☐ **abstract** (adj)   *ab-* away + *tractus* pulled

existing as an idea but not as a tangible experience : *For over a thousand years, mathematicians regarded subtracting a large number from a small one as impossible because the concept of negative numbers was too abstract.*
Form: *abstraction* = something that exists only as an idea
Root family: [tract] *retraction* (a pulling back), *protract* (to extend in time), *tractor* (vehicle that pulls farm instruments), *detract* (reduce the value of someone or something), *tractable* (manageable)

☐ **anthropology** (n)   *anthro* human + *-ology* study

the study and comparison of human cultures : *The Amazon basin has long been a focus of anthropological research because of its many isolated indigenous tribes.*
Root family: [anthro] *misanthrope* (one who distrusts all people), *philanthropy* (generosity to charitable causes), *anthropomorphic* (having human form), *anthropocentric* (pertaining to the belief that humans are the center of the universe)
Don't confuse with: *archaeology* (the study of ancient civilizations), *paleontology* (the study of fossils)

☐ **comprehensive** (adj)   *com-* together + *prehendere* to grasp

thorough and complete; covering all relevant subjects : *My doctor gave me a comprehensive physical examination.*
Synonyms: *exhaustive*, *encyclopedic*
Root family: [prehens] *reprehensible* (morally objectionable), *apprehensive* (fearful)
Don't confuse with: *comprehensible* (understandable)
Mnemonic: To avoid confusing *comprehensive* with *comprehensible*, focus on the roots and, especially, the suffixes. Recall that *–ible* or *–able* means "able to be"; for instance, *defensible* means "able to be defended." Therefore, *comprehensible* means "able to be grasped by the mind (*prehendere* = to grasp), while *comprehensive* means "encompassing (or grasping) everything relevant."

☐ **construe** (v)   *con-* together + *struere* to build

to interpret in a particular way : *Some opinion polls are unreliable because their biased phrasing encourages people to construe issues to conform to the ideology of the pollster.*
Form: *misconstrue* = to interpret incorrectly
Root family: [con-, co-, com-, col-] *conjecture* (guess), *consensus* (general agreement), *conspire* (to plot together), *coalesce* (to come together), *coherent* (forming a united whole), *compliant* (willing to obey), *confluence* (a place at which two things merge)
Root family: [stru, stroy, stry] *destroy* (put an end to by attacking), *instruct* (to teach), *industry* (manufacturing activity), *obstruct* (impede)
Don't confuse with: *construct* (to build)

☐ **discerning** (adj)   *dis-* apart + *cernere* to separate

showing a keen ability to distinguish subtle elements : *Elena has a very discerning palate for olives and can even tell in what region of Italy they were grown.*
Forms: *discern* = to recognize and distinguish, *discernment* = keen judgment, *discernible* = perceivable
Synonyms: *discriminating*, *judicious*, *astute*, *percipient*, *perspicacious*
Root family: [dis-] *disparate* (very different; variegated), *discrepancy* (a lack of compatibility between facts or claims), *disseminate* (to cast widely), *disperse* (to spread or scatter), *diffuse* (spread over a wide area)
Root family: [cern, cert, cret, cre] *ascertain* (find something out for certain), *certain* (known for sure), *certify* (formally attest or confirm), *discretion* (behavior to avoid offense or revealing private information; freedom to make decisions)

☐ **discriminating** (adj)   *dis-* apart + *crimen* judicial decision

showing good taste or judgment : *Our interior designer has a discriminating eye for bold fabrics.*
Forms: *indiscriminate* = done without careful judgment
Synonyms: *discerning*, *judicious*, *astute*, *percipient*, *perspicacious*
Root family: [dis-] *disparate* (very different; variegated), *discrepancy* (a lack of compatibility between facts or claims), *disseminate* (to cast widely), *disperse* (to spread or scatter), *disputatious* (argumentative), *dispel* (to drive away; to eliminate), *diffuse* (spread over a wide area)

Root family: [crim] *criminal* (one who commits a crime), *recrimination* (counteraccusation), *crime* (illegal act)
Usage: The word *discrimination* generally has a negative connotation because of its association with unfair practices like racial or sexual discrimination and because of its connection, via the Latin root *crimen* (judicial decision) with words like *crime* and *criminal*. *Discriminating*, however, has a generally positive connotation because it is associated with an expert's judicious ability to distinguish good things from bad.

☐ *disseminate* (v)   *dis-* widely + *semen* seed

to cast (something, usually information) widely, as seed is scattered : *The rumor was disseminated almost instantaneously over the Internet.*
Form: *dissemination* = the process or act of spreading information widely
Synonyms: *promulgate, propagate, circulate*
Root family: [dis-] *disconcerting* (unsettling), *disparate* (very different; variegated), *discrepancy* (a lack of compatibility between facts or claims), *disperse* (to spread or scatter), *dispel* (to drive away; to eliminate), *diffuse* (spread over a wide area)
Root family: [semin] *seminary* (a college to prepare clergy), *seminal* (serving as a primary influence on later works), *seminar* (a discussion-based class)
Don't confuse *dissemination* with *disinformation* (incorrect or misleading information)
Mnemonic: Picture a farmer casting *seed widely* (*dis* = widely + *semen* = seed).

☐ *erudite* (adj)   *e-* not + *rudis* untrained, unwrought

having or showing great learning or knowledge : *Professor Jacoby could be engagingly erudite without seeming pompous.*
Form: *erudition* = an expression of great learning or knowledge; the quality of having great learning or knowledge
Root family: [rud] *rudiment* (a most basic element or undeveloped first form of something), *rudimentary* (basic or undeveloped), *rude* (ill-mannered)
Synonyms: *scholarly, cerebral, learned*
Don't confuse with: *eradicate* (to destroy completely)

☐ *indoctrinate* (v)   *in-* in + *docere* to teach

to teach someone to accept a set of beliefs uncritically : *The parents were concerned that the guest speaker was going to indoctrinate their children.*
Forms: *doctrine* = a set of beliefs held by a political, philosophical, or religious group
Synonyms: *proselytize, inculcate, propagandize*
Root family: [in-] *inundate* (to flood), *incisive* (showing keen judgment), *ingratiate* (to curry favor), *inherent* (existing as an inseparable element), *infiltrate* (to gain access secretly)
Root family: [doc, dox] *doctrinaire* (seeking to impose rigid doctrine), *orthodox* (conforming strictly to traditional teachings), *docile* (compliant and easy to instruct), *paradox* (a self-contradictory statement or situation)

☐ *insular* (adj)   *insula* island

isolated from cultural and intellectual influences outside one's own experience : *The farming village was too insular for Madeleine, who wanted to experience the outside world.*
Form: *insularity* = the quality of being culturally isolated
Root family: [insula] *insulation* (the state of being protected from loss of heat, electrical conduction, or unpleasant effects, or the materials or situations that provide such protection), *isolate* (to set apart from others), *island* (land mass surrounded by water), *peninsula* (land mass surrounded on three sides by water)
Mnemonic: An *insular* community is *insulated* from outside influences.

☐ *orthodox* (adj)   *orthos* right, straight + *docere* to teach

conforming strictly to traditional teachings : *Doctor Altbaum is respectfully skeptical of treatments that have not been tested via orthodox trials.*
Forms: *orthodoxy* = authorized theory or practice, *unorthodox* = straying from conventional teachings
Root family: [ortho] *orthogonal* (at right angles), *orthopedics* (the branch of medicine dealing with correcting bone and muscle deformities), *orthodontics* (the treatment of the misalignment of teeth)
Root family: [doc, dox] *doctrinaire* (seeking to impose rigid doctrine), *indoctrinate* (to teach someone to accept a set of beliefs uncritically), *docile* (compliant and easy to instruct)

☐ *pedantic* (adj)   *pedante* schoolmaster (< *pais* child)

inclined to show off one's learning or knowledge; acting like a know-it-all : *Jennifer's pedantic displays in class earned her the scorn of her classmates.*
Forms: pedant = a know-it-all; *pedantry* = the quality or practice of being a know-it-all
Root family: [ped] *pediatrician* (a children's doctor), *pedagogy* (the art of teaching)
Mnemonic: The word *pedant* derives from *pedagogue* (schoolmaster, or literally "leader of children"), so a *pedant* is anyone who acts like a know-it-all schoolmaster. Or, for a wacky visual mnemonic, picture a gigantic *pet ant* that comes to school and raises his hand all the time because he knows all the answers.
Don't confuse words that derive from *ped* (foot)—like *pedestrian*, *podiatrist*, and *pedal*—with words that derive from *pais* (child)—like *pediatrician*, *pedagogy*, and *pedant*.

☐ *peruse* (v)   *per-* thoroughly + *use* use

to read thoroughly and carefully : *Pitifully few of the congressmen perused the bill before signing it.*
Form: perusal = the act of reading thoroughly
Root family: [per-] *perfect* (as good as can be), *perpetuate* (to help to continue for an extended period of time), *perfunctory* (carried out with a minimum of effort), *perturb* (to make uncomfortable or anxious)
Don't confuse with: *carouse* (drink alcohol abundantly, merrily, and boisterously), *pursue* (to follow in order to catch or attack)
Mnemonic: It's common to mistake *perusal* with *cursory (casual) reading* when in fact it means *careful reading*. Remember that it derives from *per* which means "thoroughly," so to *peruse* means to "use thoroughly."

☐ *postulate* (v)

[POS chew late] assume the existence or truth of something as a basis for reasoning : *Copernicus postulated that the simplest explanation for planetary motion was probably the best explanation.*
Form: postulate (n) [POS chew let] = an assumption made for the purpose of reasoning
Synonyms: posit, presume, hypothesize
Don't confuse with: pustule (a small pimple)

☐ *provincial* (adj)

unsophisticated or narrow-minded; particular to the narrow views of an isolated community : *Glen's comments reflected his provincial political views rather than an understanding of the national interest.*
Form: provincialism = narrow-mindedness or lack of sophistication
Synonyms: parochial
Don't confuse with: providential (opportune; involving benevolent divine intervention)
Mnemonic: A *province* is a small region within an empire, so someone who has never been beyond his or her *province* is *provincial*.

☐ *revelation* (n)

a fact revealed in a surprising way : *The biography provided many interesting revelations.*
Form: revelatory = revealing something previously unknown
Synonym: epiphany
Don't confuse with: revelry (noisy festivities)

---

2   THE LANGUAGE OF ARGUMENT, REASONING, AND PERSUASION

☐ *advocate* (v)   *ad-* for + *vocare* to call, to give voice

[AD vo kate] to provide public support for a person, cause, or policy : *Gina is a tireless advocate for human rights and freedom.*
Form: advocate (n) [AD voh kit] = one who advocates
Root family: [ad-] *allude* (to hint at indirectly), *aspire* (to strive for a lofty goal), *adhere* (stick fast (to)), *acquiesce* (to comply reluctantly), *annul* (to declare invalid)
Root family: [voc, vok] *evocative* (bringing strong images or feelings to mind), *revoke* (to take back), *provocative* (causing anger or annoyance), *equivocate* (to speak ambiguously and noncommittally)
Mnemonic: To *advocate* is to *give voice to* (*vocare* = to call) someone or something.
Don't confuse with: abdicate = to step down from a position of power

☐ *apologist* (n)   *apo-* away + *logos* word, study

one who argues for a particular, often controversial, position : *We were surprised to discover that a few of the history professors seemed to be apologists for fascism.*
Forms: *apology* = an argument for a particular position, ***apologetics*** = the study or practice of arguing for a particular position
Synonym: *polemicist*
Root family: [apo-] ***apostasy*** (the renunciation of a religious belief), ***apocryphal*** (having doubtful authenticity)
Root family: [log] ***eulogy*** (a praising speech), ***epilogue*** (afterword), ***anthology*** (a collection of literary works)
Don't confuse with: *apologizer* (one who expresses regret); ***apologizers*** regret their positions, but ***apologists*** do not.

☐ *appease* (v)   *pais* peace

to yield to demands in order to conciliate : *We must not appease belligerent dictators.*
Form: *appeasement* = the act of conciliating
Synonyms: *propitiate*, *pacify*, *mollify*, *placate*
Root family: [pac, peas] ***pacify*** (to calm), ***pact*** (a peace agreement)
Usage: See usage note at ***pacify*** in section 4.

☐ *bolster* (v)

to strengthen or support : *The case was bolstered by the testimony of three eyewitnesses.*
Synonyms: *fortify*, *augment*, *buttress*
Don't confuse with: *booster* (one who promotes something), ***holster*** (a handgun holder)

☐ *buttress* (n) or (v)

[1] (n) a projecting support for a building, usually of stone or brick; any strong support : *Each buttress on the cathedral was over forty feet long.*
Synonym: *bulwark*
[2] (v) to provide with support or justification : *The prince's claim to the throne was buttressed by papal decree.*
Synonyms: *fortify*, *augment*, *bolster*

☐ *cajole* (v)

to persuade through flattery or coaxing : *Theo could not be cajoled into accepting the position.*
Form: *cajolery* = flattery designed to persuade
Synonyms: *wheedle*, *coax*, *inveigle*

☐ *circumlocutory* (adj)   *circum* around + *loqui* to talk

inclined to speak evasively; speaking as if to avoid the subject : *We expected the candidate to give a circumlocutory and politically correct answer to the question, but were surprised to hear her give a direct and candid response.*
Form: *circumlocution* = evasive speech
Synonym: *periphrastic* (***peri-*** around + ***phrasis*** speech)
Root family: [circum] ***circumspect*** (cautious), ***circuitous*** (roundabout)
Root family: [loqu, locu] ***loquacious*** (talkative), ***colloquial*** (conversational), ***eloquent*** (well-spoken), ***obloquy*** (verbal abuse)

☐ *circumscribe* (v)   *circum* around + *scribere* to write or draw

to define the limits of something, often an issue or problem : *Although the Reimann Hypothesis has yet to be proven, many mathematicians believe that the problem is so well circumscribed that it soon will be.*
Synonym: *encompass*
Root family: [circum] ***circumspect*** (wary, cautious)
Root family: [scrib, script] ***inscribe*** (to write on or carve into something indelibly), ***description*** (a spoken or written representation of a person, event, or object)
Don't confuse with: *circumstance* (general situation or condition), ***circumspect*** (cautious)

☐ *cohesive* (adj)   *co-* together + *haerere* to stick

forming a united whole : *A good jazz band must be cohesive, because its members must communicate instantaneously with subtle musical and gestural cues.*
Form: *cohesion* = the act of forming a united whole
Synonym: *coherent*

Root family: [con-, co-, com-, col-] *consensus* (general agreement), *conspire* (to plot together), *coalesce* (to come together), *compliant* (willing to obey), *confluence* (a place at which two things merge)

Root family: [her, hes] *adhesive* (glue-like substance), *coherent* (clear and rational), *inherent* (existing as an inseparable attribute), *adherent* (a faithful believer in a particular practice or philosophy)

Don't confuse with: *adhesive* (a glue-like substance)

Usage: See usage note at *coherent* in section 5.

☐ *conjecture* (n)   *con-* together + *ject* thrown

a guess based on incomplete information : *Our controversial conjecture on the nature of the newly discovered planet turned out to be correct.*

Form: *conjectural* = based on conjecture

Synonyms: *speculation, postulation*

Root family: [con-, co-, com-, col-] *conformist* (one who conscientiously complies with the standards of a group), *conventional* (according to common practice), *consensus* (general agreement), *conspire* (to plot together), *coalesce* (to come together), *coherent* (forming a united whole), *confluence* (a place at which two things merge)

Root family: [ject] *objective* (based on fact), *subjective* (based on opinion), *reject* (to throw back), *eject* (to throw outward)

Mnemonic: A conjecture is an idea that is "thrown together" (*con* (together) + *ject* (throw)) from incomplete evidence, rather than determined definitively.

☐ *consensus* (n)   *con-* together + *sentire* to feel

[1] general agreement : *The senators were happy to finally reach consensus on the bill.*

Synonyms: *concord, unanimity*

[2] the generally held opinion on a matter : *The consensus was that David was the better player.*

Root family: [sens, sent] *sentient* (having the ability to feel), *sensation* (the experience of feeling), *dissent* (disagreement with conventional views)

Don't confuse with: *census* (an official survey of a population), *concession* (something granted due to a demand)

☐ *contentious* (adj)

causing or likely to provoke an argument : *Carl's accusation was as contentious as it was false.*

Forms: *contend (with)* = struggle to surmount, *contend (for)* = struggle to win (something), *contention* = disagreement; an assertion made in an argument, *contentiousness* = argumentativeness

Synonyms: *belligerent, bellicose, pugnacious, truculent*

Don't confuse with: *content* (adj) (satisfied)

☐ *credulous* (adj)   *credere* to believe

willing to believe : *None of Dave's friends were credulous when he said he was going to start his own business.*

Forms: *incredulous* = unwilling to believe, *credulity* = willingness to believe, *incredulity* = skepticism

Synonyms: *gullible, ingenuous*

Root family: [cred] *credence* (acceptance as true; believability), *credit* (good faith, particularly with regard to financial loans), *credible* (believable)

☐ *criteria* (n, pl)   *kritikos* judge

principles or standards by which something is judged or decided : *The candidate did not meet our criteria for a management position.*

Form: *criterion* (n, sing) = a single standard or principle by which something is judged or decided

Root family: [crit] *critic* (one who judges the merit of something; one who expresses a negative opinion), *critique* (a detailed evaluation), *diacritic* (a symbol above or below a letter indicating its pronunciation)

Usage: Remember that *criteria* is the plural of *criterion*.

☐ *cursory* (adj)   *currere* to run

hasty and superficial : *Marco was only able to take a cursory glance at the report before making his presentation.*

Synonyms: *perfunctory, desultory*

Root family: [cur] *cursive* (written so that adjacent characters are connected), *courier* (messenger), *curriculum* (a course of study), *incur* (to become subject to something because of one's own actions), *precursor* (a forerunner; a substance from which something else is formed)

Don't confuse with: *cursive* (written such that letters run together), *curse* (a solemn utterance intended to bring harm; a swear)

Mnemonic: If you perform a *cursory* reading, you just *run* through it quickly and hastily (*currere* = to run).

☐ *debunk* (v)

to expose the falseness of a belief : *Harry Houdini debunked all of the mediums who claimed to be able to talk to his dead mother.*
Form: *debunker* = one who debunks; *bunk* = nonsense
Synonyms: *refute, invalidate*
Don't confuse *debunker* with *bunker* (reinforced underground shelter; sand hazard on a golf course).

☐ *delineate* (v)   *de-* completely + *lineare* to create with lines

to describe or portray precisely : *The committee delineated the rules by which future officers would be chosen.*
Forms: *delineation* = the process or act of describing something precisely
Root family: [line] *collinear* (on the same line), *alignment* (the process of arranging in a line), *lineage* (family tree)
Don't confuse with: *lineage* (family tree)
Usage: Because of their common root *lineare* (to create with lines), *delineate* is often confused with *outline*. But while *outline* means to sketch briefly, *delineate* means nearly the opposite: to describe *precisely and in detail*.

☐ *dispel* (v)   *dis-* away + *pellere* to force

to drive away; to eliminate a rumor, misconception, or bad feeling : *Even the trip to the fair did not dispel Jerome's sadness.*
Synonyms: *banish, allay, quell*
Root family: [dis-] *disconcerting* (unsettling), *disdain* (feeling that something is unworthy), *discredit* (harm the reputation of something or someone), *disparate* (very different; variegated), *discrepancy* (a lack of compatibility between facts or claims), *disseminate* (to cast widely), *disperse* (to spread or scatter)
Root family: [pul, pel] *expel* (to force out), *repel* (to drive back), *propel* (to exert a forward push), *compel* (to force someone to do something)
Don't confuse with: *disperse* (to scatter)

☐ *disputatious* (adj)   *dis-* apart + *putare* to reckon

[1] (of a person) fond of having heated arguments : *Ron was ostracized from the group because of his disputatious attitude.*
[2] (of a situation) likely to cause an argument : *The meetings became more disputatious over time, forcing the group to disband.*

☐ *elucidate* (v)   *lux* light

to make clear; to shed light on : *The mysterious disappearance was elucidated by the discovery of the ransom note.*
Root family [luc, lum] *lucid* (clear), *illuminate* (to shed light on), *luminary* (a person who inspires others), *translucent* (allowing light through, but not transparently)
Synonym: *explicate*
Don't confuse with: *elusive* (hard to catch)
Mnemonic: When you *elucidate* something you make it more *lucid*.

☐ *enticement* (n)

something that attracts or tempts, particularly because it offers pleasure or advantage : *The school offered an iPod as an enticement to the student who sells the most candy bars.*
Form: *entice* = to attract or tempt
Synonyms: *lure, bait*

☐ *enumerate* (v)   *e-* out + *numerus* number

to list one by one : *We calmly enumerated our complaints to the committee.*
Form: *enumeration* = the process of listing one by one
Synonym: *itemize*
Root family: [numer] *denumerable* (countable), *innumerable* (uncountably infinite), *numerous* (plentiful)
Don't confuse with: *remunerate* (to pay for services rendered)

☐ **equivocate** (v)   *equi-* same + *vocare* to call

to speak ambiguously so as to avoid commitment : *Sheila complained about her boyfriend's tendency to equivocate when the conversation turned to marriage.*
Forms: *equivocation* = the use of noncommittal language, ***equivocal*** = noncommittal, ***unequivocal*** = clear and unambiguous
Synonyms: *dither*, *waver*, *waffle*
Root family: [voc, vok] ***advocate*** (to provide vocal support (for)), ***provoke*** (to cause a strong negative response), ***revoke*** (to officially take back), ***evocative*** (having the effect of drawing out emotions or ideas), ***invoke*** (to bring to bear)
Mnemonic: Politicians frequently ***equivocate*** about issues, that is, give "equal voice" (***equi-vocare***) to both sides so as not to offend any potential voters.

☐ **exhortation** (n)   *ex-* out + *hortari* to encourage

a strong plea, usually through an urgent speech : *The mayor's exhortation that we conserve water seems to have fallen on deaf ears.*
Forms: *exhort* = to encourage vehemently
Root family: [ex-] ***extol*** (to praise highly), ***extemporaneous*** (without planning), ***exuberant*** (filled with liveliness and energy)
Don't confuse with: *extortion* (the practice of obtaining something by threat), ***excitation*** (application of energy or stimulation), ***exertion*** (great effort)
Mnemonic: In *Horton Hears a Who*, the tiny Whos living on a speck of dust ***ask Horton*** to save them. They are ***exhortin'*** when they ***ask Horton***.

☐ **exonerate** (v)   *ex-* out, from + *onus* burden

to absolve someone of blame or fault : *The testimony of the eyewitnesses exonerated the defendant.*
Synonyms: *absolve*, *acquit*, *exculpate*, *vindicate*
Root family: [onus, oner]: ***onus*** (burden), ***onerous*** (burdensome)
Don't confuse with: *exaggerate* (to overstate), ***exasperate*** (to irritate (someone))
Mnemonic: To ***exonerate*** is to take the ***burden*** (of guilt) ***from*** someone (***ex-*** = from + ***onus*** = burden).

☐ **fallacious** (adj)   *fallere* to deceive, to be untrue

based on a mistaken belief or unsound reasoning : *The argument presented by the defense is fallacious because it is founded on an invalid assumption.*
Form: *fallacy* = a mistaken belief or example of unsound reasoning
Synonyms: *specious*, *spurious*
Root family: [fall, fals] ***fallible*** (capable of making errors), ***fault*** (an unsatisfactory feature), ***fail*** (to be unsuccessful)
Don't confuse with: *ferocious* (savagely cruel), ***felicitous*** (well-chosen for the circumstances)

☐ **harangue** (n)

a lengthy and bombastic speech : *The dictator's harangues were designed to inspire fear as much as patriotism.*
Synonyms: *tirade*, *rant*, *diatribe*
Don't confuse with: *harass* (to intimidate; to bother in an aggressive and annoying way), ***heresy*** (an anti-orthodox act or belief)
Usage: See usage note at ***tirade*** in this section.
Mnemonic: Imagine a vivid scene, from your own experience, when one person was really chewing someone else out. Then imagine that the person yelling is also throwing ***meringue*** pies at him (or her), to add injury to insult.

☐ **incongruous** (adj)   *in-* not + *con* together + *ruere* to fall

not consistent with expectations or surroundings : *An incongruous football-shaped telephone sat amid the otherwise tasteful and expensive auction items.*
Form: *incongruity* = something out of place or out of keeping
Synonyms: *dissonant*, *jarring*, *anomalous*, *discordant*, *anachronistic*
Root family: [in-, im-] ***insipid*** (flavorless), ***insuperable*** (impossible to overcome), ***inert*** (lacking vigor), ***interminable*** (unending), ***innocuous*** (harmless), ***indefatigable*** (untiring)
Don't confuse with: *not congruent* (not having the same shape and size)

☐ **induce** (v)   *in-* in + *ducere* to lead

[1] to bring about : *The doctor had to induce vomiting after Helen accidentally swallowed drain cleaner.*
Synonyms: *instigate*
[2] to persuade to do something : *The clever advertisements induced many customers to come see what the store had to offer.*
Synonyms: *wheedle*, *cajole*, *coax*

[3] to derive by inductive (from specific instances to general principles) reasoning : *From my experiences in the hotel, I have induced that the people of Jamaica are unusually friendly.*
Form: *induction* = the process of drawing general conclusions from specific instances
Root family: [in-] ***inundate*** (to flood), ***infer*** (to conclude from evidence), ***incisive*** (showing keen judgment), ***ingratiate*** (to curry favor), ***inherent*** (existing as an inseparable element), ***invoke*** (to bring to bear), ***indoctrinate*** (to teach doctrine), ***infiltrate*** (to gain access secretly)
Don't confuse with: *induct* (to admit someone into an organization in a formal ceremony)

☐ ***inexorable*** (adj)

[1] (of an eventuality) unpreventable : *We cannot stop the inexorable march of time.*
Synonyms: *relentless, inevitable, irrevocable, unremitting*
[2] (of a person) impossible to persuade : *She was inexorable in her belief in the defendant's innocence.*
Form: *inexorability* = inevitability
Synonyms: *obdurate, staunch, obstinate, recalcitrant, intransigent*

☐ ***infer*** (v)   *in-* into + *ferre* to bring, to bear

to conclude from evidence : *The fossil record allows us to infer the existence of reptiles during this era.*
Form: *inference* = a conclusion drawn by reasoning from evidence; the process of reaching such a conclusion
Root family: [in-] ***inundate*** (to flood), ***incisive*** (showing keen judgment), ***ingratiate*** (to curry favor), ***inherent*** (existing as an inseparable element), ***invoke*** (to bring to bear), ***indoctrinate*** (to teach doctrine), ***induce*** (to bring about), ***infiltrate*** (to gain access secretly)
Root family: [fer] ***fertile*** (productive), ***defer*** (to put off until later; to submit to the authority of another), ***coniferous*** (cone-bearing), ***aquifer*** (rock formation that carries groundwater)
Usage: Don't use ***infer*** when you mean ***imply*** (suggest). Although a fingerprint at a crime scene might ***imply*** guilt, only a person can ***infer*** that guilt.

☐ ***insinuate*** (v)

to suggest or hint at something, usually something morally dubious : *The lawyers released the racy photographs in order to insinuate that the defendant was not as morally upright as he claimed to be.*
Form: *insinuation* = a sly hint
Don't confuse with: *instigate* (to initiate an event or action)

☐ ***intransigent*** (adj)

stubbornly unwilling to compromise or agree with someone : *The peace talks reached an impasse when the rebels became intransigent with their demands.*
Form: *intransigence* = reluctance to compromise or agree
Synonyms: *obdurate, staunch, obstinate, recalcitrant*
Don't confuse with: *intransitive* ((of a verb) not taking a direct grammatical object)
Usage: See usage note at ***tenacious*** in section 4.

☐ ***irresolute*** (adj)   *ir-* not + *re-* (intensive) + *solvere* to loosen

hesitant; showing a lack of certainty or determination : *This irresolute and inept congress seems unable to put aside its petty bickering and do what is best for the country.*
Form: *resolute* = determined and unwavering; ***resolve*** = determination to do something; ***resolution*** = determination
Synonyms: *wavering, equivocating, dithering, ambivalent*
Root family: [solv, solu] ***absolve*** (to free from blame), ***dissolve***
Don't confuse with: *low resolution*
Mnemonic: The words ***solve, solution, resolve,*** and ***resolution*** derive from the Latin *solvere* (to loosen, to break into parts). To ***solve*** a problem almost always involves analyzing it first, that is, breaking it into parts. Similarly, it's easier to make a saltwater ***solution*** if you break the salt into smaller pieces, and the ***resolution*** of your television or computer screen depends on how many pieces, or pixels, it is broken into. Because people have historically liked to institutionalize ***solutions*** to big problems, the term ***resolution*** came to mean not just the action of solving a problem (*the pact provided a temporary resolution to the conflict*), but also the formal decision that resulted from it (*the legislature passed a resolution declaring its commitment to balancing the budget*), and then the commitment required to stick to that decision (*she maintained her resolution to abstain from chocolate*).

☐ **litigious** (adj)

unreasonably prone to suing as a means of settling disputes : *I try to appease my customers whenever they are angry, because I know how litigious our society is.*
Forms: litigiousness = tendency to settle dispute with lawsuits, **litigate** = to settle a dispute with a lawsuit, **litigant** = someone involved in a lawsuit
Don't confuse litigate with mitigate (to make a situation less severe).
Mnemonic: After someone **lit** my **gate** on fire, I decided to **litigate**.

☐ **obstinate** (adj)

stubbornly refusing to change one's position : *He obstinately refused to accept the plea bargain.*
Form: obstinacy = strong reluctance to change
Synonyms: obdurate, staunch, intransigent, recalcitrant
Don't confuse with: obstreperous (noisy and difficult to control)
Usage: See usage note at **tenacious** in section 4.
Mnemonic: Imagine **Nate** the **obstetrician** stubbornly refusing to deliver a baby.

☐ **partisan** (adj)

prejudiced in favor of a particular party, typically a political one : *I don't watch cable news because it is so partisan.*
Forms: nonpartisan = unbiased, **bipartisan** = (of a legislative action) partaken by members of two different parties
Don't confuse with: partition (a process of dividing into parts; a physical barrier between areas)
Usage: See usage note at **objective** in section 18.

☐ **placate** (v)   *placare* to please

to pacify with conciliatory gestures : *The angry customer could only be placated by the offer of a full refund and a sincere apology.*
Forms: implacable = unable to be appeased
Synonyms: propitiate, conciliate, appease, mollify
Root family: [plac, plais] **complacent** (self-satisfied), **implacable** (unable to be pleased), **placid** (peaceful), **placebo** (a sugar pill used as a control in a medical experiment), **pleasant**
Don't confuse with: placid (peaceful)
Usage: See usage note at **pacify** in section 4.

☐ **precedent** (n)   *pre-* before + *cedere* to go

a previous occurrence that is used as an example, particularly in a legal context : *There are few precedents for truly interactive textbooks.*
Form: precedence = the condition of being more important, **unprecedented** = unheard of before a recent or hypothetical occurrence
Root family: [pre-] **premeditated** (planned in advance), **precocious** (having exceptional ability at an early age)
Root family: [ced, ces] **concession** (something surrendered), **recede** (move back from a previous position), **secede** (withdraw from a formal union or alliance), **proceed** (go forth)
Don't confuse with: president (head of a republican state; head of an organization)

☐ **prevalent** (adj)   *pre-* before + *valere* to have power

abundant and widespread in a particular area : *Be careful—poison ivy is prevalent in this forest.*
Form: prevail = to be victorious; to be the most powerful, **prevalence** = widespread abundance
Synonyms: prolific, profuse, copious
Root family: [pre-] **precedent** (a previous example), **premeditated** (planned in advance), **precocious** (having exceptional ability at an early age)
Root family: [val] **ambivalent** (having mixed feelings), **valence** (the power of an atom to make bonds with other atoms), **valor** (courage and nobility in the face of danger)
Don't confuse with: relevant (connected and appropriate to the matter at hand)

☐ **propensity** (n)   *pro-* forward + *pendere* to hang

a natural inclination to behave a certain way : *Warner has a propensity for needless exaggeration.*
Root family: [pro-] **protracted** (lasting longer than expected), **prophecy** (prediction), **promote** (further the progress of something; raise in rank), **progeny** (offspring), **reciprocate** (to respond in kind)

Root family: [pond, pend, pens] ***pendant*** (a piece of jewelry hanging from a necklace), ***impending*** (about to happen; imminent), ***dependent*** (requiring something or someone for support), ***appendix*** (a table or other supporting matter at the end of a book; a vestigial sac on the large intestine), ***ponderous*** (heavy)
Don't confuse with: ***preposterousness*** (absurdity)
Mnemonic: If you have a ***propensity*** for something, you are ***propelled*** toward it with great ***intensity***.

☐ ***provocative*** (adj)   *pro-* forward + *vocare* to call

[1] intended to cause a strong negative emotional response : *Daniel's protest was designed to be provocative, rather than informative.*
Form: ***provocation*** = action intended to annoy or anger
Synonyms: ***vexing, galling, incendiary, inflammatory***
[2] intended to arouse sexual desire : *The school dress code imposes severe restrictions on provocative clothing.*
Synonyms: ***alluring, seductive***
Root family: [pro-] ***protracted*** (lasting longer than expected), ***prophecy*** (prediction), ***promote*** (further the progress of something; raise in rank), ***progeny*** (offspring), ***reciprocate*** (to respond in kind)
Root family: [voc, vok] ***revoke*** (to take back), ***evocative*** (bringing strong images or emotions to mind), ***advocate*** (to give public support), ***avocation*** (hobby), ***equivocate*** (to speak ambiguously), ***vocation*** (calling; chosen career)
Don't confuse with: ***evocative*** (bringing strong images or emotions to mind)
Usage: ***Provocative*** and ***evocative*** have very similar meanings, but ***provocative*** is usually reserved to describe something that elicits emotions that are not desired or appropriate, while ***evocative*** describes something that elicits emotions to enrich an experience.

☐ ***pugnacious*** (adj)   *pugnare* to fight

quarrelsome; prone to fighting : *Senator McGinley was a pugnacious defender of his causes, but a sweet and gentle man outside of chambers.*
Form: ***pugnacity*** = belligerence; tendency to pick fights
Synonyms: ***belligerent, bellicose, contentious, truculent***
Root family: [pug] ***impugn*** (to attack as invalid or dishonest), ***pugilist*** (prize fighter), ***repugnant*** (extremely distasteful)
Mnemonic: Imagine a combative little ***pug*** dog.

☐ ***qualify*** (v)   *qualis* of what kind

[1] to moderate a statement to make it less extreme : *I should qualify my statement so that I don't seem to be advocating total anarchy.*
[2] to meet a necessary condition (for) : *Carlos qualified for the state tennis tournament.*
Form: ***qualification*** = a moderation of a previous statement; an accomplishment or quality that makes a person suitable for a position or activity
Synonyms: ***temper, moderate***
Don't confuse ***qualify*** *(a statement)* with ***qualify*** *(for a position or privilege)*.

☐ ***rebut*** (v)

to respond to an accusation by asserting or proving it false; refute : *The candidate spent as much time rebutting her opponent's accusations as she did describing her own positions.*
Form: ***rebuttal*** = an act of refutation
Synonyms: ***repudiate, discredit***
Don't confuse with: ***rebuff*** (to reject ungraciously)

☐ ***recalcitrant*** (adj)   *re-* back + *calcitrare* to kick with the heel

stubbornly uncooperative : *The entire kindergarten class was finger-painting, save for one recalcitrant toddler.*
Synonyms: ***obdurate, staunch, obstinate, intransigent, steadfast***
Root family: [re-] ***reprehensible*** (deserving of condemnation), ***recluse*** (a person who lives a solitary lifestyle), ***refute*** (to prove something false), ***revoke*** (to take back), ***renounce*** (to give up or put aside publicly), ***reciprocate*** (to respond in kind), ***resigned*** (accepting of an undesirable situation), ***regress*** (to return to a less developed state)
Don't confuse with: ***calcified*** ((as of a fossil) hardened into stone, particularly one consisting of calcium compounds)
Usage: See usage note at ***tenacious*** in section 4.
Mnemonic: What do the words ***calcium, calculator, chalk***, and ***recalcitrant*** have in common? They all derive from the Latin root ***calx***, which means "limestone," a mineral composed primarily of calcium carbonate, or "heel," perhaps because the heel is likewise very hard. From this root came ***calculus***, which means "small pebble," and ***calcitrare***, which means "to kick back

with the heel." *Calculate* derives from the practice of accounting with pebbles, and *recalcitrant* derives from the tendency of mules to kick back with their heels rather than obey.

☐ *refute* (v)   *re-* back + *futare* to beat

to prove something false : *Just because a claim has yet be refuted does not mean that it is true.*
Forms: refutation = the process of proving something wrong, *irrefutable* = proven beyond a shadow of a doubt
Synonyms: debunk, invalidate
Root family: [re-] *revoke* (to take back), *renounce* (to give up or put aside publicly), *reciprocate* (to respond in kind), *resigned* (accepting of an undesirable situation), *regress* (to return to a less developed state), *relegate* (to place in a lower rank)
Don't confuse with: refuse (to decline (something))

☐ *resolute* (adj)

unwaveringly purposeful and dutiful : *Despite the threat of violence, the marchers were resolute about making their voices heard.*
Form: resolve (n) = unwavering commitment to a principle, *resolution* = statement of determination, *irresolute* = hesitant
Synonym: steadfast
Don't confuse with: high-resolution ((of an optical device or image) exceedingly clear down to very fine details)
Usage: See usage note at *tenacious* in section 4.

☐ *rhetoric* (n)

[1] the art of persuasion through language : *He was an expert orator, skilled in rhetoric.*
Forms: rhetorical = intended for persuasive effect, *rhetorician* = one who is adept at the language of persuasion
Synonyms: argumentation, forensics, oratory, disputation
Usage: A *rhetorical question* (such as *Who would ever buy such a lousy car?*) is not merely a question that is not answered, but one whose answer is *assumed* by the speaker or writer, because that question is being used to persuade and not to inquire. That is, the question is being used for rhetorical effect.
[2] language that is persuasive but insincere or meaningless : *His speech was dismissed as mere rhetoric.*
Synonyms: bombast, grandiloquence

☐ *specious* (adj)

seemingly plausible, but actually incorrect : *Beck's specious theories are informed more by hysteria than by reason.*
Synonyms: spurious, fallacious
Don't confuse with: species (a classification of similar organisms that can interbreed)
Mnemonic: A *specious* claim is one that should make you su-*spicious*.

☐ *speculation* (n)   *specere* to look

a guess based on meager evidence : *The theory was based more on speculation than on fact.*
Forms: speculate = to form a theory without firm evidence, *speculative* = based on flimsy evidence
Synonyms: conjecture, surmise, postulation
Root family: [spec] *introspective* (meditative), *circumspect* (cautious), *inspect* (to examine closely)
Don't confuse with: inspection (close examination)

☐ *steadfast* (adj)

dutifully firm and unwavering : *The steadfast soldier held his post for days without sleeping.*
Form: steadfastness = resolute refusal to waver
Synonym: resolute
Usage: See usage note at *tenacious* in section 4.

☐ *strident* (adj)

annoyingly loud and harsh, particularly when presenting a point of view : *The political operatives were instructed to take very strident tones at the town hall meeting, to make it seem as if their views were widely held.*
Form: stridency = harshness in presenting one's views
Synonyms: vociferous
Don't confuse with: stride (to walk briskly), *trident* (a three-pronged pitchfork)
Mnemonic: Imagine a protester *striding* with a *trident* and shouting *strident* slogans during a protest march.

☐ *subjective* (adj)   *sub* under + *ject* thrown

based on personal feelings or opinions : *Movie reviews are highly subjective.*
Root family: [ject] *objective* (based on fact), *conjecture* (guess), *reject* (to throw back), *eject* (to throw outward)
Mnemonic: In late Middle English, *subjective* originally meant "submissive, as a royal *subject* to a king or queen," but evolved to mean "pertaining to the points of view that were brought by the subjects to the monarch."
Usage: In modern usage *subjective* is the opposite of *objective* (based on fact rather than opinion).

☐ *substantiate* (v)

provide evidence for : *The scientists could not substantiate their hypothesis, because they could not replicate the results of their experiment.*
Form: *substantive* = significant because it is based in reality
Synonyms: *vindicate, corroborate, authenticate*
Don't confuse with: *substandard* (less than the norm in quality)

☐ *tenuous* (adj)   *tenuare* to make thin, to stretch

flimsy; very weak or slight (esp. pertaining to a link, argument, or relationship) : *The link between lowering taxes and stimulating business is more tenuous than most people think.*
Root family: [ten] *extend* (to stretch forward), *pretend* (to act as if something is so when it is not), *pretentious* (affecting an exaggerated importance), *contend* (with) (to struggle to defeat), *attenuate* (to reduce the force or effectiveness of something)
Don't confuse with: *tense* (taut)
Mnemonic: A *tenuous* connection is a real *stretch* (*tendere* = to stretch).

☐ *tirade* (v)

a long, angry, and critical speech : *His tirades against communism are well known.*
Synonyms: *harangue, rant, diatribe*
Don't confuse with: *torrent* (a strong and sudden stream)
Usage: *Tirade, harangue, rant,* and *diatribe* are similar, but offer different shades of meaning. *Tirade* is the most general of these, describing any long, critical speech; a *harangue* is particularly bombastic, usually inflaming the passions of listeners, and is the primary tool of the demagogue; a *rant* is primarily an instrument of catharsis, allowing the speaker to blow off steam, but not necessarily persuade or do harm; a *diatribe* is more tiresome—while a *harangue* can arouse passion, and a *rant* can be entertaining to watch, a *diatribe* is neither inspiring, informative, nor entertaining.

☐ *viable* (adj)   *vivere* to live

capable of working successfully : *We did not want to invest in a company that had not yet shown that it was viable.*
Synonyms: *feasible*
Root family: [viv, vita] *convivial* (lively and friendly), *revive* (bring back to life), *vivid* (inducing clear images in the mind), *bon vivant* (a person who enjoys a lively and social lifestyle), *vivacious* (full of lively energy)
Don't confuse with: *enviable* (worthy of envy), *verifiable* (able to be proven true or accurate)

☐ *vindicate* (v)   *vin* force + *dictum* declaration

to clear of blame or suspicion : *Victor was vindicated when another suspect confessed to the crime.*
Form: *vindication* = the process of clearing someone of blame or suspicion
Synonyms: *exonerate, exculpate*
Root family: [dict] *vindictive* (vengeful), *dictatorial* (tyrannical), *dictum* (formal declaration), *benediction* (blessing), *malediction* (curse)
Don't confuse with: *vindictive* (vengeful)
Mnemonic: The words *vindictive* and *vindicate* are easy to confuse because they both derive from the Latin *vindex* (from *vin*, "force" and *dictum*, "declaration"), which means "avenger." But they describe different aspects of vengeance: to *vindicate* means "to avenge by proving innocent," while *vindictive* means "consumed with vengeance."

☐ *zealot* (n)

a fanatic; one who is uncompromising and vehement in pursuing ideals : *The party zealots had taken over the meeting, so compromise had become impossible.*
Forms: *zeal* = feeling of deep passion for an ideal, *zealous* = passionate for one's ideals
Don't confuse *zealous* (passionate) with *jealous* (envious)

3 **THE LANGUAGE OF DISSENT, CRITICISM, AND REBELLION**

☐ *adversary* (n)   *ad-* to + *vertere* to turn

a committed enemy or opponent : *The lawsuit turned former friends into adversaries.*
Forms: *adversarial* = inclined to picking fights, pugnacious, ***adverse*** = unfavorable, harmful
Synonyms: *rival*, *contender*, *antagonist*
Root family: [ad-] ***allude*** (to hint at indirectly), ***aspire*** (to strive for a lofty goal), ***adhere*** (stick fast (to)), ***advocate*** (to provide vocal support for), ***acquiesce*** (to comply reluctantly), ***annul*** (to declare invalid)
Root family: [vers, vert] ***diverse*** (various), ***diversion*** (entertainment), ***adverse*** (harmful), ***subvert*** (undermine), ***averse*** (opposed), ***versatile*** (adaptable to different functions)

☐ *antipathy* (adj)   *anti-* against + *pathos* feeling

deep-seated dislike : *Despite the long-standing antipathy between their families, Romeo and Juliet believed their love would triumph.*
Synonyms: *aversion*, *animus*, *antagonism*, *enmity*, *loathing*, *abhorrence*
Root family: [path] ***sympathy*** (feeling of sorrow for the misfortunes of another), ***pathology*** (the science of the causes and course of diseases), ***apathetic*** (lacking concern), ***empathy*** (the ability to share the feelings of others)
Don't confuse with: *apathy* (lack of concern)

☐ *audacious* (adj)

willing to take bold risks : *Desperate to score points, the audacious quarterback called a trick play against the coach's wishes.*
Form: *audacity* = boldness
Synonyms: *impudent*, *impertinent*, *insolent*, *intrepid*
Don't confuse with: *mendacious* (lying)

☐ *averse* (adj)   *ab-* away + *vertere* to turn

having a strong dislike : *Although many considered Will a daredevil, he was actually scrupulous in his planning and highly averse to senseless risk.*
Form: *aversion* = strong dislike
Synonyms: *antipathetic*
Root family: [ab-] ***abhor*** (to regard with hate and disgust), ***abstruse*** (very difficult to understand), ***absolve*** (to free from guilt or blame), ***abstemious*** (self-disciplined and restrictive with regard to consumption)
Root family: [vers, vert] ***adversary*** (enemy), ***diverse*** (various), ***diversion*** (entertainment), ***subvert*** (undermine), ***adverse*** (harmful), ***versatile*** (adaptable to different functions)
Don't confuse with: *adverse* (harmful)

☐ *belligerent* (adj)   *bellum* war

hostile and aggressive : *We might take your suggestions more seriously if you were not so belligerent when you presented them.*
Form: *belligerence* = hostility and aggression
Synonyms: *pugnacious*, *bellicose*, *contentious*, *truculent*
Root family: [bell] ***rebellion*** (act of violent resistance), ***bellicose*** (war-mongering), ***antebellum*** (characteristic of the culture in the southern United States prior to the Civil War)

☐ *berate* (v)

to scold angrily : *The coach berated us for not keeping in shape during the off-season.*
Synonyms: *reproach*, *censure*, *rebuke*, *admonish*, *chastise*, *upbraid*, *reprove*
Don't confuse with: *irate* (very angry)
Usage: See usage note at ***rebuke*** in this section.

☐ *cantankerous* (adj)

grouchy and argumentative : *Mrs. Grieves was a cantankerous old woman who would scream at us from her porch for not wearing shoes.*
Synonyms: *irascible*, *curmudgeonly*, *churlish*, *peevish*, *fractious*, *ornery*

☐ *circumspect* (adj)   *circum* around + *specere* to look

wary; cautious : *Ken's unpleasant experiences with telemarketers made him circumspect about answering the phone.*
Form: *circumspection* = caution, wariness
Synonyms: *wary, vigilant, leery, skeptical*
Root family: [circum] *circumscribe* (to define the limits of something), *circuitous* (roundabout), *circumlocution* (evasive speech)
Root family: [spec] *speculation* (guess based on insufficient evidence), *introspective* (meditative), *inspect* (to examine closely)
Don't confuse with: *circumscribe* (to define the limits of something)
Mnemonic: Those who are *circumspect* are always "looking around" (*circum* = around + *specere* = to look) to make sure they are not in danger.

☐ *clamor* (n)   *clamare* to cry out

an uproar, usually from a crowd showing disapproval : *The guards were awakened by a clamor at the gate.*
Form: *clamor* (v) = to raise an outcry, usually in a group
Root family: [clam, claim] *acclaim* (to praise publicly), *proclaim* (announce publicly and officially)
Don't confuse with: *clamber* (to climb awkwardly)

☐ *condescend* (v)   *con-* together + *de-* down + *scandere* to climb

to act superior to someone else : *Teachers should give clear instructions and not condescend to their students.*
Forms: *condescending* = acting superior or arrogant, *condescension* = looking down on others
Synonyms: *patronize, deign*
Root family: [con-, co-, com-, col-] *conventional* (according to common practice), *conjecture* (guess), *convoluted* (complicated), *coalesce* (to come together), *coherent* (forming a united whole), *confluence* (a place at which two things merge)
Root family: [de-] *deplore* (to express strong disapproval), *denounce* (declare as bad), *debase* (reduce in value), *denigrate* (criticize unfairly), *deference* (submission to the authority of another)
Root family: [scend, scal] *transcend* (to rise above something), *ascend* (to climb), *escalate* (to increase in intensity or magnitude), *echelon* (level or rank)

☐ *encroach* (v)

to intrude on a territory or domain : *The teachers were beginning to worry that the school board was encroaching on their right to teach as they see fit.*
Form: *encroachment* = intrusion on a territory or domain
Synonyms: *trespass, impinge*
Don't confuse with: *reproach* (to reprimand)

☐ *estranged* (adj)   *extra* outside of

no longer emotionally close to someone; alienated : *After being estranged for many years, the couple finally reconciled.*
Form: *estrangement* = the state of being alienated
Synonym: *alienated*
Root family: [extra] *extraneous* (irrelevant to the subject at hand), *extravagant* (excessive, particularly in spending), *extraterrestrial* (from beyond Earth)

☐ *evade* (v)   *e-* out of + *vadere* to go

to escape or avoid, usually through clever means : *The fighter pilot was able to evade the missile with his deft maneuvers.*
Forms: *evasion* = the act of escaping or avoiding, *evasive* = with the intention of cleverly avoiding something
Synonyms: *elude, avoid, skirt*
Root family: [vad, vas] *invade* (to intrude on a region and occupy it), *pervasive* (widespread)
Don't confuse with: *invade* (to intrude on a region and occupy it)

☐ *flout* (v)

openly disregard (a rule or convention) : *It was shocking how openly Gino flouted school rules.*
Synonyms: *defy, contravene, breach*
Don't confuse with: *flaunt* (to show off)
Mnemonic: Imagine a *flautist* (flute-player) playing loudly in the middle of the library, obviously *flouting* the rule of silence.

☐ *heresy* (n)

a belief or act that contradicts religious orthodoxy : *The Republican senator's vote for the tax increase was regarded as an unforgiveable heresy.*
Forms: *heretic* = a person guilty of heresy, *heretical* = having the qualities of heresy
Synonyms: *blasphemy, apostasy, heterodoxy, dissension, iconoclasm*
Don't confuse with: *harangue* (a bombastic speech)
Mnemonic: The first person in beauty school to sport a Mohawk was guilty of *hair-esy.*

☐ *iconoclast* (n)   *eikon* likeness + *klan* to break

(literally a "breaker of icons") one who attacks cherished beliefs : *The Cubist movement consisted of bold iconoclasts shattering the definition of art and reassembling its pieces in disarray.*
Synonyms: *heretic, skeptic, infidel, renegade*
Root family: [clas] *pyroclastic* relating to the breaking of rocks by volcanic eruptions)
Don't confuse with: *idiosyncrasy* (a quirky mannerism)
Mnemonic: Imagine an *iconoclast* as someone making religious *icons crash* to the floor.

☐ *indignant* (adj)   *in-* not + *dignus* worthy

angered by unjust treatment : *Perry became indignant at the suggestion that he was cheating.*
Form: *indignation* = anger at unjust treatment
Synonyms: *aggrieved, affronted, disgruntled*
Root family: [in-, im-] *insipid* (flavorless), *insuperable* (impossible to overcome), *inert* (lacking vigor), *interminable* (unending), *innocuous* (harmless), *indefatigable* (untiring), *ineffable* (inexpressible in words), *inscrutable* (beyond understanding), *impassive* (unemotional), *incongruous* (not consistent with expectations)
Root family: [dign, dain] *dignity* (state of being worthy of respect), *dignify* (to make worthy), *disdain* (contempt), *deign* (to do something that one considers beneath one's dignity)
Don't confuse with: *indigenous* (native), *indignity* (a circumstance or treatment that makes one feel humiliated)

☐ *instigate* (v)

bring about or initiate (an action or event) : *The regime instigated a brutal crackdown on intellectuals.*
Form: *instigator* = one who brings about an action or event
Synonyms: *goad* (to provoke or annoy someone into action), *incite*
Don't confuse with: *investigate* (to examine in order to determine the truth of a situation)
Usage: Although *instigate* is nearly synonymous with *cause*, it has a more negative and intentional connotation than does *cause*. A crime is *instigated* by its perpetrators, but a beautiful cirrus cloud is *caused* by ice crystals forming in the upper atmosphere.

☐ *insurgent* (n)   *in-* into + *surgere* to rise

a rebel : *We were attacked by armed insurgents.*
Form: *insurgency* = campaign of rebellion
Synonyms: *rebel, insurrectionist, subversive, incendiary*
Root family: [in-] *inundate* (to flood), *infer* (to conclude from evidence), *incisive* (showing keen judgment), *ingratiate* (to curry favor), *inherent* (existing as an inseparable element), *invoke* (to bring to bear), *indoctrinate* (to teach doctrine), *induce* (to bring about), *infiltrate* (to gain access secretly)
Root family: [surg] *resurgence* (a revival of activity or popularity), *resurrection* (the act of rising again)

☐ *malign* (v)   *malignus* tending to evil

to speak harmful untruths about : *I am disgusted by political commercials that merely malign the candidate's opponent, rather than offering constructive information.*
Synonyms: *disparage, denigrate, revile, vilify, slander*
Root family: [mal] *malignant* (disposed to causing harm or suffering), *malicious* (full of spite), *malevolence* (evil intent)
Don't confuse with: *malignant* (disposed to causing harm or suffering)

☐ *maverick* (n)

a person who thinks independently : *Lowell Weicker was a maverick Republican senator who later ran as an independent and was elected governor of Connecticut.*
Synonyms: *nonconformist, individualist, eccentric, dissident*

☐ *misanthrope* (n)   *mis* bad + *anthropos* mankind

one who dislikes and avoids humans : *Ebenezer Scrooge was a miserly and miserable misanthrope until he learned the value of friends and family.*
Form: *misanthropic* = characterized by a hatred of mankind
Synonym: *cynic* (one who believes that all people are fundamentally selfish and dishonorable)
Root family: [anthro] ***anthropology*** (the study of human cultures), ***philanthropy*** (generosity to charitable causes), ***anthropomorphic*** (having human form), ***anthropocentric*** (pertaining to the belief that humans are the center of the universe)
Don't confuse with: *malapropism* (a mistaken use of a word for a similar-sounding one, as in, *He is a vast suppository (rather than repository) of information.*)

☐ *rancor* (n)   *rancidus* stinking

deep-seated resentment : *The rancor endured from their acrimonious divorce.*
Form: *rancorous* = characterized by deep-seated resentment
Synonyms: *malice, animosity, antipathy, enmity, acrimony, vitriol*
Root family: [ranc] ***rancid*** (stinking due to staleness or rot)
Don't confuse *rancorous* with *raucous* (annoyingly noisy)

☐ *rebuke* (v)

to express sharp and stern disapproval for someone's actions : *His wife rebuked him for staying out too late.*
Synonyms: *reproach, censure, reprove, admonish, chastise, upbraid, berate*
Don't confuse with: *rebut*
Usage: There are many ways to express disapproval. To ***admonish*** is to go easy on the wrongdoer, emphasizing advice over scolding; to ***reprove*** or ***reproach*** is to criticize with a little more force, chiefly to encourage someone to stop whatever he or she is doing wrong. To ***censure*** is to scold formally and in public. To ***rebuke*** is to scold harshly and sternly, often with a tone of sharp revulsion or condescension; to ***berate*** is scold in particular harsh and unreasonable terms, with the intention of belittling.

☐ *renounce* (v)   *re-* back + *nuntiare* to announce

to give up or put aside publicly : *He renounced his membership in the club when he heard that it would not allow women as members.*
Form: *renunciation* = an act of renouncing
Synonym: *relinquish*
Root family: [re-] ***refute*** (to prove something false), ***revoke*** (to take back), ***reciprocate*** (to respond in kind), ***resigned*** (accepting of an undesirable situation), ***regress*** (to return to a less developed state), ***relegate*** (to place in a lower rank)
Root family: [nunc, nounc] ***announce*** (declare publicly), ***denounce*** (to rebuke publicly), ***enunciate*** (to pronounce clearly)

☐ *reprehensible* (adj)   *re-* back + *prehendere* to grasp

deserving of condemnation : *David's reprehensible behavior during practice earned him a benching for the next two games.*
Synonyms: *deplorable, despicable, repugnant*
Root family: [re-] ***recluse*** (a person who lives a solitary lifestyle), ***refute*** (to prove something false), ***recalcitrant*** (stubbornly uncooperative), ***revoke*** (to take back), ***renounce*** (to give up or put aside publicly), ***regress*** (to return to a less developed state), ***relegate*** (to place in a lower rank)
Root family: [prehens] ***comprehensive*** (thorough and complete), ***apprehensive*** (fearful)
Don't confuse with: *apprehensive* (fearful), ***comprehensible*** (understandable)
Mnemonic: A ***reprehensible*** act is one that any good person would want to ***take back*** (*re-* back + ***prehendere*** to grasp).

☐ *reprove* (v)

to reprimand : *The teacher reproved Jonah for insulting Caroline in front of the class.*
Form: *reproof* = a reprimand
Synonyms: *reproach, censure, rebuke, admonish, chastise, upbraid, berate*
Don't confuse with: *disprove* (to prove false), ***prove again***
Usage: See usage note at ***rebuke*** in this section.

☐ *revoke* (v)   *re-* back + *vocare* to call

to take back a formal decree, decision, or permission : *Glen's hunting license was revoked soon after the shotgun accident.*
Forms: *irrevocable* = unable to be taken back
Root family: [re-] *recluse* (a person who lives a solitary lifestyle), *refute* (to prove something false), *renounce* (to give up or put aside publicly), *reciprocate* (to respond in kind), *regress* (to return to a less developed state), *relegate* (to place in a lower rank)
Root family: [voc, vok] *evocative, advocate, provocative, equivocate*
Synonyms: *rescind, annul, countermand, repeal*

☐ *subvert* (v)   *sub-* under + *vertere* to turn

to undermine the authority or power of another : *The opposition planned to subvert the Democrats and thwart the lawmaking process.*
Forms: *subversion* = an act that serves to undermine the authority or power of another, *subversive* = having the effect or intension of undermining the authority or power of another
Synonyms: *destabilize, sabotage*
Root family: [sub-] *submissive* (meekly obedient), *surreptitious* (secret), *subjugate* (to dominate), *subterfuge* (trickery)
Root family: [vers, vert] *adversary* (enemy), *diverse* (various), *diversion* (entertainment), *adverse* (harmful), *averse* (opposed), *versatile* (adaptable to different functions)

☐ *supplant* (v)

to replace in importance or relevance : *The old economic system was supplanted by a more sustainable one.*
Synonyms: *supersede, override*

☐ *vilify* (v)   *vilis* worthless

to denounce someone bitterly : *After her callous remarks about the poor, Michelle was vilified in the press.*
Form: *vilification* = the act or process of denouncing bitterly
Synonyms: *disparage, denigrate, revile, malign, slander*
Root family: [vil] *vile* (profoundly unpleasant), *revile* (to criticize angrily)
Don't confuse with: *verify* (to demonstrate something to be true)
Mnemonic: *To vilify* is to treat someone like a *villain*. (Actually, *vilify* and *villain* have different roots, but it's a pretty good way to remember the word.)

☐ *vindictive* (adj)   *vin* force + *dictum* declaration

showing a deep desire for revenge : *The vindictive tone of the letter showed that Tom harbored deep resentments.*
Form: *vindictiveness* = desire for revenge
Synonyms: *vengeful, spiteful, rancorous*
Root family: [dict] *vindicate* (to clear of blame), *dictatorial* (tyrannical), *dictum* (an authoritative pronouncement), *benediction* (blessing), *malediction* (curse)
Don't confuse with: *vindicate* (to clear of blame), *verdict* (official ruling of a court)

4   THE LANGUAGE OF POWER AND SUBMISSION

☐ *acquiesce* (v)   *ad-* to + *quiescere* to rest

to accept an unpleasant situation or comply to a demand reluctantly : *Since the rest of the family wanted to drive to the beach, I stopped my protests and acquiesced.*
Form: *acquiescent* = being inclined to acquiesce
Root family: [ad-] *allude* (to hint at indirectly), *aspire* (to strive for a lofty goal), *adhere* (stick fast (to)), *advocate* (to provide vocal support for)
Root family: [quies, quiet] *quietude* (a state of calmness), *quiescence* (a state of dormancy), *disquiet* (anxiety)
Don't confuse with: *acquaintance* (a passing knowledge; a person one knows only slightly), *aquatic* (pertaining to water and particularly the creatures that live in it)
Mnemonic: When someone keeps badgering you noisily over and over to do something, you can make *a* (more) *quiet scene* by just *acquiescing.*

☐ *capitulate* (v)   *capit* head

to surrender; to stop resisting : *The corporation finally capitulated to the labor union's demands.*
Form: *capitulation* = the act of surrendering
Synonym: *concede*
Root family: [cap, capit] *capital* (city that serves as administrative seat), *decapitate* (remove the head), *captain* (a person in command of a team, ship, or similar organization)
Don't confuse with: *recapitulate* (or *recap*) (summarize and restate)

☐ *coerce* (v)   *co-* together + *arcere* to restrain

to force someone to do something by use of threats : *I will not be coerced into betraying my friends.*
Form: *coercion* = the act of forcing someone against his or her will
Root family: [con-, co-, com-, col-] *conformist* (one who conscientiously complies with the standards of a group, *conventional* (according to common practice), *consensus* (general agreement), *conspire* (to plot together), *coalesce* (to come together)
Root family: [erc] *exercise* (physical activity)
Don't confuse with: *co-opt* (to divert something to a role other than it was intended for), *commerce* (the activity of buying and selling)

☐ *concession* (n)   *con-* together + *cedere* to yield, to go

[1] the act of admitting reluctantly that something is true : *I will make the concession that you have a point.*
[2] something surrendered, as land or a right : *The territory was gained as a concession from a neighboring country after the war.*
Form: *concede* = to yield
Root family: [con-, co-, com-, col-] *conformist* (one who conscientiously complies with the standards of a group, *conventional* (according to common practice), *consensus* (general agreement), *conspire* (to plot together), *coalesce* (to come together), *compliant* (willing to obey), *confluence* (a place at which two things merge)
Root family: [ced, ces] *precedent* (a previous occurrence used as an example), *recede* (move back from a previous position), *secede* (withdraw from a formal union or alliance), *proceed* (go forth)
Don't confuse with: *consensus*
Don't confuse with: *concession stand.* Most people associate the word *concession* with *concession stands*, such as those that sell food at sporting events and assume that *concession* means food. However, in this context, the term *concession* refers to the fact that the owner of the venue (a company or town, perhaps), *conceded* to another party the right to sell food on its property. That is, the stadium owner granted a *concession* for someone else to run a *stand*.

☐ *contrite* (adj)   *con-* together + *tritus* rubbed

remorseful; full of regret : *Harold felt contrite after insulting Jacqueline and bought her flowers to make amends.*
Form: *contrition* = an expression or feeling of remorse
Synonyms: *penitent, chastened, rueful*
Root family: [con-, co-, com-, col-] *conformist* (one who conscientiously complies with the standards of a group, *conventional* (according to common practice), *consensus* (general agreement), *compliant* (willing to obey)
Root family: [trit] *attrition* (a wearing down via sustained attack), *trite* (worn out; overused)
Don't confuse with: *content* (adj) (satisfied), *trite* (worn out: overused)
Don't confuse *contrition* with *attrition* (a wearing down via sustained attack).
Mnemonic: The word *contrite* comes from the Latin word *contritus* which means "ground to pieces," from *con-* (together) + *terere* (to rub). This may be because the feeling of guilt—of *contrition*—feels like a grinding in the stomach.

☐ *deference* (n)   *de-* down + *ferre* to bring

respect for or submission to the authority or opinion of another : *The villagers showed their deference by removing their hats as the duke's coach passed them.*
Forms: *deferential* = showing humility and respect, *defer* (to) = to submit to the authority or opinion of another
Synonyms: *capitulation, submissiveness, acquiescence*
Root family: [de-] *decadent* (excessively self-indulgent), *derivative* (imitative of someone else's work), *deplore* (to express strong disapproval), *denounce* (declare as bad), *detract* (reduce the value of something), *debase* (reduce in value), *denigrate* (criticize unfairly), *condescend* (to act superior to someone else)
Don't confuse with: *difference* (a point or way in which things are not the same), *deferment* (postponement)

Mnemonic: To *defer* can also mean "to postpone (a decision)." It is easy to confuse the two meanings of *defer*, particularly when you are thinking about applying to college. To keep the two straight, pay attention to the preposition that follows: if you are *deferred from* a college, the decision about your acceptance has been *postponed* to a later date; however, when you *defer to* another person, you are submitting to his or her authority or opinion.

☐ *demagogue* (n)   *demos* people + *agogos* leading

a leader who persuades followers through emotional populist appeal rather than rational argument : *The nation had grown tired of its demagogues and elected a well-educated technocrat as its new leader.*
Form: *demagoguery* = speechmaking by a political leader that appeals to popular prejudices
Root family: [dem] *democracy* (government elected by and representative of the people), *demographics* (the study of human populations), *epidemic* (a widespread occurrence of a disease)
Root family: [agog] *pedagogy* (the art of teaching), *synagogue* (a Jewish house of worship)

☐ *despot* (n)   *potentia* power

a (usually cruel) ruler with absolute power : *The colonists regarded King George as a despot.*
Forms: *despotism* = the cruel exercise of absolute power, *despotic* = having the qualities of a despot
Root family: [poten] *potentate* (powerful ruler), *impotence* (ineffectiveness), *potency* (strength), *omnipotent* (all-powerful)
Don't confuse with: *depot* (a railroad or bus station, or a large storage area)

☐ *dictatorial* (adj)   *dicere* to declare

characteristic of a ruler with total power; tyrannical : *Kevin was voted out of office because the other members objected to his dictatorial style.*
Form: *dictate* (v) = to lay down authoritatively
Synonyms: *autocratic, peremptory, overweening, overbearing, imperious*
Root family: [dict] *vindictive* (vengeful), *malediction* (curse), *dictum* (command), *benediction* (blessing)

☐ *diffident* (adj)   *dis-* away + *fidere* to trust

lacking in self-confidence; shy and modest : *Kate had to overcome her natural diffidence in order to audition for the musical.*
Form: *diffidence* = lack of self-confidence
Root family: [dis-] *disconcerting* (unsettling), *dispassionate* (not influenced by strong emotions), *disparate* (very different; variegated), *discrepancy* (a lack of compatibility between facts or claims), *disseminate* (to cast widely)
Root family: [fid] *fidelity* (faithfulness), *confidence* (faith in oneself), *perfidious* (untrustworthy), *infidel* (nonbeliever)
Don't confuse with: *indifferent* (lacking concern), *different, deferent* (respectful of the authority of others)
Mnemonic: To avoid confusing it with words like *different* and *deferent*, focus on the root *fidere* (to trust): one who is *diffident* lacks *confidence.*

☐ *domineering* (adj)   *dominus* lord, master

arrogantly overbearing : *Some admired Dave's confidence, but others considered him arrogant and domineering.*
Form: *domineer* = to act in a domineering manner
Synonyms: *imperious, overbearing, dictatorial, despotic*
Root family: [domit, domin] *dominate* (to have power over), *dominion* (sovereignty; control), *domain* (an area controlled by a ruler; a specific sphere of knowledge), *predominant* (acting as the most important or dominant element), *indomitable* (unconquerable)

☐ *eminent* (adj)

famous and respected in a particular domain : *George is an eminent pediatric oncologist.*
Forms: *eminence* = fame; recognized superiority, *preeminent* = well known as being superior
Don't confuse with: *imminent* (about to happen : *The black clouds indicated that the storm was imminent*), *emanate* (to spread out from : *His confidence emanated from him like warmth from a fire*), *immanent* (inherent : *The rights of all humanity are immanent in the Constitution*)
Mnemonic: *Eminem* was one of the first *eminent* white hip hop-artists.

☐ *enthralling* (adj)   *thrall* slave

fascinating; captivating : *The circus provided an enthralling array of exotic acts.*
Forms: *enthrall* = to captivate, *enthrallment* = state of captivation
Synonyms: *enchanting, beguiling, mesmerizing*

Don't confuse with: *appalling* (shocking)

Mnemonic: *Thrall* was an old Norse word meaning "slave," so to *enthrall* someone was to acquire great power over someone, as a master over a slave.

Usage: *Enthralling*, *enchanting*, *beguiling*, and *mesmerizing* offer different shades of meaning to "captivating." *Enthralling* derives from the Norse word for "slave," so it suggests a captivation almost against one's will; *enchanting* describes captivation as if by spell or charm (see *incantation*); *beguiling* likewise suggests the power of charm, but perhaps with deceitful motives; *mesmerizing* connotes a hypnotic power, since it derives from 18th century Austrian physician Franz Anton Mesmer whose theories led to the development of hypnosis.

☐ *exploitative* (adj)

intended to take selfish advantage of a situation or person : *A free market system should allow new companies to exploit the changing demands of consumers.*

Form: *exploit* (v) [ex PLOIT] = to make full use of, often in a selfish way

Don't confuse with: *exploit* (n) [EX ploit] (a bold feat)

☐ *hierarchy* (n)   *hieros* sacred + *arkhes* ruler

a power structure in which members are ranked by status : *Helen has spent many years working her way up the hierarchy of her law firm.*

Form: *hierarchical* = pertaining to or characteristic of a hierarchy

Synonym: *pecking order*

Root family: [hiero] *hieroglyphics* (stylized and symbolic writing as found in ancient Egypt), *hieratic* (pertaining to priests)

Root family: [arch] *monarchy* (government ruled by a king or queen), *autarchy* (government ruled by an individual with absolute power), *matriarchy* (social order in which the female line of descent is predominant), *anarchist*

☐ *imperious* (adj)   *imperare* to command

bossy and domineering : *Glenda became resentful of her manager's imperious demands.*

Synonyms: *peremptory*, *overweening*, *overbearing*, *dictatorial*, *tyrannical*

Root family: [imper, emper] *imperialist* (one who believes in the value of expanding an empire), *empire* (domain of a particularly ruler), *imperial* (royal)

Don't confuse with: *impious* (lacking reverence), *impervious* (unable to be affected), *imperial* (royal)

☐ *impervious* (adj)   *im-* not + *per-* through

not able to be influenced (by) : *Jonah was seemingly impervious to the swarming gnats.*

Synonym: *insusceptible* (to)

Root family: [per-] *perspicacious* (showing keen insight), *permeable* (allowing liquids or gases to pass through), *pervasive* (widespread in a certain area)

Don't confuse with: *imperious* (domineering)

Mnemonic: A good raincoat is *impervious* to rain because it does *not* let water *through* (*im-* not + *per* through).

☐ *indelible* (adj)   *in-* not + *delere* to destroy, to eliminate

forming an enduring impression; unforgettable : *The ink created an indelible stain on my tie.*

Synonyms: *ineradicable*, *ingrained*, *enduring*

Root family: [in-, im-] *interminable* (unending), *indefatigable* (untiring), *ineffable* (inexpressible in words), *inscrutable* (beyond understanding)

Root family: [delet] *delete* (to remove completely), *deleterious* (harmful)

Don't confuse with: *inedible* (repulsive to eat)

☐ *insolent* (adj)

rude and disrespectful : *Craig grew from an insolent adolescent into a well-mannered young adult.*

Form: *insolence* = rudeness and disrespectfulness

Synonyms: *impertinent*, *impudent*

Don't confuse with: *indolent* (lazy)

Mnemonic: Picture the *insole* of your shoe making really rude and disrespectful remarks to you about your foot odor.

☐ *insubordination* (n)   *in-* not + *sub-* under + *ordinare* to rank

an act of defying authority; disobedience : *The captain was irate about the act of insubordination by his first mate.*
Forms: *subordinate* = lower in rank, *subordination* = the act of placing something in a position of lesser importance
Synonyms: *mutiny, recalcitrance*
Root family: [in-, im-] *insipid* (flavorless), *insuperable* (impossible to overcome), *inert* (lacking vigor), *interminable* (unending), *innocuous* (harmless), *ineffable* (inexpressible in words), *inscrutable* (beyond understanding)
Root family: [sub-] *submissive* (meekly obedient), *subvert* (to undermine the authority of another), *surreptitious* (secret), *subjugate* (to dominate)
Root family: [ord] *ordinal* (relating to a ranking or order), *ordain* (to decree from a high authority)
Don't confuse *subordination* with *subornation* (the act of bribing someone to perform a criminal act, especially perjury)

☐ *mandate* (n)   *manus* hand + *dare* to give

an official order or commission to do something : *We objected to our teacher's mandate that we all write our essays according to her rigid formula.*
Form: *mandatory* = required, usually by official order
Root family: [man] *manipulate* (to control skillfully), *maneuver* (a skillful movement), *manual* (done by hand rather than automatically)
Root family: [dar, don, dos, dot, dow] *donation* (charitable gift), *endow* (to donate funds to establish a position or project), *antidote* (a medicine to counteract a poison), *dose* (a recommended quantity of medicine), *anecdote* (a humorous or instructive story), *dowry* (property or money given to a husband by a bride's family), *pardon* (to forgive), *rendition* (the act of sending a foreign criminal to another country for interrogation)
Don't confuse with: *mendacious* (lying)

☐ *obtrusive* (adj)   *ob-* toward + *trudere* to push

[1] (of things) prominent in an annoying way : *Although cell phones themselves have become less physically obtrusive over time, their users have become far more obnoxious.*
Synonyms: *conspicuous, intrusive*
[2] (of people) obnoxiously intrusive : *Donna's questions seemed solicitous at first, but soon became obtrusive.*
Form: *unobtrusive* = not tending to get in the way
Synonyms: *officious, meddlesome*
Root family: [trus, trud] *extrude* (to thrust out), *abstruse* (very difficult to understand), *intruder* (one who pushes in where he or she is unwelcome)

☐ *pacify* (v)   *pax* peace

to quell the agitation of something; to make peaceful : *The lullaby seemed to pacify the crying baby.*
Form: *pacifist* = one who advocates for peace rather than war
Synonyms: *propitiate, appease, mollify, placate*
Root family: [pac, peas] *appease* (to pacify), *pact* (a peace agreement)
Usage: The words *pacify, placate, appease, propitiate, mollify,* and *conciliate* all share the meaning of "making someone feel better," but they offer different shades of meaning. To *pacify* is to calm someone down, like a crying child, but to *placate* is to pacify and gain favor at the same time. To *appease* is calm someone down by complying (perhaps reluctantly) with his or her demands, but to *propitiate* is to make a deliberate show of pleasing someone (as a god or superior). To *mollify* is to soothe, as a mother soothes an anxious child, but to *conciliate* is to win over someone who may not trust you.

☐ *pervasive* (adj)   *per-* through + *vadere* to go

widespread : *Bigotry is still pervasive in this region, and fear of outsiders is preventing its economic development.*
Form: *pervade* = to be present throughout a region or area
Root family: [per-] *perspicacious* (showing keen insight), *permeable* (allowing liquids or gases to pass through), *impervious* (not able to be influenced)
Root family: [vad] *invade* (to intrude on a region and occupy it), *evade* (to escape or avoid)
Don't confuse with: *perverse* (showing a stubborn desire to do something unacceptable)

☐ *potent* (adj)   *potentia* power

particularly powerful, influential, or effective : *Oprah's endorsement is a potent marketing tool.*
Forms: *impotent* = weak and ineffective, *potency* = strength
Synonyms: *formidable, efficacious, redoubtable*

Root family: [poten] *despot* (cruel ruler), *potentate* (powerful ruler), *omnipotent* (all-powerful)
Don't confuse with: *potable* (drinkable)

☐ *predominant* (adj)   *dominat* ruled, governed

acting as the main element or the most powerful influence : *After their demoralizing defeat, the predominant mood among the players was gloom.*
Form: *predominance* = the state of being the controlling influence
Synonyms: *paramount, foremost*
Root family: [domit, domin] *dominate* (to have power over), *dominion* (sovereignty; control), *domain* (an area controlled by a ruler; a specific sphere of knowledge), *domineering* (overbearing), *indomitable* (unconquerable)
Don't confuse with: *preeminent* (highly distinguished)

☐ *propagate* (v)

[1] to spread and promote : *The followers of Plato propagated the concept of "ideal forms" that transcended ordinary sensory experience.*
[2] to breed, as organisms : *The poison ivy propagated throughout the garden.*
Form: *propagation* = the process of spreading or breeding
Synonyms: *disseminate, promulgate*
Don't confuse with: *propaganda* (biased and misleading information used to promote a particular political cause), *prognosticate* (to foretell an event)

☐ *recluse* (n)   *re-* back + *claudere* to close

a person who lives a solitary lifestyle : *Scout and Jem Finch were fascinated by Boo Radley, a mysterious recluse who lived near them.*
Form: *reclusive* = solitary
Synonym: *hermit*
Root family: [re-] *revoke* (to take back), *renounce* (to give up or put aside publicly), *reciprocate* (to respond in kind), *resigned* (accepting of an undesirable situation), *regress* (to return to a less developed state)
Root family: [clud, clus, claus, clois] *claustrophobia* (fear of being in enclosed spaces), *cloister* (seclude as in a monastery), *exclusive* (highly restricted), *preclude* (render impossible), *secluded* (isolated)
Don't confuse *reclusive* **with** *exclusive* (highly restricted)

☐ *relinquish* (v)   *re-* (intensive) + *linquere* to abandon

to voluntarily give up : *Simmons relinquished his position in order to start his own company.*
Synonym: *renounce*
Root family: [linqu, lict] *delinquent* (failing in one's duties), *relic* (a surviving object of historical value), *derelict* (shamefully negligent in one's duties)
Don't confuse with: *distinguish* (to recognize as different)

☐ *ruthless* (adj)

without mercy : *The piranhas attacked with ruthless abandon.*
Synonyms: *callous, inhumane*

☐ *sanction* (n)   *sanctus* holy

[1] official approval : *The king gave his sanction to the agreement among the nobles.*
Form: *sanction* (v) = to give official approval to
[2] a penalty, usually one imposed by one government upon another : *The United Nations voted to impose sanctions on the rogue nation until its government freed its dissidents.*
Form: *sanction* (v) = to impose a penalty
Root family: *sanctimonious* (acting morally superior), *sanctify* (to make holy), *sanctity* (sacredness), *sanctuary* (place of refuge)
Mnemonic: *Sanction* is an unusual word because its two meanings are nearly opposite. It derives from *sanctus* (holy) and originally referred to any decree by a church representative, such as the Pope, which officially condemned or approved something. In modern usage, the positive sense (official approval) is usually intended when the words is applied in a domestic context, but in the negative sense (an official penalty) when vapplied to foreign affairs.

☐ *sequester* (v)

to isolate from outside influences : *Andrew Wiles sequestered himself for months at a time to work on proving Fermat's theorem.*
Synonyms: *cloister, seclude, segregate*
Don't confuse with: *semester* (one half of an academic year)
Mnemonic: Picture a *sequined quester* (that is, someone like Frodo Baggins or Don Quixote who is on a quest, wearing a sequined cape) who is being *sequestered* in a dungeon by an evil nemesis.

☐ *servile* (adj)   *servus* slave

[1] excessively willing to serve others : *The new intern is helpful without being servile.*
Form: *servility* = the quality or habit of being servile
Synonyms: *obsequious, sycophantic, deferential, fawning, ingratiating*
[2] pertaining to or akin to slave labor : *She accepted even the most servile task with good nature.*

☐ *subjugate* (v)   *sub-* under + *jugum* yoke (< *jungere* to join)

to bring under one's domination : *The West Indians were subjugated by the early European settlers.*
Form: *subjugation* = the act or process of dominating
Synonyms: *vanquish, subdue*
Root family: [sub-] *submissive* (meekly obedient), *subvert* (to undermine the authority of another), *surreptitious* (secret)
Root family: [junc, join] *conjunction* (a part of speech, such as *and*, *but*, or *or*, used to join clauses or terms in a list), *disjoint* (separate and nonoverlapping), *juncture* (a place where things join)
Don't confuse with: *subjunctive* (relating to the mood of verbs indicating something imagined, wished, possible, or counter to fact), *conjugate* (to give different forms of a verb)
Mnemonic: Imagine a lowly royal *subject* trapped under the *gate* outside the royal palace and being held there by the royal guards. He is clearly a victim of *subjugation*.

☐ *tenacious* (adj)   *tenere* to hold

holding fast to a position or claim; stubbornly persistent : *Reynolds is a tenacious debater and will rarely yield a single point to an opponent.*
Form: *tenacity* = stubborn persistence
Synonyms: *dogged, unflagging, obdurate, staunch, indefatigable, obstinate, intransigent*
Root family: [ten, tain] *retain* (to hold back), *abstain* (to refrain), *attention* (the process of focusing mental energy), *sustain* (to keep something going), *untenable* (not able to be defended or maintained)
Don't confuse *tenacity* with *temerity* (boldness).
Usage: You can be stubborn in many ways. If you are *tenacious*, you "hold fast" to a position (*tenax* = holding tight) like a pit bull holding on to a bone. When you refuse to change your mind even in the face of substantial evidence, you are being *obstinate*. If you refuse to compromise with or accommodate another person or position, you are *intransigent*. When you "kick back" at someone who is trying to guide you or change your mind, you are being *recalcitrant* (*recalcitrare* = to kick back at something). If your stubbornness is an attempt to fulfill a duty or commitment, you are more noble than pigheaded, so you are *steadfast* or *resolute*.

☐ *tractable* (adj)   *tractare* to pull, to handle

easily managed or influenced : *The children proved to be more tractable after they had been given their afternoon snack.*
Form: *intractable* = difficult to manage
Root family: [tract] *abstract* (lacking concrete existence), *protract* (to extend in time), *tractor* (vehicle that pulls farm instruments), *detract* (reduce the value of someone or something)
Don't confuse with: *trackable* (able to be followed)
Mnemonic: Something *tractable* is *pull-able* (*tractare* = to pull), which means it's easy to manage, handle, or control.

☐ *unremitting* (adj)   *un-* not + *re-* back + *mittere* to send

incessant; never decreasing in intensity : *The unremitting winds threatened to tear the roof off the house.*
Form: *remit* = [1] to cease from inflicting something, [2] to send payment, [3] to refer to an authority
Synonyms: *relentless, inexorable, unabating, interminable*
Root family: [re-] *recluse* (a person who lives a solitary lifestyle), *refute* (to prove something false), *revoke* (to take back), *renounce* (to give up or put aside publicly), *reciprocate* (to respond in kind), *resigned* (accepting of an undesirable situation), *regress* (to return to a less developed state), *relegate* (to place in a lower rank)
Root family: [miss, mit] *submissive* (meekly obedient), *dismiss* (send away), *intermittent*

☐ **usurper** (n)

one who forcibly takes a position of power : *Henry was the usurper of his uncle's throne.*
Forms: usurp = to take power by force, **usurpation** = act of usurping
Don't confuse usurpation with **usury** (the practice of charging excessively high interest rates for loans)

5 THE LANGUAGE OF LANGUAGE AND LITERATURE

☐ **allude** (v)   *ad-* to + *ludere* to play

to hint at indirectly : *Many of the* Harry Potter *novels allude to events that occurred in previous books.*
Form: allusion = an indirect reference
Root family: [ad-] **aspire** (to strive for a lofty goal), **adhere** (stick fast (to)), **advocate** (to provide vocal support for), **acquiesce** (to comply reluctantly), **annul** (to declare invalid)
Root family: [lud, lus] **collusion** (a secret understanding that has a harmful purpose), **delude** (to make someone believe something that is not true), **illusion** (something that gives a false impression of reality), **ludicrous** (foolish and ridiculous)
Don't confuse with: elude (to avoid a pursuer skillfully)
Don't confuse allusion with **illusion** (a false idea or perception)

☐ **analogy** (n)

a correspondence between two things based on structural similarity : *To explain the behavior of a magnetic field, our physics professor used the analogy of a field of wheat.*
Forms: analogous = similar in terms of general structure, **analog** = something that is regarded as structurally similar to another thing
Don't confuse with: apology (argument for a particular position)

☐ **anecdote** (n)

a short amusing or informative story : *My grandfather told many funny anecdotes about life on a submarine.*
Form: anecdotal = pertaining to or deriving from an anecdote
Don't confuse with: antidote (a medicine taken to counteract a poison)

☐ **anthology** (n)   *anthos* flower + *logia* collection

a published collection of writings : *Several of the poems in the anthology were chosen for national awards.*
Synonym: chrestomathy (an instructive collection of passages)
Don't confuse with: anthropology (the study of human cultures)

☐ **bombastic** (adj)

(pertaining to speech) pompous and blustery, with little meaning : *Some cable news shows have replaced reputable journalists with bombastic blowhards.*
Form: bombast = pompous, blustery speech
Synonyms: pompous, turgid, orotund

☐ **coherent** (adj)   *co-* together + *haerere* to stick

[1] clear, rational and consistent : *David could not construct a coherent sentence, so we couldn't understand his point.*
[2] forming a united whole : *The several tribes joined to form a coherent fighting force.*
Forms: coherence = the quality of being clear and rational; the quality of forming a whole, **incoherent** = unclear or irrational; lacking coherence
Synonym: cohesive
Root family: [con-, co-, com-, col-] **conformist** (one who conscientiously complies with the standards of a group, **conventional** (according to common practice), **consensus** (general agreement), **conspire** (to plot together), **coalesce** (to come together), **confluence** (a place at which two things merge)
Root family: [her, hes] **adhesive** (glue-like substance), **cohesive** (forming a united whole), **inherent** (existing as an inseparable attribute), **adherent** (a faithful believer in a particular practice or philosophy)
Usage: Coherent and **cohesive** derive from the same roots and are synonyms as long as they are used to mean "forming a whole." However, **coherent** is more commonly used to mean "clear, rational and consistent," whereas **cohesive** is the preferred adjective for describing things that form a whole.

☐ **colloquial** (adj)   *co-* together + *loqui* to talk

pertaining to informal, conversational speech : *The teacher said that my essay was well reasoned, but that I should avoid colloquial terms like "totally" in a formal paper.*
Forms: colloquy = casual conversation, **colloquialism** = a word or phrase commonly heard in casual, but not formal, conversation
Synonym: vernacular
Root family: [loqu, locu] **loquacious** (talkative), **eloquent** (well-spoken), **circumlocutory** (inclined to speak evasively), **obloquy** (verbal abuse)
Mnemonic: A fancy word for casual conversation is **colloquy** (*co-* together + *loqui* to talk), so **colloquial** language is the language you use when talking to friends, but not when giving a formal speech or writing a formal essay.

☐ **derivative** (adj)   *de-* down + *rivus* stream

imitative of someone else's work and therefore unoriginal : *The judges suggested that Daria's version of the song was too derivative and suggested that she try to make it more original.*
Root family: [de-] **decadent** (excessively self-indulgent), **deplore** (to express strong disapproval), **denounce** (declare as bad), **detract** (reduce the value of something), **debase** (reduce in value), **denigrate** (criticize unfairly), **deference** (submission to the authority of another), **condescend** (to act superior to someone else)
Root family: [riv] **river** (a large stream), **arrival** (coming)

☐ **eclectic** (adj)   *ex-* out + *legere* to choose

deriving from a variety of sources : *Ted has very eclectic tastes in music, ranging from country to jazz to reggae.*
Root family: [lect] **elect** (to choose by voting), **select** (to choose carefully), **delectable** (very tasty)
Don't confuse with: **electric** (powered by electricity), **ecstatic** (extremely happy)

☐ **eloquent** (adj)   *loqui* to talk

articulate and well spoken : *The jury was clearly persuaded by the attorney's eloquent summary.*
Form: eloquence = fluency in speaking or writing
Root family: [loqu, locu] **loquacious** (talkative), **colloquial** (conversational), **circumlocutory** (inclined to speak evasively), **obloquy** (verbal abuse)
Don't confuse with: **elegant** (graceful and stylish)
Mnemonic: Avoid confusing **eloquent** and **elegant** by focusing on the root **loqu**, meaning "talk." A dress can be **elegant**, but it certainly can't be **eloquent** because it can't talk.

☐ **epilogue** (n)   *epi-* upon, in addition + *logos* words

a section at the end of a novel or play that explains the conclusion : *The epilogue explained that the protagonist never remarried.*
Root family: [epi-] **epigram** (a pithy saying), **epidemic** (a widespread disease)
Root family: [log] **eulogy** (a praising speech, usually for a deceased person)
Don't confuse with: **monologue** (a long speech in a play)

☐ **evocative** (adj)   *e-* out + *vocare* to call

tending to draw out strong feelings, ideas, or sensations : *Gabriel Garcia Marquez's magical novels are as evocative as they are disorienting.*
Forms: evoke = to draw out an idea, emotion, or sensation; to elicit, **evocation** = the process of bringing a feeling or idea into the conscious mind
Root family: [e-, ex-] **extol** (to praise highly), **extemporaneous** (without planning), **exuberant** (filled with liveliness and energy), **elusive** (difficult to catch or achieve), **exorbitant** (excessive)
Root family: [voc, vok] **advocate** (to speak out for), **revoke** (to take back), **provocative** (causing anger or annoyance), **equivocate** (to speak ambiguously and noncommittally)
Don't confuse with: **provocative** (causing anger or annoyance)

☐ **irony** (n)

a situation that directly contradicts expectations : *Rose considered it a delicious irony that her accountant friend Teri miscalculated the waiter's tip so egregiously.*
Form: ironic = contradicting expectations, often humorously
Don't confuse with: **iron** (a strong, hard, magnetic metal). Although **irony** can be used as an adjective to mean "like iron," it is best to avoid this usage because of the confusion with the adjective, which has an entirely different origin.

Usage: It is common to confuse *irony* with *interesting coincidence*, but they are not the same thing. Dying on one's birthday may well be an interesting coincidence, but it is certainly not *ironic*, because death is no less expected on one's birthday than on any other day. *Dramatic irony* is a literary device in which the audience is aware of an important fact that is unknown to one or more of the characters in a play.

☐ *laconic* (adj)   *Laconia* Sparta

inclined to use very few words : *Harold was so laconic at parties that few knew that he was an articulate and celebrated writer.*
Synonyms: *taciturn, reticent*
Mnemonic: *Sparta*, the martial city-state of ancient Greece, was known for its disciplined warrior culture. Hence, *spartan* has come to mean "disciplined, austere, or strict." From the Latin word for Sparta, *Laconia*, we get *laconic*, meaning "inclined to use very few words," because Spartans, unlike the Athenians, who were educated in philosophy, poetry, and oration, were not considered particularly well spoken.

☐ *lament* (v)

to mourn or express deep regret : *Our friends lamented the loss of our old playground.*
Forms: *lamentable* = regrettable, *lamentation* = a passionate expression of mourning
Synonyms: *rue, deplore*

☐ *loquacious* (adj)   *loqui* to talk

talkative; tending to chatter : *Although Anita is well liked, she is a bit too loquacious to be a good listener.*
Form: *loquacity* = the quality of being loquacious
Synonyms: *garrulous, voluble*
Root family: *colloquial* (conversational), *eloquent* (well-spoken), *circumlocutory* (inclined to speak evasively)

☐ *melodrama* (n)   *melos* music + drama

sensational drama designed to appeal to the emotions : *I prefer realistic crime dramas to melodramas like soap operas.*
Form: *melodramatic* = excessively dramatic
Root family: [melo] *melodious* (tuneful)

☐ *platitude* (n)

an overused proverb : *My father bored us with his platitudes about hard work and sacrifice.*
Synonym: *banality, bromide, inanity, cliché*
Don't confuse with: *platypus* (a semiaquatic egg-laying mammal)
Mnemonic: Imagine a *platypus* with an *attitude* spouting inane *platitudes* like "Don't put all your eggs in one basket!"

☐ *poignant* (adj)   *pungere* to prick

emotionally moving; keenly distressing : *The climax of the movie was so poignant that virtually the entire audience was reduced to tears.*
Form: *poignancy* = the quality of being emotionally moving
Synonyms: *moving, affecting, plaintive*
Root family: [punc, pung, poign] *punctilious* (scrupulously attentive to rules), *punctual* (on time), *compunction* (sharp feeling of guilt), *puncture* (to pierce), *pungent* (sharp tasting or smelling)
Don't confuse with: *pugnacious*
Mnemonic: *Poignant* derive from *pungere* (to prick) because sharp emotions often elicit a sharp physical sensation, like a poke in the stomach.

☐ *satiric* (adj)

employing humor, irony, or ridicule to poke fun at something : *The skit was a satiric jab at the gridlocked congress.*
Forms: *satire* = humor, irony, or ridicule used to poke fun at something, *satirize* = to poke fun at something with satire, *satirical* = satiric
**Don't confuse *satire* with *satyr* (in Greek mythology, a lustful, drunken god with a horse's ears and tail)

☐ *verbose* (adj)   *verbum* word

excessively wordy : *Sadly, many academics cannot distinguish intelligent prose from that which is merely verbose.*
Synonyms: *prolix, discursive*
Root family: [verb] *verbatim* (word for word), *proverb* (a pithy, well-known saying)

6 THE LANGUAGE OF JUDGMENT

☐ *ambivalent* (adj)   *ambi-* both + *valere* to be strong

having mixed feelings about something : *She was surprisingly ambivalent about attending her own birthday party.*
Form: *ambivalence* = lack of conviction on an issue
Root family: [ambi-] *ambiguous* (vague), *ambidextrous* (able to use both hands skillfully)
Root family: [val] *prevalent* (widespread and abundant), *valor* (bravery)
Don't confuse with: *ambiguous* (vague; having multiple meanings)

☐ *arbitrary* (adj)   *arbiter* judge

based on personal whim, rather than reason : *His coworkers resented his imperious and arbitrary decision-making style.*
Root family: [arbit] *arbitration* (the process of submitting a dispute to a judge), *arbiter* (a judge with absolute power)
Usage: The word *arbitrary* is sometimes misused as a synonym for *random*, as in *The shells were scattered on the beach in an arbitrary pattern.* This is a misuse of the term, because *arbitrary* derives from *arbiter*, meaning "judge," so it should only be used to describe a decision or the result of a decision.

☐ *arbitrate* (v)   *arbiter* judge

to serve as a neutral third-party judge in a dispute : *My mother arbitrated a resolution to the fight between my sister and me.*
Forms: *arbitration* = the process of resolving a dispute via a neutral third party, *arbiter* = one who serves as a judge in a dispute
Synonyms: *adjudicate, mediate*
Don't confuse with: *arbitrary* (based on whim rather than reason)
Mnemonic: Picture a judge *arbitrating* on an *Arby's tray*.

☐ *carping* (adj)

constantly finding fault, particularly about trivial matters : *April's constant carping about the movie forced me to walk out of the theater.*
Synonyms: *caviling, grousing, griping*
Don't confuse with: *carp* (n) (a freshwater fish)
Mnemonic: Imagine an annoying patron at a restaurant *carping* about the *carp* she's been served: *It's too dry! It smells fishy!*

☐ *censor* (v)   *censere* to assess

to edit out or repress objectionable material : *The prisoners' outgoing letters were being censored by the prison officials.*
Form: *censorious* = severely critical of others
Synonyms: *expurgate, bowdlerize*
Root family: [cens] *census* (the official tally of a population), *censure* (to express formal disapproval)
Don't confuse with: *censure* (to express formal disapproval)

☐ *censure* (v)   *censere* to assess

to express formal disapproval of someone's behavior : *The senator was censured for her misconduct, but was permitted to stay in office.*
Synonyms: *chastise, rebuke, upbraid, reprove, reproach*
Don't confuse with: *censor* (to edit out objectionable material)
Usage: See usage note at *rebuke* in section 3.

☐ *clemency* (n)   *clemens* mildness

leniency, particularly in judicial sentencing : *The judge showed clemency because the convict showed great remorse for his actions.*
Synonyms: *mercy, compassion*
Root family: [clemen] *inclement* (stormy)

☐ *conformist* (n)   *con-* together + *form*

one who conscientiously complies with the standards of a group : *I'd rather be an individualist than a conformist.*
Forms: *conformity* = compliance with the standards of a group, *nonconformist* = an individualist
Synonym: *traditionalist*
Root family: [con-, co-, com-, col-] *conventional* (according to common practice), *conjecture* (guess), *convoluted* (complicated), *consensus* (general agreement), *conspire* (to plot together), *coalesce* (to come together), *coherent* (forming a united whole), *compliant* (willing to obey), *confluence* (a place at which two things merge)
Root family: [form] *reformist* (supporting gradual change rather than revolution), *formality* (rigid observance of conventional rules), *deformation* (change of form; distortion)

☐ *contempt* (n)

sharp disgust for something deemed unworthy : *Her contempt for Mr. Jones was so deep that she would not even acknowledge his presence.*
Forms: *contemptible* = worthy of contempt, *contemptuous* = filled with contempt
Synonyms: *scorn, disdain, derision, disparagement*
Usage: See usage note at *disdain* in this section.

☐ *cynic* (n)

one who believes that humans are essentially selfish : *Warren was such a cynic that he mistrusted every word of praise from his teachers.*
Forms: *cynical* = distrustful of the goodwill of others, *cynicism* = belief that everyone is essentially selfish
Don't confuse with: *skeptic* (one who doubts)

☐ *demeaning* (adj)

causing a loss of respect or dignity : *The student protest did not elevate the debate, but instead reduced it to a demeaning travesty of intellectual discourse.*
Synonyms: *degrading, abject*
Don't confuse with: *demeanor* (general bearing or behavior)

☐ *denounce* (v)   *de-* down + *nuntiare* declare

publicly declare as bad or evil : *She was denounced for making a racist slur.*
Forms: *denunciation* = the act of denouncing
Synonyms: *censure, revile, malign*
Root family: [de-] *decadent* (excessively self-indulgent), *derivative* (imitative of someone else's work), *deplore* (to express strong disapproval), *detract* (reduce the value of something), *debase* (reduce in value), *denigrate* (criticize unfairly), *deference* (submission to the authority of another), *condescend* (to act superior to someone else)
Root family: [nunc, nounc] *renounce* (to give up or put aside publicly), *announce* (make a formal declaration), *enunciate* (state clearly), *pronounce* (sound a word in a particular way)
Don't confuse with: *renounce* (to disavow)

☐ *depraved* (adj)

immoral or wicked : *The murderer showed depraved indifference to human life.*
Form: *depravity* = moral corruption
Synonyms: *corrupt, degenerate, debased, nefarious, iniquitous*
Don't confuse with: *deprived* (denied of the benefit of something, particularly basic amenities and cultural advantages)

☐ *derision* (n)

mockery; contemptuous ridicule : *The derision Phil received in the locker room scarred him for life.*
Forms: *derisive* = filled with derision, *deride* = express contempt for; ridicule
Synonyms: *scorn, disdain, contempt, disparagement*
Usage: See usage note at *disdain* in this section.

☐ *disdain* (n)   *dis-* not + *dignus* worthy

feeling that something or someone is unworthy : *I could feel only disdain for Glen's self-serving apology.*
Synonyms: *scorn, contempt, derision, disparagement*
Root family: [dis-] *disconcerting* (unsettling), *discredit* (harm the reputation of something or someone), *discernment* (the ability to make fine distinctions), *dispassionate* (not influenced by strong emotions), *disparate* (very different; variegated), *discrepancy* (a lack of compatibility between facts or claims), *disseminate* (to cast widely), *disperse* (to spread or scatter), *disputatious* (argumentative), *dispel* (to drive away; to eliminate), *diffident* (lacking in self-confidence), *diffuse* (spread over a wide area)
Root family: [dign] *dignify* (to make worthy), *indignant* (angry about unjust treatment), *deign* (to do something that one considers beneath one's dignity)
Usage: *Disdain, contempt, derision, disparagement,* and *denigration* are similar, but offer different shades of meaning. *Disdain* includes a feeling of social superiority; *contempt* includes a particularly acute disgust; *derision* suggests not just a contemptuous feeling but also an outright verbal attack; *disparagement* suggests a long-term campaign to bring someone or something down; and *denigration* involves unjustly harsh criticism.

☐ **dogmatic** (adj)

proclaiming an inflexible adherence to religious or political principles : *Some reporters spend too much time spouting dogmatic opinions rather than providing objective analysis.*
Forms: dogma = rigid doctrines of a religion or philosophy, **dogmatist** = a dogmatic person
Synonyms: peremptory, imperious, doctrinaire
Don't confuse with: pragmatic (concerned with practical, rather than idealistic, considerations)
Mnemonic: Imagine a robot dog (**dog-a-matic**) barking out political beliefs.

☐ **extol** (v)   *ex-* out + *tol* ring out

to praise enthusiastically : *She extolled the technical beauty of Chopin's etudes.*
Synonyms: acclaim, exalt, eulogize
Don't confuse with: exhort (to strongly encourage someone to do something)

☐ **futile** (adj)   *futilis* leaky (< *fundere* to pour)

doomed to fail; pointless : *All attempts to defeat me are futile!*
Form: futility = pointlessness
Root family: [fus, fund, found] **confuse** (to cause to become perplexed), **confound** (to fail to distinguish different elements), **diffuse** (spread over a wide area), **fusion** (the process of joining two things into a single entity), **profuse** (abundant), **transfusion** (a transfer, usually of blood, from one person or animal to another), **refuse** (to reject)
Don't confuse with: utile (advantageous)

☐ **inane** (adj)

silly, stupid : *I find most reality shows to be an inane waste of time.*
Forms: inanity = a silly act, **inaneness** = the quality of being inane
Synonyms: fatuous, asinine, vapid, puerile
Don't confuse with: insane (mentally ill)

☐ **irreverent** (adj)   *ir-* not + *re-* (intensive) + *vereri* to respect

showing no respect for things that are ordinarily given respect : *The comedy troupe performed an irreverent sketch that thoroughly insulted the Vice President.*
Form: reverent = very respectful
Synonyms: impudent, flippant, insolent
Root family: [ir-, in-, im-] **insipid** (flavorless), **insuperable** (impossible to overcome), **inert** (lacking vigor), **interminable** (unending), **innocuous** (harmless), **ineffable** (inexpressible in words), **inscrutable** (beyond understanding), **impassive** (unemotional), **incongruous** (not consistent with expectations)
Root family: [rever] **reverend** (a title for a member of the clergy), **reverential** (highly respectful)
Don't confuse with: irrelevant (not appropriate to the matter at hand)

☐ **mundane** (adj)   *mundus* world

dull and uninteresting : *She wanted to escape her mundane existence.*
Synonyms: humdrum, monotonous, prosaic

☐ **punitive** (adj)   *punire* to punish

intended to punish : *The court imposed punitive damages to discourage such reckless behavior in the future.*
Form: impunity = exemption from punishment
Synonyms: retributive, disciplinary
Root family: [puni, peni] **punish** (to impose a penalty for an offense), **penitence** (remorse for an offense), **penitentiary** (prison), **penalty** (punishment), **penal** (related to prison or punishment)
Don't confuse with: putative (generally considered to be)
Don't confuse impunity with immunity (the ability to resist infection) or **impugn** (to attack as invalid)
Mnemonic: Punitive damages are those imposed on someone in court as a **punishment** to discourage behavior.

☐ **repudiate** (v)

to refuse association with : *I repudiate those governments that deny people equal protection under the law.*
Form: repudiation = the act of repudiating something
Synonyms: renounce, abjure
Don't confuse with: reputed (generally believed), **reputation** (the generally held value judgments about a person)

☐ *skeptical* (adj)

inclined to doubt; not easily convinced : *I was skeptical of Dawn's claim that she could talk to the dead.*
Forms: *skeptic* = a skeptical person, *skepticism* = quality of being skeptical
Don't confuse with: *cynical* (distrustful of others), *septic* (infected with bacteria)
Usage: Students commonly confuse *skeptical* with *cynical*, but they are very different words. *Skeptical* describes a questioning attitude toward *claims*, while *cynical* describes a negative attitude toward *people*.

7   THE LANGUAGE OF EXTREMISM AND EXAGGERATION

☐ *embellish* (v)   *bellus* beautiful

to make a story more interesting by fabricating or exaggerating entertaining details; to decorate; *Paul always embellishes his stories with false intrigue.*
Form: *embellishment* = a decorative detail; a detail added to a story to make it more entertaining
Synonyms: *festoon, gild, embroider*

☐ *eradicate* (v)   *e-* out + *radix* root

to eliminate completely : *By the 1960s, the Polk vaccine had virtually eradicated polio in North America.*
Form: *eradicable* = capable of being completely destroyed
Root family: [radic] *radical* (affecting fundamental change), *radish* (a pungent edible root)
Synonyms: *annihilate, abolish*

☐ *hyperbole* (n)   *hyper* above, beyond

exaggeration for persuasive effect: *The author's claim that there was a "literacy crisis" in America was dismissed as hyperbole.*
Form: *hyperbolic* = exaggerated
Root family: [hyper] *hyperactive* (excessively active), *hyperventilate* (to breathe too quickly)
Don't confuse with: *hyperbola* (a two-part geometric curve).
Mnemonic: It's interesting to note that three of the "conic sections" you may have studied in math class—the *ellipse*, the *hyperbola*, and the *parabola*—correspond to three literary terms:

- *ellipsis* (*elleipein* to leave out) = the omission of language from a quotation or of words that are implied in a sentence, or the symbol (...) indicating such an omission
- *hyperbole* (*huperbole* excess) = exaggerated comments
- *parable* (*parabola* comparison) = a story used to illustrate a moral lesson

The names of the curves are derived from their "eccentricities": a conic with an eccentricity less than 1 is "deficient," hence the name "ellipse"; a conic with an eccentricity greater than 1 is "excessive," hence the name "hyperbola"; and a conic with an eccentricity of exactly 1 is "comparable," hence the name "parabola."

☐ *indulgent* (adj)

excessively generous or lenient : *Her mother was strict, but her grandmother was indulgent.*
Forms: *indulge (in)* = allow oneself to enjoy the pleasure of, *indulgence* = an act of indulging
Don't confuse with: *indolent* (lazy)

☐ *superfluous* (adj)   *super* above + *fluere* to flow

unnecessary, excessive : *After a week of celebrations, the anniversary ball seemed superfluous.*
Form: *superfluity* = an excessive amount
Root family: [super] *insuperable* (impossible to overcome), *superlative* (of the highest degree or quality), *superficial* (on the surface only), *supercilious* (haughty and pompous)
Root family: [flu] *fluent* (able to flow freely; easily conversant in a language or field), *affluent* (wealthy), *confluence* (a place where two things flow together)

☐ *unstinting* (adj)

without reservations; given liberally : *She was unstinting in her support for animal rights.*
Form: *stint* = to give only sparingly
Synonyms: *unsparing, magnanimous, munificent, profuse*
Mnemonic: The verbs *stint, stump* and *stunt* (to retard the progress of, as in *Smoking stunts your growth.*) derive from the same Germanic root. So one who is *unstinting* does not have a stunted sense of generosity.

8 THE LANGUAGE OF CARE AND RESTRAINT

☐ *ameliorate* (v)

to make a situation better : *The recent highway improvements have done much to ameliorate many of commuters' biggest concerns.*
Synonym: *mitigate*
Don't confuse with: *emancipate* (to free from bondage)
Usage: See usage note at *mitigate* in section 17.
Mnemonic: Imagine *Eeyore* from *Winnie the Pooh* who finally gets a cake after he thinks everyone has forgotten his birthday. The cake is *a meal Eeyore ate* which *ameliorated* his depression.

☐ *assuage* (v)

to make something unpleasant less intense : *The news story was intended to sensationalize the epidemic rather than assuage people's fears about it.*
Synonyms: *mitigate, palliate, attenuate, allay, ameliorate*
Don't confuse with: *dissuade* (to persuade someone not to do something)
Usage: See usage note at *mitigate* in section 17.

☐ *curtail* (v)   *curtus* short

to cut back; to impose a restriction on an activity : *The library committee decided to curtail its expenses until it balanced its budget.*
Synonyms: *pare, retrench, curb*
Root family: [curt] *curt* (rudely abrupt)
Mnemonic: If you *cut* off the *tail* of a beaver, it will really *curtail* its abilities.

☐ *equanimity* (n)   *equa* same + *anima* spirit, mind

evenness of temper : *During the lockdown drill, our teacher's equanimity helped assuage the fears of several students.*
Synonyms: *composure, imperturbability, sangfroid, equability*
Root family: [equa, equi-] *equilateral* (having equal sides), *equilibrium* (a state of balance between opposing forces or trends)
Root family: [anim] *magnanimous* (generous), *pusillanimous* (cowardly)
Don't confuse with: *equity* (fairness)

☐ *fastidious* (adj)

showing great attention to details, particularly in matters of cleanliness : *Julia is fastidious about her food, making sure that the vegetables never touch the meat on her plate.*
Forms: *fastidiousness* = the quality of being fastidious
Synonyms: *scrupulous, meticulous, punctilious*
Usage: See usage note at *scrupulous* in this section.

☐ *impassive* (adj)   *in-* not + *passivus* suffered

unemotional; calm : *Despite all the turmoil, Randall was able to remain impassive.*
Form: *impassivity* = a state of calmness and restraint from emotion
Synonyms: *stoic, dispassionate, forbearing, phlegmatic, stolid*
Root family: [in-, im-] *insipid* (flavorless), *insuperable* (impossible to overcome), *inert* (lacking vigor), *interminable* (unending), *indefatigable* (untiring), *inscrutable* (beyond understanding), *incongruous* (not consistent with expectations)
Don't confuse with: *impassioned* (passionate), *impasse* (deadlock; point beyond which passage is impossible)
Mnemonic/Usage: Strangely, *impassive* and *passive* are closer to being synonyms than antonyms. As they are most commonly used, both suggest a *lack* of activity or emotion. To make things even more confusing, the similar-sounding words *passionate* and *impassioned*, while also seeming to be opposites of each other, actually both mean "full of emotion," essentially the *opposite* of *impassive* or *passive*. If this distinction is vexing for you, remember that a *sieve* lets things pass through, so the *–sive* words, *passive* and *impassive*, describe someone who lets things pass easily, without getting too emotional about them.

☐ *meticulous* (adj)

showing finicky attention to details and precision : *A meticulous baker, she often measures her ingredients twice before combining any of them.*
Form: *meticulousness* = attention to details and precision
Synonyms: *scrupulous, fastidious, punctilious*
Usage: See usage note at *scrupulous* in this section.

☐ *nonchalant* (adj)

calm and unconcerned, often inappropriately so : *My lab partner took a nonchalant approach to the experiment and almost caused a dangerous explosion.*
Form: *nonchalance* = lack of concern or enthusiasm
Synonyms: *blithe, blasé, dispassionate, apathetic, indifferent, insouciant*
Usage: A *nonchalant* person is usually putting on airs, but a *blithe* person is innocently unself-conscious. One who is *blasé* has usually become *jaded* to the point of *indifference*. One who is *dispassionate* is adopting a neutral attitude in order to render an objective judgment. One who is *apathetic* typically has neither airs, innocence, nor *judicious* motive.

☐ *parsimony* (n)   *parcere* to be sparing

extreme reluctance to spend money, use unnecessary language, or expend resources : *Mastering the art of haiku requires mastering the art of parsimony.*
Form: *parsimonious* (adj) = extremely reluctant to spend money, use unnecessary language, or expend resources

☐ *placid* (adj)   *placere* to please

[1] (of a person or animal) calm and unexcitable : *I chose to ride the most placid horse.*
[2] (of a place) calm and peaceful : *The chateau was a placid retreat from the city.*
Forms: *placidity* (n) = calmness; peacefulness
Root family: [plac] *placate, implacable* (unable to be pleased), *complacent*
Don't confuse with: *passive* (permitting things to happen without resistance or involvement), *platitude* (a trite proverb)

☐ *refurbish* (v)

to renovate; to restore to good condition : *David studied for weeks to refurbish his conversational Italian before traveling to Rome.*
Don't confuse with: *refurnish* (to restock with furniture)

☐ *rejuvenate* (v)   *juvenis* young

to restore the vitality of : *She felt rejuvenated after her trip to the mountains.*
Synonym: *revitalize*
Root family: [juven] *juvenile* (immature)

☐ *reticent* (adj)   *re-* (intensive) + *tacere* to be silent

unwilling to speak or express one's feelings : *When the conversation turned to her college years, Sheila became uncharacteristically reticent.*
Forms: *reticence* = unwillingness to speak or reveal one's feelings or thoughts
Root family: [tice, tace] *tacit* (unspoken, but understood, as a *tacit agreement*), *taciturn* (quiet and reserved)
Usage: Do not confuse *reticent* with *reluctant*. For instance, *He was reticent to talk about his experiences* is redundant. The correct phrasing is *He was reluctant to talk about his experiences* or *He was reticent about his experiences*.

☐ *scrupulous* (adj)

[1] diligent and attentive to details : *George is a scrupulous researcher.*
Synonyms: *meticulous, fastidious*
[2] concerned with moral correctness : *He is too scrupulous to consider cheating on his taxes.*
Forms: *scruples* = concerns about moral rectitude, *unscrupulous* = lacking in moral character
Don't confuse with: *scrutinize* (to examine closely)
Usage: *Scrupulous, meticulous, fastidious,* and *punctilious* are nearly synonymous, but each offers a different shade of meaning. *Scrupulous* suggests an exactitude combined with high moral standards; *meticulous* suggests a finicky precision, often but

not necessarily about trivial things; *fastidious* suggests a precision born of a compulsive neatness; and *punctilious* suggests an extreme attention to rules, such as etiquette.

Mnemonic: Think of the most precise and detailed-oriented person you know (or the most moral person you know) *pulling* on a *screw*.

☐ **sedate** (adj)   *sedere* to sit

calm, to the point of being dull : *Small-town life was too sedate for Maia.*

Forms: *sedate* (v) = to calm or put to sleep with drugs, ***sedative*** = a drug used to sedate

Root family: [sed, sid] *sedentary*, *dissident* (one who opposes official policy), *assiduous* (hardworking), *insidious* (subtly dangerous), *preside* (to sit in a position of authority), *reside* (to live in a particular location), *sediment* (material that settles to the bottom of a liquid or body of water, particularly a river)

Don't confuse with: *sedition* (incitement to rebellion)

☐ **stoic** (adj)

enduring hardship without complaint : *William remained stoic throughout the funeral.*

Form: *stoicism* = the belief that emotions are the enemy of reason

Synonyms: *dispassionate*, *forbearing*, *phlegmatic*, *stolid*, *impassive*

Don't confuse *stoicism* with *solecism* (an error in grammar or usage, particularly a tactless one) or *solipsism* (the belief that nothing exists except for oneself)

Mnemonic: Stoicism was a Hellenic school of philosophy founded by Zeno of Citium (and which met at the "painted porch"—Stoa Poikile—from which the school got its name) who taught that emotions were incompatible with reasoning and so cultivated a systematic detachment.

☐ **succinct** (adj)   *cingere* to cinch, as with a belt

expressed clearly and concisely : *The documentary was prefaced with a succinct description of the 15-year study it chronicled.*

Form: *succinctness* = the quality of being brief and to the point

Root family: [cinc] *cinch* (to gird with a belt), *precinct* (an administrative district)

Mnemonic: The connection between *succinct* and *precinct* comes in the idea of "cinching" or "encircling" (*cingere* = to cinch or encircle). When you make something more *succinct*, you make it "smaller and tighter" much as cinching a girdle around your waist would make you smaller and tighter. A *precinct* is a well-defined (or well "encircled") district.

☐ **temperance** (n)   *temperare* to restrain

self-control with regard to consumption : *After years of gluttonous behavior, he has learned remarkable temperance.*

Forms: *temper* = to moderate or act as a moderating force, ***temperate*** = showing moderation, ***intemperate*** = lacking self-control

Root family: [temper] *temperature* (degree of heat), *temperament* (disposition or degree of personal restraint)

Don't confuse the *tempe-* words that derive from *temperare* (to restrain) with the *tempo-* words that derive from *tempus* (time), like *extemporaneous*, *temporize* (to delay making a decision), and *contemporary* ((adj) modern; (n) one who lives during the same time period as another).

Mnemonic: The Temperance Movement in the 19th century was designed to curb excessive consumption of alcohol and ultimately led to the Prohibition Era.

To avoid confusing the cognate words *temperance*, *temperament*, and *temperature*, notice how they are all related to the root word *temperare* (to restrain): *temperance* is essentially one's "ability to restrain oneself"; *temperament* refers to much the same thing but has been generalized to encompass emotional dispositions in general; *temperature* was originally a synonym of *temperament* but lent its sense of "degree of emotional heat" to the scientific term for "degree of physical heat."

☐ **vigilant** (adj)   *vigil* awake

watchful for danger or difficulties : *We must remain vigilant against tyranny.*

Form: *vigilance* = watchfulness

Synonyms: *circumspect*, *wary*, *leery*

Root family: [vigil] *vigilante* (one who takes the law into his or her own hands); *vigil* (a prayerful period in the night)

Forms: *dispute* = a heated argument, ***disputant*** = a person involved in a heated argument, ***disputation*** = the art of debate

Root family: [dis-] *disconcerting* (unsettling), *disdain* (feeling that something is unworthy), *discredit* (harm the reputation of something or someone), *diffident* (lacking in self-confidence)

Root family: [put] *compute* (to calculate), *reputation* (social standing), *impute* (to attribute)

9 THE LANGUAGE OF FREEDOM

☐ **anarchist** (n)   *an-* without + *arkhos* ruler

one who believes in freedom from government : *The anarchists wanted to protest the summit but had difficulty organizing themselves.*
Forms: anarchy = absence of governmental rule, **anarchism** = the belief in freedom from government, **anarchic** = lacking systematic government
Root family: [arch] **monarchy** (government ruled by a king or queen), **autarchy** (government ruled by an individual with absolute power), **matriarchy** (social order in which the female line of descent is predominant), **hierarchy** (a ranked system of organization)
Don't confuse anarchic (lacking government) with **archaic** (old and outdated)
Usage: Don't use **anarchy** to mean **chaos** unless it refers to chaos that results directly from a rejection of authority.

☐ **capricious** (adj)

prone to unpredictable behavior : *Her decisions seemed more capricious than reasoned.*
Forms: capriciousness = unpredictability of mood or behavior, **caprice** = a sudden and unaccountable change of behavior
Synonyms: fickle, volatile, whimsical, arbitrary
Don't confuse with: capris (close-fitting calf-length pants), **capiche** ((from Italian *capisci*) slang for "do you understand?")

☐ **emancipate** (v)

to free from bondage : *The prisoners of war were finally emancipated by the liberating army.*
Form: emancipation = the act of freeing those in bondage, **emancipator** = one who sets prisoners free
Synonyms: unfetter, liberate
Don't confuse with: emaciate (to make abnormally thin and weak)

☐ **extemporaneous** (adj)   *ex-* out of + *tempor* time

improvised; performed without preparation : *The senator's extemporaneous speech was surprisingly coherent and very well received.*
Form: extemporize (v) = to improvise
Root family: [tempor] **temporize** (to delay making a decision), **contemporary** ((adj) modern; (n) one who lives during the same time period as another)
Don't confuse with: temporize (to delay making a decision), **contemporaneous** (occurring or existing at the same time)
Mnemonic: If you must make a speech but you are **out of time** (**ex tempor**) to plan it, you must **extemporize**.

☐ **extricate** (v)   *ex-* out + *tricae* perplexities

to free from a constraint or difficult situation : *We found it difficult to extricate ourselves from our duties.*
Synonyms: disentangle, extract
Root family: [tric] **intricate** (complex), **trick**
Don't confuse with: explicate (to analyze and develop (an idea) in detail)

☐ **impetuous** (adj)   *im-* toward + *petere* to drive

done without careful thought or planning; spontaneous : *David's jocular and impetuous nature made him the most popular player in the locker room, but it often caused problems on the field.*
Form: impetuousness = tendency to be impetuous
Synonyms: whimsical, impulsive, capricious
Root family: [im-] **impugn** (to call into question), **impetus** (energizing force), **impute** (to attribute something to someone)
Root family: [pet] **impetus** (driving force), **perpetuate** (to help continue for an extended period), **petulant** (childishly ill-tempered)
Don't confuse with: impetus (driving force), **petulant** (childishly ill-tempered)

☐ **mercurial** (adj)

inclined to unpredictable mood swings : *He was a brilliant but mercurial composer, susceptible to manic bouts of productivity and debilitating depression.*
Synonyms: volatile, capricious, temperamental
Mnemonic: A **mercurial** personality runs hot and cold, up and down, like the **mercury** in a thermometer.

☐ **unfettered** (adj)   *feter* foot (< *ped* foot)

freed from harsh restraints : *Shawn finally felt unfettered from her oppressive relationship.*
Forms: *fetter* = (n) chain or manacle used to restrain a prisoner; (v) to restrain the feet with manacles, *unfetter* = to free from restraint
Synonyms: *liberated, uninhibited, rampant, unbridled, emancipated*
Mnemonic: Someone who is *fettered* has his *feet tied* up in chains.

10 THE LANGUAGE OF CHANGE AND FORCE

☐ **catalyst** (n)   *kata-* down, fall + *luein* loosen

something that stimulates and expedites a process, often a chemical one : *Coach Johnson's speech was the catalyst that turned our football season around.*
Form: *catalyze* = to cause (a process) to accelerate, *catalytic* = acting as or relating to a catalyst, *catalysis* = the acceleration of a process via a catalyst
Root family: [cata] *cataclysm* (a violent natural event), *catastrophe* (disaster), *catapult* (a machine for heaving heavy objects), *cataract* (a waterfall), *category* (a class under which many elements "fall")
Don't confuse with: *cataclysm* (a violent natural event)
Mnemonic: The word *catalyst* (*kata-* down + *luein* loosen) may have come from the idea of a single event, like a shifting stone, causing snow or rocks to cascade into an avalanche.

☐ **disperse** (v)   *dis-* apart + *spargere* to scatter or sprinkle

to spread or scatter over a wide area : *The crowd soon dispersed after it was announced that the band had left the stadium.*
Form: *dispersion* = scattering over a wide area
Root family: [dis-] *discernment* (the ability to make fine distinctions), *disparate* (very different; variegated), *discrepancy* (a lack of compatibility between facts or claims), *disseminate* (to cast widely), *dispel* (to drive away; to eliminate), *diffuse* (spread over a wide area)
Root family: [spers] *aspersion* (a derogatory remark), *interspersed* (distributed at intervals)
Don't confuse with: *dispense* (supply, distribute, or provide), *diverse* (showing great variety)

☐ **ephemeral** (adj)

lasting a very short time : *Designers try to capture the most ephemeral trends.*
Forms: *ephemera* (plural of *ephemeron*) = things that last only a short time : *The trappings of fame are mere ephemera.*
Synonyms: *fleeting, transient, evanescent*
Don't confuse with: *ethereal* (delicate and sublime, as an ether)

☐ **impetus** (n)   *im-* toward + *petere* to strive after

the force that makes something move or energizes a process : *The coach's speech provided the impetus for the team to redouble its efforts in the second half.*
Root family: [im-] *impugn* (to call into question), *impute* (to attribute something to someone)
Root family: [pet] *impetuous* (spontaneous and without planning), *perpetuate* (to help continue for an extended period), *petulant* (childishly ill-tempered)
Don't confuse with: *impious* (not devoutly religious), *impish* (mischievous)
Mnemonic: Imagine an *imp* (a mischievous child) poking you (*impaling* you?) in the back and giving you the *impetus* to run faster.

☐ **intermittent** (adj)   *inter-* between + *mittere* to send

occurring at irregular intervals; not continuous : *The sound of intermittent gunfire revealed that the peace accord was a fragile one.*
Forms: *intermit* (v) = to postpone, *intermittence* = the quality of being intermittent
Root family: [inter-] *intervene* (to come between to alter events), *international* (pertaining to one or more countries)
Root family: [miss, mit] *submissive* (meekly obedient), *dismiss* (send away), *unremitting* (not letting up)
Don't confuse with: *interminable* (unending)

☐ **mutable** (adj)   *mutare* to change

changeable : *Her moods are as mutable as the weather.*
Forms: immutable = unchangeable, **mutability** = changeability
Synonyms: protean, fickle, mercurial
Root family: [mut] **commute** (to travel to and from work; to reduce a criminal sentence; to rearrange numbers that are being added or multiplied), **mutation** (a change in the structure of a gene, or the result of that change), **permutation** (rearrangement)
Don't confuse with: mute (to silence)
Mnemonic: Something that is **malleable** can be shaped by a **mallet**, like clay or a soft metal can.

☐ **ossify** (adj)   *os* bone + *-ify* to make

to turn into bone; to become stagnant or rigid : *Julia could feel her creative impulses ossify as she became inured to the bureaucratic regulations of her job.*
Synonym: stagnate
Don't confuse with: oscillate (swing back and forth)
Mnemonic: The Latin **os**, meaning "bone," can be found in a few medical terms you might be familiar with, like **osteoarthritis** (degeneration of the bone that causes pain in joints) or **osteoporosis** (the gradual weakening of the bones from loss of tissue due to hormonal changes). Therefore, to **ossify** is to "make into bone."

☐ **precipitous** (adj)   *praecipitare* to throw headlong

[1] dangerously high or steep : *It was a precipitous drop to the lake.*
[2] (of a decline) sudden and dramatic : *The merger led to a precipitous decline in the company's stock value.*
[3] (also *precipitate* [pre sip eh TET]) hasty : *The announcement of the layoffs, unfortunately, was precipitous (or precipitate).*
Form: precipice = steep rock face or cliff
Don't confuse with: precipitation (rain, snow, sleet, or hail)
Mnemonic: The nouns **precipitation** (rain, snow, sleet, or hail), **precipice** (high cliff), and **precipitousness** (hastiness) all derive from the Latin **praecipitare**, (to throw headlong), from **prae-** (before) + **caput** (head). Notice how they all pertain to the action of "throwing down" in different ways.
Usage: See usage note at **expedite** in section 14.

☐ **synthesis** (n)   *syn-* together + *tithenai* to place

the act of combining elements into a whole, as ideas into a system, or simpler elements into a compound : *The concert was a synthesis of modern dance, jazz, and slam poetry*
Forms: synthesize = to create something by combining elements, **synthetic** = formed by human agency via assembling chemical components
Root family: [thes, thet, them] **thesis** (a theory proposed as a premise), **antithesis** (a theory presented to oppose a given thesis), **prosthesis** (an artificial body part), **epithet** (an adjective or descriptive phrase referring to a defining quality of a person or thing, such as *lionhearted* in *Richard the Lionhearted*), **anathema** (something that is vehemently disliked)

☐ **transient** (adj)   *trans* to a different place + *ire* to go

lasting a short period of time : *Selena's sense of satisfaction was transient.*
Forms: transience = impermanence, **transitory** = transient, **transient** (n) = a homeless person
Synonyms: fleeting, ephemeral, evanescent
Root family: [trans-] **transcend** (to rise above), **transportation** (means of carrying from place to place), **translation** (the act or result of expressing something in a different language)
Don't confuse with: intransigent (stubbornly unwilling to change one's views)

☐ **volatile** (adj)   *volare* to fly

prone to unpredictable, rapid, and undesirable changes or displays of emotion; explosive : *The convergence of the opposing protest marches created a volatile and dangerous situation.*
Synonyms: incendiary, inflammatory
Root family: [vol] **volley** (an exchange of tennis shots; a series of utterances; a flurry of projectiles)
Don't confuse with: versatile
Mnemonic: In chemistry, a **volatile** liquid (such as gasoline) is one that evaporates very quickly and, often, one whose vapors are flammable or explosive. The vapors "fly" (**volare** = to fly) from the liquid, just as **volatile** situations tend to "fly" out of control.

11 THE LANGUAGE OF DULLNESS AND STASIS

☐ **banal** (adj)

lacking in originality; dull and boring : *Ironically, even the most exciting car chases have become banal cinematic devices.*
Form: banality = an overused saying or device
Synonyms: trite, hackneyed, vapid, platitudinous
Mnemonic: Today's romantic comedies are so **banal** that we should **ban all** of them.

☐ **conventional** (adj)   *con-* together + *venire* to come

according to common practice : *It's not a conventional love story.*
Forms: convene = come together in a group; **convention** = standard way of doing something; **unconventional** = demonstrating original thinking
Root family: [con-, co-, com-, col-] **conformist** (one who conscientiously complies with the standards of a group, **conjecture** (guess), **convoluted** (complicated), **consensus** (general agreement), **conspire** (to plot together), **coalesce** (to come together), **coherent** (forming a united whole), **compliant** (willing to obey), **confluence** (a place at which two things merge)
Root family: [ven, vene, vent] **intervene** (to come between to alter events), **venture** (daring undertaking), **revenue** (income), **circumvent** (to avoid by finding a way around)

☐ **homogeneous** (adj)   *homo* same + *gen* kind

consisting of parts or members all of the same kind : *The club was a homogeneous band of like-minded thinkers.*
Root family: [gen] **indigenous** (native), **progenitor** (the first in a family tree), **heterogeneous** (diverse in character or content), **disingenuous** (not sincere or candid)
Don't confuse with: homogenous (having a common biological lineage or structure)

☐ **indigenous** (adj)   *indi-* into + *gignere* to be born

native; occurring naturally in a particular place : *There are over twenty different tribes indigenous to this river valley.*
Synonyms: native, aboriginal
Root family: [gen] **progeny** (offspring), **disingenuous** (not candid or sincere), **progenitor** (the first in a family tree), **heterogeneous** (diverse in character or content), **homogeneous** (consisting of parts or members all of the same kind)
Don't confuse with: ingenious (brilliant), **indignant** (showing anger at unfair treatment)
Mnemonic: The phrase **indigenous** people refers to a tribe **born into** (**indi-** into + **gignere** to be born) a particular area.

☐ **insipid** (adj)   *in-* not + *sapere* to taste

lacking vigor or interest, flavorless : *His latest album drones with insipid songs.*
Root family: [in-, im-] **insuperable** (impossible to overcome), **inert** (lacking vigor), **interminable** (unending), **innocuous** (harmless), **indefatigable** (untiring), **ineffable** (inexpressible in words), **inscrutable** (beyond understanding), **impassive** (unemotional), **incongruous** (not consistent with expectations)
Root family: [sap, sav] **sapid** (flavorful), **savor** (taste and enjoy thoroughly), **savory** (having a flavorful spiciness or saltiness)
Mnemonic: It would be **insane** to **sip** such an **insipid** soup.
Don't confuse with: insidious (subtly harmful or dangerous)

☐ **languish** (v)

to lack energy; to grow weak : *My favorite baseball team has been languishing in last place for two weeks now.*
Forms: languor = a state of weakness or stillness, **languid** = lacking in energy; weak
Synonyms: atrophy, wither
Don't confuse with: language (a symbolic means of communication), **anguish** (great distress)
Mnemonic: When your favorite team is **languishing**, it can cause you **long anguish**.

☐ **prosaic** (adj)   *prosa* straightforward discourse

[1] commonplace : *The envoy's duties in Paris were less romantic and more prosaic than she had hoped.*
[2] lacking poetic beauty : *The band's arrangements are powerful, but their lyrics are prosaic.*
Synonyms: workaday, tedious, pedestrian, mundane
Mnemonic: Your writing might become **prosaic** and less creative if you take too much **Prozac** (the antidepressant drug).
Don't confuse with: mosaic (a picture produced by arranging colorful tiles or pieces of glass).

☐ **protracted** (adj)   *pro-* forward + *tractus* pulled

lasting longer than desired or expected : *The interview turned into a protracted debate about bigotry.*
Form: protract = to prolong
Root family: [pro-] **prophecy** (prediction), **promote** (further the progress of something; raise in rank) **progeny** (offspring), **reciprocate** (to respond in kind)
Root family: [tract] **tractable** (manageable), **abstract** (lacking a concrete existence), **detract** (to reduce the value of something)

☐ **stagnant** (adj)   *stare* to stand

[1] (of a pool of water or the air in a confined space) unmoving and hence having an unpleasant smell : *The stagnant air of the gym made us feel sick.*
[2] sluggish : *The economy has been stagnant for years.*
Forms: stagnate = to become stagnant, **stagnation** = the state of being or becoming stagnant
Root family: [stan, stat, stag, stas, stab] **stasis** (a period of inactivity), **constant** (unchanging), **stable** (resistant to movement or failure), **apostasy** (heresy)

12   THE LANGUAGE OF TRUTH, TRUTHFULNESS, AND BEAUTY

☐ **aesthetic** (adj)   *aistheta* perceptible things

concerned with the appreciation of beauty or art : *The painting gave aesthetic pleasure.*
Forms: aesthete = one who has or pretends to have special aesthetic sense, **aesthetics** = the principles or study of beauty and art
Root family: [esthe] **anesthetic** (a substance that reduces sensitivity to pain), **synesthesia** (stimulation of one sense modality by another, such as seeing colors while hearing music)
Don't confuse with: ascetic (a person who practices strict religious self-discipline), **prosthetic** (pertaining to an artificial limb or other body part)

☐ **candid** (adj)   *candidus* white

honest and straightforward : *The president gave a very candid interview just one month after leaving office.*
Form: candor = honesty and forthrightness
Synonyms: frank, ingenuous
Mnemonic: *Candid* derives from the Latin **candidus**, which means "white," because white has long been associated with purity and honesty. The related word, **candidate**, derives from the fact that, in ancient Rome, candidates for office wore white togas. In naming his title character **Candide**, Voltaire was emphasizing his pure, ingenuous nature.

☐ **fallible** (adj)   *fallere* to deceive

capable of making mistakes or errors : *I was crestfallen to discover that my father was fallible.*
Forms: infallible = incapable of making errors
Root family: [fall, fals] **fallacy** (a mistaken belief), **fault** (an unsatisfactory feature), **fail** (to be unsuccessful)

☐ **incontrovertible** (adj)   *in-* not + *contra-* against + *vertere* to turn

unable to be disputed; beyond controversy : *The proof of the theorem was incontrovertible.*
Forms: controvertible = able to be disputed, **controversy** = dispute
Synonyms: irrefutable, indubitable, unassailable, airtight
Root family: [in-, im-] **insipid** (flavorless), **insuperable** (impossible to overcome), **inert** (lacking vigor), **interminable** (unending), **innocuous** (harmless), **incongruous** (not consistent with expectations)
Don't confuse controvertible with convertible (able to be changed in form or function)

☐ **introspective** (adj)   *intro-* into + *specere* to look at

inclined to look inward; meditative : *Unlike most artists, Warhol eschewed the introspective lifestyle and in fact reveled in his life of celebrity.*
Form: introspection = the act of self-examination
Synonyms: reflective, meditative, pensive
Root family: [spec] **speculation** (guess based on insufficient evidence), **circumspect** (cautious), **inspect** (to examine closely)
Don't confuse with: retrospective (looking back in time)

☐ *rectify* (v)   *rectus* right

to make correct; to put right : *The journalist rectified her error by publishing a retraction.*
Synonyms: *amend, emend, redress, remedy*
Root family: [rect] *correct* (right), *rectangle* (quadrilateral with four right angles), *direct* (by the shortest path)

☐ *sublime* (adj)   *sub-* just beneath + *limen* threshold

supremely excellent or beautiful : *The pâté was a sublime complement to the homemade bread.*
Root family: [sub-] *submissive* (meekly obedient), *subvert* (to undermine the authority of another), *surreptitious* (secret), *subjugate* (to dominate)
Root family: [lim] *limit* (the point beyond which something may not pass), *eliminate* (completely remove), *subliminal* (below the threshold of perception), *sublimate* (to alter a crude impulse so as to make it more culturally or socially acceptable)
Don't confuse with *subliminal*. Although both words derive from the Latin roots meaning "below the threshold," *subliminal* means "below the threshold of perception," while *sublime* means "near the threshold of heaven."
Don't confuse with *sublimate*. To *sublimate* a lowly impulse, such as hatred or sexual desire, means to literally "raise it up" (since the *limen*, or threshold, of a doorway includes the top part, then bringing something *sub limen*, just below the threshold, involves raising it up), that is, to channel the energy that would otherwise be dedicated to that impulse into a more culturally and socially acceptable behavior. In chemistry, a substance *sublimates* when it transforms from a solid directly to a gas, without passing through the liquid phase.

13 THE LANGUAGE OF DECEIT, ERROR, AND CONFUSION

☐ *anachronism* (n)   *ana-* backward or mixed up + *chronos* time

something out of place in time, especially something that is outdated : *The modern-sounding dialogue was conspicuously anachronistic for a movie set in the 1920s.*
Root family: [ana-] *anagram* (a rearrangement of the letters in a word or phrase to make another word or phrase)
Root family: [chron] *synchronize* (to make to happen simultaneously or at the same pace), *chronological* (in proper time order)
Don't confuse with: *anarchic* (lacking government)
Mnemonic: Since *Anna Karenina* is set in the 19th century, *Anna's chronograph* (wristwatch) would be very *anachronistic*.

☐ *belie* (v)

[1] to fail to give a true impression of something : *David's bluster belies his lack of self-confidence.*
[2] to betray; to show to be untrue : *The evidence belies the defendant's claim.*
Mnemonic: To *belie* something is to *be* a *lie* about something (meaning [1]) or to show it to *be* a *lie* (meaning [2]).

☐ *chicanery* (n)

devious trickery or evasion : *Unlike most politicians, she discusses tax policies openly, rather than using chicanery to hide her true motives and affiliations.*
Synonyms: *ruse, machination*
Don't confuse with: *chimera* (something unrealistic or hopelessly wishful)
Mnemonic: Imagine a *chick* doing magic in a *cannery*.

☐ *circuitous* (adj)   *circum* around + *ire* to go

indirect; roundabout : *We took a circuitous route to the cabin because the main highway was closed.*
Synonyms: *meandering, tortuous, serpentine*
Root family: [circum] *circumscribe* (to define the limits of something), *circumspect* (wary), *circumlocution* (evasive speech)

☐ *confound* (v)   *con-* together + *fundere* to pour

[1] to cause someone to become confused : *She was confounded by the puzzle for many weeks.*
Synonyms: *befuddle, baffle*
[2] to confuse two elements as being one : *We should not confound patriotism and loyalty to the government.*
Root family: [con-, co-, com-, col-] *consensus* (general agreement), *conspire* (to plot together), *coalesce* (to come together), *coherent* (forming a united whole), *confluence* (a place at which two things merge)

Root family: [fus, fund, found] *confuse* (to cause to become perplexed), *effusive* (freely expressive), *fusion* (the process of joining two things into a single entity), *profuse* (abundant), *transfusion* (a transfer, usually of blood, from one person or animal to another), *refuse* (to reject), *diffuse* (spread out over a large area)

Don't confuse with: *compound* (to make something worse : *Don't compound the problem.*)

☐ *convoluted* (adj)   *con-* together + *volutus* rolled

(1) (of an argument or story) complicated and difficult to follow : *The account the witness provided was so convoluted that the jury could not follow it.*

(2) intricately folded : *The human cortex is a convoluted shell of interconnected neurons.*

Form: *convolution* = a deep fold, esp. one of many; something complex and difficult to understand

Synonyms: *tortuous, byzantine*

Root family: [con-, co-, com-, col-] *conformist* (one who conscientiously complies with the standards of a group, *coherent* (forming a united whole), *compliant* (willing to obey), *confluence* (a place at which two things merge)

Root family: [vol] *revolution* (one complete rotation; a complete political overthrow), *involved* ("rolled up in"), *voluble* (fluently talkative)

☐ *digress* (v)   *di-* away + *gradi* to walk

stray from the topic in speaking or writing : *Powell digressed for several pages to describe the history of the village he was visiting.*

Forms: *digression* = an act of digressing, *digressive* = prone to digression; having the characteristics of a digression

Root family: [grad, gress] *progress* (forward movement), *regressive* (moving backward), *egress* (exit)

Don't confuse with: *regress* (to return to a less developed state)

☐ *disingenuous* (adj)   *dis-* away + *in-* in + *gignere* to be born

not candid or sincere; deceitful : *The senator's disingenuous comments were just another example of political posturing.*

Form: *ingénue* = a naive and innocent person, *ingenuous* = innocent and naive

Synonyms: *duplicitous, mendacious*

Root family: [dis-] *disconcerting* (unsettling), *disdain* (feeling that something is unworthy), *discredit* (harm the reputation of something or someone), *dispel* (to drive away; to eliminate)

Root family: [in-] *inundate* (to flood), *infer* (to conclude from evidence), *incisive* (showing keen judgment), *ingratiate* (to curry favor), *innate* (inborn)

Root family: [gen] *indigenous* (native), *progenitor* (the first in a family tree), *heterogeneous* (diverse in character or content), *homogeneous* (consisting of parts or members all of the same kind)

Don't confuse *ingenuous* (innocent and naive) with *ingenious* (brilliant) or *not genuine*.

Mnemonic: An *ingénue* is someone who is as innocent and naive as a baby (*in* + *genuus* born), so to be *ingenuous* means to be innocent and naive. Therefore, to be *disingenuous* is to be the opposite: deceitful and full of guile.

☐ *dubious* (adj)   *dubium* doubt

[1] questionable : *That is a dubious claim, bordering on the absurd.*

Synonyms: *controvertible, suspect*

[2] doubting : *I'm dubious that our team will be able to come back and win.*

Forms: *dubiousness* = doubtfulness

Synonyms: *vacillating*

Root family: [dub] *indubitable* (without a doubt), *doubt*

☐ *duplicity* (n)   *duplicitas* twofold

deceitfulness; double-dealing : *He considered a career as a spy but wondered whether he had the skill or moral flexibility to engage in such duplicity.*

Form: *duplicitous* = deceitful

Synonyms: *chicanery, subterfuge, treachery, perfidy*

Root family: [dupl, duo] *duplicate* (to make a copy), *duplex* (a two-floor apartment building), *dual* (twofold)

Don't confuse with: *duplication* (the process of making a copy)

☐ *guile* (n)

cunning or slyness in attaining a goal : *David Rohde was able to use guile and patience to escape his Taliban captors.*

Form: *guileless* = innocent; incapable of deceit

Synonyms: *cunning, artfulness, wiles*

Don't confuse with: *guise* (outward appearance)

☐ **inept** (adj)   *in-* not + *aptus* well suited

unskilled; clumsy : *Todd's awkward joke was a sincere but inept attempt to lighten the mood.*
Form: ineptitude = clumsiness; lack of skill
Synonyms: feckless, maladroit, bumbling, ineffectual
Root family: [in-, im-] **insipid** (flavorless), **insuperable** (impossible to overcome), **inert** (lacking vigor), **interminable** (unending), **incongruous** (not consistent with expectations)
Root family: [apt, ept] **aptitude** (natural skill), **adapt** (to make to fit a new situation or use), **adept** (skillful)
Don't confuse with: inapt (inappropriate or unsuitable to the situation)

☐ **machination** (n)   *machina* contrivance

a plot or scheme : *Dawn's artful machinations succeeded in gaining her the title of class president.*
Root family: [mech, mach] **machine** (apparatus), **mechanical** (pertaining to the workings of a machine)
Mnemonic: In *Austin Powers: International Man of Mystery*, Dr. Evil's **machinations** involve building a doomsday **machine**, "Project Vulcan," in order to hold the world's **nations** hostage.
Usage: A **deus ex machina** ("god in the machine") is an unexpected and highly implausible plot twist in a novel or play that magically saves a seemingly hopeless situation.

☐ **perjure** (v)   *per-* (negative) + *jurare* to swear

to lie under oath : *Martha Stewart's conviction for conspiracy to commit perjury landed her six months in prison.*
Form: perjury = the act of lying under oath
Root family: [jur] **jurisprudence** (the study of law), **abjure** (to swear off; renounce), **adjure** (to command solemnly), **conjure** (to create, as if by magic), **jurisdiction** (the power to make official decisions)
Root family: [dict] **vindictive** (vengeful), **dictatorial** (tyrannical), **malediction** (curse), **benediction** (blessing)
Don't confuse with: modicum (a small amount)

☐ **spurious** (adj)

false or fake; not what it seems to be (esp. as applied to claims or theories) : *The stories about Jordan's career as a spy were spurious, generated by his friends' wild imaginations.*
Synonyms: specious, fallacious
Don't confuse with: furious (very angry), **spurned** (jilted, rejected)
Mnemonic: Imagine a **spurious** cowboy in fake tinfoil **spurs**.

☐ **subterfuge** (n)   *sub-* beneath + *fugere* to flee

a trick or expedient used to escape a consequence or achieve a goal : *Max's subterfuge involved three alibis and a full-scale replica of himself.*
Synonyms: ruse, chicanery
Root family: [sub-] **submissive** (meekly obedient), **subvert** (to undermine the authority of another), **subjugate** (to dominate)
Root family: [fug] **fugitive** (one who is fleeing arrest), **refugee** (one fleeing strife or persecution), **refuge** (safe haven), **centrifugal** (moving away from the center)
Mnemonic: Imagine the Joker using a **sub to** flee (**fugere** = to flee) from Batman.

☐ **surreptitious** (adj)   *sub-* under, secretly + *rapere* to seize

kept secret because it is objectionable : *Charlotte was upset when she heard about her husband's surreptitious affair.*
Synonyms: clandestine, furtive, stealthy
Root family: [sub-] **submissive** (meekly obedient), **subvert** (to undermine the authority of another), **subjugate** (to dominate)
Root family: [rap, rav] **rapacious** (extremely greedy), **ravenous** (extremely hungry), **ravage** (to bring destruction to)
Don't confuse with: superfluous (unnecessary)

☐ **treacherous** (adj)

[1] characterized by or guilty of betrayal : *Benedict Arnold's treacherous actions are etched in our national history.*
Form: treachery = abject betrayal
Synonyms: traitorous, duplicitous, perfidious
[2] hazardous : *The ocean currents here are very treacherous.*
Synonyms: perilous, precarious
Don't confuse with: tortuous (full of twists and turns), **lecherous** (showing excessive sexual desire), **trenchant** (cutting and incisive)

☐ **unscrupulous** (adj)

dishonest; showing no moral principles : *The broker's unscrupulous dealings only came to light after he had stolen several million dollars of his client's money.*
Form: ***scrupulous*** = very concerned with avoiding sin or rule-breaking
Synonyms: ***reprobate, unethical, corrupt, venal***
Usage: Although ***scrupulous*** is primarily used to mean "attentive to rules and details," whether or not those rules are moral ones, ***unscrupulous*** refers exclusively to a lack of moral principles.

☐ **vex** (v)

to make to feel annoyed or frustrated : *I am constantly vexed by my inability to remember the names of all of your friends.*
Form: ***vexation*** = state of confusion or frustration
Synonyms: ***nettle, exasperate, pique, gall***
Don't confuse with: ***hex*** (a spell or curse)

14 | THE LANGUAGE OF CREATIVITY AND PRODUCTIVITY

☐ **assiduous** (adj)

showing great care and perseverance : *He was assiduous in his research, checking every reference and tracing its history.*
Synonyms: ***diligent, industrious, sedulous***
Don't confuse with: ***deciduous*** ((of tree) shedding its leaves annually), ***arduous*** ((of a task) requiring strenuous effort)
Mnemonic: Imagine a hardworking scientist mixing ***acid*** in two (***duo***) beakers.

☐ **efficacy** (n)   *facere* to do, to make

the ability to produce the intended result : *The efficacy of the new medicine could hardly be denied.*
Forms: ***efficacious*** = effective, ***inefficacious*** = ineffective
Root family: [fic, fac, fec, -ify] ***facile*** (simplistic), ***munificent*** (generous), ***diversify*** (to make more varied), ***ossify*** (to turn into bone), ***proficient*** (competent or skilled)
Don't confuse with: ***efficiency*** (quality of achieving substantial results with a minimum of energy)
Usage: A process or instrument that works ***efficaciously*** performs its task particularly well. One that works ***efficiently***, on the other hand, performs its task at least adequately, but with minimal expense or input.

☐ **expedite** (v)   *ex-* out + *ped* foot

(of a process) to make happen more quickly or efficiently : *We could expedite deliveries by streamlining our method of dispatching the trucks.*
Form: ***expeditious*** = done with speed and efficiency
Synonyms: ***precipitate, facilitate***
Root family: [e-, ex-] ***extol*** (to praise highly), ***extemporaneous*** (without planning), ***exuberant*** (filled with liveliness and energy), ***elusive*** (difficult to catch or achieve), ***exorbitant*** (excessive), ***evocative*** (drawing out strong emotions, ideas, or feelings)
Root family: [ped] ***pedestrian*** (ordinary), ***impede*** (to hinder or obstruct)
Mnemonic: It is interesting to note that ***impede*** and ***expedite*** both derive from ***ped***, the Latin root for "foot." ***Impede***, literally "bind the feet," means to hinder or delay, whereas ***expedite***, literally "free the feet," means to make happen more quickly.
Usage: Although ***expedite***, ***precipitate***, and ***facilitate*** are similar, they differ in certain important aspects. To ***expedite*** a process is to make it happen faster and more efficiently, whereas to ***facilitate*** a process is to make it *easier* on the person or people involved. The verb ***precipitate*** applies more to an *event* than a *process*; it is to make the event happen more quickly, although it would likely have happened on its own.
Don't confuse with: ***expedition***. The words ***expedite*** and ***expedition*** derive from the same roots but have very different meanings. To ***expedite*** is to "free the feet," but to go on an ***expedition*** is to "go out on foot."
Don't confuse ***expeditious*** (done with speed and efficiency) with ***expedient*** (convenient and practical, but perhaps improper or immoral).

☐ **facilitate** (v)   *facilis* easy (< *facere* to do or make)

to make easier : *A team of clinicians was assembled to facilitate the development of the new vaccine.*
Forms: ***facile*** = simplistic, ***facilitator*** = one who makes a process easier, ***facility*** = a natural ability; ease

Root family: [fac, fec, fic] **benefactor** (one who provides a benefit), **munificent** (generous)
Don't confuse *facility* with *felicity* (intense happiness).
Don't confuse *facile* with *vassal* (a feudal landowner) or *docile* (submissive).
Usage: See usage note at *expedite* in this section.

☐ **flourish** (v)   *florere* to flower

to grow vigorously; prosper : *The arts and letters flourished during the Harlem Renaissance.*
Don't confuse with: *florid* (characterized by flowery language), **flourish** (n) (an extravagant action, usually done to attract attention : *The dance number concluded with a flourish of backflips*)
Mnemonic: The noun *flourish* and the verb *flourish* both derive from *florere* (to flower) but have distinct meanings. A *flourish* is a "flowery or extravagant display to attract attention," whereas to *flourish* means to "blossom like a flower." *Florid* also derives from *florere* but means "characterized by flowery language."

☐ **lineage** (n)   *lineare* to create with lines

descent from an ancestor : *In most medieval European societies, one's social status was decided by family lineage.*
Synonyms: *pedigree, ancestry, genealogy*
Root family: [line] **collinear** (on the same line), **alignment** (the process of arranging in a line), **delineate** (to describe precisely)
Don't confuse with: *delineate* (to describe precisely)

☐ **prodigious** (adj)   *prodigus* lavish

great in size or degree : *The team consumed prodigious amounts of pizza after the game.*
Forms: *prodigiously* = abundantly
Synonyms: *copious*
Root family: [prodigi] **prodigy** (a young person with exceptional talent), **prodigal** (tending to spend money recklessly)

☐ **profuse** (adj)   *pro-* forward + *fusus* poured

very abundantly offered or available : *Even the profuse offerings of cards and flowers did not assuage his grief.*
Form: *profusion* = an abundance
Synonyms: *prolific, prevalent, copious*
Root family: [pro-] **protracted** (lasting longer than expected), **prophecy** (prediction), **promote** (further the progress of something; raise in rank), **progeny** (offspring), **reciprocate** (to respond in kind)
Root family: [fus, fund, found] **confuse** (to cause to become perplexed), **confound** (to fail to distinguish different elements), **diffuse** (spread over a wide area), **fusion** (the process of joining two things into a single entity), **effusive** (freely expressive), **transfusion** (a transfer, usually of blood, from one person or animal to another), **refuse** (to reject)
Don't confuse with: *refuse* (to indicate unwillingness to accept something)

☐ **progeny** (n)   *pro-* forward + *gignere* to create

the collective descendants of one ancestor : *The family trust was established to ensure the well-being of the billionaire's progeny.*
Form: *progenitor* = the primary ancestor of a collection of descendants
Synonyms: *offspring, brood, scions*
Root family: [pro-] **protracted** (lasting longer than expected), **prophecy** (prediction), **promote** (further the progress of something; raise in rank), **reciprocate** (to respond in kind)
Root family: [gen] **indigenous** (native), **homogeneous** (uniform), **heterogeneous** (diverse in character)
Don't confuse *progenitor* with *prognosticator* (one who foretells or attempts to foretell future events).
Mnemonic: Think of someone named *Jenny* you know, and then imagine a *profuse* number of them in the lower branches of a family tree (*progeny* = *pro*fuse *Jennys*).

☐ **proliferate** (v)

to increase rapidly in numbers or extent : *Bootlegging proliferated during the era of Prohibition to satisfy the demand for alcohol.*
Form: *proliferation* = a rapid increase in numbers or extent
Synonyms: *burgeon, mushroom*

☐ **prolific** (adj)

[1] highly productive : *Johann Strauss was a prolific composer of waltzes.*
Synonyms: *fertile fecund*
[2] plentiful : *The mountain laurel is prolific along the side of the highway.*

Forms: *proliferate* = to multiply or reproduce rapidly
Synonyms: *copious, profuse, prevalent*
Don't confuse with: *prophetic* (accurately predictive of the future)

☐ **vigor** (n)

good health and physical strength : *The therapy helped him regain the vigor of his youth.*
Forms: *invigorating* = giving energy or strength, *vigorous* = full of energy and strength
Synonyms: *robustness, hardiness, virility*
Don't confuse with: *rigor* (thoroughness or strictness)
Don't confuse with: *erudite* (scholarly)

15 THE LANGUAGE OF MYSTERY, SURPRISE, ADVENTURE, AND DISCOVERY

☐ **ambiguous** (adj)   *ambi-* both + *agere* to do

having more than one meaning or interpretation : *In her poem, the meaning of the cloak is intentionally ambiguous.*
Form: *ambiguity* = quality of having more than one interpretation
Synonym: *equivocal*
Root family: [ambi-, amphi-] *ambidextrous* (able to use both hands skillfully), *ambivalent* (having mixed feelings), *amphibian* (an animal that lives partially in water and partially on land), *amphitheater* (an outdoor theater with seats surrounding (on *both* sides of) the stage)
Don't confuse with: *ambivalent* (having mixed feelings)

☐ **anomaly** (n)

something that deviates from the norm or expectation : *Astronomers scan the night sky looking for anomalies such as radiation bursts or unusual planetary motions.*
Form: *anomalous* = out of the norm
Synonyms: *incongruity, aberration*
Don't confuse with: *animosity* (strong hostility)
Don't confuse *anomalous* **with** *anonymous* (unnamed).

☐ **diversion** (n)   *di-* away + *vertere* to turn

[1] an entertaining activity to distract one from everyday concerns : *In the mountains, our diversions include hiking, fishing, and reading.*
Form: *diverting* = entertaining
[2] an action intended to distract someone : *I will create a diversion while you sneak into the house.*
Form: *divert* = to cause something, such as traffic or a river, to change course; to distract someone's attention from something
Root family: [di-, dis-] *discredit* (harm the reputation of something or someone), *dispassionate* (not influenced by strong emotions), *disparate* (very different; variegated), *discrepancy* (a lack of compatibility between facts or claims), *disseminate* (to cast widely), *disperse* (to spread or scatter), *disputatious* (argumentative), *diffident* (lacking in self-confidence), *diffuse* (spread over a wide area)
Root family: [vers, vert] *adversary* (enemy), *diverse* (various), *adverse* (harmful), *subvert* (undermine), *averse* (opposed), *versatile* (adaptable to different functions)
Don't confuse with: *diverse* (various)

☐ **divulge** (v)   *di-* widely + *vulgare* to make public

to make widely known, particularly information that was previously kept private : *I cannot divulge the information that was discussed in our private meeting.*
Form: *divulgence* = the act of making something widely known
Root family: [dis-, di-] *disparate* (very different; variegated), *discrepancy* (a lack of compatibility between facts or claims), *disperse* (to spread or scatter), *diffuse* (spread over a wide area)
Root family: [vulg] *vulgar* (crude and unrefined)
Don't confuse *divulgence* **with** *indulgence* (an act of being excessively generous or lenient)

☐ **elusive** (adj)   *e-* out + *ludere* to play

difficult to catch, find, understand, or achieve : *The snow leopard is one of nature's most beautiful yet elusive creatures, rarely seen by human eyes.*
Form: *elude* = to evade capture or understanding
Synonyms: *evasive, impalpable, intangible*
Root family: [e-, ex-] *extol* (to praise highly), *extemporaneous* (without planning), *exuberant* (filled with liveliness and energy)
Root family: [lud, lus] *collusion* (a secret understanding that has a harmful purpose), *delude* (to make someone believe something that is not true), *illusion* (something that gives a false impression of reality), *ludicrous* (foolish and ridiculous), *allusion* (to hint at indirectly)
Don't confuse with: *illusory* (giving a false impression), *allusive* (providing or pertaining to an indirect hint)

☐ **empirical** (adj)

pertaining to or based on observation or experience : *Although string theory provides elegant mathematical solutions to many vexing problems in physics, it lacks any empirical evidence.*
Form: *empiricism* = the belief that all knowledge is derived from sensory experience
Mnemonic: Imagine an *empire* in which everyone, especially the *emperor*, is a scientist, with telescopes on every rooftop and chemistry labs in every basement, where they constantly gather *empirical* data.

☐ **enigma** (n)

someone or something that is difficult to understand : *King Lear's motivation remains an enigma.*
Form: *enigmatic* = difficult to understand
Synonyms: *conundrum, quandary, riddle*

☐ **idiosyncrasy** (n)   *idios* unique + *syn* with + *krasis* mixture

a mannerism or quirk peculiar to an individual : *One of the stranger idiosyncrasies of professional athletes is their tendency to refer to themselves in the second or third person during interviews.*
Form: *idiosyncratic* = quirky
Synonyms: *quirk, peculiarity, eccentricity, mannerism, foible*
Root family: [idio] *idiom* (a common phrase that has a nonliteral meaning, such as "at the end of your rope"), *idiot* (stupid person)
Don't confuse with: *ideology* (a system of ideals central to the political power of a group), *iconoclast* (one who attacks cherished beliefs), *idiotic* (stupid)

☐ **inscrutable** (adj)   *in-* not + *scrutari* to search

beyond understanding : *I find quantum physics to be almost as inscrutable as the motivations of my girlfriend.*
Synonyms: *enigmatic, abstruse*
Root family: [in-, im-] *insipid* (flavorless), *insuperable* (impossible to overcome), *inert* (lacking vigor), *interminable* (unending), *innocuous* (harmless), *indefatigable* (untiring), *ineffable* (inexpressible in words), *impassive* (unemotional), *incongruous* (not consistent with expectations)
Root family: [scrut] *scrutinize* (to examine closely)
Don't confuse with: *unscrupulous* (showing no moral principles)
Mnemonic: Something that is *inscrutable* is *un-scrutinize-able*, that is, it's impossible to examine closely because it is beyond our understanding.

☐ **intrepid** (adj)   *in-* not + *trepidus* alarmed

fearless and adventurous : *The intrepid explorers set out for the summit.*
Root family: [in-, im-] *insipid* (flavorless), *insuperable* (impossible to overcome), *inert* (lacking vigor), *interminable* (unending), *innocuous* (harmless), *indefatigable* (untiring), *ineffable* (inexpressible in words), *inscrutable* (beyond understanding), *impassive* (unemotional), *incongruous* (not consistent with expectations)
Root family: [trepid] *trepidation* (fear)
Synonyms: *undaunted, stouthearted*
Don't confuse with: *insipid* (flavorless; uninteresting)
Mnemonic: The aircraft carrier *Intrepid*, now a museum moored off of Manhattan, is an impressive ship that represents the fearlessness of the U.S. Navy.

☐ **nebulous** (adj)   *nebula* mist

vague; hazy; having the form of a cloud : *The ghost appeared first as a nebulous near-human form.*
Synonyms: *amorphous*, *obscure*

☐ **paradox** (n)   *para-* distinct from, beside + *doxa* teaching

a logically self-contradictory statement or state of affairs : *It seemed to be a paradox that light could behave both as a wave and as a particle.*
Root family: [para-] *paralegal* (a lawyer's assistant), *parallel* (next to and aligned with), *paramedic* (a first aid professional)
Root family: [doc, dox] *doctrinaire* (seeking to impose rigid doctrine), *orthodox* (conforming strictly to traditional teachings), *docile* (compliant and easy to instruct)
Don't confuse with: *paradigm* (a worldview; a typical model or example)

16 THE LANGUAGE OF HARM, DEFICIT, AND DECLINE

☐ **adverse** (adj)   *ad-* to + *vertere* to turn

harmful to success or progress : *The short holiday season has had an adverse effect on sales.*
Form: *adversity* = misfortune or difficulties, usually over an extended period
Synonyms: *inauspicious*, *detrimental*, *deleterious*
Root family: [ad-] *adhere* (stick fast (to)), *advocate* (to provide vocal support for), *annul* (to declare invalid)
Root family: [vers, vert] *adversary* (enemy), *diverse* (various), *diversion* (entertainment), *subvert* (undermine), *averse* (opposed), *versatile* (adaptable to different functions)
Don't confuse with: *averse* (opposed)

☐ **archaic** (adj)   *archaios* old

old and outdated : *My cell phone, which didn't even have Internet access, seemed archaic compared to Kris's tiny smartphone.*
Synonyms: *outmoded*, *outdated*, *anachronistic*, *obsolete*
Root family: [arch] *archaeology* (the study of ancient civilizations and their artifacts), *archetype* (a very typical example)
Don't confuse with: *anarchic* (having no hierarchical government)

☐ **bane** (n)

a cause of great and persistent distress : *The bane of the traveling salesman is the time spent away from family and friends.*
Form: *baneful* = causing great distress
Synonyms: *scourge*, *blight*, *affliction*
Mnemonic: For farmers, **ban**ning the **rain** would be a great **bane** for their livelihood.

☐ **dearth** (n)

an utter lack of something : *I am disappointed by the dearth of good jazz clubs in this city.*
Synonym: *paucity*
Don't confuse with: *death*, *dirge* (a funereal song), *mirth* (good-natured amusement)
Mnemonic: The words **dearth** and **dear** (expensive) derive from the same root. If there is a **dearth** of something desired, then it is likely to be very **dear**.

☐ **debilitating** (adj)

causing someone or something to become weak : *What seemed like a slight ankle sprain soon turned into a debilitating injury.*
Forms: *debilitate* = to make weak or infirm, *debility* = a weakness or infirmity
Synonyms: *incapacitating*, *enervating*
Don't confuse with: *rehabilitate* (to restore to health)

☐ **deleterious** (adj)   *delere* to destroy, to eliminate

very harmful : *Prolonged and hopeless poverty has a very deleterious effect on children.*
Synonyms: *detrimental*, *injurious*, *adverse*
Root family: [delet] *delete* (to remove completely), *indelible* (forming an enduring impression)
Mnemonic: Imagine how **deleterious** it would be to your grade if you accidentally **deleted** the research paper that you had spent over a month researching and writing.

☐ **enervate** (v)   *e-* out of + *nervus* sinew, strength

to drain of energy or strength : *The arduous hike enervated the boys, who decided to rest for the night.*
Forms: enervation = the process of draining something of strength; weakness, **enervated** = weakened
Synonyms: debilitate, enfeeble
Don't confuse with: energize (to fill with energy), **enumerate** (to list numerically), **innervate** *(to supply an organ or body part with nerves)*
Mnemonic: To avoid confusing **enervate** with **energize**, focus on the roots *e-* (out) and *nervus* (sinew, strength or muscle): to **enervate** is to weaken, as if by removing the muscle fibers from one's body. Gross? Yes, but vivid enough to remember.

☐ **exacerbate** (v)   *ex-* (making) + *acerbus* bitter

to make a situation worse : *The lawsuit only exacerbated the animosity between the neighbors.*
Synonyms: aggravate, compound, inflame
Root family: [acer, acu] **acrid** (pungent), **acerbic** (having a bitter taste), **acrimonious** (defined by bitter feelings), **acute** (keen, as pain or ability)
Don't confuse with: exaggerate (to overstate)

☐ **insidious** (v)   *in-* on + *sedere* to sit

having a harmful effect, but in a subtle way : *Many viral diseases are insidious, remaining dormant for months or even years before symptoms are expressed.*
Synonyms: stealthy, surreptitious, treacherous
Root family: [in-] **inundate** (to flood), **infer** (to conclude from evidence), **incisive** (showing keen judgment), **ingratiate** (to curry favor), **inherent** (existing as an inseparable element), **invoke** (to bring to bear), **indoctrinate** (to teach doctrine), **induce** (to bring about), **infiltrate** (to gain access secretly)
Root family: [sed, sid] **sedentary** (inactive), **dissident** (one who opposes official policy), **assiduous** (hard working), **sedate** (calm), **preside** (to sit in a position of authority), **reside** (to live in a particular location), **sediment** (material that settles to the bottom of a liquid or body of water, particularly a river)
Don't confuse with: invidious (causing resentment)
Mnemonic: An **insidious** disease lurks **inside us** until it decides to pounce.

☐ **malevolence** (n)   *male* evil + *volent* wishing

evil intent : *The villain eyed his victim with malevolence.*
Form: malevolent = with evil intent
Synonyms: maliciousness, rancor
Root family: [mal] **malignant** (disposed to causing harm or suffering), **malicious** (full of spite), **malign** (to speak about someone in a spiteful manner)
Root family: [vole] **benevolent** (kindly), **volition** (free will), **voluntary** (performed by choice)

☐ **obsolete** (adj)

outdated; no longer in production : *Mr. King still types all of his manuscripts on an obsolete Corona typewriter.*
Forms: obsolesce = to become obsolete, **obsolescence** = the state of being obsolete
Synonyms: outmoded, outdated, anachronistic, archaic

☐ **regress** (v)   *re-* back + *gressus* walking

to return to a less developed state : *As he got angrier, Gary seemed to regress into childhood, and began kicking his feet and pouting like a toddler.*
Form: regression = the process of moving toward a less developed state, **regressive** = moving backward or toward a less developed state
Root family: [re-] **reprehensible** (deserving of condemnation), **refute** (to prove something false), **revoke** (to take back), **renounce** (to give up or put aside publicly), **relegate** (to place in a lower rank)
Root family: [grad, gress] **progress** (forward movement), **egress** (exit), **digress** (to stray from the topic)

☐ **vestige** (n)

[VEST idge] a trace of something that no longer exists : *The archaeologists wondered whether this small clay shard was a vestige of a once-great civilization.*

Form: *vestigial* = remaining as a trace of something long since gone
Synonyms: *remnant*, *relic*, *residue*
Don't confuse with: *vestment* (clothing), *prestige* [press TEEGE] (widespread respect)

☐ **virulent** (adj)   *virus* poison

bitterly hostile; extremely harmful : *The speech was an incoherent and virulent diatribe against the dangers of socialism.*
Form: *virulence* = ability to cause extreme harm; poisonousness
Synonyms: *toxic*, *pernicious*
Root family: [viru] *virus* (a nucleic acid molecule that acts as an infective agent)
Don't confuse with: *violent* (involving physical force to hurt or damage)

17 THE LANGUAGE OF KINDNESS, FAVOR, AND BENEFIT

☐ **affable** (adj)

friendly and good-natured : *Gena is so affable that she will surely make new friends at camp.*
Form: *affability* = friendliness and good nature
Synonyms: *amiable*, *genial*, *gregarious*
Don't confuse with: *ineffable* (unable to be described in words)
Mnemonic: An *affable* person is *able* to *laugh* easily (*affable* = *laugh-able*) which makes him or her very easy to like. But be careful not to confuse *affable* with *laughable* (ridiculous to the point of being amusing).

☐ **alleviate** (v)   *ad-* to + *levare* to lift

to make something, such as suffering, less severe : *She regretted that she could not alleviate her friend's pain.*
Synonyms: *mitigate*, *palliate*, *attenuate*, *allay*, *assuage*
Root family: [ad-] *allude* (to hint at indirectly), *aspire* (to strive for a lofty goal), *adhere* (stick fast (to)), *advocate* (to provide vocal support for), *acquiesce* (to comply reluctantly)
Root family: [lev] *levity* (good-natured humor), *elevate* (to lift), *relevant* (raised to an important level), *relieve* (to lift a burden from another)
Don't confuse with: *abbreviate* (to make shorter)

☐ **altruistic** (adj)   *alter* other

selfless; putting the concerns of others before one's own : *Only the most altruistic doctors can tolerate the hardships of running disease clinics in poor communities.*
Form: *altruism* = the belief in or practice of putting the concern of others before one's own
Root family: [alter] *altercation* (a noisy fight), *alter* (to change or cause to change), *alternate* (to occur in turn repeatedly, *adulterate* (to render (something) inferior, usually by adding something to it), *alter ego* (alternative personality)
Mnemonic: An *altruistic* person puts others (*alter* = other) before himself or herself, and is *always true* to the idea of charity.

☐ **amicable** (adj)   *amicus* friend

showing goodwill and a spirit of friendliness : *I hope we can reach an amicable settlement.*
Root family: [ami] *amiable* (friendly), *inimical* (antagonistic), *enmity* (hostility or active opposition)
Don't confuse with: *applicable* (relevant or appropriate)
Usage: Although *amicable* and *amiable* derive from the same roots, *amicable* is more commonly used to describe friendly *situations*, while *amiable* is more commonly used to describe friendly *people*.

☐ **auspicious** (adj)   *avis* bird + *specere* to look

conducive to success; favorable to a positive outcome : *The rainstorm did not provide an auspicious start to the wedding ceremony.*
Form: *inauspicious* = not favorable
Synonyms: *propitious*, *opportune*, *felicitous*
Root family: [spic, spec] *introspective* (reflective), *speculation* (guess based on insufficient evidence), *circumspect* (cautious), *inspect* (to examine closely)

Don't confuse with: *suspicious* (showing cautious distrust), *vicious* (cruel)

Mnemonic: *Auspicious* derives from the Latin *avis* (bird) and *specere* (to look) because in mid-16th-century Europe it was believed that observing particular birds in flight was a favorable sign in divination. From this meaning of "favorable omen," we also get the word *auspice*, which means "patronage or support," as in *The study was conducted under the auspices of the Labor Board.*

☐ *benefactor* (n)   *bene* good + *facere* to do or make

one who gives money to benefit a person or cause : *The letter acknowledged the many benefactors who had helped the Arts Society stay afloat in trying economic times.*

Synonyms: *patron*, *sponsor*

Root family: [ben, bon] *beneficiary* (one who receives a benefit), *benevolent* (kindly), *benign* (harmless)

Root family: [fac, fec, fic] *facile* (simplistic), *munificent* (generous)

Don't confuse with: *beneficiary* (one who receives a benefit)

☐ *beneficiary* (n)   *bene* good + *facere* to do or make

one who receives a benefit : *Wayne was the beneficiary of his friend's generosity.*

Synonym: *legatee*

Root family: [ben, bon] *benefactor* (one who provides a benefit), *benevolent* (kindly), *benign* (harmless)

Root family: [fac, fec, fic] *facile* (simplistic), *munificent* (generous)

Don't confuse with: *benefactor* (one who provides a benefit)

☐ *benevolent* (adj)   *bene* good + *velle* to wish

kindly; well meaning : *She was a benevolent queen, attentive to the needs of all of her subjects.*

Form: *benevolence* = kindness

Synonyms: *altruistic*, *philanthropic*, *magnanimous*

Root family: [ben, bon] *beneficiary* (one who receives a benefit), *benefactor* (one who provides a benefit)

Root family: [vol] *malevolent* (having evil intent), *volition* (free will), *voluntary* (performed by choice)

Mnemonic: English words containing *vol* can be confusing because they can derive from three different Latin roots: *velle* ((to wish) (from which we get *malevolent* (having evil intent) and *benevolent*), *volare* ((to fly) from which we get *volatile* and *volley* (to throw at a target)), or *volvere* ((to roll) from which we get *convoluted* and *revolution* (a complete turn)).

☐ *benign* (adj)   *bene* good + *genus* born

gentle; causing no harm : *Rather than rousing indignation, Senator Paulson's concession speech was benign and gracious.*

Synonyms: *innocuous*, *anodyne*

Root family: [ben, bon] *beneficiary* (one who receives a benefit), *benevolent* (kindly), *benefactor* (one who provides a benefit)

Don't confuse with: *benighted* (in a woeful state of ignorance, literally "in the darkness of night")

☐ *complement* (v) or (n)   *com-* (intensive) + *plere* to fill

[1] (v) to add to something to make it complete or perfect : *The savory sautéed spinach complemented the rich and dense portobello mushroom to make the perfect side dish.*

[2] (n) something that completes a whole : *Calculus is an important complement to the study of physics.*

Forms: *complementary* = acting to form a complete or perfect whole

Root family: [ple] *deplete* (to use the supply of), *replete* (filled to the fullest extent)

Don't confuse with: *compliment* (to say something kind about someone else)

☐ *conciliatory* (adj)   *concilium* council

likely to appease or to bring people together in goodwill : *The student exchange was intended as a conciliatory gesture between the formerly antagonistic countries.*

Forms: *conciliate* = to appease or to gain goodwill, *conciliation* = the act of appeasing or gaining goodwill

Synonyms: *appeasing*, *mollifying*, *placatory*, *propitiatory*

Root family: [concilium] *council* (an advisory or legislative body)

Usage: See usage note at *pacify* in section 4.

Mnemonic: The verb *conciliate* derives from the Latin *concilium*, which means "an assembly or council." If you know anything about how modern city councils work, you know that a lot of compromise and appeasement—a lot of *conciliation*—is often needed to get people from different backgrounds, temperaments, and political parties to work together.

☐ *decorum* (n)   *decorus* showing good taste

dignified and tasteful behavior : *Please show some decorum while we are touring the palace.*
Forms: *decorous* = in keeping with good taste and propriety, ***indecorum*** = lack of decorum, ***indecorous*** = lacking in decorum
Synonyms: *propriety, etiquette, protocol*
Root family: [deco, dec] ***decoration*** (ornamentation), ***decent*** (conforming to standards of appropriate behavior), ***decor*** (the furnishing and decoration of a home)
Don't confuse with: *decor* (the furnishing and decoration of a home). To avoid confusing these, you might remember that the ***um*** in decorum is like the ***um*** in ***human***; only ***humans*** can show ***decorum***, while only homes have ***decor***.

☐ *empathy* (n)   *pathos* feeling

the ability to understand and share the feelings of another : *Dawn has a great empathy for fellow cancer survivors.*
Forms: *empathize* = to understand and share the feelings of others, ***empathetic*** = able to empathize
Root family: [path] ***sympathy*** (feeling of sorrow for the misfortunes of another), ***pathology*** (the science of the causes and course of diseases), ***apathetic*** (lacking concern), ***antipathy*** (animosity)

☐ *eulogy* (n)   *eu* good + *logos* word

a praising speech, particularly for one who is deceased : *Glen's eulogy was touching yet humorous.*
Form: *eulogize* = to recite or write a eulogy
Synonyms: *accolade, paean, encomium*
Root family: [eu] ***euthanasia*** (mercy killing), ***euphonious*** (pleasant sounding), ***euphoria*** (extreme happiness), ***euphemism*** (a mild term or phrase intended to replace a harsher one)
Don't confuse *eulogize* with ***euthanize*** (to put a person or animal to death humanely)

☐ *euphemism* (n)   *eu* good + *pheme* speaking

a mild term or phrase intended to replace a harsh, embarrassing, or unpleasant one : *Senators are adept at inserting euphemisms like "patriot" into the names of their bills to divert the public's attention from the true nature of the laws.*
Form: *euphemistic* = pertaining to the use of euphemisms; having the qualities of euphemism
Root family: [eu] ***euthanasia*** (mercy killing), ***euphonious*** (pleasant sounding), ***euphoria*** (extreme happiness), ***eulogy*** (a praising speech, usually for the deceased)
Root family: [phem] ***blasphemy*** (speaking profanely about holy things), ***dysphemism*** (a deliberately derogatory or unpleasant term or phrase), ***prophecy*** (significant prediction of the future)
Don't confuse with: *euphoria* (extreme happiness)

☐ *innocuous* (adj)   *in-* not + *nocuus* harmful

not harmful or offensive : *The interviewer asked only innocuous questions rather than probing into more interesting topics.*
Synonyms: *benign, anodyne*
Root family: [in-, im-] ***insipid*** (flavorless), ***insuperable*** (impossible to overcome), ***inert*** (lacking vigor), ***interminable*** (unending), ***indefatigable*** (untiring), ***ineffable*** (inexpressible in words), ***inscrutable*** (beyond understanding), ***impassive*** (unemotional), ***incongruous*** (not consistent with expectations)
Root family: [nocu, noxi] ***innocent*** (not guilty), ***noxious*** (harmful), ***obnoxious*** (rudely unpleasant)

☐ *mitigate* (v)

to make less serious or severe : *The effects of hurricanes can be mitigated by the presence of a thriving barrier island system.*
Forms: *mitigating* = serving to make less serious or severe, ***unmitigated*** = without redeeming qualities
Synonyms: *palliate, attenuate, allay, assuage*
Don't confuse with: *litigate* (to file and execute a lawsuit), ***migrate*** (to move from one habitat to another, usually according to the season)
Usage: While ***pacify, placate, appease, propitiate***, and ***conciliate*** all describe things done to *people*, words like ***palliate***, ***mollify***, and ***assuage*** generally apply to *feelings*, and words like ***mitigate*** and ***ameliorate*** can pertain to *situations* as well as *feelings*.
Mnemonic: Judges or juries often consider ***mitigating*** circumstances before sentencing someone who has been convicted of a crime. Assaulting someone who is perceived as a threat is not as serious as assaulting someone without provocation, so the threatening could be a ***mitigating*** circumstance that reduces the sentence for assault.

☐ *mollify* (v)   *mollis* soft

to appease someone's anger or anxiety : *The tax bill was taken off of the agenda to mollify the angry citizens.*
Form: *mollification* = the process of appeasing anger or anxiety
Synonyms: *propitiate, conciliate, placate, appease*
Root family: [moll] *emollient* (an agent that softens skin), *mollusk* (an invertebrate with a soft unsegmented body, usually protected by a shell)
Don't confuse with: *mortify* (to make to feel embarrassed or humiliated)
Usage: See usage note at *pacify* in section 4.
Mnemonic: Imagine someone you know named *Molly* trying to settle down an angry friend.

☐ *obliging* (adj)   *ob-* toward + *ligare* to bind

eager to help : *The bellhops were very obliging to those who were good tippers.*
Root family: [lig] *ligament* (a band of connective tissue), *obligatory* (mandatory; necessary to do), *religion* (belief in a supernatural power which obligates one to perform rituals)
Don't confuse with: *obligatory* (mandatory; necessary to do)
Mnemonic: When you feel *obliged* to do something for something, you feel *bound* to do it (*ob-* to + *ligare* to bind). It is *obligatory* (mandatory; necessary to do). If you always feel *bound* to your responsibility to help others, you are *obliging*.

☐ *propriety* (n)   *proprius* one's own

conformity to standards of proper behavior : *As representatives of our school, we must conduct ourselves with the utmost propriety.*
Form: *impropriety* = improper behavior
Root family: [prop] *appropriate* (adj) (proper of suitable to the circumstances); (v) (to take something that doesn't belong to you for your own use, typically without the owner's permission : *The Spanish appropriated many of the discoveries of the Mayans as their own*), *proprietor* (the legal owner of a business)
Don't confuse with: *proprietor* (the legal owner of a business)
Mnemonic: Although *proprietor* and *propriety* are easily confused, they derive from different aspects of the root word *proprius* (one's own). A *proprietor* is the legal owner of a small business, but *propriety* is the respect with which one treats *one's own* family and tribe.

☐ *reciprocate* (v)   *re-* back + *pro-* forward

to respond to an action or gesture by doing something in kind : *If you act kindly to strangers, they are likely to reciprocate.*
Forms: *reciprocal* = done in return, ***reciprocity*** = the practice of acting with mutual benefit
Root family: [re-] *recluse* (a person who lives a solitary lifestyle), *refute* (to prove something false), *revoke* (to take back), *renounce* (to give up or put aside publicly), *regress* (to return to a less developed state)
Root family: [pro-] *protracted* (lasting longer than expected), *prophecy* (prediction), *promote* (further the progress of something; raise in rank), *progeny* (offspring)

☐ *refinement* (n)   *finire* to finish

[1] elegance in taste and manners : *Jerrod has all the refinement one would expect of a world traveler.*
[2] the process of bringing to a purer state : *Crude oil must undergo refinement before it can be used as fuel.*
Forms: *refined* = cultured and well-mannered, ***refine*** = to make more cultured, ***unrefined*** = uncultured or unimproved
Don't confuse *refine* with *define* (to set forth the meaning of something).

☐ *solicitous* (adj)   *citus* set in motion

showing interest or concern : *Lisa's office mates became solicitous when they heard that her daughter was ill.*
Forms: *solicitude* = care or concern for someone or something, ***solicit*** = to ask (someone) for something
Root family: [cit] *excite* (to elicit energetic feelings in someone; to energize something), *incite* (to encourage violence or illicit behavior), *resuscitate* (to bring back to life)
Usage: Many Americans assume that *solicitous* has a negative connotation because *solicitations* (requests for money or other donations) can be annoying. However, *solicitude* is not badgering but sincere concern. This meaning is conveyed more accurately in the British definition of *solicitor* as "an attorney who assists a client," rather than the American definition of "one who requests donations."
Don't confuse with: *solicitor* (one who requests donations for charity; (in the U.K.) an attorney)

☐ *symbiosis* (n)   *sym-* together + *bio* life

a mutually beneficial relationship between different species : *One example of symbiosis is the relationship between the clownfish and the sea anemone, whereby the clownfish receives protection from its enemies and the anemone receives food.*
Form: *symbiotic* = characterized by symbiosis
Root family: [sym] *sympathy* (compassion), *symmetry* (a geometric correspondence among similar parts)
Root family: [bio] *biology* (the study of living things), *biodegradable* (able to decompose into nutrients for living things)
Don't confuse with: *symbolic* (pertaining to the use of symbols)

☐ *tactful* (adj)   *tactus* sense of touch

showing sensitivity to the needs of others with difficult private issues : *Jerry Springer rarely shows any desire to be tactful about his guests' embarrassing personal problems.*
Forms: *tact* = sensitivity to the needs of others with difficult private issues, ***tactless*** = utterly without tact
Synonyms: *politic, discreet, judicious, decorous*
Root family: [tang, tact, ting, tig, tag, teg] *tactile* (pertaining to the sense of touch), *tangential* (barely related to the topic), *tangible* (touchable), *contact* (to touch, or get in touch with), *contagious* (spreadable, as a disease, via close contact), *contiguous* (physically touching or bordering, as *the contiguous 48 states*), *integrity* (the quality of wholeness or wholesomeness; moral uprightness)
Don't confuse with: *tacky* (showing poor taste)

☐ *utility* (n)   *utilis* useful

the state of being useful : *When searching for a new car, the Kearns were clearly more interested in utility than beauty.*
Form: *utilitarian* = designed to be useful rather than attractive; pragmatic, ***utile*** = advantageous, ***utilize*** = to use effectively
Don't confuse with: *futility* (pointlessness)

18 THE LANGUAGE OF WISDOM, STRENGTH, AND SKILL

☐ *adroit* (adj)   *a droit* as to the right (Fr < L *dexter* right)

skillful : *He was such an adroit salesman that he could sell ice cubes to polar bears.*
Form: *adroitness* = skillfulness
Synonyms: *adept, dexterous, deft, proficient*
Root family: [dext, droit] *dexterity* (skill), *ambidextrous* (having skill in using either hand)
Mnemonic: French speakers will recognize the word ***adroit*** from the French phrase ***a droit***, "to the right." This continues a trend in Romance languages to associate right-handedness with skill and the left-handedness with awkwardness or deceit. For instance, the French word ***gauche***, "left," in English means "socially inept." Similarly, the Latin word ***dexter***, "on the right," is the root of ***dexterity*** (skill) and ***ambidextrous*** (skilled in using both hands), and the Latin word ***sinister***, "left," has come to mean "malevolent" in English.

☐ *astute* (adj)

having or showing keen insight : *The announcers made many astute comments about the game.*
Synonyms: *sagacious, prudent, shrewd, canny, incisive*
Don't confuse with: *acute* (keen, as pain or ability)
Usage: Although ***astute, sagacious, prudent, judicious, shrewd, canny***, and ***incisive*** are similar, they offer different shades of meaning. ***Astute*** comes from the Latin ***astutus*** (craft), so an ***astute*** person is likely to have acquired keen insight through careful study; a ***sagacious*** person, however, is likely to have acquired this insight from the benefit of age and trial; a ***prudent*** person is both wise and conservative; a ***judicious*** person is a keen overall adjudicator, whether he or she has acquired that ability through study, age, or trial; a ***shrewd*** or ***canny*** person is insightful and even a bit cunning, particularly in pursuit of a goal like power, compromise, or money; an ***incisive*** commentator has the power to "cut" (***cis*** = cut) to the heart of the matter.

☐ *discernment* (n)   *dis-* apart + *cernere* to distinguish

the ability to make sound judgments and fine distinctions : *Becoming a master oenologist requires not only discernment but also constant study of wines and how they are produced.*
Forms: *discern* = to perceive something as being distinct from other things, ***discerning*** = having a keen ability to make fine distinctions

Synonyms: *perspicacity, percipience*
Root family: [dis-] *disparate* (very different; variegated), *discrepancy* (a lack of compatibility between facts or claims), *disseminate* (to cast widely), *disperse* (to spread or scatter), *dispel* (to drive away; to eliminate), *diffuse* (spread over a wide area)
Root family: [cern, cert] *ascertain* (find something out for certain), *certain* (known for sure), *certify* (formally attest or confirm)

☐ *discretion* (n)   *discretus* separate

sensitivity in dealing with others, particularly in not causing offense : *The teacher showed admirable discretion in not revealing the students' grades out loud.*
Forms: *discreet* = careful in not causing offense, *discretionary* = subject to a particular judgment, *indiscreet* = not careful to avoid offense
Synonyms: *tact, tactfulness*
Don't confuse *discreet* with *discrete* (individually distinct : *The program is broken down into 12 discrete steps.*)

☐ *ethics* (n)   *ethos* customs, behavior

[1] a set of moral principles : *His ethics were dubious.*
[2] the study of moral principles : *David failed his course in medical ethics.*
Forms: *ethicist* = one who studies ethics (*ethologists* study animal behavior), *ethic* = moral principles relating to a specific group or field (*puritan ethic*), *ethical* = morally correct; pertaining to ethics

☐ *exacting* (adj)   *ex-* (intensive) + *agere* to perform

making great demands on one's skills : *Rock climbing is a very exacting task.*
Form: *exact* (v) = to demand and obtain, usually as a payment : *Caesar exacted a tax on all Roman citizens.*
Root family: [agi, age, act] *agent* (someone or something that produces a desired effect), *agenda* (list of items to be accomplished at a meeting), *agile* (able to move quickly and skillfully), *exigent* (pressing; placing demands on someone or something), *inactive* (not active)
Usage: *Exacting* does not mean *exact* (adj). Both words derive from *exigere* (to drive out), but the adjective *exact* derives from a more recent Latin word, *exactus* (precise).

☐ *exemplar* (n)   *exemplum* sample (< *ex-* out + *emere* to take)

someone or something serving as an ideal example of something : *William "Boss" Tweed stands as the exemplar of American political corruption and greed.*
Form: *exemplary* = serving as an excellent example
Synonyms: *apotheosis, nonpareil, paragon*
Root family: [e-, ex-] *extol* (to praise highly), *extemporaneous* (without planning), *exuberant* (filled with liveliness and energy), *elusive* (difficult to catch or achieve)
Root family: [emp, empt, sumpt] *consumption* (the process of eating or using resources), *presumptuous* (failing to observe appropriate limits of behavior), *preempt* (take action to prevent another event from happening), *peremptory* (insisting on immediate attention), *sumptuous* (splendid and abundant)

☐ *lithe* (adj)

limber and graceful : *The dancers resembled nothing so much as rippling water as their lithe bodies undulated rhythmically.*
Synonyms: *agile, supple, limber, lissome*
Don't confuse with: *loathe* (to hate), *blithe* (carefree), *lathe* (a rotating machine for shaping wood)
Mnemonic: *Lithe* dancers can *lightly writhe*, like weightless strips of silk waving in the breeze.

☐ *objective* (adj)

focused on fact rather than opinion : *A good journalist must try to remain objective even when covering emotionally poignant stories.*
Form: *objectivity* = the state of being objective
Synonyms: *impartial, dispassionate, disinterested, nonpartisan*
Usage: Although *objective, impartial, dispassionate, disinterested,* and *nonpartisan* are similar, they offer different shades of meaning. A scientist or journalist should be *objective*, that is, focused on facts (*objects*), to the exclusion of opinions, in the pursuit of gathering and analyzing information; a good judge should be *impartial*, that is, lacking any bias for or against any of the disputants (legal *parties*); a wise judge is also *dispassionate*, that is, actively discounting his or her feelings (*passions*) in favor of the facts; a *disinterested* judge avoids considerations of personal advantage (*interest*); and a fair-minded politician is *nonpartisan*, that is, inclined to elevate pragmatic concerns over political ideology (the *party* line).
Usage: In modern usage *objective* is the opposite of *subjective* (based on opinion rather than fact).

☐ *pragmatic* (adj)   *pragma* deed

concerned with practical rather than idealistic considerations : *Her choice of car was more pragmatic than aesthetic.*
Forms: *pragmatism* = belief that practical qualities are more important than idealistic ones, ***pragmatist*** = a pragmatic person
Don't confuse with: *dogmatic*
Usage: *Pragmatic* and *practical* have very similar meanings and origins, but while a pair of shoes might be *practical* (suitable to and effective for general purposes), only people can be *pragmatic*. *Pragmatic* can describe a frame of mind or a method, but not a thing.

☐ *proficient* (adj)   *pro-* for + *facere* to do or make

competent or skilled in a particular task : *He is a proficient drummer, if not an exceptionally talented one.*
Form: *proficiency* = skill in a particular task
Synonyms: *adept, adroit, deft, dexterous*
Root family: [pro-] *protracted* (lasting longer than expected), ***prophecy*** (prediction), ***promote*** (further the progress of something; raise in rank), ***progeny*** (offspring), ***reciprocate*** (to respond in kind)
Root family: [fic, fac, fec, -ify] *facile* (simplistic), ***munificent*** (generous), ***diversify*** (to make more varied), ***ossify*** (to turn into bone), ***efficacy*** (ability to produce the intended result)

☐ *sagacious* (adj)

having or showing good judgment and discernment : *We needed the sagacious mind of Uncle Ted to help us resolve our differences.*
Forms: *sagacity* = wisdom and discernment, ***sage*** = a wise person
Synonyms: *astute, prudent, judicious, shrewd, canny, incisive*
Usage: See usage note at *astute* in this section.

☐ *valor* (n)   *valere* to be strong

courage and nobility in the face of danger : *His valor on the battlefield earned him the Congressional Medal of Honor.*
Form: *valiant* = courageous
Root family: [val] *prevalent* (widespread and abundant), ***ambivalent*** (having mixed feelings), ***valence*** (the power of an atom to make bonds with other atoms)
Don't confuse with: *pallor* an unhealthy pale appearance

19 THE LANGUAGE OF CAPITAL AND WEALTH

☐ *avarice* (n)

extreme greed : *David was repulsed by the avarice that thrived on Wall Street in the 1990s.*
Form: *avaricious* = extremely greedy
Synonyms: *cupidity, rapacity, covetousness*
Don't confuse *avaricious* with ***vicious*** (deliberately cruel or violent), ***auspicious*** (favorable), or ***avatar*** (a worldly incarnation of a god; a moving icon representing a person in cyberspace)
Mnemonic: Someone who is ***avaricious*** wants to ***have all riches***.

☐ *bourgeois* (adj)   *burgus* castle, fortified town

pertaining to or characteristic of the conventional and materialistic life of the middle class : *He rebelled against the stultifying bourgeois lifestyle and yearned for the life of a bohemian.*
Form: *bourgeoisie* = the middle class
Synonyms: *conventional*
Root family: [burg] *burg* (city or town), ***borough*** (an administrative district, as or within a town or city), ***burglar*** (one who breaks into homes to rob them (< *burgier* to pillage a town))

☐ *decadent* (adj)   *de-* down + *cadere* to fall

excessively self-indulgent : *I decided that since I had adhered strictly to my diet for two months, I could be decadent at the wedding.*
Form: *decadence* = excessive self-indulgence
Root family: [de-] *denounce* (declare as bad), ***detract*** (reduce the value of something), ***debase*** (reduce in value), ***denigrate*** (criticize unfairly), ***deference*** (submission to the authority of another), ***condescend*** (to act superior to someone else)

Root family: [cide, cade, cas, cay] *accident* (an unintentional, unexpected, and unfortunate incident), *cadence* (the rising and falling inflection of the voice), *coincide* (to occur at the same time), *cascade* (small waterfall), *recidivism* (falling back into a life of crime)

☐ *exorbitant* (adj)   *ex-* out + *orbita* track, course

excessive ; exceeding the bounds of propriety or reason : *She charged an exorbitant fee for only a few hours' work.*
Synonym: *prohibitive*
Root family: [e-, ex-] *extol* (to praise highly), *extemporaneous* (without planning), *exuberant* (filled with liveliness and energy), *elusive* (difficult to catch or achieve)
Root family: [orb] *orbit* (elliptical path of a satellite)

☐ *frugal* (adj)

reluctant to spend money or expend resources : *He was too frugal to even pay for a cab ride home.*
Form: *frugality* = thriftiness; reluctance to expend resources
Synonyms: *miserly, stingy*

☐ *indigent* (adj) or (n)

[1] (adj) poor; needy : *We've donated the proceeds to a charity that provides food and shelter to the indigent of our city.*
Synonyms: *impecunious, destitute, insolvent, penurious*
[2] (n) a poor and homeless person : *Fewer indigents can be found on the streets since the city opened the new shelter and soup kitchen.*
Form: *indigence* = poverty
Don't confuse with: *indigenous* (native)
Mnemonic: During the Depression, homeless wanderers may have been disparaged as hobos or *indigents*, but many of them might have just considered themselves *inde*pendent *gent*lemen.

☐ *lavish* (adj) or (v)

[1] (adj) extravagant or elaborate : *It was a lavish affair, elegant to the last detail.*
[2] (v) to give in extravagant quantities : *His aunts lavished little Stephen with attention.*
Don't confuse with: *slavish* (like or characteristic of a slave)

☐ *lucrative* (adj)   *lucrum* profit

highly profitable : *He abandoned his lucrative banking job for a more fulfilling career in teaching.*
Synonyms: *remunerative, gainful*
Root family: [lucr] *lucre* (profit, usually that which is ill-gotten)

☐ *mercenary* (adj) or (n)   *merces* payment

[1] (adj) primarily concerned with making money : *When our CEO left for a higher-paying job after only six months, he was rightly castigated for being mercenary.*
Synonyms: *acquisitive, venal, avaricious, covetous*
[2] (n) a soldier who fights for money rather than patriotism; a person concerned primarily with making money rather than with personal integrity : *The general preferred to work with dedicated soldiers rather than mercenaries.*
Synonym: *soldier of fortune*
Root family: [merc] *merchant* (s trader or store owner), *mercantilism* (belief in the benefits of profitable trading), *commerce* (the activity of buying and selling), *merchandise* (goods that are bought and sold)

☐ *opulent* (adj)

ostentatiously rich or lavish : *Jay Gatsby threw opulent parties at his elegant mansion.*
Form: *opulence* = lavishness
Synonyms: *grandiose, ritzy, splendid*
Don't confuse with: *opalescent* (exhibiting a milky iridescence, as an opal)

☐ *ostentatious* (adj)   *ostens* presented for display

intended to attract attention; characterized by vulgar and pretentious display : *We decorated our house tastefully, avoiding the ostentatious Christmas displays that were so common in town.*

Form: *ostentation* = pretentious and vulgar display
Synonyms: *pretentious*, *flamboyant*, *gaudy*, *ornate*, *garish*
Root family: [osten] *ostensible* (appearing to be true, but not necessarily so)
Don't confuse with: *austere*

☐ *prodigal* (adj)   *prodigus* lavish

tending to spend resources wastefully : *A prodigal manager can squander a year's worth of careful savings in just a few weeks.*
Form: *prodigality* = wastefulness
Synonyms: *profligate*, *spendthrift*, *improvident*
Root family: [prodigi] *prodigy* (a young person with exceptional talent), *prodigious* (great in size or degree)
Mnemonic: The Biblical story of the *prodigal* son is about a son who squanders all of his inheritance and later comes to regret it.

☐ *remuneration* (n)   *munero* to share, to give a gift

payment for services : *We were unhappy with the remuneration we received for the hard work we put into the project.*
Forms: *remunerate* = to pay someone for services, *remunerative* = pertaining to payment for services
Synonyms: *recompense*, *reimbursement*, *compensation*
Root family: [muni, muner] *immunity* (resistance to an infection or toxin), *munificent* (generous)
Don't confuse with: *enumeration* (listing in numerical order)
Mnemonic: *Remuneration* is received *money* for your *action.*

☐ *squander* (v)

to waste recklessly, particularly money or opportunity : *We must not squander this opportunity to get our financial house in order.*
Don't confuse with: *wander* (roam)

20 THE LANGUAGE OF PASSION, EMOTION, AND SENSATION

☐ *abash* (v)

to cause to feel embarrassed or ashamed : *I was abashed at the sight of her photograph.*
Form: *abashed* = embarrassed, *unabashed* = confidently unashamed
Don't confuse with: *bash* ((v) hit forcefully; (n) a lively party)
Mnemonic: *Abash* means to make *bashful.*

☐ *alacrity* (n)

cheerful eagerness : *Howard accepted our invitation to brunch with alacrity.*
Synonyms: *ardor*, *fervor*, *dispatch*
Don't confuse with: *anachronism* (something out of place in time), *clarity* (clearness)

☐ *apathy* (n)   *a-* without + *pathos* suffering, emotion

lack of interest or concern : *Although Glen was happy and excited about the trip, Philip's glum apathy tempered everyone's mood.*
Form: *apathetic* = lacking interest or concern
Synonyms: *indifference*, *dispassion*, *languor*
Root family: [a-, an-] *amorphous* (lacking definite shape), *anarchy* (lack of hierarchical government)
Root family: [path, pati, pass] *sympathy* (feeling of sorrow for the misfortunes of another), *pathology* (the science of the causes and course of diseases), *empathy* (the ability to share the feelings of others), *antipathy* (hostility)
Don't confuse with: *antipathy* (hostility)

☐ *apprehensive* (adj)   *prehendere* to grasp, to seize

anxious that something bad might happen : *Kyra was apprehensive about entering the abandoned house.*
Form: *apprehension* = fear that something bad might happen; the taking of a criminal suspect into custody
Synonyms: *fretful*, *disquieted*
Root family: [prehens] *comprehensive* (thorough and complete), *reprehensible* (morally objectionable)
Don't confuse with: *comprehensive* (thorough and complete)

Mnemonic: The word **apprehend**, deriving as it does from the Latin **prehendere**, meaning "to grasp or seize," means "to arrest" (*apprehend a criminal*) or "to perceive or understand superficially" (*apprehend danger*). **Apprehensive**, however, does not derive from either of those meanings, but rather the idea of being "seized" with fear.

☐ *ardor* (n)   *ardere* to burn

enthusiasm; passion : *He has maintained the same ardor for campaigning as he had when he first ran for office.*
Form: *ardent* = passionate
Root family: [ard, ars] *arsonist* (one who illegally sets fires)
Don't confuse with: *arbor* (a shady alcove covered by trees or climbing plants), *barter* (exchange of goods or services for payment instead of money)
Mnemonic: *Ardor* is a **burning** passion (*ardere* = to burn).

☐ *callous* (adj)

emotionally insensitive to the suffering of others : *He showed callous disregard of the pain that we were going through.*
Form: *callousness* = disregard for the suffering of others
Synonyms: *ruthless, inhumane, sadistic*
Don't confuse with: *callowness* (immaturity)

☐ *catharsis* (n)

the process of purging unwanted or unhealthy emotions : *After a frustrating day at the office, kickboxing class offers a welcome catharsis.*
Form: *cathartic* = providing an elimination of unwanted emotions
Synonyms: *purgation, venting*
Don't confuse with: *catheter* (a tube inserted into the body to remove fluid), *catechism* (a summary of questions and answers summarizing the principles of the Christian religion)

☐ *complacent* (adj)   *com-* (intensive) + *placent* pleasing

smugly and uncritically satisfied with one's situation : *A nation should not be complacent about its security.*
Form: *complacency* = smug self-satisfaction
Root family: [plac] *placate* (to appease), *implacable* (unable to be pleased), *placid* (peaceful)
Don't confuse with: *complaisant* (willing to please)
Mnemonic: One who is *complacent* is satisfied with his or her *place* in the world, but one who is *complaisant* wants to *please* (*plais*).

☐ *ebullient* (adj)   *e-* out + *bullire* to boil

full of cheerful energy : *Jennifer was ebullient about her acceptance to Brown.*
Form: *ebullience* = cheerful energy
Don't confuse with: *emollient* (a skin softening agent)
Mnemonic: Someone who is *ebullient* lets the joy *bubble out* (*e-* out + *bullire* to boil).

☐ *effusive* (adj)   *e-* out + *fusus* poured

freely expressive, particularly of emotions; pouring out : *Julie was effusive in her greeting, hugging each of us like a mother bear.*
Forms: *effusion* = an outpouring, usually of emotion
Root family: [fus, fund, found] *confuse* (to cause to become perplexed), *confound* (to fail to distinguish different elements), *diffuse* (spread out over a large area), *fusion* (the process of joining two things into a single entity), *profuse* (abundant), *transfusion* (a transfer, usually of blood, from one person or animal to another), *refuse* (to reject)
Don't confuse with: *elusive* (difficult to find, catch, or achieve)

☐ *fervent* (adj)   *fervere* to be hot

displaying a passionate intensity : *The protest rally was punctuated by several fervent speeches.*
Form: *fervor* = intense and passionate feeling
Synonyms: *vehement, zealous, fervid*
Root family: [ferv] *effervescent* (bubbly), *fervid* (passionate), *fever* (elevated body temperature due to infection; state of nervous excitement)
Don't confuse with: *fever* (elevated body temperature due to infection; state of nervous excitement)
Mnemonic/Usage: Although *fervent* doesn't mean exactly the same thing as *feverish*, both words derive from the same Latin root and both share the meaning of "intense feeling." In the case of *fervent*, the feeling is primarily emotional, but in *feverish*, the feeling is primarily physical.

☐ *forlorn* (adj)

pitifully sad and lonely : *The city was filled with forlorn souls with unfulfilled dreams.*
Synonyms: *despondent, disconsolate, abject, melancholy*
Don't confuse with: *foregone* (predetermined)

☐ *grudging* (adj)   grouchier to grumble

given reluctantly or resentfully : *Although his opponents hate to compete against him, they give him grudging respect.*
Root family: [grudg, grouch] *grouchy* (irritable and bad-tempered), *begrudge* (to envy someone's enjoyment of something)
Don't confuse with: *dredging* (cleaning a riverbed by scooping)

☐ *indifferent* (adj)

having no particular concern or interest : *The king was indifferent to the suffering of his own people.*
Form: *indifference* = lack of concern or interest
Synonyms: *insouciant, nonchalant, dispassionate, apathetic*
Don't confuse with: *not different*
Mnemonic: People tend to be *indifferent* about those things that they think make *no difference* in the world.
Usage: See usage note at *nonchalant* in section 8.

☐ *inhibited* (adj)

reluctant to act or restrained from acting in a natural way, usually because of self-consciousness : *Faith felt inhibited in front of her classmates, but was very much a free spirit with her friends.*
Forms: *inhibit* = to restrain or hinder, *inhibition* = self-conscious reluctance to behave naturally, *uninhibited* = free-spirited
Synonyms: *reticent, diffident*
Don't confuse with: *inhabited* (occupied as a living space by a person, animal, or group)

☐ *palpable* (adj)   palpare to touch gently

perceivable by touch; so intense as to seem touchable : *The tension in the room was palpable.*
Form: *palpate* = to touch gently, especially to diagnose a medical condition
Mnemonic: When you go the doctor with stomach pains, the doctor *palpates* your stomach with his or her *palm* to feel the *pain*.

☐ *qualitative* (adj)

pertaining to the quality of something rather than a measurable quantity : *There has been a qualitative change in the mood of the workers ever since the new contract was signed.*

☐ *resigned* (adj)   re- back + signare to sign officially

reluctantly accepting of an undesirable situation : *We were resigned to the fact that Ms. Davis, our favorite teacher, would be absent for several weeks.*
Form: *resignation* = reluctant acceptance of an undesirable situation
Synonyms: *forbearing, stoical, acquiescent, compliant*
Root family: [re-] *recluse* (a person who lives a solitary lifestyle), *renounce* (to give up or put aside publicly), *regress* (to return to a less developed state), *relegate* (to place in a lower rank)
Root family: [sign] *consign* (to deliver into another's custody), *designate* (to appoint officially), *signature* (a person's name written as an official identification mark), *significant* (noteworthy), *assign* (to allocate officially)

☐ *vehement* (adj)   vehere to carry

showing intense feeling : *The lawyer's accusation was met with a vehement denial.*
Form: *vehemence* = intense feeling
Synonym: *ardent*
Root family: [veh, vect] *vehicle* (a mechanical transportation device; a means of expression), *vector* (a quantity with magnitude and direction; a means of transmitting disease), *convection* (the circulation of air by heating and cooling)
Don't confuse with: *violent* (physically forceful)
Mnemonic: *Vehement* sounds like *vehicle* because they both derive from the Latin verb *vehere*, "to carry": someone who is *vehement* is getting "carried away."

THE POWER ROOTS AND AFFIXES FOR THE SAT

a-, an-	without	**asymmetric**, *apathy, amoral, amorphous, anarchy*
ab-	away	**absent**, *absolve, abstemious, abhor, abstruse, abstract*
-able, -ible	(adj) able to be	**paintable**, *indomitable, malleable, insuperable, tractable, interminable*
acer, acr	bitter, sharp	**acrid**, *exacerbate, acrimonious, acerbic*
act, agi, age	to act, to perform	**action**, *exacting, agent, agenda, exigent, agile*
acu	sharp	**acute**, *acumen, acuity, acupuncture*
ad-	to, toward, for	**advance**, *advocate, aspire, allude, acquiesce, adhere*
agog	leading, teaching	**demagogue**, *pedagogy, synagogue*
agon	struggle	**agony**, *antagonistic, protagonist, agonize*
-al	(adj) like, pertaining to	**personal**, *ephemeral, comical, conventional*
	(n) the act of	**denial**, *refusal, perusal*
altr, alter, ulter	other	**alter ego**, *altruism, altercation, alternate, adulterate*
ambi-, amphi-	both	**ambidextrous**, *ambivalent, ambiguous, amphibian*
ami, amic	friend	**amiable**, *amicable, inimical, amity, enemy*
ana-	backward, mixed up	**anagram**, *anachronism, anabolism, analect*
-ance, -ence	(n) act, quality, being	**tolerance**, *reticence, temperance, nonchalance, ambivalence*
anima	life, spirit, mind	**animate**, *unanimous, magnanimous, equanimity, inanimate, pusillanimous*
ante-	before	**ante**, *antecedent, antebellum, antedeluvian, antedate, anterior*
anthro	humankind	**anthropology**, *misanthrope, philanthropist, anthropomorphism*
anti-	against	**anticlimactic**, *antipathy, antagonistic, antidote, antithesis*
apo-	away, from, not	**apology**, *apostrophe, apocryphal, apostasy, apogee, apologetics*
apt, ept	well-suited	**aptitude**, *inept, apt, adapt, adept*
arbit	judge	**arbitration**, *arbitrary, arbiter*
arch	ancient	**archaeology**, *archive, archaic, archaeopteryx*
	chief, most important	**archrival**, *architect, archipelago, archetype*
	govern, rule	**anarchy**, *monarch, hierarchy, oligarchy*
-ation	(n) act of, result of	**imitation**, *saturation, cultivation, recitation, conflagration*
audi	to hear	**auditory**, *audition, audience, auditorium, audio, audit*
auto-	self	**automatic**, *autobiography, autocracy, autotroph*
bellum, belli	war, fighting	**belligerent**, *antebellum, bellicose, rebellious*
bene, bon	good	**beneficiary**, *benign, benediction, benefactor, bon mot*
bi-	two, twice	**bisect**, *biannually, bifurcate, binomial*
bio-	life	**biology**, *biography, biome, bioluminescence, symbiosis*
cad, cid, cas	to fall	**decay**, *decadent, casualty, recidivist, cascade*
cant, chant	to sing, to recite	**incantation**, *recant, cantata, enchant, chant*
cap, capit	head	**decapitate**, *capitulation, capital, recap, chapter*
carn	flesh	**carnivore**, *carnival, reincarnation, incarnate*
cata	down, fall, precipitate	**catalyst**, *cataract, cataclysm, catastrophe, catapult*
ced, ces	to go	**proceed**, *precedent, concession, recede, secede*
cern, cert	to set apart	**discern**, *discernment, ascertain, certain, certify*
chron	time	**chronological**, *synchronize, anachronism, chronograph*

cinc	to cinch, as with a belt	*succinct, cinch, precinct*
circum	around	*circumference, circuitous, circumscribe, circumlocution, circumspect*
cis, schis	to cut, to split	*scissors, incision, precise, concise, schism, schizophrenia*
clam, claim	to cry out	*clamor, proclaim, acclaim, exclaim*
clus, clud	to close	*conclude, recluse, preclude, claustrophobia, cloistered*
co-, com-, con-	together, with (intensive)	*cooperate, conform, convention, consensus, confluence, conspire consummate, condone, conflagration, complacent*
cogn, conn	to know	*recognize, connoisseur, reconnoiter, cognizant, incognito, cognoscenti*
contra-	against	*contradiction, incontrovertible, contrary, contraband, contravene*
cor, cour	heart	*cardiac, cordial, concord, discord, courage*
cred	to trust	*incredible, discredit, credence, incredulous, credible, credit*
crim	judgment, offense	*crime, discriminating, criminal, incriminate, recrimination*
crit	judge	*critic, criteria, critique, diacritic, hypocritical*
crypt, cryph	hidden	*cryptic, apocryphal, encryption, decrypt, cryptogram*
culpa	blame	*culprit, exculpate, culpable, mea culpa*
cur, cour	to run	*course, discursive, cursory, incur, precursor, courier*
de-	down, from, away	*descend, indefatigable, denigrate, detract, decadent, condescend*
deca-, deci-	ten; one-tenth	*decade, decathlon; decimeter, decimal, decibel*
delet, deli	to destroy, to eliminate	*delete, deleterious, indelible*
dem	people	*democracy, demographics, epidemic, demagogue*
dext, droit	right-handed, skilled	*dexterity, ambidextrous, adroit*
di-	apart, away	*diverge, digress, diversion, diffident, diffuse*
dia-	through	*diagonal, diameter, diaphanous, diatribe*
dic, dict	to declare	*dictate, vindictive, dictum, malediction, dictatorial*
dign, dain	worthy	*dignity, indignation, disdain, deign*
dis-	apart, away	*disband, discrepancy, discernment, disparate, disseminate, discriminate*
	against, not	*discredit, disquiet, disconcerting, disinterested, disdain*
doc, dox, doct	to teach	*indoctrinate, orthodox, docile, doctrinaire, paradox*
domin, domit	to dominate	*dominate, indomitable, domineering, predominant, domain, dominion*
duc	to lead, to carry	*conduction, induce, conduct, ductile, produce*
dupl, duo	twofold	*duplicate, duo, duplicity, duplex, dual, duality*
e-, ex-	out	*emit, evanescent, extemporaneous, emigrate, exonerate, extol*
-en	(v) to make	*harden, frighten, dampen*
	(adj) made of	*golden, woolen, wooden*
en-	cause to be, in	*endanger, entangle, enrage, envelop*
epi-	upon, in addition	*epidemic, epidermis, epicenter, epilogue*
equi, equa	the same	*equal, equanimity, equilateral, equilibrium, equivocate*
esthe	perceive, discern	*anesthetic, aesthetic, synesthesia, aesthete*
eu-	good	*eulogy, euphemism, euphonious, euphoria, eugenics*
extra-	beyond, outside	*extraneous, extraterrestrial, estranged, extravagant, extracurricular*
fac, fec, fic	to make, to do	*factory, efficacy, facilitate, facile, benefactor, munificent*
fer, pher	to bear, to carry	*fertile, infer, deference, coniferous, aquifer, pheromone*
ferv	to boil, to bubble	*effervescent, fervent, fervid, fever*

fide	faith, trust	*fidelity*, *infidel*, *perfidious*, *diffident*
flu	to flow	*fluid*, *superfluous*, *influx*, *affluent*, *fluctuate*, *confluence*
fore-	before	*foreshadow*, *foremost*, *forewarn*, *foreground*
fort, forc	strong	*force*, *fortify*, *forte*, *enforce*, *effort*, *reinforcement*
fract, frag	broken up	*fracture*, *refractory*, *fractious*, *refraction*, *fragile*, *fragment*
fug	to flee	*refugee*, *fugitive*, *centrifuge*, *refuge*, *subterfuge*
-ful	(adj) full of	*suspenseful*, *tactful*, *mirthful*, *wrongful*, *deceitful*
funct, fung	to perform	*function*, *perfunctory*, *defunct*, *dysfunctional*, *fungible*
fus, found	to pour	*effusive*, *diffuse*, *profuse*, *confound*, *confuse*, *refuse*
gen	race, kind	*homogeneous*, *progenitor*, *heterogeneous*, *indigenous*
	to create, to be born	*generate*, *genetic*, *disingenuous*, *progeny*, *congenital*
geo-	earth	*geography*, *geology*, *geometry*
grad, gress	to walk	*progress*, *digress*, *regress*, *egress*
grand	great	*grandeur*, *grandiose*, *grandiloquent*, *aggrandize*
graph	write, draw, study	*geography*, *biography*, *orthography*, *cartography*, *demographics*
grat	pleasing, thankful	*gratitude*, *gratuitous*, *gratuity*, *ingrate*, *ingratiate*
greg	flock	*congregation*, *gregarious*, *aggregate*
her, hes	to stick	*adhesive*, *adherent*, *cohesive*, *inherent*, *coherent*
-hood	(n) state of being	*childhood*, *statehood*, *adulthood*
hyper	over, above	*hyperactive*, *hyperbole*, *hyperventilate*, *hyperextend*
hypo	under	*hyposensitive*, *hypoglycemic*, *hypochondria*, *hypothesis*, *hypothalamus*
idio	unique	*idiosyncrasy*, *idiom*, *idiot*
-ify	to make	*solidify*, *ossify*, *vilify*, *fortify*, *diversify*, *edify*, *petrify*
imper, emper	to command	*imperial*, *imperious*, *empire*, *imperative*
in-, ir-, il-, im-	not	*irrelevant*, *inert*, *intractable*, *insuperable*, *inscrutable*, *incongruous*
	in, into, toward	*intrude*, *inundate*, *infer*, *incisive*, *insurgent*, *impetuous*, *indoctrinate*
inter-	between, among	*international*, *intervene*, *interloper*, *intermittent*
intro-	into	*introspective*, *introduction*, *introverted*
ir	anger	*irritated*, *irascible*, *irate*, *ire*
-ism	(n) belief, quality of	*realism*, *fatalism*, *pragmatism*, *polytheism*, *narcissism*
-ist	(n) one who is or does	*pacifist*, *conformist*, *narcissist*, *pragmatist*
-ity	(n) quality, instance of	*curiosity*, *futility*, *adversity*, *celebrity*, *passivity*
-ive	(adj) quality	*offensive*, *obtrusive*, *corrective*, *ruminative*, *evocative*, *elective*
-ize	(v) to make	*polarize*, *satirize*, *fraternize*, *lionize*, *scrutinize*, *civilize*, *sanitize*
ject	throw	*eject*, *conjecture*, *objective*, *subjective*, *reject*
jud	judge	*judiciary*, *judicious*, *adjudicate*, *prejudice*
jur, jus	to give an oath	*perjury*, *abjure*, *conjure*
	right, law	*justice*, *jurisdiction*, *injury*, *jurisprudence*, *injustice*
lect, leg, lig	to choose	*select*, *elect*, *eclectic*, *eligible*, *collect*, *recollect*
leg	lawful	*legal*, *relegate*, *delegate*, *privilege*, *allege*, *legacy*
-less	(adj) without	*painless*, *listless*, *relentless*, *ruthless*, *dauntless*
lev	to raise	*levitation*, *alleviate*, *levity*, *elevate*, *relieve*
lig	to bind	*ligament*, *obliging*, *ligature*, *obligatory*
linqu, lict	to abandon	*relinquish*, *delinquent*, *relic*, *derelict*, *reliquary*

line	to create with lines	*linear*, *lineage*, *delineate*, *collinear*, *align*
locu, loqu	to talk	*eloquent*, *colloquial*, *circumlocution*, *grandiloquent*, *loquacious*
-logy, -logue	study, discourse	*geology*, *apologist*, *eulogy*, *chronology*, *anthology*, *epilogue*
luc, lum	light	*illuminate*, *lucid*, *elucidate*, *luminous*, *translucent*
lud, lus	to be playful	*ludicrous*, *allude*, *collude*, *illusion*, *delude*
mag, maj, max	great	*magnificent*, *magnanimous*, *maxim*, *majesty*, *magnitude*
mal	bad, badly	*malicious*, *malevolent*, *malady*, *malediction*, *malign*, *maladjusted*, *malodorous*
med, mod	middle	*median*, *medium*, *modicum*, *mediocre*, *mediation*
-ment	act of, state of being	*resentment*, *enticement*, *discernment*, *refinement*, *bereavement*
merc	payment	*commerce*, *mercenary*, *commercial*, *mercantilism*, *merchandise*
meta-	change, beyond	*metaphysics*, *metamorphose*, *metabolism*
mis-	wrong	*mistake*, *misapprehension*, *misprint*, *misfit*, *mislead*
mit, miss	to send	*mission*, *intermittent*, *unremitting*, *submit*, *emit*, *permit*
moll	soft	*mollusk*, *mollify*, *emollient*
mono-	one	*monotone*, *monolith*, *monotonous*, *monologue*, *monopoly*
morph	shape	*metamorphosis*, *amorphous*, *polymorphic*, *morphology*
multi-	many	*multiply*, *multinational*, *multicolor*
muni, muner	to share	*community*, *munificent*, *immunity*, *remuneration*, *commune*
mut	to change	*mutation*, *commute*, *immutable*
nat, nas, nai	born	*prenatal*, *innate*, *natural*, *nascent*, *renaissance*
-ness	(n) quality of, state of	*soreness*, *callousness*, *boldness*, *fondness*
noc, nox	harmful	*noxious*, *innocuous*, *obnoxious*, *innocent*
nom, nomen, nym	name	*nominate*, *ignominious*, *pseudonym*, *anonymous*, *nomenclature*
non-	not	*nonfiction*, *nonprofit*, *nonsense*
null, nihil	nothing	*nil*, *nihilism*, *annul*, *annihilate*
nunc, nounc	to declare	*announce*, *denounce*, *renounce*, *enunciate*, *pronounce*
omni-	all	*omnivore*, *omnipresent*, *omniscient*, *omnipotent*
onus, oner	burden	*onus*, *exonerate*, *onerous*
ortho	right, straight, strict	*orthodontist*, *orthodox*, *orthogonal*, *orthopedics*
-ous	(adj) full of	*gracious*, *voracious*, *garrulous*, *superfluous*, *gratuitous*, *homogeneous*
pac, peas	peace	*pacify*, *appease*, *pact*, *pacifist*
palp	to touch	*palpate*, *palpable*, *palpitate*
pan-	everything, all	*panorama*, *pandemic*, *pantheon*, *panoply*, *panacea*
para-	beside, distinct from	*parallel*, *paradox*, *paradigm*, *paralegal*, *paramedic*
path, pass	to suffer	*passion*, *sympathy*, *empathy*, *apathetic*, *antipathy*, *dispassionate*, *patient*
patr	father	*patriarch*, *patronize*, *compatriot*, *patronage*
pecc	to sin	*impeccable*, *peccadillo*, *peccant*
ped	child	*pediatrician*, *pedagogy*, *pedantic*
ped, pod	foot	*pedestrian*, *podiatrist*, *impede*, *expedite*
pel, pul	to drive, to force	*repel*, *compulsion*, *impulsive*, *repulsive*, *dispel*
per-	through, throughout	*permeable*, *impervious*, *permit*, *permeate*, *pervasive*
	thoroughly	*perfect*, *peruse*, *perturb*, *perpetuate*, *perfunctory*

peri-	around	*perimeter, peripheral, peripatetic, perihelion*
pet	to drive	*impetus, impetuous, perpetuate, petulant*
phem, phes	way of speaking	*euphemism, dysphemism, blasphemy, prophesy*
pher, phor	to carry, to convey	*euphoria, metaphor, peripheral, semaphore*
phila	attraction, interest	*bibliophile, philanthropy, philosophy, hydrophilic*
phon	voice, sound	*phonetic, microphone, phonics, symphony, cacophony*
phren, fren	mind, delirium	*frenzy, frenetic, phrenology, schizophrenia, frantic*
plac	to please	*placate, placid, implacable, complacent*
plaud, plaus	to clap, show approval	*applaud, plausible, plaudits, explode*
ple	to fill	*complete, complement, deplete, replete, supplement, compliant*
plic, ply	to fold	*complicated, complicit, explication, implication*
pol	city, citizen	*metropolis, cosmopolitan, policy, politics, police, polite*
pond, pend	weight, hanging	*pendant, ponderous, impending, propensity, pendulum, dependent*
pos	to place	*position, juxtapose, posit, disposition, appose, oppose*
post-	after	*postscript, postdoctoral, posthumous*
poten	strength, power	*potent, impotent, despot, potentate, omnipotent, potency*
pre-	before	*precede, premonition, precedent, prescience, premeditated, precocious*
prehens	to grasp	*comprehend, apprehensive, reprehensible, prehensile, comprehensive*
pro-	forward	*propel, protracted, reciprocate, provocative, prophecy, progeny, profuse*
prodig	lavish	*prodigious, prodigal, prodigy*
proper, propr	one's own	*property, propriety, expropriation, proprietor, appropriate*
pug, pugn	to fight	*pugnacious, impugn, pugilist, repugnant*
punct, pung	point, sharp	*punctual, punctilious, poignant, punctuation, punctilio*
	to prick	*puncture, compunction*
puni, peni	to punish	*punish, penitent, punitive, penitentiary, punishment*
quies, quiet	to rest	*quiet, quietude, acquiesce, quiescence, disquiet*
radic	root	*radical, eradicate, radish*
rap, rav, rept	to seize	*enrapt, rapture, surreptitious, rapacious, ravenous, ravage*
re-	back	*return, reciprocate, revoke, recluse, refute, renounce*
	again	*repaint, reconsider, replenish, resurgence*
rect	right, straight	*correct, rectify, direct, rectangle*
rud	untrained	*rude, erudite, rudiment, rudimentary*
rupt	broken	*rupture, erupt, interrupt, corrupt*
sacer, secr	to make holy	*sacred, sacrifice, sacrilege, sacrosanct, consecrate*
sanct	holy	*sanctify, sanction, sanctuary, sacrosanct, sanctimonious*
sang	blood	*sanguinary, consanguineous, sanguine, sangfroid*
sap, sav, sip	to taste	*savory, insipid, savor, sapid*
sat	full	*satisfy, saturate, insatiable, sated*
scend, scal	to climb	*descend, condescend, scale, ascend, transcend, escalate, echelon*
scien	to know	*science, conscience, omniscience, prescient, conscious*
scrib, script	to write or draw	*script, circumscribe, prescribe, proscribe, inscription*
sed	to sit, to settle	*sediment, sedentary, sedate, assiduous, insidious*
semi-	half	*semicircle, semiannual, semiconductor, semi*

semin	seed	*seminal*, seminary, disseminate, seminar
sent, sens	to feel	*sense*, sentient, sensation, consensus, dissent
sequ, secu	to follow	*sequel*, sequence, obsequious, inconsequential, consecutive, consequence
-ship	(n) quality of, ability	*friendship*, hardship, workmanship, kinship
solv, solu	to loosen	*dissolve*, absolve, irresolute, resolve, solution
-some	(adj) causing, tending	*fearsome*, worrisome, bothersome
son	sound	*sonic*, dissonance, assonance, consonant, resonate
spect, spic	to look	*inspect*, introspective, circumspect, conspicuous, speculation
spir	to breathe	*respiration*, aspire, conspire, expire
spers	to scatter or sprinkle	*disperse*, aspersion, interspersed
stat, stag, stan	to stand, to stay	*stationary*, stagnate, static, constant, apostasy
strait, strict	to bind, to confine	*strict*, constrict, stringent, straitened, strangle, restriction, distress
stru, stroy, stry	to build	*construct*, construe, destroy, industry, obstruct
sub-	under	*submarine*, surreptitious, subjugate, subvert, subdued, somber
sum	highest	*summit*, consummate, summa cum laude, summary
super-	over, above	*superior*, superlative, superfluous, supercilious, insuperable
surg, surr	to rise	*surge*, insurgent, resurrection, resurgence
sym-, syn-	together, same	*synthesize*, synchronize, symbiosis, sympathy, idiosyncrasy, synonym
tace, taci	to be silent	*tacit*, reticent, taciturn
tang, tact, tag	to touch	*tangible*, tangential, tactile, integral, tactful
tele-	from a distance	*teleport*, telephone, telekinesis, telecast, telemetry
temper	to restrain	*temperate*, temperance, temper, temperature
tempo	time	*tempo*, extemporaneous, contemporary, temporary
ten	to stretch, to make thin	*extend*, tense, tenuous, attenuate, pretentious
ten, tain	to hold	*retain*, tenacious, obtain, retention, untenable, detention
term	to end	*terminate*, interminable, indeterminate, exterminate, terminal
terr	earth	*terrestrial*, disinter, extraterrestrial, subterranean, terrain
thes, thet, them	to construct	*synthesis*, prosthesis, epithet, anathema
-tion, -sion	(n) action	*discussion*, incantation, revelation, convention
	(n) quality, state	*discretion*, consternation, trepidation
tract	to pull	*tractor*, extract, abstract, tractable, protracted, retract, detractor
trans-	to a different place	*transport*, transient, transplant, transcribe
	across, through	*transparent*, translucent, transcend, transaction
trit	rubbed, worn	*trite*, attrition, contrite, detritus
troph	nourishment	*autotroph*, atrophy, eutrophic, allotrophic
trunc, trench	to cut	*truncate*, trenchant, truncheon, trunks
trus, trud	to push	*intrude*, abstruse, extrude, obtrusive, intrusive
turb	to disturb	*disturb*, perturb, turbulence
un-	not	*unspoken*, unassuming, unfettered, unstinting, unabridged
umbra	shade	*umbrella*, somber, adumbrate, umbrage, penumbra
unda, ound	wave	*undulate*, inundate, abundance, abound, redundant
under-	beneath	*underground*, undernourished, undermine, underestimate
uni-	one	*unified*, universe, uniformity, united, unilateral, unanimity
vac, void	empty, void	*vacuum*, vacuous, evacuate, devoid, avoid

vad, **vas**	to go	*evade*, *pervasive*, *invade*
vag	wandering	*vagrant*, *vague*, *vagabond*, *vagary*
val, **vail**	to be strong	*valid*, *ambivalent*, *prevalent*, *valor*
van, **vain**	gone, empty	*vanish*, *vain*, *evanescent*
vehe, **vect**	to carry	*vehicle*, *vehement*, *vector*, *convect*
vene, **vent**	to come	*convention*, *intervention*, *conventional*, *circumvent*, *prevent*
ver	true	*verify*, *verisimilitude*, *verities*, *aver*
verb	word	*verbal*, *verbatim*, *verbose*, *proverb*, *verbiage*
vert, **vers**	to turn	*convert*, *diversion*, *diverse*, *aversion*, *versatility*, *adversary*, *vertex*
vid, **vis**	to see	*invisible*, *revision*, *individual*, *video*
vigil	awake	*vigilant*, *vigil*, *invigilate*, *vigilante*
vil	worthless	*vile*, *vilify*, *reviled*
vinc, **vanq**, **vict**	to conquer	*victory*, *vanquish*, *invincible*, *convince*, *conviction*, *evict*
viva, **vita**	to live	*revive*, *viable*, *convivial*, *vivid*, *vivacious*
voc, **vok**	to call, to give voice to	*vocal*, *advocate*, *revoke*, *vociferous*, *provocative*, *equivocate*, *evocative*
vol	(> *volvere*) to roll	*revolve*, *revolution*, *convoluted*, *evolve*, *volume*, *voluble*
	(> *velle*) to wish	*volunteer*, *volition*, *benevolent*, *malevolent*
	(> *volare*) to fly	*volatile*, *volley*
vor	to devour	*carnivore*, *omnivore*, *voracious*, *herbivore*

CHAPTER 4

THE SAT WRITING AND LANGUAGE TEST: THE TEN ESSENTIAL RULES

The SAT Writing and Language Test

What is the SAT Writing and Language test?

The SAT includes a 35-minute Writing and Language test designed to assess your

proficiency in revising and editing a range of texts in a variety of content areas, both academic and career related, for expression of ideas and for conformity to the conventions of Standard Written English grammar, usage and punctuation.

The Writing and Language test consists of four passages, each 400–450 words long, in the categories of careers, social studies, humanities, and science. (For an example of the Writing and Language test, look at Section 2 of the Diagnostic Test in Chapter 2.) You are to analyze underlined portions of each passage and to determine whether they need to be revised according to the standards of

- parallel structure
- verb, modifier, and pronoun agreement
- standard idiom
- logical comparisons
- word choice
- verb tense, mood, and voice
- logical transitions
- coordination of ideas
- punctuation

You are also asked more general editorial questions, such as

- whether a certain sentence adds to or detracts from the cohesiveness of a paragraph
- where a new sentence should be placed for maximum effectiveness
- whether a particular passage or paragraph has the effect the author intends

How is it used?

Colleges use your SAT Writing and Language test score as a measure of your ability to write clearly and effectively. Good writing skills are essential to success in the liberal arts and sciences. The Writing and Language test score represents one-half of your Evidence-Based Reading and Writing Score. The other half of this score comes from the Reading test.

Sound intimidating? It's not.

There are really only 10 rules to learn in order to ace the SAT Writing and Language test, and the 33 lessons in this chapter will give you the knowledge and practice you need to master all of them.

Rule 1: Don't Sweat the Small Stuff

Lesson 1: Know the seven things to *NOT* worry about

1. Don't worry about split infinitives

Which is correct?

>   A.   *Here are seven things to **not** worry about.*
>   B.   *Here are seven things **not** to worry about.*

Sentence A includes a **split infinitive**: the infinitive *to worry* has an adverb (*not*) wedged inside it. Although the SAT probably won't test your skill for "unsplitting" infinitives, you should still do it as a matter of politeness to the grammar scolds, for whom they are the verbal equivalent of chewing aluminum foil. You can usually just shift the adverb over a little bit, as in sentence B, and make everyone happy.

　　But sometimes it's not so easy to unsplit infinitives without destroying the tone or meaning of the sentence. For instance, try unsplitting the infinitive in *The company plans to more than double its revenue next year.* Or, better yet, just don't worry about it, since it won't be on the SAT.

2. Don't worry (too much) about *who* vs. *whom*

Which is correct?

>   A.   *To **who** should I give your condolences?*
>   B.   *To **whom** should I give your condolences?*

The *who/whom* distinction is the same as the *he/him* and *they/them* distinction: the first pronoun in each pair has the **subjective case** (Lesson 21), and so is used as the *subject* of a verb, and the second has the **objective case**, and so is used as the *object* of a verb or preposition. Since the pronoun in the sentence above is the object of the preposition *to*, sentence B is correct.

　　Notice, however, that the pronoun *you* can be used as either a subject *or* an object. It represents a "merger" between the subjective *thou* and the objective *thee* from Elizabethan English. (Remember Shakespeare?) Likewise, *whom* seems to be in the process of merging with *who*. For instance, even Standard English allows a sentence like *Who are you talking to?* rather than insisting on the rather uptight-sounding *To whom are you talking?*

　　The bottom line? Chances are, your SAT won't ask you to choose between *who* and *whom*. But if it does, just remember that the *who/whom* distinction is the same as the *they/them* and *he/him* distinctions. And if you're still stuck, just go with *who*.

3. Don't worry about *that* vs. *which*

Which is correct?

>   A.   *Second Federal is the only bank in town **which** does not finance commercial mortgages.*

>   B.   *Second Federal is the only bank in town **that** does not finance commercial mortgages.*

Technically, sentence B is correct because the phrase *that does not finance commercial mortgages* is a "restrictive clause," that is, it modifies the noun *bank* by attaching a defining characteristic to it. If a modifying clause is "restrictive" (that is, it conveys defining information about the noun), it should use *that*. Alternately, if the clause is "nonrestrictive" (that is, it conveys incidental or nondefining information about the noun), it should use *which*. Helpful tip: nonrestrictive modifying clauses are almost always preceded by a comma, as in *The speech, which lasted only three minutes, secured her reputation as a master orator.*

　　Bottom line: the SAT will probably not expect you to distinguish restrictive from nonrestrictive clauses, so don't stress out about *that* versus *which* on the SAT.

4. Don't worry about starting sentences with *Because*, *And*, or *But*

Which is correct?

>   A.   *Because we don't know when Jennie will arrive, we can't make dinner reservations yet.*
>   B.   *We can't make dinner reservations yet because we don't know when Jennie will arrive.*

Ms. Bumthistle (everyone's fifth grade English teacher) probably told you that it's a cardinal sin to start a sentence with *Because*, *And*, or *But*. But it's not nice to lie to children. In fact, either sentence above is fine. The SAT frequently includes perfectly good sentences that start with *Because*. But if you want to avoid annoying the Ms. Bumthistles of the world, avoid the practice in your own writing if it's not too much trouble.

5. Don't worry about disappearing *that*s

Which is correct?

>   A.   *I really love the sweater you gave me.*
>   B.   *I really love the sweater **that** you gave me.*

Both of the sentences above are acceptable in Standard Written English. So, if *that* isn't necessary, why would we ever include it? Because it takes some of the burden away from *sweater*, which is an object in the first clause (*I really love the sweater*) as well as an object of the second clause (*You gave me [the sweater]*). By including *that*, we separate the two ideas more clearly. But since very few people are confused by the dual role of *sweater* in the first sentence, *that* is not strictly necessary.

　　Bottom line: don't worry about a missing *that*, as long as the resulting sentence still makes sense.

6. Don't worry about "parallel ellipsis"

Which is correct?

A. *The Republicans reacted to the speech with sustained applause; the Democrats, however, reacted to it with studied silence.*

B. *The Republicans reacted to the speech with sustained applause; the Democrats, studied silence.*

Both of the sentences above are grammatically correct. Sentence B, however, is more concise because it takes advantage of "parallel ellipsis." Ellipsis simply means the omission of words that are implied by context. In this case, the parallel structure of the two clauses allows the reader to "fill in" the missing words.

When you read a sentence like B, you might think that the missing words are a grammatical mistake. But if the context clearly implies the missing words, you can leave them out.

You might notice that, in sentence B, the comma plays an unusual role. Usually, commas are used to separate items in a list, to separate modifying phrases from clauses, or (with conjunctions) to separate clauses. Here, however, the comma is analogous to the apostrophe in *can't*: just as the apostrophe holds the place of the missing letters from *cannot*, so the comma in sentence B holds the place of the missing words (*however, reacted to it with*) from sentence A. Without that comma to suggest the ellipsis, the sentence would sound very strange indeed.

7. Don't worry (too much) about *good* versus *well* or *bad* versus *badly*

Which is correct?

A. *Peter performed **good**.*
B. *Peter performed **well**.*

Here, *performed* is an action verb. Any word that modifies the manner of an action verb is an *adverb*. Since *good* cannot function as an adverb in Standard English, only choice B is correct.

Which is correct?

C. *I don't feel **good**.*
D. *I don't feel **well**.*

Here, *feel* is a linking verb rather than an action verb: that is, it links the subject to an essential adjective, as in *The sky **is** blue*. So does this mean that C is right and D is wrong? No—they are both grammatically and semantically correct, since *well* can also act as an adjective, meaning "in good health." The two sentences are essentially equivalent to *I am not [feeling] good* and *I am not well*.

Which is correct?

E. *I feel **bad** for you.*
F. *I feel **badly** for you.*

Here, despite what your know-it-all friends might say, E is correct and F is wrong, since *badly* can only function as an adverb. Saying *I feel bad for you* is like saying *I feel sorry for you*. You wouldn't say *I feel sorrily for you*, would you?

It's important to know the difference between adjectives and adverbs (Lesson 14), and between action verbs and linking verbs.

But the SAT is probably not going to ask you about *good* versus *well* or *bad* versus *badly*.

Rule 2: Strengthen the Core

Lesson 2: Identify your clauses, modifiers, and conjunctions

The first and most important step in analyzing sentences is **identifying clauses.**

Every sentence contains at least one **clause,** which consists of a **subject** and a **predicate.** The subject is the **noun** or **pronoun** that is "doing" the verb, and the predicate consists of a **verb** and its **complements** (such as direct objects, indirect objects, verb modifiers, or predicate adjectives).

The **subject-verb** unit of any clause conveys the **core idea** of that clause. For instance, if we take the sentence

As the sun slowly set, the desperation of the sailors revealed itself in their sullen glances.

and isolate just the subject and verb, we still retain the core idea:

*The **desperation revealed** itself.*

Consider these two sentences:

A. *Go!*
B. *Although generally regarded as the most daunting course in the undergraduate science curriculum, Introduction to Organic Chemistry not only provides a necessary foundation in the principles of physical chemistry, but also introduces students to important experimental methods at the heart of today's most promising areas of medical research.*

Sentence A is the shortest in the English language. It has everything necessary to convey a complete thought: a verb (*go*) and its subject (the implied subject *you*). Since it is in the **imperative mood** (Lesson 30), the subject is assumed to be the person being addressed and does not need to be stated.

So here's how we can analyze sentence A:

[You] [go]!

[Implied subject] [verb]!

> Sentences can also **elaborate** the main clause with **modifiers** or **link** clauses with **conjunctions.**

Sentence B is a bit more complicated. The main clause includes a compound predicate, so it combines two statements with the same subject into one sentence:

Introduction to Organic Chemistry . . . provides a necessary foundation in the principles of physical chemistry . . .

Introduction to Organic Chemistry . . . introduces students to important experimental methods at the heart today's most promising areas of medical research.

These two clauses are linked by a **conjunction phrase** (*not only . . . but also*), and are preceded by a **subordinating conjunction** (*Although*) followed by a **modifying (participial) phrase** (*generally regarded as the most daunting course in the undergraduate science curriculum*). We'll talk more about conjunctions in Lessons 6 and 10 and about participial phrases in Lesson 12.

So here's how you should analyze sentence B:

[Although] [generally regarded as the most daunting course in the undergraduate science curriculum], *[**Introduction to Organic Chemistry**] [not only]* *[**provides a necessary foundation in the principles of physical chemistry**], [but also] [**introduces students to important experimental methods at the heart today's most promising areas of medical research.**]*

[Subordinating conjunction] [participial phrase], [**subject**], [conjunction part 1] [**predicate 1**] [conjunction part 2] [**predicate 2**].

If this analysis seems confusing now, don't worry. We'll explain all of these terms in the lessons to come. For now, focus on identifying **clauses** (the words in bold in the sentence above) because they are the **core** of any sentence. Distinguishing clauses from the rest of the sentence is the first step to becoming a stronger reader and writer.

Lesson 3: Trim every sentence to analyze its core

Consider this sentence:

My chief concern with this budget, which has otherwise been well considered, are the drastic cuts in school funds.

How does it sound? It may sound a little bit off, but why, and how do we improve it? This is where **trimming** comes in.

> Diagnosing and improving sentences requires mastering the skill of **trimming**: reducing the sentence to its **core**, or its essential elements, then analyzing that core.
>
> This is based on a very important rule of grammar: **every sentence must "work" even when its prepositional phrases, interrupters, and other modifiers are eliminated.** That is, it still must convey a grammatically complete idea.

Step 1: Cross out all nonessential prepositional phrases.

A **preposition** is any word that can be used to complete any sentence like these:

The squirrel ran _____ the tree. (e.g. up, to, around, from, in, by, on, into, etc.)

I went to the party _____ a brain surgeon. (e.g., as, with, for, etc.)

Democracy is government _____ the people. (e.g., for, of, by, etc.)

A **prepositional phrase** is the preposition plus the noun phrase that follows it, such as *from sea to shining sea*, *in the beginning*, and *for the money*.

Our sentence has two nonessential prepositional phrases that we can eliminate:

My chief concern ~~with this budget~~, which has otherwise been well considered, are the drastic cuts ~~in school funds~~.

Step 2: Cross out all interrupting modifiers.

Interrupting modifiers are generally easy to spot because they come between commas or dashes. The sentence should always hold together even when the interrupting modifiers are removed:

My chief concern ~~with this budget, which has otherwise been well considered~~, are the drastic cuts ~~in school funds~~.

Step 3: Cross out any other nonessential modifiers.

Once you learn to identify **participial phrases** (Lesson 12), **appositives** (Lesson 13), and more mundane modifiers like **adjectives** and **adverbs** (Lesson 14), you can trim them from all of your sentences, as well, with one exception: **predicate adjectives**, such as *tired* in the sentence *Karen was tired*, without which the sentence doesn't convey an idea. In our sentence, *chief* and *drastic* can go:

My ~~chief~~ concern ~~with this budget, which has otherwise been well considered~~, are the ~~drastic~~ cuts ~~in school funds~~.

So now we have the core:

My concern are the cuts.

Obviously, the subject and verb **disagree** (Lesson 4): *concern* is a singular subject, but *are* is a plural verb. So you may just want to change the verb: *My concern is the cuts*. But that's no good either, because now the sentence has a **number shift** (Lesson 11): the singular *concern* is equated with the plural *cuts*.

These problems point to an even deeper problem: the most essential part of the sentence, the verb, is very weak. Forms of the verb *to be*, like *is, are, was,* and *were*, are among the weakest verbs in English.

> To improve your writing, first focus on **strengthening and clarifying your verbs**.

This sentence is clearly indicating disapproval, so a more personal subject like *I* and a strong verb of disapproval like *object* would strengthen the sentence:

Although the budget is otherwise well considered, I object to its drastic cuts in school funds.

Notice that this revision not only corrects the grammatical problems, but it also makes the sentence stronger, clearer, and more concise.

Exercise 1: Trimming and Strengthening Sentences

Trim each of the following sentences and correct any verb problems.

1. The team of advisors, arriving slightly ahead of schedule, were met at the airport by the Assistant Prime Minister.

2. The flock of birds darting over the roiling lake look like an opalescent whirlwind.

3. Carmen, not to mention her unsympathetic sisters, were unaffected by David's pleas.

4. Juggling the demands of school, family, and work often seem too much for a young mother to bear.

5. Others on the committee, like chairman Sanders, is concerned about the lack of attention given to school safety.

6. Every one of my friends, including the boys, has supported my decision.

7. The fact that human institutions have been responsible for so many atrocities have forced some historians to adopt a cynical perspective on human nature.

    Trim each sentence. Then revise it to make it clear and concise, changing the subject and verb, if necessary.

8. The progression of a society, or at least that popularly regarded as advancements, are a result of gradual modifications, not sudden drastic overhaul.

    Trimmed: _____

    Revised: _____

    _____

9. The development of the new country's government and social institutions were affected in a negative regard by the lack of cohesiveness within the revolutionary army.

    Trimmed: _____

    Revised: _____

    _____

10. This report is intended for presenting arguments in opposition to what I took to be the less than optimal response of the administration to the most recent crises in the Middle East.

    Trimmed: _____

    Revised: _____

    _____

Lesson 4: Make sure your verbs agree with their subjects

Which is correct?

  A. *Data gathered through polling **is** not as reliable as data gathered objectively.*

  B. *Data gathered through polling **are** not as reliable as data gathered objectively.*

If we trim sentence A, we get

  Data ~~gathered through polling~~ is not as reliable ~~as data gathered objectively~~.

The subject, *data*, is plural, so the verb should be *are*. Sentence B is correct.

A few Latin plurals are frequently mistaken for singulars. Don't make that mistake.

Singular	Plural	Correct Sentence
bacterium	*bacteria*	*The bacteria **are** multiplying rapidly.*
continuum	*continua*	*The continua of space and time **are** related.*
criterion	*criteria*	*Your criteria **are** hard to meet.*
curriculum	*curricula*	*The competing curricula **were** scrutinized.*
datum	*data*	*The data on the drive **have** been corrupted.*
medium	*media*	*The media **have** largely ignored this story.*
phenomenon	*phenomena*	*Such phenomena **are** surprisingly common.*

Which is correct?

  C. *Behind every successful work of art **lies** countless hours of toil and trial.*

  D. *Behind every successful work of art **lie** countless hours of toil and trial.*

If we trim sentence C, we get

  ~~Behind every successful work of art~~ lies countless hours ~~of toil and trial~~.

Here, the subject and verb are **inverted**: the subject *hours* comes after the verb *lies*. When we "un-invert" the clause, the subject-verb disagreement is obvious: *hours lies* should be changed to *hours lie*. Therefore, sentence D is correct.

An **inverted clause**, where the verb comes before the subject, usually begins with the **dummy subject** *there*, as in *There is* or *There are*, or is preceded by a prepositional phrase.

Every inverted clause can be "un-inverted" by removing any dummy subject and rearranging the phrases. Un-inverting these sentences will help you to spot any subject-verb disagreements.

Inverted: [*There*] [*are*] [*over twenty applicants*] [*applying for the job*].

Un-inverted: [*Over twenty applicants*] [*are*] [*applying for the job*].

Inverted: [*Behind every successful work of art*] [*lie*] [*countless hours of toil and trial*].

Un-inverted: [*Countless hours of toil and trial*] [*lie*] [*behind every successful work of art*].

Which is correct?

  E. *One or two of my classmates **has** a strong chance of winning an award.*

  F. *One or two of my classmates **have** a strong chance of winning an award.*

If we trim sentence E, we get

  One or two ~~of my classmates~~ has a strong chance ~~of winning an award~~.

Is the subject, *One or two*, singular or plural? In these ambiguous situations, it helps to remember the **law of**

proximity: the essential noun (that is, not one in a prepositional phrase) that is closer to the verb gets priority. Here, since *two* is closer to the verb, the subject is regarded as plural. Therefore, sentence F is correct.

If a subject takes the form *a or b*, it is assumed to take the number of *b*.

Exercise 2: Subject-Verb Agreement

Choose the correct verb form.

1. The flock of geese (was/were) startled by the shotgun blast.

2. The data on my computer (was/were) lost when the hard drive failed.

3. Neither of the twins (is/are) allergic to penicillin.

4. Much of what I hear in those lectures (go/goes) in one ear and out the other.

5. Amy, like her friends Jamie and Jen, (wants/want) to go to Mount Holyoke College.

6. Among the lilies and wildflowers (were/was) one solitary rose.

7. Either the chairperson or her assistants (is/are) going to have to make the decision.

8. There (is/are) hardly even a speck of dirt left on the carpet.

9. In every teaspoon of soil (are/is) over two million tiny microorganisms.

10. There (is/are), in my opinion, far too few primary physicians working in this district.

11. Beyond that hill (is/are) hundreds of bison.

12. Never before (have/has) there been such voices heard on the public airwaves.

13. Every player on both teams (was/were) at the press conference after the game.

14. There (has/have) been a theater and a toy store in the mall ever since it opened.

15. There (is/are) a great many production problems to iron out before show time.

16. The proceeds from the sale of every auctioned item (goes/go) to charity.

17. There (is/are) more than three years remaining on her contract.

18. Neither of the girls (was/were) frightened by the small animals that scurried past their tent.

19. This technology, developed by the military for field communications, (have/has) become essential to private industry as well.

20. Every player on both teams (was/were) concerned about the goalie's injury.

21. The company's sponsorship of mentorship programs (has/have) garnered many accolades from other philanthropic organizations.

22. Neither the children nor their parents (utter/utters) a word when Mrs. Denny tells her stories.

23. How important (is/are) strength training and cardiovascular training to your daily fitness regimen?

Rule 3: Organize the Ideas in Your Paragraphs

Lesson 5: Present your ideas cohesively and with a consistent tone

What's wrong with this paragraph?

> *The politics of hydraulic fracturing, or "fracking," have obscured both the dangers and the benefits of this new technology. Opponents suggest that the high-pressure fluid used to fracture deep rock formations may contain carcinogens that may seep into groundwater, and that fracking induces earthquakes. Supporters point out that this activity is taking place well below even the deepest aquifers and is well sealed off from human water supplies. The technical term for earthquakes is seismic activity, and the fractures are pretty small, really: only about 1 millimeter or less.*

The paragraph starts off well, with a clear topic sentence about the politics of fracking. It then gives a quick summary of the two positions on the topic. With the last sentence, however, the paragraph begins to lose its focus and tone: the phrase *pretty small, really* is too conversational for the tone of this paragraph, and the ideas in the last sentence are not tied logically to the ongoing discussion. Here's a revision that more effectively links to the previous sentence:

> *They also point out that the seismic activity induced by fracking is minimal: the vast majority of the fractures it induces are less than 1 millimeter wide.*

Every **effective** prose paragraph should

- be focused on a topic sentence that develops the central idea of the passage
- explain or illustrate any significant claims
- avoid irrelevant commentary
- maintain a consistent and appropriate tone

Lesson 6: Coordinate your clauses effectively and avoid commas splices

Which is better?

A. *Despite being a best-selling author, Brian Greene is a professor of physics, he is also cofounder of the World Science Festival, and this event draws nearly half a million people each year.*

B. *Cofounded by best-selling author and professor of physics Brian Greene, the World Science Festival draws nearly half a million people each year.*

It's not too hard to see that sentence B seems clearer and more logical than sentence A, but why? The answer is **coordination**. Both sentences contain the same four ideas, but sentence B coordinates those ideas more effectively. Sentence A contains three independent clauses:

. . . Brian Greene is a professor of physics . . .

. . . [Brian Greene] is also cofounder of the World Science Festival . . .

. . . [the World Science Festival] draws nearly half a million people each year . . .

So the reader is left confused: what is the central idea of this sentence? Brian Greene's professorship? His festival? The popularity of the festival? Even worse, the **preposition** *Despite* doesn't make sense, since being a best-selling author doesn't interfere in any obvious way with being a physics professor.

Sentence B, in contrast, packages these ideas to make them easier to digest. The first two ideas are **subordinated** in a **participial phrase**, and the third idea is emphasized as the **independent clause**.

In a **well-coordinated** sentence,

- the central idea is expressed in the main **independent clause**
- secondary ideas are expressed in **subordinate clauses** or **modifying phrases**
- ideas are linked with logically appropriate **conjunctions**, **prepositions**, and **adverbs**

Notice also that the second comma in sentence A is a **comma splice**, joining two independent clauses. That's a no-no.

Avoid **comma splices**. A comma splice is the error of joining two **independent clauses** with only a comma:

Comma splice (wrong):   *We were having a great time, T.J. played his guitar.*

Independent clauses can be joined in one sentence in one of three acceptable ways:

Comma-conjunction: *We were having a great time, but T.J. played his guitar.*

Semicolon: *We were having a great time; T.J. played his guitar.*

Colon: *We were having a great time: T.J. played his guitar.*

Semicolons are used to join two ideas when the second **supports or extends** the first. **Colons** are used to join two ideas when the second **explains or specifies** the first. The first sentence indicates that T.J.'s guitar *didn't help* the mood; the second indicates that T.J.'s guitar *didn't hurt* the mood; the third indicates that T.J.'s guitar *explained* the mood.

Exercise 3: Coordinating Clauses

Join each set of sentences into a single well-coordinated sentence.

1. H. K. Schaffer's latest movie has received widespread critical acclaim. She directed the movie. It is the third movie that she has directed. She is the daughter of famous screenwriter George Schaffer. Her latest movie is a comedy entitled *The Return*.

2. Scientists have made an important discovery. The scientists who made the discovery are a team from universities and research institutions from all over the world. The discovery concerns a region of the brain called the prefrontal cortex. The scientists have discovered that this region governs impulse control in humans. Studying this region of the brain can help scientists learn more about criminal behavior.

Rewrite the following sentences so that the clauses coordinate logically and concisely.

3. Electric cars may not be as environmentally friendly as they are widely regarded, so the electricity they use actually comes from fossil fuels; that electricity is produced in power plants that often burn coal or other fossil fuels and that burning often produces enormous amounts of greenhouse emissions.

5. We are motivated by our principles; our principles change all the time, though: our experiences and our priorities evolve as we grow.

4. Although regular exercise is good for your muscles, it is also good for your heart, so it is good for your brain too by keeping it well oxygenated and the increased oxygenation helps it work more efficiently.

Lesson 7: Give your reader helpful transitions, especially between paragraphs

Consider this transition between paragraphs:

> . . . and so we should be respectful of other people, even those with whom we disagree, while always striving to eliminate inequities and abuses of power.
>
> To Kill a Mockingbird *was written by Harper Lee and published in 1960. It portrays the fictional town of Maycomb, Alabama . . .*

The end of the first paragraph makes a bold claim: that we should strive *to eliminate inequities and abuses of power.* But the next paragraph abruptly shifts to mundane facts about the publication of a particular book. Although readers who are familiar with *To Kill a Mockingbird* might have an idea why this author is mentioning it, the author does not provide any helpful transitions to guide the reader into the new paragraph and indicate how the new paragraph connects with previous one. Consider this revision:

> . . . and so we should be respectful of other people, even those with whom we disagree, while always striving to eliminate inequities and abuses of power.
>
> *In* To Kill a Mockingbird *(1960), Harper Lee depicts a fictional town, Maycomb, Alabama, that is tainted by such inequities and abuses . . .*

Now we understand the reference better because the author has provided a **helpful paragraph transition.** The phrase *such inequities and abuses* demonstrates clearly that the events in *To Kill a Mockingbird* will illustrate the importance of fighting inequities and abuse, and therefore exemplify the thesis from the previous paragraph.

Provide your readers with helpful paragraph transitions to clarify the links between topic ideas. Keep in mind the common **transitional words and phrases** below.

To extend an idea

indeed	*furthermore*	*moreover*	*in fact*
further	*also*	*beyond that*	*additionally*

To illustrate or specify an idea

for example	*for instance*	*in particular*	*namely*
such as	*especially*	*to illustrate*	*specifically*

To make a comparison or contrast

similarly	*likewise*	*actually*	*nevertheless*
however	*although*	*despite*	*on the other hand*

To show consequence

as a result	*so*	*thus*	*subsequently*
therefore	*hence*	*accordingly*	*for this reason*

To provide explanation or reason

this is because	*since*	*thus*	*the reason is that*
how	*because*	*why*	*as*

Lesson 8: Make your cross-references clear

Consider these sentences from our "fracking" essay:

> . . . *The opponents of fracking are correct to ask questions about the safety and sustainability of this process. Could it poison the local water supply with carcinogens? Can we spare the vast amount of injection water it requires? Can we safely recycle its wastewater? Could it be introducing more methane into the water supply than would naturally be present? Could it be causing potentially dangerous seismic activity? But this also must be followed by careful, scientific, and impartial investigation, not mere fear-mongering.*

Each of the five questioning sentences contains the pronoun *it*, which makes a "cross-reference" to a noun in the first sentence, namely, *fracking* (or, equivalently, *process*). The last sentence also includes a cross-referencing pronoun, *this*. But to what does it refer? It doesn't seem to be referring to fracking anymore; that wouldn't make sense. Nor does it make sense to refer to the other singular nouns in previous sentences, like *methane*, *water supply*, or *seismic activity*. So the reader may be left a bit confused. Here, we need to revise to clarify the cross-reference:

> But **this questioning** must be followed by careful, scientific, and impartial investigation, not mere fear-mongering.

When referring to concepts introduced in previous sentences, using **pronouns** will often help you be concise, but **make sure your cross-references are clear**. Sometimes clarity may require you to replace the "cross-referencing" pronouns with more precise nouns.

Exercise 4: Effective Transitions and Cross-References

Rewrite the second sentence in each pair, providing an effective transition and clarifying any cross-references.

1. . . . Modern biologists have tried for decades to explore the relationship between ancient humans and Neanderthals, but analyzing DNA from prehistoric hominids has until recently proven very difficult.

   The "clean room" at the Max Planck Institute in Germany is like those used in the manufacturing of computer chips or space telescopes, solving the issue by preventing contamination from dust particles so that biologists can extract and examine minute bits of DNA from 400,000-year-old hominid bones.

2. . . . As satisfying as it may be to punish wrongdoers, the real impetus behind tough sentencing laws is the belief that they actually deter crime.

   The treatment so many prisoners receive in state and federal penitentiaries, including humiliation and loss of autonomy, only exacerbates any short- or long-term psychological issues that make them susceptible to antisocial and criminal impulses, according to evidence.

3. . . . It's easy to understand, in a society as complex, diverse, and bureaucratic as ours, how some citizens could develop a deep distrust of governmental institutions.

   The willingness to equate all governmental institutions with tyranny is an enormously dangerous one that can only impede human moral, economic, and cultural progress.

Rule 4: Use Parallel Structure

Lesson 9: Understand the Law of Parallelism

Which is better?

A. *In the '70s and '80s, high school math teachers taught almost exclusively by lecture; today, more cooperative and project-based methods are likely to be employed.*

B. *In the '70s and '80s, high school math teachers taught almost exclusively by lecture; today, they are more likely to use cooperative and project-based methods.*

Which is better?

C. *Ms. Kelly always tried to provide clear instructions that showed respect and were fair to all of her students.*

D. *Ms. Kelly always tried to provide instructions that were clear, respectful, and fair to all of her students.*

Sentences A and C don't seem glaringly wrong, but B and D sound a bit better. Why? **Parallelism.**

The Law of Parallelism

When a sentence includes a list, contrast, or comparison, the items being listed, contrasted, or compared should have the **same grammatical form**.

Sentence A contains two clauses that contrast teaching in the '70s and '80s with teaching today. However, the comparison is not parallel: the first sentence is in the **active voice**, but the second is in the **passive voice** (Lesson 29). Sentence B reads more smoothly because both clauses are in the active voice, which aligns the subjects and clarifies the contrast.

Sentence C ascribes three adjectives to Ms. Kelly's instructions, but not in a parallel form. Sentence D clarifies the central idea by putting these adjectives in a clear and parallel list.

Lesson 10: Watch for standard parallel constructions

Which is better?

A.   *It seems sometimes that our representatives would rather generate sound bites for their partisans instead of working to solve our social and economic problems.*

B.   *It seems sometimes that our representatives would rather generate sound bites for their partisans than solve our social and economic problems.*

The problem in sentence A is hard for most readers to catch. It may take a few readings before you notice it.

The word *rather* indicates that the sentence is making a contrast. Such a contrast requires a **standard parallel construction**: *rather X than Y.* When you see the word *rather*, you should expect the word *than* to appear soon afterward. But in sentence A, not only does *than* not appear, but the two words from *X* and *Y* that should be parallel are not: *generate* is a present-tense verb, but *working* is a gerund. Sentence B makes the correction, and creates the parallel construction *rather generate . . . than solve.*

Use the following **standard parallel constructions** precisely. When you use any of these phrases, use the precise wording, and make sure *X* and *Y* are parallel.

rather X than Y	*X more than Y*	*neither X nor Y*	*X is like Y*
prefer X to Y	*either X or Y*	*both X and Y*	*the more X, the more Y*
less X than Y	*not so much X as Y*	*not X but Y*	*the better X, the better Y*

Lesson 11: Avoid number shifts

> If a sentence equates two things, those things should have the **same number**.

Which is better?

    A. *Everyone enjoyed their meal.*
    B. *Everyone enjoyed his or her meal.*
    C. *They all enjoyed their meals.*

Sentence A commits a **number shift**: the pronoun *their* is plural, but its antecedent *everyone* is singular. Additionally, the object *meal* is singular, which doesn't make sense—are multiple people sharing a single meal? One way to correct this problem is by changing *their* to the singular *his or her*, as in sentence B. But this phrase is needlessly awkward. Sentence C avoids both problems, so it is the best of the three.

Consider this sentence:

The problem with this plan is all of the permits we would have to file before starting the project.

If we trim it a bit, we get

The problem ~~with this plan~~ is all of the permits we would have to file ~~before starting the project~~.

Again, we have a number shift: the singular *problem* is equated with the plural *all of the permits*. We could try to fix the problem by pluralizing the subject:

The problems with this plan are all of the permits we would have to file before starting the project.

But that sounds very strange. The best revision strengthens the verb to avoid the number shift:

Filing all of the permits required by this plan will probably delay the project.

Exercise 5: Parallel Structure

Rewrite each sentence to improve its parallel structure.

1. The candidate's platform included tax code reform, an improved school system, and reviving good relations with the unions.

2. Good study practices are not so much about working hard, but rather how well you use your time.

3. The more you get to know her, the more likely it is that you will like her.

4. The food here is not only exceptionally fresh, but its price is also very reasonable.

5. The financial crisis of 2007 was exacerbated by the esoteric nature of certain financial instruments, skittish investors, and the lack of awareness of regulators.

6. Ms. Bennett is appreciated by her colleagues because she is very supportive and has a lot of knowledge.

7. I can't decide whether I should give Maria the tickets, or Caitlyn.

8. The United States experienced a contraction in wealth, an increase in risk spreads, and the credit markets were deteriorating.

9. I prefer the romantic virtuosity of Liszt, as opposed to Chopin's emotional accessibility.

10. The festival draws crowds from across the country that come not so much for the music but rather because of the spirit of free expression.

Rule 5: Use Modifiers Effectively
Lesson 12: Don't let your participles dangle

Which is correct?

A. *Widely considered one of the most challenging pieces for piano, Franz Liszt stretched the boundaries of musical technique with his* Etude no. 5.

B. *Widely considered one the most challenging pieces for piano, Franz Liszt's* Etude no. 5 *stretches the boundaries of musical technique.*

Sentence A includes a **dangling participle**. The **past participle** *considered* requires a subject. Since **participial phrases** don't include their own subjects, they must "borrow" them from the main clause. What is the subject of the participle? That is, what, exactly, is *considered one of the most challenging pieces for piano*? Surely not Franz Liszt—he is the composer. It is *Etude no. 5.* Because the subject of the main clause should also be the subject of the participial phrase, the correct choice is B.

> When a **participial phrase** begins a sentence, its subject should be the subject of the main clause that follows. Otherwise, it is called a **dangling participle**.

What are **participles**, anyway?

Participles are verb forms, like *broken* and *thinking,* that cannot stand by themselves as verbs. They are only part of the verb, hence the name "participle." Notice, for instance, that we can't say

*She **broken** the plate.*

*We **thinking** about you.*

Each participle requires a helping verb to complete the verb phrase and make a sensible clause:

*She **has broken** the plate.*

*We **were thinking** about you.*

Present participles like *eating, fighting,* and *interrupting* always end in *-ing.* **Past participles**, however, fall under two categories: "regular" past participles like *straightened* and *pushed* end in *-ed,* but "irregular" past participles can take many forms, like *fought, been, eaten, swum,* and *seen.* For a list of some common irregular forms, see Lesson 25.

In English, we use present participles (with the helping verb *to be*) in verbs with the **progressive aspect** (Lesson 23), such as *I am eating* and *I had been eating.* We use past participles (with the helping verb *to have*) in verbs with the **consequential aspect** (Lesson 23) such as *I have eaten* and *I had eaten.*

When participles appear without their helping verbs, they act as adjectives, and their phrases are called **participial phrases**. Here are some more examples:

*When **designing a user interface**, software engineers should focus on simplicity.*

***Although pleased with her victory**, Angela knew that she still had more work to do.*

Lesson 13: Know where to place your modifiers

Which is correct?

    A. *In an emergency, I am amazed at how calm Marco can be.*

    B. *I am amazed at how calm Marco can be in an emergency.*

What does the **prepositional phrase** *in an emergency* modify? It answers the question *When can Marco be calm?* rather than *When can I be amazed?* Since it modifies the second verb rather than the first verb, B is the better choice.

> Any modifier or modifying phrase should be placed as close (or "proximate") as possible to the word it modifies without disrupting the sentence. This is called the **Law of Proximity**. Modifiers or modifying phrases that violate this rule are called **misplaced modifiers**.

Which is correct?

    C. *A splendid example of synthetic cubism, Picasso painted* Three Musicians *in the summer of 1924.*

    D. *Picasso painted* Three Musicians, *a splendid example of synthetic cubism, in the summer of 1924.*

What does the **appositive phrase** *a splendid example of synthetic cubism* modify? It answers the question *What is* The Three Musicians? rather than *Who was Picasso?* Since it modifies the second noun, not the first, choice D is correct.

Which is correct?

    E. *To illustrate his point, we watched Mr. Genovese take out a giant boa constrictor.*

    F. *We watched Mr. Genovese take out a giant boa constrictor to illustrate his point.*

What does the **infinitive phrase** *to illustrate his point* modify? It answers the question *Why did he take it out?* rather than *Why did we watch it?* Since it modifies the second verb rather than the first, choice F is correct.

Exercise 6: Dangling and Misplaced Modifiers

Rewrite each underlined portion, if necessary, to correct any dangling or misplaced modifiers.

1. <u>Rounding the bend</u>, the pub of my dreams finally came into view.

2. Although emotionally drained, <u>Martha's creative instinct compelled her</u> to keep writing.

3. Determined to avenge his friend, <u>the sword was unsheathed by Claudius</u>.

4. <u>To find a good Thai restaurant, there are a lot of apps and websites to help you.</u>

5. <u>Even with a sprained ankle, the coach forced Adam</u> back into the game.

6. <u>We found my lost earrings walking back to my car</u>.

7. Lacking any real sailing skills, <u>David's primary concern was</u> keeping the boat upright.

8. Already exhausted from the day's climb, <u>the looming storm forced the hikers to pitch an early camp</u>.

9. Thinking that her friends were behind her, <u>it frightened Allison</u> to realize that she was alone.

10. <u>Without being aware of it</u>, termites can infest your home unless you take proper precautions.

11. <u>Always regarded as a dutiful mother, we were surprised to hear Carol</u> complaining about domestic life.

12. <u>To get a good jump out of the starting blocks, sprinters say that proper hip positioning is essential</u>.

13. Seeking ways to reduce the budget deficit, <u>proposals for cutbacks are being considered by the town council</u>.

14. Although unhappy with the tone of the debate, <u>the senator's plan was</u> to remain calm and rational.

15. <u>Famous for its visual arts scene, Portland's</u> musical culture is also a source of local pride.

16. Without seeming to move a muscle, <u>the coin disappeared instantly from the magician's hand</u>.

17. <u>To maintain good health, physicians recommend both vigorous exercise and disciplined eating</u>.

18. After searching for months for the perfect rug, <u>one appeared as we were exploring a garage sale</u>.

Lesson 14: Don't confuse adjectives and adverbs

Which is correct?

A. *I was impressed by how poised he was and how cogent his argument was presented.*

B. *I was impressed by how poised he was and how cogent his argument was.*

C. *I was impressed by how poised he was and how cogently he presented his argument.*

At first, reading, sentence A seems to follow the law of parallelism: it follows the formula *I was impressed by* *A and B*, and the phrases *how poised* and *how cogent* have the same form. However, the adjective in the second phrase is misused: we cannot say *his argument was presented cogent*, but rather *his argument was presented cogently*. Action verbs like *presented* can only be modified by **adverbs**, not **adjectives**. Sentence B corrects the modifier error but uses stilted phrasing. Sentence C, the best of the three, although less strictly parallel than sentence B, corrects the modifier error in A and the stiffness of sentence B.

Don't use an adjective to do the job of an adverb. Many popular advertisements grab your attention by replacing adverbs with adjectives, as in *Think different, Eat fresh, Shine bright*, and *Live strong*. But in Standard English, **adjectives** are strictly **noun modifiers**. If you want to modify a verb (or an adjective or another adverb), only an **adverb** will do. Most adverbs end in *-ly* (as in *profoundly, quickly*, and *desperately*), but many common ones do not.

Common **adverbs** that do NOT end in *-ly*:

> *always, away, ever, never, there, here, so, too, yet, very*

Common **adjectives** that DO end in *-ly*:

> *lovely, lonely, motherly, neighborly, friendly, costly, beastly, lively, womanly, likely, scholarly*

Common words that can serve EITHER as **adjectives** or **adverbs**:

	Adjective	**Adverb**
very	*I drove that very car.*	*It is very hot.*
well	*The cat is not well.*	*She performed well.*
fast	*She is a fast reader.*	*Don't go so fast.*
straight	*It was a straight shot.*	*I can't shoot straight.*
just	*It was a just decision.*	*She just arrived.*
late	*We had a late lunch.*	*It happened late in the day.*
low	*You have set a low bar.*	*Don't sink so low.*
high	*I have high standards.*	*I can't jump very high.*
hard	*That test was hard.*	*Don't push so hard.*

If you have trouble deciding between using an adjective and using an adverb, ask: "What question does this word answer?" If it is a question about a noun or pronoun, the modifier must be an adjective. If it is a question about a verb, adjective, or another adverb, the modifier must be an adverb.

Lesson 15: Know when to use -er, -est, more, and most

Which is correct?

A. *I don't know which is most troubling: your apathy or your incompetence.*
B. *I don't know which is more troubling: your apathy or your incompetence.*

Sentence A is comparing only two things: *apathy* and *incompetence*, so it must use the **comparative** form, *more*, instead of *most*. Sentence B is correct.

> If a sentence compares two things at a time (we call this a **binary** comparison), it must use a **comparative adjective**, that is, one that use -*er* or *more*. If the sentence singles out one thing from a group of three or more, it must use a **superlative adjective**, that is, one that uses -*est* or *most*.

Which is correct?

C. *Your dog couldn't be adorabler.*
D. *Your dog couldn't be more adorable.*

Which is correct?

E. *Incorporating the company was more simple than I expected.*
F. *Incorporating the company was simpler than I expected.*

When do we use -*er*, and when do we use *more*? The rule is actually pretty straightforward.

> If an adjective has just one or two syllables, it usually takes the -*er* suffix (e.g., *faster, stronger, sillier*), but if it has more than two syllables, it usually takes *more* (e.g., *more beautiful, more outrageous, more desperate*).
>
> However, monosyllabic past participles, when used as adjectives, also tend to take *more* rather than -*er*: we say *more set in his ways* rather than *setter in his ways*, *more shocked* rather than *shockeder*, and *more tired* rather than *tireder*.
>
> *Fun* is another interesting exception. Although something that is comparatively *funny* is *funnier*, something that is comparatively *fun* is *more fun*. For some reason, Standard English has decided against *funner*.

So, in the sample sentences, choices D and F are correct.

Which is correct?

G. *Please hold the baby gentler next time.*
H. *Please hold the baby more gently next time.*

Here, the problem with sentence G is the problem we discussed in Lesson 14: an adjective is being used where an adverb is required. Since the modifier is answering the question "How should one hold the baby?" it is answering a question about the verb *hold*, and therefore should take the adverbial form *more gently*.

Which is correct?

J. *Annie is the most unique person I know.*
K. *Annie is unique.*

The adjective *unique* is known as an "absolute" or "superlative" adjective. It comes from the Latin *uni*, meaning "one," and it means "one of a kind." Therefore, tacking on *most* is redundant. Sentence K makes the same point without the redundancy.

> Don't modify absolutes like *perfect, unique, singular,* or *obliterated* unless you are trying to be ironic.

Exercise 7: Using Modifiers Correctly

Correct any modifier problems in the sentences below.

1. In the second debate, the councilwoman made her points much stronger than she did in the first one.

2. My shirt smelled foully after rugby practice.

3. We never usually get to go on such exotic vacations.

4. My father is the most patient of my parents, but my mother is more knowledgeable about relationships.

5. The sixth graders weren't hardly interested in going to the museum after school.

6. I can run a marathon easier than I can swim three miles.

7. As you revise your essay, try to express your thoughts clearer and develop your ideas more.

8. The chemistry final was much more easy than the last two chapter tests.

9. Caroline's sculpture was the most unique among the entries.

10. These cost-cutting measures won't barely address the budget deficit.

11. The teacher never told us about the test until the day before.

12. Students never usually verify the "facts" they use in their research papers.

Rule 6: Make Your Comparisons Clear and Precise

Lesson 16: Make sure your comparisons are logical

Which is correct?

    A.   *Not only is Anna the captain, but she also practices harder than anyone on the track team.*

    B.   *Not only is Anna the captain, but she also practices harder than anyone else on the track team.*

Anna cannot work harder than she herself does, and she is on the track team, so the first comparison is **illogical**. It is logical, however, to say that she works harder than *anyone else on the track team*, so sentence B is correct.

Which is correct?

    C.   *The turnout for this year's art festival was even better than last year.*

    D.   *The turnout for this year's art festival was even better than the turnout for last year's festival.*

The phrase *even better* indicates a comparison, but between what two things? In sentence C, this year's *turnout* is being compared to *last year*. This is another type of **illogical comparison** called a **category error**: the two things being compared are not comparable things. Sentence D corrects this error because *the turnout for last year's festival* is in the same category as *the turnout for this year's festival*. Since this is an "apples-to-apples" comparison, sentence D is correct.

Make sure all of your comparisons are **logical comparisons**.

- Make sure that equivalent things are not treated as non-equivalent things. (For instance, Anna can't practice harder than herself.)
- Make sure that non-comparable things are not treated as comparable things (For instance, this year's turnout can't be compared to last year, but it can be compared to last year's turnout.)

Lesson 17: Know how to use *less/fewer, many/much,* or *amount/number*

Which is best?

A. *To decrease the amount of violent conflicts among rival fans, the concession stands will sell less alcoholic drinks during the game.*

B. *To decrease the number of violent conflicts among rival fans, the concession stands will sell fewer alcoholic drinks during the game.*

C. *To decrease the amount of violence among rival fans, the concession stands will sell less alcohol during the game.*

The terms *less, much,* and *amount* apply generally to **uncountable or continuous quantities** like *traffic, money,* and *food.* The terms *fewer, many,* and *number* apply generally to **countable and discrete quantities** like *cars, dollars,* and *pizzas.*

But what if the quantities are **countable and continuous**, like *miles, gallons,* or *miles per gallon?* For instance, would you say *This car gets fewer miles per gallon* or *This car gets less miles per gallon?* The answer depends on whether the context suggests you should emphasize the quantity's **countability** (in which case you should use *fewer*) or its **continuity** (in which case you should use *less*). Of course, you could avoid the problem altogether by saying *This car is less efficient.*

Sentence A is problematic because it uses *amount* and *less* in reference to countable and discrete quantities, *conflicts* and *alcoholic drinks.* Sentence B corrects the problem by switching to *number* and *fewer,* but sentence C, which changes the quantities themselves to *violence* and *alcohol,* sounds more natural. The SAT will not expect you to choose between choices B and C on a multiple-choice question, because technically both are correct.

Exercise 8: Making Logical Comparisons

Correct any illogical comparisons in the sentences below.

1. The show was universally praised by critics, who said consistently that it was more intelligent and provocative than anything on the air.

2. Team unity and a strong work ethic were the key to their success.

3. Mathematics lessons in Japanese classrooms, unlike American classrooms, are often focused on solving a single complex problem rather than many simplistic problems.

4. The hybrid electric-combustion engines of the new cars are much quieter than conventional cars.

5. To the critics of the time, the surrealists were regarded as being as inscrutable, if not more so, than the Dadaists.

6. Modernist poetry was far less accessible to the readers of its time than was Shakespeare.

7. Her suitcase would not close because she had packed too much of her towels into it.

8. The year-end bonus was equally divided between Parker, Alyssa, and me.

9. Many students wanted to be a lifeguard at the club.

10. The toughest thing about her class is you have to do so much homework every night.

Rule 7: Make Sure Your Pronouns Are Clear and Precise

Lesson 18: Make sure your pronouns agree with their antecedents

Which is correct?

A. *Our financial team strictly maintains the confidentiality of their clients.*
B. *Our financial team strictly maintains the confidentiality of its clients.*
C. *Our financial counselors strictly maintain the confidentiality of their clients.*

> Every **definite pronoun** like *it*, *him*, *herself*, and *their* takes the place of a noun or pronoun called the **antecedent**. Every definite pronoun must **agree** in number (singular or plural) and category.

In sentence A, the definite pronoun, *their*, is plural, but the antecedent, *team*, is singular. This is a **number** disagreement. (At least it is in Standard American English; in Standard British English, collective nouns like *team*, *crowd*, and *committee* are treated as plurals.) Sentence B corrects this problem but introduces a subtle number shift and implies (probably incorrectly) that the entire team shares its clients. Sentence C corrects both problems and so is the best choice.

Which is correct?

D. *Sabrina, surprisingly, was the one that broke the silence.*
E. *Sabrina, surprisingly, was the one who broke the silence.*

Which is correct?

F. *The filibuster is a strategy where senators can extend debate in order to prevent a vote.*
G. *The filibuster is a strategy in which senators can extend debate in order to prevent a vote.*

> **Interrogative pronouns** are the pronouns we use to ask questions, like *who*, *what*, *where*, and *when*. When these pronouns are not used to ask questions, they serve as **definite pronouns** that refer to the nouns that immediately precede them (that is, they serve as **appositives**). Like all definite pronouns, they must agree in category with their antecedents.
>
> | Interrogative Pronoun | Antecedent Category |
> |---|---|
> | *where* | *place* |
> | *who* | *person* |
> | *when* | *time* |
> | *how* | *explanation* |
> | *why* | *reason* |
> | *what* | *thing or concept* |

The pronouns in sentence D and sentence F both disagree in **category** with their antecedents: Sabrina is a person, not a thing, so *who* is a more appropriate pronoun than *that*. The filibuster is a procedure, not a place, so *which* is a more appropriate pronoun than *where*.

Lesson 19: Avoid ambiguous pronouns

What is wrong with the following sentences?

A. *The coach told Mike that he was going to miss the next game.*

B. *The main difference between scientific thinking and ideological thinking is that it gives evidence priority over belief.*

Both of these sentences are ambiguous. In sentence A, who will miss the game, *Mike* or *the coach*?

In sentence B, which way of thinking gives evidence priority, *scientific thinking* or *ideological thinking*? Both sentences should be revised to eliminate **ambiguous pronouns**.

C. *The coach said that he would bench Mike for the next game.*

D. *Scientific thinking, unlike ideological thinking, gives evidence priority over belief.*

Lesson 20: Maintain consistency with your pronouns

Which is correct?

A. *My wife and I enjoy attending our school reunions because you meet so many interesting people there.*

B. *My wife and I enjoy attending our school reunions because we meet so many interesting people there.*

The pronoun references in sentence A are inconsistent: the generic pronoun *you* conflicts with the personal explanation indicated by the context, so the use of *we* in sentence B is more appropriate.

Which is correct?

C. *The flying squirrel uses its patagium—a membrane extending from the wrist to the ankle—as a parachute to help them glide safely out of the reach of predators.*

D. *The flying squirrel uses its patagium—a membrane extending from the wrist to the ankle—as a parachute to help it glide safely out of the reach of predators.*

Sentence C commits a **pronoun shift**. The pronoun referring to the *flying squirrel* has shifted from *its* to *them*. Sentence D makes the correction.

Watch your pronouns to make sure that they don't **shift**. Once you choose a pronoun to refer to a particular antecedent, stick with it.

Exercise 9: Using Pronouns

Circle all pronouns and rewrite to correct any pronoun errors.

1. This is one of those times in a game where an undisciplined player can lose focus or forget about strategy.

2. If a student wants to learn the meaning of a word, begin by learning its relevant context.

3. Caroline passed the phone to Julia, but she couldn't bring herself to speak.

4. Not wanting to be the one that slowed the team down, David dropped out of the race.

5. Brown is committed to assisting their students by providing him or her with any necessary financial aid.

6. The media ignored the reports because it didn't consider them newsworthy.

7. No one that has been through the first week of boot camp ever believes that they will make it through the entire six weeks.

8. Although one should never read carelessly, you should move briskly through the page to maintain focus on the purpose behind the text.

9. Neither Jack nor Ted thought that their team could lose the game, even when he began missing his shots.

10. Students sometimes aren't ready to handle the extra work that is required when his or her courses become more demanding.

11. I enjoy reading stories where underdogs eventually triumph.

12. Everyone will be expected to do their share to prepare the camp for visitor's day.

13. The museum received so many donations that they surpassed their fund-raising goal for the year.

14. The judges usually give the trophy to the performer that makes the fewest mistakes.

15. We have configured the pool so that each swimmer will have a lane to themselves.

16. Who was the player that hit the home run?

Lesson 21: Use the correct pronoun case

Each of these sentences contains one pronoun error. Can you find it?

A. *As the waiter was talking to Jenna and I, he showed us the tattoo on his neck.*
B. *I don't know anyone who can run a campaign more effectively than her.*
C. *Although Carl said he wasn't hungry, the first one at the buffet was him.*
D. *The team voted and selected myself as the next captain.*

These pronoun errors are called errors in **case**. Here are the corrections:

E. *As the waiter was talking to Jenna and me, he showed us the tattoo on his neck.*
F. *I don't know anyone who can run a campaign more effectively than she can.*
G. *Although Carl said he wasn't hungry, he was the first one at the buffet.*
H. *The team voted and selected me as the next captain.*

The **case** of a pronoun refers to its relationship to the verb. If a pronoun serves as or is equated with the **subject** of a verb, it takes the **subjective case**. If it serves as the **direct or indirect object** of the verb, it takes that **objective case**. If the **object** of the verb has the same referent as the **subject**, then it takes the **reflexive case**. If it indicates possession, it takes the **possessive case**.

Subjective case	Objective case	Reflexive case	Possessive case
I, he, she, we, they, who	*me, him, her, us, them, whom*	*myself, himself, herself ourselves, themselves*	*my/mine, his, her/hers, our/ours, their/theirs*

In sentence A, the pronoun *I* is the object of the prepositional phrase *to Jenna and I*, and so it requires the objective case, as in sentence E. In sentence B, the comparative phrase *more effectively* is adverbial, indicating that the comparison is between verbs in the clauses *who can run* and *she [can run]*, so the pronoun *her* should be changed to the subjective case, as in sentence F.

In sentence C, the verb *was* is a **linking verb**, which means that the pronoun *him* is being "equated" with the subject *one*, and therefore should be changed to the subjective case, as in sentence G. (Notice, also, that sentence G "inverts" the main clause from sentence C so that it is parallel with the first clause.) Sentence D abuses the **reflexive case**, which is the subject of our next lesson.

Lesson 22: Don't abuse reflexive pronouns

Which is correct?

A. *Either Caroline or myself will open the account this week.*

B. *Either Caroline or I will open the account this week.*

A reflective pronoun should only be used as

- the object of a verb when it is identical to the subject:

    e.g., *I did it all by myself. She cut herself.*

- an emphatic **appositive** (Lesson 13): *I myself would never do such a thing.*

Do NOT use reflexive pronouns as ordinary subjects or objects.

Since *myself* is part of the subject phrase, it must take the subjective case; therefore sentence B is correct.

Exercise 10: Pronoun Case

Circle the correct pronoun in each sentence.

1. The climb was much easier for Camille than it was for Jeff and (I/me/myself).

2. The other contestants did not seem as confident as (he/him/himself).

3. (Us/We) detectives are always careful to follow every lead.

4. Every student should make (his or her/their) own study plan.

5. The administrators never seem to listen to the opinions of (us/we) students.

6. Jim gave control of the project to Fiona and (me/myself/I).

7. The university presented the honor to David and (he/him/himself).

8. Justine and (me/I/myself) have always been closest friends.

9. There is no point in (our/us) delaying the tests any longer.

10. It seems quite clear that you and (I/me) will have to work together to solve this problem.

11. It might be difficult for (him and me/he and I) to agree on a topic.

12. (We/Us) and the other new members debated the issue for over two hours.

13. The owners of the club offered my wife and (I/me/myself) a free bottle of wine with dinner.

14. No other member of the team could outrun (I/me/myself).

15. The teachers were getting tired of (him/his) constantly falling asleep in class.

16. Major League ballparks have always held a special attraction for Dave and (I/me).

17. I am concerned about (you/your) taking so much time off work.

Rule 8: Make Your Verbs Clear and Precise
Lesson 23: Know how to use the consequential or "perfect" aspect

Which is correct?

A. *It doesn't really matter now, because I have been to the mountaintop.*

B. *It doesn't really matter now, because I was on the mountaintop.*

C. *It doesn't really matter now, because I went to the mountaintop.*

Why do sentences B and C sound so uninspiring in comparison to sentence A (adapted from Martin Luther King Jr.'s last speech)? They fall flat because they destroy the meaning conveyed by the *tense* and *aspect* of the verb in sentence A. The **tense** of a verb indicates its place in time: past, present, or future, but the **aspect** of a verb indicates how its action or status extends to the subject.

	Tense	Aspect
*I **have been** to the mountaintop.*	Present	Consequential (or "perfect")
*I **went** to the mountaintop.*	Past	Simple (isolated action)

Sentence A is obviously about *who King is now as a consequence of a previous event*, not simply about *what he did in the past*. In other words, it requires the **present tense** and the **consequential (or "perfect") aspect**. Sentences B and C destroy this essential meaning by putting the verb in the **simple past tense**.

The **aspect** of a verb indicates how its action or status extends to the subject, and is generally independent of tense. For instance, a present tense verb can have many different aspects:

I eat.	=	I am in the habit of eating. (Habitual aspect)
I am eating.	=	I am in the process of eating. (Progressive aspect)
I have to eat.	=	I feel compelled to eat. (Compulsive aspect)
I have eaten.	=	My current status is the consequence of previous eating. (Consequential or "perfect" aspect)
I have been eating.	=	My current status is the consequence of previous eating, and I am still eating. (Consequential and progressive aspects)

Grammatical forms of the consequential (or "perfect") aspect:

Present perfect	*has/have* + past participle	e.g., *I **have eaten**.*
Past perfect	*had* + past participle	e.g., *They **had** never **smoked**.*
Future perfect	*will have* + past participle	e.g., *By Friday, we **will have completed** the project.*

Use the **consequential (or "perfect") aspect** (e.g., *have taken, had taken, will have taken*) when you want to indicate that a status is the **consequence** of a *previous action or status*.

I have eaten.	=	My current status is the consequence of previous eating.
They had never smoked.	=	Their status at that point in the past was the consequence of previous non-smoking.
By Friday, we will have completed the project.	=	Our status next Friday will be the consequence of the fact that we completed the project.

Lesson 24: Know how to express historical facts and general ideas

Which is correct?

  A. *In his book* Walden, *Thoreau* **provided** *a manifesto for self-reliance.*

  B. *In his book* Walden, *Thoreau* **provides** *a manifesto for self-reliance.*

Which is correct?

  C. *The ancient Greek philosopher Zeno* **taught** *that motion* **was** *an illusion.*

  D. *The ancient Greek philosopher Zeno* **taught** *that motion* **is** *an illusion.*

  E. *The ancient Greek philosopher Zeno* **teaches** *that motion* **was** *an illusion.*

  F. *The ancient Greek philosopher Zeno* **teaches** *that motion* **is** *an illusion.*

Because both Zeno and Thoreau are long dead, the first version of each sentence, with past tense verbs, may seem correct. However, it is important to ask: do these sentences indicate **historical facts** or **general ideas**?

> In Standard English, historical facts take the past tense, but statements about general ideas and references to the content of widely available artistic works usually take the present tense. In an ambiguous case, such as when referring to an idea that has been refuted over the course of history, choose the tense that emphasizes the appropriate quality: use the present tense if you intend to emphasize its "idea-ness," but use the past tense if you intend to emphasize the fact that it is "history."

For the first pair of sentences, context is everything. If the sentence were part of a paragraph discussing Thoreau's life or the history of Transcendentalism, it would be a statement of historical fact, and so choice A would be preferred. If, however, this sentence were part of a discussion of the *ideas* in *Walden*, then sentence B would be correct.

The second sentence includes two clauses. The first refers to the *historical* fact that Zeno was a teacher, and the second refers to a *general idea* about motion. If you wish to emphasize the "idea-ness" of the second clause, then sentence D is the best choice. If you wish to emphasize the fact that this claim is "history" (that is, no longer believed), then sentence C is the best choice.

Lesson 25: Watch for irregular verbs

Which is correct?

A. *Peter was in pain after the run because he had **tore** his Achilles tendon.*
B. *Peter was in pain after the run because he had **torn** his Achilles tendon.*

The verb in the second clause takes the **consequential** (or "perfect") **aspect** (Lesson 24), which requires the past participle *torn*, not *tore*. The verb *to tear* is an **irregular verb**, which means that its past participle is not an *-ed* form of the verb. The correct sentence is B.

Here is a list of some common irregular verbs. Remember that verbs in the consequential or "perfect" aspect require the **past participle form**, not the **past tense form**. For instance, *I have drank* is the wrong form; *I have drunk* is correct.

Infinitive form	Past Tense	Past Participle
to arise	arose	arisen
to awaken	awoke	awoken
to beat	beat	beaten
to begin	began	begun
to blow	blew	blown
to break	broke	broken
to burst	burst	burst
to cast	cast	cast
to come	came	come
to creep	crept	crept
to do	did	done
to draw	drew	drawn
to drink	drank	drunk
to drive	drove	driven
to forsake	forsook	forsaken
to get	got	got, gotten
to go	went	gone

Infinitive form	Past Tense	Past Participle
to hurt	hurt	hurt
to kneel	kneeled, knelt	knelt
to know	knew	known
to lay (to put in place)	laid	laid
to lie (to recline)	lay	lain
to ride	rode	ridden
to run	ran	run
to shrink	shrank	shrunk, shrunken
to sink	sank	sunk
to speak	spoke	spoken
to spring	sprang	sprung
to swim	swam	swum
to take	took	taken
to tear	tore	torn
to write	wrote	written

Exercise 11: Verb Tenses and Aspects

Circle the verb form(s) that make each sentence coherent.

1. This morning, Ryan (came/has come/comes) to work with bags under his eyes because he (stayed/had stayed/was staying) up all last night.

2. Already, and without (spending/having spent) so much as an hour on research, Dale (wrote/has written/will write) the first draft of her essay.

3. (Developing/Having developed) the first hydrogen cell automobile, the team (hoped/had hoped) to reveal it to the world at the technology exposition.

4. Right after school, we (went/had gone) to Mario's for pizza.

5. Surprisingly, *Catcher in the Rye* (is/was/would be) the only full-length novel that the late J. D. Salinger ever (has published/published/will have published).

6. (Finding/Having found) no evidence against the accused, the detectives (had/had had) to release him.

7. (Being/Having been) captured by the rebels, David soon (began/had begun) to fear he would never escape.

8. When I (arrived/had arrived) home from the museum, I (started/had started/will start) to plan my art project.

9. By the time the committee (adjourned/had adjourned), it (voted/had voted) on all four key proposals.

10. As the seventh inning stretch began, we (did not score/had not scored) a single run.

11. In *To Kill a Mockingbird*, Harper Lee (uses/used/has used) the character of Dill Harris, whom she (bases/based/has based) on her real-life friend Truman Capote, to embody youthful innocence and imagination.

12. That evening, we (had/had had) a lovely meal with the group with whom we (hiked/had hiked) all afternoon.

13. (Walking/Having walked) all night, this morning we (were/had been) desperate to find a resting spot.

14. By the time I am done with finals, I (will write/will have written) four major papers.

15. (Winning/Having won) her previous three races, Anna (was/had been) confident that she (will win/would win) the next one as well.

16. It surprised us to learn that Venus (is/was/had been) almost the same size as Earth.

17. Buyers often (worry/have worried/will worry) too much about finding a low mortgage rate, and (forget/have forgotten/will forget) to scrutinize the terms of the contract.

18. I am qualified for this job because I (completed/have completed/had completed) two courses in digital marketing.

19. During the time of the ancient Greeks, many physicians (believed/had believed) that illnesses (are caused/were caused) by imbalances in bodily fluids.

20. Students (often worry/will often worry) excessively about grades and not enough about understanding.

Rule 9: Make the Rest of Your Sentence Clear and Precise
Lesson 26: Avoid redundancy

Which is correct?

A. *With only seconds remaining left to go in the game, Michael grabbed the ball and sped quickly down the court.*

B. *With only seconds to go in the game, Michael grabbed the ball and sped down the court.*

Notice that sentence A does not convey any idea that is not also conveyed in sentence B. Therefore, the three words that have been removed are **redundant**. Sentence B is better because it obeys the Law of Parsimony.

The Law of Parsimony

All else being equal, shorter is better.

Only one of *remaining*, *left*, or *to go* is necessary, because they all have the same meaning. Also, since *sped* means *moved quickly*, the adverb *quickly* is redundant.

Lesson 27: Avoid diction errors

Which sentence is best?

- A. *The news about the court's ruling extended quickly throughout the Internet.*
- B. *The news about the court's ruling scattered quickly throughout the Internet.*
- C. *The news about the court's ruling propagated quickly throughout the Internet.*
- D. *The news about the court's ruling expanded quickly throughout the Internet.*

None of these sentences is grammatically wrong, but sentence A sounds odd. The word *extended* is not quite right for this context. From the Latin *tendere* which means "to stretch," *extend* applies to things, like baseball games or necks, that are made to go beyond their typical lengths. But *news*, unlike a baseball game or a neck, does not have a "typical length," so trying to apply the verb *extend* to it is a **diction error**: the inappropriate use of a word.

Sentence B sounds a bit better, but *scatter* applies to a bunch of individual things, like seeds or mice, that are suddenly moving away from their group. Since this *news* is a single fact, not many individual items in a bunch, *scattered* doesn't quite work, either.

Sentence C uses *propagated*, which means *spread or promoted, as an idea or theory*. Since *news* spreads very much as an idea or theory does, the verb is being used appropriately.

Sentence D uses *expanded*, which, like *extended*, typically refers to something growing beyond its typical size or limit. Since *news* doesn't have a typical size or limit, *expanded* is not quite the right word.

Which sentence is correct?

- E. *We interviewed about thirty perspective candidates for the job.*
- F. *We interviewed about thirty prospective candidates for the job.*

The diction error in sentence E is a **"sound-alike"** error. The word *perspective* is a noun meaning "point of view," but the sentence clearly calls for an adjective describing the candidates. *Prospective* is an adjective meaning "expected to play a particular role or to achieve a particular goal in the future," which is certainly appropriate in describing a job candidate.

Common "sound-alikes"

accept (v) = to agree to take <*accept* an offer>
except (prep) = not including <*every day* **except** *Sunday*>
except (v) = exclude <*present company* **excepted**>

adapt (v) = to make suitable for a particular purpose <***adapted** to a new use*>
adopt (v) = to choose as one's own <***adopt** a child*>
adept (adj) = highly skilled <*an **adept** player*>

affect (v) = to influence <*it **affected** me deeply*>
effect (n) = result or consequence <*had a good **effect***>

allude (v) = to make a subtle or indirect reference (to) <*he **alluded** to their first meeting*>
elude (v) = to escape from; to avoid <***elude** capture*>

allusion (n) = a subtle reference <*an **allusion** to Othello*>
illusion (n) = misconception or misperception <*optical **illusion***>

ambivalent (adj) = having conflicting feelings (about) <*I feel **ambivalent** about going to the party*>
ambiguous (adj) = unclear or having more than one interpretation <*an **ambiguous** signal*>

cite (v) = to credit as a source of information <***cite** an article*>; to commend for meritorious action <***cited** for bravery*>
site (n) = location where a particular activity occurs <*the **site** of the battle*>
sight (v) = to see at a specific location <*she was **sighted** in the crowd*>

compliment (n) = a praising personal comment <*compliments are always appreciated*>
complement (n) = something that completes or makes a whole <*Brie is a fine complement to this wine*>

council (n) = a committee <*the executive council*>
counsel (v) = to give advice <*he counseled me wisely*>

discrete (adj) = distinct <*dozens of discrete parts*>
discreet (adj) = prudently modest in revealing information <*please be discreet about our meeting*>

elicit (v) = to bring out or to call forth <*the joke elicited uncomfortable laughter*>
illicit (adj) = unlawful <*illicit activities*>

eminent (adj) = prominent and distinguished <*an eminent historian*>
imminent (adj) = about to happen <*imminent doom*>

flaunt (v) = to show (something) off <*if you've got it, flaunt it*>
flout (v) = to show disregard for <*flout the rules*>

gambit (n) = a careful strategy or an opening move <*a bold gambit*>
gamut (n) = the complete range <*run the gamut*>

imply (v) = to suggest or hint at <*a handshake implies agreement*>
infer (v) = to draw a conclusion from evidence <*we can infer hostile intent*>

morale (n) (mor-AL) = shared enthusiasm for and dedication to a goal <*the team's morale was high*>
moral (n) (MOR-al) = lesson or principle about good behavior <*the story had a nice moral*>

phase (n) = stage in a process <*third phase of the project*>
faze (n) = to disturb (someone's) composure <*fazed by the interruption*>

precede (v) = to come before <*thunder is always preceded by lightning*>
proceed (v) (pro-CEED) = to go on, usually after a pause (*pro-* forward) <*proceed with the task*>
proceeds (n) (PRO-ceeds) = funds received from a venture <*proceeds from the raffle*>

principal (n) = head of a school <*principal Skinner is well liked*>; the initial investment in an interest-bearing
             account <*many investments risk a loss of principal*>
principle (n) = guiding rule <*the principle of the matter*>

reticent (adj) = reserved or reluctant to talk freely <*she has been reticent in therapy*>
reluctant (adj) = disinclined to do something <*reluctant to reveal personal information*>

Exercise 12: Diction Problems

Choose the best word in the sentences below.

1. Even the most trivial news seems to (affect/effect) the stock price immediately.

2. Even the most aggressive pesticides could not (delete/remove/eradicate/abolish) the beetles.

3. The (moral/morale) of the troops was at an all-time low during the Christmas season.

4. That scarf really (compliments/complements) your outfit.

5. Many well-trained oenologists can (separate/ distinguish/acknowledge/certify) the tastes of dozens of different grapes.

6. The article emphasized the low voter turnout in order to (imply/infer) that the senator may not have been elected by a true majority.

7. The justices can debate a case for weeks before a formal ruling is (appointed/specified/chosen/ predetermined/given/designated).

8. It may be years before we understand how pollution from the new power plant might (affect/effect) the regional environment.

9. The negotiations became very (apprehensive/ tense/neurotic/fretful/anxious) when the topic of old tribal conflicts was broached.

10. Heather was the (principal/principle) author of the study that was recently published in a prominent scientific magazine.

11. Although enormously popular among filmgoers, the movie was soundly (disparaged/confronted/ molested/eradicated/charged/impaired) by critics.

12. The words and images in advertisements are carefully chosen to subtly (propel/compel/extort/ oppress/oblige) consumers into buying things they may not want.

13. Try as they might, the hikers could not find the (antidote/anecdote) to the snake venom.

14. The acid solution was so potent that we had to (dilute/delude) it with water before we could use it safely.

15. Annie's project (excelled/overshadowed/outstripped/exceeded/preceded) all of our expectations.

16. Originally built for a small tractor, the engine had to be (correlated/attuned/converted/reoriented/ improved) for use as a boat motor.

17. As someone committed to fairness in education, she could not accept the (iniquity/inequity) of the admissions policy.

18. Although most of the manuscripts were signed by their authors, some were written (anonymously/ unanimously).

19. It was hard for the comic to (elicit/illicit) even the slightest laugh from the crowd.

20. We needed to (adapt/adopt/adept) the play to make it appropriate for younger audiences.

21. Darryl's self-esteem (enlarged/blossomed/multiplied/escalated/proliferated) once she found a peer group that shared her interests.

22. She thought she should be (discreet/discrete) about their relationship.

23. The (council/counsel) will decide how to finance the new city park.

24. Rather than obeying the coach, Richard always tries to (flaunt/flout) the team rules.

25. His knowledge of sports runs the (gamut/gambit) from table tennis to arena football.

26. The jury should not (infer/imply) guilt from the defendant's refusal to answer these questions.

27. The builders had to (truncate/curtail/lower/ belittle/subside) their work during the evening hours after the neighbors filed a complaint.

28. Rather than eliminate the department all at once, they decided to (faze/phase) it out gradually.

29. Barking dogs can often signal (imminent/eminent) danger.

30. After our vacation, we decided to (proceed/precede) with the plan.

31. Recent diplomatic efforts have focused on (defusing/declining/dwindling/degrading/discounting) the conflict by promoting nonconfrontational dialogue of all sorts.

32. I always felt (reticent/reluctant) to talk in class.

33. The democratically elected government has been forcefully (shifted/substituted/exchanged/supplanted) by a military cabal.

34. The police officer was (cited/sighted) for her efforts in the hostage rescue.

Eliminate any redundant words or phrases in the paragraph below.

35. When we look back to past history, we see that whenever a new innovation is introduced for the first time, people rarely accept the whole entire concept, at least not right away. If and when something threatens the ways of the past, people don't easily accept this new concept. Societies necessarily need stability because consistency and predictability make people feel comfortable and minimize conflict. Even when technology gives us a more efficient method, we often continue on with our older, less efficient ways. For instance, it's not uncommon to see people using e-mail for quick communications while at the same time they could have just texted to accomplish the same thing. If we take a moment to pause and consider for a second, it doesn't take much to see we can see that we can communicate more efficiently by text. And there are even some traditionalists who like the old way of doing things and will write letters on paper, which requires killing trees!

Lesson 28: Avoid errors in idiom

What is the difference between these two sentences?

   A.   *If you want to make friends, you should go on in the party.*

   B.   *If you want to make friends, you should go in on the party.*

These sentences use different **semantic idioms**, and so give very different advice. When you tell someone to *go on in*, you are giving him or her casual permission to enter, so sentence A says that casually inserting yourself into a social situation can make you more likeable. When you ask someone to *go in on* something, you are asking him or her to contribute money to the effort, so sentence B says that the folks throwing the party would like you more if you kicked in a few bucks. A semantic idiom is a common phrase with an established meaning, like *push through, on fire, see the light*, or *go in on*, that differs from its literal meaning.

> Errors in **idiom** are usually "wrong preposition" errors. In some idiomatic phrases, the choice of preposition is essential to the meaning: for instance, *breaking up, breaking down, breaking in*, and *breaking out* are all very different activities. In other idiomatic phrases, such as the **standard parallel constructions** described in Lesson 10, the preposition is simply a matter of convention. For instance, the sentence *Thai food is very different than Cantonese food* contains an error in syntactical idiom. The preposition *than* should only be used with comparative adjectives, as in *smaller than, faster than*, and *harder than*. But *different* is not a comparative adjective and instead takes the preposition *from*. We should say *Thai food is very different from Cantonese food.*

Which is correct?

   C.   *Effective therapy depends both on consistent adherence to the protocol as well as regular recalibration of the medication dosage.*

   D.   *Effective therapy depends both on consistent adherence to the protocol and regular recalibration of the medication dosage.*

   E.   *Effective therapy depends on both consistent adherence to the protocol and regular recalibration of the medication dosage.*

Sentence C uses the word *both*, which can either be followed by a simple plural noun (*both legs, both kinds*) or a prepositional phrase (*both of them*) or be part of a **standard parallel construction**, *both X and Y*, which we saw in Lesson 10. A standard parallel construction is a **syntactical idiom**, that is, a rigid way of phrasing relationships between ideas. Notice that the phrasing in sentence C—*both X as well as Y*—is **nonidiomatic**. The phrasing in D is idiomatic but **nonparallel** (Lesson 9): *X* is a prepositional phrase but *Y* is a noun phrase. Sentence E is both idiomatic and parallel, and is the best choice.

> When writing formally, remember to **ESP: eliminate superfluous prepositions**. We often use "extra" prepositions in informal speech, such as the redundant prepositions in *climb up, fall down*, and *fight against*. Notice how eliminating the unnecessary prepositions in these sentences makes them sound more "proper":
>
> *Her superior skill and strength helped her to dominate over her opponents.*
>
> *Many of our neighbors helped out with the renovation of the old firehouse.*
>
> *You don't want to miss out on all the fun.*
>
> *Their attempt to extract out the harmful chemicals was unsuccessful.*

Exercise 13: Errors in Idiom

Choose the correct preposition, or "none" if none is required.

1. I prefer the soft light of an incandescent bulb (to/over/more than/*none*) the harsh light of some fluorescent bulbs.

2. We all agreed (on/with/about/*none*) a plan to go skiing rather than hiking.

3. The defendant would not agree (to/on/with/about) the plea bargain.

4. We found dozens of old photographs hidden (in/*none*) between the pages.

5. Good study habits are necessary (to/for/in/*none*) academic success.

6. The new house color is not very different (from/than/to/*none*) the old one.

7. Margot was angry (with/about/at/*none*) Brian for not telling her that he was leaving.

8. They were both angry (about/at/with/*none*) the boys' behavior.

9. A lawyer should review the contract to see that it complies (with/in/about/to/*none*) the laws of your state.

10. The interview provided insight (about/into/for/*none*) the creative process of great directors.

11. We were very angry (about/with/at/against/*none*) him for ignoring our phone calls.

12. We all agreed (with/on/to/about/*none*) the high quality of the food.

13. Her tests include questions that seem very different (than/from/of/*none*) those that we see in the homework.

14. When she arrived on campus, she felt truly independent (of/from/*none*) her parents for the first time.

15. We were very angry (about/at/with/*none*) the exorbitant price of gasoline at the corner gas station.

16. It was hard not to agree (to/about/with/*none*) her offer of a free evening of babysitting.

17. I arrived at the meeting too late to raise my objection (against/to/of/*none*) the proposal.

18. If we don't act soon, we may miss (out on/*none*) the opportunity to lock in the lowest rates.

Lesson 29: Know how to use the active and passive voices

Which is better?

> A. *I broke the paddle.*
> B. *The paddle was broken by me.*

Sentence A and sentence B make the same statement, but in different **voices**: sentence A uses the **active voice** and sentence B uses the **passive voice**. In the active voice, the subject is the "actor" of the action, but in the passive voice, it is not.

> For most declarative statements in which the actor is known, the **active voice** (e.g., *I kicked the ball*) is clearer and more direct than the **passive voice** (e.g., *The ball was kicked by me*).

Which is better?

> C. *Henry ate all of his steak, but his vegetables were uneaten.*
> D. *Henry ate all of his steak but none of his vegetables.*

In sentence C, the first clause is active, but the second is passive. This is not only a violation of the **Law of Parallelism** (Lesson 9), but also a subtle evasion: who failed to eat the vegetables? Sentence D is more parallel, clear, and direct.

Overusing the passive voice not only makes your sentences wordier, but also often indicates **evasiveness**, because the passive voice does not require the actor. For instance, a statement like *I made a mistake* cannot be construed as an evasion of responsibility when phrased in the active voice. However, the passive voice form *A mistake was made by me*, when "trimmed" (Lesson 3) becomes *A mistake was made*, which is clearly evasive.

Which is better?

> E. *Although we enjoyed the hike to the peak, on the way down mosquitoes bit us, a thunderstorm drenched us, and countless thorns scratched us.*
> F. *Although we enjoyed the hike to the peak, on the way down we were bitten by mosquitoes, drenched by a thunderstorm, and scratched by countless thorns.*

In sentence E, all three clauses at the end of the sentence are parallel and active, yet the sentence sounds strange. In sentence F introducing the passive voice improves the sentence by creating another level of parallelism, because now all four clauses have the same subject: *we enjoyed . . . we were bitten . . . [we were] drenched . . . [we were] scratched.*

> Sometimes parallel structure requires using the passive voice.

Lesson 30: Understand your moods

Which is correct?

  A. *If I was more patient, I would become a good violinist.*
  B. *If I were more patient, I can become a good violinist.*
  C. *If I were more patient, I could become a good violinist.*

These sentences are **conditionals**, which take the form *"If X, then Y"* or simply *"If X, Y"* where *X* is a clause called the **hypothesis** and *Y* is a clause called the **conclusion**. The hypothesis takes different forms depending on whether it is **occasional**, **unlikely**, or **counterfactual**. The hypothesis here is **unlikely or wishful** and the conclusion indicates a **possibility**, so, as our discussion below will clarify, only sentence C has the correct form.

If the hypothesis is **occasional** or **likely**, then it takes the **indicative mood**; that is, it is stated as a fact. For instance, theorems in mathematics and logic and statements about common consequences take this form:

  If two sides of a triangle are congruent, then the two base angles are also congruent.

  If I eat too much, I will have a hard time sleeping.

  If you turn the switch, the light will go on.

If the hypothesis is **present counterfactual**, that is, it is unlikely or wishful, then it takes the **present subjunctive mood.** (Notice that a present subjunctive hypothesis, if it does not use the verb *to be*, can take the same form as the **simple past tense**.)

  If I had a million dollars, I would buy a new house.

  If Kate could tolerate the noise, she would come to the club with us.

  If I were taller, I would play in the NBA.

If the hypothesis is **past counterfactual**, that is, it contradicts a state or event in the past, then it takes the **past subjunctive mood.** (Notice that a counterfactual hypothesis takes the same form as the **past consequential**, and the counterfactual conclusion takes the **consequential aspect** (Lesson 23).)

  If I had caught the ball, we would have won the game.

  If I had been more studious in college, I could have graduated cum laude.

Counterfactuals can also include indirect commands, wishes, expressions of doubt, hypothetical consequences, and suggestions, all of which take the **subjunctive mood.**

> A **mood** is a verb category that indicates whether a clause is a factual statement (**indicative mood**, as in *I went to the park*), a direct command (**imperative mood**, as in *Go to the park!*), a question (**interrogative mood**, as in *Did you go to the park?*), or a counterfactual (**subjunctive mood**, as in *I should have gone to the park*).

Verbs that are in the subjunctive mood often require a **subjunctive auxiliary**, otherwise known as a "verb modal."

Subjunctive auxiliary	indicates	example
Can	present ability	*I can play the piano.*
Could	present possibility	*I could be losing my eyesight.*
Could	past ability	*I remember when I could run.*
Could	past permission	*Last year, we could use the pool.*
May	present permission	*You may enter.*
May	present possibility	*That may be true.*
Might	likelihood	*I might go fishing later.*
Might	purpose	*I took a nap so I might be rested.*
Must	compulsion	*I must have that dress.*
Should	suggestion	*You should eat more.*
Should	likelihood	*The train should arrive soon.*
Will	future inevitability	*Your day will come.*
Would	conditional conclusion	*If I had tried harder, I would have won.*
Would	inclination	*I would eat that.*
Would	past inevitability	*They said I would never walk again.*

The verb *to be* can sometimes take its subjective form without an auxiliary:

<u>Subjunctive forms of the verb *to be*</u>

*If I **were** faster, I could play wide receiver.*	(unlikely)
*He plays as if he **were** never injured.*	(counterfactual)
*I wish I **were** ten pounds lighter.*	(wishful)
*He asked that we **be** there exactly at 6.*	(indirect command)

Which is correct?

A. *If we would have left earlier, we would not have been caught the storm.*

B. *If we had left earlier, we would not have been caught the storm.*

Again, sentence A is a conditional with a **counterfactual** hypothesis, indicating that a nonfactual condition would have a particular result. However, the auxiliary *would* indicates a conditional conclusion, not a conditional hypothesis. The counterfactual hypothesis takes the same form as the **past consequential** (Lesson 23), *had left*, as in sentence B.

Exercise 14: Mood and Voice

Circle the correct verb form in each of the following sentences.

1. If our wide receiver (was/were) a little faster, he would get more open in the secondary.

2. As a matter of fact, Theo (was/would have been) only six years old when the Civil War (had begun/ began).

3. Denny would be more successful if only he (promoted/would promote) himself more aggressively.

4. The brochure suggested that we (are/be/would be) at the camp first thing in the morning.

5. I wish that my horse (were/was) not so lethargic this morning.

6. If the goalie (would have/had) lifted his glove even slightly, the puck (would have gotten/would get) through.

7. He acted as though the concert hall (was/were) filled with screaming fans.

8. I wish that summer camp (was/were) two weeks longer.

9. If the class (would have/had) voted against it, we would not have purchased the new gerbil cage.

10. We doubted that Joanna (will/would/might) get the part, since she was sick during her audition.

11. If I (were/was/had been) in Paris, I would probably be spending most of my time at the *Louvre*.

12. If I (might have/would have/had) known that the food was so good here, I (would have come/would come/came) sooner.

13. The coach demanded that we (would be/be/should be/were) in bed by eleven o'clock.

14. Yvonne acted as if she (was/were) the only customer in the restaurant.

15. Gina wished that she (had/would have/will have) chosen the red dress instead of the pink one.

16. The professor spoke to us as if he (was/were) an ancient Athenian general.

17. I (would have wanted/wanted) to (have seen/see) the countryside, but I was sick in bed for the entire vacation.

18. Had I found his wallet, I (would have/had/will have) returned it to him immediately.

19. If only the doctor (had/would have) told me to cut back on eating red meat, I (would have/should have) complied.

Rule 10: Know How to Punctuate

Lesson 31: Know how to use apostrophes

Which is correct?

A. *Its hard to know when you're dog has reached the limit of it's stamina if your not checking it regularly during your run.*

B. *It's hard to know when your dog has reached the limit of its stamina if you're not checking it regularly during your run.*

C. *It's hard to know when you're dog has reached the limit of it's stamina if you're not checking it regularly during you're run.*

Apostrophes serve two main functions: to indicate missing letters in a **contraction** as in *can't* (from *cannot*), and to indicate **possession**, as in *we went to Jacob's house*.

When turning a singular noun into a possessive adjective, simply add *'s*, as in *the committee's decision*. If the noun is a plural ending in *s*, simply add an apostrophe, as in *the sisters' relationship*.

Several common contractions are homophones (sound-alikes) of possessives, and so the two are commonly confused. Fortunately, there is a simple rule to keep them straight: the contraction always gets the apostrophe:

<u>contraction</u>	<u>possessive</u>
it's (it is)	*its*
you're (you are)	*your*
who's (who is)	*whose*
they're (they are)	*their*

Notice that sentence B above is the only one of the three that uses apostrophes correctly and avoids the *its/it's* and *your/you're* confusion.

Lesson 32: Know how to use commas

What is wrong with these sentences?

    A. *The subject that intimidates me the most, is calculus.*

    B. *I could not help Justine with her project, I had just begun a new job.*

    C. *As we passed through Springfield, Massachusetts we stopped at the Basketball Hall of Fame.*

    D. *We will be discussing my favorite poem, "Leaves of Grass," next semester.*

    E. *I would like to thank my parents, God and Ayn Rand.*

Sentence A suffers from the **stray comma syndrome**. Simply put, the comma doesn't belong. Chuck it.

> The primary job of the comma is as a separator. It is used to separate
>
> - items in a list (e.g., *He was fat, dumb, and lazy.*)
> - coordinate adjectives (e.g., *She gave a droning, uninspired speech.*)
> - modifying phrases from the main clause (e.g., *In summary, I am appalled.*)
> - dependent clauses that precede independent clauses (e.g., *Whenever I try, I fail.*)
> - (with a conjunction) independent clauses from other independent clauses (e.g., *I think, therefore I am.*)
>
> It can also be used to
>
> - introduce a quotation (e.g., *Tom said, "I ain't goin' where I ain't needed."*)
> - format an address or date (e.g., *Saturday, July 19, 2014*; *Cleveland, Ohio*)
> - to signal an addressee in dialogue or colloquial prose (e.g., *Get going, buster!*)

Sentence B commits a **comma splice** (Lesson 6). Two independent clauses cannot be joined with just a comma. Either change the comma to a colon or semicolon, or insert a conjunction:

> *I could not help Justine with her project, because I had just begun a new job.*

Sentence C omits the comma after the state name. It should read

> *As we passed through Springfield, Massachusetts, we stopped at the Basketball Hall of Fame.*

Notice that this treats *Massachusetts* as an **interrupter** (Lesson 3), which is fine because the sentence reads correctly even when it is omitted.

> Substantial modifying phrases in the middle of a sentence are called **interrupting modifiers** (Lesson 3) and should be separated from the main clause by commas. Remember that **a sentence should read properly even when the interrupters have been removed.**

In sentence D, the title of the poem works the same way as the state name in sentence C. It is a specifying modifier and requires commas before and after:

> *We will be discussing my favorite poem, "Leaves of Grass," next semester.*

> When a comma follows a title or phrase in quotes, the comma must precede the end quote.

Sentence E omits the **serial comma**, the comma that separates the second-to-last item in a list from the conjunction *and*. The serial comma is almost universally accepted as proper and necessary in Standard American English, because without it sentence E becomes absurd. In this apocryphal dedication of a book, the lack of a serial comma makes it seem like the author believes she is the offspring of a deity and a childless woman. Of course, the author intends her dedication as a list of four, not two:

> *I would like to thank my parents, God, and Ayn Rand.*

Two notable authorities that do not accept this rule are the *New York Times* and the *AP (Associated Press) Stylebook*, which recommend against the Oxford comma except to prevent an ambiguity such as that in sentence E.

> The use of the **serial comma** (the second comma in the phrase *A, B, and C*) in Standard American Usage is still a matter of debate and therefore will almost certainly not be tested on the SAT.

Lesson 33: Know how to use dashes

What is wrong with this sentence?

   A.   *The best that they could do—at least without a splint, was to set the broken bone and wait for help to arrive.*

The **dash** (or, as it is sometimes known, the **em dash**) is used to insert an abrupt break in thought in the middle or at the end of a sentence. If the break comes in the middle, then two dashes signify the beginning and the end of the interruption. In this case, the end of the interruption is indicated by a comma, where it should be a dash:

   The best that they could do—at least without a splint— was to set the broken bone and wait for help to arrive.

If the interruption is not much of a departure from the main idea, then commas will work also:

   The best that they could do, at least without a splint, was to set the broken bone and wait for help to arrive.

The punctuation on the two sides of an interrupter must be identical: either both em dashes or both commas.

Exercise 15: Punctuation

Correct any errors in punctuation (apostrophes, commas, dashes, colons, and semicolons) in the following sentences.

1. Truman Capote's nonfiction book, *In Cold Blood* is considered the first, greatest true crime novel.

2. I could not see clearly, until my eyes adjusted to the bright lights.

3. Runners, who step out of they're lanes during the first lap, will be disqualified.

4. Contrary to popular belief water will reach it's boiling point more slowly, when its under greater pressure.

5. In my opinion the most interesting part of the trip, was the river cruise.

6. Its easy to see, even on the dreariest of days—how Paris has earned it's reputation as the City of Love.

7. Having decided to postpone her college education Jill began looking for a job.

8. Regardless of who's phone rings the entire class will be punished for any disruption.

9. Isabella sprained her ankle, now she won't be able to practice for several weeks.

10. If you can't take care of you're own dog don't expect me to pay for it's grooming.

11. Don't expect this to be cheap, perfection has it's price.

12. What disappoints me most, is that you didn't even tell me you were leaving.

13. I told you, don't go near the street!

14. I remember that, *The Monkey's Paw*, was my favorite short story in the ninth grade.

15. The DVD's that they just received, don't seem to work in they're player.

16. A cyclotron, like the one Ernest Lawrence built at Berkeley—accelerates particles in a spiral path.

CHAPTER 4 ANSWER KEY

Exercise 1

1. *The team ~~were~~ was met.*
2. *The flock ~~took~~ looks like a whirlwind.*
3. *Carmen ~~were~~ was unaffected.*
4. *Juggling ~~seem~~ seems too much.*
5. *Others ~~is~~ are concerned.*
6. *Every one has supported my decision.* (correct)
7. *The fact ~~have~~ has forced some historians . . .*
8. *The progression are a result of gradual modifications, not sudden overhaul.* The subject and verb disagree, but more important, they are weak and unclear. Revision: *We progress more by small increments than by major upheavals.*
9. *The development were affected by the lack.* The subject and verb disagree, but more important, they are weak and unclear. Revision: *The discord within the revolutionary army hindered social and political development.*
10. *This report is intended.* Very uninformative subject and verb. Revision: *The administration responded poorly to the most recent crises in the Middle East.*

Exercise 2

1. *was*
2. *were*
3. *is*
4. *goes*
5. *wants*
6. *was*
7. *are*
8. *is*
9. *are*
10. *are*
11. *are*
12. *have*
13. *was*
14. *have*
15. *are*
16. *go*
17. *are*
18. *was*
19. *has*
20. *was*
21. *has*
22. *utter*
23. *are*

Exercise 3

1. *The comedy* The Return, *the third and latest movie directed by H. K. Schaffer, daughter of famed screenwriter George Schaffer, has received widespread critical acclaim.*
2. *An international team of scientists has discovered that the prefrontal cortex governs impulse control in humans, providing an important insight into criminal behavior.*
3. *Although electric cars are widely considered to be environmentally friendly, the electricity they use often comes from power plants that burn coal or other fossil fuels, which generate copious greenhouse emissions.*
4. *Regular exercise not only strengthens your muscles and heart, but also oxygenates your brain, helping it work more efficiently.*
5. *Although we are motivated by our principles, those principles change as our experiences transform our priorities.*

Exercise 4

1. *One of their greatest challenges, DNA contamination, has recently been overcome at the Max Planck Institute in Germany, where biologists have developed a "clean room," like those used in manufacturing computer chips and space telescopes, to examine minute bits of genetic material from 400,000-year-old hominid bones.*
2. *However, evidence suggests that the loss of autonomy and frequent humiliation that prisoners receive only aggravates the crime problem by exacerbating any short- or long-term psychological issues that make them susceptible to antisocial and criminal impulses.*
3. *Nevertheless, the willingness to equate all governmental institutions with tyranny is an enormously dangerous one that can only impede moral, economic, and cultural progress.*

Exercise 5

1. *. . . reforming the tax code, improving the schools, and reviving good relations . . .*
2. *. . . but about using your time well.*
3. *. . . the more you will like her.*
4. *. . . but also very reasonably priced.*
5. *. . . exacerbated by esoteric financial instruments, skittish investors, and oblivious regulators.*
6. *. . . is very supportive and knowledgeable.*
7. *. . . give the tickets to Maria or to Caitlyn.*
8. *. . . experienced contracting wealth, increasing risk spreads, and deteriorating credit markets.*
9. *I prefer the romantic virtuosity of Liszt to the emotional accessibility of Chopin.*
10. *. . . not so much for the music as for the spirit of free expression.*

Exercise 6

1. *As I rounded the bend*
2. *Martha was compelled by her creative instinct*
3. *Claudius unsheathed his sword*

4. *There are a lot of apps and websites to help you find a good Thai restaurant.*
5. *Even though Adam had a sprained ankle, the coach forced him*
6. *As we walked back to the car, we found my lost earrings.*
7. *David was concerned primarily with*
8. *the hikers pitched an early camp because of the looming storm*
9. *Allison was frightened*
10. *Without your being aware of it*
11. *We were surprised to hear Carol, whom we always regarded as a dutiful mother,*
12. *Sprinters say that proper hip positioning is essential to getting a good jump out of the starting blocks.*
13. *the town council is considering proposals for cutbacks*
14. *the senator planned*
15. *Although Portland is famous for its visual arts scene, its*
16. *the magician made the coin disappear instantly*
17. *Physicians recommend both vigorous exercise and disciplined eating for maintaining good health.*
18. *we saw one at a garage sale*

Exercise 7

1. *much stronger → much more strongly*
2. *foully → foul*
3. *never usually → rarely*
4. *most → more*

5. *weren't hardly → weren't*
6. *easier → more easily*
7. *clearer → more clearly*
8. *more easy → easier*
9. *the most unique → unique*
10. *won't barely → won't*
11. *never told → didn't tell*
12. *never usually → rarely*

Exercise 8

1. *anything → anything else*
2. *key → keys*
3. *American classrooms → those in American classrooms*
4. *conventional cars → those of conventional cars*
5. *as inscrutable, if not more so, than → as inscrutable as, if not more inscrutable than,*
6. *Shakespeare → Shakespeare's poetry*
7. *much → many*
8. *between → among*
9. *a lifeguard → lifeguards*
10. *is you have → is having*

Exercise 9

1. *where → when*
2. *a student wants → you want (or begin → he or she should begin)*
3. *she → Julia (or Caroline)*
4. *that → who*
5. *their → its, him or her → them*
6. *it → they*
7. *that → who, they → he or she*
8. *one → you (or you → one)*

9. *he → Jack (or Ted or whoever was missing the shots)*
10. *his or her → their*
11. *where → in which*
12. *Everyone → They all (or their → his or her)*
13. *they → it*
14. *that → who*
15. *each swimmer → all swimmers (or themselves → himself or herself)*
16. *that → who*

Exercise 10

1. *me*
2. *he (did)*
3. *We*
4. *his or her*
5. *us*
6. *me*
7. *him*
8. *I*
9. *our*
10. *I*
11. *him and me*
12. *We*
13. *me*
14. *me*
15. *his*
16. *me*
17. *your*

Exercise 11

1. *came, had stayed*
2. *having spent, has written*
3. *Having developed, hoped*
4. *went*
5. *is, published*
6. *Having found, had*
7. *Having been, began*
8. *arrived, started*
9. *adjourned, had voted*
10. *had not scored*
11. *uses, based*
12. *had, had hiked*
13. *Having walked, were*
14. *will have written*

15. *Having won, was, would win*
16. *is*
17. *worry, forget*
18. *have completed*
19. *believed, were caused*
20. *often worry*

Exercise 12

1. *affect*
2. *eradicate*
3. *morale*
4. *complements*
5. *distinguish*
6. *imply*
7. *given*
8. *affect*
9. *tense*
10. *principal*
11. *disparaged*
12. *compel*
13. *antidote*
14. *dilute*
15. *exceeded*
16. *converted*
17. *inequity*
18. *anonymously*
19. *elicit*
20. *adapt*
21. *blossomed*
22. *discreet*
23. *council*
24. *flout*
25. *gamut*
26. *infer*
27. *curtail*
28. *phase*
29. *imminent*
30. *proceed*
31. *defusing*
32. *reluctant*
33. *supplanted*
34. *cited*
35. *redundancies: back, past, new, for the first time, entire, If and, necessarily, consistency and, on, at the same time, to accomplish the same thing, If we take a moment to pause and consider for a second*

Exercise 13

1. *to*
2. *on*
3. *to*
4. none
5. *to (or for)*
6. *from*
7. *with*
8. *about*
9. *with*
10. *into*
11. *with*
12. *about*
13. *from*
14. *of*
15. *about*
16. *to*
17. *to*
18. none

Exercise 14

1. *were*
2. *was, began*

3. *would promote*
4. *be*
5. *were*
6. *had, would have gotten*
7. *were*
8. *were*
9. *had*
10. *would*
11. *were*
12. *had, would have come*
13. *be*
14. *were*
15. *had*
16. *were*
17. *wanted, see*
18. *would have*
19. *had, would have*

Exercise 15

1. *. . . book,* In Cold Blood, *is considered*

the first and the greatest . . .
2. delete the comma
3. *Runners who step out of their lanes during the first lap will be disqualified.*
4. *. . . belief, water will reach its boiling point more slowly when it's . . .*
5. *. . . opinion, the most interesting part of the trip was . . .*
6. *It's easy to see, even on the dreariest of days, how Paris has earned its . . .*
7. *. . . college education, Jill . . .*
8. *. . . whose phone rings, the entire class . . .*
9. *. . . ankle; now she . . .*

10. *. . . your own dog, don't expect me to pay for its grooming.*
11. *Don't expect this to be cheap; perfection has its price.*
12. delete the comma
13. *I told you: don't . . .*
14. delete both commas
15. *The DVDs that they just received don't seem to work in their player.*
16. *cyclotron—like the one Ernest Lawrence built at Berkeley— accelerates . . .*

CHAPTER 5

THE SAT READING TEST

The SAT Reading Test

What is the SAT Reading test?

The SAT includes a 65-minute Reading test designed to assess your

> *proficiency in reading and comprehending a broad range of high-quality, appropriately challenging literary and informational texts in the content areas of U.S. and world literature, history/social studies, and science.*

The SAT Reading test consists of four passages, each 500–750 words long. (For an example of the Reading test, look at Section 1 of the Diagnostic Test in Chapter 2.) You are to read the passages and answer multiple-choice questions about

- the purpose and main idea of the passage
- the meaning and purpose of particular words and phrases in context
- the inferences that can be justifiably drawn from the passage
- the tone and attitude conveyed by the author

Additionally, some passages with a common theme are paired and accompanied by questions about

- points of agreement or disagreement between the paired passages
- differences in tone or emphasis between the paired passages

Also, some of the passages will be accompanied by tables or graphs and questions about

- how to interpret the data represented in the table or graph
- how to incorporate these data appropriately into the passage

How is it used?

Colleges use your SAT Reading test score as a measure of your ability to perform demanding college-level reading tasks. The SAT Reading test score represents one-half of your Evidence-Based Reading and Writing score. The other half of this score comes from the Writing and Language test.

Sound intimidating? It's not.

There are only four rules of analytical reading to learn in order to ace the SAT Reading test, and the 12 lessons in this chapter will give you the knowledge and practice you need to master all of them.

The Core Analytical Reading Skills

Lesson 1: Learn to read analytically

Which is correct?

A. *The SAT Reading test is primarily a test of your multiple-choice test-taking skill.*

B. *The SAT Reading test is primarily a test of your analytical reading skill.*

C. *The SAT Reading test is primarily a test of your literary reading skill.*

Although basic test-taking skills are helpful, they won't get you very far. Acing the SAT Reading test requires solid **analytical reading skills**, that is, the ability to **extract the key information** from any passage and **to identify its evidence**. Specifically, you should be able to read any SAT passage on any topic and determine its

- purpose
- central idea
- structure
- functional elements
- tone

It's important to remember that the SAT Reading test is *not a literary skills test*. You may spend a lot of time in English class learning to

- explore connections between a text and its cultural context

- evaluate the emotional effect of a literary piece
- explore abstract ideas that are implicit in a work, such as "the concept of utopia"
- find examples of symbolism, foreshadowing, and other subtle and figurative literary elements

But these literary skills, while important for your enjoyment and edification, are not tested by the SAT Reading test.

Although it is helpful to know a few important **test-taking skills**, just knowing these tricks won't get you very far. The SAT Reading test is essentially a test of **analytical reading skill**, *not* **literary reading skills**.

According to the College Board, the SAT Reading test is **evidence-based**. That is, it specifically assesses your ability to justify your responses with **literal evidence** from the passage and **quantitative evidence** from associated tables or graphs. Therefore, be ready to supply the **evidence** for any answers you give.

Lesson 2: Get your mind right

Which is correct?

A. *The SAT Reading passages are chosen to be as difficult and boring as possible.*

B. *The SAT Reading passages are chosen because they represent the kinds of prose students are most likely to encounter in a college liberal arts curriculum.*

The answer, despite popular belief, is B. The SAT Reading passages are not chosen by sadists. They are selected to represent the kind of reading you will do in college. Don't begin the SAT Reading Test with the attitude, "Oh no, not another tedious and pointless SAT reading passage!" This will only sabotage your performance by creating a negative self-fulfilling prophecy.

How well you do on the SAT Reading test depends very much on the mindset you bring to the test.

If you expect a passage to be tedious and pointless, it will be, because you will miss its interesting key points. If instead you expect to learn something new and interesting, you will remain more focused and engaged and attack the questions much more confidently and accurately.

Keep an open mind and—we promise—you'll learn something new from every SAT you take.

How do you avoid "spacing out?"

Many students occasionally "space out" on high-pressure reading tests like the SAT: their eyes scan over the words, but the words don't go in the brain. The best way to avoid space-outs is to **master the skills of active reading**. When your brain is active and engaged, it can't "space out." The heart of active reading is focusing on the **analytical questions** that we will discuss in the upcoming lessons.

The Three Key Questions

Lesson 3: Ask, "What is the purpose of this passage?"

To comprehend a passage analytically, you must first categorize it in terms of which three categories?

A. *Fiction, nonfiction, or poetry*
B. *Exposition, rhetoric, or narrative*
C. *History, science, or humanities*

The correct answer is B. Don't worry so much about whether the passage is fiction or nonfiction, or if the topic is unfamiliar to you. You need a plan of attack for any passage the SAT throws your way. Strong analytical reading begins with asking, **"What is the overall purpose of this passage?"** Any well-written piece of prose has one of three possible purposes corresponding to the following categories:

- **Expository prose** presents **objective information** and is organized around a **guiding question**, such as "What happened in the Battle of Bull Run?" or "What is polarized light, and what is it used for?" Examples of expository prose include news articles and science textbooks.
- **Rhetorical prose** presents **an author's personal point of view** and is organized around a **thesis**, such as "We have an exaggerated perception of gang violence," or "Hiking is good for the soul." Examples of rhetorical prose include Op-Ed essays, blog posts, and some magazine articles.
- **Narrative prose** presents **a fictional or nonfictional story** and is organized around a **protagonist and a transformative struggle**, such as "Jean Valjean struggles to redeem himself," or "King Lear struggles to establish a legacy." Examples of narrative prose include memoirs, short stories, biographies, and novels.

As you read any SAT Reading passage, first ask, **"What is its overall purpose: to present objective information** (expository), **to present a point of view** (rhetorical), **or to tell a story** (narrative)**?"**

You can often determine overall purpose from the introduction or the first paragraph. For instance, if a passage is described as a *discussion* or *description*, it's likely to be expository. If it is described as a *speech* or an *essay*, it's probably rhetorical. If it is described as an excerpt from a *memoir* or *novel*, then it's probably narrative.

But **be careful**. Authors often combine different modes of prose. For instance, an essay arguing for tougher gun laws (rhetorical purpose) might tell a heart-wrenching story (narrative element) to make the point. Similarly, a short story (narrative purpose) might include a lengthy description (expository element) of the town in which it is set.

Always confirm your theory about purpose by carefully reading the final paragraph. If the final paragraph focuses on describing an interesting fact, the passage is probably expository. If it focuses on a proposal, evaluation, or suggestion, the passage is probably rhetorical. If it describes a person's resolution of a problem, the passage is probably a narrative. **Most passages confirm their overall purpose in the final paragraph.**

Lesson 4: Ask, "What is the central idea of this passage?"

What is the best way to determine the central idea of a passage?

    A. *Read the first paragraph, which always summarizes the main idea.*

    B. *Read the topic sentence of the final paragraph.*

    C. *It depends on the passage type and structure.*

The correct answer is C. Although the first and last paragraphs often contain key information, sometimes the first paragraph or two simply provide background information or summarize a misconception to be refuted. Sometimes a passage doesn't get around to the central idea until the third or fourth paragraph.

> **Once you have determined the general purpose of the passage, focus immediately on finding the central idea.** The purpose and central idea are intimately linked.
>
> - The central idea of any **expository essay** is a **guiding question**, such as "What is the carbon cycle?"
> - The central idea of any **rhetorical essay** is a **thesis**, such as "Perseverance is more important to success than skill is."
> - The central idea of any **narrative** is the **protagonist's transformative struggle**, such as "The narrator discovers how to be an artist."
>
> **The central idea is often, but not always, revealed at the beginning of the passage and reinforced at the end of the passage.** Sometimes your first guess about the main idea, based on the first paragraph, may be wrong and need to be revised.

Consider this excerpt and the question that follows:

Without some appreciation of common large numbers, it's impossible to react with the proper skepticism to terrifying reports that more than a million American kids are kidnapped each year, or with the proper sobriety to a warhead carrying a megaton of explosive power—the equivalent of a million tons (or two billion pounds) of TNT.

And if you don't have some feeling for probabilities, automobile accidents might seem a relatively minor problem of local travel, whereas being killed by terrorists might seem to be a major risk when going overseas. As often observed, however, the 45,000 people killed annually on American roads are approximately equal in number to all American dead in the Vietnam War. On the other hand, the seventeen Americans killed by terrorists in 1985 were among the 28 million of us who traveled abroad that year—that's one chance in 1.6 million of becoming a victim . . .

The primary purpose of this passage is to

    A) warn against the dangers associated with daily living in the United States

    B) compare the costs of war-related activities to the costs of domestic activities

    C) discuss common misunderstandings about statistical data

    D) propose solutions to some problems in American domestic and foreign policy

Most students get this question wrong, because they focus too much on **specific details** and not enough on **overall purpose** and **logical structure**.

So what is the central idea in this passage? If you look at some of the passage details, such as the references to car accidents and kidnapping, you might be reminded of *the dangers associated with daily living* or the *cost of domestic activities* or even *domestic policy problems*. If you notice the references to warheads, the Vietnam War, and terrorism, you might be reminded of *war-related activities* or *American foreign policy problems*. For these reasons, choices A, B, and D might all seem like good answers.

But they are all wrong.

Consider choice A. Is kidnapping mentioned in order to *warn against danger*? No: the author says that the *proper* response to the *terrifying reports that more than a million American kids are kidnapped each year* is not fear and caution, but *skepticism*. In fact, his point is that if we had *some appreciation of common large numbers*, we would see that this statistic is preposterous.

How about choice B? The statement that *the 45,000 people killed annually on American roads are approximately equal in number to all American dead in the Vietnam War* seems to be comparing *the costs of war-related activities to the costs of domestic activities*. But is this the *primary purpose of the passage*? No, this statistic is mentioned only to make a broader point: that it is irrational to fear terrorism more than daily driving, and that this irrationality is due, in least in part, to our lack of *feeling about probabilities*.

Now look at choice D. Does the passage *propose any solutions* to the problems of kidnapping, terrorism, nuclear weapons, car accidents, or war? Certainly not in these first two paragraphs. More important, these paragraphs suggest a very different overall purpose.

The point of these first two paragraphs is that *[w]ithout some appreciation of common large numbers* and a *feeling for probabilities*, we will overreact to some dangers and underreact to others. In other words, there is some danger inherent in our *common misunderstandings about statistical data*. Therefore, the best answer is choice C.

How to attack purpose questions

Many SAT Reading questions ask about the **purpose** of particular words, phrases, or references. Here are some examples:

> The author uses the word "debacle" (line 3) in order to emphasize her belief that . . .

> The quotation in lines 42–51 primarily serves to . . .

To attack these questions, first remind yourself of the **overall purpose and central idea** of the passage, and remember that **every portion of the passage must help convey the central idea of the passage.**

Consider this question about the "innumeracy" passage that is the source of the earlier quote:

> The author mentions the work of Drs. Kronlund and Phillips (lines 53–58) primarily in order to
>
> A) warn against the risks of certain medical procedures
>
> B) highlight a promising medical breakthrough
>
> C) demonstrate the fallibility of medical experts
>
> D) dispute a common medical theory

Even without reading lines 53–58, you can see which choices don't fit with the overall purpose and central idea that we identified in the previous question. Since the primary purpose of this passage is to "discuss common misunderstandings about statistical data," the reference to *the work of Drs. Kronlund and Phillips* must serve this primary purpose in some way. Choices B and D are not strongly connected to the understanding of statistical data. Choices A and C, however, are plausible answers because *warning against risks* often involves understanding the data that show the likelihood of those risks, and *the fallibility of medical experts* might include their inability to understand and interpret statistics (which is precisely the main theme of the essay).

Exercise 1

*This passage is adapted from John Allen Paulos,
Innumeracy ©1988 Hill and Wang, a division of Farrar,
Straus and Giroux, LLC. Paulos is a mathematician dis-
cussing the role of mathematics in American culture.*

Line
Without some appreciation of common large
numbers, it's impossible to react with the proper
skepticism to terrifying reports that more than a
million American kids are kidnapped each year,
5 or with the proper sobriety to a warhead carrying
a megaton of explosive power—the equivalent of
a million tons (or two billion pounds) of TNT.
    And if you don't have some feeling for
probabilities, automobile accidents might
10 seem a relatively minor problem of local travel,
whereas being killed by terrorists might seem
to be a major risk when going overseas. As often
observed, however, the 45,000 people killed
annually on American roads are approximately
15 equal in number to all American dead in the
Vietnam War. On the other hand, the seventeen Americans killed by terrorists in 1985 were
among the 28 million of us who traveled abroad
that year—that's one chance in 1.6 million of
20 becoming a victim. Compare that with these
annual rates in the United States: one chance in
68,000 of choking to death; one chance in 75,000
of dying in a bicycle crash; one chance in 20,000
of drowning; and one chance in only 5,300 of
25 dying in a car crash.
    Confronted with these large numbers and
with the correspondingly small probabilities
associated with them, the innumerate will inevitably respond with the non sequitur, "Yes, but
30 what if you're that one," and then nod knowingly,
as if they've demolished your argument with
penetrating insight. This tendency to personalize

is a characteristic of many who suffer from innumeracy. Equally typical is a tendency to equate
35 the risk from some obscure and exotic malady
with the chances of suffering from heart and
circulatory disease, from which about 12,000
Americans die each week.
    There's a joke I like that's marginally
40 relevant. An old married couple in their nineties
contact a divorce lawyer, who pleads with them
to stay together. "Why get divorced now after sev-
enty years of marriage?" The little old lady finally
pipes up in a creaky voice: "We wanted to wait
45 until the children were dead."
    A feeling for what quantities or time spans
are appropriate in various contexts is essential
to getting the joke. Slipping between millions
and billions or between billions and trillions
50 should in this sense be equally funny, but it isn't,
because we too often lack an intuitive grasp for
these numbers.
    A recent study by Drs. Kronlund and Phillips
of the University of Washington showed that
55 most doctors' assessments of the risks of various
operations, procedures, and medications (even
in their own specialties) were way off the mark,
often by several orders of magnitude. I once
had a conversation with a doctor who, within
60 approximately 20 minutes, stated that a certain
procedure he was contemplating (a) had a one-
chance-in-a-million risk associated with it;
(b) was 99 percent safe; and (c) usually went
quite well. Given the fact that so many doctors
65 seem to believe that there must be at least eleven
people in the waiting room if they're to avoid
being idle, I'm not surprised at this new evidence
of their innumeracy.

1

The primary purpose of this passage is to

A) warn against the dangers associated with daily
living in the United States

B) compare the costs of war-related activities to
the costs of domestic activities

C) discuss common misunderstandings about
statistical data

D) propose solutions to some problems in
American domestic and foreign policy

2

The author regards the "reports" (line 3) with an
attitude of

A) journalistic objectivity

B) informed incredulity

C) intense alarm

D) lighthearted humor

3

The activities listed in lines 21–25 serve primarily as examples of

A) underappreciated dangers

B) intolerable risks

C) medical priorities

D) policy failures

4

The passage includes all of the following EXCEPT

A) ad hominem

B) verifiable statistics

C) amusing illustration

D) social assessment

5

In line 32, the author's use of the word "penetrating" is an example of

A) subtle euphemism

B) deliberate hyperbole

C) sincere acclamation

D) ironic sarcasm

6

In line 32, "personalize" most nearly means

A) customize decoratively

B) describe insultingly

C) represent humanely

D) interpret out of context

7

The passage suggests that the "exotic malady" (line 35) is an example of

A) a delusion that is slowly being dispelled

B) a risk that is wildly overestimated

C) a peril that is rapidly growing

D) a disease that defies conventional treatment

8

Which choice provides the best evidence for the answer to the previous question?

A) Lines 1–7 ("Without some . . . of TNT")

B) Lines 12–16 ("As often . . . War")

C) Lines 39–40 ("There's a joke . . . relevant")

D) Lines 58–64 ("I once . . . quite well")

9

The author mentions the work of Drs. Kronlund and Phillips (lines 53–58) primarily in order to

A) warn against the risks of certain medical procedures

B) highlight a promising medical breakthrough

C) demonstrate the fallibility of medical experts

D) dispute a common medical theory

Lesson 5: Ask, "What is the structure of this passage?"

Passage adapted from Cleveland Hickman, Larry Roberts, and Allan Larson, Integrated Principles of Zoology. ©2001 The McGraw-Hill Companies.

Here is a sample SAT Reading passage, with some notes about its **functional structure**.

In ancient times, people commonly believed that new life could arise not only by parental reproduction, but also, on occasion, by spontaneous generation from nonliving material. For example, frogs appeared to arise from damp earth, mice from putrefied matter, insects from dew, and maggots from decaying meat. Warmth, moisture, sunlight, and even starlight often were mentioned as factors that encouraged spontaneous generation of living organisms.

Misconception about the origin of life: spontaneous generation.

One of the early efforts to synthesize organisms in the laboratory can be seen in a recipe for making mice given by the Belgian plant nutritionist Jean Baptiste van Helmont (1648):

Example of this misconception: recipe for synthesizing adult mice from soiled underwear.

. . . press a piece of underwear soiled with sweat together with some wheat in an open jar, after about 21 days the odor changes and the ferment. . . . changes the wheat into mice . . . not small mice, not even miniature adults or aborted mice, but adult mice emerge!

In 1861, Louis Pasteur demonstrated that, in fact, living organisms cannot so easily arise spontaneously from nonliving matter. In his experiments, Pasteur introduced fermentable material into a flask with a long S-shaped neck that was open to the air. The flask and its contents were boiled to kill any microorganisms, then cooled and left undisturbed. No fermentation could occur because new microorganisms could not enter through the neck. But when the neck was removed, microorganisms in the air could enter the fermentable material and proliferate. Thus, Pasteur showed that life came from previously existing organisms and their reproductive elements, such as eggs and spores or, in the case of van Helmont's "recipe," adult mice that crept into the jar. Announcing his results to the French Academy, Pasteur proclaimed, "Never will the doctrine of spontaneous generation arise from this mortal blow."

Refutation of theory of spontaneous generation by a clever experiment.

But Pasteur, for all his brilliance, wasn't entirely correct. The first "life," if we can call it that, appears to have assembled over the course of millions of years of random collisions of nonliving molecules in the chemical-rich cauldron of early earth, until, by chance, very basic self-replicating units formed. These first self-replicating units, which arose almost 4 billion years ago, are most likely the ancestors we share with every living thing on earth today. But with no scientist to witness it, how can we know that the dawn of life happened that way? The evidence is embedded in the complex molecules common to all living things—DNA, RNA, proteins, lipids, hormones—which can be painstakingly traced back to simpler chemicals that most likely preceded them in the family tree. Even more profoundly, astrophysicists can now trace the building blocks of life—carbon, nitrogen, and oxygen—to a spectacular birth inside ancient exploding stars!

Implication of rare biogenesis over millions of years: it seems to have happened only once, so all life is related.

To read analytically, you must pay attention to the functional structure of the passage. In other words, think about how **each paragraph** serves the central idea.

Notice that, in the passage above, the notes indicate that the first paragraph *describes a misconception*, the second *provides an example of that misconception*, the third *provides a refutation of that misconception*, and the fourth *describes an implication of the corrected theory*. All of these paragraphs serve the central purpose of *describing the history and implications of a biological theory*.

The **structure** of a passage depends very much on its **purpose.**

Expository essays can be structured in many possible ways in order to answer the guiding question. They may include background information, illustrations of concepts, examples of general claims, relevant data, anecdotes, or discussions of implications. Of course, any of these elements may be omitted, supplemented, or rearranged.

Narratives have a fairly consistent structure: (1) the struggle is introduced, (2) the struggle is developed, and (3) the struggle is resolved, transforming the protagonist. The details may differ dramatically from narrative to narrative, but the overall structure probably will not.

Rhetorical essays can also be structured in many possible ways. A **rhetorical argument** is likely to describe a position, then refute it with a counterargument. A **rhetorical narrative** tells a story in order to highlight a particular point of view. Rhetorical essay can include paragraphs dedicated to logical analysis of a claim, explanation, illustration, discussion of implications, modification of a claim, and so on.

Exercise 2

This passage is adapted from Cleveland Hickman, Larry Roberts, and Allan Larson, Integrated Principles of Zoology. *©2001 The McGraw-Hill Companies.*

Line   In ancient times, people commonly believed that new life could arise not only by parental reproduction, but also, on occasion, by sponta-neous generation from nonliving material. For
5   example, frogs appeared to arise from damp earth, mice from putrefied matter, insects from dew, and maggots from decaying meat. Warmth, moisture, sunlight, and even starlight often were mentioned as factors that encouraged spontaneous genera-
10 tion of living organisms.

    One of the early efforts to synthesize organ-isms in the laboratory can be seen in a recipe for making mice given by the Belgian plant nutri-tionist Jean Baptiste van Helmont (1648):
15   . . . press a piece of underwear soiled with sweat together with some wheat in an open jar, after about 21 days the odor changes and the ferment. . . . changes the wheat into mice . . . not small mice, not even miniature adults or aborted
20 mice, but adult mice emerge!

    In 1861, Louis Pasteur demonstrated that, in fact, living organisms cannot so easily arise spontaneously from nonliving matter. In his experiments, Pasteur introduced fermentable
25 material into a flask with a long S-shaped neck that was open to the air. The flask and its contents were boiled to kill any microorganisms, then cooled and left undisturbed. No fermentation could occur because new microorganisms could
30 not enter through the neck. But when the neck was removed, microorganisms in the air could enter the fermentable material and proliferate. Thus, Pasteur showed that life came from previ-ously existing organisms and their reproductive
35 elements, such as eggs and spores or, in the case of van Helmont's "recipe," adult mice that crept into the jar. Announcing his results to the French Academy, Pasteur proclaimed, "Never will the doctrine of spontaneous generation arise from
40 this mortal blow."

    But Pasteur, for all his brilliance, wasn't entirely correct. The first "life," if we can call it that, appears to have assembled over the course of millions of years of random collisions of
45 nonliving molecules in the chemical-rich caul-dron of early Earth, until, by chance, very basic self-replicating units formed. These first self-replicating units, which arose almost 4 billion years ago, are most likely the ancestors we share
50 with every living thing on earth today. But with no scientist to witness it, how can we know that the dawn of life happened that way? The evidence is embedded in the complex molecules common to all living things—DNA, RNA, proteins, lipids, hor
55 mones—which can be painstakingly traced back to simpler chemicals that most likely preceded them in the family tree. Even more profoundly, astrophysicists can now trace the building blocks of life—carbon, nitrogen, and oxygen—to a spec
60 tacular birth inside ancient exploding stars!

1

The author regards the examples listed in lines 5–7 as

A) scientific frauds

B) astonishing discoveries

C) faulty conclusions

D) quaint traditions

2

Which choice provides the best evidence for the answer to the previous question?

A) Lines 1–4 ("In ancient . . . material")

B) Lines 7–10 ("Warmth . . . organisms")

C) Lines 21–23 ("In 1861 . . . matter")

D) Lines 30–32 ("But when . . . proliferate")

3

Louis Pasteur would most likely fault the "recipe" described in lines 15–20 for its lack of

A) scientific controls

B) quantitative precision

C) fermentable material

D) airborne microorganisms

4

In line 40, "mortal" most nearly means

A) human

B) earthly

C) bitter

D) fatal

5

The final paragraph suggests that Pasteur was mistaken about

A) the chemical composition of living cells

B) the possibility of life arising from nonliving matter

C) when the earliest forms of life arose on Earth

D) the existence of a common ancestor to all living things

6

In line 46, "basic" most nearly means

A) innate

B) quintessential

C) easily understood

D) rudimentary

7

In the final paragraph, the author characterizes the early earth primarily as

A) idyllic

B) mysterious

C) perilous

D) chaotic

8

Which best describes the content and organization of the passage as a whole?

A) the account of a discovery followed by a discussion of its practical applications

B) the description of a common belief followed by a presentation of the evidence refuting it

C) the illustration of a complex theory followed by a consideration of its inadequacies

D) the story of the struggles of a scientist followed by an appreciation of his legacy

The Three Secondary Questions

Lesson 6: Ask, "How does the author use language?"

Good writers choose their words carefully. Each word should serve a purpose in conveying an idea or tone to the reader. Often, SAT Reading questions ask you to determine the meaning or tone of particular words or phrases based on context.

How to attack word-in-context questions

Word-in-context questions test your "verbal inference" skills, that is, your ability to determine the meanings of words by how they are used in context. Here's an example:

> In line 24, the word "decline" most nearly means . . .

The word *decline* isn't really a **challenging** word. Instead, it's an **ambiguous** word. That is, it has a variety of possible meanings. It can mean "politely refuse," "diminish in strength," or "move downward." Its meaning depends on its context.

To attack a word-in-context question, reread the sentence in which the word is used, recalling the purpose of that paragraph and the specific meaning of that sentence. Then think of a word or phrase you could replace the word with without altering the meaning of the sentence, and then find its best match among the choices.

Check your answer by rereading the sentence with the replacement word or phrase. Make sure the resulting sentence sounds okay, that is, it conveys the proper meaning and tone, and it follows Standard English idiom.

Consider question 4 in Exercise 2:

4. In line 40, "mortal" most nearly means

A) human

B) earthly

C) bitter

D) fatal

We can use the word *mortal* in many different ways. In *Socrates is merely mortal*, it means "human." In *The coffin contained our dog's mortal remains*, it means "earthly."

In *They were mortal enemies*, it means "bitter." In *The infection turned out to be a mortal one*, it means "fatal." So answering this question requires knowing more than the definition of *mortal*; it requires understanding the context of this particular sentence. When Pasteur said, *"Never will the doctrine of spontaneous generation arise from this mortal blow,"* he meant that the doctrine is as dead as an opponent who has been struck with a sword. Therefore, in this context, *mortal* means "fatal," and the correct answer is D.

How to attack tone questions

The SAT Reading question will sometimes ask about the **tone or attitude** conveyed by the passage as a whole or in particular words or phrases. Here are some examples:

> The author's attitude toward the "critics" (line 22) can best be described as

> The tone of lines 13–16 ("It was not until. . . . emergency") is one of

When attacking tone questions, make sure to first recall the *overall* tone of the passage, and think about how the specified portion fits the overall tone. For instance, imagine that a question asks about the tone of a discussion about "voodoo practices." In an expository essay about Caribbean anthropology, this discussion may have an "objective" tone. In a rhetorical essay about the dangers of superstitious behavior, it may have a "disdainful" tone. In a narrative about a woman's fond recollections of her grandmother's rituals, it may have an "affectionate" tone. **Don't assume that the author's attitude toward a topic matches your own.**

Before choosing an answer that suggests a very strong tone, like "alarmism," "glorification," or "disgust," **make sure that you can justify your choice with literal evidence from the passage**.

When answering tone or attitude questions, **pay attention to the voice of the speaker**. Does the line in question represent the opinion of the author, or the opinion of someone else? Does it represent a point of view the author agrees with, or disagrees with?

Consider question 7 in Exercise 2:

7. In the final paragraph, the author characterizes the early Earth primarily as

   A) idyllic

   B) mysterious

   C) perilous

   D) chaotic

The passage is Exercise 2 is an **expository essay**, and therefore has an **objective overall purpose**. This means that the **author's point of view** is not at issue here. However, the author may still use language to convey tone. In the final paragraph, early Earth is described as a *chemical-rich cauldron* in which, *by chance*, the first self-replicating chemical units were formed. Although this is obviously not a portrayal of an *idyllic* ("blissful") scene, a *chemical-rich cauldron* could certainly be *mysterious*, *perilous*, or *chaotic*. So which tone does the author primarily mean to convey?

To answer this question, as with so many SAT Reading questions, we must step back and look at the bigger picture. The point of this paragraph is that the earliest life most likely arose from the hot, seething, bubbling mixture of gas and liquid that pervaded the earth billions of years ago. In other words, the author describes a *chaotic* world. He is not portraying early Earth as *mysterious*, because he is claiming to understand important aspects of that ancient environment. He is also not portraying the early Earth as *perilous*, because no creatures yet existed to suffer its dangers.

Exercise 3

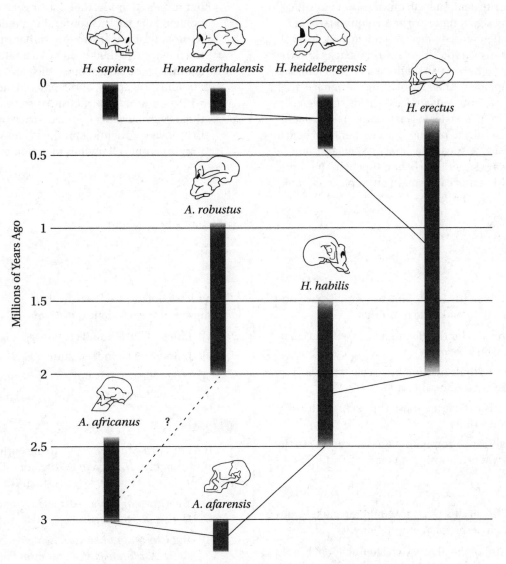

Hominid Family Tree

©2015 Christopher F. Black and College Hill Coaching.

This passage is adapted from John R. Skoyles and Dorion Sagan, *Up from Dragons*. ©2002 The McGraw-Hill Companies. Here, the authors discuss the evolution of human intelligence.

Line

We are a bright species. We have gone into space and walked on the moon. Yet you would never have guessed that if you traveled back to between 100,000 and 40,000 years ago. At
5 that time our *Homo sapiens* ancestors and Neanderthals (*Homo neanderthalensis*) coexisted. Neanderthals were like us but physically stronger, with large bones and teeth, protruding brows and face, and hardly a chin. Perhaps
10 what we lacked in brawn we made up for in

brains. But for most of our history, our species was not bright enough to act very differently from the Neanderthals, let alone be more successful than they were. Only around 40,000 to
15 32,000 years ago, in Western Asia and Europe, did Neanderthal people disappear, to be replaced by our species.

Why did we coexist with Neanderthals for 60,000 years—a far longer case of hominids living
20 side by side than any other in human history? And why did we eventually win out? Brains alone cannot provide the answer, as Neanderthals may in fact have had the larger ones. Perhaps they lacked the long vocal chamber needed for speech. Equal
25 certainty exists among those who study the base

of their skulls that they did and that they did not. If they did lack one, then this could be the explanation, but maybe not, since even without a voice box, gestures can communicate, as can be seen
30 among the deaf. Indeed, hunters find advantages in using sign language (speech sounds would warn off potential prey), and not just while hunting but in everyday life. Anthropologists find that hunter-gatherers use sophisticated sign languages
35 to complement their speech. Sign language might even have other advantages—evidence even suggests that it is easier to learn than speech: deaf children start to pick up signs earlier than hearing ones learn to speak. So "spoken speech" is not
40 in all ways superior to "signed speech." It is not something that can explain our replacement of the Neanderthals.

The reason we—anatomically modern humans—won out lies, we suspect, not in being
45 brighter or better able to speak but in our very physical frailty and our resulting need to exploit our minds. Neanderthals, stronger than us, did not need to take this route. They could survive with their physical strength rather than tapping
50 the potential of their brains. An analogy is with countries: the richest ones, such as Switzerland, Finland, Singapore, and Japan, are not blessed with, but rather lack, natural resources. Without them, they have been forced to use their brains
55 to innovate, providing products and services ranging from cell phones to diplomacy.

1

The authors use the phrase "equal certainty" (lines 24–25) to make the point that

A) the reason for the Neanderthals' extinction is now well known

B) Neanderthals may not have coexisted with modern humans after all

C) scientists disagree about the vocal ability of Neanderthals

D) the ability to communicate is necessary to the survival of a hunting species

2

The authors of this passage would most likely agree with which of the following statements?

A) anthropological research should adopt higher standards of evidence

B) physical weakness is not necessarily a disadvantage in the fight for survival

C) Neanderthals lacked the vocal ability to develop sophisticated language

D) modern humans could not have achieved as much without the help of the Neanderthals

3

Which choice provides the best evidence for the answer to the previous question?

A) Lines 24–26 ("Equal certainty . . . did not")

B) Lines 30–33 ("Indeed, hunters . . . everyday life")

C) Lines 40–42 ("It is not . . . the Neanderthals")

D) Lines 43–47 ("The reason . . . our minds")

4

The term *Cro-Magnon* refers to the earliest members of the species *H. sapiens*. Which of following statements is most justified by the diagram in Figure 1?

A) The *Cro-Magnon* are direct descendants of *H. neanderthalensis*.

B) The *Cro-Magnon* and *H. heidelbergensis* both share *A. afarensis* as a common ancestor.

C) Competition with the *Cro-Magnon* led to the extinction of *H. erectus*.

D) The *Cro-Magnon* and *A. robustus* both descended from *H. habilis*.

5

If the fossil record indicated in the accompanying diagram is assumed to be accurate and complete, what is the longest period of time that any single hominid species lived on the earth?

A) 1,000,000 years

B) 1,250,000 years

C) 1,750,000 years

D) 2,000,000 years

6

Which of the following best describes how the diagram supports the main argument of this passage?

A) It shows that hominid species have existed for over 2,000,000 years.

B) It shows that *H. neanderthalensis* had a long vocal chamber.

C) It shows that *H. sapiens* and *H. neanderthalensis* both existed in the period between 100,000 and 40,000 years ago.

D) It shows that *H. sapiens* and *H. neanderthalensis* had a common ancestor.

7

The authors mention that "hunter-gatherers use sophisticated sign language" (line 34) primarily in order to

A) refute a common misconception about hunter-gatherers

B) specify the mechanism by which modern humans came to replace Neanderthals

C) bolster their claim about the larger brain size of Neanderthals

D) suggest that long vocal chambers might not provide a decisive evolutionary advantage

8

In line 49, "tapping" most nearly means

A) exploiting

B) exhausting

C) nominating

D) monitoring

9

The authors mention "cell phones" and "diplomacy" (line 56) primarily as examples of

A) universally admired commercial products

B) effective means of global communication

C) goods and services based on intellectual resources

D) activities that require little physical strength

Lesson 7: Ask, "How does the author use evidence?"

Always be ready to justify your answer to any SAT Reading question, and to answer **literal evidence** questions and **quantitative evidence** questions.

How to attack literal evidence questions

Literal evidence questions are of the form

> Which choice provides the best evidence for the answer to the previous question?

Every literal evidence question asks you to find a specific line in the passage that directly supports the point in the previous question. Make sure that the evidence you cite in the passage is **clear, direct evidence**, and does not require any broad inferences or dramatic leap of logic.

Consider questions 1 and 2 in Exercise 2:

1. The author regards the examples listed in lines 5–7 as

    A) scientific frauds

    B) astonishing discoveries

    C) faulty conclusions

    D) quaint traditions

2. Which choice provides the best evidence for the answer to the previous question?

    A) Lines 1–4 ("In ancient . . . material")

    B) Lines 7–10 ("Warmth . . . organisms")

    C) Lines 21–23 ("In 1861 . . . matter")

    D) Lines 30–32 ("But when . . . proliferate")

Lines 5–7 list the following examples: *frogs appeared to arise from damp earth, mice from putrefied matter, insects from dew, and maggots from decaying meat.* In line 1, the author indicates that these are things that *people commonly believed* in ancient times. But the passage then goes on to explain that these beliefs are mistaken, and that life in fact does not arise that way. Therefore, the answer to question 1 is C: *faulty conclusions.*

What literal evidence best shows that the author regards these statements as *faulty conclusions*? In lines 21–23, the author states that *in fact, living organisms cannot so easily arise from nonliving matter.* Notice that this is a **clear, direct statement** that the author regards the beliefs listed in lines 5–7 as *faulty conclusions.* Therefore, the correct answer to question 2 is C. Choice A is incorrect because lines 1–4 simply state that ancient people believed these things, not that the author disagrees. Choice B is incorrect because lines 7–10 just give details about these beliefs, but no indication that the author doesn't share them. Choice D is incorrect because lines 30–32 just give a detail about Pasteur's experiment, and no direct indication that the author disagrees with the list of beliefs.

Consider questions 2 and 3 in Exercise 3:

2. The authors of this passage would most likely agree with which of the following statements?

    A) anthropological research should adopt higher standards of evidence

    B) physical weakness is not necessarily a disadvantage in the fight for survival

    C) Neanderthals lacked the vocal ability to develop sophisticated language

    D) modern humans could not have achieved as much without the help of the Neanderthals

3. Which choice provides the best evidence for the answer to the previous question?

    A) Lines 24–26 ("Equal certainty . . . did not")

    B) Lines 30–33 ("Indeed, hunters . . . everyday life")

    C) Lines 40–42 ("It is not . . . the Neanderthals")

    D) Lines 43–47 ("The reason . . . our minds")

The answer to question 2 is B: *physical weakness is not necessarily a disadvantage in the fight for survival.* How do we know? Because this is a direct implication of the main thesis that humans came to dominate the Neanderthals by taking advantage of their intellectual abilities rather than relying on their physical strength.

Where is the best literal evidence for this? In lines 43–47, where the authors state their main thesis: *The reason we—anatomically modern humans—won out lies, we sus-pect, not in being brighter or better able to speak but in our very physical frailty and our resulting need to exploit our minds.* Therefore, the correct answer to question 3 is choice D. Choice A is incorrect because this sentence merely states that scientists disagree about the length of the Neanderthal vocal chamber. Choice B is incorrect because this sentence merely states that hunters some-times find it helpful to communicate silently. Choice C is incorrect because this sentence merely states that the ability to speak cannot explain our dominance over the Neanderthals.

How to attack quantitative evidence questions

Quantitative evidence questions ask about the content of graphs, tables, or diagrams that may be associated with the passage. Here are some examples:

> Which claim about the United States prison population is best supported by the graph in Figure 1?

> Which of the following best describes how Figure 1 supports the main argument of this passage?

As with literal evidence questions, quantita-tive evidence questions require you to identify the **clear and direct** evidence contained in the graph, table, or diagram.

When interpreting data, remember that **correla-tion does not imply causation**: the mere fact that quantity B goes up at the same time that (or soon after) quantity A goes up does **not** mean that A *causes* B.

Consider questions 4, 5, and 6 in Exercise 3:

4. The term *Cro-Magnon* refers to the earliest mem-bers of the species *H. sapiens*. Which of following statements is most justified by the diagram in Figure 1?

   A) The *Cro-Magnon* are direct descendants of H. neanderthalensis.

   B) The *Cro-Magnon* and *H. heidelbergensis* both share *A. afarensis* as a common ancestor.

   C) Competition with the *Cro-Magnon* led to the extinction of *H. erectus*.

   D) The *Cro-Magnon* and *A. robustus* both descended from *H. habilis*.

5. If the fossil record indicated in the diagram in Figure 1 is assumed to be accurate and complete, what is the longest period of time that any single hominid species lived on the earth?

   A) 1,000,000 years

   B) 1,250,000 years

   C) 1,750,000 years

   D) 2,000,000 years

6. Which of the following best describes how Figure 1 supports the main argument of this passage?

   A) It shows that hominid species have existed for over 2,000,000 years.

   B) It shows that *H. neanderthalensis* had a long vocal chamber.

   C) It shows that *H. sapiens* and *H. neanderthalensis* both existed between 100,000 and 40,000 years ago.

   D) It shows that *H. sapiens* and *H. neanderthalensis* had a common ancestor.

The figure shows a "family tree" of hominid species going back approximately 3 million years. The vertical bars represent the approximate time periods in which each species lived (according to the fossil record), and lines between species indicate the most likely lines of heritage. The dotted line in the lower left portion of the diagram indicates some uncertainty about whether or not *A. robustus* descended from *A. africanus*.

The correct answer to question 4 is B. The undot-ted lines in the diagram indicate that *H. sapiens* (which includes the *Cro-Magnon*) descended from *H. heidel-bergensis*, which descended from *H. erectus*, which descended from *H. habilis*, which descended from *A. afarensis*. Therefore, the *Cro-Magnon* and *H. heidelber-gensis* both share *A. afarensis* as a common ancestor. Choice A is incorrect because the diagram shows no line of descent from *H. neanderthalensis* to *H. sapiens*. Choice C is incorrect because the diagram contains no information about the reasons for extinction. Choice D is incorrect because there is no line of descent from *H. habilis* to *A. robustus*.

The correct answer to question 5 is C. The longest vertical bar for any hominid species is that for *H. erectus*, which begins at about the 2-million-year mark and ends at about the 250,000-year mark. Subtracting these two values gives us a time span of about 1,750,000 years.

The correct answer to question 6 is C. Although statements A and D are both valid conclusions based on the information in the diagram, neither of these facts supports the main argument of the passage, which is found in lines 43–47: *The reason we—anatomically modern humans—won out [in our competition with the Neanderthals] lies, we suspect, not in being brighter or better able to speak but in our very physical frailty and our resulting need to exploit our minds.* Therefore, the argument rests on the fact that *H. sapiens* coexisted with *H. neanderthalensis*. The diagram clearly shows that both species lived in the period between approximately 100,000 years ago and 40,000 years ago, and so could have been in direct competition. It also shows that *H. neanderthalensis* appears to have gone extinct, because its vertical bar does not reach all the way up to the 0 mark.

Lesson 8: Ask, "How does the author use rhetorical devices?"

The SAT Reading test may ask you about the **rhetorical effect** of particular sections of the passage. These questions test your ability to recognize particular **rhetorical and literary devices** that the author may use to persuade the reader.

---

16 Basic Stylistic and Rhetorical Devices

An **ad hominem** is an attack "on the person" rather than an attack on his or her ideas or reasoning. For example, *Her political opinions can't be trusted because she is just an actress* is not an argument, but merely an ad hominem.

An **allusion** is an implicit reference to something. For example, the statement *He's gone down the rabbit hole* is an allusion to the bizarre and fanciful episodes in the story *Alice in Wonderland*.

An **analogy** is an illustrative comparison between things that have a similar function or structure. For example, the levels of processing in a computer provide an analogy for understanding levels of processing in the human brain.

An **anecdote** is an illustrative story. For example, a story about a friend whose headache went away after he stood on his head for ten minutes is anecdotal evidence, not scientific evidence, for the health benefits of inversion.

An **aphorism** is a widely accepted truth. For example, the aphorism *If it ain't broke, don't fix it* can provide a concise argument against spending a lot of money on a new program. Aphorisms are also called **maxims**, **adages**, or **proverbs**.

An **appeal to authority** is a suggestion that the reader should agree with an idea because a respected authority happens to believe it. For example: *The world's greatest scientist, Sir Isaac Newton, believed that iron could be turned into gold, so who are we to question the idea?*

An **appeal to emotion** is an attempt to persuade the reader through an emotionally charged anecdote or allusion. For example, a story about an infuriating experience with an insurance salesman may be an effective way to argue against aggressive sales tactics.

Characterization is the use of imagery, diction, or description to convey a particular attitude toward a person, thing, or idea. For example, referring to a proposal as a *scheme* characterizes it as being deceitful.

A **euphemism** is a term that makes something seem more positive than it is. For example, salespersons or political canvassers often use the term *courtesy call* as a euphemism for an unwanted disruption.

Hyperbole is deliberate exaggeration for persuasive effect. For example, saying that *Molly's comma usage is a catastrophe* is almost certainly hyperbole.

Irony is a deliberate reversal of expectations in order to surprise a reader. For example, Christopher Hitchens justified his attitude toward free will by using irony: *I believe in free will, because I have no other choice.*

A **metaphor** is an application of a word or phrase to something it doesn't literally apply to. For example, calling a refusal a *slap in the face* uses metaphor to emphasize its harshness.

Rhetorical **parallelism** is the use of repeated grammatical form to emphasize a point. For example, John F. Kennedy used parallelism in his inaugural address when he said *we shall pay any price, bear any burden, meet any hardship, support any friend, oppose any foe to assure the survival and the success of liberty.*

Personification is the attribution of personal qualities to something that is not a person. For example, we are using rhetorical personification when we say that an idea is *on its last legs* or *gave its last gasp.*

A **simile** is a comparison using *like* or *as*. For instance, Irena Dunn used rhetorical simile when she said *A woman without a man is like a fish without a bicycle.*

An **understatement** encourages the reader to complete a point by suggesting that it is less significant than it obviously is. For instance, it's quite an understatement to say that *Donald Trump is a tad self-absorbed.*

Consider questions 4 and 5 from Exercise 1:

4. The passage includes all of the following EXCEPT

    A) ad hominem

    B) verifiable statistics

    C) amusing illustration

    D) social assessment

5. In line 32, the author's use of the word "penetrating" is an example of

    A) subtle euphemism

    B) deliberate hyperbole

    C) sincere acclamation

    D) ironic sarcasm

The correct answer to question 4 is A: *ad hominem*. Although the passage criticizes widespread innumeracy, at no point does the author attack anyone personally. Choice B is incorrect because the author uses verifiable statistics liberally in the first, second, third, and sixth paragraphs. Choice C is incorrect because the joke

described in the fourth paragraph is an *amusing illustration*. Choice D is incorrect because the passage makes a *social assessment* in lines 32–34 when he states that *[t]his tendency to personalize is a characteristic of many who suffer from innumeracy*, and again in lines 52–53 when he states that *we too often lack an intuitive grasp for these numbers*.

The correct answer to question 5 is D: *ironic sarcasm*. The author states that *the innumerate will inevitably respond with the non sequitur, "Yes, but what if you're that one," and then nod knowingly, as if they've demolished your argument with penetrating insight* (lines 28–32). In other words, the *penetrating insight* is really not *penetrating* at all: it is a *non sequitur* (a statement that does not follow logically from the premises). The author is using the word *penetrating* ironically and sarcastically. Choice A is incorrect, because the author is not using the word *penetrating* to make the insight seem more positive than it is. In fact, he is criticizing, not euphemizing. Choice B is incorrect because the author is not using exaggeration for rhetorical effect. Choice C is incorrect because *penetrating* is not intended as an *acclamation* (word of praise).

Advanced SAT Reading Techniques

Lesson 9: Master the "preemptive attack" strategies

Which is the best way to attack SAT Reading *passages*?

    A. *Read the **questions** first, then go back to the passage and look for the answers to those particular questions.*

    B. *Read the **passage** first, with the key questions in mind, then attack the questions with the passage summary in mind.*

Which is the best way to attack SAT Reading *questions*?

    C. *Read the question, check any line references, then read all of the choices, crossing out the "unreasonable" answers, then choose the most reasonable choice that remains.*

    D. *Read the question, check any line references, then answer it in your own mind before looking at any of the choices, then choose the answer that best matches yours.*

These two questions have been roundly debated in the SAT prep industry for decades. I've seen hundreds of students use all of these strategies, and in my experience, the most reliable attack strategy is the **"preemptive attack" strategy**.

The "preemptive attack" strategy for SAT Reading

- **Attack the passage before it attacks you**. Some test takers try to outsmart the SAT Reading Test by reading the questions first before reading the passage, so they have a "head start." The problem with this strategy is that **it forces you to read inefficiently and incompletely by wasting time on details, thereby putting you at a disadvantage on "main purpose" or "main idea" questions.** If, instead, you read with your attention on **purpose**, **central idea**, and **structure**, you will be more prepared for any reading question the SAT may throw at you.

- **Attack the question before it traps you**. That is, formulate your own answer to each reading question before looking at the answer choices. Some test takers think they are saving time by reading the answer choices immediately after reading each question. The problem with this strategy is that **those who read the answer choices too soon tend to fall for the "traps."**

The "traps" are the wrong answer choices that are included to catch careless readers. They sound plausible because they include words or ideas that remind you of the content of the passage, but they do not answer the question correctly. If, instead, you formulate a reliable answer in mind before reading the choices, you will avoid the traps.

Consider question 9 from Exercise 3:

    9. The authors mention "cell phones" and "diplomacy" (line 56) primarily as examples of

        A) universally admired commercial products

        B) effective means of global communication

        C) goods and services based on intellectual resources

        D) activities that require little physical strength

This question can easily trip you up if you do not use the preemptive attack strategy. If you try to answer it without understanding the "big picture," you will focus on the sentences in the vicinity of line 56. This paragraph mentions that these are *products and services* (line 55) coming from *Switzerland, Finland, Singapore, and Japan* (lines 51–52), so choice A: *universally coveted commercial products* may seem reasonable. It is also obvious that *cell phones* and *diplomacy* are *effective means of global communication*, so choice B also may seem reasonable. The paragraph also mentions using *physical strength rather than tapping the potential of their brains* (lines 49–50), so choice D may seem reasonable, as well.

But all of those choices are traps.

Instead, attack this question "preemptively." First, read the passage and summarize it in terms of the three key questions: it is a **rhetorical essay** arguing for the **thesis** that *the reason [Homo sapiens won out over the Neanderthals] lies, we suspect, not in being brighter or better able to speak but in our very frailty and our resulting need to exploit our minds*. Then translate question 9 into an open-ended question: *the authors mention "cell phones" and "diplomacy" primarily as examples of* what? If these examples serve the purpose of the essay (which of course they do), then they are examples of how countries also *exploit their minds* rather than relying on natural resources. Therefore the correct answer is C: *goods and services based on intellectual resources*. Notice that choices A, B, and D don't fit at all with the purpose of the paragraph.

Exercise 4

This passage is from C. F. Black, "The Evolution of Explanation." ©2015 Christopher F. Black and College Hill Coaching. Reprinted by permission of the author.

Line   The march of human intellectual progress over the last 2,500 years has been, in brief, a journey from teleological to mechanistic explanations. We have moved, slowly and tortuously,
5   from beliefs about the "purpose" of phenomena like lightning and earthquakes to debates about which theories, equations, and mechanisms best represent them. We've deepened our understandings by strengthening our mode of explanation.
10   But we can't pat ourselves on the back just yet. We are all—even the most scientific among us—still plagued by faulty intuitions.

        We are all born teleologists. From the Latin "telos" or "goal," teleology is the act of explaining
15   phenomena in terms of their presumed purposes or desires, rather than their causes: we have brains so we can think, the sun shines so we can be warm, rain falls so we can have fresh water. Such explanations come so easily to us that we
20   find it hard to appreciate how misguided and unhelpful they are. They fail because they can't predict the future as accurately as mechanistic explanations can: the laws of chemistry predict reactions, the laws of fluid dynamics predict
25   tomorrow's weather, and the laws of physics predict when and where our interplanetary probes will land.

        Teleological explanations seem intuitive because our consciousness is a constant stream
30   of urge followed by action: we are thirsty so we get some water, we are frightened so we run away, we want to make a friend so we say hello. These urge-action connections are so constant inside of our brains that we fool ourselves into thinking
35   that they apply outside of our brains as well. We program ourselves to mistake urges for causes.

        Teleological explanations fail when we try to describe phenomena that are outside of our

skulls: rocks do not fall because they want to
40   return to the earth, tornadoes don't form because the sky gods are angry. We know now that rocks and clouds lack the mental machinery required for desire or anger. The real explanations for these phenomena are found in the mechanisms of
45   physics and meteorology.

        Still, when a friend asks you why you're not going to a party, you're not going to describe the mechanisms by which your brain processed the information, weighing rational and emotional
50   inputs in various cortical and limbic centers, and produced a decision-response. You're just going to say you don't want to go. In personal conversations, teleological explanations are fine, if crude.

        Even the most clear-minded scientist slides
55   into teleology from time to time when describing natural phenomena to laypeople. When, in a recent documentary, evolutionary biologist Neil Shubin stated that "to combat the dry air on land, reptiles evolved a new kind of skin" he wasn't
60   disavowing the theory of natural selection and embracing the belief that an animal can evolve a feature just to satisfy a need. He was merely trying to explain something complex in terms we could understand.

65   The superior accuracy of mechanistic explanations comes at a price. They are not only more complex, but also more unsettling. If I skipped the party because of electro-chemical reactions governed by the laws of physics and chemistry,
70   where is my free will?

        We will only continue our progress toward deeper understanding if we see our self-centered intuitions as obstacles rather than guides to our pursuit. If we are to cure diseases, eradicate
75   social scourges, and create a better world, we must embrace the disciplined, if counterintuitive, methods of scientific mechanism.

1

The first paragraph characterizes the "march of human intellectual progress" as

A) halting

B) inspirational

C) misguided

D) controversial

2

The first paragraph is notable primarily for its use of

A) euphemism

B) understatement

C) metaphor

D) anecdote

3

In line 3, "mechanistic" most nearly means

A) unemotional

B) automatic

C) complex

D) scientific

4

To the author, the examples in lines 16–18 ("we have brains . . . fresh water") primarily represent

A) scientific theories

B) beneficial circumstances

C) unsound beliefs

D) unintuitive phenomena

5

The author faults teleological explanations primarily for their

A) imprecision

B) intuitiveness

C) conciseness

D) impenetrability

6

Which choice provides the best evidence for the answer to the previous question?

A) Lines 3–7 ("We have moved . . . represent them")

B) Lines 19–21 ("Such explanations . . . they are")

C) Lines 21–27 ("They fail . . . will land")

D) Lines 28–32 ("Teleological explanations . . . say hello")

7

According to the author, Neil Shubin's error was that he

A) failed to appreciate the education level of his audience

B) confused purpose with cause in a scientific explanation

C) used a complex metaphor to describe a simple concept

D) did not properly define technical terms

8

The main function of the seventh paragraph (lines 65–70) is to

A) concede a drawback

B) propose an alternative

C) address an injustice

D) correct a misunderstanding

9

The tone of the final paragraph (lines 71–77) is best described as

A) beseeching

B) jocular

C) sardonic

D) journalistic

Lesson 10: Play "devil's advocate"

Strong analytical readers use the strategy of "devil's advocate," that is, they **read not just to understand the passage, but to criticize it**. Even if you are absorbed by the discussion, agree with the argument, or identify with the narrative, you will understand and appreciate it more deeply if you take a critical stance.

If the passage is **expository**, ask

How could the descriptions or explanations in this passage be clearer or more effective?

Does the author leave any relevant questions unanswered?

Is the passage logically and effectively organized?

If the passage is **rhetorical**, ask

Did the author address alternate points of view on this subject?

What kind of evidence would weaken this argument or point of view?

What could the author do to make this essay more persuasive?

If the passage is a **narrative**, ask

Is the conflict or struggle indicated clearly?

Are the characterizations effective?

Is the dialogue realistic, given the time, place, and circumstance?

The passage in Exercise 4 is a rhetorical essay, but since the topic is unfamiliar to most readers, it also contains a healthy dose of exposition. Its **rhetorical thesis** is that mechanistic explanations are more reliable, if less intuitive, than teleological explanations. The **expository guiding question** is *What are the two "modes of explanation," and what are they good for?*

So think about the critical questions for expository and rhetorical essays, and apply them to the passage in Exercise 4. How do you think the author did? Were the explanations clear? Was the analysis thorough? Was the passage organized logically? Did the author address alternate points of view? Is there evidence that could weaken its thesis? Could it have been more persuasive?

Consider questions 8 and 9 from Exercise 4:

8. The main function of the seventh paragraph (lines 65–70) is to

   A) concede a drawback
   B) propose an alternative
   C) address an injustice
   D) correct a misunderstanding

9. The tone of the final paragraph (lines 71–77) is best described as

   A) beseeching
   B) jocular
   C) sardonic
   D) journalistic

If you are reading with the "devil's advocate" questions in mind, you should notice that the seventh paragraph plays a special role. It is **acknowledging an alternate point of view**, which is that mechanistic explanations of our own decisions seem to deny the possibility of free will. Therefore, the correct answer to question 8 is A: *concede a drawback*.

Understanding the rhetorical function of the seventh paragraph makes it easier to understand the tone of the final paragraph. Since the author has **conceded a drawback** to his thesis, he must work harder to demonstrate its validity. Therefore, he uses *beseeching* language, like *only . . . if*, and *must*. Therefore, the answer to question 9 is A.

When you keep the critical questions in mind, you sharpen your reading skills by bringing higher-order reasoning to bear. You also hone the analytical skills you need to attack the SAT Essay, which asks you to write a critical analysis of a rhetorical essay.

Lesson 11: Mark up the passage

A great way to maintain your focus on an SAT Reading passage is to mark it up by underlining and annotating. But do it thoughtfully and carefully. Here are some tips for using underlining and annotating as **analytical tools**.

- **Read the entire paragraph** before underlining or annotating. You can't be sure of the overall idea and purpose until you read the entire paragraph.
- **Don't overdo it.** Underlining and annotation should be tools for comprehension, not just ways of keeping track of what you've read. Try to limit yourself to one underlined sentence or one brief note per paragraph.

- **Focus on purpose and central idea.** If you want to underline, underline only the topic sentence. If you want to annotate, note only the purpose and main idea.
- **Circle key abstractions.** Abstractions like *empiricism* and *modernism* are harder to understand than concrete objects or experiences like *hummingbirds* and *football games*. So circle the key abstractions, if only to slow down and think about them. For instance, in Exercise 4, you might circle words like *progress*, *teleological*, and *mechanistic*. If you don't stop and think about these abstractions, you can't understand the passage.

Lesson 12: Learn how to attack the paired passages

The SAT Reading Test will include **paired passages** on a common topic, followed by questions in which you may be asked to compare or contrast the perspectives, content, or tone of the passages.

When given **paired passages** on the SAT Reading Test, you may be asked to answer questions like these:

- What is the common topic of the two passages?
- How do the two passages differ in attitude or tone?

- How do the two passages differ in emphasis?
- Are there any important points of disagreement?

Read paired passages just as you would normal SAT Reading passages, but with particular attention to important differences in content, attitude, and tone.

Exercise 5

Passage 1 from Teresa Audesirk, Gerald Audesirk, and Bruce E. Byers, Biology: Life on Earth. ©2006 Pearson Education, Inc.

Passage 1

Line The study of life on Earth ultimately involves the study of the molecules of which living organisms are composed. How does photosynthesis convert the energy of sunlight into the energy of
5 sugar molecules? What is the structure of the cell membrane, and how does it function in controlling the movement of materials into and out of the cell? How do muscles contract? How do the nerve cells in your brain communicate with one
10 another? What causes cancer? To understand the answers to these questions, you must first learn about energy and matter, the properties of atoms, and how atoms interact with one another to form molecules.

Passage 2

15 The idea that photosynthesis is essential to life has long been fundamental to our understanding of Earth's biosystems. If the sun were to go out, we assumed, life would soon follow. Yet in the 1970s, scientists discovered organisms thriving in
20 deep-sea hydrothermal vents far from any solar energy. These organisms rely on bacteria that harvest energy not from light but from the chemical bonds in sulfides and other molecules in a process called chemosynthesis. Other more complex
25 organisms then incorporate the living bacteria into their tissues. Such relationships mirror the myriad complex relationships we see in the photosynthetic food chain, in which bacteria are incorporated into organisms to provide benefits
30 such as breaking down or synthesizing chemicals that the organisms' own tissues cannot.

1

Which question posed in Passage 1 most directly concerns the author of Passage 2?

A) Lines 3–5 ("How does photosynthesis . . . molecules?")

B) Lines 5–8 ("What is the structure . . . the cell?")

C) Lines 8–10 ("How do the nerve . . . one another?")

D) Line 10 ("What causes cancer?")

2

Both passages are primarily concerned with

A) the complexity of structures in living tissue

B) the origin and evolution of life on Earth

C) the chemical processes that sustain life

D) the symbiotic relationship among species

3

The questions in lines 3–10 represent

A) points of scientific controversy

B) sources of frustration to biologists

C) areas of productive inquiry

D) inspirations for recent innovations

4

The "bacteria" mentioned in line 28 are best regarded as

A) insidious infections

B) exotic parasites

C) symbiotic partners

D) rudimentary progenitors

5

The author of Passage 2 would most likely suggest that the discussion of "life on Earth" (line 1) in Passage 1 also include mention of

A) atypical sources of energy

B) long extinct life forms

C) parasitic relationships among species

D) the human role in preserving biodiversity

6

Which of the following is most representative of the "complex relationships" mentioned in line 27?

A) a species of deciduous tree competing with another species for exposure to sunlight

B) a fungus living within a grass plant that renders the grass more drought resistant

C) a human white blood cell destroying invasive bacteria in an infection

D) a mother bear protecting her cub by charging an intruder

7

In line 18, the phrase "we assumed" suggests that biologists

A) accepted a proposition uncritically

B) adopted a significant social role

C) acquired a new research technique

D) overstepped the boundaries of their expertise

Exercise 6

This passage is from Wassily Kandinsky, Concerning the Spiritual in Art. *©1997 Dover Publications. Reprinted by permission of Dover Publications. In this essay, Kandinsky (1866-1944), a Russian abstract painter, discusses the relationship between Primitivism, a movement to revive the art of ancient peoples, and Materialism, a movement that denies the existence or value of the spiritual realm.*

Line Every work of art is the child of its age and, in many cases, the mother of our emotions. It follows that each period of culture produces an art of its own which can never be repeated. Efforts
5 to revive the art-principles of the past will at best produce an art that is stillborn. It is impossible for us to live and feel as did the ancient Greeks. In the same way those who strive to follow the Greek methods in sculpture achieve only a similarity
10 of form, the work remaining soulless for all time. Such imitation is mere aping. Externally the monkey completely resembles the human being; he will sit holding a book in front of his nose, and turn over the pages with a thoughtful aspect, but
15 his actions have for him no real meaning.

There is, however, in art another kind of external similarity that is founded on a fundamental truth. When there is a similarity of inner tendency in the whole moral and spiritual
20 atmosphere, a similarity of ideals, at first closely pursued but later lost to sight, a similarity in the inner feeling of any one period to that of another, the logical result will be a revival of the external forms which served to express those inner feel-
25 ings in an earlier age. An example of this today is our sympathy, our spiritual relationship, with the Primitives. Like ourselves, these artists sought to express in their work only internal truths, renouncing in consequence all considerations
30 of external form.

This all-important spark of inner life today is at present only a spark. Our minds, which are even now only just awakening after years of materialism, are infected with the despair
35 of unbelief, of lack of purpose and ideal. The nightmare of materialism, which has turned the life of the universe into an evil, useless game, is not yet past. It holds the awakening soul still in its grip. Only a feeble light glimmers like a tiny
40 star in a vast gulf of darkness. This feeble light is but a presentiment, and the soul, when it sees it, trembles in doubt whether the light is not a dream, and the gulf of darkness reality. This doubt and the still-harsh tyranny of the material-
45 istic philosophy divide our soul sharply from that of the Primitives. Our soul rings cracked when we seem to play upon it, as does a costly vase, long buried in the earth, which is found to have a flaw when it is dug up once more. For this reason, the
50 Primitive phase, through which we are now passing, with its temporary similarity of form, can only be of short duration.

1

The passage is primarily concerned with

A) the obstacles to a particular undertaking

B) the motivation for a specialized practice

C) the origins of a philosophical debate

D) a contrast between ancient and modern techniques

2

In the first sentence, the contrast between "child" and the "mother" is primarily one of

A) immaturity versus maturity

B) creation versus creator

C) disobedience versus supervision

D) joy versus anxiety

3

In line 14, "aspect" most nearly means

A) particular feature

B) individual perspective

C) degree of feeling

D) facial expression

4

Which of the following best exemplifies the "truth" mentioned in line 18?

A) Many great artists find it difficult to achieve renown in their own lifetimes.

B) Painters and musicians from all cultures tend to eschew materialist conventions.

C) Sculptures celebrating the virtue of liberty share common features across eras.

D) It is impossible to faithfully reproduce cave paintings created in prehistoric times.

5

According to the passage, materialism affects artists primarily by

A) awakening them with a glimmer of inspiration

B) establishing their connection to an earlier time

C) denying them access to meaningful and spiritual activity

D) mocking their attempts to make a living from art

6

Which choice provides the best evidence for the answer to the previous question?

A) Lines 27–30 ("Like ourselves . . . external form")

B) Lines 31–32 ("This all-important . . . a spark")

C) Lines 38–39 ("It holds . . . grip")

D) Lines 46–49 ("Our soul rings . . . once more")

7

The author uses the phrase "trembles in doubt" (line 42) in order to emphasize his belief that

A) philosophers are unsure about the meaning of materialism

B) true artists question whether the era of materialism is truly past

C) highly creative people have only a tenuous grip on reality

D) artists are particularly susceptible to feelings of fear and obsession

8

In line 47, the "costly vase" represents

A) a materialistic aspiration

B) a finely crafted piece of art

C) a cynical attempt at forgery

D) an irretrievable frame of mind

CHAPTER 5 ANSWER KEY

Exercise 1

1. **C** The thesis of the passage is that *[w]ithout some appreciation of common large numbers* and a *feeling for probabilities*, we will overreact to some dangers and underreact to others. In other words, there is some danger inherent in our *common misunderstandings about statistical data*.

2. **B** The author regards these "reports" with *informed incredulity* because he has good reason to believe they are not accurate. He expresses this fact when he suggests that we should regard them with *skepticism* (lines 2–3). (There are only about 74 million kids in the U.S., so if 1 million kids were kidnapped every year, then about 6 kids would be kidnapped from the average American elementary school *every year*.)

3. **A** The list of activities in lines 21–25 are dangerous events that are more probable than terrorism. Therefore, they are *underappreciated dangers*.

4. **A** *Ad hominem* is personal attack. Although the passage criticizes widespread innumeracy, at no point does the author attack anyone personally. Choice B is incorrect because the author uses verifiable statistics liberally in the first, second, third, and sixth paragraphs. Choice C is incorrect because the joke described in the fourth paragraph is an *amusing illustration*. Choice D is incorrect because the passage makes a *social assessment* in lines 32–34 when he states that *[t]his tendency to personalize is a characteristic of many who suffer from innumeracy*, and again in lines 51–52 when he states that *we too often lack an intuitive grasp for these numbers*.

5. **D** The author states that *the innumerate will inevitably respond with the non sequitur, "Yes, but what if you're that one,"* and then nod knowingly, *as if they've demolished your argument with penetrating insight* (lines 28–32). In other words, the *penetrating insight* is really not *penetrating* at all: it is a *non sequitur* (a statement that does not follow logically from the premises). The author is using the word *penetrating* ironically and sarcastically. Choice A is incorrect, because the author is not using the word *penetrating* to make the insight seem more positive than it is. In fact, he is criticizing, not euphemizing. Choice B is incorrect because the author is not using exaggeration for rhetorical effect. Choice C is incorrect because *penetrating* is not intended as an *acclamation* (word of praise).

6. **D** When the author uses the phrase *this tendency to personalize*, he is referring to the *non sequitur* in the previous sentence: *"Yes, but what if you're that one,"* which is an attempt to individualize the horror of terrorism out of the context in which its probability is calculated.

7. **B** The third paragraph (lines 26–38) discusses the tendency of people to overestimate the chances of certain horrific event precisely because they are exotic and attention-grabbing. The *exotic malady* is mentioned as one such *risk that is wildly overestimated*.

8. **A** The first sentence of the passage provides direct evidence that the author believes that people commonly overestimate particular risks, such as *reports that more than a million American kids are kidnapped each year*.

9. **C** The final paragraph mentions Drs. Kronlund and Phillips because their study *showed that most doctors' assessments of the risks of various operations, procedures, and medications were way off the mark*. In other words, they were *fallible* (capable of error) with regard to their own specialties.

Exercise 2

1. **C** Lines 5–7 list the following examples: *frogs appeared to arise from damp earth, mice from putrefied matter, insects from dew, and maggots from decaying meat*. In line 1, the author indicates that these are things that *people commonly believed* in ancient times. But the passage then goes on to explain that these beliefs were mistaken, and that life in fact does not arise that way.

2. **C** In lines 22–23, the author states that *in fact, living organisms cannot so easily arise from nonliving matter*. Notice that this is a clear, direct statement that the author regards the beliefs listed in lines 5–7 as *faulty conclusions*. Therefore, the correct answer to question 2 is C. Choice A is incorrect because lines 1–4 simply state that ancient people believed these things, not that the author disagrees. Choice B is incorrect because lines 7–10 just give details about these beliefs, but no indication that the author doesn't share them. Choice D is incorrect because lines 30–32 just give a detail about Pasteur's experiment, and no direct indication that the author disagrees with the list of beliefs.

3. **A** Lines 21–40 describe Pasteur's experiment, in which he demonstrates that *living organisms*

cannot so easily arise spontaneously from nonliving matter, and that the mice in van Helmont's demonstration likely *crept into the jar.* In other words, van Helmont's recipe lacked scientific controls to keep living things out.

4. **D** When Pasteur said, *"Never will the doctrine of spontaneous generation arise from this mortal blow,"* he meant that the doctrine is as dead as an opponent who has been struck with a sword. Therefore, in this context, *mortal* means "fatal."

5. **B** The final paragraph describes how Pasteur *wasn't entirely correct* about the possibility of life arising from nonliving matter by describing the most likely scenario by which *basic self-replicating units,* the precursors of life, could have arisen from nonliving molecules in the *chemical-rich cauldron of early Earth.*

6. **D** The phrase *very basic self-replicating units* refers to the most *rudimentary* chemical building blocks of life.

7. **D** The point of this paragraph is that the earliest life most likely arose from the *chemical-rich cauldron of early Earth.* In other words, the author describes a *chaotic* world. He is not portraying early earth as *mysterious,* because he is claiming to understand important aspects of that ancient environment. He is also not portraying the early earth as *perilous,* because no creatures yet existed to suffer its dangers.

8. **B** The passage begins by describing the *common belief* that *new life could arise . . . by spontaneous generation from nonliving material* then presents evidence, in the form of Pasteur's experiment, that refutes that belief.

Exercise 3

1. **C** In saying that *[e]qual certainty exists among those [scientists] who study the base of their skulls that [Neanderthals] did [lack the long vocal chamber needed for speech] and that they did not,* the author is saying that there is considerable disagreement about the vocal abilities of Neanderthals.

2. **B** The main thesis of this passage is that humans came to dominate the Neanderthals by taking advantage of their intellectual abilities rather than relying on their physical strength. This directly implies that *physical weakness is not necessarily a disadvantage in the fight for survival.*

3. **D** In lines 43–47, the authors state their main thesis: *The reason we—anatomically modern humans—won out lies, we suspect, not in being brighter or better able to speak but in our very physical frailty and our resulting need to exploit our minds.* Choice A is incorrect because this sentence

merely states that scientists disagree about the length of the Neanderthal vocal chamber. Choice B is incorrect because this sentence merely states that hunters sometimes find it helpful to communicate silently. Choice C is incorrect because this sentence merely states that the ability to speak cannot explain our dominance over the Neanderthals.

4. **B** The solid lines in the diagram indicate that *H. sapiens* (which includes the *Cro-Magnon*) descended from *H. heidelbergensis,* which descended from *H. erectus,* which descended from *H. habilis,* which descended from *A. afarensis.* Therefore, the *Cro-Magnon* and *H. heidelbergensis* both share *A. afarensis* as a common ancestor. Choice A is incorrect because the diagram shows no line of descent from *H. neanderthalensis* to *H. sapiens.* Choice C is incorrect because the diagram contains no information about the reasons for extinction. Choice D is incorrect because there is no line of descent from *H. habilis* to *A. robustus.*

5. **C** In the diagram, the longest vertical bar for any hominid species is that for *H. erectus,* which begins at about the 2-million-year mark and ends at about the 250,000-year mark. Subtracting these two values gives us a time span of about 1,750,000 years.

6. **C** Although statements A and D are both valid conclusions based on the information in the diagram, neither of these facts supports the main thesis of the passage, which is found in lines 43–47: *The reason we—anatomically modern humans—won out [in our competition with the Neanderthals] lies, we suspect, not in being brighter or better able to speak but in our very physical frailty and our resulting need to exploit our minds.* Therefore, the argument rests on the fact that *H. sapiens* coexisted with *H. neanderthalensis.* The diagram clearly shows that both species lived in the period between approximately 100,000 years ago and 40,000 years ago, and so could have been in direct competition. It also shows that *H. neanderthalensis* appears to have gone extinct, because its vertical bar does not reach all the way up to the 0 mark.

7. **D** The author mentions that *hunter-gatherers use sophisticated sign language* to provide evidence that speech is not necessary for success in hunting, and that therefore *long vocal chambers might not provide a decisive evolutionary advantage.*

8. **A** In saying that Neanderthals *could survive with their physical strength rather than tapping the potential of their brains,* the authors are saying that, unlike *Homo sapiens,* the Neanderthals did not need to *exploit* (take advantage of) their intelligence.

9. **C** These are examples of how countries *exploit their minds* rather than relying on natural

CHAPTER 5 / THE SAT READING TEST

resources to compete with other nations economically. Therefore, the correct answer is C: *goods and services based on intellectual resources.* Notice that choices A, B, and D don't fit at all with the overall purpose of the paragraph.

Exercise 4

1. **A** The first paragraph states that the we have moved *slowly and tortuously* toward *strengthening our mode of explanation.* In other words, that the *march of human intellectual progress* has not been steady and direct, and that indeed we are still *plagued by faulty intuitions.* In other words, this progress has been *halting* (slow and hesitant).

2. **C** The first paragraph describes human intellectual progress with the metaphor of a *march.* It does not employ any *euphemism* (a word or phrase used to make something unpleasant sound less so), *understatement* (phrasing that makes something seem less intense than it is), or *anecdote* (illustrative story).

3. **D** The main idea of the passage is that *mechanistic* explanations are those *theories, equations, and mechanisms[that] best represent* physical phenomena. These are the *scientific* modes of explanation.

4. **C** The statements listed in line 16–18 are examples of *explaining phenomena in terms of their presumed purposes or desires, rather than their causes.* The passage as a whole explains how such *teleological* explanations are in fact *misguided and unhelpful* (lines 20–21). Therefore, these are *unsound beliefs.*

5. **A** The problem with teleological explanations, according to the author, is that they *can't predict the future as accurately as mechanistic explanations can* (lines 21–23). Therefore, they are *imprecise* in this regard.

6. **C** The author explains the *imprecision* of teleological explanations in lines 21–27, where he states that they *can't predict the future as accurately as mechanistic explanations can.*

7. **B** Neil Shubin is mentioned as an example of a *clear-minded scientist [who] slides into teleology from time to time when describing natural phenomena to laypeople* (lines 54–56). That is, he is *confusing purpose with cause in a scientific explanation.*

8. **A** The purpose of this paragraph is to acknowledge the *drawback* that mechanistic explanations of our own decisions seem to deny the possibility of free will, which is something that most people consider precious.

9. **A** Since the author has conceded a drawback to his thesis in his previous paragraph, this paragraph uses *beseeching* language, like *only . . . if,* and *must* to make a plea to the reader to reject teleological explanations.

Exercise 5

1. **A** Passage 2 is primarily concerned with the chemical reactions that harness energy to sustain life, specifically *photosynthesis* (line 15) and *chemosynthesis* (line 24). Therefore the question *How does photosynthesis convert the energy of sunlight into the energy of sugar molecules?* is most directly relevant to Passage 2.

2. **C** Passage 1 focuses on *the study of the molecules of which living things are composed* (lines 1–3) and how those molecules convert energy, make muscles contract, help nerve cells communicate, and so on. Passage 2 focuses on the chemical reactions that harness energy to sustain life. Therefore, both passages are primarily concerned with *the chemical processes that sustain life.*

3. **C** This list of questions represent some of the questions that guide *the study of the molecules of which living organisms are composed* (lines 1–3), therefore they are *areas of productive inquiry.* Passage 1 does not discuss any scientific controversies, innovations, or sources of frustration.

4. **C** The bacteria mentioned in line 28 are *incorporated into organisms to provide benefits.* This is a *symbiotic* relationship, in which both organisms benefit. These bacteria are not *infections* or *parasites,* because they are not doing harm, and they are not *progenitors,* because they are not the original ancestors of a species or kind.

5. **A** Since Passage 2 is focused on the recent discovery of a new way by which living organisms on Earth can harvest energy, namely chemosynthesis, its author would likely suggest that the study of life on earth include research into *atypical sources of energy.*

6. **B** The *complex relationships* mentioned in line 27 are those *in which bacteria are incorporated into organisms to provide benefits.* The choice that best resembles such a relationship is *a fungus living within a grass plant that renders the grass more drought resistant.*

7. **A** The phrase *we assumed* in line 18 refers to the belief among biologists that solar energy is required to sustain life on Earth. In other words, they accepted this proposition *uncritically,* and, it turns out, erroneously.

Exercise 6

1. **A** This rhetorical essay focus on the author's thesis that *the Primitive phase . . . can only be of short duration* (lines 51–52). The first paragraph explains how an attempt *to revive the art-principles of the past will at best produce an art that is stillborn* (lines 5–6), the second paragraph gives

a glimmer of hope to the Primitivists by stating that our *spiritual relationship with the Primitives* (lines 26–27) may lead to a *revival of the external forms* (lines 23–24). The last paragraph describes the obstacle that materialism places in the way of the Primitivist movement. Therefore, as a whole, the passage is concerned with *the obstacles to a particular undertaking*.

2. **B**   The statement *every work of art is the child of its age and, in many cases, the mother of our emotions* means that art derives from the culture in which its created, and in turn forms our emotional response to that culture. Therefore the metaphor is one of *creation versus creator*.

3. **D**   The phrase *thoughtful aspect* is used to describe the face of a monkey that is acting as if it is reading but really is not. That is, he has a *thoughtful facial expression*, but is not really thinking.

4. **C**   The *fundamental truth* described in the second paragraph is that *when there is a similarity . . . in the spiritual atmosphere, a similarity of ideals . . . the logical result will be a revival of the external forms which served to express those feelings*. In other words, the art forms will be similar if the cultural

feelings are similar. This suggests that *sculptures celebrating the virtue of liberty share common features across eras*.

5. **C**   The passage states that *[o]ur minds . . . are infected with the despair of unbelief, of lack of purpose and ideal* (lines 32–35) because of the *nightmare of materialism* (line 36). Therefore the effect of materialism is to *deny [artists] access to meaningful and spiritual activity*.

6. **C**   The best evidence for this answer comes in lines 38–39, where the author states that *[materialism] holds the awakening soul still in it its grip*.

7. **B**   The last paragraph uses the metaphor of a *feeble light* to represent the awakening soul of the artist, and the *darkness* to represent the *nightmare of materialism,* so when the author states that the soul *trembles in doubt whether the light is not a dream,* he is saying that artists are wondering whether their artistic ideals can survive the era of materialism.

8. **D**   The *costly vase* is compared to the beleaguered artist's soul, which *is found to have a flaw when it is dug up once more*. In other words, the principles and ideals of primitive art cannot be completely recovered, and so the primitive *frame of mind* is *irretrievable*.

CHAPTER 6

THE SAT ESSAY: ANALYZING ARGUMENTS

The SAT Essay

What is the SAT Essay?

The SAT includes an **optional** 50-minute Essay assignment designed to assess your

> *proficiency in writing a cogent and clear analysis of a challenging rhetorical essay written for a broad audience.*

Should you choose to accept the challenge, the SAT Essay will be the fifth and final section of your test.

The SAT Essay assignment asks you to read a 650–750 word rhetorical essay (such as a *New York Times* op-ed about the economic pros and cons of using biofuels) and to write a well-organized response that

- demonstrates an understanding of the essay's central ideas and important details
- analyzes its use of evidence, such as facts or examples, to support its claims
- critiques its use of reasoning to develop ideas to connect claims and evidence
- examines how it uses stylistic or persuasive elements, such as word choice or appeals to emotion, to add power to the ideas expressed

How is it used?

Many colleges use the SAT Essay in admissions or placement decisions. Many also regard it as an important indicator of essential skills for success in college, specifically, your ability to demonstrate understanding of complex reading assignments, to analyze arguments, and to express your thoughts in writing.

Sound intimidating? It's not.

If you have mastered the analytical reading skills discussed in Chapter 5, you already have a strong start on tackling the SAT Essay, since strong active reading of the source text is the first and most important step in the analytical writing task. There are four rules to success on the SAT Essay, and the 13 lessons in this chapter will give you the knowledge and practice you need to master all of them.

Understand the Analytical Task
Lesson 1: Fifty minutes

The SAT Essay assesses your proficiency in reading, analysis, and writing. You are given 50 minutes to read an argumentative essay and write an analysis that demonstrates your comprehension of the essay's primary and secondary ideas and your understanding of its use of evidence, language, reasoning, and rhetorical or literary elements to support those ideas. You must support your claims with evidence from the text and use critical reasoning to evaluate its rhetorical effectiveness.

So what should you do with those 50 minutes?

Reading: 15–20 minutes

Although 15–20 minutes may seem like a long time to devote to reading a 750-word essay, remember that you must do more than simply read the essay. You must **comprehend**, **analyze**, and **critique** it. In other words, you must master the "Three-Pass Approach" that we will practice in lessons 4–6. This is a fairly advanced reading technique, and you will need to devote substantial time to practicing it. Even once you've mastered it, you will still need to set aside 15–20 minutes on the SAT Essay section to read and annotate the passage thoroughly.

Organizing: 10–15 minutes

Your next task is to gather the ideas from your analyses and use them to formulate a thesis and structure for a five- or six-paragraph essay. If you have performed your first task properly and have completed your "Three-Pass" analysis, creating an outline will be much easier. We will discuss these tasks in lessons 7 and 8.

Your thesis should summarize the thesis of the essay and its secondary ideas, describe the author's main stylistic and rhetorical elements, and provide an insightful critique of the essay.

Take your time with this process, too. Don't make the mistake of writing your essay before you have articulated a thoughtful guiding question and outlined the essay as a whole.

Writing: 20–25 minutes

Next, of course, you have to write your easy. To get a high score, your essay must provide an eloquent introduction and conclusion, articulate a precise central claim about the essay, be well organized, show a logical and cohesive progression of ideas, maintain a formal style and an objective tone, and show a strong command of language. But if you've followed these steps, which we will explore in more detail below, the essay will flow naturally and easily from your analysis and outline.

Lesson 2: Learn the format of the SAT Essay

The passages you are asked to analyze present a point of view on a topic in the arts, sciences, politics, or culture. They address a broad audience, express nuanced views on complex subjects, and use evidence and logical reasoning to support their claims.

The Essay, should you choose to take it, is the fifth and final portion of the SAT. Here is a sample essay and prompt (from the diagnostic test in Chapter 2). Read it carefully to familiarize yourself with the instructions and format.

You have <u>50 minutes</u> to read the passage and write an essay in response to the prompt provided below.

As you read the passage below, consider how Steven Pinker uses

- evidence, such as facts or examples, to support his claims

- reasoning to develop ideas and connect claims and evidence

- stylistic or persuasive elements, such as word choice or appeals to emotion, to add power to the ideas expressed

Adapted from Steven Pinker, "Mind Over Mass Media." ©2010 by The New York Times. Originally published June 10, 2010.

New forms of media have always caused moral panics: the printing press, newspapers, paperbacks and television were all once denounced as threats to their consumers' brainpower and moral fiber.

So too with electronic technologies. PowerPoint, we're told, is reducing discourse to bullet points. Search engines lower our intelligence, encouraging us to skim on the surface of knowledge rather than dive to its depths. Twitter is shrinking our attention spans.

But such panics often fail reality checks. When comic books were accused of turning juveniles into delinquents in the 1950s, crime was falling to record lows, just as the denunciations of video games in the 1990s coincided with the great American crime decline. The decades of television, transistor radios and rock videos were also decades in which I.Q. scores rose continuously.

For a reality check today, take the state of science, which demands high levels of brainwork and is measured by clear benchmarks of discovery. Today, scientists are never far from their e-mail and cannot lecture without PowerPoint. If electronic media were hazardous to intelligence, the quality of science would be plummeting. Yet discoveries are multiplying like fruit flies, and progress is dizzying. Other activities in the life of the mind, like philosophy, history and cultural criticism, are likewise flourishing.

Critics of new media sometimes use science itself to press their case, citing research that shows how "experience can change the brain." But cognitive neuroscientists roll their eyes at such talk. Yes, every time we learn a fact or skill the wiring of the brain changes; it's not as if the information is stored in the pancreas. But the existence of neural plasticity does not mean the brain is a blob of clay pounded into shape by experience.

Experience does not revamp the basic information-processing capacities of the brain. Speed-reading programs have long claimed to do just that, but the verdict was rendered by Woody Allen after he read *War and Peace* in one sitting: "It was about Russia." Genuine multitasking, too, has been exposed as a myth, not just by laboratory studies but by the familiar sight of an SUV undulating between lanes as the driver cuts deals on his cell phone.

Moreover, the evidence indicates that the effects of experience are highly specific to the experiences themselves. If you train people to do one thing, they get better at doing that thing, but almost nothing else. Music doesn't make

you better at math; conjugating Latin doesn't make you more logical; brain-training games don't make you smarter. Accomplished people don't bulk up their brains with intellectual calisthenics; they immerse themselves in their fields. Novelists read lots of novels; scientists read lots of science.

The effects of consuming electronic media are also likely to be far more limited than the panic implies. Media critics write as if the brain takes on the qualities of whatever it consumes, the informational equivalent of "you are what you eat." As with primitive peoples who believe that eating fierce animals will make them fierce, they assume that watching quick cuts in rock videos turns your mental life into quick cuts or that reading bullet points and Twitter postings turns your thoughts into bullet points and Twitter postings.

Yes, the constant arrival of information packets can be distracting or addictive, especially to people with attention deficit disorder. But distraction is not a new phenomenon. The solution is not to bemoan technology but to develop strategies of self-control, as we do with every other temptation in life. Turn off e-mail or Twitter when you work, put away your BlackBerry at dinner time, ask your spouse to call you to bed at a designated hour.

And to encourage intellectual depth, don't rail at PowerPoint or Google. It's not as if habits of deep reflection, thorough research and rigorous reasoning ever came naturally to people. They must be acquired in special institutions, which we call universities, and maintained with constant upkeep, which we call analysis, criticism and debate. They are not granted by propping a heavy encyclopedia on your lap, nor are they taken away by efficient access to information on the Internet.

The new media have caught on for a reason. Knowledge is increasing exponentially; human brainpower and waking hours are not. Fortunately, the Internet and information technologies are helping us manage, search, and retrieve our collective intellectual output at different scales, from Twitter and previews to e-books and online encyclopedias. Far from making us stupid, these technologies are the only things that will keep us smart.

Write an essay in which you explain how Steven Pinker builds an argument to persuade his audience that new media are not destroying our moral and intellectual abilities. In your essay, analyze how Pinker uses one or more of the features listed in the box above (or features of your own choice) to strengthen the logic and persuasiveness of his argument. Be sure that your analysis focuses on the most relevant features of the passage.

Your essay should NOT explain whether you agree with Pinker's claims, but rather explain how Pinker builds an argument to persuade his audience.

Lesson 3: Understand the scoring rubric

Your essay will be scored based on three criteria: **reading**, **analysis**, and **writing**. Two trained readers will give your essay a score of 1 to 4 on these three criteria, and your subscore for each criterion will be the sum of these two, that is, a score from 2 to 8. Here is the official rubric for all three criteria.

SAT Essay Scoring Rubric

Score	Reading	Analysis	Writing
4	• demonstrates a thorough understanding of the source text, including its central ideas, its important details, and how they interrelate • is free of errors of fact or interpretation with regard to the text • makes skillful use of textual evidence (quotations, paraphrases, or both) to demonstrate a complete understanding of the source text	• offers an insightful analysis of the source text and demonstrates a sophisticated understanding of the analytical task • offers a thorough, well-considered evaluation of the author's use of evidence, reasoning, and/or stylistic and persuasive elements, and/or features of the student's own choosing • contains relevant, sufficient, and strategically chosen support for claims or points made • focuses consistently on those features of the text that are most relevant to addressing the task	• is cohesive and demonstrates a highly effective command of language • includes a precise central claim • includes an eloquent introduction and conclusion, and demonstrates a logical and effective progression of ideas within and among paragraphs • uses an effective variety of sentence structures, demonstrates precise word choice, and maintains a formal style and objective tone • shows a strong command of the conventions of Standard Written English and is free or virtually free of errors
3	• demonstrates effective understanding of the source text, including its central ideas and important details • is free of substantive errors of fact and interpretation with regard to the text • makes appropriate use of textual evidence (quotations, paraphrases, or both) to demonstrate an understanding of the source text	• offers an effective analysis of the source text and demonstrates an understanding of the analytical task • competently evaluates the author's use of evidence, reasoning, and/or stylistic and persuasive elements, and/or features of the student's own choosing • contains relevant and sufficient support for claims or points made • focuses primarily on those features of the text that are most relevant to addressing the task	• is mostly cohesive and demonstrates effective control of language • includes a central claim or implicit controlling idea • includes an effective introduction and conclusion, and demonstrates a clear progression of ideas within and among paragraphs • uses a variety of sentence structures, demonstrates some precise word choice, and maintains a formal style and objective tone • shows a good control of the conventions of Standard Written English and is free of significant errors that detract from the quality of writing

| 2 | • demonstrates some understanding of the source text, including its central ideas, but not of important details
• may contain errors of fact and/or interpretation with regard to the text
• makes limited and/or haphazard use of textual evidence (quotations, paraphrases, or both) to demonstrate some understanding of the source text | • offers limited analysis of the source text and demonstrates only partial understanding of the analytical task
• identifies and attempts to describe the author's use of evidence, reasoning, and/or stylistic and persuasive elements, and/or features of the student's own choosing, but merely asserts rather than explains their importance, or makes unwarranted claims
• contains little or no support for claims
• may lack a clear focus on those features of the text that are most relevant to addressing the task | • demonstrates little or no cohesion and limited skill in the use and control of language
• may lack a clear central claim or controlling idea or may deviate from the claim or idea
• lacks an effective introduction and/or conclusion
• may demonstrate some progression of ideas within paragraphs but not throughout
• has limited variety in sentence structures
• demonstrates inconsistently effective diction and deviates noticeably from a formal style and objective tone
• shows a limited control of the conventions of Standard Written English and contains errors that detract from the quality of writing and may impede understanding |
| 1 | • demonstrates little or no comprehension of the source text
• fails to show an understanding of the text's central ideas, and may include only details without reference to central ideas
• may contain numerous errors of fact or interpretation with regard to the text
• makes little or no use of textual evidence (quotations, paraphrases, or both), demonstrating little or no understanding of the source text | • offers little or no analysis or ineffective analysis of the source text and demonstrates little or no understanding of the analytic task
• identifies without explanation some aspects of the author's use of evidence, reasoning, and/or stylistic and persuasive elements
• makes unwarranted analytical claims
• contains little or no support for claims, or support is largely irrelevant
• may not focus on features of the text that are relevant to addressing the task
• offers no discernible analysis (e.g., is largely or exclusively summary) | • demonstrates little or no cohesion and inadequate skill in the use and control of language
• may lack a clear central claim or controlling idea
• lacks a recognizable introduction and conclusion, and lacks any discernible progression of ideas
• lacks variety in sentence structures, demonstrates weak diction, and may lack a formal style and objective tone
• shows a weak control of the conventions of Standard Written English and may contain numerous errors that undermine the quality of writing |

Use the "Three-Pass Approach" (15–20 minutes)

Good analytical writing begins with strong analytical reading. In this first stage of the process, which should take between 15 and 20 minutes, take the "Three-Pass Approach" to analyzing the passage.

Lesson 4: First pass: Comprehend

First, read the passage to understand its primary and secondary ideas using the skills you learned in Chapter 5. Ask: **What is the central thesis, and what claims does the author make in each paragraph to support this thesis?** Underline the key ideas, and annotate the paragraphs with very brief summaries.

Adapted from Steven Pinker, "Mind Over Mass Media." ©2010 by The New York Times. Originally published June 10, 2010.

New forms of media have always caused moral panics: the printing press, newspapers, paperbacks and television were all once denounced as threats to their consumers' brainpower and moral fiber.

So too with electronic technologies. PowerPoint, we're told, is reducing discourse to bullet points. Search engines lower our intelligence, encouraging us to skim on the surface of knowledge rather than dive to its depths. Twitter is shrinking our attention spans.

But such panics often fail reality checks. When comic books were accused of turning juveniles into delinquents in the 1950s, crime was falling to record lows, just as the denunciations of video games in the 1990s coincided with the great American crime decline. The decades of television, transistor radios and rock videos were also decades in which I.Q. scores rose continuously.

For a reality check today, take the state of science, which demands high levels of brainwork and is measured by clear benchmarks of discovery. Today, scientists are never far from their e-mail and cannot lecture without PowerPoint. If electronic media were hazardous to intelligence, the quality of science would be plummeting. Yet discoveries are multiplying like fruit flies, and progress is dizzying. Other activities in the life of the mind, like philosophy, history and cultural criticism, are likewise flourishing.

Critics of new media sometimes use science itself to press their case, citing research that shows how "experience can change the brain." But cognitive neuroscientists roll their eyes at such talk. Yes, every time we learn a fact or skill the wiring of the brain changes; it's not as if the information is stored in the pancreas. But the existence of neural plasticity does not mean the brain is a blob of clay pounded into shape by experience.

Summary

People have long worried that media make us dumb and immoral.

Today, the same is said of PowerPoint, Google, and Twitter.

But sociological evidence refutes those fears, rather than supports them.

Scientists use the media, yet are as productive as ever. The same is true with those who work in the humanities.

The "science" used to bolster these panics is weak, facile, and misleading.

CONTINUE

Experience does not revamp the basic information-processing capacities of the brain. Speed-reading programs have long claimed to do just that, but the verdict was rendered by Woody Allen after he read *War and Peace* in one sitting: "It was about Russia." Genuine multitasking, too, has been exposed as a myth, not just by laboratory studies but by the familiar sight of an SUV undulating between lanes as the driver cuts deals on his cell phone.

Moreover, the evidence indicates that the effects of experience are highly specific to the experiences themselves. If you train people to do one thing, they get better at doing that thing, but almost nothing else. Music doesn't make you better at math; conjugating Latin doesn't make you more logical; brain-training games don't make you smarter. Accomplished people don't bulk up their brains with intellectual calisthenics; they immerse themselves in their fields. Novelists read lots of novels; scientists read lots of science.

The effects of consuming electronic media are also likely to be far more limited than the panic implies. Media critics write as if the brain takes on the qualities of whatever it consumes, the informational equivalent of "you are what you eat." As with primitive peoples who believe that eating fierce animals will make them fierce, they assume that watching quick cuts in rock videos turns your mental life into quick cuts or that reading bullet points and Twitter postings turns your thoughts into bullet points and Twitter postings.

Yes, the constant arrival of information packets can be distracting or addictive, especially to people with attention deficit disorder. But distraction is not a new phenomenon. The solution is not to bemoan technology but to develop strategies of self-control, as we do with every other temptation in life. Turn off e-mail or Twitter when you work, put away your BlackBerry at dinner time, ask your spouse to call you to bed at a designated hour.

And to encourage intellectual depth, don't rail at PowerPoint or Google. It's not as if habits of deep reflection, thorough research and rigorous reasoning ever came naturally to people. They must be acquired in special institutions, which we call universities, and maintained with constant upkeep, which we call analysis, criticism and debate. They are not granted by propping a heavy encyclopedia on your lap, nor are they taken away by efficient access to information on the Internet. The new media have caught on for a reason. Knowledge is increasing exponentially; human brainpower and waking hours are not. Fortunately, the Internet and information technologies are helping us manage, search, and retrieve our collective intellectual output at different scales, from Twitter and previews to e-books and online encyclopedias. Far from making us stupid, these technologies are the only things that will keep us smart.

New media don't redesign our brains as easily as the critics suggest.

Cognitive changes require very specific training . . .

. . . so exposure to new media won't change our brains dramatically.

Instantaneous social media can be distracting, so just turn them off when you need to.

Deep intellectual skills are not eroded by quick access to information, but by practicing the skills of analysis, criticism, and debate.

Quick access to information is good.

Lesson 5: Second pass: Analyze

Next, read the passage again with a different question in mind: **How does the author use evidence, reasoning, and rhetorical devices to support the central thesis and perhaps address potential counterarguments?**

The College Board says that a strong essay must *offer insightful analysis of the source text* by examining *the author's use of evidence, reasoning, and/or stylistic elements.* Therefore, you should know the common stylistic and rhetorical devices and recognize them when you see them.

In Chapter 5, we discussed the 16 basic rhetorical and literary devices that can help you to better analyze college-level prose. Now let's revisit them, and look at 17 more devices you should look for as you analyze argumentative essays.

33 Stylistic and Rhetorical Devices for Analysis of Rhetorical Essays

An *ad hominem* is an attack "on the person" rather than an attack of his or her ideas or reasoning. For example, *Her political opinions can't be trusted because she is just an actor* is not an argument about the merits of her ideas, but merely an ad hominem.

Alliteration is the repetition of initial sounds in words to emphasize a rhetorical point. For instance, when John F. Kennedy referred to *high standards of strength and sacrifice*, he was using alliteration (notice the repeated "s" sounds) to draw his listeners into public service.

An *allusion* is an implicit reference to something, usually to a piece of literature or a well-known historical event. For example, the statement *He's gone down the rabbit hole* is an allusion to the bizarre and fanciful episodes in the story *Alice in Wonderland*, and a reference to Benedict Arnold is an allusion to historical betrayal.

Anachronism is the intentional or accidental clash between things from different historical eras. It is a form of *juxtaposition*. For instance, calling the telegraph "the Twitter of the nineteenth century" not only elicits a sonic allusion (the taps and beeps of a telegraph sound like chirping), but also employs creative anachronism.

An *analogy* is an illustrative comparison between things that have a similar function or structure, usually with the use of the words *like* or *as*. For example, the levels of processing in a computer provide an analogy for understanding levels of processing in the human brain.

An *anecdote* is an illustrative story. For example, a story about a friend whose headache went away after he stood on his head for ten minutes is anecdotal evidence, not scientific evidence, for the health benefits of inversion.

An *aphorism* is a widely accepted truth. For example, the aphorism *If it ain't broke, don't fix it* can provide a concise argument against spending a lot of money on a new program. Aphorisms are also called *maxims*, *adages*, or *proverbs*.

An *appeal to authority* is a suggestion that the reader should agree with an idea because a respected authority happens to believe it. For example: *The world's greatest scientist, Sir Isaac Newton, believed that iron could be turned into gold, so who are we to question the idea?*

An *appeal to emotion (pathos)* is an attempt to persuade the reader through an emotionally charged anecdote or allusion. For example, a story about an infuriating experience with an insurance salesman may be an effective way to argue against aggressive sales tactics.

Begging the question is the process of seeming to address a question without actually doing so, or assuming that the answer to a question is obvious when it is in fact not. For instance, asserting that *putting more guns in the hands of good people can only deter crime* is an example of begging the question. Specifically, it ignores the questions of how this would work, whether solid evidence supports the claim, and whether such a program might have dangerous unforeseen consequences.

Characterization is the use of imagery, diction, or description to convey a particular attitude toward a person, thing, or idea. For example, referring to your opponent's proposal as a *scheme* characterizes it as being deceitful, harmful, or secretive.

Concession or *qualification* is the act of acknowledging a point of argument to the opposition, perhaps as a means of moderating your thesis or to preempt potential attacks that your opponent might use against you. For instance, an argument for a tax increase might include a concession that it would place an extra burden on taxpayers, and that those taxpayers might be rightfully concerned that those revenues are spent wisely, then appease these concerns by weighing the social benefits against any perceived burdens.

Connotation refers to the emotional, historic, and sensual associations of a word. Good writers are always aware of the connotations of a word as well as its literal meaning. For instance, a proposal for a tax increase might be described as an *investment* because this word connotes growth and progress.

Didacticism is basically a fancy word for teaching. In a rhetorical essay, an author may use didacticism to instruct the reader about a technical concept that the reader might need to know to understand a concept. For instance, in an essay about the differences between natural selection and the theory of "intelligent design," an author might use didacticism to clarify the definition of terms like "scientific method," "evidentiary standards," and "hypothesis."

Ethos is a class of rhetorical devices that attempt to elicit moral sentiments in order to make a point, especially when those moral sentiments correspond to a set of shared cultural beliefs. For instance, an author may refer to *the American Spirit* or *traditional values* as an appeal to ethos in order to inspire or persuade a reader.

A *euphemism* is a term that makes something seem more positive than it is. For example, salespersons or political canvassers often use the term *courtesy call* as a euphemism for an unwanted disruption, and military technicians use the term *collateral damage* as a euphemism for human casualties.

A *foil* is a person or thing that makes someone or something else seem better by contrast. For example, a person arguing against a tax increase might use the image of a bumbling, bureaucratic tax collector as a foil, whereas the foil for someone arguing *for* the tax increase might be the image a greedy billionaire who doesn't care about the public good or about opportunities for the disadvantaged.

Guilt by association is largely regarded as a rhetorical fallacy but is frequently used in an attempt to persuade readers against an adversary. It is a fallacy because being mere association does not itself imply agreement or similarity. For instance, if a teacher mistrusts you simply because she knows that you hang around with friends who have cheated on tests, she is smearing you with guilt by association.

Hyperbole is deliberate exaggeration for persuasive effect. For example, saying that *Molly's comma usage is a catastrophe* is almost certainly hyperbole.

Imagery is the use of vivid sensory impressions in order to elicit a feeling like anger, peacefulness, beauty, wistfulness, sympathy, or the like. Keats uses visual and sonic imagery in his ode *To the Autumn* when he writes *full-grown lambs loud bleat from hilly bourn; Hedge-crickets sing; and now with treble soft; The redbreast whistles from a garden-croft*.

Induction is the process of drawing or implying broad generalizations from a few examples. *Overgeneralization* is an inductive fallacy. For instance, drawing the conclusion from a few encounters with driving instructors that *all DMV workers are impatient* is an act of induction that many would consider an unfair overgeneralization.

Irony is a deliberate reversal of expectations in order to surprise a reader, often for persuasive effect. For example, Christopher Hitchens justified his attitude toward free will by using irony: *I believe in free will, because I have no other choice.*

Logical analysis (logos) is the examination of an argument in terms of its logical support (or lack thereof). An author might use logos to refute a claim like *all politicians are liars* by pointing out an honest politician (*counterexample*) or by showing that such a claim does not follow from any logical premises (*non sequitur*). On the other hand, an author might use logos to support a claim by showing that it follows necessarily from previously accepted premises (*deduction*) or that its falsehood would lead to an absurd situation (*indirect proof* or *reductio ad absurdum*) or that it follows a well-accepted pattern (*induction*).

A *metaphor* is an application of a word or phrase to something it doesn't literally apply to. For example, calling a refusal a *slap in the face* uses metaphor to emphasize its harshness.

Rhetorical *parallelism* is the use of repeated grammatical form to emphasize a point. For example, John F. Kennedy used parallelism in his inaugural address when he said *we shall pay any price, bear any burden, meet any hardship, support any friend, oppose any foe to assure the survival and the success of liberty.*

Rhetorical *paradox* is the use of a logically self-contradictory statement to make a point. Oscar Wilde is known for such masterful examples of rhetorical paradox as *The only thing worse than being talked about is not being talked about* and *I can resist anything but temptation.*

Parody is comical and exaggerated imitation. Tina Fey is famous for her parodies of former vice-presidential candidate Sarah Palin. Many writers of persuasive essays use parody to mock the positions of their opponents.

The *persona* a writer adopts is the voice that he or she uses to establish his or her standing or personality in the argument. For instance, an author might create a very gentle and casual persona (*Don't you hate it when . . .*) or a more formal and forceful persona (*Our current political discourse must change if we are to address the existential crises our nation faces . . .*), each of which has its advantages and disadvantages in persuading readers.

Personification is the attribution of personal qualities to something that is not a person. For example, we are using rhetorical personification when we say that an idea is *on its last legs* or *gave its last gasp.*

A *polemic* is a forceful and controversial argument against a widely held position. For instance, any forceful argument against the virtue of compassion or the benefit of hard work would be considered a polemic because these values are widely accepted and have a history of forceful argumentation behind them. Christopher Hitchens and Jonathan Swift are some famous polemicists.

A *simile* is a comparison using *like* or *as*. For instance, Irena Dunn used rhetorical simile when she said *A woman without a man is like a fish without a bicycle.*

A *straw man* is an unfair misrepresentation of an opponent's position so that it can be more easily refuted. It is a common and dishonest logical fallacy. For instance, if one wanted to refute the position that *teens should be taught about responsible contraception use in order to prevent both unwanted pregnancies and the spread of potentially lethal diseases*, one might replace this position with a straw man position: *my opponent wants to give all of your kids condoms so they can go out and have as much sex as they want without worrying about any consequences.* This recharacterization of the original position is a straw man because it misstates not only the content of the actual proposal, but also the intention of the program and the consideration being given to the consequences of potentially dangerous activities.

An *understatement* encourages the reader to embrace a point by underemphasizing its intensity, which is taken to be obvious. For instance, it's an understatement to suggest that *Donald Trump is a little self-absorbed.*

This list is by no means exhaustive, but it provides a solid framework for analyzing the passage. In your second read-through, keep it simple. Just underline the sentences or phrases that use these devices, and categorize the devices in the margin.

Read the annotations in the sample analysis below and see how each underlined portion represents that particular device. Train yourself to see these devices in all of the rhetorical essays you read: newspaper op-eds, long form essays, and even your own papers.

This analysis is a critical step in writing the SAT Essay. As the scoring rubric indicates, your essay should *offer a thorough, well-considered evaluation of the author's use of evidence, reasoning, and/or stylistic and persuasive elements.*

The rubric also indicates that a good essay will contain *relevant, sufficient, and strategically chosen support for claims or points made.* This means you must **give quotations from the text that show where the author uses these particular devices and stylistic elements.**

Adapted from Steven Pinker, "Mind Over Mass Media." ©2010 by The New York Times. Originally published June 10, 2010.

Analysis

New forms of media have always caused moral panics: the printing press, newspapers, paperbacks and television were all once denounced as threats to their consumers' brainpower and moral fiber.

= examples for historical context

So too with electronic technologies. PowerPoint, we're told, is reducing discourse to bullet points. Search engines lower our intelligence, encouraging us to skim on the surface of knowledge rather than dive to its depths. Twitter is shrinking our attention spans.

= modern examples to establish extent of misconception

But such panics often fail reality checks. When comic books were accused of turning juveniles into delinquents in the 1950s, crime was falling to record lows, just as the denunciations of video games in the 1990s coincided with the great American crime decline. The decades of television, transistor radios and rock videos were also decades in which I.Q. scores rose continuously.

= historical evidence as counterpoint

For a reality check today, take the state of science, which demands high levels of brainwork and is measured by clear benchmarks of discovery. Today, scientists are never far from their e-mail and cannot lecture without PowerPoint. If electronic media were hazardous to intelligence, the quality of science would be plummeting. Yet discoveries are multiplying like fruit flies, and progress is dizzying. Other activities in the life of the mind, like philosophy, history and cultural criticism, are likewise flourishing.

= neologism (recently coined phrase)

= appeal to authority?

= reductio ad absurdum

= clever simile

Critics of new media sometimes use science itself to press their case, citing research that shows how "experience can change the brain." But cognitive neuroscientists roll their eyes at such talk. Yes, every time we learn a fact or skill the wiring of the brain changes; it's not as if the information is stored in the pancreas. But the existence of neural plasticity does not mean the brain is a blob of clay pounded into shape by experience. Experience does not revamp the basic information-processing capacities of the brain. Speed-reading programs have long claimed to do just that, but the verdict was rendered by Woody Allen after he read *War and Peace* in one sitting: "It was about Russia." Genuine multitasking, too, has been exposed as a myth, not just by laboratory studies but by the familiar sight of an SUV undulating between lanes as the driver cuts deals on his cell phone.

= qualification
= sarcasm

= metaphor

= humorous cultural allusion

= counterexample

Moreover, the evidence indicates that the effects of experience are highly specific to the experiences themselves. If you train people to do one thing, they get better at doing that thing, but almost nothing else. Music doesn't make you better at math; conjugating Latin doesn't make you more logical; brain-training games don't make you smarter. Accomplished people don't bulk up their brains with intellectual calisthenics; they

= didacticism

= examples/analogies

CONTINUE ▶

immerse themselves in their fields. Novelists read lots of novels; scientists read lots of science.

The effects of consuming electronic media are also likely to be far more limited than the panic implies. Media critics write as if the brain takes on the qualities of whatever it consumes, the informational equivalent of "you are what you eat." As with primitive peoples who believe that eating fierce animals will make them fierce, they assume that watching quick cuts in rock videos turns your mental life into quick cuts or that reading bullet points and Twitter postings turns your thoughts into bullet points and Twitter postings.

Yes, the constant arrival of information packets can be distracting or addictive, especially to people with attention deficit disorder. But distraction is not a new phenomenon. The solution is not to bemoan technology but to develop strategies of self-control, as we do with every other temptation in life. Turn off e-mail or Twitter when you work, put away your BlackBerry at dinner time, ask your spouse to call you to bed at a designated hour.

And to encourage intellectual depth, don't rail at PowerPoint or Google. It's not as if habits of deep reflection, thorough research and rigorous reasoning ever came naturally to people. They must be acquired in special institutions, which we call universities, and maintained with constant upkeep, which we call analysis, criticism and debate. They are not granted by propping a heavy encyclopedia on your lap, nor are they taken away by efficient access to information on the Internet. The new media have caught on for a reason. Knowledge is increasing exponentially; human brainpower and waking hours are not. Fortunately, the Internet and information technologies are helping us manage, search, and retrieve our collective intellectual output at different scales, from Twitter and previews to e-books and online encyclopedias. Far from making us stupid, these technologies are the only things that will keep us smart.

= appeasement

= analogy

= concession

= constructive suggestion

= exhortation

= didacticism

= optimism

Lesson 6: Third pass: Critique

In your third pass, read the passage one more time and ask: **How *effectively* does the essay use reasoning, evidence, and the stylistic and rhetorical devices I just identified?** Again, indicate your thoughts in the margins.

According to the College Board, a top-scoring essay must *"offer a thorough, well-considered **evaluation** of the author's use of evidence, reasoning, and/or stylistic elements."* That is, it is not enough to point out these elements; you must also *evaluate* them. A strong essay must also *"focus consistently on those features of the text that are most relevant to addressing the task,"* that is, it must demonstrate that you can distinguish *especially relevant* points and devices from *incidental* points and devices.

Adapted from Steven Pinker, "Mind Over Mass Media." ©2010 by The New York Times. Originally published June 10, 2010.

Evaluation

New forms of media have always caused moral panics: the printing press, newspapers, paperbacks and television were all once denounced as threats to their consumers' brainpower and moral fiber.

= concise summary of common misconception

So too with electronic technologies. PowerPoint, we're told, is reducing discourse to bullet points. Search engines lower our intelligence, encouraging us to skim on the surface of knowledge rather than dive to its depths. Twitter is shrinking our attention spans.

= effective connection to modern media

But such panics often fail reality checks. When comic books were accused of turning juveniles into delinquents in the 1950s, crime was falling to record lows, just as the denunciations of video games in the 1990s coincided with the great American crime decline. The decades of television, transistor radios and rock videos were also decades in which I.Q. scores rose continuously.

= effectively abrupt change of tone to introduce thesis

= relevant summary of evidence, but lacking detail

For a reality check today, take the state of science, which demands high levels of brainwork and is measured by clear benchmarks of discovery. Today, scientists are never far from their e-mail and cannot lecture without PowerPoint. If electronic media were hazardous to intelligence, the quality of science would be plummeting. Yet discoveries are multiplying like fruit flies, and progress is dizzying. Other activities in the life of the mind, like philosophy, history and cultural criticism, are likewise flourishing.

= good use of *reductio ad absurdum*

= unsubstantiated claim

Critics of new media sometimes use science itself to press their case, citing research that shows how "experience can change the brain." But cognitive neuroscientists roll their eyes at such talk. Yes, every time we learn a fact or skill the wiring of the brain changes; it's not as if the information is stored in the pancreas. But the existence of neural plasticity does not mean the brain is a blob of clay pounded into shape by experience. Experience does not revamp the basic information-processing capacities of the brain. Speed-reading programs have long claimed to do just that, but the verdict

= logical examination of counterargument

= possible straw man?

= unsubstantiated claim

= welcome comic relief

was rendered by Woody Allen after he read *War and Peace* in one sitting: "It was about Russia." Genuine multitasking, too, has been exposed as a myth, not just by laboratory studies but by the familiar sight of an SUV undulating between lanes as the driver cuts deals on his cell phone.

= good example

Moreover, the evidence indicates that the effects of experience are highly specific to the experiences themselves. If you train people to do one thing, they get better at doing that thing, but almost nothing else. Music doesn't make you better at math; conjugating Latin doesn't make you more logical; brain-training games don't make you smarter. Accomplished people don't bulk up their brains with intellectual calisthenics; they immerse themselves in their fields. Novelists read lots of novels; scientists read lots of science.

= pathos (inspires anger and contempt)

= intriguing, but unsubstantiated claims—what is the evidence?

The effects of consuming electronic media are also likely to be far more limited than the panic implies. Media critics write as if the brain takes on the qualities of whatever it consumes, the informational equivalent of "you are what you eat." As with primitive peoples who believe that eating fierce animals will make them fierce, they assume that watching quick cuts in rock videos turns your mental life into quick cuts or that reading bullet points and Twitter postings turns your thoughts into bullet points and Twitter postings.

= fair comparison?

Yes, the constant arrival of information packets can be distracting or addictive, especially to people with attention deficit disorder. But distraction is not a new phenomenon. The solution is not to bemoan technology but to develop strategies of self-control, as we do with every other temptation in life. Turn off e-mail or Twitter when you work, put away your BlackBerry at dinner time, ask your spouse to call you to bed at a designated hour.

= important concession

= welcome practical advice

And to encourage intellectual depth, don't rail at PowerPoint or Google. It's not as if habits of deep reflection, thorough research and rigorous reasoning ever came naturally to people. They must be acquired in special institutions, which we call universities, and maintained with constant upkeep, which we call analysis, criticism and debate. They are not granted by propping a heavy encyclopedia on your lap, nor are they taken away by efficient access to information on the Internet. The new media have caught on for a reason. Knowledge is increasing exponentially; human brainpower and waking hours are not. Fortunately, the Internet and information technologies are helping us manage, search, and retrieve our collective intellectual output at different scales, from Twitter and previews to e-books and online encyclopedias. Far from making us stupid, these technologies are the only things that will keep us smart.

= good use of ethos, encouraging us to aspire to "intellectual depth"

= appreciation of a common concern

= effective use of juxtaposition in concluding statement

Organize Your Thoughts (10–15 minutes)

After you've finished your three passes, it's time to organize your thoughts. You need to have something interesting to write about and a coherent way to express it. This stage of the process involves **constructing a thesis** and **outlining the entire essay**.

Lesson 7: Construct a precise, thorough, and insightful thesis

According to the College Board, a good thesis for your SAT Essay is **precise**, **thorough**, and **insightful**. That is, it conveys a thoughtful central idea that demonstrates that you (1) thoroughly understand the text, (2) have analyzed its essential rhetorical and stylistic elements, and (3) have evaluated those elements for effectiveness.

Take your time when composing your thesis. Choose your words carefully and make sure you capture the key elements listed above. You will probably need more than one sentence to accomplish everything you need in a good thesis paragraph. Consider this first draft for our thesis:

Draft 1

In his essay, "Mind Over Mass Media," Steven Pinker looks at new forms of media. His thesis is about the reality of modern social media and the Internet. He talks about the misconceptions that cultural critics have about the relationship between modern media and the human brain.

Is it precise?

Analyze your sentences for precision by "trimming" them as we discussed in Chapter 4, Lesson 3. Trimming reduces a sentence to its **core**, that is, the phrases that convey the essential ideas. When we do this with our first draft, we get ". . . *Steven Pinker looks at new forms . . . . His thesis is about the reality . . . . He talks about the misconceptions . . . ."* Are the verbs strong and clear? Are the objects concrete and precise? Not really. Let's look back at our notes and use quotations from the passage to make these sentences more precise.

Draft 2

In his essay, "Mind Over Mass Media," Steven Pinker ~~looks at~~ examines the "moral panics" about the supposed moral and cognitive declines caused by new forms of media. His thesis is ~~about the reality of modern social~~ media and the Internet that "such panics often fail reality checks." He ~~talks about~~ effectively analyzes the misconceptions that cultural critics have about the relationship between modern media and the human brain.

Notice that this revision better specifies *what* Pinker is examining in his essay by more precisely articulating his thesis, even including a quotation.

Is it thorough?

Although our second draft provides more detail about Pinker's thesis, this draft still lacks detail about his essay's rhetorical and stylistic elements. It could be more thorough. Let's look back at our notes and add some details about these elements.

Draft 3

*In his essay, "Mind Over Mass Media," Steven Pinker examines the "moral panics" about the supposed moral and cognitive declines caused by new forms of media. His thesis, ~~is~~ that "such panics often fail reality checks," **is supported with historical examples, logical analysis, illustrative images, and touches of humor.** He **provides scientific context for his claims, and** effectively analyzes the misconceptions that cultural critics have about the relationship between modern media and the human brain.*

Note that this revision more thoroughly explains *how* Pinker makes his points by specifying rhetorical and stylistic devices.

Is it insightful?

An insightful essay provides a unique perspective on and evaluation of the source text. Although the SAT Essay instructions say that your response *should NOT explain whether you agree with the author's claims*, the official SAT Essay scoring rubric states that a high-scoring essay must *offer a thorough, well-considered evaluation of the author's use of evidence, reasoning, and/or stylistic elements, and/or features of the student's own choosing*. In other words, don't say *whether you agree* with the source text, but explain *how well it performs the persuasive task*.

Think of it this way: a good movie or restaurant reviewer shouldn't just say "Don't go to that movie because I hate car chases," or "Don't go to that restaurant because I don't like spicy food," because a reader might actually like car chases or spicy food. Instead, a good reviewer describes the cinematic aspects of the movie or culinary aspects of the food to help the *reader* make a better decision. Similarly, your essay should give your reader enough information to decide for himself or herself whether Pinker's essay is strong.

Our current draft is lacking some of these insights, so let's add a few.

Draft 4

In his essay, "Mind Over Mass Media," Steven Pinker examines the "moral panics" about the supposed moral and cognitive declines caused by new forms of media. **His essay provides a measure of balance to our sometimes hysterical discussions of social media and instantaneous digital information.** *His thesis, that "such panics often fail reality checks," is supported with historical examples, logical analysis, illustrative images, and touches of humor. He provides scientific context for his claims, and effectively analyzes the misconceptions that cultural critics have about the relationship between modern media and the human brain.* **Although his argument could have been bolstered with more specific scientific support, his essay as a whole effectively argues for a reprieve from the hysteria about intellectual and moral decline allegedly caused by Twitter and Facebook.**

Notice that this revision insightfully evaluates *how effectively* Pinker makes his points.

Lesson 8: Outline your essay

Once you've composed your thesis, outline the rest of your essay. Plan to write between five and seven paragraphs.

Our thesis paragraph draws the reader in by *beginning* to answer the question *How does Steven Pinker's Essay, "Mind Over Mass Media," establish a point of view about the effects of modern media and information technologies?* by summarizing Pinker's thesis, describing his rhetorical and stylistic techniques, and evaluating the effectiveness of his writing.

The rest of the essay should focus on **supporting those points** and **discussing their relevance**.

Outline

1. *Pinker's essay examines the "moral panics" about new media and information technologies supposedly causing cognitive and moral decline, and argues for a reprieve from the hysteria.*
2. *Pinker effectively uses historical examples to support his thesis.*
3. *Pinker uses logical analysis to refute the opposing viewpoint.*
4. *Pinker uses psychological research to explain how misguided our worries about new media are.*
5. *Pinker attempts to refute his critics with an analogy between modern critics and the thinking of ancient peoples.*
6. *Pinker provides constructive advice for those prone to distraction by new media.*
7. *Pinker concludes with a hopeful view of new media and information technologies.*

Write the Essay (20–25 minutes)

Lesson 9: Use strong verbs

According to the College Board, a strong essay *demonstrates a highly effective command of language*. As we discussed in Lesson 7, strong sentences contain **strong verbs**. Strengthen your verbs by **minimizing weak verbs** (like *to be, to have, to make,* and *to do*) and **minimizing passive verbs**.

Minimize weak verbs by upgrading "lurkers"

Look at a recent essay you've written and circle all of the verbs. Are more than one-third of your verbs *to be* verbs (*is, are, was, were*)? If so, strengthen your verbs. You cannot maintain a strong discussion if you overuse weak verbs like *to be, to have,* and *to do.*

To strengthen your sentences, upgrade any **lurkers**—the words in your sentence that aren't verbs, but should be. Consider this sentence:

*This action **is in violation of** our company's confidentiality policy.*

It revolves around a very weak verb. But the noun *violation* is a lurker. Let's upgrade it to verb status:

*This action **violates** our company's confidentiality policy.*

Notice how this small change "punches up" the sentence.

Here are some more examples of how upgrading the lurkers can strengthen a sentence:

Weak: *My failure on the test **was** reflective of the fact of my not having studied.*

Stronger: *I **failed** the test because I **didn't study**.*

Here, we've upgraded the lurkers *reflective* (adjective) and *having studied* (participle). Notice that this change not only strengthens the verbs and clarifies the sentence, but also unclutters the sentence by eliminating the prepositional phrases *on the test, of the fact,* and *of my not having studied.*

Weak: *The fact of the governor's ignoring the protestors **made** them resentful of him.*

Stronger: *The protestors **resented** the fact that the governor **ignored** them.*

We've upgraded the lurkers *ignoring* (gerund) and *resentful* (adjective). Again, notice that strengthening the sentence also unclutters it of unnecessary prepositional phrases.

Weak: *The mice **had** a tendency to overeat when they **had** a lack of this hormone.*

Stronger: *The mice **overate** when they **lacked** this hormone.*

We've upgraded the lurkers *to overeat* (infinitive) and *lack* (noun).

Activate your passive verbs

> What is the difference between these two sentences?

The rebel army made its bold maneuver under the cloak of darkness.

The bold maneuver was made by the rebel army under the cloak of darkness.

These two sentences say essentially the same thing, but the first sentence is in the **active voice** whereas the second is in the **passive voice**. In the **active voice**, the subject of the sentence is the "actor" of the verb, but in the **passive voice**, the subject is *not* the actor. (The *maneuver* did not *make* anything, so *maneuver* is not the *actor* of the verb *made* in the second sentence, even though it is the subject.) Notice that the second sentence is weaker for two reasons: it's heavier (it has more words) *and* it's slower (it takes more time to get to the point).

But there's an even better reason to avoid passive voice verbs: they can make you sound deceitful. Consider this classic passive-voice sentence:

Mistakes were made.

Who made them? Thanks to the passive voice, we don't need to say. We can avoid responsibility.

> Although you may sometimes need to use the **passive voice**, avoid it when you can. The **active voice** is clearer and stronger, and it encourages you to articulate essential details (like "who did it") for your reader.

Weak: *The entire project **was completed by** Joe in less than a week.*

Stronger: *Joe **completed** the entire project in less than a week.*

Lesson 10: Use concrete and personal nouns

> Strong writers use **concrete and personal nouns**, even when discussing abstract ideas. Readers identify more strongly with people and things than they do with abstractions like *being* and *potential*.

You may have noticed that strengthening our verbs in Lesson 9 also had the extra benefit of strengthening our nouns:

Weak: *My **failure** on the **test** was reflective of the **fact** of my not **having studied**.*

Stronger: *I failed the **test** because I didn't study.*

In the first sentence, 75% of the nouns (*failure, fact*, and *having studied*) are abstract, but in the second, the nouns and pronouns (*I, test, I*) are personal and concrete.

Weak: *The **fact** of the governor's **ignoring** the **protestors** made **them** resentful of **him**.*

Stronger: *The **protestors** resented the **fact** that the **governor** ignored **them**.*

By upgrading the gerund *ignoring* to a verb, we reduced the number of abstract nouns in the sentence by 50%. Even better, we upgraded the subject from an abstract noun (*fact*) to a concrete and personal one (*protestors*).

Lesson 11: Explain and connect your ideas

According to the College Board, a strong essay *demonstrates a sophisticated understanding* of the source text and *demonstrates a logical and effective progression of ideas*. Therefore, **explain** each of your ideas and **connect** them with each other and with your central claim.

Explain your ideas

Don't merely state your ideas: *explain* them clearly enough so that your reader can easily follow your analysis.

Weak: *Pinker attempts to refute his critics with analogy.*

Stronger: *Pinker attempts to refute cultural critics by drawing an analogy between their reasoning and the faulty reasoning of "primitive peoples" who believe that "eating fierce animals will make them fierce."*

Good explanations often include words like **by** (*our team slowed down the game by using a full-court press*), **because** (*we won because we executed our game plan flawlessly*), or **therefore** (*we slowed down their offense; therefore, we were able to manage the game more effectively*).

Be careful, however, of overusing using phrases like **because of** and **due to**. These phrases tend to produce weak explanations because they link to *noun phrases* rather than *clauses*. Clauses are more explanatory because they include verbs and therefore convey more information.

Weak: *The essay works **because of** its imagery.*

Stronger: *The essay works **because** its images evoke powerful ideas that support the thesis.*

Notice that avoiding the *of* forces the writer to provide a *clause* instead of just a *noun phrase* and therefore give a more substantial explanation.

Connect your ideas with clear cross-references

In Chapter 4, Lesson 8, we discussed the importance of making strong **cross-references** in analytical or rhetorical essays, that is, connecting ideas to establish a clear chain of reasoning. **Use your pronouns carefully**, particularly when they refer to ideas mentioned in previous sentences. Make sure your pronouns have clear antecedents.

Consider these sentences:

Davis makes the important point that defense lawyers sometimes must represent clients whom they know are guilty, not only because these lawyers take an oath to uphold their clients' right to an adequate defense, but also because firms cannot survive financially if they accept only the obviously innocent as clients. This troubles many who want to pursue criminal law.

What does the pronoun *This* in the second sentence refer to? What *troubles many who want to study criminal law*? Is it the fact that Davis is making this point? Is it the moral implications of lawyers representing the guilty? Is it the technical difficulty of lawyers representing the guilty? Is it the financial challenges of maintaining a viable law practice? Is it all of these? The ambiguity of this pronoun obscures the discussion and makes the reader work harder to follow it. Clarify your references so that your train of thought is easy to follow.

*Davis makes the important point that defense lawyers sometimes must represent clients whom they know are guilty, not only because these lawyers take an oath to uphold their clients' right to an adequate defense, but also because firms cannot survive financially if they accept only the obviously innocent as clients. **Such moral and financial dilemmas** trouble many who want to pursue criminal law.*

Connect your ideas with logical transitions

As you move from idea to idea—within a sentence, between sentences, or between paragraphs—always consider the logical relationship between these ideas, and make these connections clear to your reader. The logical "connectors" include words and phrases like

for example	*furthermore*	*moreover*	*alternatively*
therefore	*however*	*first, second, third*	*otherwise*
because	*although*	*nevertheless*	*subsequently*
commensurately	*hence*	*thereby*	*as a consequence*

Lesson 12: Choose your words carefully

According to the College Board, a strong essay *demonstrates precise word choice*. **Chapter 3, "The Language of Ideas," provides exactly the vocabulary you need to articulate your ideas clearly and precisely.** Spend some time with the vocabulary in Chapter 3 to familiarize yourself with words like *consensus, conjecture, criteria, comprehensive, cohesive, circumscribe,* and *construe* that are at the heart of the "analytical task."

Choose *precise* words over *pretentious* ones. You won't get extra points for using obscure words when you could use simple ones.

Pretentious: *An astute scribe should always eschew superfluous grandiloquence.*

Precise: *A good writer uses big words only when necessary.*

Lesson 13: Pay attention to sentence structure

According to the College Board, a strong essay *uses an effective variety of sentence structures.* Short sentences have impact; long sentences have weight. Good writers realize this and structure their sentences to fit their purpose.

Consider this paragraph:

Medical interns are overworked. They are constantly asked to do a lot with very little sleep. They are chronically exhausted as a result. They can make mistakes that are dangerous and even potentially deadly.

What is so dreary about it? The sentences all have the same structure. Consider this revision:

Constantly overworked and given very little time to sleep, medical interns are chronically exhausted. These conditions can lead them to make dangerous and even deadly mistakes.

Your readers won't appreciate your profound ideas if they are stupefied by unvarying sentences. Now consider these sentences:

Gun advocates tell us that "guns don't kill people; people kill people." On the surface, this statement seems obviously true. However, analysis of the assumptions and implications of this statement shows clearly that even its most ardent believers can't possibly believe it.

Now consider this alternative:

Gun advocates tell us that "guns don't kill people; people kill people." On the surface, this statement seems obviously true. It's not.

Which is better? The first provides more information, but the second provides more impact. Good writers always think about the length of their sentences. Long sentences are often necessary for articulating complex ideas, but short sentences are better for emphasizing important points. Choose wisely.

Sample Essay

Analysis of Pinker's "Mind Over Mass Media"

In his essay, "Mind Over Mass Media," Steven Pinker examines the "moral panics" about the supposed moral and cognitive declines caused by new forms of media. His essay provides a measure of balance to our sometimes hysterical discussions of social media and instantaneous digital information. His thesis, that "such panics often fail reality checks," is supported with historical examples, logical analysis, illustrative images, and touches of humor. He provides scientific context for his claims and effectively analyzes the misconceptions that cultural critics have about the relationship between modern media and the human brain. Although his argument could have been bolstered with more specific scientific support, his essay as a whole effectively argues for a reprieve from the hysteria about intellectual and moral decline allegedly caused by Twitter and Facebook.

Pinker addresses common misconceptions with historical evidence: "When comic books were accused of turning juveniles into delinquents in the 1950s, crime was falling to record lows, just as the denunciations of video games in the 1990s coincided with the great American crime decline." Here, Pinker is suggesting that sociological and psychological evidence refutes claims of social decline.

Pinker effectively uses indirect proof or "reductio ad absurdum" in his third paragraph: "If electronic media were hazardous to intelligence, the quality of science would be plummeting. Yet discoveries are multiplying like fruit flies, and progress is dizzying. Other activities in the life of the mind, like philosophy, history and cultural criticism, are likewise flourishing." Unfortunately, Pinker does not provide substantial evidence to bolster these claims. He fails to address the common counterclaim that much of the "science" published on the Internet is flimsy, and the "cultural criticism" lazy.

Pinker then grounds his argument with reference to evidence from psychological research. To Pinker, the claim that "information can change the brain" is facile ("it's not as if the information is stored in the pancreas") and misleading ("the existence of neural plasticity does not mean the brain is a blob of clay pounded into shape by experience"). Rather, Pinker suggests, "the effects of experience are highly specific to the experiences themselves . . . Music doesn't make you better at math; conjugating Latin doesn't make you more logical; brain-training games don't make you smarter." Unfortunately, Pinker here seems to mistake assertion for argumentation. He is directly contradicting the claims of thousands of music and Latin teachers, as well as dozens of Lumosity commercials. But he is only gainsaying. Here again, we might expect some data to support his points.

Next, Pinker attempts to refute cultural critics by drawing an analogy between their reasoning and the faulty reasoning of "primitive peoples" who believe that "eating fierce animals will make them fierce." He likens this to the thinking of modern observers who believe that "reading bullet points and Twitter postings turns your thoughts into bullet points and Twitter postings." But of course just because one line of reasoning parallels another does not mean that both are equally incorrect. Here again, Pinker's argument would benefit from information about the actual cognitive effects of reading Twitter feeds.

Next, Pinker provides a concession to his opponents: "Yes, the constant arrival of information packets can be distracting or addictive, especially to people with attention deficit disorder." But here again, even in conceding a point, Pinker doesn't quite offer the information a reader might want: How significant is this distraction or addiction, and does it have any harmful long-term effects? We don't get this information, but we do get some welcome practical advice: "Turn off e-mail or Twitter when you work . . ." We get even more substantial advice in the next paragraph: to cultivate "intellectual depth" we must avail ourselves of "special institutions, which we call universities" and engage in "analysis, criticism, and debate." But why, a reader might wonder, should we moderate our use of electronic media if it doesn't have any real harmful effects, and indeed, as he says in his conclusion, these media "are the only things that will keep us smart?"

Finally, Pinker ends with a broader perspective and a note of hope: "the Internet and information technologies are helping us manage, search, and retrieve our collective intellectual output . . . Far from making us stupid, these technologies are the only things that will keep us smart." Perhaps Pinker is right, but his argument would be stronger with more substantial quantitative evidence and more direct refutation of our real concerns about how the Internet might be changing our brains.

Scoring

Reading—8 (both readers gave it a score of 4 out of 4)

This response demonstrates extremely thorough comprehension of Pinker's essay through skillful use of summary, paraphrase, and direct quotations. The author summarizes Pinker's central thesis and modes of persuasion (*His thesis, that "such panics often fail reality checks," is supported with historical examples, logical analysis, illustrative images, and touches of humor*) and shows a clear understanding of Pinker's supporting ideas and overall tone (*He provides historical and scientific context for his claims and effectively analyzes the misconceptions that cultural critics have about the relationship between modern media and the human brain. . . . Pinker ends with a broader perspective and a note of hope*). Each quotation is accompanied by insightful commentary that demonstrates that this author thoroughly understands Pinker's central and secondary ideas, and even recognizes when Pinker seems occasionally to fall short of his own purpose.

Analysis—8 (both readers gave it a score of 4 out of 4)

This response provides a thoughtful and critical analysis of Pinker's essay and demonstrates a sophisticated understanding of the analytical task. The author has identified Pinker's primary modes of expression (*historical examples, logical analysis, illustrative images, and touches of humor*) and has even provided a detailed examination of Pinker's preferred logical method, reductio ad absurdum, with a discussion of several examples. Perhaps even more impressively, the author indicates where Pinker's evidence falls short, providing critical analysis and suggesting alternatives (*Unfortunately, Pinker does not provide substantial evidence to bolster these claims. He fails to address the common counterclaim that much of the "science" published on the Internet is flimsy, and the "cultural criticism" lazy. . . . Pinker here seems to mistake assertion for argumentation. . . . Here again, Pinker's argument would benefit from information about the actual cognitive effects of reading Twitter feeds*). Overall, the author's analysis of Pinker's essays demonstrates a thorough understanding not only of the rhetorical task that Pinker has set for himself, but also the means by which it is best accomplished.

Writing—8 (both readers gave it a score of 4 out of 4)

This response shows a masterful use of language and sentence structure to establish a clear and insightful central claim (*Although his argument could have been bolstered with more specific scientific support, his essay as a whole effectively argues for a reprieve from the hysteria about intellectual and moral decline allegedly caused by Twitter and Facebook*). The response maintains a consistent focus on this central claim and supports it with a well-developed and cohesive analysis of Pinker's essay. The author demonstrates effective verb choice (*effectively analyzes the misconceptions . . . . He likens this to the thinking of modern observers*) and a strong grasp of relevant analytical terms such as *reduction ad absurdum*, *facile*, *sociological and psychological evidence*, *counterclaim*, *assertion*, *argumentation*, and *gainsaying*. The response is well developed, progressing from general claim to specific analysis to considered evaluation. Largely free from grammatical error, this response demonstrates strong command of language and proficiency in writing.

THE SAT MATH TEST: THE HEART OF ALGEBRA

The SAT Math: Heart of Algebra

Why is algebra so important on the SAT Math test?

About 36% (21 out of 58) of the SAT Math questions fall under the category called the "Heart of Algebra." Questions in this category test your ability to

> *analyze, fluently solve, and create linear equations, inequalities, [and] systems of equations using multiple techniques.*

These questions will also assess your skill in

> *interpreting the interplay between graphical and algebraic representations [and] solving as a process of reasoning.*

The specific topics include

- creating and solving linear equations in one and two variables
- graphing and interpreting linear equations
- creating, interpreting, and solving linear systems
- graphing and solving inequalities and systems of inequalities
- interpreting and solving algebraic word problems

Why are these skills important?

Algebra is an essential tool of quantitative analysis not only in math but also in subjects like engineering, the physical sciences, and economics. When describing the relationships between or among different quantities, or exploring the nature of unknown quantities, algebra provides essential tools for analyzing and solving problems. Most colleges consider fluency in algebra to be a vital prerequisite to a college-level liberal arts curriculum.

Sound intimidating? It's not.

If you take the time to master the four core skills presented in these 13 lessons, you will gain the knowledge and practice you need to master even the toughest SAT Math "Heart of Algebra" questions.

Skill 1: Working with Expressions
Lesson 1: Using algebraic expressions

To solve tough SAT math problems, you must be fluent in defining, manipulating, and analyzing algebraic expressions.

Corrine drives to her office at an average speed of 50 miles per hour. When she returns home by the same route, the traffic is lighter and she averages 60 miles per hour. If her trip home is 10 minutes shorter than her trip to her office, what is the distance, in miles, from Corrine's home to her office?

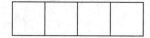

(*Medium-hard*) Why does everyone hate "word problems" like this one? For most of us, the problem is that the equations aren't "set up" for us—we have to set them up ourselves, which can be a pain in the neck. But we can make these problems much easier by breaking them down into clear steps.

Key Steps to Solving Tough Algebraic Problems

Solving tough problems in mathematics and science frequently involves four essential steps:

1. identify the relevant quantities in the situation
2. express those quantities with algebraic expressions
3. translate the facts of the problem situation into equations involving those expressions
4. analyze and solve those equations

Step 1. Identify: In this problem, there are six relevant quantities:

- the speed from home to work
- the distance from home to work
- the time it takes to get from home to work
- the speed from work to home
- the distance from work to home
- the time it takes to get from work to home

This may seem like a lot, but as we will see, keeping track of them is quite manageable.

Step 2. Express: The problem gives us enough information to express all six quantities in terms of only two "unknowns." If d is the distance, in miles, from her home to her office, and t is the time, in hours, it takes her to get home from the office, then we can express our six quantities, respectively, as

To Office	From Office
50 mph	60 mph
d miles	d miles
$t + 1/6$ hours (10 minutes = 1/6)	t hours

Step 3. Translate: To translate the facts of this problem into equations, we must know the formula *distance = average speed × time*. Applying this to each trip gives us

To Office	From Office
$d = 50(t + 1/6)$	$d = 60(t)$

Step 4. Analyze and Solve: We have now reduced the problem to a "two by two system," that is, two equations with two unknowns. Since the number of equations equals the number of unknowns, we should be able to solve for those unknowns. (In Lessons 12 and 13, we will review these concepts and techniques.) Since the unknown d is isolated in both equations, substitution is simple:

1. Substitute for d: $\qquad\qquad 50(t + 1/6) = 60(t)$
2. Distribute: $\qquad\qquad 50t + 50/6 = 60t$
3. Subtract 50t: $\qquad\qquad 50/6 = 10t$
4. Divide by 10: $\qquad\qquad 5/6 = t$

Since t represents the time it took Corrine to return home, in hours, this means it took her 5/6 hours (or 50 minutes) to get from her office to her home, and 5/6 hour + 1/6 hour = 1 hour to get to her office from home. But remember, the question asks for the *distance* from her home to her office, which we can find by substituting into either of our equations:

$$50(5/6 + 1/6) \quad \text{or} \quad 60(5/6) = 50 \text{ miles}$$

Lesson 2: The Laws of Arithmetic

When expressing or simplifying a quantity, you frequently have many options. For instance, the expression $4x^2 - 12x$ can also be expressed as $4x(x - 3)$. Similarly, 3.2 can be expressed as 16/5 or 3 ⅕ or 32/10. Which way is better? It depends on what you want to do with the expression. Different forms of an expression can reveal different characteristics of that quantity or the equation in which it appears. To gain fluency in expressing quantities, you must understand the **Laws of Arithmetic.**

What is the value of $\dfrac{3+6\times2}{2\times4}+\dfrac{5-1}{2\times1^3}$?

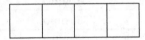

To simplify complex expressions, you must know the Order of Operations:

PG-ER-MD-AS

Step 1: **PG** (**parentheses** and other **grouping** symbols, from innermost to outermost and left to right)

Since this expression contains no parentheses, we don't have to worry about "grouped" operations, right? Wrong! Remember that **fraction bars and radicals are "grouping symbols" just like parentheses are.**

In other words, we can think of this expression as

$$\frac{(3+6\times2)}{(2\times4)}+\frac{(5-1)}{(2\times1^3)}$$

If a set of parentheses contains only one operation, then we simply do that operation:

$$\frac{(3+6\times2)}{8}+\frac{4}{(2\times1^3)}$$

If it contains more than one operation, then we must move on to the next step.

Step 2: **ER** (**exponents** and **roots**, from innermost to outermost and left to right)

Do any of the parentheses contain exponents or roots? Yes, so we must perform that operation next:

$$\frac{(3+6\times2)}{8}+\frac{4}{(2\times1)}$$

Step 3: **MD** (**multiplication** and **division**, from left to right)

Next, we do any multiplication inside the parentheses:

$$\frac{(3+12)}{8}+\frac{4}{2}$$

Step 4: **AS** (**addition** and **subtraction**, from left to right)

Now we do any addition and subtraction left in the parentheses:

$$\frac{15}{8}+\frac{4}{2}$$

Once all the "grouped" operations are completed, we run through the order of operations once again to finish up. Exponents or roots? No. Multiplication or division? Yes:

$$1.875 + 2$$

Addition or subtraction? Yes: $1.875 + 2 = 3.875$

What is the sum of the first 100 positive integers?

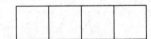

(*Hard*) Here, following the order of operations would be, shall we say, less than convenient: it would require 99 computations. Even with a calculator, it would be a pain. But here is a much simpler method:

Original expression:	$1 + 2 + 3 + 4 + \cdots + 97 + 98 + 99 + 100$
Rearrange and regroup:	$(1 + 100) + (2 + 99) + (3 + 98) + \cdots + (50 + 51)$
Simplify:	$(101) + (101) + (101) + \cdots + (101)$
Since we have 50 pairs, this equals:	$50(101)$
Simplify:	$5{,}050$

This gives us *exactly the same result* as the order of operations would give, but with just a few simple calculations. How did we do it? By using three more laws of arithmetic: the **commutative law of addition**, the **associative law of addition**, and the **distributive law of multiplication over addition.**

Use the Laws of Arithmetic to simplify expressions or reveal their properties.

The Commutative Law of Addition

When adding, order doesn't matter.

e.g., $3 + 8 + 17 + 12 = 3 + 17 + 12 + 8$

The Commutative Law of Multiplication

When multiplying, order doesn't matter.

e.g., $2 \times 16 \times 50 \times 3 = 3 \times 16 \times 50 \times 2$

The Associative Law of Addition

When adding, grouping doesn't matter.

e.g., $1 + 100 + 2 + 99 + 3 + 98 + \cdots + 50 + 51 = (1 + 100) + (2 + 99) + (3 + 98) + \cdots + (50 + 51)$

The Associative Law of Multiplication

When multiplying, grouping doesn't matter.

e.g., $1 \times 2 \times 3 \times 4 \times 5 = (1 \times 2 \times 3) \times (4 \times 5)$

The Distributive Law of Multiplication over Addition

When multiplying by a grouped sum, you don't have to do the grouped sum first; you can multiply first, as long as you distribute the multiplication over the entire sum.

e.g., $5(20 + 7) = 5 \times 20 + 5 \times 7 = 100 + 35 = 135$

Which of the following is equivalent to $3(3^4 \times 5^3)$? [No calculator]

A) $3(3^4) \times 3(5^3)$

B) $9^4 + 15^3$

C) $9^4 \times 15^3$

D) $3^5 \times 5^3$

Before making your choice, check the laws of arithmetic; don't make up your own laws. Which laws of arithmetic can we use? Since the expression is a product, we can use the **commutative law of multiplication** and jumble up the terms, or the **associative law of multiplication** and regroup the terms any way we want (or not at all). Using the associative law gives us

$3(3^4 \times 5^3) = (3 \times 3^4) \times 5^3 = 3^5 \times 5^3$ Therefore, the correct answer is (D).

Don't "over-distribute."

Were you tempted to choose (A), (B), or (C) in the question above? If so, you are not alone. You are simply the victim of one of the most common mistakes in algebra: over-distribution. It comes from a misinterpretation of the Law of Distribution. The correct law is

When multiplying by a grouped sum, you don't have to do the grouped sum first; you can multiply first, as long as you distribute the multiplication over the entire sum.

It is *not*

If something is outside parentheses, just bring it inside and distribute.

Look at these examples of "over-distribution" and verify that they are incorrect:

$3(2 \times 5)$ is **not** equal to $(3 \times 2) + (3 \times 5)$ or $(3 \times 2) \times (3 \times 5)$

$(2 + 3)^2$ is **not** equal to $2^2 + 3^2$

If $x \neq 0$, which of the following equals $\dfrac{3x^2 + 6x + 9x^2}{3x}$?

A) $2x + \dfrac{1}{2}$

B) $4x + \dfrac{1}{2}$

C) $2x^2 + 2$

D) $4x + 2$

(*Medium*)

$$\dfrac{3x^2 + 6x + 9x^2}{3x}$$

Commutative Law of Addition:

$$\dfrac{3x^2 + 9x^2 + 6x}{3x}$$

Associative Law of Addition:

$$\dfrac{(3x^2 + 9x^2) + 6x}{3x}$$

Distributive Law:

$$\dfrac{(3 + 9)x^2 + 6x}{3x} = \dfrac{12x^2 + 6x}{3x}$$

Division by a number is multiplication by its reciprocal:

$$\dfrac{1}{3x}(12x^2 + 6x)$$

Distributive Law:

$$\dfrac{12x^2}{3x} + \dfrac{6x}{3x} = 4x + 2$$

So the correct answer is (D). Look at each step carefully and notice how each one uses a particular Law of Arithmetic. In particular, notice that the "combining of like terms" in steps 1–3 is really an example of commuting, associating, and (un)distributing. Even more interesting, notice that steps 4–5 show that division distributes just like multiplication does.

You can also distribute division over addition just as you can distribute multiplication.

$$\text{e.g.,} \quad \frac{25a + 5ab}{5b} = \frac{25a}{5b} + \frac{5ab}{5b} = \frac{5a}{b} + a$$

How many distinct values of x are solutions to the equation $x^2 + 4 = -4x$?

A) none

B) one

C) two

D) three

(*Medium*) You might recognize that this equation is a **quadratic equation** (which we will discuss in much more detail in Chapter 9) and remember that such equations *usually* have two distinct solutions, but *not always*, so we must look at this equation more carefully.

1. Add $4x$: $x^2 + 4x + 4 = 0$
2. Since $4x = 2x + 2x$: $x^2 + 2x + 2x + 4 = 0$

Step 2 might seem a bit mysterious. Why did we write $4x$ as $2x + 2x$? Here we are using the **Product-Sum Method** for factoring quadratics, which is explained in a bit more detail in Chapter 9, Lesson 4. For now, though, just notice that each step follows a particular Law of Arithmetic.

3. Associative Law of Addition: $(x^2 + 2x) + (2x + 4) = 0$
4. Distributive Law: $x(x + 2) + 2(x + 2) = 0$
5. Distributive Law: $(x + 2)(x + 2) = 0$

If the product of two numbers is 0, then one of those numbers must be 0. (This is the **Zero Product Property**.) Therefore $x + 2 = 0$ and so $x = -2$. Since the other factor is the same, we only get one solution to this equation, and the answer is (B).

To check the equation in step 5, we can FOIL the product of binomials on the left side to make sure we get the same expression we had back in step 1: $(x + 2)(x + 2) = x^2 + 4x + 4$, which is precisely the expression we started with in step 1, confirming that our work is correct.

This means that the factoring process in steps 2–5 can be thought of as un-FOILing. We will look at this method of factoring more carefully in Chapter 9.

Make sure you know how to FOIL and un-FOIL.

FOILing is simply the shortcut for multiplying two binomials, which requires applying the distributive law twice. For example:

	$(x + 4)(x - 5)$
F (product of the two "first" terms):	$x \times x = x^2$
O (product of the two "outside" terms):	$x \times -5 = -5x$
I (product of the two "inside" terms):	$4 \times x = 4x$
L (product of the two "last" terms):	$4 \times -5 = -20$
F + O + I + L:	$x^2 + -5x + 4x + -20 = x^2 - x - 20$

Exercise Set 1 (No Calculator)

1

$(1 - (1 - (1 - 2))) - (1 - (1 - (1 - 3))) =$

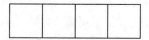

2

When 14 is subtracted from 6 times a number, 40 is left. What is half the number?

3

Four consecutive even numbers have a sum of 76. What is the greatest of these numbers?

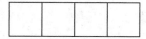

4

If $\dfrac{5x}{2} + 3 = 7$, then $10x + 12 =$

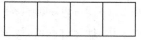

5

What number decreased by 7 equals the opposite of five times the number?

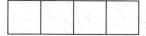

6

If $5d + 12 = 24$, then $5d - 12 =$

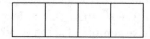

7

If $\dfrac{2y^2}{5} = y^2$, then $y + 5 =$

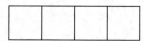

8

The product of x and y is 36. If both x and y are integers, then what is the least possible value of $x - y$?

A) -37

B) -36

C) -35

D) -9

9

If a factory can manufacture b computer screens in n days at a cost of c dollars per screen, then which of the following represents the total cost, in dollars, of the computer screens that can be manufactured, at that rate, in m days?

A) $\dfrac{bcm}{n}$

B) $\dfrac{bmn}{c}$

C) $\dfrac{mc}{bn}$

D) $\dfrac{bc}{mn}$

10

Which of the following is equivalent to $5x(2x \times 3) - 5x^2$ for all real values of x?

A) $5x^2 + 15x$

B) $25x^2$

C) $5x^2 - 15x$

D) $10x^2 \times 15x - 5x^2$

11

The symbol **O** represents one of the fundamental operators: $+$, $-$, $\times$, or $\div$. If $(x \, \mathbf{O} \, y) \times (y \, \mathbf{O} \, x) = 1$ for all positive values of x and y, then **O** can represent

A) $+$

B) $\times$

C) $-$

D) $\div$

Exercise Set 1 (Calculator)

12

The difference of two numbers is 4 and their sum is 14. What is their product?

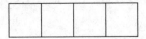

13

If $x + y - 1 = 1 - (1 - x)$, what is the value of y?

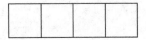

14

If $3x^2 + 2x = 40$, then $15x^2 + 10x =$

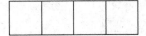

15

Ellen is currently twice as old as Maria, but in 6 years, Maria will be 2/3 as old as Ellen. How old is Ellen now?

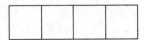

16

If $2x - 2y = 5$ and $x + y = 6$, what is the value of $x^2 - y^2$?

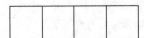

17

On a typical day, a restaurant sells n grilled cheese sandwiches for p dollars each. Today, however, the manager reduced the price of grilled cheese sandwiches by 30% and as a result sold 50% more of them than usual. Which of the following represents the revenue for today's grilled cheese sandwich sales, in dollars?

A) $0.5np - 0.3$

B) $1.05np$

C) $1.20np$

D) $1.50np$

18

For all real numbers x and y, $4x(x) - 3xy(2x) =$

A) $12x^2y(x - 2y)$

B) $2x^2(2 - 3y)$

C) $2x^2(2 + 3y)$

D) $4xy(x - 3y)$

19

If $a = 60(99)^{99} + 30(99)^{99}$, $b = 99^{100}$, and $c = 90(90)^{99}$, then which of the following expresses the correct ordering of a, b, and c?

A) $c < b < a$

B) $b < c < a$

C) $a < b < c$

D) $c < a < b$

20

Which of the following statements must be true for all values of x, y, and z?

   I. $(x + y) + z = (z + y) + x$

   II. $(x - y) - z = (z - y) - x$

   III. $(x \div y) \div z = (z \div y) \div x$

A) I only

B) I and II only

C) I and III only

D) II and III only

21

Carlos began with twice as much money as David had. After Carlos gave $12 to David, Carlos still had $10 more than David. How much money did they have <u>combined</u> at the start?

A) $34

B) $68

C) $102

D) $108

EXERCISE SET 1 ANSWER KEY

No Calculator

1. 1

$$(1 - (1 - (1 - 2))) - (1 - (1 - (1 - 3)))$$

Parentheses:	$(1 - (1 - (-1))) - (1 - (1 - (-2)))$
Next parentheses:	$(1 - (2)) - (1 - (3))$
Next parentheses:	$(-1) - (-2)$
Subtract:	$-1 + 2 = 1$

2. 9/2 or 4.5 $\qquad 6x - 14 = 40$

Add 14:	$6x = 54$
Divide by 6:	$x = 9$
Multiply by $\dfrac{1}{2}$:	$\dfrac{1}{2}x = \dfrac{9}{2}$

3. 22 Let n be the least of these numbers. The sum of four consecutive even numbers is therefore $n + (n + 2) + (n + 4) + (n + 6) = 76$.

Simplify:	$4n + 12 = 76$
Subtract 12:	$4n = 64$
Divide by 4:	$n = 16$

Therefore the largest of these numbers is $16 + 6 = 22$.

4. 28 $\qquad\qquad\qquad \dfrac{5}{2}x + 3 = 7$

Multiply by 4:	$10x + 12 = 28$

5. 7/6 or 1.16 or 1.17 $\qquad x - 7 = -5x$

Subtract x:	$-7 = -6x$
Divide by -6:	$\dfrac{7}{6} = x$

6. 0 $\qquad\qquad\qquad\qquad 5d + 12 = 24$

Subtract 24:	$5d - 12 = 0$

7. 5 $\qquad\qquad\qquad\qquad \dfrac{2y^2}{5} = y^2$

Subtract y^2:	$-\dfrac{3y^2}{5} = 0$
Multiply by $-5/3$:	$y^2 = 0$
Take square root:	$y = 0$
Add 5:	$y + 5 = 5$

8. C If $xy = 36$ and x and y are integers, then x and y are both factors of 36. In order to minimize the value of $x - y$, we must find the greatest separation between x and y. The greatest separation between a factor pair is $1 - 36 = -35$.

9. A We should regard this as a "conversion" problem from m *days* into a corresponding number of *dollars*.

$$m \text{ days} \times \frac{b \text{ screens}}{n \text{ days}} \times \frac{c \text{ dollars}}{1 \text{ screen}} = \frac{bcm}{n}$$

10. B Original expression: $\qquad 5x(2x \times 3) - 5x^2$

Parentheses:	$5x(6x) - 5x^2$
Multiply:	$30x^2 - 5x^2$
Subtract:	$25x^2$

Remember: The Law of Distribution does *not* apply in the first step, because the grouped expression doesn't include addition or subtraction.

11. D The simplest approach is perhaps to choose simple values for x and y, like 2 and 3, and see which operator yields a true equation. Since $(2 \div 3) \times (3 \div 2) = 1$, the answer is (D).

Calculator

12. 45 $\qquad\qquad\qquad\qquad a - b = 4$

$$a + b = 14$$

Add equations:	$2a = 18$
Divide by 2:	$a = 9$
Substitute $a = 9$:	$9 + b = 14$
Subtract 9:	$b = 5$
Evaluate ab:	$ab = 9 \times 5 = 45$

13. 1 $\qquad\qquad x + y - 1 = 1 - (1 - x)$

Distribute:	$x + y - 1 = 1 - 1 + x$
Subtract x:	$y - 1 = 1 - 1$
Simplify:	$y - 1 = 0$
Add 1:	$y = 1$

14. 200 $\qquad\qquad\qquad 3x^2 + 2x = 40$

Multiply by 5:	$15x^2 + 10x = 200$

15. 12 Let $e =$ Ellen's current age and $m =$ Maria's current age.

Ellen is twice as old as Maria:	$e = 2m$
In 6 years, Maria will be 2/3 as old as Ellen:	$m + 6 = \dfrac{2}{3}(e + 6)$
Substitute $e = 2m$:	$m + 6 = \dfrac{2}{3}(2m + 6)$
Multiply by 3:	$3m + 18 = 2(2m + 6)$
Distribute:	$3m + 18 = 4m + 12$
Subtract $3m$ and 12:	$6 = m$

Therefore $e = 2m = 2(6) = 12$.

16. **15** First equation: $2x - 2y = 5$

Divide by 2: $x - y = 2.5$
Second equation: $x + y = 6$
Multiply: $(x - y)(x + y) = x^2 - y^2 = (2.5)(6) = 15$

Alternately, we could solve the system using either substitution or linear combination and get $x = 4.25$ and $y = 1.75$, and evaluate $x^2 - y^2 = (4.25)^2 - (1.75)^2 = 18.0625 - 3.0625 = 15$.

17. **B** The revenue is equal to the number of items sold times the price per item. If the restaurant typically sells n sandwiches per day, but today sold 50% more, it sold $1.5n$ sandwiches. If the price p was reduced 30%, today's price is $0.70p$. Therefore, the total revenue is $(1.5n)(0.70p) = 1.05np$.

18. **B** $4x(x) - 3xy(2x)$

Multiply: $4x^2 - 6x^2y$
Largest common factor: $2x^2(2 - 3y)$

19. **D** Although a calculator is permitted for this question, most calculators will give an "overflow error" when trying to calculate numbers like 99^{100}, because they're just too large. However, comparing these numbers is straightforward if we can express them in a common format.

$a = 60(99)^{99} + 30(99)^{99}$ $= 90(99)^{99}$
$b = 99^{100}$ $= 99(99)^{99}$
$c = 90(90)^{99}$ $= 90(90)^{99}$

20. **A** Only statement I is true, by the Commutative and Associative Laws of Addition. Choosing simple values like $x = 1$, $y = 2$, and $z = 3$ will demonstrate that statements II and III do not yield true equations.

21. **C** Let $x =$ the number of dollars David had to start. If Carlos started with twice as much money as David, then Carlos started with $2x$ dollars. After Carlos gave David $12, Carlos had $2x - 12$ dollars and David had $x + 12$ dollars. If Carlos still had $10 more than David, then

$$2x - 12 = 10 + x + 12$$

Simplify: $2x - 12 = x + 22$
Add 12: $2x = x + 34$
Subtract x: $x = 34$

Therefore, David started with $34 and Carlos started with $2(\$34) = \$68$, so they had $\$34 + \$68 = \$102$ combined to start.

Lesson 3: Simplifying expressions and operations

If x and y are positive numbers and $3x - 2y = 7$, what is the value of $\dfrac{2y+7}{6x}$?

A) $\dfrac{1}{7}$

B) $\dfrac{1}{3}$

C) $\dfrac{2}{7}$

D) $\dfrac{1}{2}$

(*Easy*) Working with algebraic equations doesn't always mean "solving for x." Notice that this particular question doesn't ask for the values of x or y, but rather for the value of a more complicated expression. This may seem harder, but it's actually pretty simple if you understand the Law of Substitution

The Law of Substitution

If two expressions are equal, then you may substitute one for the other at any point in the problem.

How does this help us here? Notice that if we simply add $2y$ to both sides of the equation, we get

$$3x - 2y = 7$$

Add $2y$: $\qquad\qquad\qquad\qquad\qquad 3x = 2y + 7$

Therefore, by the Law of Substitution, we can substitute $3x$ for $2y + 7$ or vice-versa. Since $2y + 7$ appears in the expression we are asked to evaluate, it makes sense to replace it with $3x$:

$$\dfrac{2y+7}{6x}$$

Substitute $3x$ for $2y + 7$: $\qquad\qquad \dfrac{3x}{6x}$

Simplify: $\qquad\qquad\qquad\qquad\quad \dfrac{1}{2}$

When a question asks you to analyze a complex expression, don't be intimidated. Look for simple relationships that allow you to simplify them using techniques like the Law of Substitution.

Increasing a positive number x by 25% and then decreasing the result by 50% is equivalent to dividing x by what number?

A) 1.333

B) 1.5

C) 1.6

D) 1.625

(*Medium*) Increasing a quantity by 25% is equivalent to multiplying it by 1.25, because the final amount is 125% of the original amount (Chapter 8, Lesson 8). Decreasing a quantity by 50% is equivalent to multiplying it by .5, because the final amount is 50% of the original amount. Therefore, performing both changes is equivalent to multiplying by 1.25×0.50, or 0.625, which is equal to 5/8. But the question asks us for the equivalent *division*. Here, we need to remember a simple rule: **multiplying by a number is equivalent to dividing by its reciprocal**. Therefore, multiplying by 5/8 is the same as dividing by 8/5, which is 1.6. Therefore, the correct answer is (C).

Every operation can be expressed in terms of its inverse operation.

Adding (x)	is equivalent to	subtracting ($-x$).
Subtracting (x)	is equivalent to	adding ($-x$).
Multiplying by (x)	is equivalent to	dividing by $\left(\dfrac{1}{x}\right)$.
Dividing by $\left(\dfrac{x}{y}\right)$	is equivalent to	multiplying by $\left(\dfrac{y}{x}\right)$.
Taking the nth root of a number	is equivalent to	raising the number to the $\left(\dfrac{1}{n}\right)$th power.

And here are two more handy equivalences:

| Increasing a number by x% | is equivalent to | multiplying that number by $\left(1+\dfrac{x}{100}\right)$. |
| Decreasing a number by x% | is equivalent to | multiplying that number by $\left(1-\dfrac{x}{100}\right)$. |

If $\dfrac{m^2-n^2}{2m-2n}=\dfrac{9}{2}$ what is the value of $m+n$?

(*Easy*) When a problem includes a complicated expression, we should try to simplify it, but always keep an eye on what the question is asking. In this case, simplifying to find the value of $m+n$ requires knowing some factoring identities.

Useful factoring identities

The difference of squares equals the product of conjugates: $x^2-y^2=(x+y)(x-y)$

Perfect square polynomials: $x^2+2ax+a^2=(x+a)(x+a)$

$x^2-2ax+a^2=(x-a)(x-a)$

The first of these identities helps us factor our numerator: $\dfrac{m^2-n^2}{2m-2n}=\dfrac{9}{2}$

Factor numerator and denominator: $\dfrac{(m+n)(m-n)}{2(m-n)}=\dfrac{9}{2}$

Cancel common factors: $\dfrac{(m+n)}{2}=\dfrac{9}{2}$

Multiply by 2: $m+n=9$

Lesson 4: Using conversion as a problem-solving tool

Niko is 27 inches shorter than his father, who is 5 feet 10 inches tall. How tall is Niko? (1 foot = 12 inches)

A) 3 feet 4 inches

B) 3 feet 6 inches

C) 3 feet 7 inches

D) 3 feet 10 inches

(*Easy*) Solving this problem requires **unit conversions**. To convert inches to feet, we multiply by the conversion factor (1 foot/12 inches). To convert feet to inches, we multiply by its reciprocal (12 inches/1 foot). If Niko's father is 5 feet 10 inches tall, he is 5 feet × (12 inches/1 foot) + 10 inches = 70 inches tall. If Niko is 27 inches shorter, he is 70 − 27 = 43 inches tall, which is equivalent to 43 inches × (1 foot/12 inches) = 3 7/12 feet, or 3 feet 7 inches, so the correct answer is (C).

Conversion factors as problem-solving tools

A **conversion factor** is simply a fraction in which the quantities in the numerator and the denominator represent equal quantities. Sometimes the equivalence is **universal**—for instance, 1 pound is **always** equal to 16 ounces—and sometimes it is **problem-specific**—for instance when a machine pump waters at a rate 3 gallons per hour, 1 hour of pumping is "equal" to 3 gallons being pumped.

If a factory can manufacture b computer screens in n days at a cost of c dollars per screen, then which of the following represents the total cost, in dollars, of the computer screens that can be manufactured, at that rate, in m days?

A) $\dfrac{bcm}{n}$

B) $\dfrac{bmn}{c}$

C) $\dfrac{mc}{bn}$

D) $\dfrac{bc}{mn}$

(*Medium*) This problem, from the previous exercise set, can be solved in several different ways. One method is to simply choose values for the unknowns and turn the problem into an arithmetic problem instead of an algebra problem. But here we will look at it as a *conversion* problem.

We can think of this problem as being a "conversion" from a quantity of *days* to an equivalent quantity of *dollars*. We are given that this factory is working for m days, so we write this quantity down, including the units, and we multiply by the conversion factors until we get dollars:

$$m\,\text{days} \times \frac{b\,\text{screens}}{n\,\text{days}} \times \frac{c\,\text{dollars}}{1\,\text{screen}} = \frac{bcm}{n}\,\text{dollars}$$

So the correct answer is (A).

Exercise Set 2 (No Calculator)

1

If bag A weighs 4 pounds 5 ounces and bag B weighs 6 pounds 2 ounces, how much heavier, in <u>ounces</u>, is bag B than bag A? (1 pound = 16 ounces)

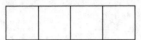

2

If $\dfrac{3a+b}{b}=\dfrac{7}{5}$, what is the value of $\dfrac{a}{b}$?

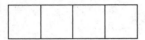

3

If $x - 2y = 10$ and $x \neq 0$, what is the value of $\dfrac{2x}{y+5}$?

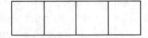

4

If $a - b = 4$ and $a^2 - b^2 = 3$, what is the value of $a + b$?

5

If 6 gricks are equivalent to 5 merts, then 2 merts are equivalent to how many gricks?

6

If the function $\{x\}$ is defined by the equation $\{x\} = (1 - x)^2$, what is the value of $\{\{4\}\}$?

7

If $\dfrac{a+b}{b}=3$ and $\dfrac{a+c}{c}=5$, what is the value of $\dfrac{b}{c}$?

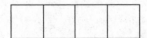

8

$$(x - 9)(x - a) = x^2 - 4ax + b$$

In the equation above, a and b are constants. If the equation is true for all values of x, what is the value of b?

A) −27

B) −12

C) 12

D) 27

9

If $\dfrac{5}{x}+\dfrac{7}{5}=1$, what is the value of x?

A) $-\dfrac{25}{2}$

B) −7

C) $-\dfrac{24}{7}$

D) $-\dfrac{7}{5}$

10

$$(p + 2)^2 = (p - 5)^2$$

The equation above is true for which of the following values of p?

A) −2 and 5

B) 2 and −5

C) 1.5 only

D) 5 only

11

If $\dfrac{3x}{m-nx}=2$ for all positive values of m and n, then which of the following is equal to x?

A) $\dfrac{2m-2n}{3}$

B) $\dfrac{2m-3}{2n}$

C) $\dfrac{3+2n}{2m}$

D) $\dfrac{2m}{3+2n}$

Exercise Set 2 (Calculator)

12

Let m be a positive real number. Increasing m by 60% then decreasing the result by 50% is equivalent to dividing m by what number?

13

What is the sum of the first 50 positive even integers?

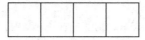

14

Three years ago, Nora was half as old as Mary is now. If Mary is four years older than Nora, how old is Mary now?

15

If 2/3 of the seats at a football stadium were filled at the beginning of the game, and at halftime 1,000 spectators left, leaving 3/7 of the seats filled, what is the total number of seats in the stadium?

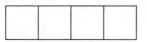

16

If three candy bars and two gumdrops cost $2.20, and four candy bars and two gumdrops cost $2.80, what is the cost, in dollars, of one gumdrop?

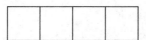

17

If $\dfrac{x^2 - 2x + 1}{2 - 2x} = -3$, what is the value of $x - 1$?

18

Subtracting 3 from a number and then multiplying this result by 4 is equivalent to multiplying the original number by 4 and then subtracting what number?

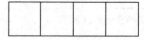

19

In a poker game, a blue chip is worth 2 dollars more than a red chip, and a red chip is worth 2 dollars more than a green chip. If 5 green chips are worth m dollars, then which of the following represents the value, in dollars, of 10 blue chips and 5 red chips?

A) $50 + 3m$

B) $18 + 60m$

C) $40 + 3m$

D) $28 + 20m$

20

A train travels at an average speed of 50 miles per hour for the first 100 miles of a 200-mile trip, and at an average of 75 miles per hour for final 100 miles. What is the train's average speed for the entire trip?

A) 58.5 mph

B) 60.0 mph

C) 62.5 mph

D) 63.5 mph

21

Which of the following is equivalent to $3m(m^2 \times 2m)$ for all real values of m?

A) $3m^2 + 6m$

B) $3m^2 \times 6m$

C) $3m^3 \times 6m^2$

D) $6m^4$

22

If the cost of living in a certain city increased by 20% in the 10 years from 1980 to 1990, and increased by 50% in the 20 years from 1980 to 2000, what was the percent increase in the cost of living from 1990 to 2000?

A) 15%

B) 20%

C) 25%

D) 30%

EXERCISE SET 2 ANSWER KEY

No Calculator

1. **29** 4 pounds 5 ounces $= 4(16) + 5 = 69$ ounces, and 6 pounds 2 ounces $= 6(16) + 2 = 98$ ounces. Therefore, bag B weighs $98 - 69 = 29$ ounces more.

2. **2/15 or .133**

$$\frac{3a+b}{b} = \frac{7}{5}$$

Distribute division:

$$\frac{3a}{b} + \frac{b}{b} = \frac{7}{5}$$

Simplify:

$$\frac{3a}{b} + 1 = \frac{7}{5}$$

Subtract 1:

$$\frac{3a}{b} = \frac{2}{5}$$

Divide by 3:

$$\frac{a}{b} = \frac{2}{15}$$

3. **4** Expression to be evaluated:

$$\frac{2x}{y+5}$$

Given equation: $x - 2y = 10$

Add $2y$: $x = 2y + 10$

Substitute $x = 2y + 10$:

$$\frac{2(2y+10)}{y+5}$$

Simplify:

$$\frac{4y+20}{y+5}$$

Factor and simplify:

$$\frac{4(y+5)}{y+5} = 4$$

4. **¾ or .75** $a^2 - b^2 = 3$

Factor: $(a-b)(a+b) = 3$

Substitute $a - b = 4$: $4(a+b) = 3$

Divide by 4:

$$a + b = \frac{3}{4}$$

5. **12/5 or 2.4** $2\text{ merts} \times \dfrac{6\text{ gricks}}{5\text{ merts}} = \dfrac{12}{5}\text{ gricks}$

6. **64**

$$\{4\} = (1-4)^2 = (-3)^2 = 9$$
$$\{\{4\}\} = (1 - \{4\})^2 = (1-9)^2 = (-8)^2 = 64$$

7. **2** Given equation:

$$\frac{a+b}{b} = 3$$

Distribute division:

$$\frac{a}{b} + 1 = 3$$

Subtract 1:

$$\frac{a}{b} = 2$$

Reciprocate:

$$\frac{b}{a} = \frac{1}{2}$$

Given equation:

$$\frac{a+c}{c} = 5$$

Distribute division:

$$\frac{a}{c} + 1 = 5$$

Subtract 1:

$$\frac{a}{c} = 4$$

Multiply:

$$\frac{b}{c} = \left(\frac{b}{a}\right)\left(\frac{a}{c}\right) = \left(\frac{1}{2}\right)(4) = 2$$

8. **D** Given: $(x-9)(x-a) = x^2 - 4ax + b$

FOIL: $x^2 - ax - 9x + 9a = x^2 - 4ax + b$

Simplify: $x^2 - (a+9)x + 9a = x^2 - 4ax + b$

If this equation is true for all x, then the coefficients of corresponding terms must be equal, so $a + 9 = 4a$

Subtract a: $9 = 3a$

Divide by 3: $3 = a$

Therefore $b = 9a = 9(3) = 27$.

9. **A** Given equation:

$$\frac{5}{x} + \frac{7}{5} = 1$$

Multiply by $5x$: $25 + 7x = 5x$

Subtract $7x$: $25 = -2x$

Divide by -2:

$$-\frac{25}{2} = x$$

10. **C** Given equation: $(p+2)^2 = (p-5)^2$

FOIL: $p^2 + 4p + 4 = p^2 - 10p + 25$

Subtract p^2: $4p + 4 = -10p + 25$

Add $10p$: $14p + 4 = 25$

Subtract 4: $14p = 21$

Divide by 14: $p = 1.5$

11. **D** Given equation:

$$\frac{3x}{m-nx} = 2$$

Multiply by $m - nx$: $3x = 2(m - nx)$

Distribute: $3x = 2m - 2nx$

Add $2nx$: $3x + 2nx = 2m$

Factor out x: $x(3 + 2n) = 2m$

Divide by $3 + 2n$:

$$x = \frac{2m}{3+2n}$$

Calculator

12. **1.25**   Increasing a number by 60% is equivalent to multiplying it by 1.60, and decreasing a number by 50% is equivalent to multiplying it by 0.50. Therefore, performing both changes in succession is equivalent to multiplying by $1.60 \times 0.50 = 0.80$. Multiplying by 0.80 is equivalent to dividing by its reciprocal: $1/(0.80) = 1.25$.

---

13. **2,550**   The sum of the first 50 positive integers is $2 + 4 + 6 + 8 + \cdots + 100$. As with the example is Lesson 2, these numbers can be regrouped into 25 pairs of numbers each of which has a sum of $2 + 100 = 102$. Therefore, their sum is $25(102) = 2,550$.

---

14. **14**   Let $n =$ Nora's age now, and $m =$ Mary's age now. If 3 years ago, Nora was half as old

as Mary is now:	$n - 3 = \dfrac{1}{2}m$
If Mary is 4 years older than Nora:	$m = 4 + n$
Subtract 4:	$m - 4 = n$
Substitute $n = m - 4$:	$m - 4 - 3 = \dfrac{1}{2}m$
Simplify:	$m - 7 = \dfrac{1}{2}m$
Multiply by 2:	$2m - 14 = m$
Subtract m and add 14:	$m = 14$

---

15. **4,200**   Let $x =$ the total number of seats in the

stadium.	$\dfrac{2}{3}x - 1,000 = \dfrac{3}{7}x$
Subtract $\dfrac{3}{7}x$:	$\dfrac{2}{3}x - \dfrac{3}{7}x - 1,000 = 0$
Add 1,000:	$\dfrac{2}{3}x - \dfrac{3}{7}x = 1,000$
Combine like terms:	$\dfrac{5}{21}x = 1,000$
Multiply by $\dfrac{21}{5}$:	$x = \dfrac{21,000}{5} = 4,200$

---

16. **0.20**   Let $g =$ the cost, in dollars, of one gumdrop, and $c =$ the cost, in dollars, of one candy bar.

	$4c + 2g = 2.80$
	$3c + 2g = 2.20$
Subtract:	$c = 0.60$
Substitute $c = 0.60$:	$4(0.60) + 2g = 2.80$
Simplify:	$2.40 + 2g = 2.80$
Subtract 2.40:	$2g = 0.40$
Divide by 2:	$g = 0.20$

---

17. **6** $\dfrac{x^2 - 2x + 1}{2 - 2x} = -3$

Factor:	$\dfrac{(x-1)(x-1)}{2(1-x)} = -3$
Multiply by -1:	$\dfrac{(x-1)(x-1)}{2(x-1)} = -3$
Simplify:	$\dfrac{x-1}{2} = 3$
Multiply by 2:	$x - 1 = 6$

---

18. **12**   We can just choose a number to work with, like 10. If we subtract 3 from this number then multiply the result by 4, we get $4(10 - 3) = 28$. If we multiply it by 4 and then subtract a mystery number, we get $4(10) - x = 40 - x$.

	$28 = 40 - x$
Subtract 40:	$-12 = -x$
Multiply by -1:	$12 = x$

---

19. **A**   If 5 green chips are worth m dollars, then each green chip is worth $m/5$ dollars. If a red chip is worth 2 dollars more than a green chip, then each red chip is worth $m/5 + 2$ dollars. If each blue chip is worth 2 dollars more than a red chip, then each blue chip is worth $m/5 + 4$ dollars. Therefore, 10 blue chips and 5 red chips are worth $10(m/5 + 4) + 5(m/5 + 2) = 2m + 40 + m + 10 = 3m + 50$ dollars.

---

20. **B**   The average speed is equal to the total distance divided by the total time. The total distance is 200 miles. The time for the first hundred miles is (100 miles/50 mph) = 2 hours, and the time for the second hundred miles is (100 miles/75 mph) = 4/3 hours. Therefore the total time of the trip is $2 + 4/3 = 10/3$ hours, and the average speed is

$$\frac{200}{\dfrac{10}{3}} = 200 \times \frac{3}{10} = 60 \text{ mph}$$

---

21. **D** $3m(m^2 \times 2m)$

Parentheses:	$3m(2m^3)$
Multiply:	$6m^4$

---

22. **C**   Assume the cost of living in 1980 was $100. If this increased by 20% from 1980 to 1990, then the cost of living in 1990 was 1.20($100) = $120. If the increase from 1980 to 2000 was 50%, then the cost of living in 2000 was 1.50($100) = $150. The percent increase from 1990 to 2000 is therefore

$$\frac{150 - 120}{120} \times 100\% = \frac{30}{120} \times 100\% = 25\%$$

Skill 2: Working with Linear Equations

Lesson 5: Constructing and interpreting linear equations

The Horizon Resort charges $150 per night for a single room, and a one-time valet parking fee of $35. There is a 6.5% state tax on the room charges, but no tax on the valet parking fee. Which of the following equations represents the total charges in dollars, c, for a single room, valet parking, and taxes, for a stay of n nights at The Horizon Resort?

A) $c = (150 + 0.065n) + 35$

B) $c = 1.065(150n) + 35$

C) $c = 1.065(150n + 35)$

D) $c = 1.065(150 + 35)n$

(*Medium*) This question asks us explicitly to set up an equation to express a mathematical relationship in a word problem. Usually, this is just the first step in analyzing the situation more deeply, for instance, finding particular values of the variables that satisfy certain conditions, or interpreting the meanings of terms or coefficients in the equation, but this problem only asks us to set up the equation.

When translating verbal information into an equation, it's helpful to take small steps. First, since the room charge is $150 per night, the charge for n nights is $150n$. If a 6.5% tax is added to this, the room charge becomes $150n + 0.065(150n) = 1.065(150n)$. The $35 valet parking charge is added separately, and not taxed, so the total charges are $1.065(150n) + 35$, and the correct answer is (B). Notice that this equation shows **a linear relationship** between c and n.

> When setting up equations from word problems, **try to classify the relationship** (that is, linear, quadratic, exponential) **between the variables**, so that you can check that the equation is of the correct form. In this lesson, we will focus only on **linear relationships**, that is, relationships that can be expressed in the form $y = mx + b$.

Which of the following represents the equation of the line with an x-intercept of 6 that passes through the point (4, 4)?

A) $y = -\dfrac{1}{2}x + 6$

B) $y = 2x - 4$

C) $y = -2x + 12$

D) $y = -2x + 6$

(*Easy*) This question asks you to construct the equation of a line given some facts about its graph. Start by drawing a graph (on the xy-plane) of the given information in the space next to the question. It also helps to know something about the different forms of linear equations and what they reveal about the graph of the line.

Graph of a line in the xy-plane

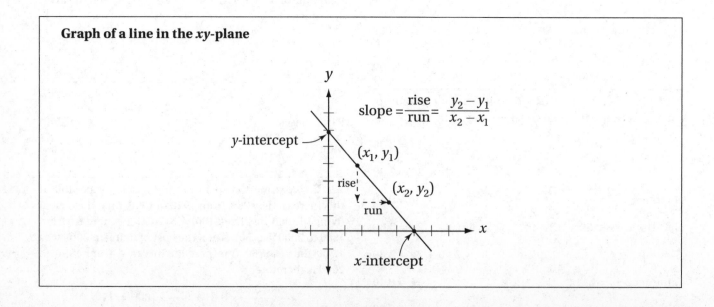

$$\text{slope} = \frac{\text{rise}}{\text{run}} = \frac{y_2 - y_1}{x_2 - x_1}$$

Forms of linear equations

Slope-intercept form: $y = mx + b$ **Features:** slope $= m$, y-intercept $= b$

Standard form: $ax + by = c$ **Features:** slope $= -a/b$, y-intercept $= c/b$, x-intercept $= c/a$

Point-slope form: $y - y_1 = m(x - x_1)$ **Features:** slope $= m$, point on line $= (x_1, y_1)$

In this problem, we are given two points on the line: $(4, 4)$ and the x-intercept $(6, 0)$. We can calculate the slope using the slope formula above: slope $= (4 - 0)/(4 - 6) = (4)/(-2) = -2$. If we use this slope and the point $(6, 0)$, we can set up the equation in point-slope form:

Point-slope form of equation: $y - 0 = -2(x - 6)$

Simplify and distribute: $y = -2x + 12$

This is the equation in (C). Notice that this equation is in **slope-intercept form**, and reveals that this line also has a y-intercept of 12. Check this fact against your diagram, and also check that both given points, $(4, 4)$ and $(6, 0)$, satisfy this equation.

Lesson 6: Solving equations with the Laws of Equality

If $\dfrac{1}{x} + \dfrac{2}{3x} = 4$, what is the value of x?

A) $\dfrac{7}{5}$

B) $\dfrac{3}{5}$

C) $\dfrac{5}{12}$

D) $\dfrac{1}{6}$

(*Medium*) At first glance, this doesn't look like a linear equation. But one simple move reveals that it is:

$$\frac{1}{x} + \frac{2}{3x} = 4$$

Multiply both sides by $3x$: $3x\left(\dfrac{1}{x} + \dfrac{2}{3x}\right) = 3x(4)$

Distribute and simplify: $3 + 2 = 12x$

Divide by 12: $5/12 = x$

As this shows, sometimes solving equations requires a clever use of the **Laws of Equality.**

The Laws of Equality

Every equation is a balanced scale, and the Laws of Equality are simply the rules for "keeping the scale balanced," that is, deducing *other* true equations. In a nutshell, the Laws of Equality say that

1. You may make changes to any equation, as long as you follow rules 2 and 3.
2. Whatever you do to one side of the equation, you must do to the other.
3. You may not perform undefined operations (like dividing by 0), or operations that have more than one possible result (like taking a square root).

If $x^2 = y^2$, then which of the following must be true?

    I. $x = y$

    II. $x = \dfrac{y^2}{x}$

    III. $x = |y|$

A) none

B) I only

C) I and II only

D) I, II and III

(*Medium-hard*) This question tests your skills of **deductive logic**. Notice it is not asking which statements *can* be true, but rather which *must be true*. It seems that if we "unsquare" both sides of the original equation, we get the equation in I. If we divide the original equation by x on both sides, we get the equation in II. Does this mean that statements I and II are necessarily true? No, because we violated rule 3 in both cases. If $x^2 = y^2$, it does not follow that $x = y$. Notice that x could be 2 and y could be -2. These values certainly satisfy the original equation, but they do not satisfy the equations in I or III. They do, however, satisfy the equation in II, because $2 = (-2)^2/2$. However, statement II is still not necessarily true. What if x and y were both 0? This would satisfy the original equation, but $0 \neq (0)^2/(0)$ because $0/0$ is *undefined*. Therefore, the correct answer is (A).

This example teaches us two lessons:

1. **Before taking the square root of both sides of an equation, remember that every positive number has <u>two</u> square roots.** For instance the square root of 9 is 3 or -3.
2. **Before dividing both sides of an equation by an unknown, make sure it can't equal 0.**

Lesson 7: Making and analyzing graphs of linear equations

If m is a constant greater than 1, which of the following could be the graph in the xy-plane of $x + my + m = 0$?

A)

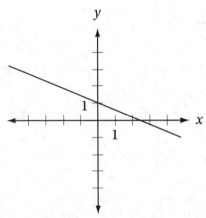

B)

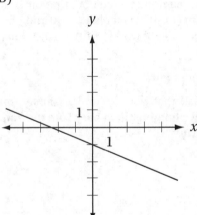

C)

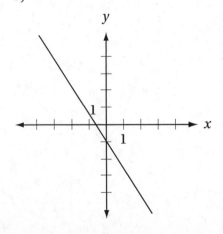

D)

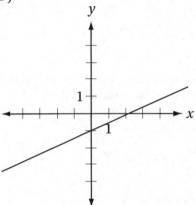

(*Medium-hard*) First, we should try to get the equation into a more useful form. Let's try the slope-intercept ($y = mx + b$) form:

$$x + my + m = 0$$

Subtract x and m: $\qquad\qquad my = -x - m$

Divide by m: $\qquad\qquad y = \left(-\dfrac{1}{m}\right)x - 1$

This shows that the line has a slope of $-1/m$ and a y-intercept of -1. Since the problem tells us that m is greater than 1, we know that the slope ($-1/m$) must be between -1 and 0. The only graph that satisfies these conditions is (B).

Thinking about slopes

It's helpful to think of slope as **the amount a line goes up (or down) for each step it takes to the right. Lines with a positive slope slant *upward* to the right, lines with a negative slope slant *downward* to the right, and lines with a 0 slope are *horizontal*.** For instance, a line with slope -3 moves *down* 3 units for every unit step to the right.

Parallel and perpendicular lines

- **Parallel lines have equal slopes.**
- **Perpendicular lines have slopes that are opposite reciprocals of each other.** That is, if one line has a slope of a/b, its perpendicular has a slope of $-b/a$.

The points $A(10, 4)$ and $B(-2, k)$ are 13 units apart. Which of the following equations could describe the line that contains points A and B?

A)　$13x + 12y = 178$

B)　$5x + 12y = 98$

C)　$5x - 12y = 98$

D)　$5x - 13y = -2$

(*Hard*) Drawing a diagram will help us analyze this problem. Although we don't know precisely where point B is, we know it is somewhere on the line $x = -2$. This gives us the following picture:

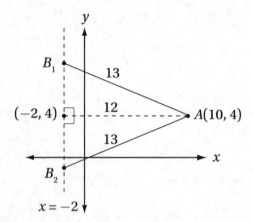

Next, notice that all of the equations given in the choices are in "standard" form, and in standard form the slope of the line is $-a/b$. Therefore, the slopes of these lines are, respectively, (A) $-13/12$, (B) $-5/12$, (C) $5/12$, and (D) $5/13$. Therefore, finding the slope of the line should help us choose the correct equation.

Looking at the diagram more closely, notice that it includes two right triangles, and we can find the missing side of each one using the Pythagorean Theorem, or just by noticing that they are both 5-12-13 right triangles ($5^2 + 12^2 = 13^2$). Putting this information into the diagram shows us that B can therefore be at $(-2, 9)$ or $(-2, -1)$.

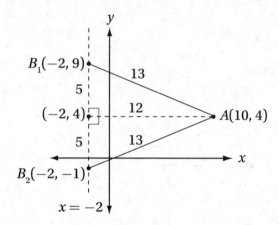

Therefore, the slope (rise/run) of the line containing B_1 is $-5/12$, and the slope of the line containing B_2 is $5/12$. This means that our answer is either (B) or (C). How do we choose between them? Just remember that the line must contain the point $(10, 4)$. If you plug $x = 10$ and $y = 4$ into these equations, only (B) works: $5(10) + 4(12) = 98$.

Checking your work

Always check that your solutions satisfy your equations by **plugging them back into the equations to verify**.

Exercise Set 3 (No Calculator)

1

If $x - 2(1 - x) = 5$, what is the value of x?

2

If $f(x) = -2x + 8$, and $f(k) = -10$, what is the value of k?

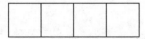

3

What is the slope of the line that contains the points $(-2, 3)$ and $(4, 5)$?

4

What is the slope of the line described by the equation $\dfrac{1}{x} + \dfrac{1}{2x} = \dfrac{5}{y}$?

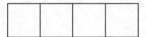

5

Line l is perpendicular to the line described by the equation $5x + 11y = 16$. What is the slope of line l?

6

If $\dfrac{x+1}{10} + \dfrac{2x}{5} = 1$, what is the value of x?

7

What is the y-intercept of the line containing the points $(3, 7)$ and $(6, 3)$?

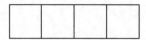

8

In the xy-plane, the graph of $y = h(x)$ is a line with slope -2. If $h(3) = 1$ and $h(b) = -9$, what is the value of b?

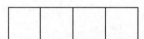

9

If a train maintains a constant speed of 60 miles per hour, it can travel 4 miles per gallon of diesel fuel. If this train begins a trip with a full 200 gallon tank of diesel fuel, and maintains a speed of 60 miles per hour, which of the following equations represents the number of gallons, g, left in the tank t hours into the trip?

A) $g = \dfrac{200 - 60t}{4}$

B) $g = 200 - \dfrac{1}{15t}$

C) $g = 200 - 15t$

D) $g = 200 - \dfrac{1}{15}t$

10

The points $A(2, 3)$ and $B(m, 11)$, are 10 units apart. Which of the following equations could describe the line that contains points A and B?

A) $8x + 6y = 11$

B) $8x - 6y = -2$

C) $6x + 8y = 36$

D) $6x - 8y = -12$

11

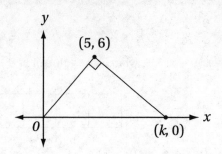

The figure above shows a right triangle with vertices at the origin, $(5, 6)$ and $(k, 0)$. What is the value of k?

A) $\dfrac{19}{3}$

B) $\dfrac{58}{5}$

C) $\dfrac{26}{3}$

D) $\dfrac{61}{5}$

Exercise Set 3 (Calculator)

12

If the points (2, 4), (5, k), and (8, 20) are on the same line, what is the value of k?

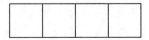

13

Line l has a slope of 3 and a y-intercept of -4. What is its x-intercept?

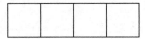

14

If $f(-1) = 1$ and $f(3) = 2$ and f is a linear function, what is the slope of the graph $y = f(x)$?

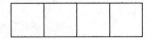

15

If $f(-1) = 1$ and $f(3) = 2$ and f is a linear function, what is $f(5)$?

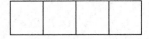

16

In the xy-plane, the graph of line n has an x-intercept of $2b$ and an y-intercept of $-8b$, where $b \neq 0$. What is the slope of line n?

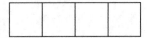

17

If $\dfrac{2}{x} + \dfrac{2}{5x} = 4$, what is the value of x?

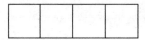

18

If the line $3x - 2y = 12$ is graphed in the xy-plane, what is its x-intercept?

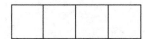

19

If the graphs of the equations $5x - 2y = 5$ and $6x + ky = 9$ are perpendicular, what is the value of k?

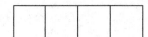

20

The net profit for the sales of a product is equal to the total revenue from the sales of that product minus the total cost for the sales of that product. If a particular model of calculator sells for \$98, and the cost for making and selling n of these calculators is \$$(35n + 120,000)$, which of the following equations expresses the net profit in dollars, P, for making and selling n of these calculators?

A) $P = 63n - 120,000$

B) $P = 63n + 120,000$

C) $P = 63(n - 120,000)$

D) $P = 63(n + 120,000)$

21

Which of the following represents the equation of the line with an x-intercept of 5 and a y-intercept of 6?

A) $y - 6 = -\dfrac{6}{5}(x - 5)$

B) $y - 6 = -\dfrac{5}{6}(x - 5)$

C) $y - 6 = -\dfrac{6}{5}x$

D) $y - 6 = -\dfrac{5}{6}x$

22

x	2	3	4
$f(x)$	a	8	b

The table above shows several ordered pairs corresponding to the linear function f. What is the value of $a + b$?

A) 12

B) 16

C) 20

D) It cannot be determined from the information given.

EXERCISE SET 3 ANSWER KEY

Part 1: No Calculator

1. 7/3 or 2.33
$$x - 2(1 - x) = 5$$

Distribute: $\qquad x - 2 + 2x = 5$

Simplify: $\qquad 3x - 2 = 5$

Add 2: $\qquad 3x = 7$

Divide by 3: $\qquad x = 7/3$

---

2. 9
$$f(k) = -2k + 8 = -10$$

Subtract 8: $\qquad -2k = -18$

Divide by −2: $\qquad k = 9$

---

3. 1/3 or .333
$$\text{slope} = \frac{5 - 3}{4 - (-2)} = \frac{2}{6} = \frac{1}{3}$$

---

4. 10/3 or 3.33
$$\frac{1}{x} + \frac{1}{2x} = \frac{5}{y}$$

Multiply by $2xy$: $\qquad \dfrac{2xy}{x} + \dfrac{2xy}{2x} = \dfrac{10xy}{y}$

Simplify: $\qquad 2y + y = 10x$

Simplify: $\qquad 3y = 10x$

Divide by 3: $\qquad y = \dfrac{10}{3}x$

---

5. 11/5 or 2.2 The slope of the given line is −5/11, so the slope of the line perpendicular to it is 11/5.

---

6. 9/5 or 1.8
$$\frac{x + 1}{10} + \frac{2x}{5} = 1$$

Multiply by 10: $\qquad (x + 1) + 4x = 10$

Simplify: $\qquad 5x + 1 = 10$

Subtract 1: $\qquad 5x = 9$

Divide by 5: $\qquad x = 9/5$

---

7. 11 There are a variety of ways of solving this problem, but perhaps the simplest is to draw a quick sketch:

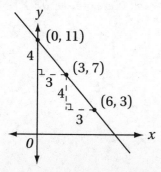

Notice that to get from (6, 3) to (3, 7) we must go left 3 units and up 4 units (in other words, the slope is −4/3). If we simply repeat this from (3, 7), we arrive at the y-intercept, which is (0, 11).

---

8. 8 This line has a slope of −2 and contains the points (3, 1) and (b, −9). Therefore $-2 = \dfrac{-9 - 1}{b - 3}$

Simplify: $\qquad -2 = \dfrac{-10}{b - 3}$

Multiply by $b - 3$: $\qquad -2b + 6 = -10$

Subtract 6: $\qquad -2b = -16$

Divide by −2: $\qquad b = 8$

---

9. C Since the tanks starts with 200 gallons, the amount it has left is 200 − the number of gallons used. The number of gallons used is

$$t \text{ hours} \times \frac{60 \text{ miles}}{1 \text{ hour}} \times \frac{1 \text{ gallon}}{4 \text{ miles}} = 15t \text{ gallons}$$

---

10. B Once again, a quick sketch can be very helpful. Notice that traveling from point

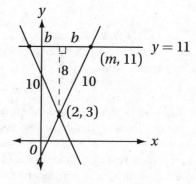

$A(2, 3)$ to point $B(m, 11)$ requires going up 8 units and right (or left) some unknown distance b. We can find b with the

Pythagorean Theorem: $\qquad 8^2 + b^2 = 10^2$

Simplify: $\qquad 64 + b^2 = 100$

Subtract 64: $\qquad b^2 = 36$

Take the square root: $\qquad b = 6$

Therefore, m is either $2 - 6 = -4$ or $2 + 6 = 8$, and the slope of this line is either $8/6 = 4/3$ or $8/(-6) = -4/3$. The only equation among the choices that is satisfied by the ordered pair (2, 3) and has a slope of either 4/3 or −4/3 is (B).

11. **D**   Recall that the slopes of perpendicular lines are opposite reciprocals. The slope of the segment from (0, 0) to (5, 6) is 6/5, so the slope of its perpendicular is −5/6.

Therefore $\dfrac{6-0}{5-k}=-\dfrac{5}{6}$

Cross-multiply: $-36=5(5-k)$
Distribute: $-36=25-5k$
Subtract 25: $-61=-5k$
Divide by −5: $61/5=k$

Part 2: Calculator

12. **12**   The slope of this line is $\dfrac{20-4}{8-2}=\dfrac{16}{6}=\dfrac{8}{3}$,

therefore, $\dfrac{k-4}{5-2}=\dfrac{8}{3}$

Cross-multiply: $3k-12=24$

Add 12: $3k=36$

Divide by 3: $k=12$

13. **4/3 or 1.33**   Since the slope and y-intercept are given, it is easy to express the linear equation in slope-intercept form: $y=3x-4$.

The x-intercept is the value of x on the line for which $y=0$: $0=3x-4$

Add 4: $4=3x$

Divide by 3: $4/3=x$

14. **¼ or .25**   The line contains the points (−1, 1) and (3, 2), so its slope is $\dfrac{2-1}{3-(-1)}=\dfrac{1}{4}$

15. **5/2 or 2.5**   Although we could solve this problem by deriving the linear equation, it is perhaps easier to take advantage of the result from question 14. The slope of 1/4 means that the y-coordinate of any point on the line increases by 1/3 each time the x-coordinate increases by 1. Since the x-coordinate increases by 2 between $f(3)$ and $f(5)$, the y-coordinate must therefore increase by 2(1/4) = 1/2, so $f(5)=2+½=2.5$.

16. **4**   The line contains the points (2b, 0) and (0, −8b); therefore, it has a slope of $\dfrac{0-(-8b)}{2b-0}=\dfrac{8b}{2b}=4$.

17. **3/5 or .6** $\dfrac{2}{x}+\dfrac{2}{5x}=4$

Multiply by 5x: $10+2=20x$
Simplify: $12=20x$
Divide by 20: $x=12/20=3/5$

18. **4**   The x-intercept is the value of x for which $y=0$: $3x-2(0)=12$
Simplify: $3x=12$
Divide by 3: $x=4$

19. **15**   Recall that the slope of a line in standard form $ax+by=c$ is $-a/b$. Therefore, the slope of $5x-2y=5$ is 5/2 and the slope of $6x+ky=9$ is $-6/k$. If these lines are perpendicular, then their slopes are opposite reciprocals:

                                        $\dfrac{k}{6}=\dfrac{5}{2}$

Multiply by 6: $k=30/2=15$

20. **A**   The total revenue for selling n calculators at \$98 each is \$98n the cost for making and selling n calculators is \$(35n + 120,000). Therefore the profit is \$(98n − 35n − 120,000) = 63n − 120,000 dollars.

21. **C**   This line contains the points (5, 0) and (0, 6) and therefore has a slope of $\dfrac{0-6}{5-0}=-\dfrac{6}{5}$.

Since its y-intercept is 6, its slope-intercept form is

$y=-\dfrac{6}{5}x+6$ or, subtracting 6 from both sides,

$y-6=-\dfrac{6}{5}x$

22. **B**   Since f is a linear function, it has a slope that we can call m. Recall that it's often useful to think of the slope of a line as the "unit change," that is, the amount that y changes each time x increases by 1. Since the x values increase by 1 with each step in our table, the y values must therefore increase by m with each step. This means that $a=8-m$ and $b=8+m$. Therefore, $a+b=8-m+8+m=16$.

Skill 3: Working with Inequalities and Absolute Values

Lesson 8: Understanding inequalities and absolute values

On the real number line, a number, b, is more than twice as far from -3 as it is from 3. Which of the following equations can be solved to find all possible values of b?

A) $|b - 3| > 2|b + 3|$

B) $|b + 3| > 2|b - 3|$

C) $2|b - 3| > |b + 3|$

D) $2|b + 3| > |b - 3|$

Distance and absolute value

The absolute value of a number x, written as $|x|$, means its distance from 0 on the number line. In fact, we can use absolute value to represent the distance between *any* two numbers.

$|x - a|$ means the distance between x and a on the number line.

Notice that this works no matter which number is greater. For instance, the distance between 2 and 7 is $|2 - 7| = |-5| = 5$, which is the same as the distance between 7 and 2: $|7 - 2| = |5| = 5$.

Notice that an expression like $|x + a|$ is equivalent to $|x - (-a)|$, which means that $|x + a|$ can be translated as the distance between x and $-a$.

(*Medium-hard*) We can use this definition to translate the problem. The key is to translate the statement "b is more than twice as far from -3 as it is from 3" into a statement about **distances**: "The distance between b and -3 is more than twice the distance between b and 3." Notice how easily this translates into an inequality:

(*The distance between b and -3) is more than (twice the distance between b and 3*)

$$|b - (-3)| > 2|b - 3|$$

$$|b + 3| > 2|b - 3|$$

which is choice (B).

Lesson 9: Solving inequalities with the Laws of Inequality

If $-\frac{1}{2} < -2x + 1 < -\frac{1}{3}$, what is one possible value of x?

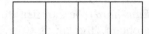

(Easy) This kind of inequality is called a "sandwich inequality" because the expression in the middle is between the other two, like meat between slices of bread. Working with inequalities like this one requires understanding the **Laws of *Inequality***.

The Laws of Inequality

Every inequality is a "tipped" scale, and the Laws of Inequality are simply the rules for "keeping the scale tipped the right way," that is, deducing *other* true inequalities that follow from the original one. In a nutshell, the Laws of Inequality say that

1. You may make changes to any inequality, as long as you follow rules 2, 3 and 4.
2. Whatever you do to one side of the inequality, you must do to the other.
3. You may not perform undefined operations (like dividing by 0), or operations that have more than one possible result (like taking a square root).
4. If you multiply or divide both sides by a negative number, you must "switch" the direction of the inequality. This is because multiplying or dividing by a negative number involves a *reflection* over the origin on the number line, and this reflection requires the "switch":

So we can solve the sandwich inequality by applying the correct laws of inequality: $-\frac{1}{2} < -2x + 1 < -\frac{1}{3}$

Multiply by -6 (the common denominator) and "switch:" $3 > 12x - 6 > 2$

Add 6: $9 > 12x > 8$

Divide by 12: $0.75 > x > 0.66 \ldots$

Therefore, any value greater than 0.666 but less than 0.750 is correct.

Which of the following must be true if $\frac{a}{b} \le -3$?

A) $a \le -3b$

B) $a \ge -3b$

C) $a \le -3b < 0$ or $a \ge -3b > 0$

D) $a \le -3b < 0$ or $a \ge -3b > 0$

(Hard) We might be tempted to multiply both sides of the inequality by b and get the inequality in (A). But this would be incorrect because it would ignore rule 4. We need to consider the possibility that *b might be negative*. Let's think about possible solutions to the original inequality. Notice that $a = 10$ and $b = -2$ gives a possible solution, because $10/(-2) = -5 \le -3$. But this would *not* satisfy the inequality in (A): 10 is *not* less than or equal to $(-3)(-2) = 6$.

To solve this inequality, we will need to consider two distinct possible conditions:

Condition 1: If $b > 0$, then $a \le -3b$ and therefore $a \le -3b < 0$

Condition 2: If $b < 0$, then $a \ge -3b$ and therefore $a \ge -3b > 0$

which is the answer in choice (D).

Lesson 10: Graphing inequalities

On the real number line, a number, b, is more than twice as far from -3 as it is from 3. Which of the following graphs represents all possible values of b?

A)

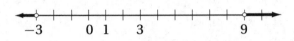

B)

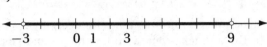

C)

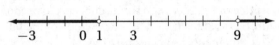

D)

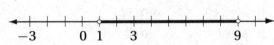

(Medium) We saw this scenario in Lesson 8, but now we are asked to graph the solution. Recall from Lesson 8 that this relationship is expressed by the inequality

$|b + 3| > 2|b - 3|$. How do we translate this into a graph? The simplest way to start is to visualize the number line, and to think about a related, but simpler, question: *What if b is exactly twice as far from -3 as it is from 3?* A little guessing and checking should reveal that two points work:

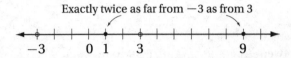

Exactly twice as far from -3 as from 3

Notice that 9 works because 3 is the midpoint between -3 and 9, and 1 works because it is 2/3 of the way from -3 to 3. Also, you can confirm that both numbers satisfy the equation $|b + 3| = 2|b - 3|$. These two points now divide the line into three parts: everything less than 1, everything between 1 and 9, and everything greater than 9. A little bit of checking (just pick a number from each portion and plug it into our inequality) confirms that only the numbers in the middle portion satisfy our inequality, so the correct graph is the one in choice (D).

When graphing inequalities, it often helps to start with the graph of the **corresponding equation** and work from there. **The graph of the equation usually provides the boundaries for the graph of the inequality.**

Exercise Set 4 (No Calculator)

1

What positive number is twice as far from 10 as it is from 1?

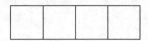

2

If the points $(2, a)$ and $(14, b)$ are 20 units apart, what is $|a - b|$?

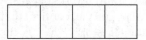

3

What is the least integer n for which $0 < \dfrac{4}{n} < \dfrac{5}{9}$?

4

If $|x + 4| = |x - 5|$, what is the value of x?

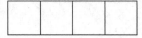

5

What is the greatest integer value of n such that $-\dfrac{n}{21} > -\dfrac{1}{2}$?

6

What is the only integer b for which $\dfrac{1}{b} > \dfrac{3}{11}$ and $3b \geq 7.5$?

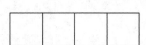

7

If $(b + 2)^2 = (b - 5)^2$, what is the value of b?

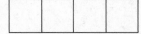

8

Which of the following statements is equivalent to the statement $-4 < 2x \leq 2$?

A) $x > -2$ and $x \leq 1$

B) $x < -2$ or $x \geq 1$

C) $x \geq -2$ and $x < 1$

D) $x \leq -2$ or $x > 1$

9

The annual profit from the sales of an item is equal to the annual revenue minus the annual cost for that item. The revenue from that item is equal to the number of units sold times the price per unit. If n units of a portable heart monitor were sold in 2012 at a price of \$65 each, and the annual cost to produce n units was \$(20,000 + 10n)$, then which of the following statements indicates that the total profit for this heart monitor in 2012 was greater than \$500,000?

A) $500,000 < 55n - 20,000$

B) $500,000 > 55n - 20,000$

C) $500,000 < 55n + 20,000n$

D) $500,000 < 75n - 20,000n$

10

Colin can read a maximum of 25 pages an hour. If he has been reading a 250 page book for h hours, where $h < 10$, and has p pages left to read, which of the following expresses the relationship between p and h?

A) $250 - p \leq \dfrac{25}{h}$

B) $250 \geq p + \dfrac{25}{h}$

C) $250 - p \leq 25h$

D) $250 + 25h \leq p$

11

On the real number line, a number, x, is more than 4 times as far from 10 as it is from 40. Which of the following statements describes all possible values of x?

A) $x < 34$ or $x > 50$

B) $x > 40$

C) $34 < x < 50$

D) $32.5 < x < 160$

Exercise Set 4 (Calculator)

12

If $a < 0$ and $|a - 5| = 7$, what is $|a|$?

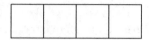

13

If n is a positive integer and $16 > |6 - 3n| > 19$, what is the value of n?

14

What is the only integer n such that $20 - 2n > 5$ and $\dfrac{2n}{3} > 4$?

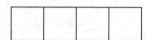

15

What is the smallest number that is as far from 9.25 as 3 is from −1.5?

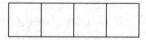

16

If $|2x + 1| = 2|k - x|$, for all values of x, what is the value of $|k|$?

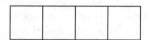

17

Which of the following is equivalent to the statement $|x - 2| < 1$?

A) $x < 3$

B) $x < -1$

C) $1 < x < 3$

D) $-1 < x < 3$

18

If the average (arithmetic mean) of a and b is greater than the average (arithmetic mean) of c and $2b$, which of the following must be true?

A) $b > 0$

B) $a > b$

C) $a > b + c$

D) $a + c > b$

19

Of the statements below, which is equivalent to the statement "The distance from x to 1 is greater than the distance from x to 3?

A) $1 < x < 3$

B) $x > 2$

C) $x < 2$

D) $x - 1 > 3$

20

Which of the following is equivalent to the statement $4x^2 \geq 9$?

A) $2x > 3$

B) $x \geq 1.5$ or $x \leq -1.5$

C) $|x| > 2$

D) $-1.5 \leq x \leq 1.5$

21

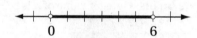

The graph above indicates the complete solution set to which of the following statements?

A) $|x - 3| > 3$

B) $|x| < 6$

C) $|x - 6| < 6$

D) $|x - 3| < 3$

22

Which of the following is true for all real values of x?

A) $|x| > 0$

B) $x < 2$ or $x > 1$

C) $x > -2$ or $x < -3$

D) $x^2 - 1 > 0$

EXERCISE SET 4 ANSWER KEY

No Calculator

1. **4** It is helpful to plot these values on the number line and think:

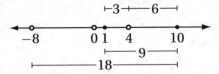

The distance between 1 and 10 is 9, so clearly the number that is 9 more units to the left of 1, namely -8, is twice as far from 10 as it is from 1. However, this is a negative number so it can't be our answer. There is one other number that is twice as far from 10 as it is from 1: the number that is 1/3 the distance from 1 to 10. This number is 4, which is 3 units from 1 and 6 units from 10.

---

2. **16** From the Distance Formula,

$$(2 - 14)^2 + (a - b)^2 = 20^2$$

Simplify: $\qquad\qquad 144 + (a - b)^2 = 400$

Subtract 144: $\qquad\qquad (a - b)^2 = 256$

Square root: $\qquad\qquad |a - b| = 16$

---

3. **8** $\qquad\qquad\qquad\qquad 0 < \dfrac{4}{n} < \dfrac{5}{9}$

Since n must be positive for this statement to be true, we can multiply by $9n$ without having to "swap" the inequality symbols:

$$0 < 36 < 5n$$

Divide by 5: $\qquad\qquad\qquad 0 < 7.2 < n$

Therefore, the smallest integer value of n is 8.

---

4. **½ or .5** Two numbers, a and b, have the same absolute value only if they are equal or opposites. Clearly $x + 4$ and $x - 5$ cannot be equal, since $x - 5$ is 9 less than $x + 4$. Therefore they must be opposites.

$$x + 4 = -(x - 5)$$

Distribute: $\qquad\qquad x + 4 = -x + 5$

Add x: $\qquad\qquad\qquad 2x + 4 = 5$

Subtract 4: $\qquad\qquad\qquad 2x = 1$

Divide by 2: $\qquad\qquad\qquad x = 1/2$

---

5. **10** $\qquad\qquad\qquad\qquad -\dfrac{n}{21} > -\dfrac{1}{2}$

Multiply by -42 and "swap:" $\qquad 2n < 21$

Divide by 2: $\qquad\qquad\qquad n < 10.5$

Therefore, the greatest possible integer value of n is 10.

---

6. **3** $\qquad\qquad\qquad\qquad\qquad 3b \geq 7.5$

Divide by 3: $\qquad\qquad\qquad\qquad b \geq 2.5$

$$\dfrac{1}{b} > \dfrac{3}{11}$$

Since b is greater than or equal to 2.5, it is positive, so we can multiply both sides by $11b$ without "swapping" the inequality:

$$11 > 3b$$

Divide by 3: $\qquad\qquad\qquad\qquad 3.67 > b$

The only integer between 2.5 and 3.67 is 3.

---

7. **3/2 or 1.5** $\qquad\qquad (b + 2)^2 = (b - 5)^2$

FOIL: $\qquad b^2 + 4b + 4 = b^2 - 10b + 25$

Subtract b^2: $\qquad\qquad 4b + 4 = -10b + 25$

Add $10b$: $\qquad\qquad\qquad 14b + 4 = 25$

Subtract 4: $\qquad\qquad\qquad 14b = 21$

Divide by 14: $\qquad\qquad\qquad b = 1.5$

---

8. **A** $\qquad\qquad\qquad\qquad -4 < 2x \leq 2$

Divide by 2: $\qquad\qquad\qquad -2 < x \leq 1$

which is equivalent to $-2 < x$ and $x \leq 1$.

---

9. **A** The profit is the revenue minus the cost: $65n - (20{,}000 + 10n) = 55n - 20{,}000$.

---

10. **C** If Colin can read a maximum of 25 pages an hour, then in h hours he can read a maximum of $25h$ pages. If he has p pages left in a 250-page book, he has read $250 - p$ pages. Since it has taken him h hours to read these $250 - p$ pages, $250 - p \leq 25h$.

---

11. **C** $\qquad\qquad\qquad\qquad |x - 10| > 4|x - 40|$

It helps to sketch the number line and divide is into three sections: the numbers less than 10, the numbers between 10 and 40, and the numbers greater than 40.

CASE 1: $x < 10$. It should be clear that all numbers less than 10 are closer to 10 than they are to 40, so this set contains no solutions.

CASE 2: $10 < x \leq 40$. If x is between 10 and 40, $x - 10$ is positive and $x - 40$ is negative, so $|x - 10| = x - 10$ and $|x - 40| = -(x - 40)$.

$$|x - 10| > 4|x - 40|$$

Substitute: $\qquad\qquad x - 10 > -4(x - 40)$

Distribute: $\qquad\qquad x - 10 > -4x + 160$

Add $4x$: $\qquad\qquad\qquad 5x - 10 > 160$

Add 10: $\qquad\qquad\qquad 5x > 170$

Divide by 5: $\qquad\qquad\qquad x > 34$

So this gives us $34 < x \leq 40$.

CASE 3: $x > 40$. If x is greater than 40, then both $x - 10$ and $x - 40$ are positive, so $|x - 10| = x - 10$ and $|x - 40| = x - 40$.

	$|x - 10| > 4|x - 40|$
Substitute:	$x - 10 > 4(x - 40)$
Distribute:	$x - 10 > 4x - 160$
Add 10:	$x > 4x - 150$
Subtract $4x$:	$-3x > -150$
Divide by -3 and "swap:"	$x < 50$

So this gives us $40 < x < 50$. When we combine this with the solutions from CASE 2, we get $34 < x < 50$.

Calculator

12. 2 If $|a - 5| = 7$, then either $a - 5 = 7$ or $a - 5 = -7$, so either $a = 12$ or $a = -2$. Since $a < 0$, a must be -2, and $|-2| = 2$.

---

13. 8 CASE 1: If $6 - 3n$ is positive, then

$|6 - 3n| = 6 - 3n$, so	$16 > 6 - 3n > 19$
Subtract 6:	$10 > -3n > 13$
Divide by -3 and "swap:"	$-10/3 < n < -13/3$

But this contradicts the fact that n is positive.

CASE 2: If $6 - 3n$ is negative, then

$|6 - 3n| = -(6 - 3n)$, so	$16 > -(6 - 3n) > 19$
Distribute:	$16 > -6 + 3n > 19$
Add 6:	$22 > 3n > 25$
Divide by 3:	$7.33 > n > 8.33$

And the only integer in this range is $n = 8$.

---

14. 7

	$20 - 2n > 5$
Subtract 20:	$-2n > -15$
Divide by -2 and "swap:"	$n < 7.5$
	$\dfrac{2n}{3} > 4$
Multiply by 3:	$2n > 12$
Divide by 2:	$n > 6$

Since n must be an integer between 6 and 7.5, $n = 7$.

---

15. 4.75 The distance from 3 to -1.5 is $|3 - (-1.5)|$ $= 4.5$. Therefore the two numbers that are 4.5 away from 9.25 are $9.25 + 4.5 = 13.75$ and $9.25 - 4.5 = 4.75$.

---

16. ½ or .5 If the equation is true for all values of x, let's choose a convenient value for x,

like $x = 1$.

	$|2x + 1| = 2|k - x|$
Substitute $x = 1$:	$|2(1) + 1| = 2|k - 1|$
Simplify:	$3 = 2|k - 1|$
Divide by 2:	$1.5 = |k - 1|$
Therefore	$\pm 1.5 = k - 1$
Add 1:	$k = 2.5$ or -0.5
Now try $x = 0$:	$|2(0) + 1| = 2|k - 0|$
Simplify:	$1 = 2|k|$
Divide by 2:	$0.5 = |k|$
Therefore	$\pm 0.5 = k$

Therefore, $k = -0.5$ and so $|k| = |-0.5| = 0.5$.

---

17. C Recall that the expression $|x - 2|$ means "the distance from x to 2," so the statement $|x - 2| < 1$ means "The distance from x to 2 is less than 1." Therefore, the solution set is all of the numbers that are less than 1 unit away from 2, which are all the numbers between 1 and 3.

---

18. C

	$\dfrac{a + b}{2} > \dfrac{c + 2b}{2}$
Multiply by 2:	$a + b > c + 2b$
Subtract b:	$a > c + b$

---

19. B The formal translation of this statement is $|x - 1| > |x - 3|$, which we can solve algebraically by considering three cases: (I) $x \leq 1$, (II) $1 < x \leq 3$, and (III) $x > 3$, but it is probably easier to just graph the number line and notice that the midpoint between 1 and 3, that is, 2, is the point at which the distance to 1 and the distance to 3 are equal. Therefore, the points that are farther from 1 than from 3 are simply the points to the right of this midpoint, or $x > 2$.

---

20. B

	$4x^2 \geq 9$
Take square root:	$|2x| \geq 3$
If $x > 0$:	$2x \geq 3$
Divide by 2:	$x \geq 1.5$
If $x < 0$:	$2x \leq -3$
Divide by 2:	$x \leq -1.5$

---

21. D Notice that the midpoint of the segment shown is 3, and the graph shows all points that are less than 3 units in either direction. Therefore, $|x - 3| < 3$.

---

22. B (A) is untrue if $x = 0$, (C) is untrue for $x = -2$, and (D) is untrue if $x = 0.5$. But (B) is true for any real number.

Skill 4: Working with Linear Systems
Lesson 11: Constructing, graphing, and interpreting linear systems

A **system of equations** is just a set of equations that apply simultaneously to a given problem situation. Solving for the system means finding all sets of values for the unknowns that make *all* of the equations true. Systems of equations can be analyzed both algebraically (by exploring the equations) or geometrically (by exploring the graphs).

Two high school teachers took their classes on a field trip to a museum. One class spent $154 for admission for 20 students and 3 adults, and the other class spent $188 for admission for 24 students and 4 adults. Which of the following systems of equations could be solved to determine the price of a single student admission, s, and the price of a single adult admission, a, in dollars?

A) $a + s = 51$

   $44s + 7a = 342$

B) $20s + 3a = 154$

   $24s + 4a = 188$

C) $\dfrac{20}{s} + \dfrac{3}{a} = 154$

   $\dfrac{24}{s} + \dfrac{4}{a} = 188$

D) $20 + 24 = s$

   $3 + 4 = a$

(*Medium*) This problem can be described with a **two-by-two system of equations**, that is, two equations with two unknowns. The two equations come from two facts: one class spent $154 for admission and the other class spent $188 for admission. The cost of 20 student admissions and 3 adult admissions is $20s + 3a$, so the first equation is $20s + 3a = 154$. Similarly, the equation for the other class is $24s + 4a = 188$, so the correct answer is (B).

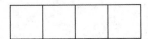

$$y = 2x - 3$$

$$y = -2x + 17$$

If the solutions to the two equations above are graphed in the xy-plane, what is the y-coordinate of the point at which the graphs intersect?

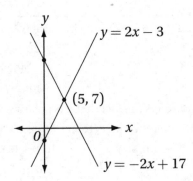

(*Easy*) Since the equations of both lines are given in slope-intercept form, we could graph the two lines in the xy-plane to find their point of intersection.

Therefore, the point (5, 7) gives us the only solution to this system, and so the answer to the original question is 7.

Alternately, (as we will see in Lesson 13) we can just add the corresponding sides of the two equations together to get $2y = 14$, which yields $y = 7$.

The solution of a two-by-two system of equations can be visualized as the **intersection of their graphs in the xy-plane**.

If the graphs are parallel lines, or other non-intersecting graphs, then the system **has no solution**. If the graphs intersect multiple times, then the system **has multiple solutions**.

$$y - 4x = 6$$

$$16x = 4y + k$$

For what value of k does the system of equations above have at least one solution?

A) -32

B) -30

C) -24

D) -20

(*Medium*) This is a two-by-two system of linear equations, and so its solution is the intersection of those two lines. If we convert them to slope-intercept form, we get $y = 4x + 6$ and $y = 4x - k/4$, which reveals that these two lines have the same slope. This means that they are either parallel lines or identical lines. Two lines with the same slope can intersect only if they are the same line, and therefore $-k/4 = 6$ and $k = -24$.

Lesson 12: Solving systems by substitution

Let's go back to the second linear system from Lesson 11. This system can also be solved with a simple application of the Law of Substitution.

$$y = 2x - 3$$
$$y = -2x + 17$$

1. Substitute for y: $2x - 3 = -2x + 17$

2. Add $2x$: $4x - 3 = 17$

3. Add 3: $4x = 20$

4. Divide by 4: $x = 5$

5. Plug into either original
   equation to find y: $y = 2(5) - 3$ or $-2(5) + 17 = 7$

> When one of the equations in a system is already solved for one variable (or when it's relatively easy to solve it for one variable), then substituting for this variable in the other equation often makes it easier to solve the system.

$$3x + y = 3y + 4$$
$$x + 4y = 6$$

Based on the system of equations above what is the value of the product xy?

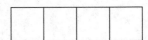

(*Medium*) This system is not quite as tidy as the previous one, but we can still solve it by using the Law of Substitution.

$$3x + y = 3y + 4$$
$$x + 4y = 6$$

Subtract $4y$ from second equation to
isolate x: $x = -4y + 6$

Substitute for x in first
equation: $3(-4y + 6) + y = 3y + 4$

Simplify left side: $-11y + 18 = 3y + 4$

Add $11y$ and subtract 4: $14 = 14y$

Divide by 14: $1 = y$

Substitute $y = 1$ to find x: $x = -4(1) + 6 = 2$

Evaluate xy: $xy = (2)(1) = 2$

Lesson 13: Solving systems by linear combination

$$3x + 6y = 18$$
$$3x + 4y = 6$$

Based on the system of equations above, what is the value of y?

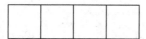

(*Easy*) Although this system can be solved by substitution (try it as an exercise), the setup of these equations suggests a much easier method, known as *linear combination*. It's based on a simple idea:

The Law of Combination

If $a = b$ and $c = d$, then $a + c = b + d$, $a - c = b - d$, and $ac = bd$

In other words, you should always feel free to add, subtract, or multiply the corresponding sides of two equations to make a new equation.

If we apply this rule to our system, notice that we can easily eliminate x from the system by just subtracting the equations:

$$3x + 6y = 18$$
$$- (3x + 4y = 6)$$
$$\overline{ 2y = 12}$$

Divide by 2: $\qquad\qquad\qquad\qquad y = 6$

$$3x - y = 20$$
$$2x + 4y = 7$$

Based on the system of equations above, what is the value of $x - 5y$?

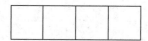

(*Medium*) This question looks tougher than the previous one, because it's not just asking for x or y. It seems that the question requires us to solve the system for x *and* y and then to plug these values into the expression $x - 5y$ and evaluate. We could do that, but there is a much simpler method. Notice that a simple combination gives us the expression the question is asking for.

$$3x - y = 20$$
Subtract equations: $\qquad\dfrac{- (2x + 4y = 7)}{x - 5y = 13}$

Using Linear Combination

When you're given a system of equations on the SAT, **always notice carefully what the question is asking you to evaluate**. Even if it appears to be the value of a complicated expression, often you can find it with a simple combination of the given equations.

Exercise Set 5 (No Calculator)

1

If $3x + 2y = 72$, and $y = 3x$, what is the value of x?

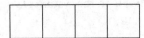

2

If $2a - 7b = 10$ and $2a + 7b = 2$, what is the value of $4a^2 - 49b^2$?

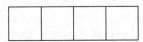

3

If the lines $y = -4x - 3$ and $y = -3x - b$ intersect at the point $(-1, c)$, what is the value of b?

4

If the lines $4x + 5y = 13$ and $4y + kx = 2$ are parallel, what is the value of k?

5

If the lines $4x + 5y = 13$ and $6y - kx = 6$ are perpendicular, what is the value of k?

6

$$\frac{2a}{b} = \frac{1}{3}$$

$$\frac{c}{b} + 1 = \frac{5}{3}$$

Based on the system of equations above, what is the value of $\frac{a}{c}$?

7

If $ab = -4$ and $abc = 12$, what is the value of $\frac{c}{ab}$?

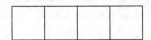

8

If a and b are constants and the graphs of the lines $2x - 3y = 8$ and $ax + by = 2$ are perpendicular, then what is the value of $\frac{3a}{b}$?

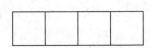

9

$$5x - y = 11$$
$$2x - 2y = 9$$

Based on the system of equations above, what is the value of $3x + y$?

A) −2

B) 0

C) 2

D) 4

10

Two numbers have a difference of 4 and a sum of −7. What is their product?

A) −33

B) −10.25

C) 8.25

D) 10.25

11

It costs Emma p dollars to make each of her custom bracelets, which she sells for m dollars apiece. She makes a profit of $60 if she makes and sells 5 of these bracelets, but she only makes a profit of $10 if she makes 5 bracelets but only sells 4 of them. How much does it cost Emma to make each bracelet?

A) $36

B) $38

C) $48

D) $50

Exercise Set 5 (Calculator)

12

If $2y = x + 1$ and $4x + 6y = 0$, then $y =$

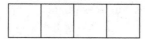

13

If $6x + 7y = \dfrac{4}{5}$ and $6x - 7y = \dfrac{6}{5}$, then $y =$

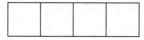

$$2x - 5y = 20$$
$$10x - 25y = 4k$$

14

For what value of k does the system of equations above have at least one solution?

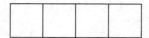

15

At the beginning of the week, the ratio of cats to dogs at Glenna's Pet Store was 4 to 5. By the end of the week, the number of cats had doubled, while the number of dogs had increased by 12. If the ratio of cats to dogs at the end of the week was 1 to 1, how many cats did the store have at the <u>beginning</u> of the week?

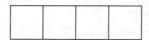

16

Jenny originally had twice as many friendship bracelets as Emilie. After Jenny gave Emilie 5 of her friendship bracelets, Jenny still had 10 more than Emilie. How many friendship bracelets did Jenny have originally?

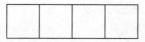

17

The average (arithmetic mean) of x and y is 14. If the value of x is doubled and the value of y is tripled, the average (arithmetic mean) of the two numbers remains the same. What is the value of x?

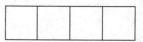

18

$$7m + 10n = 7$$
$$6m + 9n = 1$$

Based on the system of equations above, what is the value of $4m + 4n$?

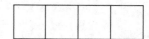

19

In the xy-plane, perpendicular lines a and b intersect at the point $(2, 2)$. If line a contains the point $(7, 1)$, which of the following points is on line b?

A) $(0, 1)$

B) $(4, 5)$

C) $(7, 3)$

D) $(3, 7)$

20

Which of the following pairs of equations has no solution in common?

A) $2x - 3y = 1$ and $6x - 9y = 3$

B) $y = 4x$ and $y = -4x$

C) $2x - 3y = 1$ and $6x - 9y = 2$

D) $y = 4x$ and $2y - 8x = 0$

21

In the xy-plane, the line l is perpendicular to the line described by the equation $\dfrac{1}{x} + \dfrac{1}{2y} = \dfrac{1}{y}$. What is the slope of line l?

A) -2

B) $-\dfrac{1}{2}$

C) $\dfrac{1}{2}$

D) 2

EXERCISE SET 5 ANSWER KEY

No Calculator

1. 8

$$3x + 2y = 72$$

Substitute $y = 3x$: $\quad 3x + 2(3x) = 72$

Simplify: $\quad 9x = 72$

Divide by 9: $\quad x = 8$

---

2. 20

$$4a^2 - 49b^2$$

Factor: $\quad (2a - 7b)(2a + 7b)$

Substitute: $\quad (10)(2) = 20$

---

3. 2

$$y = -4x - 3$$

Substitute $x = -1, y = c$: $\quad c = -4(-1) - 3$

Simplify: $\quad c = 1$

Other equation: $\quad y = -3x - b$

Substitute $x = -1, y = 1$: $\quad 1 = -3(-1) - b$

Simplify: $\quad 1 = 3 - b$

Subtract 3: $\quad -2 = -b$

Divide by -1: $\quad 2 = b$

---

4. 3.2 or 16/5 Parallel lines must have equal slopes. The slope of $4x + 5y = 13$ is $-4/5$, and the slope of $4y + kx = 2$ is $-k/4$.

$$\frac{-4}{5} = \frac{-k}{4}$$

Cross-multiply: $\quad -5k = -16$

Divide by -5: $\quad k = 16/5 = 3.2$

---

5. 7.5 or 15/2 Perpendicular line have slopes that are opposite reciprocals. The slope of $4x + 5y = 13$ is $-4/5$, and the slope of $6y - kx = 6$ is $k/6$.

$$\frac{-4}{5} = \frac{-6}{k}$$

Cross-multiply: $\quad -4k = -30$

Divide by -4: $\quad k = 7.5$

---

6. .25 or ¼ First equation: $\quad \dfrac{2a}{b} = \dfrac{1}{3}$

Divide by 2: $\quad \dfrac{a}{b} = \dfrac{1}{6}$

Second equation: $\quad \dfrac{c}{b} + 1 = \dfrac{5}{3}$

Subtract 1: $\quad \dfrac{c}{b} = \dfrac{2}{3}$

Reciprocate: $\quad \dfrac{b}{c} = \dfrac{3}{2}$

Multiply: $\quad \left(\dfrac{a}{b}\right)\left(\dfrac{a}{b}\right) = \dfrac{a}{c} = \left(\dfrac{1}{6}\right)\left(\dfrac{3}{2}\right) = \dfrac{3}{12} = \dfrac{1}{4}$

---

7. .75 or ¾

$$abc = 12$$

Substitute $ab = -4$: $\quad (-4)c = 12$

Divide by -4: $\quad c = -3$

Expression to evaluate: $\quad \dfrac{c}{ab}$

Substitute $c = -3$ and $ab = -4$: $\quad \dfrac{c}{ab} = \dfrac{-3}{-4} = \dfrac{3}{4}$

---

8. 4.5 or 9/2 The slope of $2x - 3y = 8$ is 2/3, and the slope of $ax + by = 2$ is $-a/b$. If the two lines are perpendicular, then the slopes are

opposite reciprocals: $\quad \dfrac{2}{3} = \dfrac{b}{a}$

Reciprocate: $\quad \dfrac{a}{b} = \dfrac{3}{2}$

Multiply by 3: $\quad \dfrac{3a}{b} = \dfrac{9}{2}$

---

9. C

$$5x - y = 11$$
$$2x - 2y = 9$$

Subtract equations: $\quad 3x + y = 2$

---

10. C

$$a - b = 4$$
$$a + b = -7$$

Add equations: $\quad 2a = -3$

Divide by 2: $\quad a = -1.5$

Substitute $a = -1.5$: $\quad -1.5 + b = -7$

Add 1.5: $\quad b = -7 + 1.5 = -5.5$

Evaluate product: $\quad ab = (-1.5)(-5.5) = 8.25$

---

11. B Let $c =$ the cost to make each one of Emma's bracelets.

$$5m - 5c = 60$$
$$4m - 5c = 10$$

Subtract: $\quad m = 50$

Substitute $m = 50$: $\quad 5(50) - 5c = 60$

Simplify: $\quad 250 - 5c = 60$

Subtract 250: $\quad -5c = -190$

Divide by -5: $\quad c = 38$

Calculator

12. 2/7 or .286 or .285

$$2y = x + 1$$

Subtract 1: $\quad 2y - 1 = x$

Given: $\quad 4x + 6y = 0$

Substitute $x = 2y - 1$: $\quad 4(2y - 1) + 6y = 0$

Distribute: $\quad 8y - 4 + 6y = 0$

Simplify: $14y - 4 = 0$

Add 4: $14y = 4$

Divide by 14: $y = 4/14 = 2/7$

---

13. **1/6 or .166 or .167** $6x + 7y = \dfrac{4}{5}$

                                                       $6x - 7y = \dfrac{6}{5}$

Add equations: $12x = 2$

Divide by 12: $x = 2/12 = 1/6$

---

14. **25**   The slope of $2x - 5y = 20$ is 2/5. The slope of $10x - 25y = 4k$ is 10/25 = 2/5. Since the two lines have the same slope, they have no points of intersection unless they are the same line. $2x - 5y = 20$

                                                       $10x - 25y = 4k$

Multiply first equation by 5: $10x - 25y = 100$

Therefore, $4k = 100$ and so $k = 25$.

---

15. **16**   If the original ratio of cats to dogs is 4 to 5, then we can say there were $4n$ cats and $5n$ dogs to start. At the end of the week, therefore, there were $8n$ cats and $5n + 12$ dogs. If this ratio was 1:1, then $8n = 5n + 12$

Subtract $5n$: $3n = 12$

Divide by 3: $n = 4$

Therefore, there were $4n = 4(4) = 16$ cats at the beginning of the week.

---

16. **40**   Let $x =$ the number of friendship bracelets Emilie had to start. This means that Jenny originally had $2x$ bracelets. After Jenny gave 5 of them to Emilie, Jenny had $2x - 5$ and Emilie had $x + 5$. If Jenny still had 10 more than Emilie, then $2x - 5 = 10 + (x + 5)$

Simplify: $2x - 5 = x + 15$

Subtract x and add 5: $x = 20$

This means that Jenny had $2x = 2(20) = 40$ to start.

---

17. **56** $\dfrac{x+y}{2} = 14$

Multiply by 2: $x + y = 28$

If x is doubled and y is tripled, the average

remains the same: $\dfrac{2x+3y}{2} = 14$

Multiply by 2: $2x + 3y = 28$

Previous equation: $x + y = 28$

Multiply by 3: $3x + 3y = 84$

Other equation: $2x + 3y = 28$

Subtract equations: $x = 56$

---

18. **24** $7m + 10n = 7$

                                                       $6m + 9n = 1$

Subtract equations: $m + n = 6$

Multiply by 4: $4m + 4n = 24$

---

19. **D**   Line a contains the points (2, 2) and (7, 1); therefore, it has a slope of $\dfrac{2-1}{2-7} = -\dfrac{1}{5}$. If line b is perpendicular to line a, then it must have a slope of 5 (the opposite reciprocal of $-1/5$). You might find it helpful to sketch the line with slope 5 through the point (2, 2), and confirm that is passes through the point (3, 7), which is one unit to the right and one 5 units up.

---

20. **C**   In order for two lines in the xy-plane to have no points in common, they must be parallel and nonidentical. The only two such lines among these choices are $2x - 3y = 1$ and $6x - 9y = 2$, which both have a slope of 2/3, but have different y-intercepts of $-1/3$ and $-2/9$.

---

21. **A** $\dfrac{1}{x} + \dfrac{1}{2y} = \dfrac{1}{y}$

Multiply by $2xy$: $2y + x = 2x$

Subtract x: $2y = x$

Divide by 2: $y = \dfrac{1}{2}x$

This line has a slope of 1/2, so the perpendicular must have a slope of -2.

CHAPTER 8

THE SAT MATH TEST: PROBLEM SOLVING AND DATA ANALYSIS

The SAT Math: Problem Solving and Data Analysis

Why is problem-solving and data analysis important on the SAT Math test?

About 26% (15 out of 58 points) of the SAT Math questions fall under the category of Problem Solving and Data Analysis. Questions in this category test your ability to

create a representation of a problem, consider the units involved, attend to the meaning of quantities, and [apply reasoning about] ratios, rates, and proportional relationships.

They also assess your skill in

interpreting and synthesizing data, [as well as identifying] quantitative measures of center, the overall pattern, and any striking deviations from the overall pattern in different data sets.

The specific topics include

- using rates, ratios, and proportional relationships to solve problems
- evaluating and analyzing data gathering methods
- calculate and use statistics of "central tendency" like mean, median, and mode
- basic measures of data "spread" such as standard deviation, range, and confidence intervals
- solving problems concerning percentages and percent change
- analyzing scatterplots, pie graphs, tables, histograms, and other graphs
- exploring linear, quadratic, and exponential relationships in data

How are these skills used?

Analyzing and drawing inferences from data are core skills not only in mathematics and the physical sciences, but also in social sciences such as psychology, sociology, and economics. Since these subjects constitute a substantial portion of any liberal arts curriculum, colleges consider these to be essential college preparatory skills.

Sound intimidating? It's not.

If you take the time to master the four core skills presented in these 16 lessons, you will gain the knowledge and practice you need to master SAT Math problem-solving and data analysis questions.

Skill 1: Working with Data
Lesson 1: Working with averages (arithmetic means)

The average (arithmetic mean) of four numbers is 15. If one of the numbers is 18, what is the average (arithmetic mean) of the remaining three numbers?

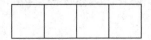

The **average (arithmetic mean)** of any set of numbers is calculated with the formula

$$average = \frac{sum}{\#\,of\,numbers}$$

But it is helpful to notice that this form can take two other forms:

$$sum = average \times \#\,of\,numbers$$

$$\#\,of\,numbers = \frac{sum}{average}$$

(*Medium*) In this problem, we are given the average of the set and the number of numbers in the set. So we can use the formula *sum* = *average* × *# of numbers* to find the

sum of these numbers: $15 \times 4 = 60$. If one of these numbers is 18, then the sum of the remaining three numbers is $60 - 18 = 42$. Using the first formula above gives us an average of $42/3 = 14$.

Ms. Aguila's class, which has 20 students, scored an average of 90% on a test. Mr. Bowle's class, which has 30 students, scored an average of 80% on the same test. What was the combined average score for the two classes? (Disregard the % symbol when gridding. For instance, enter 74% as 74.)

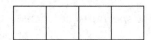

(*Medium*) Can we just take the average of the scores for the two classes, and say the overall average is $(90+80)/2 = 85$? No, because there are more students in the second class, so we can't "weigh" the two classes equally. Using the formula above we can calculate the sum of all of the scores in both classes. In Ms. Aguila's class, the sum of the scores is $90 \times 20 = 1,800$, and the sum of the scores in Mr. Bowe's class is $80 \times 30 = 2,400$. Therefore, the sum of all of the scores in the two classes combined is $1,800 + 2,400 = 4,200$. Since there are 50 students altogether in the two classes, the combined average is $4,200/50 = 84$.

Lesson 2: Working with medians and modes

The median of 1, 6, 8, and k is 5. What is the average (arithmetic mean) of these four numbers?

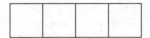

The **median** of any set of numbers is the number that divides the **ordered set** into two equal sets. In other words, half of the numbers should be **less than or equal to** the median, and half the numbers should be **greater than or equal to** the median. To find a median,

1. Put the numbers in increasing (or decreasing) order.
2. If there are an odd number of numbers, the median is the middle number.
3. If there are an even number of numbers, the median is the average of the *two* middle numbers.

(*Medium*) Using this definition we can find the value of k. The tricky part is step 1, since we don't know where k should be when we put the numbers in order. Clearly, however, there are only four possibilities to consider.

If k is the least of these numbers, then the correct ordering is k, 1, 6, 8. Since there are an even number of numbers, the median is the average of the middle two: $(1 + 6)/2 = 3.5$. But this contradicts the given fact that the median is 5, so that doesn't work. Putting k in the next slot gives us an order of 1, k, 6, 8. In this case, the median would be $(k + 6)/2$.

$$\frac{k+6}{2} = 5$$

Multiply by 2: $\quad\quad\quad\quad\quad\quad\quad\quad k + 6 = 10$
Subtract 6: $\quad\quad\quad\quad\quad\quad\quad\quad\quad\quad k = 4$

Notice that this confirms our assumption that k is between 1 and 6, so k must equal 4. Now we must find the average of these four numbers: $(1 + 4 + 6 + 8)/2 = 19/2 = 9.5$.

Roll	Frequency
1	10
2	a
3	b
4	7
5	9
6	9

The table above shows the results of 50 rolls of a die, with two missing values labeled a and b. If the mode of these 50 rolls is 2, what is the greatest possible average (arithmetic mean) value of these rolls?

The **mode** of a set of numbers is the number that appears the **most frequently**. This means that not every set of numbers has a mode. For instance, in the set 1, 1, 2, 3, 4, the mode is 1, but the set 1, 2, 3, 4 does not have a mode, because every numbers occurs once.

(*Hard*) This data set has 50 numbers, each representing a roll of a die. If the mode is 2, then 2 is the most frequent roll. Since the table above shows that the highest known frequency is 10 (for a roll of 1), then a (the number of times a 2 was rolled) must be at least 11. We also know that the total number of rolls is 50, so $10 + a + b + 7 + 9 + 9 = 50$, and therefore $a + b = 15$. The question asks us to find the *greatest possible average* of these rolls, so we want to maximize the *sum* of all of the rolls. This means that we want b (the number of times a 3 was rolled) to be as great as possible. Since $b = 15 - a$, then the greatest b can be is $15 - 11 = 4$. Therefore $a = 11$ and $b = 4$. Now we have to find the average of these 50 numbers: $[(1)(10) + (2)(11) + (3)(4) + (4)(7) + (5)(9) + (6)(9)]/50 = (10 + 22 + 12 + 28 + 45 + 54)/50 = 3.42$.

Lesson 3: Understanding data spread

The SAT Math test may occasionally ask you about the "spread" of a set of data. You will **NOT** have to calculate technical statistics like **variance**, **standard deviation**, or **margin of error**, but you **might** be asked to answer more basic questions about the "spread" of a set of data, as in the questions below.

The "range" of a set of data is defined as the absolute difference between the least value and the greatest value in the set. If five positive integers have an average (arithmetic mean) of 10, what is the greatest possible "range" of this set?

(*Medium-hard*) If five numbers have an average of 10, then their sum must be $5 \times 10 = 50$. If we want the greatest possible "range," then we must maximize one of these numbers by minimizing the sum of the *other* numbers. Since the smallest positive integer is 1, we can minimize the sum of the other four numbers by setting them all equal to 1. This gives us $1 + 1 + 1 + 1 + x = 50$, so $x = 46$. This gives us a maximum "range" of $46 - 1 = 45$.

The "absolute deviation" of a number in a set is the absolute difference between that number and the average (arithmetic mean) of the set. The "average absolute deviation" of a set is the average (arithmetic mean) of all of the absolute deviations in the set. Which of the following sets has the greatest "average absolute deviation?"

A) 2, 2, 2, 2

B) 2, 3, 4, 5

C) 4, 4, 5, 5

D) 4, 4, 4, 5

(*Medium*) When a question introduces a new term, **read its definition carefully**—several times, if necessary. This question gives us *two* new terms. To understand these terms, let's apply them to a simple set of numbers, such as the set in choice (A). The average of this set is 2; therefore, the "absolute deviation" of each of these numbers is its "absolute difference" from 2, which is 0 for each number. The "average absolute deviation" of the entire set is defined as the average of these "absolute deviations," which is, of course, $(0 + 0 + 0 + 0)/4 = 0$.

Notice that the "average absolute deviation" of a number set is a measure of "spread." Since the numbers in (A) are bunched up as tightly as possible, their "average absolute deviation" is 0. Now let's look at the remaining choices. Which seems to have the greatest "spread?" Once you've made your guess, do the calculations and see if you're right. For confirmation, you should find that the "average absolute deviations" are (A) 0, (B) 1, (C) 0.5, and (D) 0.375. Therefore, the correct answer is (B).

Lesson 4: Variations and drawing inferences from data

The variables x and y **vary directly** if they have a **constant ratio**, that is,

$$\frac{y}{x} = k \text{ or } y = kx \quad \text{(where } k \text{ is a constant)}$$

The variables x and y **vary inversely** if they have a **constant product**, that is,

$$xy = k \text{ or } y = \frac{k}{x} \quad \text{(where } k \text{ is a constant)}$$

x	y
1	5
2	20

Given the ordered pairs in the table above, which of the following could be true?

A) y varies directly as x

B) y varies inversely as x

C) y varies directly as the square of x

D) y varies inversely as the square of x

(*Medium-hard*) Using the definitions above, we can see whether y and x vary directly or inversely. Do they have a **constant ratio**? No: $5/1 \neq 20/2$. Therefore, they do not vary directly and (A) is incorrect. Do they have a **constant product**? No: $1 \times 5 \neq 2 \times 20$. Therefore, they do not vary inversely, and (B) is incorrect. To check (C), we must ask: do y and x^2 have a constant ratio? Yes: $5/(1)^2 = 20/(2)^2 = 5$, therefore the correct answer is (C).

If y varies **directly** as x, then the graph of their relation in the xy-plane is a **line through the origin**:

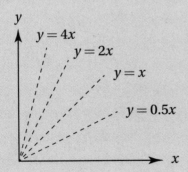

If y varies **inversely** as x, then the graph of their relation in the xy-plane is a **hyperbola that approaches, but does not touch, the x- and y-axes**:

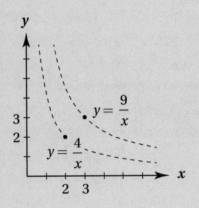

x	y
2	12
4	96

The variables x and y are related by an equation of the form $y = Ax^n$ where A and n are both positive real numbers. Based on the data in the table above, what is the value of y when $x = 3$?

A) 40.5

B) 46.0

C) 54.0

D) 64.0

(*Medium*) In order to find the value of y when $x = 3$, we must find the specific equation relating x and y. We can find the values of A and n in the equation $y = Ax^n$ by first plugging in the values from the table. Plugging in the first ordered pair gives us $12 = A(2)^n$ and plugging in the second ordered pair gives us $96 = A(4)^n$.

$$96 = A(4)^n$$
$$12 = A(2)^n$$

Divide the corresponding sides:

$$\frac{96}{12} = \frac{4^n}{2^n}$$

Simplify:

$$8 = 2^n$$

Substitute $8 = 2^3$:

$$2^3 = 2^n \text{ and so } n = 3$$

(Notice that this means that y varies directly as x^3.)

Substitute $n = 3$ into either equation:

$$12 = A(2)^3$$

Simplify:

$$12 = 8A$$

Divide by 8:

$$1.5 = A$$

Therefore, the equation that relates x and y is $y = 1.5x^3$. Finally, we find y when $x = 3$ by substituting into the equation: $y = 1.5(3)^3 = 1.5(27) = 40.5$, so the correct answer is (A).

Exercise Set 1 (No Calculator)

1

The "range" of a set of data is defined as the absolute difference between the least value and the greatest value in the set. Four positive integers have an average (arithmetic mean) of 7.5.

a. What is the greatest possible range of this set?

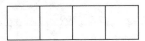

b. What is the least possible range of this set?

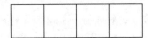

2

If the median of 2, 4, 6, and b is 4.2, what is the average (arithmetic mean) of these four numbers?

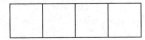

3

The average (arithmetic mean) of 2, 5, 8 and k is 0. What is the median of these numbers?

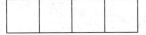

4

A set of numbers has a sum of 48 and an average of 6. How many numbers are in the set?

5

If the average (arithmetic mean) of 4 and x is equal to the average (arithmetic mean) of 2, 8, and x, what is the value of x?

6

The median of a set of 22 consecutive even integers is 25. What is the largest number in the set?

7

If p varies inversely as q and $p = 4$ when $q = 6$, the which of the following is another solution for p and q?

A) $p = 8$ and $q = 12$

B) $p = 8$ and $q = 10$

C) $p = 12$ and $q = 1$

D) $p = 12$ and $q = 2$

8

A set of n numbers has an average (arithmetic mean) of $3k$ and a sum of $12m$, where k and m are both positive. Which of the following is equivalent to n?

A) $\dfrac{4m}{k}$ B) $\dfrac{4k}{m}$ C) $\dfrac{k}{4m}$

D) $\dfrac{m}{4k}$

9

If y varies inversely as the square of x, then when x is multiplied by 4, y will be

A) divided by 16

B) divided by 2

C) multiplied by 2

D) multiplied by 16

10

Let $f(x, y) = Ax^2y^3$ where A is a constant. If $f(a, b) = 10$, what is the value of $f(2a, 2b)$?

A) 100

B) 260

C) 320

D) 500

11

A set of four integers has a mode of 7 and a median of 4. What is the greatest possible average (arithmetic mean) of this set?

A) 3.50

B) 3.75

C) 4.00

D) 4.25

Exercise Set 1 (Calculator)

12

Four positive integers have a mode of 4 and a median of 3. What is their sum?

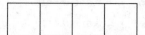

13

Five different integers have an average (arithmetic mean) of 10. If none is less than 5, what is the greatest possible value of one of these integers?

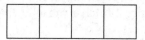

14

If b varies inversely as a, and $b = 0.5$ when $a = 32$, then for how many ordered pairs (a, b) are a and b both positive integers?

15

The median of 11 consecutive integers is 28. What is the least of these integers?

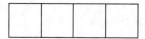

16

If $y = Ax^3$ and $y = 108$ when $x = 3$, then for what value of x does $y = 62.5$?

17

A set of four positive integers has a median of 2 and a mode of 2. If the average (arithmetic mean) of this set is 3, what is the largest possible number in the set?

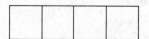

18

If y varies inversely as x and the graph of their relation in the xy-plane passes through the point (2, 15), what is the value of y when $x = 4$?

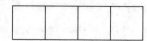

19

Roll	Frequency
1	4
2	5
3	4
4	6
5	5
6	6

A six-sided die was rolled 30 times and the results tabulated above. What is the difference between the average (arithmetic mean) of the rolls and the median of the rolls?

A) 0.1

B) 0.2

C) 0.3

D) 0.4

20

If y varies inversely as the square of x, and $y = 4$ when $x = 2$, then what is the value of y when $x = 3$?

A) $\dfrac{16}{9}$

B) $\dfrac{8}{3}$

C) 3

D) 9

21

At a fixed temperature, the volume of a sample of gas varies inversely as the pressure of the gas. If the pressure of a sample of gas at a fixed temperature is increased by 50%, by what percent is the volume decreased?

A) 25%

B) $33\frac{1}{3}$%

C) 50%

D) $66\frac{2}{3}$%

22

If the graph of $y = f(x)$ in the xy-plane contains the points (4, 3) and (16, 6), which of the following could be true?

A) y varies directly as the square of x

B) y varies inversely as the square of x

C) y varies directly as the square root of x

D) y varies inversely as the square root of x

EXERCISE SET 1 ANSWER KEY

No Calculator

1a. 26   If the average of 4 numbers is 7.5, they must have a sum of $4 \times 7.5 = 30$. To maximize the range, we must maximize one of the numbers by minimizing the other 3 by setting them all equal to 1 (the smallest positive integer). The numbers therefore are 1, 1, 1, and 27, and the range is $27 - 1 = 26$.

1b. 1   To minimize the range, we "cluster" the numbers as closely together as possible. The tightest cluster of integers with a sum of 30 is 7, 7, 8, and 8, which gives a range of $8 - 7 = 1$.

2. 4.1   If the set contains four numbers, its median is the average of the middle two numbers, so the middle two numbers must have a sum of $(2)(4.2) = 8.4$. Thus the four numbers must be 2, 4, 4.4, and 6. (Notice that the question did not say that all numbers were integers.) The average of these is $16.4/4 = 4.1$.

3. 3.5   If the average of these numbers is 0, their sum must be $(4)(0) = 0$, and therefore $k = -15$ and the numbers, in increasing order, are -15, 2, 5, and 8. The median is $(2 + 5)/2 = 3.5$.

4. 8 $6 = 48/n$, so $n = 8$.

5. 8

$$\frac{4 + x}{2} = \frac{2 + 8 + x}{3}$$

Cross-multiply: $12 + 3x = 20 + 2x$
Subtract $2x$ and 12: $x = 8$

6. 46   The median divides the set into two equal parts, so 11 of these numbers must be less than 25 and 11 must be greater than 25. Since they are consecutive even integers, the 11 numbers above the median must be 26, 28, 30, 32, . . . 46.

7. D   If p and q vary inversely, their product is a constant. $4 \times 6 = 24$, and the only other pair with a product equal to 24 is (D) 12 and 2.

8. A $n = sum/average = 12m/3k = 4m/k$

9. A   The equation relating x and y is $y = k/x^2$. If $x = 1$, then $y = k$. If x is multiplied by 4, then $x = 4$ and $y = k/16$, so y has been divided by 16.

10. C $f(a, b) = Aa^2b^3 = 10$. $f(2a, 2b) = A(2a)^2(2b)^3 = 32(Aa^2b^3) = 32(10) = 320$.

11. B   If this set has a mode of 7, then at least two of the numbers are 7. If the median is 4, then the two middle numbers must have a sum of $(2)(4) = 8$. Therefore the two middle numbers are 1 and 7, and the sequence must be n, 1, 7, 7. To maximize the average, we must maximize n, but n can't be 1, because then the set would not have a mode of 7. It must be the next lower integer, 0, and the average is $(0 + 1 + 7 + 7)/4 = 3.75$.

Calculator

12. 11   The only four numbers that satisfy these conditions are 1, 2, 4, and 4.

13. 24   If the average of five numbers is 10, their sum is $5 \times 10 = 50$. To maximize one, we must minimize the sum of the other four. If none is less than five, and all are different integers, they are 5, 6, 7, 8, and 24.

14. 5   If the variables vary inversely, their product is constant. $(0.5)(32) = 16$. The only pairs of positive integers with a product of 16 are (1, 16), (2, 8), (4, 4), (8, 2), and (16, 1).

15. 23   If the middle number is 28, there are five numbers less than 28, and five greater. Since they are consecutive integers, the least is $28 - 5 = 23$.

16. 2.5   Since $108 = A(3)^3$, $A = 4$, so if $62.5 = 4x^3$, $x = 2.5$.

17. 7   At least two of the integers must be 2 and none can be less than 1. If the sum must be $4 \times 3 = 12$, the set including the largest possible number is 1, 2, 2, and 7.

18. 7.5   The product of x and y is $2 \times 15 = 30$, so $y = 30/4 = 7.5$.

19. C   Average $= (1 \times 4 + 2 \times 5 + 3 \times 4 + 4 \times 6 + 5 \times 5 + 6 \times 6)/30 = 3.7$. Median $=$ average of 15th and 16th roll: $(4 + 4)/2 = 4$. $4 - 3.7 = 0.3$.

20. A y and x^2 must have a constant product of $4 \times 2^2 = 16$. Therefore, $y = 16/9$.

21. **B** Pick values for the original pressure and volume, such as 2 and 3. If they vary inversely, their product is the constant $2 \times 3 = 6$. If the pressure is increased by 50%, it becomes $(1.5)(2) = 3$, and so the volume becomes $6/3 = 2$, a change of $-33\ 1/3\%$.

22. **C** For both ordered pairs, $\dfrac{y}{\sqrt{x}}$ is a constant: $\dfrac{3}{\sqrt{4}} = \dfrac{6}{\sqrt{16}} = \dfrac{3}{2}$, so y is directly proportional to the square root of x.

Skill 2: Working with Rates, Ratios, Percentages, and Proportions

Lesson 5: Rates and unit rates

On a sunny day, a 50 square meter section of solar panel array can generate an average of 1 kilowatt-hour of energy per hour over a 10-hour period. If an average household consumes 30 kilowatt-hours of energy per day, how large an array would be required to power 1,000 households on sunny days?

A) 1,500 square meters

B) 15,000 square meters

C) 150,000 square meters

D) 15,000,000 square meters

(*Medium*) This is clearly a "rate problem," because it includes two "per" quantities. When working with rates, keep two important ideas in mind:

The units for any rate can be translated to give the formula for the rate. For instance, if a word problem includes the fact that "a rocket burns fuel at a rate of 15 kilograms per second," this fact can be translated into a formula as long as we remember that *per* means *divided by*:

$$\text{rate (of fuel burning)} = \frac{\text{\# kilograms of fuel}}{\text{\# seconds}}$$

Any "rate fact" in a problem can be interpreted as a "conversion factor." For instance, if "a rocket burns fuel at a rate of 15 kilograms per second," then in the context of that problem, one second of burning *is equivalent to* 15 kilograms of fuel being burned. Therefore, as we discussed in Chapter 7, Lesson 4, we are entitled to use either of the following **conversion factors** in this problem:

$$\frac{15 \text{ kilograms}}{1 \text{ second}} \quad \text{or} \quad \frac{1 \text{ second}}{15 \text{ kilogram}}$$

Just as we did in Chapter 7, Lesson 4, we can solve this problem by just noticing that it is essentially a **conversion problem**. The question asks "how large an array (in square meters) would be required to power 1,000 households on sunny days?" So we can treat the problem as a conversion from a particular number of

households to a particular number of *square meters of solar panels*:

$$1{,}000 \text{ households} \times \frac{30 \text{ kwh/day}}{1 \text{ household}} \times \frac{1 \text{ day}}{10 \text{ sun-hours}} \times$$

$$\frac{50 \text{ square meters}}{1 \text{ kwh/sun-hour}} = 150{,}000 \text{ square meters}$$

Note very carefully how (1) all of the units on the left side of the equation cancel except for "square meters" (which is what we want), and (2) each conversion factor represents an explicit fact mentioned in the problem.

Many rate problems can be easily managed with the "rate pie":

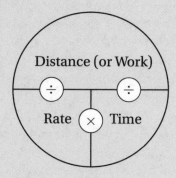

This is a simple graphical device to organize information in a rate problem. It is simply a way of expressing all three forms of the "rate equation" at once: *distance = rate × time*; *rate = distance/time*; and *time = distance/rate*. For example, if a word problem states that "Maria completes an *x*-mile bicycle race at an average speed of *z* miles per hour," your "rate pie" should look like this:

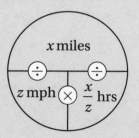

First, we plug the given values in: x miles goes in for distance, and z miles per hour goes in for rate. Then, as soon **as two of the spaces are filled, we simply perform the operation between them** (in this case division) **and put the result in the final space.** In this case, the time Maria took to complete the race was x/z hours.

A water pump for a dredging project can remove 180 gallons of water per minute, but can work only for 3 consecutive hours, at which time it requires 20 minutes of maintenance before it can be brought back online. While it is offline, a smaller pump is used in its place, which can pump 80 gallons per minute. Using this system, what is the least amount of time it would take to pump 35,800 gallons of water?

A) 3 hour 10 minutes

B) 3 hours 15 minutes

C) 3 hours 25 minutes

D) 3 hours 30 minutes

(*Hard*) If we want to pump out the water as quickly as possible, we want to use the stronger pump for the maximum three hours. To find the total amount of water pumped in that time, we do the conversion:

$$3 \text{ hours} \times \frac{60 \text{ minutes}}{1 \text{ hour}} \times \frac{180 \text{ gallons}}{1 \text{ minute}} = 32,400 \text{ gallons}$$

So after 3 hours, there are still $35,800 - 32,400 = 3,400$ gallons left to pump. At that point, the smaller pump must be used for a minimum of 20 minutes, which can pump

$$20 \text{ minutes} \times \frac{80 \text{ gallons}}{1 \text{ minute}} = 1,600 \text{ gallons}$$

which still leaves $3,400 - 1,600 = 1,800$ gallons left. Notice that we have already taken 3 hours and 20 minutes, and as yet have not finished pumping. This means that choices (A) and (B) are certainly incorrect. So how long will it take to pump the remaining 1,800 gallons? Now that we can bring the stronger pump online, it will only take 1,800 gallons $\times$ (1 minute/180 gallons) = 10 more minutes; therefore, the correct answer is (D).

Although you don't need to construct a graph of this situation to solve the problem, graphing helps show the overall picture:

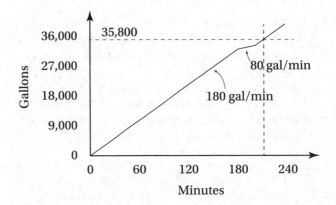

Notice that the line has a slope of 180 for the first 180 minutes, then 80 for the next 20 minutes, and then 180 for the next 180 minutes, and crosses the line $y = 35,800$ at 210 minutes.

In the graph of any linear function, y in terms of x, the slope of the line is equivalent to the **unit rate** of the function, that is, **the rate at which y increases or decreases for every unit increase in x.**

Lesson 6: Ratios: part-to-part and part-to-whole

A marathon offers $5,000 in prize money to the top three finishers. If the first-, second-, and third-place prizes are distributed in a ratio of 5:4:1, how much money, in dollars, does the second-place finisher receive?

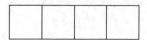

(*Easy*) When given a "part-to-part" ratio, such as 5:4:1 (which is of course, really a part-to-part-to-part ratio), it often helps to add up the parts and consider the whole. This prize is divided into $5 + 4 + 1 = 10$ equal parts, so the winner gets 5/10 of the prize money, the second-place finisher gets 4/10 of the prize money, and the third-place finisher gets 1/10 of the prize money. The second-place finisher therefore takes home $(4/10) \times \$5,000 = \$2,000$.

> If you are given a part-to-part ratio, it is often helpful to add up the parts and then divide each part by the sum. For instance, if a paint mixture is a 2:5 combination of red and yellow, respectively, the "whole" is $2 + 5 = 7$, which means that the mixture is 2/7 red and 5/7 yellow.

Bronze is an alloy (a metallic mixture) consisting of copper and tin. If 50 kg of a bronze alloy of 20% tin and 80% copper is mixed with 70 kg of a bronze alloy of 5% tin and 95% copper, what fraction, by weight, of the combined bronze alloy is tin?

A) 5/48

B) 9/80

C) 1/8

D) 1/4

(*Medium*) The combined alloy will weigh 50 kg + 70 kg = 120 kg. The total weight of the tin comes from the two separate alloys: $(0.20)(50) + (0.05)(70) = 10 + 3.5 = 13.5$ kg. Therefore the fraction of the combined alloy that is tin is 13.5/120, which simplifies to 9/80.

Exercise Set 2 (Calculator)

1

If a train travels at a constant rate of 50 miles per hour, how many minutes will it take to travel 90 miles?

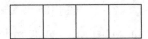

2

Two cars leave the same point simultaneously, going in the same direction along a straight, flat road, one at 35 miles per hour and the other at 50 miles per hour. After how many minutes will the cars be 5 miles apart?

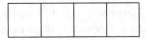

3

If a $6,000 contribution is divided among charities *A*, *B*, and *C* in a ratio of 8:5:2, respectively, how much more, in dollars, does charity *A* receive than charity *C*?

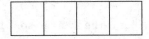

4

If a car traveling at 60 mph is chasing a car travelling at 50 mph and is ¼ mile behind, how many minutes will it take the first car to catch the second?

5

A truck's gas tank can hold 18 gallons. If the tank is 2/3 full and the truck travels for 4 hours at 60 miles per hour until it runs out of gas, what is the efficiency of the truck, in miles per gallon?

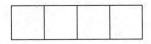

6

A motorcycle has a fuel efficiency of 60 miles per gallon when it is cruising at a speed of 50 miles per hour. How many hours can it travel at 50 miles per hour on a full tank of gas, if its tank can hold 10 gallons?

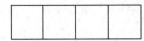

7

If the ratio of *a* to *b* is 3 to 4, and the ratio of *a* to *c* is 5 to 2, what is the ratio of *b* to *c*?

A) 3 to 10

B) 3 to 5

C) 5 to 3

D) 10 to 3

8

A paint mixture consists of a 3:2:11 ratio of red, violet, and white, respectively. How many ounces of violet are needed to make 256 ounces of this mixture?

A) 32

B) 36

C) 46

D) 48

9

A pool that holds 20,000 gallons is ¼ full. A pump can deliver *g* gallons of water every *m* minutes. If the pumping company charges *d* dollars per minute, how much will it cost, in dollars, to fill the pool?

A) $\dfrac{5,000\,md}{g}$

B) $\dfrac{5,000\,gd}{m}$

C) $\dfrac{15,000\,md}{g}$

D) $\dfrac{5,000\,gd}{m}$

10

Yael travels to work at an average speed of 40 miles per hour and returns home by the same route at 24 miles per hour. If the total time for the round trip is 2 hours, how many miles is her trip to work?

A) 25

B) 30

C) 45

D) 60

11

A hare runs at a constant rate of a miles per hour, and a tortoise runs at a constant rate of b miles per hour, where $0 < b < a$. How many more hours will it take the tortoise to finish a race of d miles than the hare?

A) $\dfrac{a+b}{2d}$

B) $\dfrac{ad-bd}{ab}$

C) $\dfrac{b-a}{d}$

D) $\dfrac{ab-bd}{ad}$

12

Janice can edit 700 words per minute and Edward can edit 500 words per minute. If each page of text contains 800 words, how many pages can they edit, working together, in 20 minutes?

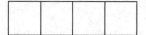

13

If a printer can print 5 pages in 20 seconds, how many pages can it print in 5 minutes?

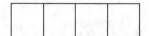

14

Traveling at 40 miles per hour, Diego can complete his daily commute in 45 minutes. How many minutes would he save if he traveled at 50 miles per hour?

15

If $\dfrac{2a}{3b} = \dfrac{1}{5}$ and $\dfrac{c}{2b} - \dfrac{1}{2}$, what is $\dfrac{a}{c}$?

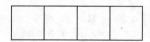

16

If a cyclist races at 30 miles per hour for 1/2 of the distance of a race, and 45 miles per hour for the final 1/2 of the distance, what is her average speed, in miles per hour, for the entire race?

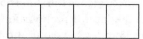

17

Anne can paint a room in 2 hours, and Barbara can paint the same room in 3 hours. If they each work the same rate when they work together as they do alone, how many hours should it take them to paint the same room if they work together?

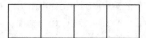

18

What is the average speed, in miles per hour, of a sprinter who runs ¼ mile in 45 seconds? (1 hour = 60 seconds)

A) 11.25

B) 13.5

C) 20

D) 22

19

A car travels d miles in t hours and arrives at its destination 3 hours late. At what average speed, in miles per hour, should the car have gone in order to arrive on time?

A) $\dfrac{t-3}{d}$

B) $\dfrac{d}{t-3}$

C) $\dfrac{d}{t} - 3$

D) $\dfrac{d-3}{t}$

20

In three separate 1-mile races, Ellen finished with times of x minutes, y minutes, and z minutes, respectively. What was her average speed, in miles per <u>hour</u>, for all three races?

A) $\dfrac{x+y+z}{3}$

B) $\dfrac{3}{x+y+z}$

C) $\dfrac{x+y+z}{180}$

D) $\dfrac{180}{x+y+z}$

21

Sylvia drove 315 miles and arrived at her destination in 9 hours. If she had driven 10 miles per hour faster, how many hours would she have saved on the trip?

A) 1.75 hours

B) 2.00 hours

C) 2.25 hours

D) 2.50 hours

EXERCISE SET 2 ANSWER KEY

1. **108** *time = distance/rate* = 90 miles/50 mph = 1.8 hours = 1.8 hour × 60 min/hour = 108 minutes.

2. **20** The fast car is moving ahead of the slow car at a rate of 50 − 35 = 15 mph, and so it will be 5 miles ahead after 5 ÷ 15 = 1/3 hour = 20 minutes.

3. **2,400** Since 8 + 5 + 2 = 15, charity *A* receives 8/15 of the contribution, and charity *C* receives 2/15. The difference is 6/15, or 2/5, of the total, which is (2/5)($6,000) = $2,400.

4. **1.5** Since the faster car is catching up to the slower car at 60 − 50 = 10 mph, it will take (1/4 mile)/(10 mph) = 1/40 hours = 60/40 minutes = 1.5 minutes.

5. **20** The tank contains (2/3)(18) = 12 gallons, and travels (4 hours)(60 mph) = 240 miles, so its efficiency is 240/12 = 20 miles per gallon.

6. **12** With 10 gallons of gas and an efficiency of 60 miles per gallon, the car can travel 10 × 60 = 600 miles. At 50 miles an hour this would take 600/50 = 12 hours.

7. **D** $\dfrac{b}{c} = \dfrac{b}{a} \times \dfrac{a}{c} = \dfrac{4}{3} \times \dfrac{5}{2} = \dfrac{10}{3}$

8. **A** According to the ratio, the mixture is 2/(3 + 2 + 11) = 2/16 = 1/8 violet. Therefore 256 ounces of the mixture would contain (1/8)(256) = 32 ounces of violet paint.

9. **C** If the pool is ¼ full, it requires (3/4)(20,000) = 15,000 more gallons.

$$15{,}000 \text{ gallons} \times \dfrac{m \text{ minutes}}{g \text{ gallons}} \times \dfrac{d \text{ dollars}}{1 \text{ minute}}$$

$$= \dfrac{15{,}000\, md}{g} \text{ dollars.}$$

10. **B** Let *x* = the distance, in miles, from home to work. Since *time = distance/rate*, it takes Yael *x*/40 hours to get to work and *x*/24 hours to get home.

$$\dfrac{x}{40} + \dfrac{x}{24} = 2$$

Simplify:
$$\dfrac{x}{15} = 2$$

Multiply by 15:
$$x = 30 \text{ miles}$$

11. **B** The tortoise would take *d*/*b* hours to complete the race, and the hare would take *d*/*a* hours to complete the race, so the tortoise would take $\dfrac{d}{a} - \dfrac{d}{a} = \dfrac{ad}{ab} - \dfrac{bd}{ab} = \dfrac{ad - bd}{ab}$ hours longer.

12. **30** Together they can edit 700 + 500 = 1,200 words per minute, so in 20 minutes they can edit

$$20 \text{ minutes} \times \dfrac{1{,}200 \text{ words}}{1 \text{ minute}} \times \dfrac{1 \text{ page}}{800 \text{ words}} = 30 \text{ pages}$$

13. **75** If the printer can print 5 pages in 20 seconds, it can print 15 pages in 1 minute, and therefore 15 × 5 = 75 pages in 5 minutes.

14. **9** Since 45 minutes is ¾ hour, Diego's daily commute is 40 × ¾ = 30 miles. If he traveled at 50 mph it would take him 30/50 = 3/5 hours = 36 minutes, so he would save 45 − 36 = 9 minutes.

15. **3/10 or 0.3**

$$\dfrac{2a}{3b} \times \dfrac{2b}{c} = \dfrac{1}{5} \times \dfrac{2}{1}$$

Simplify:
$$\dfrac{4a}{3c} = \dfrac{2}{5}$$

Multiply by ¾:
$$\dfrac{a}{c} = \dfrac{2}{5} \times \dfrac{3}{4} = \dfrac{3}{10}$$

16. **36** Pick a convenient length for the race, such as 180 miles (which is a multiple of both 30 and 45). The first half of the race would therefore be 90 miles, which would take 90 miles ÷ 30 mph = 3 hours, and the second half would take 90 miles ÷ 45 mph = 2 hours. Therefore, the entire race would take 3 + 2 = 5 hours, and the cyclist's average speed would therefore be 180 miles ÷ 5 hours = 36 miles per hour.

17. **1.2 or 6/5** Anne's rate is 1/2 room per hour, and Barbara's rate is 1/3 room per hour, so together their rate is 1/3 + 1/2 = 5/6 room per hour. Therefore, painting one room should take (1 room)/(5/6 room per hour) = 6/5 hours.

18. **C** $\dfrac{0.25\,\text{mile}}{45\,\text{seconds}} \times \dfrac{3{,}600\,\text{seconds}}{1\,\text{hour}} = 20\,\text{mph}$

19. **B** In order to arrive on time, it would have to travel the d miles in $t - 3$ hours, which would require a speed of $d/(t - 3)$ mph.

20. **D** $\dfrac{3\,\text{miles}}{x + y + z\,\text{minutes}} \times \dfrac{60\,\text{minutes}}{1\,\text{hour}} = \dfrac{180}{x + y + z}\,\text{mph}$

21. **B** Sylvia traveled at $315/9 = 35$ miles per hour. If she had traveled at $35 + 10 = 45$ miles per hour, she would have arrived in $315/45 = 7$ hours, thereby saving 2 hours.

Lesson 7: Interpreting percent problems

What number is 5 percent of 36?

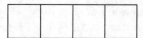

When interpreting word problems, remember that **statements about quantities can usually be translated into equations or inequalities**. Here's a simple translation key:

is/is equal to	means	$=$
of	means	$\times$
what/what number	means	x
per	means	$\div$
percent	means	$\div 100$

(*Easy*) Notice that this enables us to translate the question into an equation, which can be solved to get the answer:

What number is 5 percent of 36?
$$x \quad = (5 \div 100) \times 36 \qquad \text{so } x = 1.8$$

28 is what percent of 70?

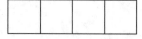

Again, let's use the glossary to translate and then solve:

28 is what percent of 70?
$$28 = \quad (x \div 100) \quad \times 70$$

Simplify:
$$28 = \frac{x}{100} \times 70 = 0.7x$$

Divide by 0.7:
$$40 = x$$

What number is 120% greater than 50?

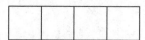

To **increase a number by x%**, just multiply it by $\left(1 + \dfrac{x}{100}\right)$. To **decrease a number by x%**, just multiply it by $\left(1 - \dfrac{x}{100}\right)$. For instance, to increase a number by 20%, just multiply by 1.20 (because the final quantity is 120% of the original quantity, and to decrease a number by 20%, just multiply by 0.80 (because the final quantity is 80% of the original quantity).

(*Easy*) If we increase a number by 120%, the resulting number is 100% + 120% = 220% of the original number. Therefore, the number that is 120% greater than 50 is $2.20 \times 50 = 110$.

Lesson 8: Percent change

A shirt has a marked retail price of $80, but is on sale at a 20% discount. If a customer has a coupon for 10% off of the sale price, and if the sales tax is 5%, what is the final price of this shirt, including all discounts and tax?

A) $58.80

B) $60.00

C) $60.48

D) $61.60

(*Medium*) To find the final price, we must perform three changes: decrease by 20%, decrease by 10%, and increase by 5%. This gives us (1.05)(0.90)(0.80)($80) = $60.48, so the answer is (C). Notice that, since multiplication is *commutative*, it doesn't matter in what order we perform the three changes; the result will still be the same.

If a population of bacteria increases from 100 to 250, what is the percent increase in this population?

A) 60%

B) 67%

C) 150%

D) 250%

To find the percent change in a quantity, just use the formula

$$percent\,change = \frac{final\,amount - initial\,amount}{initial\,amount} \times 100\%$$

Notice that any "percent change" is a "percent of the initial amount," which explains why the initial amount s the value in the denominator.

(*Easy*) If we know this formula, this question is straightforward: the percent change is (250 − 100)/100 × 100% = 150%, choice (C). If you mistakenly use 250 as the denominator, you would get an answer of (A) 60%, which is incorrect.

Lesson 9: Working with proportions and scales

On a scale blueprint, the drawing of a rectangular patio has dimensions 5 cm by 7.5 cm. If the longer side of the actual patio measures 21 feet, what is the area, in square feet, of the actual patio?

A)   157.5 square feet

B)   294.0 square feet

C)   356.5 square feet

D)   442.0 square feet

(*Medium*) In a scale drawing, all lengths are **proportional** to the corresponding lengths in real life. That is, the lengths in the drawing and the corresponding lengths in real life should all be in the **same ratio**. We can set up a proportion here to find the shorter side of the patio, x.

$$\frac{7.5\,\text{cm}}{21\,\text{feet}} = \frac{5\,\text{cm}}{x\,\text{feet}}$$

When working with proportions, remember the two **laws of proportions**.

The Law of Cross-Multiplication

If two ratios are equal, then their "cross-products" must also be equal.

$$\text{If } \frac{a}{b} = \frac{c}{d} \text{ then } ad = bc.$$

The Law of Cross-Swapping

If two ratios are equal, then their "cross-swapped" ratios must also be equal.

$$\text{If } \frac{a}{b} = \frac{c}{d}, \text{ then } \frac{d}{b} = \frac{c}{a} \text{ and } \frac{a}{c} = \frac{b}{d}.$$

$$\frac{7.5\,\text{cm}}{21\,\text{feet}} = \frac{5\,\text{cm}}{x\,\text{feet}}$$

Cross-multiply: $7.5x = 105$

Divide by 7.5: $x = 14$

Therefore, the patio has dimensions 21 feet by 14 feet, and so it has an area of $(21)(14) = 294$ square feet. The correct answer is (B).

Exercise Set 3 (Calculator)

1

What number is 150% of 30?

2

If the areas of two circles are in the ratio of 4:9, the circumference of the larger circle is how many times the circumference of the smaller circle?

3

What number is 30% less than 70?

4

What number is the same percent of 36 as 5 is of 24?

5

David's motorcycle uses 2/5 of a gallon of gasoline to travel 8 miles. At this rate, how many miles can it travel on 5 gallons of gasoline?

6

The retail price of a shirt is $60, but it is on sale at a 20% discount and you have an additional 20% off coupon. If there is also a 5% sales tax, is the final cost of the shirt?

A) $34.20

B) $36.48

C) $37.80

D) $40.32

7

If the price of a house increased from $40,000 to $120,000, what is the percent increase in price?

A) 67%

B) 80%

C) 200%

D) 300%

8

At a student meeting, the ratio of athletes to non athletes is 3:2, and among the athletes the ratio of males to females is 3:5. What percent of the students at this meeting are female athletes?

A) 22.5%

B) 25%

C) 27.5%

D) 37.5%

9

To make a certain purple dye, red dye and blue dye are mixed in a ratio of 3:4. To make a certain orange dye, red dye and yellow dye are mixed in a ratio of 3:2. If equal amounts of the purple and orange dye are mixed, what fraction of the new mixture is red dye?

A) $\dfrac{9}{20}$

B) $\dfrac{1}{2}$

C) $\dfrac{18}{35}$

D) $\dfrac{27}{40}$

10

If the price of a stock declined by 30% in one year and increased by 80% the next year, by what percent did the price increase over the two-year period?

A) 24%

B) 26%

C) 50%

D) 500

11

A farmer has an annual budget of $1,200 for barley seed, with which he can plant 30 acres of barley. If next year the cost per pound of the seed is projected to decrease by 20%, how many acres will he be able to afford to plant next year on the same budget?

A) 24

B) 25

C) 36

D) 37.5

12

If x is $\frac{2}{3}$% of 90, what is the value of $\frac{2}{3} - x$?

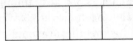

13

If n is 300% less than $\frac{5}{2}$, what is the value of $|n|$?

14

The cost of a pack of batteries, after a 5% sales tax, is $8.40. What was the price before tax, in dollars?

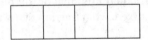

15

If the price of a sweater is marked down from $80 to $68, what is the percent discount? (Ignore the % symbol when gridding.)

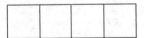

16

Three numbers, a, b, and c, are all positive. If b is 30% greater than a, and c is 40% greater than b, what is the value of $\frac{c}{a}$?

17

If the width of a rectangle decreases by 20%, by what percent must the length increase in order for the total area of the rectangle to double? (Ignore the % symbol when gridding.)

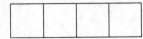

18

Two middle school classes take a vote on the destination for a class trip. Class A has 25 students, 56% of whom voted to go to St. Louis. Class B has n students, 60% of whom voted to go to St. Louis. If 57.5% of the two classes combined voted to go to St. Louis, what is the value of n?

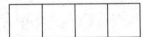

19

If 12 ounces of a 30% salt solution are mixed with 24 ounces of a 60% salt solution, what is the percent concentration of salt in the mixture?

A) 45%

B) 48%

C) 50%

D) 54%

20

If the length of a rectangle is doubled but its width is decreased by 10%, by what percent does its area increase?

A) 80%

B) 90%

C) 180%

D) 190%

21

The freshman class at Hillside High School has 45 more girls than boys. If the class has n boys, what percent of the freshman class are girls?

A) $\dfrac{n+45}{2n+45}\%$

B) $\dfrac{100n}{2n+45}\%$

C) $\dfrac{100(n+45)}{2n+45}\%$

D) $\dfrac{100n}{n+45}\%$

22

If the population of town B is 50% greater than the population of town A, and the population of town C is 20% greater than the population of town A, then what percent greater is the population of town B than the population of town C?

A) 20%

B) 25%

C) 30%

D) 40

EXERCISE SET 3 ANSWER KEY

1. **45** $1.50 \times 30 = 45$

2. **1.5** Imagine that the areas are 4π and 9π. Since the area of a circle is πr^2, their radii are 2 and 3, and their circumferences are $2(2)\pi = 4\pi$ and $2(3)\pi = 6\pi$, and $6\pi \div 4\pi = 1.5$.

3. **49** $70 - 0.30(70) = 0.70(70) = 49$.

4. **7.5**

$$\frac{x}{36} = \frac{5}{24}$$

Cross multiply: $24x = 180$
Divide by 24: $x = 7.5$

5. **100**

$$\frac{\frac{2}{5}\text{gallon}}{8 \text{ miles}} = \frac{5 \text{ gallons}}{x \text{ miles}}$$

Cross multiply: $\frac{2}{5}x = 40$

Multiply by 5/2: $x = 100$

6. **D** $1.05 \times 0.80 \times 0.80 \times \$60 = \$40.32$

7. **C** $(120{,}000 - 40{,}000)/40{,}000 \times 100\% = 200\%$

8. **D** The fraction of students who are athletes is $3/(2 + 3) = 3/5$, and the fraction of these who are females is $5/(3 + 5) = 5/8$. Therefore the portion who are female athletes is $3/5 \times 5/8 = 3/8 = 37.5\%$.

9. **C** The purple dye is $3/(3 + 4) = 3/7$ red, and the orange dye is $3/(3 + 2) = 3/5$ red. Therefore, a half-purple, half-orange dye is $(1/2)(3/7) + (1/2)(3/5) = 3/14 + 3/10 = 18/35$ red.

10. **B** If the price of the stock were originally, say, $100, then after this two-year period its price would be $(0.70)(1.80)(\$100) = \$126$, which is a 26% increase.

11. **D** The quantity of barley seed is proportional to the acreage it can cover. The cost of seed for each acre of barley was originally $\$1{,}200/30 = \$40$ per acre. The next year, after the 20% decrease, the price would be $(0.80)(\$40) = \$32$ per acre. With the same budget, the farmer can therefore plant $1{,}200/32 = 37.5$ acres of barley.

12. **1/15 or 0.067 or 0.066**

$$\frac{2}{3}\% \text{ of } 90 = \frac{2}{3} \div 100 \times 90 = \frac{180}{300} = \frac{3}{5}$$

$$\frac{2}{3} - x = \frac{2}{3} - \frac{3}{5} = \frac{1}{15}$$

13. **5** $n = \left|\frac{5}{2} - (3)\left(\frac{5}{2}\right)\right| = \left|-\frac{10}{2}\right| = 5$

14. **8.00** Let x be the price before tax:

$$1.05x = \$8.40$$

Divide by 1.05: $x = \$8.00$

15. **15** $(68 - 80)/80 = -0.15$

16. **1.82** $b = 1.30a$ and $c = 1.40b$, so $c = 1.40(1.30a) = 1.82a$. Therefore $c/a = 1.82a/a = 1.82$.

17. **150** For convenience, pick the dimensions of the rectangle to be 10 and 10. (This is of course a square, but remember that a square *is* a rectangle!) This means that the original area is $10 \times 10 = 100$. If the width decreases by 20%, the new width is $(0.80)(10) = 8$. Let the new length be x. Since the new rectangle has double the area, $8x = 200$, and so $x = 25$. This is an increase of $(25 - 10)/10 \times 100\% = 150\%$.

18. **15** The total number of "St. Louis votes" can be expressed in two ways, so we can set up an equation to solve for n: $(0.56)(25) + (0.60)n = 0.575(25 + n)$
Simplify: $14 + 0.6n = 14.375 + 0.575n$
Subtract 14 and .575n: $0.025n = 0.375$
Divide by .025: $n = 15$

19. **C** The total amount of salt in the mixture is $(.30)(12) + (.60)(24) = 18$, and the total weight of the mixture is $12 + 24 = 36$ ounces, so the percent salt is $18/36 = 50\%$.

20. **A** If the original dimensions are w and l, the original area is wl. If the length is doubled and the width decreased by 10%, the new area is $(0.9l)(2w) = 1.8wl$, which is an increase of 80%.

21. **C** The number of girls in the class is $n + 45$, and the total number of students is $n + n + 45$, so the percent of girls is $\dfrac{n + 45}{2n + 45} \times 100\%$.

22. **B** B is 50% greater than A: $B = 1.5A$
C is 20% greater than A: $C = 1.2A$
Divide by 1.2: $0.8\overline{3}C = A$
Substitute: $B = 1.5(0.8\overline{3}C)$
Simplify: $B = 1.25C$

Skill 3: Working with Tables of Data
Lesson 10: Using tables as problem-solving tools

A table can be useful for organizing information that falls into categories. Even if a problem does not include a table, ask yourself: **does the information in this problem fall into non-overlapping categories?** If so, consider setting up a table with the categories as row or column labels.

A committee determines that it will meet on the Thursday after the third Monday of every month. What is the latest date of the month on which this meeting could fall?

A) the 17th

B) the 18nd

C) the 24rd

D) the 25th

(*Medium*) A calendar, which of course is a kind of table, can be handy here. But how do we fill in the numbers? Since we want the *latest* date of the month possible, we need to find the latest date on which the third Monday could fall. A little trial-and-error should reveal that the latest the *first* Monday could fall is the 7th.

S	M	T	W	Th	F	S
	1					
	7	8				
	14					
	21	22	23	24		

Since there are seven days per week, the second Monday must be the 14th and the third must be the 21st. Therefore the meeting will be three days later, on Thursday the 24th. We don't have to complete the entire calendar page to solve the problem.

Sam is considering buying a car, and has two models to choose from. Model N has a sticker price that is 25% higher than that of Model P, but he will receive $1,500 in trade-in credit from the Model N dealer and only $1,000 in trade-in credit from the Model P dealer. Even after the trade-in credits are applied to both cars, Model N is still $2,000 more expensive than Model P (before taxes and fees). What is the sticker price of Model N?

A) $10,000

B) $12,000

C) $12,500

D) $13,000

(*Medium*) Again, this problem does not give us a table, but the fact that we must keep track of two car models and two prices per car model (sticker price and post trade-in price) suggests that a table might be useful.

	Sticker Price	After Trade-In
Model N	$1.25x$	$1.25x - 1,500$
Model P	x	$x - 1,000$

Since Model N has a sticker price that is 25% higher than that of Model P, if the sticker price of Model P is x, then the sticker price for Model N is $1.25x$. The respective costs after trade-in, then, are $1.25x - 1,500$ and $x - 1,000$. Now we must solve for x by setting up an equation, which comes from the fact that, even after the trade-in, Model N is still $2,000 more expensive. Therefore $1.25x - 1500 = (x - 1,000) + 2,000$.

Simplify: $1.25x - 1,500 = x + 1,000$

Add 1,500 and subtract x: $0.25x = 2,500$

Divide by 0.25: $x = 10,000$

Now, keep in mind that the question is asking for the sticker price of Model N, not Model P. Therefore the correct answer is $(1.25)(10,000) = 12,500$.

Lesson 11: Finding conditional probabilities and population fractions

OPINION ON PROPOSAL 547

	Approve	Disapprove	No Opinion	Total
Female	120	42	38	200
Male	98	40	62	200
Total	218	82	100	400

According to the results of the poll indicated in the table above, what percent of those who expressed an opinion on the proposal were female?

A) 52%

B) 54%

C) 68%

D) 81%

(*Medium*) This question asks us to find a **population fraction**, that is, a part-to-whole fraction. This question is almost identical to asking a **conditional probability** question, namely: *if a poll subject who expressed an opinion on Proposal 547 is chosen at random, what is the probability that the person is female?*

> The probability of an event is a part-to-whole ratio, and therefore can have only a value from 0 to 1. An event with probability 0 is impossible, and an event with probability 1 is certain.

The table indicates that the total number of respondents who expressed an opinion is $218 + 82 = 300$. Of these, $120 + 42 = 162$ are women, and therefore the percent of these that are women is $162/300 \times 100\% = 54\%$. Alternately, we could say that if a respondent expressing an opinion were chosen at random, that person would have a 0.54 probability of being female.

Lesson 12: Analyzing variable relations with tables

In Lesson 4 we used tables to identify direct and inverse variations between variables, but ordered pairs of variables can have many other relationships as well.

> Tables—along with graphs and equations—are important tools for analyzing functional relationships between variables. When given an equation expressing y in terms of x, you should know how to generate a table of ordered pairs and use that table to graph the relationship. Alternately, you should learn to analyze the properties of a function from that table of values.

Even if our equation is complicated, like

$$f(x) = \frac{x^3 - x}{2x + 4}$$

we can just pick values for x, like -3, -2, -1, 0, 1, 2, and 3, use these to calculate the corresponding values of y (or $f(x)$) and create a table of ordered pairs

x	y
-3	12
-2	no sol.
-1	0
0	0
1	0
2	3/4
3	12/5

which we can then use to plot points on a graph.

x	y
2	10
5	b
10	34

If the variables x and y in the table above have a linear relationship, what is the value of b?

A) 19

B) 20

C) 21

D) 22

(*Medium*) One way to approach this question is to use the fact that, in a linear relation, the y increases in proportion to the change in x. This rate of increase is the slope of the line. Taking the first and third ordered pairs, it seems that when x increases by $10 - 2 = 8$, y in turn increases by $34 - 10 = 24$. Therefore, the slope of the line is $24/8 = 3$. That is, every time the x coordinate increases by 1, the y coordinate increases by 3. Now looking at the first and second ordered pairs, since x is increasing by $5 - 2 = 3$, y must increase by $3(3) = 9$, and so b is equal to $10 + 9 = 19$, and the correct answer is (A).

Another way to look at it is that we have solved the proportion $\dfrac{34 - 10}{10 - 2} = \dfrac{b - 10}{5 - 2}$:

Simplify:	$\dfrac{24}{8} = \dfrac{b - 10}{3}$
Cross multiply:	$72 = 8b - 80$
Add 80:	$152 = 8b$
Divide by 8:	$19 = b$

Exercise Set 4 (Calculator)

1

BACTERIA CULTURE POPULATION

Minutes	0	1	2	3
Culture A	520	720	920	1,120
Culture B	500	600	720	864

Which of the following equations best expresses the population, P, of bacteria culture A, as a function of t, in minutes?

A) $P = 200t + 520$

B) $P = 520(1.4)^t$

C) $P = 2,000(t - 0.5)^2$

D) $P = 520t + 200$

2

Which of the following equations best expresses the population, P, of bacteria culture B, as a function of t, in minutes?

A) $P = 100t + 500$

B) $P = 500(1.2)^t$

C) $P = 2,000(t - 0.5)^2$

D) $P = 500t + 100$

3

After 2 minutes, the population of culture A is what percent greater than the population of culture B?

A) 16.7%

B) 20.0%

C) 27.8%

D) 127.8%

4

If culture A continues to grow at a constant rate, at what time should its population reach 2,000?

A) 7 minutes 4 seconds

B) 7 minutes 24 seconds

C) 7 minutes 40 seconds

D) 8 minutes 20 seconds

5

By what percent did the population of culture B increase over the first 3 minutes?

A) 36.4%

B) 42.1%

C) 72.8%

D) 172.8%

Questions 6–8 refer to the following information

TALENT SHOW TICKETS

	Adult	Child	Senior	Student
Tickets Sold	84	40	16	110
Total Revenue	$630	$200	$96	$495

6

According to the table above, how much is the price of one senior ticket?

A) $4.00

B) $6.00

C) $12.00

D) $16.00

7

How much more is the cost of one adult ticket than the cost of one student ticket?

A) $0.50

B) $1.50

C) $2.50

D) $3.00

8

Which is closest to the average (arithmetic mean) price of the 250 tickets sold?

A) $5.54

B) $5.59

C) $5.68

D) $5.72

▲

9

What is the median price of the 250 tickets sold?

A) $5.00

B) $5.50

C) $5.75

D) $6.00

10

If a meeting must take place on the third Tuesday of the month, what is the earliest date of the month on which it could take place?

A) the 14th

B) the 15th

C) the 22nd

D) the 27th

11

What is the latest date of the month on which the meeting could take place?

A) the 13th

B) the 14th

C) the 21st

D) the 26th

▼

Questions 12–21 refer to the following information

U.S. ENERGY CONSUMPTION
(Quadrillion BTU (QBTU))

	Fossil Fuels	Nuclear	Non-nuclear Renewables	Total
1950	31.63	0.00	2.98	34.61
1970	63.52	0.24	4.07	67.84
1990	72.33	6.10	6.04	84.47
2010	81.11	8.43	8.09	97.63

12

From 1970 to 1990, the percent increase in the U.S. consumption of nuclear energy was closest to

A) 96%

B) 240%

C) 2,400%

D) 3,400%

13

In a pie graph representing total U.S. energy consumption in 2010, the sector representing non nuclear renewables would have a central angle measuring approximately

A) 8°

B) 12°

C) 24°

D) 30°

14

Nuclear energy and renewable energy are often grouped together in the category "non-greenhouse" energy. In 1970, approximately what percent of non-greenhouse energy was nuclear?

A) 0.4%

B) 5.6%

C) 5.9%

D) 6.4%

15

In 2010 what percent of non-greenhouse energy consumption was nuclear?

A) 9%

B) 29%

C) 49%

D) 51%

16

In the four years shown, what percent of the total energy consumed was due to non-nuclear renewables?

A) 5.6%

B) 6.8%

C) 7.4%

D) 7.9%

17

What was the percent increase in fossil fuel energy consumption between 1950 and 2010?

A) 28%

B) 61%

C) 124%

D) 156%

18

The "renewability index" is defined as the fraction of total U.S. energy consumption that comes from non-nuclear renewable energy. What was the percent increase in the renewability index from 1970 to 2010?

A) 17%

B) 37%

C) 47%

D) 99%

19

For how many of the years shown above did fossil fuels account for less than 90% of the annual U.S. energy consumption?

A) One

B) Two

C) Three

D) Four

20

Between 1950 and 2010, the average annual rate of increase in the consumption of non-nuclear renewable energy was closest to

A) 0.085 QBTU/yr

B) 0.128 QBTU/yr

C) 1.70 QBTU/yr

D) 2.27 QBTU/yr

21

Between 1970 and 2010, the annual consumption of fossil fuels in the U.S. increased nearly linearly. If this linear trend were to continue, which of the following is closest to the level of U.S. fossil fuel consumption we would expect for 2035 (in quadrillion BTUs)?

A) 90

B) 91

C) 92

D) 93

EXERCISE SET 4 ANSWER KEY

1. **A** According to the table, the population of culture A increases by 200 bacteria every minute, indicating a linear relationship with a slope of 200. (Remember that the slope of a function is equivalent to its **unit rate of change**.) Choice (A) is the only option that indicates a line with slope 200.

2. **B** The table indicates that culture B is not increasing linearly, since the population difference from minute to minute is not constant, but increasing. This rules out choices (A) and (D). By substituting $t = 0$, $t = 1$ and $t = 2$, we can see that only the function in (B) gives the correct populations. Notice that the base of the exponential, 1.2, indicates that the population grows by 20% each minute.

3. **C** At the 2 minute mark, the populations are 920 and 720, respectively, so culture A has a population that is $(920 - 720)/720 \times 100\% = 27.8\%$ greater.

4. **B** If we use the population equation (see question 1), we can solve for t. Plugging in 2,000 for P gives us $2,000 = 200t + 520$, which gives a solution of $t = 7.4$ minutes. Since 0.4 minutes equals $0.4 \times 60 = 24$ seconds, the time elapsed is 7 minutes 24 seconds.

5. **C** In the first 3 minutes, culture B grew from 500 to 864 bacteria, which is an increase of $(864 - 500)/500 \times 100\% = 72.8\%$.

6. **B** The total revenue for each ticket type equals the price per ticket times the number of tickets sold. Therefore, the price for each senior ticket is $96 \div 16 = \$6$.

7. **D** One adult ticket costs $\$630 \div 84 = \$7.50$, and one student ticket costs $\$495 \div 110 = \$4.50$, so each adult ticket costs $3 more.

8. **C** The average price per ticket equals the total revenue for all tickets divided by the number of tickets: $(\$630 + \$200 + \$96 + \$495)/250 = \$5.684$.

9. **A** The median price of 250 tickets is the average of the prices of the 125th and 126th tickets, if the price for each ticket is listed in increasing order. The ticket prices, in increasing order, are $4.50 for students (110 tickets), $5.00 for children (40 tickets), $6.00 for seniors (16 tickets), and $7.50 for adults (84 tickets). With this ordering, the 125th and 126th price are both $5.00.

10. **B** The earliest the first Tuesday could be is the 1st, so the earliest the third Tuesday could be is the 15th.

11. **C** The latest the first Tuesday could be is the 7th, so the latest the third Tuesday could be is the 21st.

12. **C** In 1970, nuclear energy consumption was 0.24, and in 1990 it was 6.10. This represents an increase of $(6.10 - 0.24)/0.24 \times 100\% = 2,442\%$.

13. **D** In 2010, non nuclear renewables accounted for $8.09/97.63 \times 100\% = 8.3\%$ of consumption, which would correspond to a $0.083 \times 360° = 29.88°$ central angle.

14. **B** In 1970, the total "non-greenhouse" energy was $0.24 + 4.07 = 4.31$. Therefore the percent that was nuclear is $0.24/4.31 \times 100\% = 5.6\%$.

15. **D** In 2010, this percent was $8.43/(8.43 + 8.09) \times 100\% = 51\%$.

16. **C** The total non nuclear renewable energy consumption for the four years is $2.98 + 4.07 + 6.04 + 8.09 = 21.18$, and the total energy consumption is $34.61 + 67.84 + 84.47 + 97.63 = 284.55$. Therefore the percent is $21.18/284.55 \times 100\% = 7.4\%$.

17. **D** In 1950, fossil fuel consumption was 31.63, and in 2010 it was 81.11. This is an increase of $(81.11 - 31.63)/31.63 \times 100\% = 156\%$.

18. **B** In 1970, the renewability index was $4.07/67.84 = 0.060$, and in 2010 it was $8.09/97.63 = .082$. This is a percent increase of $(0.082 - 0.060)/0.060 \times 100\% = 37\%$.

19. **B** In 1990, the percent of consumption from fossil fuels was $72.33/84.47 \times 100\% = 85.6\%$, and in 2010 it was $81.11/97.62 \times 100\% = 83.1\%$.

20. **A** The annual rate of increase is the total increase divided by the time span in years. The total increase is $8.09 - 2.98 = 5.11$. Over a 60-year span, this gives a rate of $5.11/60 = 0.085$.

21. **C** In the 40 year span from 1970 to 2010, fossil fuel consumption increased at a rate of $(81.11 - 63.52)/40 = 0.44$ QBTU/Yr. In 25 more years at this rate, the consumption should be $81.11 + 25(0.44) = 92.11$ QBTU.

Skill 4: Working with Graphs of Data
Lesson 13: Working with scatterplots

Scatterplots are graphs of ordered pairs that represent data points. They are very useful for showing relationships between variables that do *not* vary in a highly predictable way.

PARTICULATE MATTER, 2004–2012

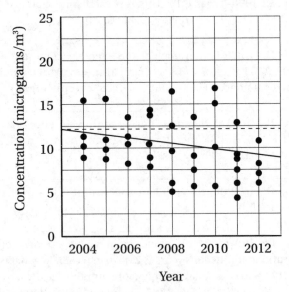

Particulate matter is a class of air pollutants. The scatterplot above shows 40 readings for particulate matter concentration, in micrograms per cubic meter, for a particular metropolitan area over 9 years. Based on the line of best fit shown, which of the following is closest to the average yearly decrease in particulate matter concentration?

A) 0.32 micrograms/m³ per year

B) 0.64 micrograms/m³ per year

C) 3.2 micrograms/m³ per year

D) 6.4 micrograms/m³ per year

A **line of best fit** is simply a line that "hugs" the data in a scatterplot better than any other line. In a statistics course, you will learn how to calculate a line of best fit precisely (or your calculator can do it for you), but the SAT will only expect you to use lines of best fit to make inferences about general trends in data or to find "expected values."

(*Medium*) In this problem, the line of best fit shows a general downward trend in the data, even though the data are fairly widely scattered. To find the "average yearly decrease" in particulate matter concentration, we simply have to find the slope of this line. To get the most accurate estimate for slope, we should take points on the line that are far apart. The leftmost endpoint seems to be at (2003, 12), and the rightmost endpoint seems to be at (2013, 9). This gives us a slope of $(9 - 12)/(2013 - 2003) = -3/10 = -0.3$ micrograms/m³ per year, so the correct answer is (A).

According to the line of best fit to the data above, which of the following is closest to the percent decrease in average particulate matter concentration from 2007 to 2012?

A) 9%

B) 18%

C) 36%

D) 60%

(*Medium-hard*) This question is similar to the previous one, but notice the two important differences: first, it is asking us to compare two *specific* years, and it is asking us to calculate the *percent decrease* rather than the *rate of decrease*, so we will need the percent change formula from Lesson 8. The line of best fit gives a value of about 11 in 2007 and about 9 in 2012. Therefore the percent change is $(9 - 11)/11 \times 100\% = -18\%$, and the correct answer is (B).

If the Environmental Protection Agency's air quality standard is 12 micrograms of particulate matter per cubic meter, as shown with the dotted line, what percent of these data fall above this standard?

A) 11%

B) 14.5%

C) 27.5%

D) 35%

(*Easy*) This question is simply asking for a part-to-whole ratio expressed as a percentage. There are 40 total data points (as the problem states), and 14 of them lie above the line: $14/40 \times 100\% = 35\%$, so the correct answer is (D).

Lesson 14: Linear and non linear relationships

Sometimes the SAT Math test will ask you to draw inferences from graphs that are non-linear. Even if a graph is not linear, you should still be able to draw inferences based on the points on that graph. For instance, you should be able to find the average rate of change between two points by finding the slope of the line segment connecting them, or compare the rate of growth of one curve to that of another curve.

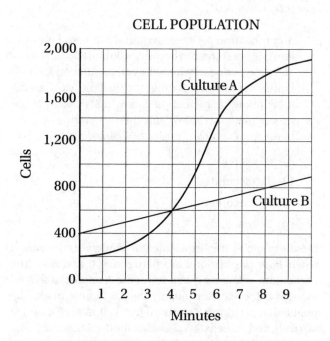

CELL POPULATION

The graph above shows the number of cells in two separate bacterial cultures as a function of time. How much time elapsed between the point when the two cultures had equal population and the point when the population of culture A was twice that of culture B?

A)   2 minutes

B)   3 minutes

C)   4 minutes

D)   5 minutes

(*Medium*) The time when the two populations are equal is easy to find: it's where the two curves intersect, at the 4-minute mark. The four answer choices tell us where to look next on the graph. Since choice (A) is 2 minutes, we should find the populations at the $4 + 2 = 6$-minute mark. At 6 minutes, culture B has a population of 700 and culture A has a population of 1,400, which of course is twice as great, and therefore the answer is (A).

How much longer did it take culture B to double its original population than it took culture A?

A)   2 minutes

B)   3 minutes

C)   4 minutes

D)   5 minutes

(*Medium*) Culture A has a starting population of 200 and doubles its population to 400 at the 3-minute mark. Culture B has a starting population of 400 and doubles its population to 800 at the 8-minute mark. Therefore, culture B took $8 - 3 = 5$ more minutes to double its population, and the correct answer is (D).

Lesson 15: Drawing inferences from graphs

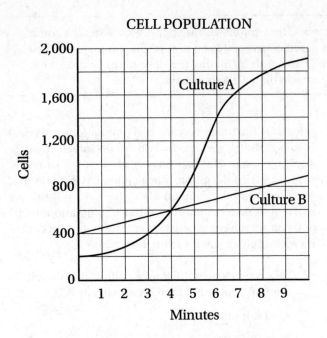

CELL POPULATION

If culture B were to continue its linear growth, how many <u>more</u> minutes (beyond the 10 minutes shown in the graph) would be required for culture B to reach 1,500 cells?

A) 9 minutes

B) 12 minutes

C) 13.5 minutes

D) 15 minutes

(*Medium*) By taking any two points on the line for culture B, for instance (0,400) and (4,600), we can calculate the slope of the line, which equals the **unit rate of growth**: $(600 - 400)/(4 - 0) = 50$ cells per minute. Since culture B contains 900 cells at the 10 minute mark, it would take $600/50 = 12$ more minutes to reach 1,500 cells, and the correct answer is (B).

A particular experiment requires that both culture A and culture B contain between 400 and 800 cells each. The time period in which the cell population for both cultures is within this range is called the "experimental window." Which of the following is closest to the "experimental window" for the two cultures shown in the graph above? (1 minute = 60 seconds)

A) 95 seconds

B) 120 seconds

C) 165 seconds

D) 240 seconds

(*Medium-hard*) The "experimental window" is the period when *both* populations are between 400 and 800. The population of culture A hits 400 at the 3-minute mark and exceeds 800 cells after roughly the 4.6-minute mark. The population of culture B starts off (at the 0-minute mark) at 400 cells, and exceeds 800 cells after the 8-minute mark. The overlapping period is between 3 minutes and 4.6 minutes, for a period of roughly 1.6 minutes or $1.6 \times 60 = 96$ seconds; therefore, the correct answer is (A).

Lesson 16: Working with pie graphs

We've all seen pie graphs. They are convenient ways of representing part-to-part and part-to-whole relationships. On the SAT Math test, you may be asked to analyze the features of pie graphs in some detail, or to discuss the features of a hypothetical pie graph.

When analyzing pie graphs, remember this helpful formula:

$$\frac{part}{whole} = \frac{degrees\ in\ sector}{360°}$$

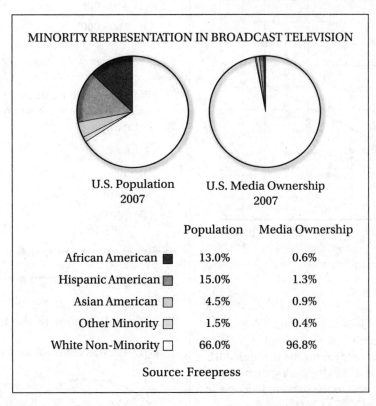

MINORITY REPRESENTATION IN BROADCAST TELEVISION

U.S. Population
2007

U.S. Media Ownership
2007

		Population	Media Ownership
African American	■	13.0%	0.6%
Hispanic American	■	15.0%	1.3%
Asian American	▢	4.5%	0.9%
Other Minority	▢	1.5%	0.4%
White Non-Minority	▢	66.0%	96.8%

Source: Freepress

In the diagram above, which of the following is closest to the measure of the central angle of the sector representing total minority ownership of U.S. broadcast television media in 2007?

A) 3°

B) 8°

C) 12°

D) 15°

(*Easy*) According to the graphic, the total minority ownership of television media in 2007 was 0.6% + 1.3% + 0.9% + 0.4% = 3.2%. Therefore the central of the sector representing this portion measures 0.032 × 360° = 11.52°, so the correct answer is (C).

Maria is constructing a pie graph to represent the expenses for her project, consisting of three expense categories: marketing, design, and development. She knows that the marketing expenses are $12,000 and the design expenses are $30,000, but the development expense could range anywhere from $30,000 to $48,000. Based on this information, which of the following could be the measure of the central angle of the sector representing marketing expenses?

A) 36°

B) 54°

C) 62°

D) 70°

(*Medium-hard*) The measure of the central angle of the sector depends on the part-to-whole ratio, so we need to calculate the maximum and minimum part-to-whole ratio for the marketing expenses, the marketing expenses are fixed at $12,000, but the total expenses could range from $12,000 + $30,000 + $30,000 = $72,000 to $12,000 + $30,000 + $48,000 = $90,000. This means that the part-to-whole ratio for marketing could range from 12,000/90,000 = 0.133 to 12,000/72,000 = 0.167. Therefore the central angle for the marketing sector can measure anywhere from 0.133 × 360° = 48° to 0.167 × 360° = 60°. The only choice in this range is (B) 54°.

Exercise Set 5 (Calculator)

Questions 1–4 refer to the following information

ANNUAL REVENUE PER STORE

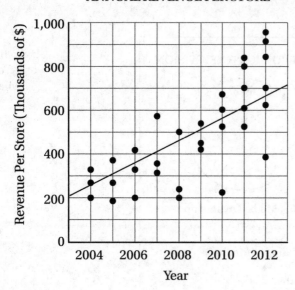

1

The scatterplot above shows the annual revenue for all of the individual retail stores operated by a clothing company for each year from 2004 through 2012. Based on the line of best fit to the data shown, which of the following is closest to the percent increase in revenue per store from 2005 to 2011?

A) 50%

B) 100%

C) 120%

D) 300%

2

In 2006, the total combined revenue for all stores was closest to

A) $350,000

B) $480,000

C) $700,000

D) $950,000

3

From 2009 to 2010, the total combined revenue for all stores increased by approximately

A) $50,000

B) $200,000

C) $400,000

D) $600,000

4

Between 2006 and 2012, what was the percent increase in the total number of retail stores for this company?

A) 45%

B) 50%

C) 100%

D) 200%

Questions 5–9 refer to the following information

UNITED STATES FEDERAL BUDGET—FISCAL YEAR 2010

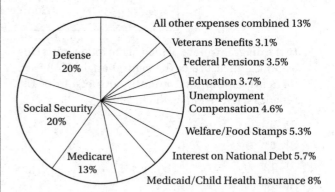

All other expenses combined 13%
Veterans Benefits 3.1%
Federal Pensions 3.5%
Education 3.7%
Unemployment Compensation 4.6%
Welfare/Food Stamps 5.3%
Interest on National Debt 5.7%
Medicaid/Child Health Insurance 8%

Defense 20%
Social Security 20%
Medicare 13%

5

The chart above shows the allocation of $3.5 trillion in U.S. federal expenses for 2010. What were the total 2010 expenditures on Defense?

A) $700 billion

B) $70 billion

C) $7 billion

D) $700 million

6

What is the measure of the central angle for the sector representing Medicare expenses?

A) 13.0°

B) 45.5°

C) 46.8°

D) 48.2°

7

If Interest on National Debt expenses were to decrease by $20 billion from their 2010 levels, this would represent a percent decrease of approximately

A) 6%

B) 10%

C) 12%

D) 15%

8

How much more did the United States spend in 2010 on Interest on National Debt than on Education?

A) $2 billion

B) $7.0 billion

C) $20 billion

D) $70 billion

9

If 50% of the budget for Federal Pensions were to be reallocated as Social Security expenses, the size of the Social Security budget would increase by what percent?

A) 1.75%

B) 8.75%

C) 17.75%

D) 21.75%

Questions 10–17 refer to the following information

PRESCHOOL BLOOD LEAD LEVELS VS. VIOLENT CRIME RATES IN THE UNITED STATES
(23-Year Lag)

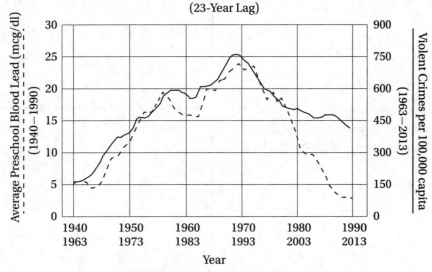

Year

Source: Rick Nevin, *Lead Poisoning and the Bell Curve*, 2012

10

According to the graph above, in 1970 the number of violent crimes per 100,000 capita in the United States was closest to

A) 25

B) 375

C) 700

D) 750

11

In 1970 the average preschool blood lead level, in mcg/dL, was closest to

A) 10

B) 12

C) 23

D) 25

12

The percent decline in violent crime from 1993 to 2013 is closest to

A) 11%

B) 35%

C) 47%

D) 88%

13

From 1970 to 1990, the average annual rate of decline in preschool blood lead levels, in mcg/dL per year, was approximately

A) 1

B) 5

C) 15

D) 17

14

Which of the following 10-year spans saw the greatest percent increase in preschool blood lead levels?

A) 1945–1955

B) 1955–1965

C) 1965–1975

D) 1975–1985

15

Which of the following five-year spans saw the greatest percent increase in violent crime?

A) 1963–1968

B) 1968–1973

C) 1973–1978

D) 1978–1983

16

Approximately how many years did it take for average preschool blood lead levels to return to their 1950 levels?

A) 25

B) 30

C) 35

D) 40

17

For approximately how many years between 1963 and 2013 was the violent crime rate in the United States greater than 375 crimes per 100,000 capita?

A) 25

B) 30

C) 37

D) 42

EXERCISE SET 5 ANSWER KEY

1. **C** In 2005, the revenue per store, according to the line of best fit, was about $300,000, and in 2012 it was about $650,000, so the percent change is (650,000 − 300,000)/300,000 × 100% = 116.67%, which is closest to (C) 120%.

2. **D** In 2006, the data points show that there were 3 stores, with revenue of roughly $200,000, $330,000, and $420,000, for a total of $950,000.

3. **D** In 2009, the combined revenue for the three stores was approximately $420,000 + $450,000 + $550,000 = $1,420,000. In 2010, the combined revenue for four stores was approximately $220,000 + $520,000 + $600,000 + $675,000 = $2,015,000, for an increase of about $595,000.

4. **C** In 2006 there were 3 stores and in 2012 there were 6 stores, which is an increase of (6 − 3)/3 × 100% = 100%.

5. **A** The chart shows that 20% of the expense budget went to defense, which equals 0.2 × $3,500,000,000,000 = $700 billion.

6. **C** Medicare accounts for 13% of expenses, so the sector angle is 0.13 × 360° = 46.8°.

7. **B** The Interest on National Debt in 2010 was 0.057 × $3.5 trillion = $199.5 billion, so a decrease of $20 billion would be 20/199.5 × 100% = 10%.

8. **D** The difference between Interest on National Debt and Education is 5.7% − 3.7% = 2%, and 0.02 × $3.5 trillion = $70 billion.

9. **B** The Social Security budget in 2010 was 0.20 × $3.5 trillion = $700 billion. 50% of the Federal Pensions budget is 0.5 × 0.035 × $3.5 billion = $61.25 billion. This would be an increase of 61.25/700 × 100% = 8.75%.

10. **B** The vertical axis label on the left shows that the violent crime trend is indicated by the *solid* curve and the *bottom* time series (1963–2013). For this curve, 1970 is slightly to the left of the vertical line at 1973, which shows values clearly between 300 and 450.

11. **C** The vertical axis label on the left shows that the preschool blood lead trend is indicated by the *dashed* curve and the *top* time series (1940–1990).

12. **C** In 1993, the violent crime rate was 750, and in 2013 it was about 400. The percent decrease is therefore (400 − 750)/750 × 100% = 46.7%

13. **A** In 1970, the blood lead levels were about 23 and in 1990, they were about 3. The rate of decline is therefore (23 − 3)/(1990 − 1970) = 1 mcg/dL per year.

14. **A** From 1945–1955 preschool blood lead levels increased from about 5 to about 17, a percent increase of (17 − 5)/5 × 100% = 240%.

15. **A** The question asks for the greatest *percent* increase, not the greatest *net* increase in violent crime. Notice that the *net* increase from 1963–1968 (from roughly 150 to 250) seems to be slightly less than net increase from 1968–1973 (from roughly 250 to 375), the *percent* increase from 1963–1968 (+67%) is clearly greater than that from 1968–1973 (+50%).

16. **B** In 1950, blood lead levels were about 12 mcg/dL, and they did not return to this level until 1980.

17. **D** The graph indicates that from about 1970 to 2013, the violent crime rate was above 375 crimes per 100,000 capita.

CHAPTER 9

THE SAT MATH: ADVANCED MATHEMATICS

The SAT Math: Advanced Mathematics

Why are the Advanced Mathematics topics important on the SAT Math test?

About 27% (16 out of 58 points) of the SAT Math questions are Advanced Mathematics questions. Questions in this category are about

understanding of the structure of expressions and the ability to analyze, manipulate, and rewrite these expressions. This includes an understanding of the key parts of expressions, such as terms, factors, and coefficients, and the ability to interpret complicated expressions made up of these components.

It will also assess your skill in

rewriting expressions, identifying equivalent forms of expressions, and understanding the purpose of different forms.

The specific topics include

- solving, graphing, and analyzing quadratic equations
- solving equations with radicals that may include extraneous solutions
- solving systems including linear and quadratic equations
- creating exponential or quadratic functions from their properties
- calculating with and simplifying rational expressions
- analyzing radicals and exponentials with rational exponents
- creating equivalent forms of expressions to reveal their properties
- working with compositions and transformations of functions
- analyzing higher-order polynomial functions, particularly in terms of their factors and zeros

How is it used?

Fluency in these topics in advanced math is essential to success in postsecondary mathematics, science, engineering, and technology. Since these subjects constitute a portion of any liberal arts curriculum, and a substantial portion of any STEM (science, technology, engineering, or mathematics) program, colleges consider these to be essential college preparatory skills for potential STEM majors.

Sound intimidating? It's not.

If you take the time to master the four core skills presented in these 14 lessons, you will gain the knowledge and practice you need to master SAT Advanced Math questions.

Skill 1: Understanding Functions

Lesson 1: What is a function?

A function is just a "recipe" for turning any "input" number into another number, called the "output" number. The input number is usually called x, and the output number is $f(x)$ or y. For instance, the function $f(x) = 3x^2 + 2$ is a three-step recipe for turning any input number, x, into another number, $f(x)$, by the following steps: (1) square x, (2) multiply this result by 3, and (3) add 2 to this result. The final result is called $f(x)$ or y.

If $f(2x) = x + 2$ for all values of x, which of the following equals $f(x)$?

A) $\dfrac{x+2}{2}$

B) $\dfrac{x}{2} + 2$

C) $\dfrac{x-2}{2}$

D) $2x - 2$

(*Medium*) Let's use the "function-as-recipe" idea. The equation tells us that f is a function that turns an input of $2x$ into $x + 2$. What steps would we need to take to accomplish this?

Input value:	$2x$
1. Divide by 2:	x
2. Add 2:	$x + 2$

Therefore, f is a two-step function that takes an input, divides it by 2, and then adds 2. Therefore, $f(x)$ equals the result when an input of x is put through the same steps, which yields (B) $f(x) = \dfrac{x}{2} + 2$.

Another way to think about this problem is to pick a value for x, like $x = 1$. Substituting this into the given equation gives us $f(2(1)) = 1 + 2$, or $f(2) = 3$. Therefore, the correct function must take an input of 2 and turn it into 3. If we substitute $x = 2$ into all of the choices, we get (A) $f(2) = 2$, (B) $f(2) = 3$, (C) $f(2) = 0$, and (D) $f(2) = -1$. Clearly, the only function that gives the correct output is (B).

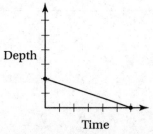

The graph above shows the depth of water in a right cylindrical tank as a function of time as the tank drains. Which of the following represents the graph

of the situation in which the tank starts with twice as much water as the original tank had, and the water drains at three times the original rate?

A)
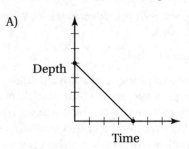

B)
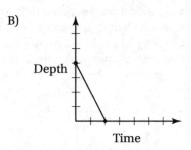

C)
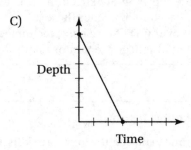

D)
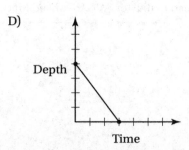

(*Medium*) Although no increments are shown on the axes (so, for instance, the tick marks on the *time* axis could indicate minutes, or hours, or days, or any other time unit, and the tick marks on the *depth* axis could represent meters, or centimeters, or any other depth unit), we do know that **the point at which the axes cross is the origin**, or the point (0, 0). The given graph shows that the tank starts at 2 depth units and drains completely after 6 time units. In other words, the tank drains at 1/3 of a depth unit per time unit. (Remember from Chapter 8 that **the slope equals the unit rate of change**.) In the new graph, then, the tank should start at a depth of $2 \times 2 = 4$ depth units, and it should drain at $3 \times 1/3 = 1$ depth unit per time unit. In other words, it should take 4 time units for the tanks to drain completely. The only graph that shows this correctly is (A).

Lesson 2: Functions as graphs, equations, or tables

Make sure you're fluent in expressing functions in three ways: as **graphs** in the xy-plane, **equations** in functional notation, or **tables** of ordered pairs. Also, make sure you can go from one format to another. **Every input-output $(x - y)$ pair can be represented in any of these three ways**. For instance, if the function g turns an input value of -2 into an output value of 4, we can translate this in three ways:

- The graph of $y = g(x)$ in the xy-plane contains the point $(-2, 4)$.
- $g(-2) = 4$
- In a table of ordered pairs for the function, $x = -2$ is paired with $y = 4$.

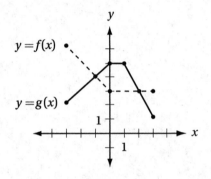

The graphs of functions f and g are shown above for $-3 \le x \le 3$. Which of the following describes the set of all x for which $f(x) \le g(x)$?

A) $x \ge -3$

B) $-3 \le x \le -1$ or $2 \le x \le 3$

C) $-1 \le x \le 2$

D) $3 \le x \le 5$

(*Easy*) The key to this problem is understanding what the statement $f(x) \le g(x)$ means. Since $f(x)$ and $g(x)$ are the y-values of the respective functions, $f(x)$ is less than or equal to $g(x)$ wherever the graphs cross or the graph of $g(x)$ is above the graph of $f(x)$. The two graphs cross at the points $(-1, 4)$ and $(2, 3)$, and $g(x)$ is above $f(x)$ at every point in between, so the correct answer is (C) $-1 \le x \le 2$.

	$g(x)$	$h(x)$
1	2	-9
2	4	-6
3	6	-3
4	8	0
5	10	3
6	12	6
7	14	9
8	16	12
9	18	15

Given the table of values for functions g and h above, for what value of x must $g(h(x)) = 6$?

A) 2

B) 5

C) 6

D) 12

(*Medium-hard*) The notation $g(h(x)) = 6$ means that when the input number, x, is put into the function h, and this result is then placed into function g, the result is 6. Working backward, we should ask: what input to g would yield an output of 6? According to the table, only an input of 3 into g would yield an output of 6. This means that $h(x) = 3$. So what input into h would yield an output of 3? Consulting the table again, we can see that $g(5) = 3$, and therefore $x = 5$ and the correct answer is (B).

Lesson 3: Compositions and transformations of functions

The notation $f(g(x))$ indicates the **composition** of two functions, g and f. The number x is put into the function g and this result is put into the function f and the result is called $f(g(x))$.

If $f(x) = x + 2$ and $f(g(1)) = 6$, which of the following could be $g(x)$?

A) $g(x) = 3x$

B) $g(x) = x + 3$

C) $g(x) = x - 3$

D) $g(x) = 2x + 1$

(*Medium-hard*) The notation $f(g(1)) = 6$ indicates that the number 1 is placed into function g, then the result is placed into function f, and the result is an output of 6.

Given equation: $\qquad\qquad f(g(1)) = 6$

Use the given definition of f: $\qquad g(1) + 2 = 6$

Subtract 2: $\qquad\qquad\qquad g(1) = 4$

In other words, g is function that gives an output of 4 when its input is 1. The only function among the choices that has this property is (B) $g(x) = x + 3$.

If $f(x) = x^2 + 1$ and $g(f(x)) = 2x^2 + 4$ for all values of x, which of the following expresses $g(x)$?

A) $g(x) = 2x + 1$

B) $g(x) = 2x + 2$

C) $g(x) = 2x + 3$

D) $g(x) = 2x^2 + 1$

(*Medium-hard*) As with the previous question, it helps to use the law of substitution to simplify the problem. By the definition of f, $g(f(x)) = g(x^2 + 1) = 2x^2 + 4$. Therefore, the function g turns an input of $x^2 + 1$ into an output of $2x^2 + 4$. What series of steps would accomplish this?

Starting expression: $\qquad\qquad x^2 + 1$

Multiply by 2: $\qquad\qquad\qquad 2x^2 + 2$

Add 2: $\qquad\qquad\qquad\qquad\quad 2x^2 + 4$

Therefore, g is a two-step function that takes an input, multiplies it by 2, and adds 2, which is the function in choice (B).

When the function $y = g(x)$ is graphed in the xy-plane, it has a minimum value at the point $(1, -2)$. What is the maximum value of the function $h(x) = -3g(x) - 1$?

A) 4

B) 5

C) 6

D) 7

(*Medium*) The graph of $y = h(x) = -3g(x) - 1$ is the graph of g after it has been stretched vertically by a factor of 3, reflected over the x-axis, and then shifted down 1 unit. This would transform the minimum value point of $(1, -2)$ to a *maximum* value point on the new graph at $(1, -3(-2) - 1)$ or $(1, 5)$, so the correct answer is (B).

Function Transformations

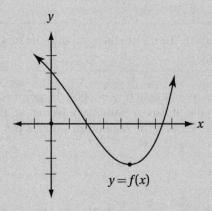

$$y = f(x)$$

If the function $y = f(x)$ is graphed in the xy-plane (as in the example above), then the following represent **transformations** of function f.

The graph of $y = f(x + k)$, where k is a positive number, is the graph of $y = f(x)$ **shifted left k units.**

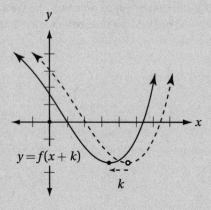

$$y = f(x + k)$$

The graph of $y = f(x - k)$, where k is a positive number, is the graph of $y = f(x)$ **shifted right k units.**

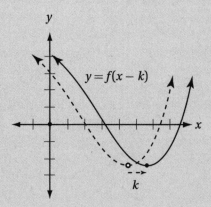

$$y = f(x - k)$$

The graph of $y = f(x) + k$, where k is a positive number, is the graph of $y = f(x)$ **shifted up k units.**

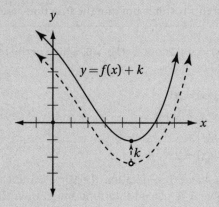

$$y = f(x) + k$$

The graph of $y = kf(x)$ is the graph of $y = f(x)$ **stretched vertically by a factor of k** (if $k > 1$) or **shrunk vertically by a factor of k** (if $k < 1$).

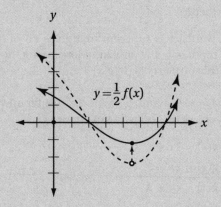

$$y = \frac{1}{2}f(x)$$

The graph of $y = -f(x)$ is the graph of $y = f(x)$ **reflected over the x-axis.**

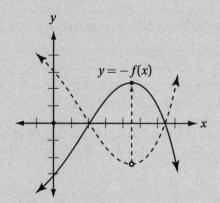

$$y = -f(x)$$

Exercise Set 1 (Calculator)

1

If $f(x) = x^2 + x + k$, where k is a constant, and $f(2) = 10$, what is the value of $f(-2)$?

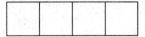

2

The minimum value of the function $y = h(x)$ corresponds to the point $(-3, 2)$ on the xy-plane. What is the maximum value of $g(x) = 6 - h(x + 2)$?

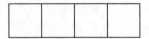

3

The function g is defined by the equation $g(x) = ax + b$, where a and b are constants. If $g(1) = 7$ and $g(3) = 6$, what is the value of $g(-5)$?

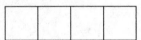

4

Let the function h be defined by the equation $h(x) = f(g(x))$ where $f(x) = x^2 - 1$ and $g(x) = x + 5$. What is the value of $h(2)$?

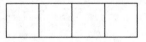

▼

Questions 5–9 refer to the table below.

x	$f(x)$	$k(x)$
1	3	5
2	4	6
3	5	1
4	6	2
5	1	3
6	2	4

5

According to the table above, $f(3) =$

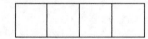

6

According to the table above, $f(k(6)) =$

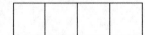

7

According to the table above, $k(k(6)) =$

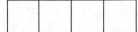

8

According to the table above, if $k(f(x)) = 5$, then what is the value of x?

9

Which of the following is true for all values of x indicated in the earlier table?

A) $f(k(x)) - k(f(x)) = 0$

B) $f(k(x)) + k(f(x)) = x$

C) $f(k(x)) - k(f(x)) = x$

D) $f(k(x)) + k(f(x)) = 0$

▲

10

If $g(x - 1) = x^2 + 1$, which of the following is equal to $g(x)$?

A) $x^2 + 2$

B) $x^2 + 2x$

C) $x^2 + 2x + 1$

D) $x^2 + 2x + 2$

11

If $h(x) = \dfrac{x+1}{2}$ and $f(x) = (x - 1)^2$, then which of the following is equal to $f(h(x))$ for all x?

A) $\dfrac{x^2 - 2x + 2}{2}$

B) $\dfrac{x^2 - 2x + 2}{4}$

C) $\dfrac{x^2 - 2x + 1}{2}$

D) $\dfrac{x^2 - 2x + 1}{4}$

Exercise Set 1 (No Calculator)

Questions 12–19 are based on the graph below.

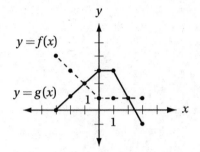

12

What is the value of $g(-1)$?

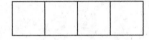

13

What is the value of $g(f(3))$?

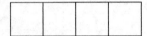

14

What is the value of $f(g(3))$?

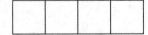

15

If $g(f(x)) = -1$, what is the value of $x + 10$?

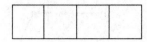

16

If $f(k) + g(k) = 0$, what is the value of k?

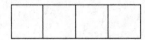

17

If $f(a) = g(a)$, where $a < 0$, and $f(b) = g(b)$, where $b > 0$, what is the value of $a + b$?

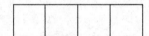

18

Let $h(x) = f(x) \times g(x)$. What is the maximum value of $h(x)$ if $-3 \le x \le 3$?

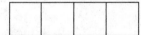

19

Which of the following graphs represents the function $y = f(x) + g(x)$?

A)

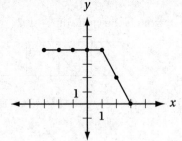

B)

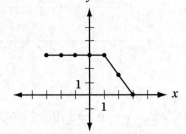

C)

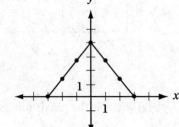

D)

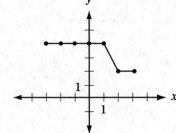

EXERCISE SET 1 ANSWER KEY

Calculator

1. 6 $f(2) = 2^2 + 2 + k = 10$, so $6 + k = 10$ and $k = 4$. Therefore, $f(-2) = (-2)^2 + (-2) + 4 = 6$.

2. 4 The graph of the function $g(x) = 6 - h(x + 2)$ is the graph of h after (1) a shift 2 units to the left, (2) a reflection over the x-axis, and (3) a shift 6 units up. If we perform these transformations on the point $(-3, 2)$, we get the point $(-5, 4)$, and so the maximum value of g is 4 when $x = -5$.

3. 10

	$g(3) = a(3) + b = 6$
	$g(1) = a(1) + b = 7$
Subtract the equations:	$2a = -1$
Divide by 2:	$a = -0.5$
Substitute to find b:	$-0.5 + b = 7$
Add 0.5:	$b = 7.5$
Therefore	$g(x) = -0.5x + 7.5$
	$g(-5) = -0.5(-5) + 7.5 = 10$

4. 48 $h(2) = f(g(2)) = f(2 + 5) = f(7) = (7)^2 - 1 = 48$

5. 5 $f(3) = 5$

6. 6 $f(k(6)) = f(4) = 6$

7. 2 $k(k(6)) = k(4) = 2$

8. 5 According to the table, the only input into k that yields an output of 5 is 1. Therefore, $f(x)$ must be 1, and the only input into f that yields an output of 1 is $x = 5$.

9. A Examination of the table reveals that, for all given values of x, $f(g(x)) = x$ and $g(f(x)) = x$. (This means that f and k are **inverse functions**, that is, they "undo" each other.) This implies that $f(k(x)) - k(f(x)) = x - x = 0$.

10. D One way to approach this question is to pick a new variable, z, such that $z = x - 1$ and therefore $x = z + 1$.

Original equation:	$g(x - 1) = x^2 + 1$
Substitute $z = x - 1$:	$g(z) = (z + 1)^2 + 1$
FOIL:	$g(z) = z^2 + 2z + 1 + 1$
Simplify:	$g(z) = z^2 + 2z + 2$
Therefore	$g(x) = x^2 + 2x + 2$

11. D

$$f(h(x)) = f\left(\frac{x+1}{2}\right) = \left(\frac{x+1}{2} - 1\right)^2$$

$$= \left(\frac{x+1}{2} - \frac{2}{2}\right)^2 = \left(\frac{x-1}{2}\right)^2$$

$$= \frac{x^2 - 2x + 1}{4}$$

No Calculator

12. 2 The graph of g contains the point $(-1, 2)$, therefore $g(-1) = 2$.

13. 3 The graph of f contains the point $(3, 1)$; therefore, $f(3) = 1$, and so $g(f(3)) = g(1)$. Since the graph of g contains the point $(1, 3)$, $g(1) = 3$.

14. 2 The graph of g contains the point $(3, -1)$; therefore, $g(3) = -1$, and so $f(g(3)) = f(-1)$. Since the graph of f contains the point $(-1, 2)$, $f(-1) = 2$.

15. 8 The only input to function g that yields an output of -1 is 3. Therefore, if $g(f(x)) = -1$, $f(x)$ must equal 3. The only input to f that yields an output of 3 is -2, therefore $x = -2$ and $x + 10 = 8$.

16. 3 The only input for which f and g give outputs that are opposites is 3, because $f(3) = 1$ and $g(x) = -1$.

17. 1 The two points at which the graphs of g and f cross are $(-1, 2)$ and $(2, 1)$. Therefore, $a = -1$ and $b = 2$ and so $a + b = 1$.

18. 4 $h(x) = f(x) \times g(x)$ has a maximum value when $x = -1$, where $f(1) \times g(1) = 2 \times 2 = 4$.

19. A To graph $y = f(x) + g(x)$, we must simply "plot points" by choosing values of x and finding the corresponding y-values. For instance, if $x = -3$, $y = f(3) + g(3) = 4 + 0 = 4$, so the new graph must contain the point $(-3, 4)$. Continuing in this manner for $x = -2$, $x = -1$, and so on yields the graph in (A).

Skill 2: Working with Quadratics and Other Polynomials
Lesson 4: Adding, multiplying, and factoring polynomials

A **quadratic expression** is a second-degree polynomial, that is, an expression of the form $ax^2 + bx + c$. The SAT Math test may ask you to analyze quadratic expressions and equations, as well as higher-order polynomials.

To **factor a simple quadratic expression**, first see if it fits any of the basic factoring formulas below.

Difference of Squares:

$$x^2 - a^2 = (x + a)(x - a)$$

Perfect Square Trinomials:

$$x^2 + 2ax + a^2 = (x + a)(x + a) = (x + a)^2$$

$$x^2 - 2ax + a^2 = (x - a)(x - a) = (x - a)^2$$

Which of the following is a factor of $x^2 + 8x + 16$?

A) $x - 4$

B) $x - 8$

C) $x + 4$

D) $x + 8$

(*Easy*) Notice that this quadratic fits the pattern $x^2 + 2ax + a^2$ and therefore can be factored using the second formula above: $x^2 + 8x + 16 = (x + 4)(x + 4)$. Therefore, the correct answer is (C).

To **factor a more complex quadratic expression**, use the **Product-Sum Method** illustrated below.

Which of the following is a factor of $6x^2 + 7x + 2$?

A) $3x - 2$

B) $3x + 2$

C) $3x - 1$

D) $3x + 1$

(*Medium*) First notice that this is a quadratic expression in which $a = 6$, $b = 7$, and $c = 2$. Now we can factor this expression using the **Product-Sum Method**.

Step 1: Call ac the **product number** ($6 \times 2 = 12$), and b the **sum number** (7).

Step 2: Find the two numbers with a product equal to the **product number** and a sum equal to the **sum number**. What two numbers have a product

of 12 and a sum of 7? A little guessing and checking should reveal that the numbers are 3 and 4.

Step 3: Rewrite the original quadratic, but expand the middle term in terms of the sum you just found: $6x^2 + 7x + 2 = 6x^2 + (3x + 4x) + 2$

Step 4: Use the associative law of addition to group the first two terms together and the last two terms together: $6x^2 + (3x + 4x) + 2 = (6x^2 + 3x) + (4x + 2)$

Step 5: Factor out the greatest common factor from each pair.
$(6x^2 + 3x) + (4x + 2) = 3x(2x + 1) + 2(2x + 1)$
If we do this correctly, the binomial factors will be the same.

Step 6: Factor out the common binomial factor.
$(3x + 2)(2x + 1)$

Step 7: FOIL this result to confirm that it is equivalent to the original quadratic.

Therefore, the correct answer is (B).

Alternately, we could "test" each choice as a potential factor of $6x^2 + 7x + 2$ until we find one that works. For instance, we can test choice (A) by trying to find another binomial factor that when multiplied by $(3x - 2)$ gives a product of $6x^2 + 7x + 2$. The best guess would be $(2x - 1)$, because the product of the two first terms ($3x \times 2x$) gives us the correct first term, $6x^2$, and the product of the two last terms (-2×-1) gives us the correct last term, 2. Now we FOIL the two binomials completely to see if we get the correct middle term: $(3x - 2)(2x - 1) = 6x^2 - 3x - 4x + 2 = 6x^2 - 7x + 2$, which has an incorrect middle term ($-7x$ instead of $7x$). The fact that this is the *opposite sign* of the correct middle term suggests that we need only change the binomial from subtraction to addition, which gives us an answer of (B) $3x + 2$.

To **add or subtract polynomials**, simply **combine** like terms.

Expression to be simplified:

$$(3x^4 + 5x^3 - 2x + 2) - (x^4 - 5x^3 + 2x^2 + 6)$$

Distribute to eliminate parentheses:

$$3x^4 + 5x^3 - 2x + 2 - x^4 + 5x^3 - 2x^2 - 6$$

Combine like terms:

$$(3x^4 - x^4) + (5x^3 + 5x^3) - 2x^2 - 2x + (2 - 6)$$

Simplify:

$$2x^4 + 10x^3 - 2x^2 - 2x - 4$$

Which of the following is equivalent to $2x(x + 1) - x^2(x + 1)$ for all values of x?

A) $x^2 + x$

B) $x^3 - x^2 + 2x$

C) $-x^3 + x^2 + 2x$

D) $-x^3 + x^2 + 2x + 1$

(*Easy*) Original expression: $\qquad 2x(x + 1) - x^2(x + 1)$

Distribute: $\qquad\qquad\qquad 2x^2 + 2x - x^3 - x^2$

Combine like terms: $\qquad\qquad -x^3 + x^2 + 2x$

Therefore, the correct answer is (C).

> When **multiplying binomials**, remember to **FOIL**.

Expression to be multiplied: $\qquad (ax + b)(cx + d)$

F (product of the two "first" terms): $\qquad ax \times cx = (ac)x^2$

O (product of the two "outside" terms): $\qquad ax \times d = (ad)x$

I (product of the two "inside" terms): $\qquad b \times cx = (bc)x$

L (product of the two "last" terms): $\qquad b \times d = bd$

F + O + I + L: $\qquad (ac)x^2 + (ad)x + (bc)x + bd$

Which of the following is equivalent to $(2x - 7)(3x + 1)$ for all values of x?

A) $6x^2 - 7$

B) $6x^2 + 5x - 7$

C) $6x^2 - 21x - 7$

D) $6x^2 - 19x - 7$

(*Easy*) Original expression: $\qquad (2x - 7)(3x + 1)$

FOIL: $\qquad (2x)(3x) + (2x)(1) +$
$\qquad\qquad (-7)(3x) + (-7)(1)$

Simplify: $\qquad 6x^2 + 2x - 21x - 7$

Combine like terms: $\qquad 6x^2 - 19x - 7$

Therefore, the correct answer is (D).

> To **multiply two polynomials**, remember to **distribute** each term in the first polynomial to each term in the second polynomial, then simplify. FOILing is just a special example of this kind of distribution.

Expression to be simplified: $\quad (2x^2 - x + 2) \times (x^3 + x - 1)$

Distribute: $\qquad (2x^2)(x^3) + (2x^2)(x) - (2x^2)(1) - (x)(x^3) -$
$\qquad\qquad (x)(x) + (x)(1) + (2)(x^3) + (2)(x) - (2)(1)$

Simplify: $\qquad 2x^5 + 2x^3 - 2x^2 - x^4 - x^2 + x + 2x^3 + 2x - 2$

Combine like terms: $\qquad 2x^5 - x^4 + 4x^3 - 3x^2 + 3x - 2$

Lesson 5: Solving quadratic equations

> **To solve factorable quadratic equations**, first use the Laws of Equality to set one side of the equation to 0, then factor and use the **Zero Product Property**.
>
> > **Zero Product Property:** If the product of any set of numbers is 0, then at least one of those numbers must be 0.

Which of the following is a solution to the equation $8 - x^2 = -2x$?

A) -4

B) -3

C) -2

D) -1

We could just plug in each number in the choices to the equation until we find one that works. But it's good to know the general method for finding both solutions. In this case, the fact that the numbers in the choices are all integers suggests that this quadratic is factorable.

Equation to be solved: $8 - x^2 = -2x$

Subtract 8 and add x^2: $0 = x^2 - 2x - 8$

Factor using the Product-Sum Method: $0 = (x - 4)(x + 2)$

Use Zero Product Property: $x - 4 = 0$ or $x + 2 = 0$, so $x = 4$ or -2

> **To solve tougher quadratic equations**, first use the Laws of Equality to set one side of the equation to 0, then use the **Quadratic Formula**.
>
> > **Quadratic Formula:** If $ax^2 + bx + c = 0$,
> >
> > then $x = \dfrac{-b \pm \sqrt{b^2 - 4ac}}{2a}$
>
> The equation $ax^2 + bx + c = 0$ has **no real solutions** if $b^2 - 4ac < 0$. This is because the square root of a negative number is not a real number.

Which of the following is a solution to the equation $3x^2 = 4x + 2$?

A) $\dfrac{4 - \sqrt{10}}{6}$

B) $\dfrac{2 - \sqrt{10}}{6}$

C) $\dfrac{2 - \sqrt{10}}{4}$

D) $\dfrac{2 - \sqrt{10}}{3}$

(*Medium*) Although we could just plug the numbers in the choices back into the equation to see which one works, it's a bit of a pain to do that with such obnoxious numbers. The ugliness of these numbers also tells us that this quadratic is not easily factorable. Therefore, it's probably best to use the Quadratic Formula.

Equation to be solved: $3x^2 = 4x + 2$

Subtract 4x and 2 to set right side to 0: $3x^2 - 4x - 2 = 0$

Use Quadratic Formula:

$$x = \frac{4 \pm \sqrt{(-4)^2 - 4(3)(-2)}}{2(3)} = \frac{4 \pm \sqrt{16 + 24}}{6}$$

$$= \frac{4 \pm \sqrt{40}}{6} = \frac{4 \pm 2\sqrt{10}}{6} = \frac{2 \pm \sqrt{10}}{3}$$

Therefore, the correct answer is (D).

If $x > 0$ and $x^2 - 5x = 6$, what is the value of x?

(*Medium*)   Equation to be solved: $x^2 - 5x = 6$

Subtract 6 to set one side to 0: $x^2 - 5x - 6 = 0$

Factor using the Product-Sum Method: $(x - 6)(x + 1) = 0$

Use the Zero Product Property: $x = 6$ or $x = -1$

Since the problem states that $x > 0$, the correct answer is 6.

Alternately, we could have used the Quadratic Formula on the equation $x^2 - 5x - 6 = 0$:

$$\frac{-b \pm \sqrt{b^2 - 4ac}}{2a} = \frac{5 \pm \sqrt{(-5)^2 - 4(1)(-6)}}{2(1)}$$

$$= \frac{5 \pm \sqrt{49}}{2} = \frac{5 \pm 7}{2} = 6 \text{ or } -1$$

If a quadratic equation has the form $x^2 + bx + c = 0$, the zeros of the quadratic must have a sum of $-b$ and a product of c.

This is because if $a = 1$, the quadratic formula gives solutions of $\dfrac{-b + \sqrt{b^2 - 4c}}{2}$ and $\dfrac{-b + \sqrt{b^2 - 4c}}{2}$.

Sum of zeros:

$$\frac{-b + \sqrt{b^2 - 4c}}{2} + \frac{-b - \sqrt{b^2 - 4c}}{2}$$

$$= \frac{-b + \sqrt{b^2 - 4c} + -b - \sqrt{b^2 - 4c}}{2}$$

$$= \frac{-2b}{2} = -b$$

Product of zeros:

$$\frac{-b + \sqrt{b^2 - 4c}}{2} \times \frac{-b - \sqrt{b^2 - 4c}}{2}$$

$$= \frac{(-b)^2 - (b^2 - 4c)}{4} = \frac{b^2 - b^2 + 4c}{4}$$

$$= \frac{4c}{4} = c$$

If one of the solutions to the equation $2x^2 - 7x + k = 0$ is $x = 5$, what is the other possible value of x?

A) $-\dfrac{3}{2}$

B) $-\dfrac{2}{3}$

C) $\dfrac{2}{3}$

D) $\dfrac{3}{2}$

(*Medium-hard*) We can start by substituting $x = 5$ into the original equation and solving:

Original equation:	$2x^2 - 7x + k = 0$
Substitute $x = 5$:	$2(5)^2 - 7(5) + k = 0$
Simplify:	$15 + k = 0$
Subtract 15:	$k = -15$
Rewrite original equation with $k = -15$:	$2x^2 - 7x - 15 = 0$
Factor with Product-Sum Method:	$(2x + 3)(x - 5) = 0$
Use Zero Product Property:	$x = -3/2$ or 5

Therefore, the correct answer is (A).

Alternately, we can save a bit of time and effort by using the theorem above.

Original equation:	$2x^2 - 7x + k = 0$
Divide by 2:	$x^2 - \dfrac{7}{2}x + \dfrac{k}{2} = 0$

Since the quadratic is now in the form $x^2 + bx + c = 0$, we know that the sum of the solutions must be 7/2, or 3.5. Therefore, if one of the solutions is 5, the other must be $3.5 - 5 = -1.5$, or $-3/2$.

Lesson 6: Analyzing the graphs of quadratic functions

The graph of any quadratic function in the xy-plane, that is, a function of the form $y = f(x) = ax^2 + bx + c$, has the following important features:

- It is a parabola with a vertical axis of symmetry at $x = -\dfrac{b}{2a}$.
- The y-intercept is c, since $f(0) = a(0)^2 + b(0) + c = c$.
- If it crosses the x-axis, it does so at the points $\left(\dfrac{-b + \sqrt{b^2 - 4ac}}{2a}, 0 \right)$ and $\left(\dfrac{-b - \sqrt{b^2 - 4ac}}{2a}, 0 \right)$.
- If a is positive, the parabola is "open up," and if a is negative, it is "open down."
- If the quadratic is in the form $y = a(x - h)^2 + k$, then the vertex of the parabola is (h, k).

The graph of the quadratic function $y = g(x)$ in the xy-plane is a parabola with vertex at $(3, -2)$. If this graph also passes through the origin, which of the following must equal 0?

A) $g(4)$

B) $g(5)$

C) $g(6)$

D) $g(7)$

(*Medium*) It's helpful to draw a sketch of this parabola so that we can see its shape.

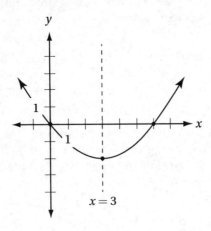

For this question, the axis of symmetry is key. Since the parabola has a vertex of $(3, -2)$, its axis of symmetry is

$x = 3$. The zeros of the parabola (the points where $y = 0$, or where the graph crosses the x-axis) must be symmetric to this line. Since the origin is 3 units to the *left* of this axis, the other zero must be three units to the *right* of the axis, or at the point $(6, 0)$. This means that $g(6)$ must equal 0, and the correct answer is (C).

Notice that we don't need to do anything complicated, like find the specific quadratic equation (which would be a pain in the neck).

When the quadratic function f is graphed in the xy-plane, its graph has a positive y-intercept and two distinct negative x-intercepts. Which of the following could be f?

A) $f(x) = -2(x + 3)(x + 1)$

B) $f(x) = 3(x + 2)^2$

C) $f(x) = -4(x - 2)(x - 3)$

D) $f(x) = (x + 1)(x + 3)$

(*Easy*) Since the functions are all given in factored form, it is easy to see where their zeros lie by using the Zero Product Property. The function in (A) has zeros (x-intercepts) at $x = -3$ and $x = -1$, which are both negative, but its y-intercept is $f(0) = -2(3)(1) = -6$, which is of course not positive. The only choice that gives two distinct x-intercepts and a positive value for $f(x)$ is choice (D) $f(x) = (x + 1)(x + 3)$, which has x-intercepts at $x = -1$ and $x = -3$, and a y-intercept at $y = 3$.

The quadratic function h is defined by the equation $h(x) = ax^2 + bx + c$, where a is a negative constant and c is a positive constant. Which of the following could be the graph of h in the xy-plane?

A)

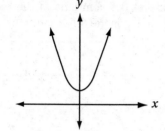

B)

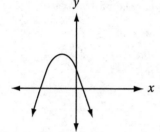

C)

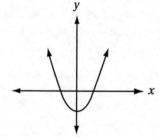

D)

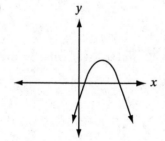

(*Easy*) The graph of $y = ax^2 + bx + c$ is an "open down" parabola if a is negative, and has a y-intercept of c. The only "open down" parabola with a positive y-intercept is choice (B).

Exercise Set 2 (No Calculator)

1

If $(x - 2)(x + 2) = 0$, then $x^2 + 10 =$

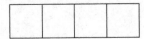

2

If $(a - 3)(a + k) = a^2 + 3a - 18$ for all values of a, what is the value of k?

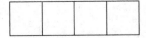

3

When the quadratic function $y = 10(x + 4)(x + 6)$ is graphed in the xy-plane, the result is a parabola with vertex at (a, b). What is the value of ab?

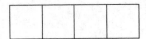

4

If the function $y = 3x^2 - kx - 12$ has a zero at $x = 3$, what is the value of k?

5

If the graph of a quadratic function in the xy-plane is a parabola that intersects the x-axis at $x = -1.2$ and $x = 4.8$, what is the x-coordinate of its vertex?

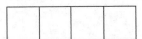

6

If the graph of $y = a(x - b)(x - 4)$ has a vertex at $(5, -3)$, what is the value of ab?

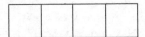

7

What is the sum of the zeros of the function $h(x) = 2x^2 - 5x - 12$?

8

If $x = -5$ is one of the solutions of the equation $0 = x^2 - ax - 12$, what is the other solution?

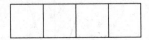

9

Which of the following is equivalent to $2a(a - 5) + 3a^2(a + 1)$ for all values of a?

A) $6a^4 - 24a^3 - 6$

B) $5a^5 + 3a^2 - 10a$

C) $3a^3 + 5a^2 - 10a$

D) $3a^3 + 2a^2 - 10a - 6$

10

Which of the following functions, when graphed in the xy-plane, has exactly one negative x-intercept and one negative y-intercept?

A) $y = -x^2 - 6x - 9$

B) $y = -x^2 + 6x - 9$

C) $y = x^2 + 6x + 9$

D) $y = x^2 - 6x + 9$

11

If $2x^2 + 8x = 42$ and $x < 0$, what is the value of x^2?

A) 4

B) 9

C) 49

D) 64

12

When the function $y = h(x) = ax^2 + bx + c$ is graphed in the xy-plane, the result is a parabola with vertex at $(4, 7)$. If $h(2) = 0$, which of the following must also equal 0?

A) $h(5)$

B) $h(6)$

C) $h(8)$

D) $h(9)$

Exercise Set 2 (Calculator)

13

If $x > 0$ and $2x^2 - 4x = 30$, what is the value of x?

14

If $x^2 + bx + 9 = 0$ has only one solution, and $b > 0$, what is the value of b?

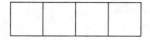

15

When $y = 5(x - 3.2)(x - 4.6)$ is graphed in the xy-plane, what is the value of the y-intercept?

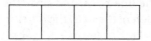

16

When $y = 5(x - 3.2)(x - 4.6)$ is graphed in the xy-plane, what is the x-coordinate of the vertex?

17

If $(2x - 1)(x + 3) + 2x = 2x^2 + kx - 3$ for all values of x, what is the value of k?

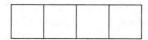

18

If $b^2 + 20b = 96$ and $b > 0$, what is the value of $b + 10$?

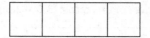

19

The graph of $y = f(x)$ in the xy-plane is a parabola with vertex at (3, 7). Which of the following must be equal to $f(-1)$?

A) $f(2)$

B) $f(4)$

C) $f(7)$

D) $f(15)$

20

Which of the following functions, when graphed in the xy-plane, has two positive x-intercepts and a negative y-intercept?

A) $y = -2(x - 1)(x + 5)$

B) $y = -2(x + 3)^2$

C) $y = -2(x - 5)^2$

D) $y = -2(x - 1)(x - 5)$

21

Which of the following equations has no real solutions?

A) $x^2 - 3x + 2 = 0$

B) $x^2 - 3x - 2 = 0$

C) $x^2 + 2x - 3 = 0$

D) $x^2 + 2x + 3 = 0$

22

The graph of the function $y = a(x + 6)(x + 8)$ has an axis of symmetry at $x = k$. What is the value of k?

A) -7

B) -6

C) 7

D) 8

23

The graph of the quadratic function $y = f(x)$ in the xy-plane is a parabola with vertex at (6, -1). Which of the following must have the same value as the y-intercept of this graph?

A) $f(-2)$

B) $f(3.5)$

C) $f(12)$

D) $f(13.5)$

EXERCISE SET 2 ANSWER KEY

No Calculator

1. 14

$$(x-2)(x+2)=0$$

FOIL: $x^2-4=0$

Add 14: $x^2+10=14$

2. 6

$$(a-3)(a+k)=a^2+3a-18$$

FOIL: $a^2+(k-3)a-3k=a^2+3a-18$

Equate coefficients: $k-3=3; -3k=-18$

Therefore $k=6$.

3. 50 By the Factor Theorem, the parabola has x-intercepts at $x=-4$ and $x=-6$. The x-coordinate of the vertex is the average of these zeros, or -5. To get the y-coordinate of the vertex, we just plug $x=-5$ back into the equation: $y=10(-5+4)(-5+6)=10(-1)(1)=-10$. Therefore $a=-5$ and $b=-10$ and so $ab=50$.

4. 5

When $x=3$, $y=0$: $0=3(3)^2-k(3)-12$

Simplify: $0=27-3k-12$

Simplify: $0=15-3k$

Add $3k$: $3k=15$

Divide by 3: $k=5$

5. 1.8 The x-coordinate of the vertex is the average of the x-intercepts (if they exist): $(-1.2+4.8)/2=3.6/2=1.8$.

6. 18 The x-coordinate of the vertex is the average of the x-intercepts (if they exist):

$$5=(b+4)/2$$

Multiply by 2: $10=b+4$

Subtract 4: $6=b$

Substitute $x=5$ and $y=-3$ into equation to find the value of a: $-3=a(5-6)(5-4)=-a$

Multiply by -1: $3=a$

Therefore, $ab=(3)(6)=18$

7. 2.5

$$0=2x^2-5x-12$$

Factor: $0=(2x+3)(x-4)$

Therefore, the zeros are $x=-3/2$ and $x=4$, which have a sum of 2.5. Alternately, you can divide the original equation by 2:

$$0=x^2-2.5x-12$$

and recall that any quadratic in the form $x^2+bx+c=0$ must have zeros that have a sum of $-b$ and a product of c. Therefore, without having to calculate the zeros, we can see that they have a sum of $-(-2.5)=2.5$.

8. 2.4 We know that one of the zeros is $x=-5$, and we want to find the other, $x=b$. We can use the Factor Theorem:

$$x^2-ax-12=(x+5)(x-b)$$

FOIL: $x^2-ax-12=x^2+(5-b)x-5b$

Since the constant terms must be equal, $12=5b$ and therefore, $b=12/5=2.4$.

9. C

$$2a(a-5)+3a^2(a+1)$$

Distribute: $2a^2-10a+3a^3+3a^2$

Collect like terms: $3a^3+5a^2-10a$

10. A Substitute $x=0$ to find the y-intercept of each graph. Only (A) and (B) yield negative y-intercepts, so (C) and (D) can be eliminated. Factoring the function in (A) yields $y=-(x+3)$, which has only a single x-intercept at $x=-3$.

11. C

$$2x^2+8x=42$$

Divide by 2: $x^2+4x=21$

Subtract 21: $x^2+4x-21=0$

Factor: $(x+7)(x-3)=0$

Therefore, $x=-7$ or 3, but since $x<0$, $x=-7$ and therefore, $x^2=(-7)^2=49$.

12. B Draw a quick sketch of the parabola. Since it has a vertex at (4, 7), it must have an axis of symmetry of $x=4$. The two zeros of the function must be symmetric to the line $x=4$, and since the zero $x=2$ is two units to the left of the axis, the other must by 2 units to the right, at $x=6$.

Calculator

13. 5

$$2x^2-4x=30$$

Divide by 2: $x^2-2x=15$

Subtract 15: $x^2-2x-15=0$

Factor: $(x-5)(x+3)=0$

Therefore, $x=5$ or -3. But since $x>0$, $x=5$.

14. 6 Let's call the one solution a. If it is the only solution, the two factors must be the same:

$$x^2+bx+9=(x-a)(x-a)$$

FOIL: $x^2+bx+9=x^2-2ax+a^2$

Therefore, $b=-2a$ and $a^2=9$. This means that $x=3$ or -3 and so $b=-2(3)=-6$ or $-2(-3)=6$. Since b must be positive, $b=6$.

15. 73.6 The y-intercept is simply the value of the function when $x=0$: $y=5(0-3.2)(0-4.6)=73.6$.

16. 3.9 The x-coordinate of the vertex is simply the average of the zeros: $(3.2+4.6)/2=3.9$.

17. 7

$$(2x-1)(x+3)+2x=2x^2+kx-3$$

FOIL: $2x^2+5x-3+2x=2x^2+kx-3$

Simplify: $2x^2+7x-3=2x^2+kx-3$

Subtract $2x^2$ and add 3: $7x=kx$

Divide by x: $7=k$

18. **14** $b^2 + 20b = 96$

Subtract 96: $b^2 + 20b - 96 = 0$

Factor: $(b - 4)(b + 24) = 0$

Therefore, $b = 4$ or -24, but if $b > 0$, then b must equal 4, and therefore, $b + 10 = 14$. Alternately, you might notice that adding 100 to both sides of the original equation gives a "perfect square trinomial" on the left side: $b^2 + 20b + 100 = 196$

Factor: $(b + 10)^2 = 196$

Take square root: $b + 10 = \pm 14$

If $b > 0$: $b + 10 = 14$

---

19. **C** Since the vertex of the parabola is at (3, 7), the axis of symmetry is $x = 3$. Since $x = -1$ is 4 units to the left of this axis, and $x = 7$ is 4 units to the right of this axis, $f(-1)$ must equal $f(7)$.

---

20. **D** $y = -2(x - 1)(x - 5)$ has x-intercepts at $x = 1$ and $x = 5$ and a y-intercept of $y = -10$. (Notice that the function in (C) has only *one* positive x-intercept at $x = 5$.)

21. **D** This one is tough. Since this question allows a calculator, you could solve this by graphing or with the Quadratic Formula. Remember that a quadratic equation has no real solution if $b^2 - 4ac < 0$. The only choice for which $b^2 - 4ac$ is negative is (D). Alternately, if you graph the left side of each equation as a function in the xy-plane (which I only advise if you have a good graphing calculator), you will see that the function in (D) never crosses the x-axis, implying that it cannot equal 0.

---

22. **A** This quadratic has zeros at $x = -6$ and $x = -8$, so its axis of symmetry is at the midpoint of the zeros, at $x = -7$.

---

23. **C** If the vertex of the parabola is at (6, -1), its axis of symmetry must be $x = 6$. The y-intercept of the function is $f(0)$, which is the value of y when $x = 0$. Since this point is 6 units to the left of the axis of symmetry, its reflection over the axis of symmetry is 6 units to the rights of the axis, at $f(12)$.

Lesson 7: Analyzing polynomial equations

> **The Factor Theorem**
>
> - If a polynomial expression has a zero (a value of x for which the polynomial equals 0) at $x = a$, it must have a factor of $(x - a)$.
> - Conversely, if a polynomial has a factor of $(x - a)$, it must have a zero at $x = a$.

The function f is defined by the equation $f(x) = x^3 - ax^2 - bx + 20$ where a and b are constants. In the xy-plane, the graph of $y = f(x)$ intersects the x-axis at the points $(-2, 0)$, $(2, 0)$, and $(p, 0)$. What is the value of p?

A) 4

B) 5

C) 10

D) 20

(*Medium-hard*) Since $x = -2$ and $x = 2$ and $x = p$ are zeros of the function (that is, they are inputs that yield an output of 0), the polynomial must have $(x + 2)$, $(x - 2)$, and $(x - p)$ as factors.

$$f(x) = x^3 - ax^2 - bx + 20 = (x + 2)(x - 2)(x - p)$$

FOIL $(x + 2)(x - 2)$: $= (x^2 - 4)(x - p)$

FOIL $(x^2 - 4)(x - p)$: $= x^3 - px^2 - 4x + 4p$

Since $x^3 - px^2 - 4x + 4p$ must be equivalent to $x^3 - ax^2 - bx + 20$, all of the corresponding coefficients must be equal. That is, $-p = -a$, $-4 = -b$, and $4p = 20$. Therefore, $p = 5$, $a = 5$, and $b = 4$, and the correct answer is (B).

Which range of values defines all of the values of x for which the function f in the previous question is positive?

A) $x < -2$ or $x > 2$

B) $-2 < x < 5$

C) $-2 < x < 2$ or $x > 5$

D) $2 < x < 5$

> When analyzing a polynomial function, you may find it very helpful to draw its graph in the $xy =$ plane. Sometimes the x-and y-intercepts are all you need to get a good picture by hand. You should also know how to use the graphing function on your calculator, when it is permitted.

(*Hard*) This question is easier to solve if we have a graph of the function. Since we know that the equation of the function is $y = (x + 2)(x - 2)(x - 5)$, we know that it has x-intercepts at $x = -2$, $x = 2$, and $x = 5$, and a y-intercept at $y = (0 + 2)(0 - 2)(0 - 5) = 20$. Therefore, the graph looks like this:

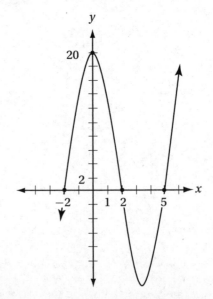

On this graph, the points where f is positive are the points above the x-axis. This corresponds to the points where x is between -2 and 2, and where x is greater than 5. Therefore, the correct answer is (C).

Lesson 8: Systems involving quadratics

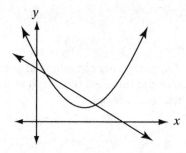

The figure above shows the graph of a system of two equations in the xy-plane. How many solutions does this system have?

A) Zero   B) One   C) Two   D) Three

(*Easy*) Finding the solutions to a system of equations means finding the ordered pairs that satisfy all of the equations simultaneously. (If you need to review how to solve systems, see Chapter 7.) If the equations are graphed, the solutions correspond to any points where all of the graphs meet. In this case, the two graphs cross in two distinct points, so the system has two solutions and the answer is (C).

$$y + 2x = 6$$
$$y = x^2 + 3x$$

Given the system above, which of the following could be the value of y?

A) 1 or −6

B) 0 or −5

C) 0 or 10

D) 4 or 18

(*Medium*) Perhaps the simplest way to solve this system is with the process of substitution, which we applied to linear systems in Chapter 7, Lesson 12.

First equation: $\qquad\qquad\qquad y + 2x = 6$

Substitute $y = x^2 + 3x$: $\qquad x^2 + 3x + 2x = 6$

Subtract 6: $\qquad\qquad\qquad x^2 + 5x - 6 = 0$

Factor with Product-Sum Method: $\quad (x + 6)(x - 1) = 0$

Apply Zero-Product Property: $\qquad\quad x = -6$ or 1

But be careful. You may be tempted to choose (A) 1 or −6, but the question asks for the value of y, not x. To find the corresponding values of y, we must plug our x-values back into one of the equations: $y = (-6)^2 + 3(-6) = 18$ or $y = (1)^2 + 3(1) = 4$; therefore, the correct answer is (D).

$$y = 1$$
$$x^2 + y^2 = 4$$
$$y = x^2$$

How many distinct ordered pairs (x, y) satisfy the three-equation system above?

A) Zero   B) One   C) Two   D) Three

(*Medium*) To find the solutions of a system means to find the ordered pairs (x, y) that satisfy all of the equations simultaneously. Although graphing this system is not too hard, it is probably simpler to solve this system algebraically.

Substitute the first equation,
$y = 1$, into the other two: $\qquad\qquad x^2 + (1)^2 = 4$
$$1 = x^2$$

Use $x^2 = 1$ to substitute into
other equation: $\qquad\qquad\qquad (1) + (1)^2 = 4$

Simplify: $\qquad\qquad\qquad\qquad\qquad 2 = 4$

Since this yields an equation that can never be true, regardless of the values of the unknowns, there is no real solution to this system, and the correct answer is (A).

If you graph this system, it will show a horizontal line, a circle, and a parabola. You will see that no point exists where all three graphs meet, indicating that the system has no solution.

Exercise Set 3 (No Calculator)

1

If $x^3 - 7x^2 + 16x - 12 = (x - a)(x - b)(x - c)$ for all values of x, what is the value of abc?

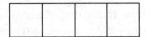

2

If $x^3 - 7x^2 + 16x - 12 = (x - a)(x - b)(x - c)$ for all values of x, what is the value of $a + b + c$?

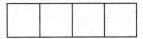

3

1. If $x^3 - 7x^2 + 16x - 12 = (x - a)(x - b)(x - c)$ for all values of x, what is the value of $ab + bc + ac$?

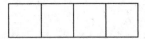

4

If $x^2 - ax + 12$ has a zero at $x = 3$, what is the value of a?

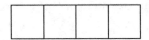

5

If $x^2 - ax + 12$ has a zero at $x = 3$, at what other value of x does it have a zero?

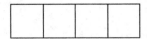

6

$$y = 4x^2 + 2$$
$$x + y = 16$$

When the two equations in the system above are graphed in the xy-plane, they intersect in the point (a, b). If $a > 0$, what is the value of a?

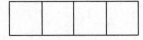

7

$$x^2 + y^2 = 9$$

Which of the following equations, if graphed in the xy-plane, would intersect the graph of the equation above in exactly one point?

A) $y = -4$

B) $y = -3$

C) $y = -1$

E) $y = 0$

8

If $g(x) = a(x + 1)(x - 2)(x - 3)$ where a is a negative constant, which of the following is greatest?

A) $g(0.5)$

B) $g(1.5)$

C) $g(2.5)$

D) $g(3.5)$

9

If $2x^2 + ax + b$ has zeros at $x = 5$ and $x = -1$, what is the value of $a + b$?

A) -18

B) -9

C) -2

D) -1

10

If the graph of the equation $y = ax^4 + bx$ in the xy-plane passes through the points $(2, 12)$ and $(-2, 4)$, what is the value of $a + b$?

A) 0.5   B) 1.5   C) 2.0

D) 2.5

11

If the function $y = 3(x^2 + 1)(x^3 - 1)(x + 2)$ is graphed in the xy-plane, in how many distinct points will it intersect the x-axis?

A) Two   B) Three   C) Four

D) Five

Exercise Set 3 (Calculator)

12

If $x^2 + y = 10x$ and $y = 25$, what is the value of x?

13

If $2x^3 - 5x - a$ has a zero at $x = 4$, what is the value of a?

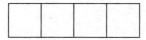

14

If $x > 0$ and $x^4 - 9x^3 - 22x^2 = 0$, what is the value of x?

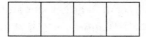

15

If d is a positive constant and the graph in the xy-plane of $y = (x^2)(x^2 + x - 72)(x - d)$ has only one positive zero, what is the value of d?

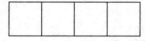

16

$$y = 2x^2 + 18$$
$$y = ax$$

In the system above, a is a positive constant. When the two equations are graphed in the xy-plane, they intersect in exactly one point. What is the value of a?

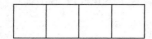

17

$$4a^2 - 5b = 16$$
$$3a^2 - 5b = 7$$

Given the system of equations above, what is the value of a^2b^2?

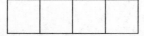

18

For how many distinct positive integer values of n is $(n - 1)(n - 9)(n - 17)$ less than 0?

A) Six
B) Seven
C) Eight
D) Nine

19

$$x^2 + 2y^2 = 44$$
$$y^2 = x - 2$$

When the two equations above are graphed in the xy-plane, they intersect in the point (h, k). What is the value of h?

A) -8
B) -6
C) 6
D) 8

20

$$m^2 + 2n = 10$$
$$2m^2 + 2n = 14$$

Given the system of equations above, which of the following could be the value of $m + n$?

A) -7
B) -2
C) 1
D) 2

21

For how many distinct values of x does $(x^2 - 4)(x - 4)^2(x^2 + 4)$ equal 0?

A) Three
B) Four
C) Five
D) Six

22

The function $f(x)$ is defined by the equation $f(x) = a(x + 2)(x - a)(x - 8)$ where a is a constant. If $f(2.5)$ is negative, which of the following could be the value of a?

A) -2
B) 0
C) 2
D) 4

EXERCISE SET 3 ANSWER KEY

No Calculator

1. **12** When the expression $(x - a)(x - b)(x - c)$ is fully distributed and simplified, it yields the expression $x^3 - (a + b + c)x^2 + (ab + bc + ac)x - abc$. If this is equivalent to $x^3 - 7x^2 + 16x - 12$ for all values of x, then all of the corresponding coefficients must be equal.

2. **7** See question 1.

3. **16** See question 1.

4. **7** If $x^2 - ax + 12 = 0$ when $x = 3$, then

$$(3)^2 - 3a + 12 = 0$$

Simplify:	$21 - 3a = 0$
Add $3a$:	$21 = 3a$
Divide by 3:	$7 = a$

5. **4** As we saw in question 4, $a = 7$.

	$x^2 - 7x + 12$
Factor:	$(x - 3)(x - 4)$

Therefore, the zeros are 3 and 4.

6. **7/4 or 1.75**

	$x + y = 16$
Subtract x:	$y = 16 - x$
Substitute:	$16 - x = 4x^2 + 2$
Subtract 16, add x:	$0 = 4x^2 + x - 14$
Factor:	$0 = (4x - 7)(x + 2)$

Therefore, $x = -2$ or 7/4, but if x must be positive, it equals 7/4.

7. **B** The graph of the given equation is a circle centered at the origin with a radius of 3. Therefore, the horizontal line at $y = -3$ just intersects it at $(0, -3)$. You can also substitute $y = -3$ into the original equation and verify that it gives exactly one solution.

8. **C** Just notice the sign of each factor for each input:
$g(0.5) = (-)(+)(-)(-) = $ negative
$g(1.5) = (-)(+)(-)(-) = $ negative
$g(2.5) = (-)(+)(+)(-) = $ positive
$g(3.5) = (-)(+)(+)(+) = $ negative
Since (C) is the only option that yields a positive value, it is the greatest.

9. **A**

	$2x^2 + ax + b$
If $x = 5$ is a zero:	$2(5)^2 + 5a + b = 0$
Subtract 50:	$5a + b = -50$
If $x = -1$ is a zero:	$2(-1)^2 + a(-1) + b = 0$
Subtract 2:	$-a + b = -2$
Multiply by -1:	$a - b = 2$
Add equations:	$6a = -48$

Divide by 6:	$a = -8$
Substitute $a = -8$:	$-8 - b = 2$
Add 8:	$-b = 10$
Multiply by -1:	$b = -10$

Therefore, $a + b = -8 + -10 = -18$.

10. **D**

Substitute (2, 12):	$12 = a(2)^4 + b(2)$
Simplify:	$16a + 2b = 12$
Substitute (−2, 4):	$4 = a(-2)^4 + b(-2)$
Simplify:	$16a - 2b = 4$
Add two equations:	$32a = 16$
Divide by 32:	$a = ½$
Substitute:	$16(1/2) + 2b = 12$
Subtract 8:	$2b = 4$
Divide by 2:	$b = 2$

Therefore, $a + b = 2.5$.

11. **A** Use the Zero Product Property. The factor $(x^2 + 1)$ cannot be zero for any value of x, $(x^3 - 1)$ is zero when $x = 1$, and $(x + 2)$ is zero when $x = -2$. Therefore, there are only two distinct points in which this graph touches the x-axis.

Calculator

12. **5** Substitute $y = 25$:

	$x^2 + 25 = 10x$
Subtract $10x$:	$x^2 - 10x + 25 = 0$
Factor:	$(x - 5)(x - 5) = 0$
Use Zero Product Property:	$x = 5$

13. **108** If $x = 4$ is a zero:

	$2(4)^3 - 5(4) - a = 0$
Simplify:	$108 - a = 0$
Add a:	$108 = a$

14. **11**

	$x^4 - 9x^3 - 22x^2 = 0$
Divide by x^2:	$x^2 - 9x - 22 = 0$
Factor:	$(x - 11)(x + 2) = 0$
Use Zero Product Property:	$x = 11$ or -2

15. **8**

	$y = (x^2)(x^2 + x - 72)(x - d)$
Factor:	$y = (x^2)(x + 9)(x - 8)(x - d)$

By the Zero Property, the zeros are $x = 0$, -9, 8, or d. Since d is positive, but there can only be one positive zero, $d = 8$.

16. **12**

	$y = 2x^2 + 18$
Substitute $y = ax$:	$ax = 2x^2 + 18$
Subtract ax:	$0 = 2x^2 - ax + 18$
Divide by 2:	$0 = x^2 - \dfrac{a}{2}x + 9$

If the graphs intersect in only one point, the system must have only one solution, so this quadratic must be a "perfect square trinomial" as discussed in Lesson 4.

$$x^2 - \frac{a}{2}x + 9 = x^2 - 2bx + b^2$$

Equate coefficients: $\qquad\qquad\qquad b^2 = 9$

$$2b = a/2$$

The only positive solution to this system is $b = 3$ and $a = 12$.

---

17. **144** $\qquad\qquad\qquad\qquad 4a^2 - 5b = 16$

$$3a^2 - 5b = 7$$

Subtract equations: $\qquad\qquad\qquad\qquad a^2 = 9$

Substitute $a^2 = 9$: $\qquad\qquad\qquad 3(9) - 5b = 7$

Subtract 27: $\qquad\qquad\qquad\qquad -5b = -20$

Divide by -5: $\qquad\qquad\qquad\qquad b = 4$

Therefore, $a^2b^2 = 9(4)^2 = 144$.

---

18. **B** In order for the product of three numbers to be negative, either all three numbers must be negative or exactly one must be negative and the others positive. Since n must be a positive integer, $n - 1$ cannot be negative, and so there must be two positive factors and one negative. The only integers that yield this result are the integers from 10 to 16, inclusive, which is a total of seven integers.

---

19. **C** $\qquad\qquad\qquad\qquad\qquad x^2 + 2y^2 = 44$

Substitute $y^2 = x - 2$: $\qquad\qquad x^2 + 2(x - 2) = 44$

Distribute: $\qquad\qquad\qquad\qquad x^2 + 2x - 4 = 44$

Subtract 44: $\qquad\qquad\qquad x^2 + 2x - 48 = 0$

Factor: $\qquad\qquad\qquad\qquad (x - 6)(x + 8) = 0$

This seems to imply that the x-coordinate of the point of intersection could be either 6 or -8, both of which are choices. Can they both be correct? No: if we substitute $x = -8$ into either equation, we get no solution, because y^2 cannot equal -8. Therefore, the correct answer is (C) 6, and the points of intersection are $(6, 2)$ and $(6, -2)$.

---

20. **C** $\qquad\qquad\qquad\qquad 2m^2 + 2n = 14$

$$m^2 + 2n = 10$$

Subtract equations: $\qquad\qquad\qquad\qquad m^2 = 4$

Take square root: $\qquad\qquad\qquad\qquad m = \pm 2$

Substitute $m^2 = 4$: $\qquad\qquad\qquad 4 + 2n = 10$

Subtract 4: $\qquad\qquad\qquad\qquad\qquad 2n = 6$

Divide by 2: $\qquad\qquad\qquad\qquad\qquad n = 3$

Therefore, $m + n = -2 + 3 = 1$ or $2 + 3 = 5$.

---

21. **A** Use the Zero Product Property. $(x^2 - 4)$ equals 0 if x is 2 or -2, $(x - 4)$ equals 0 if x is 4, and $(x^2 + 4)$ cannot equal 0. Therefore, there are exactly three distinct zeros.

---

22. **C** $\qquad f(2.5) = a(2.5 + 2)(2.5 - a)(2.5 - 8)$

Simplify: $\qquad\qquad\qquad (-24.75)(a)(2.5 - a)$

This product can only be negative if a and $(2.5 - a)$ have the same sign, which is only true for (C) $a = 2$.

Skill 3: Working with Exponentials and Radicals
Lesson 9: The Laws of Exponentials

When working with exponentials you must understand the Laws of Exponentials.

> **Law #1: If *n* is a positive integer, then x^n means the result when 1 is *multiplied* by *x* repeatedly *n* times.**

e.g., $3^5 = 1 \times 3 \times 3 \times 3 \times 3 \times 3 = 243$

You might think that it's unnecessary to include the 1 in this product, but including it will help clarify what zero, negative, and fractional exponents mean. For instance, think about the following sequence:

$$243, 81, 27, 9, 3, \_\_\_, \_\_\_, \_\_\_$$

What are the missing three terms in this sequence? With a little trial and error, you will see that the rule for getting each term is "divide the previous term by 3," and therefore the missing terms are 1, 1/3, and 1/9. But notice, also, that these terms are just the descending integer powers of 3:

$3^5 = 1 \times 3 \times 3 \times 3 \times 3 \times 3$ $= 243$

$3^4 = 1 \times 3 \times 3 \times 3 \times 3$ $= 81$

$3^3 = 1 \times 3 \times 3 \times 3$ $= 27$

$3^2 = 1 \times 3 \times 3$ $= 9$

$3^1 = 1 \times 3$ $= 3$

$3^0 = 1$ $= 1$

$3^{-1} = 1 \div 3$ $= 1/3$

$3^{-2} = 1 \div 3 \div 3$ $= 1/9$

And so on. If you explore this pattern, and patterns for the powers of other numbers, you will notice that some other laws clearly emerge.

> **Law #2: As long as *x* does not equal 0, $x^0 = 1$.**

You can think of x^0 as meaning "1 multiplied by *x* zero times, or not at all." Therefore, the result is 1.

> **Law #3: If *n* is a positive integer, then x^{-n} means the result when 1 is *divided* by *x* repeatedly *n* times.**
>
> In other words, $x^{-n} = \dfrac{1}{x^n}$.

e.g., $2^{-3} = 1 \div 2 \div 2 \div 2 = \dfrac{1}{2^3} = \dfrac{1}{8}$

> **Law #4: $x^m \times x^n = x^{m+n}$** (When multiplying exponentials with equal *bases*, **add** the *exponents*.)

e.g., $x^3 \times x^2 = (1 \times x \times x \times x) \times (1 \times x \times x)$
$= 1 \times x \times x \times x \times x \times x = x^5$

> **Law #5: $x^n \times y^n = (xy)^n$** (When multiplying exponentials with equal *exponents*, **multiply** the *bases*.)

This law follows from the Commutative and Associative Laws of Addition.

e.g., $4^3 \times 7^2 = (1 \times 4 \times 4 \times 4) \times (1 \times 7 \times 7 \times 7)$
$= 1 \times (4 \times 7) \times (4 \times 7) \times (4 \times 7)$
$= (4 \times 7)^3$

> **Law #6: $\dfrac{x^m}{x^n} = x^{m-n}$** (When dividing exponentials with equal *bases*, **subtract** the *exponents*.)

e.g., $\dfrac{x^5}{x^3} = \dfrac{1 \times x \times x \times x \times x \times x}{1 \times x \times x \times x} = 1 \times x \times x = x^2$

> **Law #7: $\dfrac{x^n}{y^n} = \left(\dfrac{x}{y}\right)^n$** (When dividing exponentials with equal *exponents*, **divide** the *bases*.)

e.g., $\dfrac{50^3}{25^3} = \left(\dfrac{50}{25}\right)^3 = 2^3 = 8$

> **Law #8: $(x^m)^n = x^{mn}$**

e.g., $(x^3)^2 = (1 \times x^3 \times x^3) = (1 \times (1 \times x \times x \times x) \times (1 \times x \times x \times x)) = 1 \times x \times x \times x \times x \times x \times x = x^6$

> **Law #9: $x^{\frac{1}{n}} = \sqrt[n]{x}$**

Proof: This follows directly from Law #8. If we raise $x^{\frac{1}{n}}$ to the nth power, by Law #8 we must get x^1 or x. The number that we must raise to the nth power in order to get x is, by definition, the "nth root of x."

Law #10: If $x > 1$ and $x^a = x^b$, then $a = b$.

Which of the following expressions is equivalent to $\dfrac{(n+n+n)(n+n+n)}{3^{-1}}$?

A) $\dfrac{n^6}{3}$

B) $3n^2$

C) $3n^6$

D) $27n^2$

(*Medium*) $\dfrac{(n+n+n)(n+n+n)}{3^{-1}}$

Simplify numerator: $\dfrac{(3n)(3n)}{3^{-1}}$

Simplify numerator
and apply Law #3 to
denominator: $\dfrac{9n^2}{\dfrac{1}{3}}$

To divide by a number is to
multiply by its reciprocal: $9n^2 \times 3 = 27n^2$

Therefore, the correct answer is (D).

Which of the following expressions is equivalent to $\dfrac{3 \times 3^{2n}}{9^n}$ for all values of n?

A) $\left(\dfrac{2}{3}\right)^n$

B) 3

C) 3^n

D) 9^{2n}

(*Medium*) Express all terms in exponential form: $\dfrac{3 \times 3^{2n}}{9^n} = \dfrac{3^1 \times 3^{2n}}{9^n}$

Apply Law #4: $\dfrac{3^{2n+1}}{9^n}$

Substitute $9 = 3^2$: $\dfrac{3^{2n+1}}{(3^2)^n}$

Apply Law #8 to the
denominator: $\dfrac{3^{2n+1}}{3^{2n}}$

Apply Law #6: $3^{2n+1-2n} = 3^1 = 3$

Therefore, the correct answer is (B).

Alternately, we can plug in various values for n and find that the expression gives a value of n no matter what.

Lesson 10: The Laws of Radicals

The radical symbol ($\sqrt{\ }$) is used to indicate roots, which are the inverse of exponentials. For instance, because $2^3 = 8$, we can say that 2 is the "third root" or "cube root" of 8 ($2 = \sqrt[3]{8}$).

Law #9 of exponentials shows us that radicals (or "roots") can be expressed as exponentials. For instance, $\sqrt[3]{8} = 8^{\frac{1}{3}}$. Therefore, we can use the Laws of Exponentials to simplify radical expressions.

e.g., $\left(2\sqrt{2x}\right)^6 = \left(2(2x)^{\frac{1}{2}}\right)^6 = (2)^6\left((2x)^{\frac{1}{2}}\right)^6$

$= (2)^6(2x)^3 = (2)^6(2)^3(x)^3 = 2^9 x^3$

Law #1: $\sqrt[n]{x} = x^{\frac{1}{n}}$ (This is just the "reflected" version of Law of Exponentials #9.)

Law #2: $\sqrt[n]{x} \times \sqrt[n]{y} = \sqrt[n]{xy}$ (This follows directly from Law of Exponentials #5.)

Law #3: $\dfrac{\sqrt[n]{x}}{\sqrt[n]{y}} = \sqrt[n]{\dfrac{x}{y}}$ (This follows directly from Law of Exponentials #7.)

Working with square roots is much easier if you **memorize the first 10 or so "perfect square integers":**

$2^2 = 4$, $3^2 = 9$, $4^2 = 16$, $5^2 = 25$, $6^2 = 36$, $7^2 = 49$, $8^2 = 64$, $9^2 = 81$, $10^2 = 100$, $11^2 = 121$, $12^2 = 144 \ldots$

This will help you both **simplify** and **estimate** radical expressions.

- If the radicand has a perfect square factor, the radical can be simplified by factoring.

  e.g., $\sqrt{72} = \sqrt{36} \times \sqrt{2} = 6\sqrt{2}$

- If a fraction has a radical in the denominator, eliminate it by multiplying numerator and denominator by the radical.

  e.g., $\dfrac{1+\sqrt{2}}{\sqrt{3}} = \dfrac{1+\sqrt{2}}{\sqrt{3}} \times \dfrac{\sqrt{3}}{\sqrt{3}} = \dfrac{\sqrt{3}+\sqrt{6}}{3}$

- To estimate the value of square roots, notice which two consecutive perfect squares the radicand lies between.

  e.g., $\sqrt{64} < \sqrt{72} < \sqrt{81}$ and therefore $8 < \sqrt{72} < 9$

Which of the following is equivalent to $\dfrac{2\sqrt{2}+4\sqrt{18}}{\sqrt{2}}$? (No calculator)

A) $6\sqrt{10}$ B) 7   C) 14   D) 19

(*Medium*) Notice that each answer choice is much simpler than the original expression. This suggests that the original expression can be simplified. Let's begin by looking at the radical expressions. If you know your perfect squares you will see that neither **radicand** (the expression inside the radical) is a perfect square, but one of the radicands—18—is a multiple of a perfect square: $18 = 2 \times 9$.

Original expression:	$\dfrac{2\sqrt{2}+4\sqrt{18}}{\sqrt{2}}$
Substitute $18 = 9 \times 2$:	$\dfrac{2\sqrt{2}+4\sqrt{9\times 2}}{\sqrt{2}}$
Apply Law #2:	$\dfrac{2\sqrt{2}+4\sqrt{9}\times\sqrt{2}}{\sqrt{2}}$
Simplify $\sqrt{9} = 3$:	$\dfrac{2\sqrt{2}+12\sqrt{2}}{\sqrt{2}} = \dfrac{14\sqrt{2}}{\sqrt{2}} = 14$

Therefore, the correct answer is (C).

If $x^2 = 4$, $y^2 = 9$, and $(x-2)(y+3) \neq 0$, what is the value of $x + y$?

A) -5 B) -1 C) 1   D) 5

Every positive number has **two distinct square roots**. For instance, both 5 and -5 are the square root of 25, because $(5)^2 = 25$ and $(-5)^2 = 25$.

However, the symbol $\sqrt{\ }$ means the **principal, or non-negative square root**, so $\sqrt{25} = 5$ and not -5.

(*Easy*) If $x^2 = 4$, then $x = \pm 2$, and if $y^2 = 9$, then $y = \pm 2$. But if $(x-2)(y+3) \neq 0$, the x cannot equal 2 and y cannot equal -3. Therefore, $x = -2$ and $y = 3$, and $x + y = 1$, so the correct answer is (C).

Lesson 11: Solving radical and exponential equations

If $\dfrac{1}{x+2} = \sqrt{2}$, what is the value of x?

A) $\dfrac{1+2\sqrt{2}}{2}$

B) $\dfrac{1-2\sqrt{2}}{2}$

C) $\dfrac{1-2\sqrt{2}}{\sqrt{2}}$

D) $\dfrac{1+2\sqrt{2}}{\sqrt{2}}$

(*Hard*)

	$\dfrac{1}{x+2} = \sqrt{2}$
Multiply by $(x+2)$:	$1 = \sqrt{2}(x+2)$
Distribute:	$1 = \sqrt{2}x + 2\sqrt{2}$
Subtract $2\sqrt{2}$:	$1 - 2\sqrt{2} = \sqrt{2}x$
Divide by $\sqrt{2}$:	$\dfrac{1+2\sqrt{2}}{\sqrt{2}} = x$

Therefore, the correct answer is (D).

If $\dfrac{1}{2^k} = 4\sqrt{2}$, what is the value of k?

A) -3

B) $-\dfrac{5}{2}$

C) $-\dfrac{3}{2}$

D) $\dfrac{7}{2}$

(*Medium-hard*)

	$\dfrac{1}{2^k} = 4\sqrt{2}$
Use Exponential Law #3:	$2^{-k} = 4\sqrt{2}$
Use Radical Law #1:	$2^{-k} = 4 \times 2^{\frac{1}{2}}$
Substitute $4 = 2^2$:	$2^{-k} = 2^2 \times 2^{\frac{1}{2}}$
Use Exponential Law #4:	$2^{-k} = 2^{\frac{5}{2}}$
If $2^a = 2^b$, then $a = b$:	$-k = \dfrac{5}{2}$
Multiply by -1:	$k = -\dfrac{5}{2}$

If $3y = \sqrt{\dfrac{2}{y}}$, what is the value of y^3?

A) $\dfrac{2}{9}$

B) $\dfrac{4}{9}$

C) $\dfrac{2}{3}$

D) $\dfrac{4}{3}$

(*Hard*)

	$3y = \sqrt{\dfrac{2}{y}}$
Use Radical Law #3:	$3y = \dfrac{\sqrt{2}}{\sqrt{y}}$
Multiply by $\sqrt{y}$:	$3y\sqrt{y} = \sqrt{2}$
Use Radical Law #1:	$3y^1 y^{\frac{1}{2}} = 2^{\frac{1}{2}}$
Use Exponential Law #4:	$3y^{\frac{3}{2}} = 2^{\frac{1}{2}}$
Divide by 3:	$y^{\frac{3}{2}} = \dfrac{2^{\frac{1}{2}}}{3}$
Square both sides:	$y^3 = \dfrac{2}{9}$

Therefore, the correct answer is (A).

Exercise Set 4 (No Calculator)

1

If $2a^2 + 3a - 5a^2 = 9$, what is the value of $a - a^2$?

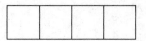

2

If $(200)(4,000) = 8 \times 10^m$, what is the value of m?

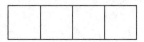

3

If $w = -10^{30}$, what is the value of $\dfrac{8w^2}{(8w)^2}$?

4

If $2^x = 10$, what is the value of $5(2^{2x}) + 2^x$?

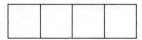

5

If $(x + 2)(x + 4)(x + 6) = 0$, what is the greatest possible value of $\dfrac{1}{2^x}$?

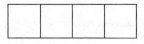

6

If $\left(4 + 4\sqrt{2}\right)^2 = a + b\sqrt{2}$, where a and b are integers, what is the value of $a + b$?

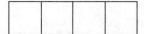

7

If $\dfrac{a}{3 + \sqrt{5}} = \dfrac{3 - \sqrt{5}}{b}$, what is the value of $(ab)^{\frac{3}{2}}$?

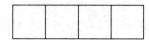

8

If $9^x = 25$, what is the value of 3^{x-1}?

A) $\dfrac{3}{25}$ B) $\dfrac{5}{3}$ C) $\dfrac{25}{3}$ D) 24

9

If $g(x, y) = \dfrac{2x}{y^3}$ and a and b are positive numbers, what is the value of $\dfrac{g(4a, 2b)}{g(a, b)}$?

A) $\dfrac{1}{4}$ B) $\dfrac{1}{2}$ C) 2   D) 4

10

Which of the following is equivalent to $\dfrac{2^n \times 2^n}{2^n \times 2}$ for all positive values of n?

A) 2   B) 2^n C) 2^{n-1}

D) 2^{2n}

11

Which of the following is equivalent to $3^m + 3^m + 3^m$ for all positive values of m?

A) 3^{m+1} B) 3^{2m} C) 3^{3m}

D) 3^{3m+1}

12

If x is a positive number and $5^x = y$, which of the following expresses $5y^2$ in terms of x?

A) 5^{2x} B) 5^{2x+1} C) 5^{3x}

D) 25^{2x}

Exercise Set 4 (Calculator)

13

If $n^2 = \sqrt{64^4}$ and $n > 0$, what is the value of n?

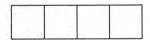

14

What is the smallest integer value of m such that $\dfrac{1}{10^m} < 0.000025$?

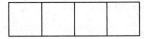

15

If $\dfrac{3}{3^{-k}} = 9\sqrt{27}$, what is the value of k?

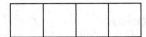

16

If $(x^m)^3(x^{m+1})^2 = x^{37}$ for all values of x, what is the value of m?

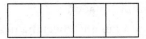

17

If $9\sqrt{12} - 4\sqrt{27} = n\sqrt{3}$, what is the value of n?

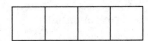

18

If $8^{\frac{1}{6}} = \left(2^{-\frac{1}{12}}\right)^{-n}$, what is the value of n?

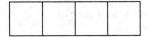

19

What is one possible value for x such that $0 < \dfrac{4}{5}x < \sqrt{x} < x$?

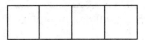

20

Which of the following is equivalent to $\dfrac{4}{2^{-2}(x+x)(x+x)}$ for all positive values of x?

A) $\dfrac{1}{x^4}$ B) $\dfrac{4}{x^2}$ C) $\dfrac{1}{4x^2}$ D) $\dfrac{16}{x^4}$

21

The square root of a certain positive number is twice the number itself. What is the number?

A) $\dfrac{1}{8}$ B) $\dfrac{1}{4}$ C) $\dfrac{1}{2}$ D) $\dfrac{1}{\sqrt{2}}$

22

Which of the following is equivalent to $\dfrac{2m\sqrt{2n} + m\sqrt{18n}}{m\sqrt{2}}$ for all positive values of m and n?

A) $3m\sqrt{3n}$

B) $5m\sqrt{2}$

C) $3\sqrt{3n}$

D) $5\sqrt{n}$

23

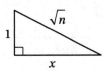

In the figure above, if $n > 1$, which of the following expresses x in terms of n?

A) $\sqrt{n^2 - 1}$

B) $\sqrt{n-1}$

C) $\sqrt{n+1}$

D) $\dfrac{\sqrt{n-1}}{2}$

EXERCISE SET 4 ANSWER KEY

No Calculator

1. 3
Simplify:
Divide by 3:

$$2a^2 + 3a - 5a^2 = 9$$
$$3a - 3a^2 = 9$$
$$a - a^2 = 3$$

2. 5 $(200)(4,000) = 800,000 = 8 \times 10^5$

3. 1/8 or .125

$$\frac{8w^2}{(8w)^2}$$

Exponential Law #5:

$$\frac{8w^2}{64w^2}$$

Cancel common factors:

$$\frac{1}{8}$$

4. 510
Exponential Law #8:
Substitute $2^x = 10$:
Simplify:

$$5(2^{2x}) + 2^x$$
$$5(2^x)^2 + 2^x$$
$$5(10)^2 + 10$$
$$5(10)^2 + 10 = 510$$

5. 64   If $(x + 2)(x + 4)(x + 6) = 0$, then $x = -2, -4$, or -6. Therefore 2^{-x} could equal 2^2, 2^4, or 2^6. The greatest of these is $2^6 = 64$.

6. 80

$$\left(4 + 4\sqrt{2}\right)^2$$

FOIL:

$$(4)^2 + 2(4)\left(4\sqrt{2}\right) + \left(4\sqrt{2}\right)^2$$

Simplify:

$$16 + 32\sqrt{2} + 32$$

Simplify:

$$48 + 32\sqrt{2}$$

Therefore $a = 48$ and $b = 32$ and $a + b = 80$.

7. 8

$$\frac{a}{3 + \sqrt{5}} = \frac{3 - \sqrt{5}}{b}$$

Cross-multiply:

$$ab = \left(3 + \sqrt{5}\right)\left(3 - \sqrt{5}\right)$$

Simplify:

$$ab = 9 - 5 = 4$$

Therefore $ab^{3/2} = 4^{3/2} = 8$

8. 5/3 or 1.66 or 1.67
Substitute $9 = 3^2$:
Exponential Law #8:
Take square root:

$$9^x = 25$$
$$(3^2)^x = 25$$
$$3^{2x} = 25$$
$$3^x = 5$$

Divide by 3:

$$\frac{3^x}{3^1} = \frac{5}{3}$$

Exponential Law #6:

$$3^{x-1} = \frac{5}{3}$$

9. B

$$\frac{g(4a, 2b)}{g(a, b)} = \frac{\dfrac{2(4a)}{(2b)^3}}{\dfrac{2a}{b^3}}$$

Simplify:

$$= \frac{2(4a)}{(2b)^3} \times \frac{b^3}{2a}$$

Simplify:

$$= \frac{8ab^3}{16ab^3} = \frac{1}{2}$$

10. C

$$\frac{2^n \times 2^n}{2^n \times 2}$$

Cancel common factor:

$$\frac{2^n}{2^1}$$

Exponential Law #6:

$$2^{n-1}$$

11. A
Combine like terms:
Exponential Law #4:

$$3^m + 3^m + 3^m$$
$$3(3^m)$$
$$3^{m+1}$$

12. B
Substitute $y = 5^x$:
Exponential Law #8:
Exponential Law #4:

$$5y^2$$
$$5(5^x)^2$$
$$5(5^{2x})$$
$$5^{2x+1}$$

Calculator

13. 64
Radical Law #1
Exponential Law #8:

$$n^2 = \sqrt{64^4}$$
$$n^2 = (64^4)^{1/2}$$
$$n^2 = 64^2$$

14. 5

$$\frac{1}{10^m} < 0.000025$$

Scientific Notation:

$$1 \times 10^{-m} < 2.5 \times 10^{-5}$$

Substitution and checking makes it clear that $m = 5$ is the smallest integer that satisfies the inequality.

15. 2.5

$$\frac{3}{3^{-k}} = 9\sqrt{27}$$

Exponential Law #6:
Simplify:
Express as exponentials:
Exponential Law #4:
Exponential Law #10:
Subtract 1:

$$3^{1-(-k)} = 9\sqrt{27}$$
$$3^{k+1} = 9 \times 3\sqrt{3}$$
$$3^{k+1} = 3^2 \times 3 \times 3^{\frac{1}{2}}$$
$$3^{k+1} = 3^{3.5}$$
$$k + 1 = 3.5$$
$$k = 2.5$$

16. 7
Exponential Law #8:
Exponential Law #4:
Exponential Law #10:
Subtract 2:
Divide by 5:

$$(x^m)^3(x^{m+1})^2 = x^{37}$$
$$(x^{3m})(x^{2m+2}) = x^{37}$$
$$x^{5m+2} = x^{37}$$
$$5m + 2 = 37$$
$$5m = 35$$
$$m = 7$$

17. 6
Factor:

$$9\sqrt{12} - 4\sqrt{27} = n\sqrt{3}$$
$$9\sqrt{4} \times \sqrt{3} - 4\sqrt{9} \times \sqrt{3} = n\sqrt{3}$$

Divide by $\sqrt{3}$:	$9\sqrt{4} - 4\sqrt{9} = n$
Simplify:	$18 - 12 = 6 = n$

---

18. **6** $8^{\frac{1}{6}} = \left(2^{-\frac{1}{12}}\right)^{-n}$

Substitute $8 = 2^3$: $(2^3)^{\frac{1}{6}} = \left(2^{-\frac{1}{12}}\right)^{-n}$

Exponential Law #8: $2^{\frac{1}{2}} = 2^{\frac{n}{12}}$

Exponential Law #10: $\dfrac{1}{2} = \dfrac{n}{12}$

Multiply by 12: $6 = n$

---

19. **$1 < x \le 1.56$** $0 < \dfrac{4}{5}x < \sqrt{x} < x$

Middle inequality: $\dfrac{4}{5}x < \sqrt{x}$

Square both sides: $\dfrac{16}{25}x^2 < x$

Divide by x: $\dfrac{16}{25}x < 1$

(Since $x > 0$, we do not "swap" the inequality.)

Multiply by 25/16: $x < \dfrac{25}{16} = 1.563$

Last inequality: $\sqrt{x} < x$

Square both sides: $x < x^2$
Divide by x: $1 < x$
Therefore, x must be both greater than 1 and less than or equal to 1.56.

---

20. **B** $\dfrac{4}{2^{-2}(x+x)(x+x)}$

Simplify: $\dfrac{4 \times 2^2}{(2x)^2}$

Simplify: $\dfrac{16}{4x^2}$

Cancel common factor: $\dfrac{4}{x^2}$

---

21. **B**   Translate: $\sqrt{x} = 2x$
Square both sides: $x = 4x^2$
Divide by $4x$: $\dfrac{1}{4} = x$

---

22. **D** $\dfrac{2m\sqrt{2n} + m\sqrt{18n}}{m\sqrt{2}}$

Factor terms: $\dfrac{2m\sqrt{2}\sqrt{n} + m\sqrt{9}\sqrt{2}\sqrt{n}}{m\sqrt{2}}$

Cancel common factors: $2\sqrt{n} + \sqrt{9}\sqrt{n}$

Combine like terms: $2\sqrt{n} + 3\sqrt{n} = 5\sqrt{n}$

---

23. **B**   Pythagorean Theorem: $1^2 + x^2 = \left(\sqrt{n}\right)^2$

Simplify: $1 + x^2 = n$
Subtract 1: $x^2 = n - 1$

Take square root: $x = \sqrt{n-1}$

Skill 4: Working with Rational Expressions

Lesson 12: Interpreting and computing with rational expressions

Which of the following is equivalent to $\dfrac{2}{x}-\dfrac{1}{x+1}$ for all x greater than 0?

A) $\dfrac{2}{x+1}$

B) $\dfrac{1}{x(x+1)}$

C) $\dfrac{x+2}{x^2+x}$

D) $\dfrac{3}{x+1}$

When adding, subtracting, multiplying, or dividing rational expressions, just follow the rules for working with fractions.

- When adding or subtracting fractions, first get a common denominator, then combine numerators.

$$\frac{x+1}{x}-\frac{x}{x-1}=\frac{(x+1)(x-1)}{(x)(x-1)}-\frac{x(x)}{(x)(x-1)}$$
$$=\frac{(x^2-1)-x^2}{(x)(x-1)}=\frac{-1}{x^2-x}=\frac{1}{x-x^2}$$
$$=\frac{1}{x(1-x)}$$

- When multiplying fractions, just multiply straight across.

$$\frac{x+1}{x}\times\frac{x}{x-1}=\frac{(x+1)(x)}{(x)(x-1)}=\frac{x+1}{x-1}$$

- To divide by a fraction, just multiply by its reciprocal.

$$\frac{x+1}{x}\div\frac{x}{x-1}=\frac{x+1}{x}\times\frac{x-1}{x}=\frac{x^2-1}{x^2}$$

(*Medium*) To simplify this difference of fractions, we must find a common denominator.

$$\frac{2}{x}-\frac{1}{x+1}=\frac{2(x+1)}{x(x+1)}-\frac{1x}{x(x+1)}=\frac{2x+2-x}{x(x+1)}=\frac{x+2}{x^2+x}$$

So the correct answer is (C).

If $\dfrac{9x^2}{3x+1}$ is equivalent to $\dfrac{1}{3x+1}+B$ for all x, which of the following is equivalent to B?

A) $3x-1$

B) $3x+1$

C) $9x^2$

D) $9x^2-1$

(*Hard*) It helps to notice that the given rational expression is "improper," but that the transformed expression is not. Recall that an "improper fraction," like 5/3, is one in which the numerator is larger than the denominator. Such fractions can also be expressed as "mixed numbers," which include an integer and a "proper fraction:" $5/3 = 1\tfrac{2}{3}$. Similarly, an "improper rational expression" is one in which the **degree** of the numerator is greater than the **degree** of the denominator. In the expression $\dfrac{9x^2}{3x+1}$, the numerator has a degree of 2 and the denominator has a degree of 1. Just as with improper fractions, we can convert this to a "mixed" expression by just doing the division:

$$
\begin{array}{r}
3x-1 \\
3x+1\overline{)9x^2+0x+0} \\
\underline{9x^2+3x} \\
-3x+0 \\
\underline{-3x-1} \\
1
\end{array}
$$

which means that $\dfrac{9x^2}{3x+1}$ equals $3x-1+\dfrac{1}{3x+1}$. Therefore, the correct answer is (A).

$$\frac{1}{x} + b = \frac{1}{y}$$

Let x represent the time, in hours, it takes pump A to fill a standard tank, and let y represent the time, in hours, it takes pump A and pump B, working together, to fill the same standard tank. If the equation above represents this situation, then b must represent

A) the time, in hours, it takes pump B, working alone, to fill the standard tank
B) the portion of the standard tank that pump B fills when the pumps work together to fill the entire standard tank
C) the rate, in standard tanks per hour, of pump B
D) the difference between the rates, in standard tanks per hour, of pump B and pump A

Rational expressions are often used to express **rates**. (Remember: *rate*, *rational*, and *ratio* all derive from the same Latin root.) When working with rational expressions that **represent real quantities**, it often helps to **think in terms of the rate-units that they represent**.

For instance, if t represents the amount of time, in hours, it takes someone to paint n rooms, then t/n represents the number of "hours per room" and n/t represents the number of "rooms per hour."

(*Medium-hard*) You may find it helpful to review Chapter 8, Lesson 5, "Rates and unit rates" before tackling this problem. We are told that x represents the number of "hours per tank" for pump A, that is, the number of hours it takes pump A to fill one standard tank. Therefore, its reciprocal, $1/x$, must represent the number of "tanks per hour" for pump A, that is, the number of tanks (or fraction of a tank) that pump A can fill in one hour. Likewise, since y represents the number of "hours per tank" when the two pumps work together, $1/y$ must represent the number of "tanks per hour" that the two pumps can fill when working together.

The essential fact in this situation is that "the rate (in tanks per hour) at which the two pumps work together must equal the sum of the rates (in tanks per hour) of the two pumps working separately." (For instance, if pump A can fill 2 tanks per hour and pump B can fill 3 tanks per hour, then working together they can fill 5 tanks per hour.)

Since the given equation essentially says, "the rate of pump A plus b = the rate of pump A and pump B working together," b must represent the rate (in tanks per hour) of pump B. Therefore, the correct answer is (C).

Lesson 13: Simplifying rational expressions

If $x = 3a$ and $a \neq 2$, which of the following is equivalent to $\dfrac{x^2 - 36}{(x-6)^2}$?

A) $\dfrac{a+2}{a-2}$

B) $\dfrac{3a+2}{3a-2}$

C) $\dfrac{3a+2}{3a}$

D) $\dfrac{9a^2 - 36}{9a^2 + 36}$

Since rational expressions are just fractions (although perhaps complicated ones), we simplify them **exactly the same way we simplify any fraction**, that is, by **cancelling common factors in the numerator and denominator** (which is equivalent to dividing by 1), or **multiplying numerator and denominator by a convenient factor** (which is equivalent to multiplying by 1).

- Factoring and cancelling common factors:

$$\frac{2x^2 - 18}{x^2 + 5x + 6} = \frac{2(x+3)(x-3)}{(x+2)(x+3)} = \frac{2(x-3)}{x+2}$$

- Multiplying by a common factor:

$$\frac{\dfrac{1}{3} + \dfrac{1}{x}}{2} = \frac{\left(\dfrac{1}{3} + \dfrac{1}{x}\right) \times 3x}{2 \times 3x} = \frac{x+3}{6x}$$

(*Medium*) This question is asking us to translate an expression in x into an expression in a, which requires making a substitution. However, it is a bit simpler if we don't substitute right away, but instead simplify the given expression:

$$\frac{x^2 - 36}{(x-6)^2}$$

Factor: $\dfrac{(x+6)(x-6)}{(x-6)(x-6)}$

Cancel common factor: $\dfrac{x+6}{x-6}$

Substitute $x = 3a$: $\dfrac{3a+6}{3a-6}$

Divide numerator and
denominator by 3: $\dfrac{a+2}{a-2}$

Therefore the answer is (A). Bonus question: Why did the question have to mention that $a \neq 2$?

If $\dfrac{2x^2 - 18}{5x^2 - 10x - 15} = \dfrac{a(x+b)}{x+1}$ for all $x > 3$, where a and b are constants, what is the value of ab?

A) $\dfrac{2}{5}$

B) $\dfrac{3}{5}$

C) $\dfrac{6}{5}$

D) $\dfrac{7}{5}$

(*Medium-hard*) The expression on the left side of the equation is obnoxious and in desperate need of simplification:

$$\frac{2x^2 - 18}{5x^2 - 10x - 15}$$

Factor: $\dfrac{2(x+3)(x-3)}{5(x+1)(x-3)}$

Cancel common factor
(okay since $x > 3$): $\dfrac{2(x+3)}{5(x+1)}$

Divide numerator and
denominator by 5: $\dfrac{\dfrac{2}{5}(x+3)}{x+1}$

This last step, which may seem strange, is important because it shows us how the two sides of the equation "match up." If this equation is to be true for "all $x > 3$" then a must equal 2/5 and b must equal 3. Therefore, $ab = (2/5)(3) = 6/5$, and the correct answer is (C). Bonus question: Why did the question mention that $x > 3$?

Lesson 14: Solving rational equations

If $x > 0$ and $\dfrac{1}{x-1} - \dfrac{1}{x+1} = 2$, what is the value of x?

[No calculator]

A) $\sqrt{2}$

B) $\sqrt{3}$

C) $\sqrt{5}$

D) $\sqrt{7}$

When solving an equation that includes fractions or rational expressions, you may find it helpful to **simplify the equation by multiplying both sides by the "common denominator"** (that is, the common multiple of the denominators).

$$\frac{x}{5} + \frac{1}{x} = 2$$

Multiply by $5x$:
$$5x \times \left(\frac{x}{5} + \frac{1}{x}\right) = 5x \times 2$$

Distribute:
$$\frac{5x^2}{5} + \frac{5x}{x} = 10x$$

Simplify:
$$x^2 + 5 = 10x$$

Notice that, in this case, the equation simplifies to a quadratic, which is relatively easy to work with.

(*Hard*) Let's apply this strategy to our equation:

$$\frac{1}{x-1} - \frac{1}{x+1} = 2$$

Multiply by $(x-1)(x+1)$:
$$(x-1)(x+1)\left(\frac{1}{x-1} - \frac{1}{x+1}\right) = 2(x-1)(x+1)$$

Distribute:
$$\frac{(x-1)(x+1)}{x-1} - \frac{(x-1)(x+1)}{x+1} = 2(x^2-1)$$

Simplify:
$$(x+1) - (x-1) = 2x^2 - 2$$

Simplify:
$$2 = 2x^2 - 2$$

Add 2:
$$4 = 2x^2$$

Divide by 2:
$$2 = x^2$$

Take the square root:
$$\pm\sqrt{2} = x$$

But since the equation states that $x > 0$, the correct answer is (A).

The function f is defined by the equation $f(x) = x^2 - 3x - 18$ and the function h is defined by the equation $h(x) = \dfrac{f(x)}{2x - 12}$. For what value of x does $h(x) = 6$?

A) -6

B) -3

C) 0

D) 9

(*Hard*) The first thing we should try to do is simplify the expression for $h(x)$.

$$h(x) = \frac{f(x)}{2x - 12}$$

Substitute $f(x) = x^2 - 3x - 18$:
$$h(x) = \frac{x^2 - 3x - 18}{2x - 12}$$

Factor using Product-Sum Method:
$$h(x) = \frac{(x+3)(x-6)}{2(x-6)}$$

Cancel common factor:
$$h(x) = \frac{x+3}{2}$$

Solve for x if $h(x) = 6$:
$$6 = \frac{x+3}{2}$$

Multiply by 2:
$$12 = x + 3$$

Subtract 3:
$$9 = x$$

Therefore, the correct answer is (D).

Exercise Set 5 (No Calculator)

1

If $\dfrac{1}{3} - \dfrac{1}{5} = \dfrac{y}{9}$, what is the value of y?

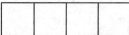

2

If $\dfrac{x}{x+1} + \dfrac{1}{x-1} = \dfrac{25}{24}$ and $x > 0$, what is the value of x?

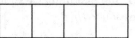

3

If $\dfrac{1}{x-2} - \dfrac{1}{x+2} = \dfrac{8}{5}$, what is the value of x^2?

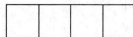

4

If $2 - \dfrac{1}{z} = -\dfrac{5}{6}$, what is the value of z?

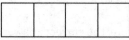

5

Let $g(x) = x^2 - 9x + 18$ and $h(x) = \dfrac{g(x)}{x-a}$, where a is a constant. If $h(4) = \dfrac{1}{12}$, what is the value of a?

6

If $\dfrac{1}{2x-2} - \dfrac{1}{2x+1} = \dfrac{a}{4x^2 - 2x - b}$ for all values of x greater than 1, what is the value of $a + b$?

7

Which of the following is equivalent to $\dfrac{2}{1-x} + \dfrac{x}{x-1}$ for all x greater than 1?

A) $\dfrac{x+2}{x^2-1}$

B) $\dfrac{x+2}{x-1}$

C) $\dfrac{x-2}{x^2-1}$

D) $\dfrac{x-2}{x-1}$

8

For how many distinct integer values of n is $\dfrac{n+5}{n+2} > 2$?

A) Zero   B) One   C) Two   D) Three

9

If $a = \dfrac{1}{4}x$ and $a > 1$, which of the following is equivalent to $\dfrac{4(x-4)^2}{4x^2 - 64}$?

A) $\dfrac{a-4}{a+4}$

B) $\dfrac{a^2-4}{a^2+4}$

C) $\dfrac{a-1}{a+1}$

D) $\dfrac{a^2-1}{a^2+1}$

Exercise Set 5 (Calculator)

10

If $\dfrac{x}{5} - \dfrac{3}{x} = 2$, what is the value of $x^2 - 10x$?

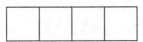

11

For how many positive integer values of k is $\dfrac{1}{10k} > 0.001$?

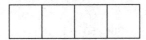

12

If $g(x) = x^2 - 9x + 18$ and $h(x) = \dfrac{g(x)}{x^2 + 3}$, what is the value of $h(9)$?

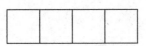

13

If $\dfrac{1}{x+1} + \dfrac{1}{x-1} = 9$, what is the value of $\dfrac{9x}{x^2 - 1}$?

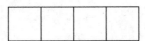

14

If $\dfrac{c}{c-1} \div \dfrac{c+1}{2c} = \dfrac{10}{c^2 - 1}$, what is the value of c^2?

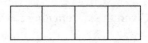

15

If $\dfrac{4x^2 + 1}{2x + 1} = 2x - 1 + \dfrac{a}{2x + 1}$ for all values of x, what is the value of a?

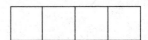

16

Which of the following is equivalent to $\dfrac{1}{b} - \dfrac{b^2}{2}$ for all positive values of b?

A) $\dfrac{b^2 - 1}{2 - b}$

B) $\dfrac{b^2 - 1}{2b}$

C) $\dfrac{b^3 - 2}{2b}$

D) $\dfrac{2 - b^3}{2b}$

17

$$\frac{1}{a} - \frac{1}{b} = 2$$

$$\frac{1}{a} + \frac{1}{b} = 8$$

Given the system above, what is the value of $a + b$?

A) $\dfrac{1}{15}$

B) $\dfrac{1}{8}$

C) $\dfrac{8}{15}$

D) $\dfrac{8}{5}$

18

If one proofreader takes n hours to edit 30 pages and another takes m hours to edit 50 pages, and together they can edit x pages per hour, which of the following equations must be true?

A) $\dfrac{30}{n} + \dfrac{50}{m} = x$

B) $\dfrac{30}{n} + \dfrac{50}{m} = \dfrac{1}{x}$

C) $\dfrac{n}{30} + \dfrac{m}{50} = x$

D) $\dfrac{n}{30} + \dfrac{m}{50} = \dfrac{1}{x}$

EXERCISE SET 5 ANSWER KEY

No Calculator

1. 6/5 or 1.2

$$\frac{1}{3} - \frac{1}{5} = \frac{y}{9}$$

Multiply by 45: $15 - 9 = 5y$
(45 is the least common multiple of the denominators.)
Simplify: $6 = 5y$
Divide by 5: $6/5 = y$

2. 7

$$\frac{x}{x+1} + \frac{1}{x-1} = \frac{25}{24}$$

Multiply by $24(x + 1)(x - 1)$:
$$24x(x - 1) + 24(x + 1) = 25(x + 1)(x - 1)$$
Distribute: $24x^2 - 24x + 24x + 24 = 25x^2 - 25$
Gather like terms: $0 = x^2 - 49$
Add 49: $49 = x^2$
Take square root: $\pm 7 = x$
Since x must be positive, $x = 7$.

3. 13/2 or 6.5

$$\frac{1}{x-2} - \frac{1}{x+2} = \frac{8}{5}$$

Multiply by $5(x - 2)(x + 2)$:
$$5(x + 2) - 5(x - 2) = 8(x - 2)(x + 2)$$
Distribute: $5x + 10 - 5x + 10 = 8x^2 - 32$
Subtract 20 and simplify: $0 = 8x^2 - 52$
Add 52: $52 = 8x^2$
Divide by 8: $52/8 = 13/2 = x^2$
Remember, the question asks for the value of x^2, not x, so don't worry about taking the square root.

4. 6/17 or .353

$$2 - \frac{1}{z} = -\frac{5}{6}$$

Multiply by $6z$: $12z - 6 = -5z$
Add $5z$ and 6: $17z = 6$
Divide by 17: $z = 6/17$

5. 28

$$h(4) = \frac{g(4)}{4 - a} = \frac{1}{12}$$

Use definition of g:
$$\frac{4^2 - 9(4) + 18}{4 - a} = \frac{1}{12}$$
Simplify:
$$\frac{-2}{4 - a} = \frac{1}{12}$$
Cross-multiply: $4 - a = -24$
Add 24 and a: $28 = a$

6. 5

$$\frac{1}{2x - 2} - \frac{1}{2x + 1}$$

Combine fractions:
$$\frac{(2x + 1) - (2x - 2)}{(2x - 2)(2x + 1)}$$
Simplify:
$$\frac{3}{4x^2 - 2x - 2}$$
Since $\dfrac{3}{4x^2 - 2x - 2}$ must equal $\dfrac{a}{4x^2 - 2x - b}$ for all values of x, $a = 3$ and $b = 2$, so $a + b = 5$.

7. D

Since $(1 - x) = -(x - 1)$:

$$\frac{2}{1 - x} + \frac{x}{x - 1} = \frac{-2}{x - 1} + \frac{x}{x - 1}$$

$$= \frac{x - 2}{x - 1}$$

8. C

$$\frac{n + 5}{n + 2} > 2$$

Recall from Chapter 7, Lesson 9, on solving inequalities, that we need to consider two conditions. First, if $n + 2$ is positive (that is, $n > -2$), we can multiply on both sides without "flipping" the inequality: $n + 5 > 2n + 4$
Subtract n and 4: $1 > n$
So n must be between -2 and 1, and the integer values of -1 and 0 are both solutions. Next, we consider the possibility $n + 2$ is negative (that is, $n < -2$), and therefore multiplying both sides by $n + 2$ requires "flipping" the inequality:

$$n + 5 < 2n + 4$$

Subtract n and 4: $1 < n$
But there are no numbers that are both less than -2 and greater than 1, so this yields no new solutions.

9. C

$$\frac{4(x - 4)^2}{4x^2 - 64}$$

Factor:
$$\frac{4(x - 4)^2}{4(x - 4)(x + 4)}$$
Cancel common factors:
$$\frac{x - 4}{x + 4}$$
Substitute $x = 4a$:
$$\frac{4a - 4}{4a + 4}$$
Cancel common factor:
$$\frac{a - 1}{a + 1}$$

Calculator

10. 15

$$\frac{x}{5} - \frac{3}{x} = 2$$

Multiply by $5x$: $x^2 - 15 = 10x$
Add 15, subtract $10x$: $x^2 - 10x = 15$
Notice that you should *not* worry about solving for x!

11. 2

$$\frac{1}{10k} > 0.001$$

Use common base: $10^{-k} > 10^{-3}$
Exponential Law #10: $-k > -3$
Multiply by -1: $k < 3$
Therefore, the two positive integer solutions are 1 and 2.

12. **3/14 or .214**

$$h(9) = \frac{g(9)}{9^2 + 3}$$

Use definition of g:

$$h(9) = \frac{9^2 - 9(9) + 18}{84}$$

Simplify:

$$h(9) = \frac{18}{84} = \frac{3}{14}$$

---

13. **81/2 or 40.5**

$$\frac{1}{x+1} + \frac{1}{x-1} = 9$$

Combine fractions:

$$\frac{(x+1) + (x+1)}{(x+1)(x-1)} = 9$$

Simplify:

$$\frac{2x}{x^2 - 1} = 9$$

Multiply by 9/2:

$$\frac{9x}{x^2 - 1} = \frac{81}{2}$$

---

14. **5**

$$\frac{c}{c-1} \div \frac{c+1}{2c} = \frac{10}{c^2 - 1}$$

Convert to ×:

$$\frac{c}{c-1} \times \frac{2c}{c+1} = \frac{10}{c^2 - 1}$$

Multiply:

$$\frac{2c^2}{c^2 - 1} = \frac{10}{c^2 - 1}$$

Multiply by $c^2 - 1$:

$$2c^2 = 10$$

Divide by 2:

$$c^2 = 5$$

---

15. **2** Notice that the right-hand side of the equation is the "proper" form of the "improper" fraction on the left, and that a is the remainder when the division of the polynomials is completed:

$$
\begin{array}{r}
2x - 1 \\
2x+1 \overline{)\, 4x^2 + 0x + 1} \\
\underline{4x^2 + 2x} \\
-2x + 1 \\
\underline{-2x - 1} \\
2
\end{array}
$$

16. **D**

$$\frac{1}{b} - \frac{b^2}{2}$$

Common denominator:

$$\frac{2}{2b} - \frac{b^3}{2b}$$

Combine:

$$\frac{2 - b^3}{2b}$$

---

17. **C**

$$\frac{1}{a} - \frac{1}{b} = 2$$

$$\frac{1}{a} + \frac{1}{b} = 8$$

Add equations:

$$\frac{2}{a} = 10$$

Multiply by a:

$$2 = 10a$$

Divide by 10:

$$1/5 = a$$

Subtract equations:

$$\frac{-2}{b} = -6$$

Multiply by $-b$:

$$2 = 6b$$

Divide by 6:

$$1/3 = b$$

Therefore, $a + b = 1/5 + 1/3 = 8/15$.

---

18. **A** The number of pages they can edit together in an hour must equal the sum of the number of pages they can edit separately. The number of pages the first proofreader can edit per hour is $30/n$, and the number of pages the second proofreader can edit per hour is $50/m$. Since they can edit x pages per hour together,

$$\frac{30}{n} + \frac{50}{m} = x.$$

NOTE: You can avoid the most common mistakes with this problem by paying attention to the units of each term. The units of two sides, as well as the unit of each term in a sum or difference, must "match." Notice that the unit for all of the terms is pages/hour.

CHAPTER 10

THE SAT MATH: ADDITIONAL TOPICS

The SAT Math: Additional Topics

What other special topics are included on the SAT Math test?

About 10% (6 out of 58 points) of the SAT Math questions are "Additional Topics" questions. These include topics like

- analyzing triangles using the Pythagorean Theorem
- graphing circles and other figures in the xy-plane
- analyzing areas, circumferences, chords, and sectors of circles
- measuring angles and arcs in radians
- working with area and volume and their formulas
- using the theorems of congruence and similarity
- working with basic trigonometric relationships including cofunction identities
- calculating with imaginary and complex numbers

Why are these topics important?

These topics from geometry, trigonometry, and advanced analysis are crucial to work in engineering, physics, architecture, and even design. Although they are not essential to every college major, they do provide tools for understanding and analyzing advanced concepts across the curriculum.

Sound intimidating? It's not.

Some of you have already spent some time in math class studying these topics. If not, the three skills described in these 12 lessons will give you the knowledge and practice you need to master them.

Skill 1: Understanding Geometric Relationships

Lesson 1: Intersecting and parallel lines

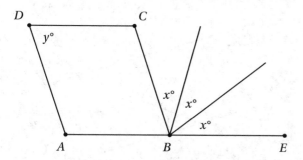

In the figure above, $ABCD$ is a parallelogram, and point B lies on $\overline{AE}$. If $x = 40$, what is the value of y?

A) 40   B) 50   C) 60   D) 70

(*Medium*) Since $ABCD$ is a parallelogram, we can take advantage of the Parallel Lines Theorem.

The Intersecting Lines Theorem

When two lines cross, four angles are formed. The vertical angles are congruent and adjacent angles are supplementary (that is, they have a sum of 180°).

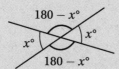

The Parallel Lines Theorem

When two parallel lines are crossed by a third line, eight angles are formed. If the third line is perpendicular to one of the parallel lines, then it's perpendicular to the other and all eight angles are right angles. Otherwise, all four acute angles are congruent, all four obtuse angles are congruent, and any acute angle is supplementary to any obtuse angle.

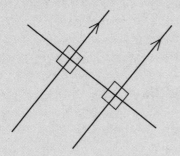

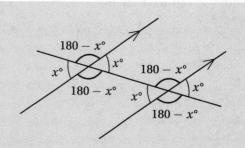

Helpful Tip

When dealing with parallel lines, especially in complicated figures, we can simplify things by considering angles in pairs. The important pairs form one of four letters: F, Z, C, or U.

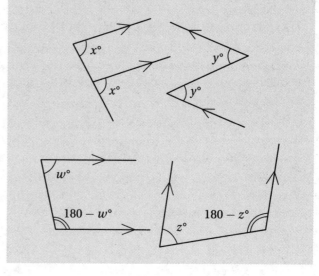

First, let's mark up the diagram with what we know from the Parallel Lines Theorem.

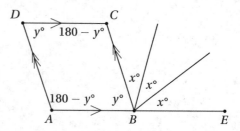

Since the pairs of opposite sides are parallel, the consecutive angles in the parallelogram must be supplementary (that is, have a sum of 180°). Notice that these pairs of consecutive angles form "U"s or "C"s as mentioned in the previous Helpful Tip. This implies that **opposite angles are congruent** in a parallelogram.

Since $\overline{ABE}$ is a straight (180°) angle:
$$y + x + x + x = 180$$
Substitute $x = 40$ and simplify: $y + 120 = 180$
Subtract 120: $y = 60$
Therefore, the correct answer is (C).

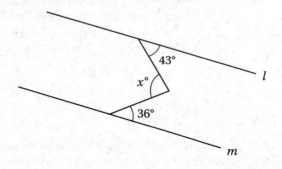

In the figure above, lines l and m are parallel. What is the value of x?

A) 43   B) 79   C) 86   D) 101

(*Hard*) Although our diagram includes parallel lines, it doesn't seem to show any of the parallel line "letter pairs" that we discussed above, because no line directly connects the parallel lines. We can fix this problem by drawing an extra line that's parallel to l and m through the vertex of the angle.

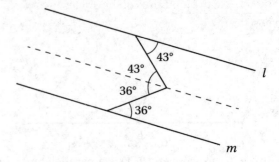

Now we have two "Z" pairs of angles (otherwise known as "alternate interior" pairs) that show that the middle angle is actually the sum of two smaller angles of 36° and 43°, and therefore, $x = 36 + 43 = 79$, and the correct answer is (B).

Lesson 2: Triangles

Angle Sum Theorem

The sum of the measures of the angles in any triangle is 180°.

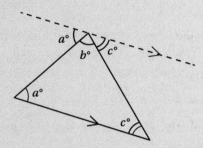

We can prove this with the "draw an extra line" trick. If we take any triangle, pick any of its vertices, and draw a line through that vertex that is parallel to the opposite side, we get a picture like the one above. Since the line we've drawn is a 180° angle, and since the "Z" angle pairs must be congruent, we've proven that $a + b + c = 180$.

Side-Angle Theorem

The largest angle in a triangle is always across from the largest side, and the smallest angle is always across from the smallest side.

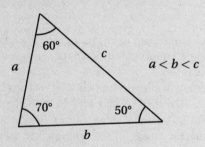

Isosceles Triangle Theorem

If two sides in a triangle are congruent, the two angles across from those sides are also congruent. Conversely, if two angles in a triangle are congruent, the two sides across from them are also congruent.

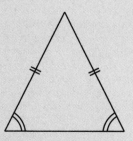

Exterior Angle Theorem

If the side of a triangle is extended beyond a vertex, it makes an exterior angle with the adjacent side. The measure of this exterior angle is equal to the sum of the two remote interior angles.

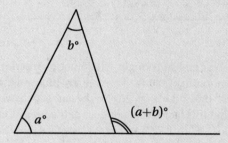

The Triangle Inequality

The sum of any two sides of a triangle must always be greater than the third side.

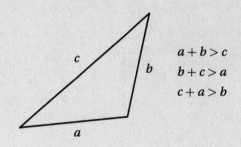

$$a + b > c$$
$$b + c > a$$
$$c + a > b$$

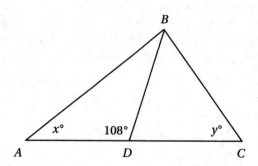

In the figure above, if $AD = DB = DC$, what is the value of $x + y$?

A) 72

B) 90

C) 96

D) 108

(*Medium*) Since angle *ADB* and angle *BDC* are supplementary and *AD* = *DB* = *DC*, we can take advantage of the Isosceles Triangle Theorem to mark up the diagram.

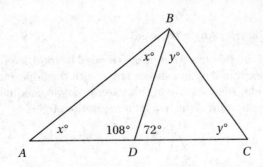

Now let's look at triangle *ABC*. Since its interior angles must have a sum of 180°, $x + x + y + y = 180$, and therefore, $2x + 2y = 180$ and $x + y = 90$. So the correct answer is (B). Notice that this fact is independent of the measures of the other two (108° and 72°) angles. As long as *AD* = *DB* = *DC*, this relationship will hold. We can see these angle relationships if we notice that these three segments could all be radii of a circle centered at *D*.

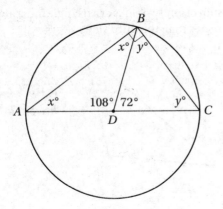

You may remember from studying geometry that any "inscribed" angle (an angle inside a circle with a vertex on the circle) intercepts an arc on the circle that is twice its measure. Since angle *ABC* is an inscribed angle that intercepts a 180° arc, it must have a measure of 90° and therefore, $x + y = 90$.

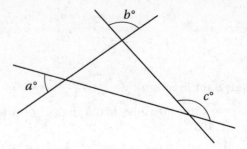

The figure above shows three intersecting lines. What is the value of *c* in terms of *a* and *b*?

A) $180 - a - b$

B) $180 - a + b$

C) $90 + b - a$

D) $a + b$

(*Easy*) First, we should notice that two of the angles are "vertical" to two interior angles of the triangle, and the other is an exterior angle.

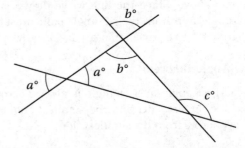

Since the *c*° angle is an exterior angle to the triangle, the Exterior Angle Theorem tells us that $c = a + b$, so the correct answer is (D).

Alternately, we could just choose reasonable values for *a* and *b*, like $a = 50$ and $b = 90$, and then analyze the diagram in terms of these values. This would imply that the interior angles of the triangle are 50°, 90°, and 40°, and *c*° would then be the measure of the supplement of 40°, which is 140°. If we then plug these values for *a* and *b* into all of the choices, the only one that yields 140 is D.

Lesson 3: The xy-plane

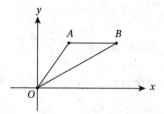

Note: Figure not drawn to scale.

In the xy-plane above, points A and B lie on the graph of the line $y = 6$. If $\overline{OB}$ has a slope of $\frac{1}{2}$ and $AB = 5$, what is the slope of $\overline{OA}$?

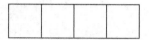

(*Medium-hard*) To analyze this diagram, we must recall the definition of slope from Chapter 7, Lesson 5.

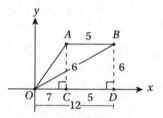

First, let's drop two perpendicular segments from A and B to points C and D, respectively, on the x-axis. Since A and B lie on the line $y = 6$, they are both 6 units from the x-axis, and so $AC = BD = 6$. Then, since the slope of OB is ½, $BD/OD = ½$, and therefore, $OD = 12$. Since $AB = 5$, $CD = 5$ also, and therefore, $OC = 12 - 5 = 7$. (Don't worry that $\overline{OC}$ looks shorter than $\overline{CD}$ in the diagram. Remember, the figure is not drawn to scale!) This gives us everything we need to find the slope of $\overline{OA}$, which connects $(0, 0)$ to $(7, 6)$. By the slope formula from Chapter 7, Lesson 5, slope $= (6 - 0)/(7 - 0) = 6/7 = 0.857$.

Working in the Coordinate Plane

Finding Segment Midpoints. To find the coordinates of a **midpoint**, just average the coordinates of the **endpoints**.

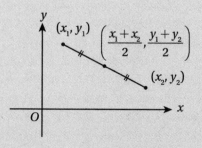

Finding Slopes. To find the **slope** of a line in the xy-plane from any two points on the line, use the **slope formula**.

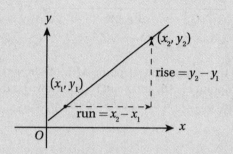

$$\text{slope} = \frac{\text{rise}}{\text{run}} = \frac{y_2 - y_1}{x_2 - x_1}$$

Finding Areas. Remember that the **area** of a figure is just the number of **unit squares** that fit inside it. You don't always need to use a special formula to find the area of a figure. Even for very complicated shapes, you can sometimes find the area just by counting squares.

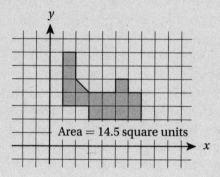

Area = 14.5 square units

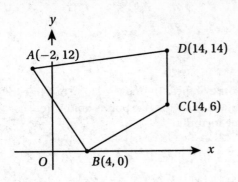

In the figure above, point M (not shown) is the midpoint of $\overline{AB}$ and point N (not shown) is the midpoint of $\overline{CD}$. What is the slope of $\overline{MN}$?

(*Medium*) To find the midpoint of a segment, we just need to take the average of the endpoints. Point M, the midpoint of $\overline{AB}$, therefore has coordinates

$\left(\dfrac{-2+4}{2}, \dfrac{12+0}{2}\right) = (1,6)$, and point N, the midpoint

of $\overline{CD}$, has coordinates $\left(\dfrac{14+14}{2}, \dfrac{6+14}{2}\right) = (14,10)$.

By the Slope Formula, then, the slope of $\overline{MN}$ is

$\dfrac{10-6}{14-1} = \dfrac{4}{13} = 0.307$ or 0.308.

Lesson 4: The Pythagorean Theorem and the Distance Formula

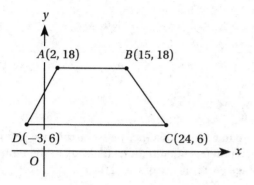

What is the perimeter of quadrilateral *ABCD* in the figure above?

(*Medium*) The perimeter of a figure is the distance around its edges. It's easy to find the lengths of $\overline{AB}$ and $\overline{DC}$ because they are horizontal. The length of a horizontal segment is just the difference between the *x*-coordinates of its endpoints. The length of $\overline{AB}$ is $15 - 2 = 13$, and the length of $\overline{DC}$ is $24 - (-3) = 27$. To find the lengths of $\overline{AD}$ and $\overline{BC}$, we can drop two vertical lines from points *A* and *B* to the bottom edge. This shows that $\overline{AD}$ and $\overline{BC}$ are hypotenuses of two right triangles as shown in the figure below.

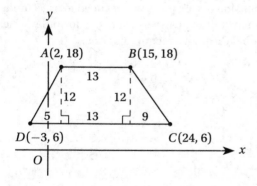

(Take a minute to confirm the lengths of all the segments for yourself.) With this information, we can find *AD* and *BC* by the Pythagorean Theorem.

The Pythagorean Theorem

If *a*, *b*, and *c* represent the sides of a right triangle in which *c* is the longest side (the hypotenuse),

$$a^2 + b^2 = c^2$$

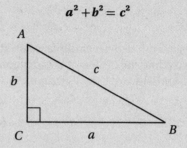

Special Right Triangles

The SAT Math test expects you to be familiar with four families of special right triangles: **45°-45°-90° triangles, 30°-60°-90° triangles, 3-4-5 triangles**, and **5-12-13 triangles**. Take some time to familiarize yourself with these particular side-side relationships and side-angle relationships so that you can use these relationships when you recognize these triangles in SAT Math questions.

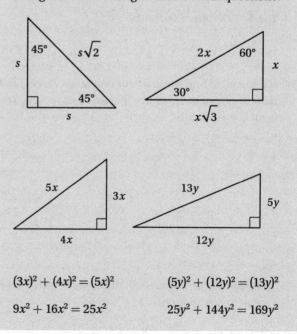

$(3x)^2 + (4x)^2 = (5x)^2$ $(5y)^2 + (12y)^2 = (13y)^2$

$9x^2 + 16x^2 = 25x^2$ $25y^2 + 144y^2 = 169y^2$

So, according to our diagram: $AD^2 = 5^2 + 12^2 = 169$ Take the square root: $AD = 13$

$BC^2 = 9^2 + 12^2 = 225$

Notice that triangle on the left is a 5-12-13 special right triangle, and the triangle on the right is a 3-4-5 special right triangle. Noticing these relationships provides a shortcut to using the Pythagorean Theorem.

$BC = 15$

Therefore, the perimeter of $ABCD$ is $13 + 15 + 27 + 13 = 68$.

The Distance Formula

$$d = \sqrt{(x_2 - x_1)^2 + (y_2 - y_1)^2}$$

We can generalize the technique we used in the previous problem to find the distance between *any* two points in the *xy*-plane. Just think of this distance as the length of the hypotenuse of a right triangle, as in the figure below. In other words, the Pythagorean Theorem and the Distance Formula are one and the same.

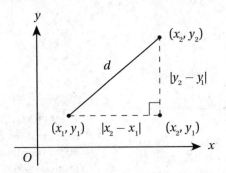

By the Pythagorean Theorem: $|x_2 - x_1|^2 + |y_2 - y_1|^2 = d^2$

Take the square root: $d = \sqrt{(x_2 - x_1)^2 + (y_2 - y_1)^2}$

The 3-D Distance Formula

$$d = \sqrt{(x_2 - x_1)^2 + (y_2 - y_1)^2 + (z_2 - z_1)^2}$$

If we need to find the distance between two points in three-dimensional *xyz*-space, we just need to use a modified version of the distance formula that includes the extra *z*-dimension. You can see where this formula comes from if you imagine trying to find the length of the longest diagonal through a rectangular box.

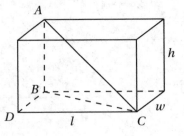

The length of this diagonal, AC, is also the hypotenuse of right triangle ABC, and so its length is given by the Pythagorean Theorem.

Pythagorean Theorem for ABC: $AC = \sqrt{(AB)^2 + (BC)^2}$

Pythagorean Theorem for BDC: $(BC)^2 = (BD)^2 + (DC)^2$

Substitute: $AC = \sqrt{(AB)^2 + (BD)^2 + (DC)^2}$

Since $AB = h$, $BD = w$, and $DC = l$ $AC = \sqrt{l^2 + w^2 + h^2}$

Exercise Set 1: Geometry (No Calculator)

1

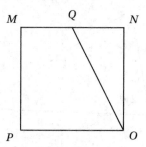

In the figure above, *MNOP* is a square and *Q* is the midpoint of $\overline{MN}$. If $QO = \dfrac{\sqrt{20}}{3}$, what is the area of square *MNOP*?

2

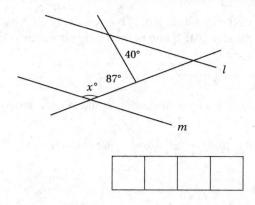

Lines *l* and *m* are parallel in the figure above. What is the value of *x*?

3

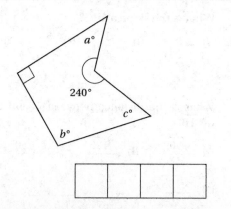

In the figure above, what is the value of $a + b + c$?

4

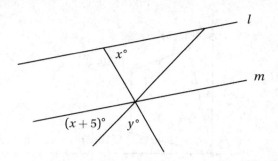

Lines *l* and *m* are parallel in the figure above. Which of the following expresses the value of *y* in terms of *x*?

A) $95 - 2x$

B) $165 - 2x$

C) $175 - 2x$

D) $185 - 2x$

5

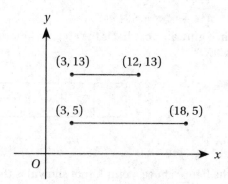

In the figure above, what is the distance between the midpoints (not shown) of the two line segments?

A) $\sqrt{68}$ B) $\sqrt{73}$ C) $\sqrt{76}$

D) $\sqrt{78}$

6

What is the perimeter of an equilateral triangle inscribed in a circle with circumference 24π?

A) $36\sqrt{2}$ B) $30\sqrt{3}$

C) $36\sqrt{3}$ D) $24\sqrt{6}$

Exercise Set 1: Geometry (Calculator)

Questions 7–9 are based on the figure below.

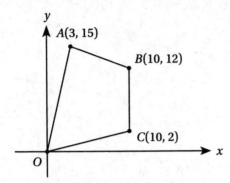

Note: Figure not drawn to scale.

7

In the figure above, what is the perimeter of quadri-lateral *ABCO*, to the nearest integer?

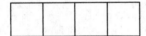

8

In the figure above, what is the area, in square units, of *ABCO*?

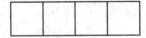

9

In the figure above, point *K* (not shown) is the mid-point of $\overline{OA}$, and point *M* (not shown) is the midpoint of $\overline{AB}$. What is the slope of $\overline{KM}$?

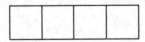

10

In the *xy*-plane, point *H* has coordinates (2, 1) and point *J* has coordinates (11, 13). If $\overline{HK}$ is parallel to the *x*-axis and $\overline{JK}$ is parallel to the *y*-axis, what it the perimeter of triangle *HJK*?

11

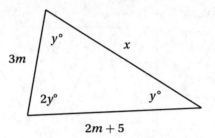

Note: Figure not drawn to scale.

In the figure above, what is the value of *x*?

A) $5\sqrt{2}$ B) $5\sqrt{3}$ C) $15\sqrt{2}$ D) $15\sqrt{3}$

Questions 12–15 are based on the situation described below.

In the *xy*-plane, *ABCD* is a square. Point *A* has coor-dinates (−1, 2) and point *B* has coordinates (3, 5).

12

Which of the following could be the coordinates of *C*?

A) (0, 9)   B) (6, 0)   C) (2, −2)   D) (−4, 6)

13

What is the area of square *ABCD*?

A) 25   B) 28   C) 30   D) 32

14

What is the slope of $\overline{BC}$?

A) $-\dfrac{4}{3}$ B) $-\dfrac{3}{4}$ C) $\dfrac{3}{4}$ D) $\dfrac{4}{3}$

15

What is the distance between *C* and the midpoint of $\overline{AB}$?

A) $\dfrac{\sqrt{50}}{4}$ B) $\dfrac{\sqrt{125}}{4}$ C) $\dfrac{\sqrt{50}}{2}$

D) $\dfrac{\sqrt{125}}{2}$

EXERCISE SET 1: GEOMETRY ANSWER KEY

No Calculator

1. 16/9 or 1.77 or 1.78 If we define x as the length of $\overline{QN}$, then the length of one side of the square is $2x$, and so the area of square $MNOP$ is $(2x)(2x) = 4x^2$. To find this value, we can apply the Pythagorean Theorem to right triangle QNO:

$$x^2 + (2x)^2 = \left(\frac{\sqrt{20}}{3}\right)^2$$

Simplify:

$$5x^2 = \frac{20}{9}$$

Divide by 5:

$$x^2 = \frac{20}{45} = \frac{4}{9}$$

Multiply by 4:

$$4x^2 = \frac{16}{9} = 1.77 \text{ or } 1.78$$

2. 133 The key is to notice simple relationships between angles until we get around to x.

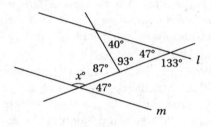

3. 210 Draw three lines as shown:

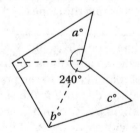

Since the polygon divides into 3 triangles, the sum of its internal angles is $(3)(180°) = 540°$. Therefore $a + b + c + 240 + 90 = 540$, and so $a + b + c = 210$.

4. C Using the Crossed Lines Theorem and the Parallel Lines Theorem, we can mark up the diagram like this:

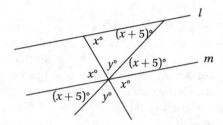

This shows that $x + y + x + 5 = 180$, and so $y = 175 - 2x$.

5. B The midpoint of the top segment is $\left(\frac{3 + 12}{2}, \frac{13 + 13}{2}\right) = \left(\frac{15}{2}, 13\right)$, and the midpoint of the bottom segment is $\left(\frac{3 + 18}{2}, \frac{5 + 5}{2}\right) = \left(\frac{21}{2}, 5\right)$, therefore, the distance between them is

$$\sqrt{\left(\frac{21}{2} - \frac{15}{2}\right)^2 + (13 - 5)^2} = \sqrt{3^2 + 8^2} = \sqrt{73}$$

6. C To solve this problem we must draw a diagram and find the relationship between the radius of the circle and the sides of the triangle. By the Isosceles Triangle Theorem, if all three sides of a triangle are congruent, then all three angles must be congruent. Since these angles also must have a sum of 180°, they must each be 60°. If we draw the bisectors of each of these angles, we divide the triangle into six smaller triangles. These smaller triangles are congruent 30°-60°-90° triangles, as shown here:

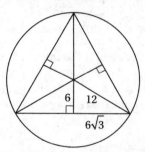

Since the circumference of the circle $(2\pi r)$ is 24π, its radius is 12. Since each of the hypotenuses of our right triangles is also a radius of the circle, we can find all of the sides of these triangles using the 30°-60°-90° relationships. Each side of the equilateral triangle is therefore $2(6\sqrt{3}) = 12\sqrt{3}$, and its perimeter is therefore

$$2(12\sqrt{3}) = 36\sqrt{3}.$$

Calculator

7. **43** Using the distance formula, we can calculate the lengths of each segment. $OA = \sqrt{234} \approx 15.30$, $AB = \sqrt{58} \approx 7.61$, $BC = 10$, and $OC = \sqrt{104} \approx 10.20$. Therefore, the perimeter is approximately $15.30 + 7.61 + 10 + 10.20 = 43.11$, which rounds to 43.

8. **107** Since we do not have a formula that directly calculates the area of such an odd-shaped quadrilateral, we must analyze its area in terms of simpler shapes. The simplest way to do this is by drawing a box around it. This turns the area of interest into a rectangle minus three right triangles, all of which have areas that can be easily calculated.

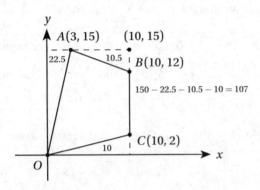

9. **6/5 or 1.2** The midpoint of $\overline{OA}$ is (1.5, 7.5) and the midpoint of $\overline{AB}$ is (6.5, 13.5); therefore, the slope of the segment between them is 6/5.

10. **36** If point K is on the same horizontal line as (2, 1), it must have a y-coordinate of 1, and if it is on the same vertical line as (11, 13), it must have an x-coordinate of 11. Therefore, K is the point (11, 1), and so $HK = 9$, $JK = 12$, and $HJ = \sqrt{9^2 + 12^2} = \sqrt{225} = 15$. Notice that it is a 3-4-5 triangle!

11. **C** Since the sum of the interior angles of any triangle is 180°, $y + y + 2y = 4y = 180$, and therefore $y = 45$. Therefore, this is a 45°-45°-90° right triangle. Since two angles are equal, the two opposite sides must also be equal, so $3m = 2m + 5$ and so $m = 5$ and the two legs each

have measure 15. Using the Pythagorean Theorem or the 45°-45°-90° shortcut, we can see that $x = 15\sqrt{2}$.

12. **A** The key to questions 12 through 15 is a good diagram in the xy-plane that represents the given information:

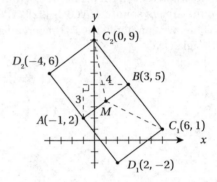

If $ABCD$ is a square, then the points A, B, C, and D must appear *in that order* around the square. Notice that to get from point A to point B, we must move 4 units to the right and 3 units up. This means that, in order to get to point C along a perpendicular of the same length, we must go either *3 units right and 4 units down*, or *3 units left and 4 units up*. This puts us either at (6, 1) or (0, 9).

13. **A** The diagram shows that AB is the length of the hypotenuse of a right triangle with legs 3 and 4. You should recognize this as the special 3-4-5 right triangle. If $AB = 5$, then the area of the square is $5^2 = 25$.

14. **A** Notice that the slope of $\overline{BC}$ is the same regardless of which option we choose for C. In either case, the slope formula tells us that the slope is $-4/3$.

15. **D** The midpoint of $\overline{AB}$ (point M above) is (1, 3.5). We can use the distance formula to find the distance between this point and either of the possible locations of C. (Notice that the distance is the same either way.) Alternately, we might notice that MC is the hypotenuse of a right triangle with legs 5 and 2.5. Either way, we get a value of $\dfrac{\sqrt{125}}{2}$.

Lesson 5: Circles

Which of the following equations represents a circle in the *xy*-plane that passes through the point (1, 5) and has a center of (3, 2)?

A) $(x - 3)^2 + (y - 2)^2 = \sqrt{13}$

B) $(x - 3)^2 + (y - 2)^2 = 13$

C) $(x - 1)^2 + (y - 5)^2 = 13$

D) $(x - 3)^2 + (y - 2)^2 = 25$

Equations of Circles

$$(x - h)^2 + (y - k)^2 = r^2$$

A circle is defined as the set of all points in a plane that are a fixed distance, *r*, from a fixed point, (*h, k*). The distance *r* is called the **radius** and (*h, k*) is the **center**.

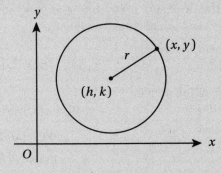

Therefore, by the Distance Formula, any point (*x, y*) on the circle must satisfy the equation

$$r = \sqrt{(x - h)^2 + (y - k)^2}$$

or $(x - h)^2 + (y - k)^2 = r^2$

(*Easy*) Since our circle has a center at (3, 2), its equation must have the form $(x - 3)^2 + (y - 2)^2 = r^2$, which eliminates choice (C). To find *r*, the radius, we simply have to find the distance between the center and any point on the circle. By the distance formula, this is $\sqrt{(3 - 1)^2 + (2 - 5)^2} = \sqrt{4 + 9} = \sqrt{13}$, and therefore, $r^2 = \left(\sqrt{13}\right)^2 = 13$. The correct answer is (B). If you chose (A), keep in mind that the equation for a circle has r^2 on the right side, not *r*.

What is the area, in square centimeters, of a circle with circumference of 16π centimeters?

A) 8π

B) 16π

C) 32π

D) 64π

(*Easy*) If the circumference of the circle is 16π centimeters: $2\pi r = 16\pi$

Divide by 2π: $r = 8$

Therefore, by the area formula: $\text{Area} = \pi r^2 = \pi(8)^2 = 64\pi$

So the correct answer is (D).

Circumference of a Circle

$$\text{circumference} = \pi d = 2\pi r$$

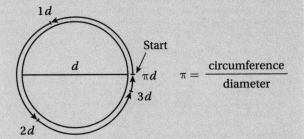

The number π ($\approx$ 3.14159 . . .) is defined as the number of diameters it takes to get around a circle. Put another way, π is the ratio of the circumference of any circle to its diameter. Since any diameter is twice the radius,

$$\pi = \frac{\text{circumference}}{\text{diameter}} = \frac{\text{circumference}}{2r} \text{ and so}$$

circumference = 2π*r*

Area of a Circle

$$A = \pi r^2$$

If we cut any circle into tiny enough sectors, and reassemble them as shown below, we can create a parallelogram-like shape that has a height of *r* and a length that is half of the circumference, or π*r*.

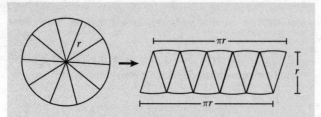

Since the area of any parallelogram is equal to its base times its height, the area of a circle is $(\pi r)(r) = \pi r^2$.

Tangents to Circles

A tangent line to a curve is a line that touches the curve without crossing it. **A tangent line to any circle is perpendicular to the radius at the point of tangency.**

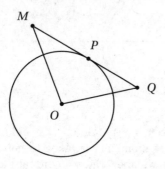

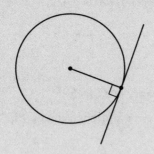

In the figure above, $\overline{MQ}$ is tangent to the circle at point P, $MO = \sqrt{269}$, and $OQ = \sqrt{244}$. If the circle has an area of 100π, what is the area of triangle MOQ?

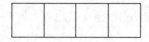

(*Hard*) The first thing we should do is draw radius $\overline{OP}$. Since this is a radius to the point of tangency, it is perpendicular to the tangent. We should also write in the given measures.

The area of the circle is 100π: $\pi(OP)^2 = 100\pi$

Divide by π: $(OP)^2 = 100$

Take square root: $OP = 10$

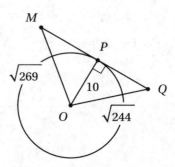

Notice that $\overline{OP}$ is the height of triangle MOQ if $\overline{MQ}$ is taken as its base. If we can find the length of base $\overline{MQ}$, we can simply use the triangle angle formula $A = \dfrac{bh}{2}$.

To find MQ, we can use the Pythagorean Theorem to find MP and PQ and just add them together.

Pythagorean Theorem for
triangle OPM: $10^2 + (MP)^2 = \left(\sqrt{269}\right)^2$

Pythagorean Theorem for
triangle OPQ: $10^2 + (PQ)^2 = \left(\sqrt{244}\right)^2$

Simplify: $100 + (MP)^2 = 269$

                                     $100 + (PQ)^2 = 244$

Subtract 100: $(MP)^2 = 169$

                                          $(PQ)^2 = 144$

Take square root: $MP = 13$

                                             $PQ = 12$

Therefore $MQ =$
$MP + PQ =$
$13 + 12 = 25$, so: Area of $MOQ = \dfrac{bh}{2} = \dfrac{25 \times 10}{2} = 125$

Lesson 6: Radians, chords, arcs, and sectors

What is the degree measure of an angle that measures 4.5 radians?

A) $4.5\pi^\circ$ B) $\dfrac{\pi^\circ}{40}$ C) $\dfrac{810^\circ}{\pi}$ D) $\dfrac{4\pi^\circ}{9}$

(*Medium*) Although many students will get this question wrong, it is very simple if you know how to convert radians to degrees. All we need to do to convert any radian measure to a degree measure is to multiply it by the conversion factor $\dfrac{180^\circ}{\pi \text{ radians}}$ (as explained below).

Therefore, $4.5 \text{ radians} = 4.5 \text{ radians} \times \dfrac{180^\circ}{\pi \text{ radians}} = \dfrac{810^\circ}{\pi}$, and the correct answer is (C).

The Radian

A **radian** is simply the radius of a circle used as a "measuring stick" for an arc on the circle and for its corresponding central angle.

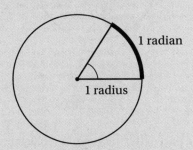

Because *circumference* $= 2\pi r$, a full rotation of 360° equals 2π radians, and 180° equals π radians.

Therefore, we may use $\dfrac{\pi \text{ radians}}{180^\circ}$ as a conversion factor to convert a degree measure to radians, and $\dfrac{180^\circ}{\pi \text{ radians}}$ as a conversion factor to convert a radian measure to degrees.

$$30^\circ = 30^\circ \times \frac{\pi \text{ radians}}{180^\circ} = \frac{\pi}{6} \text{ radians}$$

$$45^\circ = 45^\circ \times \frac{\pi \text{ radians}}{180^\circ} = \frac{\pi}{4} \text{ radians}$$

$$60^\circ = 60^\circ \times \frac{\pi \text{ radians}}{180^\circ} = \frac{\pi}{3} \text{ radians}$$

$$90^\circ = 90^\circ \times \frac{\pi \text{ radians}}{180^\circ} = \frac{\pi}{2} \text{ radians}$$

$$\pi \text{ radians} = \pi \times \frac{180^\circ}{\pi \text{ radians}} = 180^\circ$$

$$\frac{3\pi}{2} \text{ radians} = \frac{3\pi}{2} \times \frac{180^\circ}{\pi \text{ radians}} = 270^\circ$$

$$2\pi \text{ radians} = 2\pi \times \frac{180^\circ}{\pi \text{ radians}} = 360^\circ$$

Take some time to memorize the radian measures of the common degree measures above. Put them on flashcards and study them until you've mastered them.

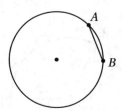

The circle above has an area of 100π square centimeters. If chord $\overline{AB}$ is 8 centimeters long, how far, in centimeters, is $\overline{AB}$ from the center of the circle?

A) 6   B) 8   C) $\sqrt{72}$ D) $\sqrt{84}$

(*Medium*) First, let's draw three extra line segments:

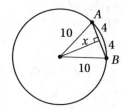

Since $\pi r^2 = 100\pi$, $r = 10$. If we draw a perpendicular from the center to the chord, the length of this segment is the distance from the center to the chord. This segment also bisects the chord, dividing it into two equal segments of 4 centimeters each. This allows us to use the Pythagorean Theorem to find this distance: $4^2 + x^2 = 10^2$

Simplify:	$16 + x^2 = 100$
Subtract 16:	$x^2 = 84$
Take square root:	$x = \sqrt{84}$

Therefore, the correct answer is (D).

Chords

A **chord** is any line segment that connects two points on a circle. The longest chord in a circle is its **diameter**, which passes through the center.

The perpendicular segment from the center of the circle to a chord always bisects that chord.

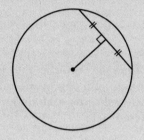

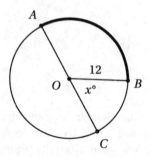

Note: Figure not drawn to scale.

In the figure above, AC is a diameter of the circle with center O, $OB = 12$, and the length of arc AB is 7π. What is the value of x?

A)   60

B)   72

C)   75

D)   78

(*Medium*) Since the circle has a radius of 12, its circumference is $2\pi(12) = 24\pi$. Since AC is a diameter, then the measure of arc AC is half the circumference, or 12π. If the length of arc AB is 7π, then the length of arc BC is $12\pi - 7\pi = 5\pi$. Since the central angle of $x°$ is the same fraction of 360° as its arc BC is to the entire circumference,

$$\frac{x}{360} = \frac{5\pi}{24\pi}$$

| Cross multiply: | $24\pi x = 1{,}800\pi$ |
| Divide by 24π: | $x = 75$ |

Therefore, the correct answer is (C).

Arcs and Sectors

An **arc** is a continuous part of the circumference of a circle. Every arc has a corresponding **central angle**. The **ratio of an arc length to the circumference is equal to the ratio of its central angle to 360° (or, in radians, 2π).**

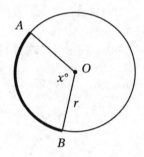

$$\frac{m\widehat{AB}}{2\pi r} = \frac{x}{360}$$

A **sector** is a part of the interior of a circle bounded by an arc and two radii. **The ratio of a sector area to the area of the circle is equal to the ratio of its central angle to 360° (or, in radians, 2π).**

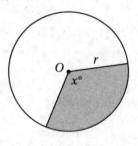

$$\frac{\text{area of sector}}{\pi r^2} = \frac{x}{360}$$

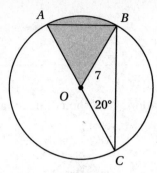

Note: Figure not drawn to scale.

In the figure above, *AC* is a diameter of the circle with center *O*, *OB* = 7, and the measure of *ACB* is 20°. What is the area of the shaded sector?

A) $\dfrac{14\pi}{12}$ B) $\dfrac{14\pi}{9}$ C) $\dfrac{49\pi}{12}$

D) $\dfrac{49\pi}{9}$

(*Medium-Hard*) Since $\overline{OA}$, $\overline{OB}$, and $\overline{OC}$ are all radii, triangles *AOB* and *BOC* are isosceles. Therefore, we can analyze the diagram with the Isosceles Triangle Theorem and the Angle Sum Theorem:

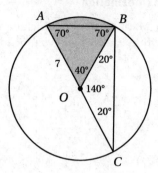

Since the central angle of the sector is 40°, the area of the sector is 40°/360° = 1/9 the area of the circle. Since the area of the circle is $\pi(7)^2 = 49\pi$, the area of the sector is $49\pi/9$ square units. Therefore, the correct answer is (D).

Lesson 7: Areas and volumes

Reference Information

Every SAT Math section will include the following **Reference Information**. Take some time to familiarize yourself with these area and volume formulas.

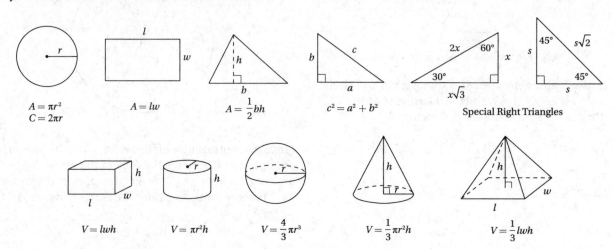

$A = \pi r^2$
$C = 2\pi r$

$A = lw$

$A = \dfrac{1}{2}bh$

$c^2 = a^2 + b^2$

Special Right Triangles

$V = lwh$

$V = \pi r^2 h$

$V = \dfrac{4}{3}\pi r^3$

$V = \dfrac{1}{3}\pi r^2 h$

$V = \dfrac{1}{3}lwh$

The number of degrees of arc in a circle is 360.
The number of radians of arc in a circle is 2π.
The sum of the measures in degrees of the angles of a triangle is 180.

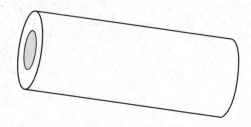

The figure above shows a wooden cylindrical tube with a length of 10 centimeters and a diameter of 4 centimeters with a cylindrical hole with a diameter of 2 centimeters that extends 40% of the length of the tube. The tube is closed on the end opposite to the hole. The density of the wood is 4.2 grams per cubic centimeter. What is the mass of this tube, to the nearest gram? (Recall that *mass = density × volume*)

A) 151 grams

B) 343 grams

C) 468 grams

D) 475 grams

(*Medium*) To find the mass of the tube, we must multiply its density by its volume. To find its volume, we must subtract the volume of cylindrical hole from the volume of the wooden cylinder. The large cylinder has a radius of 2 (remember, the *diameter* is 4 and so the radius is $4 \div 2 = 2$) and a length of 10, so its volume is $\pi(2)^2(10) = 40\pi$. The cylindrical hole has a radius of 1 (because its diameter is 2) and a length of $(0.40)(10) = 4$, so the volume of the hole is $\pi(1)^2(4) = 4\pi$. Therefore the total volume of the closed tube is $40\pi - 4\pi = 36\pi \approx 113.1$. Since the mass is equal to the volume times the density, its mass is $(113.1)(4.2) = 475$ grams, so the correct answer is (D).

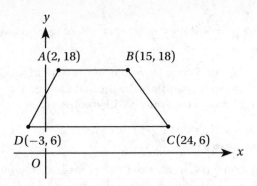

What is the area, in square units, of quadrilateral *ABCD* above?

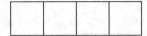

(*Medium*) You might remember this figure from Lesson 4, in which we found its perimeter. Now we are asked to find its area. Unfortunately, we are not given any formula for calculating the area of this kind of quadrilateral. (You might remember that its technical name is a **trapezoid**, but in fact we don't need to know anything special about trapezoids to solve this problem.) In such situations, it helps to remember the **Strange Area Rule**.

Strange Area Rule

When asked to find a "strange area," that is, the area of a region for which you do not have a simple formula, **try to analyze the region into the *sum* or the *difference* of simpler shapes.**

In this case, we can look at this area in two different ways: as a rectangle *plus* two right triangles, or as a bigger rectangle *minus* two right triangles:

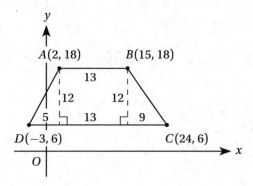

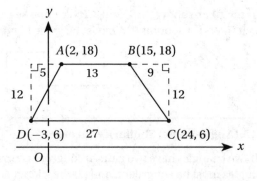

We should get the same result from either method. With the first method, the area of the trapezoid is the area of the rectangle plus the areas of two right triangles. This gives us a total area of $(12)(13) + (1/2)(5)(12) + (1/2)(9)(12) = 156 + 30 + 54 = 240$. With the second method, the area of the trapezoid is the area of the large rectangle minus the areas of the two right triangles. This gives us a total area of $(12)(27) - (1/2)(5)(12) - (1/2)(9)(12) = 324 - 30 - 54 = 240$. Bingo!

Lesson 8: Similar figures

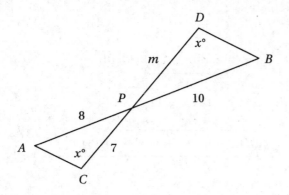

In the figure above, $\overline{AB}$ and $\overline{CD}$ are line segments that intersect at point P. What is the value of m?

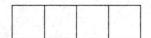

(*Medium*) The key to this question is noticing that the two triangles are **similar**. That is, that they are the same shape, although they may be different sizes.

Similarity

In geometry, *similar* really just means *the same shape*. Two figures are similar if and only if all pairs of corresponding angles are congruent, and all pairs of corresponding sides are proportional.

Helpful Tip

Always be on the lookout for similar triangles in SAT Math diagrams!

AA (Angle-Angle) Similarity Theorem

If two triangles have two pairs of congruent corresponding angles, then (1) the remaining pair of corresponding angles must be congruent, and (2) the triangles must be similar.

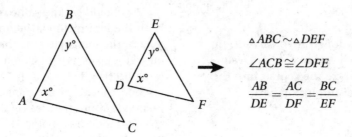

SAS (Side-Angle-Side) Similarity Theorem

If two triangles have two pairs of proportional corresponding sides, and the corresponding angles between those sides are also congruent, then the triangles must be similar.

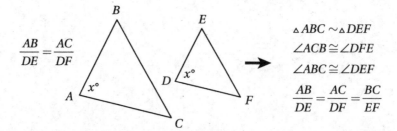

Perimeters, Areas, and Volumes of Similar Figures

If two polygons are similar with corresponding sides in ratio of $a{:}b$, then the corresponding **perimeters** of those figures have a ratio of $a{:}b$ and their corresponding **areas** have a ratio of $a^2{:}b^2$. If two solids have corresponding lengths in a ratio of $a{:}b$, then their **volumes** have a ratio of $a^3{:}b^3$.

Coming back to our diagram, if $\overline{AB}$ and $\overline{CD}$ intersect at point P, the Crossed Lines Theorem tells us that $\angle APC$ and $\angle BPD$ must be congruent, and so, by the AA Theorem, $\triangle APC \sim \triangle BPD$. Therefore, the corresponding sides are proportional:

$$\frac{8}{10} = \frac{7}{m}$$

Cross multiply:

$$8m = 70$$

Divide by 8:

$$m = 70/8 = 8.75$$

Exercise Set 2: Geometry (No Calculator)

1

A cereal company sells oatmeal in two sizes of cylindrical containers. The radius of the larger container is twice that of the smaller, and the height of the larger container is 50% greater than the smaller. If the smaller container holds 10 ounces of oatmeal, how many ounces can the larger container hold?

2

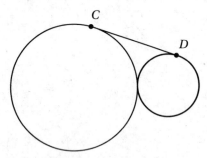

Note: Figure not drawn to scale.

In the figure above, $\overline{CD}$ is tangent to both circles, which are tangent to each other. If the smaller circle has a circumference of 4π and the larger circle has a circumference of 16π, what is the length of $\overline{CD}$?

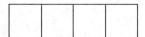

3

What is the area, in square inches, of a circle with diameter $6\pi^2$ inches?

A) $9\pi^4$ B) $9\pi^5$ C) $36\pi^4$ D) $36\pi^5$

4

What is the length of the longest line segment that connects two vertices of a rectangular box that is 6 units wide, 4 units long, and 2 units tall?

A) $\sqrt{12}$ B) $\sqrt{48}$ C) $\sqrt{56}$

D) $\sqrt{58}$

5

Which of the following equations represents a circle in the xy-plane that intersects the x-axis at $(3, 0)$ and $(9, 0)$?

A) $(x - 6)^2 + (y - 4)^2 = 25$

B) $(x - 3)^2 + (y - 9)^2 = 25$

C) $(x - 6)^2 + (y - 4)^2 = 36$

D) $(x - 3)^2 + (y - 9)^2 = 36$

6

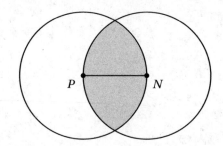

In the figure above, P and N are the centers of the circles and $PN = 6$. What is the area of the shaded region?

A) $18\pi - 9\sqrt{3}$ B) $24\pi - 9\sqrt{3}$

C) $24\pi - 18\sqrt{3}$ D) $36\pi - 18\sqrt{3}$

7

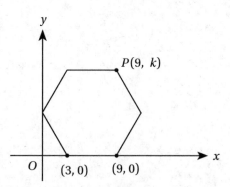

The diagram above shows a hexagon with all sides congruent and all angles congruent. What is the value of k?

A) $6\sqrt{2}$ B) $6\sqrt{3}$ C) $12\sqrt{2}$ D) $12\sqrt{3}$

Exercise Set 2: Geometry (Calculator)

8

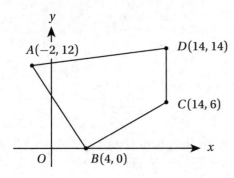

What is the area, in square units, of the quadrilateral above?

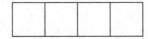

9

What is the degree measure, to the nearest whole degree, of an angle that measures 5.6 radians?

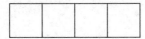

10

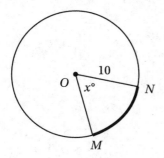

In the figure above, arc $\overset{\frown}{MN}$ has a length of 11.5. To the nearest integer, what is the value of x?

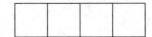

11

The Great Pyramid in Giza, Egypt, has a height of 140 meters and a volume of 2.6 million cubic meters. If a scale model of the Great Pyramid is to be built that is 2 meters high, what will be the volume, in cubic meters, of this model?

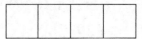

12

Which of the following equations defines a circle that is tangent to the y-axis?

A) $(x - 2)^2 + (y + 3)^2 = 2$

B) $(x - 2)^2 + (y + 3)^2 = 3$

C) $(x - 2)^2 + (y + 3)^2 = 4$

D) $(x - 2)^2 + (y + 3)^2 = 9$

▼

Questions 13 and 14 refer to the diagram below.

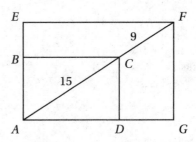

The figure above shows two rectangles that share a common vertex, and $\overline{AF}$ is a line segment that passes through C.

13

What is the ratio of the area of rectangle $ABCD$ to the area of rectangle $AEFG$?

A) 3:5

B) 9:25

C) 5:8

D) 25:64

14

If $CD = 9$, what is the perimeter of rectangle $AEFG$?

A) 67.2

B) 72.6

C) 76.2

D) 78.6

15

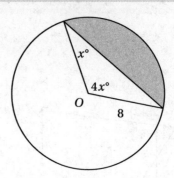

Point O is the center of the circle above. What is the area of the shaded region?

A) $\dfrac{64\pi}{3} - 16\sqrt{3}$

B) $\dfrac{16\pi}{3} - 8\sqrt{3}$

C) $\dfrac{64\pi}{3} - 12\sqrt{3}$

D) $\dfrac{64\pi}{3} - 8\sqrt{3}$

EXERCISE SET 2: GEOMETRY ANSWER KEY

No Calculator

1. **60** If the smaller cylinder has a radius of r and a height of h, its volume is $\pi r^2 h$. The larger cylinder therefore must have a radius of $2r$ and a height of $1.5h$, and a volume of $\pi(2r)^2(1.5h) = 6\pi r^2 h$. Since this is 6 times the volume of the smaller cylinder, it must hold $10 \times 6 = 60$ ounces of oatmeal.

2. **8** First, let's draw the radii to the points of tangency, the segment joining the centers, and the segment from the center of the smaller circle that is perpendicular to the radius of the larger circle. Since the tangent segment is perpendicular to the radii, these segments form a rectangle and a right triangle.

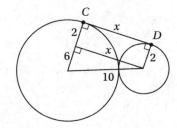

Since the circumference of the smaller circle is 4π, its radius is 2, and since the circumference of the larger circle is 16π, its radius is 8. The hypotenuse of the right triangle is the sum of the two radii: $2 + 8 = 10$. One of the legs of the right triangle is the difference of the two radii: $8 - 2 = 6$.

Pythagorean Theorem:	$x^2 + 6^2 = 10^2$
Simplify:	$x^2 + 36 = 100$
Subtract 36:	$x^2 = 64$
Take square root:	$x = 8$

3. **B**

Diameter $= 2r$:	$2r = 6\pi^2$
Divide by 2:	$r = 3\pi^2$
Area formula:	$\pi r^2 = \pi(3\pi^2)^2$
Simplify:	$\pi r^2 = \pi(9\pi^4)$
Simplify:	$\pi r^2 = 9\pi^5$

4. **C** From the 3-D Distance Formula back in Lesson 4, the length of the diagonal is $\sqrt{6^2 + 4^2 + 2^2} = \sqrt{36 + 16 + 4} = \sqrt{56}$

5. **A** All of the equations are clearly equations of circles, so our only task is to verify that one of these equations is satisfied by both point (3, 0) and point (9, 0). Simply by plugging these coordinates into the equations, we can verify that only the equation in (A) is true for both points: $(3-6)^2 + (0-4)^2 = 25$ and $(9-6)^2 + (0-4)^2 = 25$.

6. **C** In this problem, we have to take advantage of the Strange Area Rule from Lesson 7. First we should draw the segments from P and N to the points of intersection. Since each of these segments is a radius, they have equal measure (6), and form two equilateral 60°-60°-60° triangles.

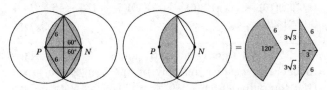

The shaded region is composed of two circle "segments," each of which is a sector minus a triangle, as shown in the figure above. The sector, since it has a 120° central angle, has an area 1/3 of the whole circle, or $(1/3)(\pi(6)^2) = 12\pi$ and the triangle has area $3(3\sqrt{3}) = 9\sqrt{3}$. Therefore, the shaded region has an area of $(2)(12\pi - 9\sqrt{3}) = 24\pi - 18\sqrt{3}$.

7. **B** Each side of the hexagon has length $9 - 3 = 6$. Each interior angle of a regular hexagon has measure $(6-2)(180°)/6 = 120°$, so the segments shown form two 30°-60°-90° triangles with lengths shown below.

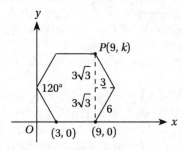

Therefore, $k = 3\sqrt{3} + 3\sqrt{3} = 6\sqrt{3}$.

Calculator

8. 142   First, let's draw a rectangle around the figure as shown.

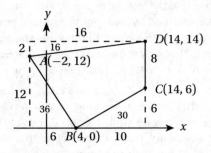

This shows that the area we want is the area of the rectangle minus the areas of the three triangles: $(16)(14) - (1/2)(2)(16) - (1/2)(12)(6) - (1/2)(10)(6) = 224 - 16 - 36 - 30 = 142$.

9. 321   To convert any angle from radians to degrees, we just multiply by the conversion factor $(180°)/(\pi \text{ radians})$. $5.6 \times 180°/\pi = 320.86 \approx 321°$.

10. 66   In a circle with radius 10, and arc of length 11.5 has a radian measure of $11.5/10 = 1.15$ radians. In degrees, this equals $1.15 \times 180°/\pi = 65.89° \approx 66°$.

11. 7.58   If two similar solids have sides in ratio of $a{:}b$, then their volumes are in a ratio of $a^3{:}b^3$. The ratio of the heights is $140{:}2 = 70{:}1$, so the ratio of volumes is $70^3{:}1^3 = 343{,}000{:}1$. This means that the volume of the model is $2{,}600{,}000 \div 343{,}000 \approx 7.58$ cubic meters.

12. C   As a quick sketch will verify, in order for a circle to be tangent to the y-axis, its radius must equal the absolute value of the x-coordinate of its center. Since the center of each square is $(2, -3)$, the radius must be 2. The only circle with a radius of 2 is (C).

13. D   By the AA Theorem, triangle ACD is similar to triangle AFG, and so rectangle $ABCD$ is similar to rectangle $AEFG$. The ratio of the corresponding sides is equal to the ratio of their diagonals, which is $15{:}24 = 5{:}8$. Therefore, the ratio of their areas is $5^2{:}8^2 = 25{:}64$

14. A   If $CD = 9$, we can find AD by the Pythagorean Theorem. $(AD)^2 + (CD)^2 = (AC)^2$

Substitute: $(AD)^2 + 9^2 = 15^2$
Simplify: $(AD)^2 + 81 = 225$
Subtract 81: $(AD)^2 = 144$
Take square root: $AD = 12$

This means that the perimeter of $ABCD$ is $12 + 9 + 12 + 9 = 42$. Since the ratio of the perimeters of similar figures equals the ratio of corresponding sides, $\dfrac{42}{p} = \dfrac{5}{8}$

Cross multiply: $5p = 336$
Divide by 5: $p = 67.2$

15. A   The two radii and the chord form an isosceles triangle. $x + x + 4x = 180$

Simplify: $6x = 180$
Divide by 6: $x = 30$

Therefore, the diagram should look like this:

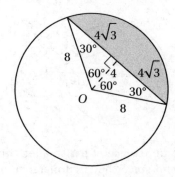

As we saw in question 6, this portion of the circle is called a "segment," and we find its area by taking the area of the sector minus the area of the triangle. The sector has area $(120/360)(\pi 8^2) = 64\pi/3$, and the triangle has area $(1/2)(8\sqrt{3})(4) = 16\sqrt{3}$, so the segment has an area of $64\pi/3 - 16\sqrt{3}$.

Skill 2: Understanding Basic Trigonometry

Lesson 9: The basic trigonometric functions

Which of these is equivalent to $\cos\dfrac{\pi}{4} - \sin\dfrac{\pi}{6}$? (No calculator)

A) $\dfrac{1 - \sqrt{3}}{2}$

B) $\dfrac{\sqrt{2} - \sqrt{3}}{2}$

C) $\dfrac{\sqrt{2} - 1}{2}$

D) $\dfrac{\sqrt{3} - \sqrt{2}}{2}$

The Basic Trigonometric Functions

Any of the three basic trigonometric functions, like all functions, takes an input number and transforms it into an output number. A trigonometric function takes an angle, θ, as an input and constructs a right triangle with θ as one of its acute angles. The output is then the ratio of two sides of that triangle as defined by the mnemonic SOH-CAH-TOA.

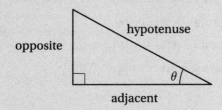

$$\sin\theta = \frac{\text{opposite}}{\text{hypotenuse}} \qquad \cos\theta = \frac{\text{adjacent}}{\text{hypotenuse}}$$

$$\tan\theta = \frac{\text{opposite}}{\text{adjacent}}$$

But these definitions are limited, because they only work when θ is an acute angle. What if it's a larger angle, like 135°, or even a negative angle, like −20°? To find the trigonometric ratios for these angles, we use the **unit circle**.

The Unit Circle

The unit circle is just a circle with radius 1 centered at the origin of the xy-plane. When using the unit circle, all angles must be in **standard position, that is, with vertex at the origin and measured counterclockwise from the positive x-axis** (just like the angle θ in the following figure).

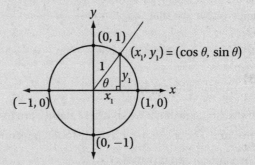

When an angle, θ, is in standard position, its terminal ray intersects the unit circle in the point (x_1, y_1). If we drop a vertical line segment from this point to the x-axis, we form a right triangle with legs of length x_1 and y_1 and a hypotenuse of length 1 (as shown above).

So now let's go back to the definitions of the basic trigonometric functions. In terms of this right triangle, what are the sine, cosine, and tangent of θ?

$$\sin\theta = \frac{\text{opposite}}{\text{hypotenuse}} = \frac{y_1}{1} = y_1$$

$$\cos\theta = \frac{\text{adjacent}}{\text{hypotenuse}} = \frac{x_1}{1} = x_1$$

$$\tan\theta = \frac{\text{opposite}}{\text{adjacent}} = \frac{y_1}{x_1}$$

This suggests three important theorems:

- The **sine** of any angle is the **y-coordinate** of its corresponding point on the unit circle.
- The **cosine** of any angle is the **x-coordinate** of its corresponding point on the unit circle.
- The **tangent** of any angle is the **ratio of the y-coordinate to the x-coordinate** of its corresponding point on the unit circle.

(*Medium-hard*) First, you may find it useful to convert the angles to degree measures using the conversion factor ($180°/\pi$ radians). This gives us $\pi/4$ radians $= 45°$ and $\pi/6$ radians $= 30°$. We should recognize these as angles in two Special Right Triangles:

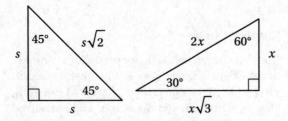

Using the definitions for sine and cosine above, these triangles show us that $\cos 45° = \dfrac{s}{s\sqrt{2}} = \dfrac{1}{\sqrt{2}} = \dfrac{\sqrt{2}}{2}$ and $\sin 30° = \dfrac{x}{2x} = \dfrac{1}{2}$. Therefore, $\cos\dfrac{\pi}{4} - \sin\dfrac{\pi}{6} = \dfrac{\sqrt{2}}{2} - \dfrac{1}{2} = \dfrac{\sqrt{2}-1}{2}$ and the correct answer is (C).

If $\sin x = a$ and $\sin z = -a$, where x and z are in radians, and $\dfrac{\pi}{2} < x < \pi$, which of the following could be the value of z in terms of x?

A) $\pi - x$

B) $x - \pi$

C) $2\pi + x$

D) $x - \dfrac{\pi}{2}$

(*Hard*) The statement $\dfrac{\pi}{2} < x < \pi$ indicates that x is an angle in quadrant II, where the sine (the y-value of the points on the unit circle) is positive. Let's draw

this situation on the unit circle so we can visualize it. (We don't want to confuse the *angles* called x and y in the problem with the x-coordinates and y-coordinates in the xy-plane. For this reason, let's label the terminal rays for the angles "angle x" and "angle z.") Recall that the sine of any angle is the y-coordinate of the point on the unit circle that corresponds to that angle. If $\sin x = a$, then a is the y-coordinate of the point on the unit circle that corresponds to "angle x," as shown in the diagram. If $\sin z = -a$, then $-a$ is the y-coordinate of the point on the unit circle that corresponds to "angle z." There are two possible locations for "angle z" as shown in the diagram.

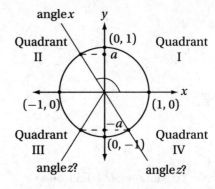

At this point, it may be easiest to simply pick a value for "angle x" that is between $\pi/2$ (≈ 1.57) and π (≈ 3.14), such as $x = 2$. Since $\sin 2 \approx 0.909$ (remember to put your calculator into "radian mode"), $a = 0.909$. Now we just need to find which angle among the choices has a sine of -0.909

A) $\sin(\pi - 2) = 0.909$

B) $\sin(2 - \pi) = -0.909$

C) $\sin(2\pi + 2) = 0.909$

D) $\sin(2 - \pi/2) = 0.416$

Therefore, the correct answer is (B).

The Pythagorean Identity

$$\sin^2 x + \cos^2 x = 1 \text{ for all values of } x$$

An **identity** is an algebraic equation that is true for all values of the unknown, and not just for particular values. We can prove the **Pythagorean Identity** by just applying the Pythagorean Theorem to our right triangle and thinking about the trigonometric ratios.

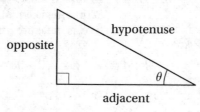

Apply Pythagorean Theorem: $\qquad\qquad\qquad\qquad\qquad$ (opposite)^2 + (adjacent)^2 = (hypotenuse)^2

Divide by (hypotenuse)^2: $\qquad\qquad\qquad\qquad\qquad \left(\dfrac{\text{opposite}}{\text{hypotenuse}}\right)^2 + \left(\dfrac{\text{adjacent}}{\text{hypotenuse}}\right)^2 = \left(\dfrac{\text{hypotenuse}}{\text{hypotenuse}}\right)^2$

Simplify using trig definitions: $\qquad\qquad\qquad\qquad\qquad\qquad\qquad\qquad \sin^2\theta + \cos^2\theta = 1$

If b is an angle measure such that $\sin b = \dfrac{1}{3\cos b}$, what is the value of $(\sin b - \cos b)^2$?

A) $\dfrac{1}{3}$

B) $\dfrac{\sqrt{2}}{3}$

C) $\dfrac{\sqrt{3}-1}{3}$

D) $\dfrac{\sqrt{3}+\sqrt{2}}{3}$

(*Medium*) The expression we are trying to evaluate includes squared trigonometric ratios, so we will probably have to take advantage of the Pythagorean Identity.

Expression to evaluate: $\qquad\qquad\qquad (\sin b - \cos b)^2$

FOIL: $\qquad\qquad\qquad \sin^2 b - 2\sin b \cos b + \cos^2 b$

Rearrange using Commutative Law of Addition: $\qquad \sin^2 b + \cos^2 b - 2\sin b \cos b$

Substitute $\sin^2 b + \cos^2 b = 1$: $\qquad\qquad 1 - 2\sin b \cos b$

Now we'll have to find the value of $\sin b \cos b$, which we can find with the given equation.

Given equation: $\qquad\qquad\qquad\qquad \sin b = \dfrac{1}{3\cos b}$

Multiply by $\cos b$: $\qquad\qquad\qquad\qquad \sin b \cos b = \dfrac{1}{3}$

Substitute $\sin b \cos b = \dfrac{1}{3}$

into original expression: $\quad 1 - 2\sin b \cos b = 1 - 2 \times \dfrac{1}{3} = \dfrac{1}{3}$

So the correct answer is (A).

Lesson 10: The trigonometry of complementary angles

If $\sin y = \dfrac{a}{b}$ and $0 < y < \dfrac{\pi}{2}$, which of the following

is equal to $\sin\left(\dfrac{\pi}{2} - y\right)$?

A) $\dfrac{\sqrt{a^2 - b^2}}{a}$

B) $\dfrac{\sqrt{b^2 - a^2}}{a}$

C) $\dfrac{\sqrt{a^2 - b^2}}{b}$

D) $\dfrac{\sqrt{b^2 - a^2}}{b}$

Trigonometry of Complementary Angles

$$\sin\left(\frac{\pi}{2} - x\right) = \cos x$$

$$\cos\left(\frac{\pi}{2} - x\right) = \sin x$$

The two acute angles in a right triangle are **complements** of one another, that is, they have a sum of 90° (or, in radians, $\dfrac{\pi}{2}$). So, if one of the angles has a radian measure of x, the other has a measure of $\dfrac{\pi}{2} - x$.

If we look at the trigonometric ratios for this new angle, we see that these ratios are related to the trigonometric ratios of its complement by the following rule: **The trigonometric ratio of any angle equals the *cofunction* of its *complement*.**

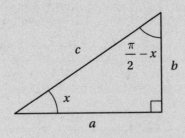

$$\sin\left(\frac{\pi}{2} - x\right) = \frac{a}{c} = \cos x$$

$$\cos\left(\frac{\pi}{2} - x\right) = \frac{b}{c} = \sin x$$

(*Medium-hard*) Let's start by drawing a picture of this situation. Since y is the measure of an acute angle, we can imagine it as the interior angle of a right triangle. Since its sine is equal to a/b, we can say that the opposite side has measure a and the hypotenuse has measure b.

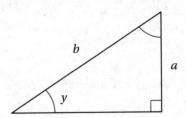

Now we can find the length of the remaining leg (let's call it k) in terms of a and b using the Pythagorean Theorem:

$$k^2 + a^2 = b^2$$

Subtract a^2:

$$k^2 = b^2 - a^2$$

Take the square root:

$$k = \sqrt{b^2 - a^2}$$

Also, we know that the other acute angle has a measure of $\dfrac{\pi}{2} - y$, so let's complete the picture:

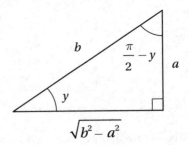

Now, finding the value of $\sin\left(\dfrac{\pi}{2} - y\right)$ is just a matter of using the definition of sine: SOH.

$$\sin\left(\frac{\pi}{2} - y\right) = \frac{\sqrt{b^2 - a^2}}{b}$$

So the correct answer is (D).

Exercise Set 3: Trigonometry (No Calculator)

1

What is the greatest possible value of f if
$f(x) = \dfrac{8 \sin 2x}{2} - \dfrac{1}{2}?$

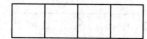

2

If $\cos\left(\dfrac{\pi}{3}\right) = a$, what is the value of $\left(\dfrac{a}{3}\right)^2?$

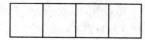

3

If $(\sin x - \cos x)^2 = 0.83$, what is the value of $(\sin x + \cos x)^2?$

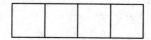

4

Which of the following is equivalent to $\dfrac{\sin\left(\dfrac{\pi}{6}\right)}{\cos\left(\dfrac{\pi}{3}\right)}?$

A) $\dfrac{1}{\sqrt{6}}$ B) $\dfrac{1}{\sqrt{3}}$ C) $\dfrac{\sqrt{3}}{\sqrt{2}}$ D) 1

5

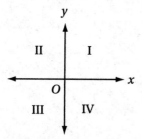

If $\sin\theta < 0$ and $\sin\theta \cos\theta < 0$, then θ must be in which quadrant of the figure above?

A) I   B) II   C) III   D) IV

6

If $\sin x = \dfrac{a}{b}$ and $0 < x < \dfrac{\pi}{2}$, which of the following expressions is equal to $\dfrac{b}{a}?$

A) $\sin\left(\dfrac{1}{x}\right)$

B) $\dfrac{1}{\cos\left(\dfrac{\pi}{2} - x\right)}$

C) $1 - \sin^2 x$

D) $\sin\left(\dfrac{\pi}{2} - x\right)$

7

If $\sin b = a$, which of the following could be the value of $\cos(b + \pi)?$

A) $\sqrt{a^2 - 1}$

B) $a^2 - 1$

C) $-\sqrt{1 - a^2}$

D) $1 - a^2$

8

If $0 < x < \dfrac{\pi}{2}$ and $\dfrac{\cos x}{1 - \sin^2 x} = \dfrac{3}{2}$, what is the value of $\cos x?$

A) $\dfrac{1}{9}$

B) $\dfrac{1}{3}$

C) $\dfrac{4}{9}$

D) $\dfrac{2}{3}$

EXERCISE SET 3: TRIGONOMETRY ANSWER KEY

No Calculator

1. **7/2 or 3.5** The discussion in Lesson 9 about the definition of the sine function and the unit circle made it clear that the value of the sine function ranges from -1 to 1. Therefore, the maximum value of $\dfrac{8\sin 2x}{2} - \dfrac{1}{2}$ is $\dfrac{8(1)}{2} - \dfrac{1}{2} = \dfrac{7}{2}$ or 3.5.

2. **1/36 or .027 or .028** An radian measure of $\pi/3$ is equivalent to $60°$. If you haven't memorized the fact that $\cos(60°) = \frac{1}{2}$, you can derive it from the Reference Information at the beginning of every SAT Math section, which includes the $30°$-$60°$-$90°$ special right triangle. Since $a = \frac{1}{2}$, $(a/3)^2 = (1/6)^2 = 1/36$.

3. **1.17**

	$(\sin x - \cos x)^2 = 0.83$
FOIL:	$\sin^2 x - 2\sin x \cos x + \cos^2 x = 0.83$
Regroup:	$\sin^2 x + \cos^2 x - 2\sin x \cos x = 0.83$
Simplify:	$1 - 2\sin x \cos x = 0.83$
Subtract 1:	$-2\sin x \cos x = -0.17$
Multiply by -1:	$2\sin x \cos x = 0.17$
Evaluate this expression:	$(\sin x + \cos x)^2$
FOIL:	$\sin^2 x + 2\sin x \cos x + \cos^2 x$
Regroup:	$\sin^2 x + \cos^2 x + 2\sin x \cos x$
Substitute:	$1 + 0.17 = 1.17$

4. **D** $\sin(\pi/6) = \frac{1}{2}$ and $\cos(\pi/3) = \frac{1}{2}$, so $\sin(\pi/6)/\cos(\pi/3) = 1$.

5. **D** If $\sin\theta < 0$, then θ must be either in quadrant III or in quadrant IV. (Remember that sine corresponds to the y-coordinates on the unit circle, so it is negative in those quadrants where the y-coordinates are negative.) If $\sin\theta \cos\theta < 0$, then $\cos\theta$ must be positive (because a negative times a positive is a negative). Since $\cos\theta$ is only positive in quadrants I and IV (because cosine corresponds to the x-coordinates on the unit circle), θ must be in quadrant IV

6. **B** First, notice that a/b and b/a are reciprocals. Next, we can use the identity in Lesson 10 that $\sin x = \cos\left(\dfrac{\pi}{2} - x\right)$ to see that choice (B) is just the reciprocal of $\sin x$. Alternately, we can just choose a value of x, like $x = 1$, and evaluate $\sin 1 = 0.841$. The correct answer is the expression that gives a value equal to the reciprocal of 0.841, which is $1/0.841 = 1.19$. Plugging in $x = 1$ gives (A) 0.841, (B) 1.19, (C) 0.292, (D) 0.540.

7. **C** Recall from the Pythagorean Identity that $\cos b = \pm\sqrt{1 - \sin^2 b}$. Substituting $\sin b = a$ gives $\cos b = \pm\sqrt{1 - a^2}$. The angle $b + \pi$ is the reflection of angle b through the origin, so $\cos(b + \pi)$ is the opposite of $\cos b$, which means that $\cos(b + \pi) = \pm\sqrt{1 - a^2}$.

8. **D** Recall from the Pythagorean Identity that $\cos^2 x = 1 - \sin^2 x$.

	$\dfrac{\cos x}{1 - \sin^2 x} = \dfrac{3}{2}$
Substitute $\cos^2 x = 1 - \sin^2 x$:	$\dfrac{\cos x}{\cos^2 x} = \dfrac{3}{2}$
Cancel common factor:	$\dfrac{1}{\cos x} = \dfrac{3}{2}$
Reciprocate:	$\cos x = \dfrac{2}{3}$

Skill 3: Understanding Complex Numbers

Lesson 11: Understanding the imaginary number *i* and the complex plane

Imaginary Numbers

$$i = \sqrt{-1}$$

The **imaginary number** *i* is defined as the principal square root of −1.

The square root of a negative number is not on the real number line, because the square of a real number cannot be negative. Therefore, the square roots of negative numbers must reside on their own number line, which we call the **"imaginary axis,"** which is perpendicular to the real axis, intersecting it at the origin. The plane defined by the real axis and the imaginary axis is called the **complex plane**.

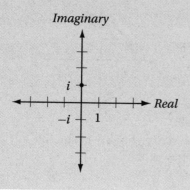

Given that $i = \sqrt{-1}$, which of the following is equal to $\dfrac{1}{i^3}$?

A) *i*

B) −*i*

C) 1

D) −1

(*Medium-hard*) To answer this question, we just need to know the basic exponent rules and the definition of *i*.

Original expression: $\dfrac{1}{i^3}$

Factor: $\dfrac{1}{i^2 \times i^1}$

Substitute $i^2 = -1$ $-\dfrac{1}{i}$

Multiply by *i*/*i*: $-\dfrac{i}{i^2}$

Substitute $i^2 = -1$: $-(-i) = i$

Therefore, the correct answer is (A).

Lesson 12: Adding, multiplying, dividing, and simplifying complex numbers

Complex Numbers

The sum of a real number and an imaginary number is called a **complex number**. All complex numbers can be expressed in the form $a + bi$ where a and b are real numbers and $i = \sqrt{-1}$.

Every complex number $a + bi$ corresponds to the point (a, b) on the complex plane.

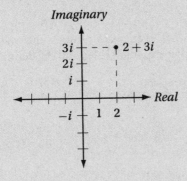

Adding Complex Numbers

To add complex numbers, just combine "like" terms.

Original expression:	$(3 - 2i) + (2 + 6i)$
Regroup with Commutative and Associative Laws of Addition:	$(3 + 2) + (-2i + 6i)$
Simplify:	$5 + 4i$

Multiplying Complex Numbers

To multiply complex numbers, just FOIL and combine like terms.

Original expression:	$(3 - 2i)(2 + 6i)$
FOIL:	$(3)(2) + (3)(6i) + (-2i)(2) + (-2i)(6i)$
Simplify:	$6 + 18i - 4i - 12i^2$
Substitute $i^2 = -1$:	$6 + 18i - 4i - 12(-1)$
Combine like terms:	$18 + 14i$

Dividing Complex Numbers

To divide complex numbers, express the quotient as a fraction, multiply numerator and denominator by the **complex conjugate** of the denominator, and simplify. The **complex conjugate** of $a + bi$ is $a - bi$.

Original expression:	$\dfrac{2 + i}{3 - i}$

Multiply numerator and denominator by conjugate of denominator: $\dfrac{(2 + i)(3 + i)}{(3 - i)(3 + i)}$

FOIL: $\dfrac{6 + 2i + 3i + i^2}{9 + 3i - 3i - i^2}$

Simplify: $\dfrac{5 + 5i}{10}$

Distribute division: $\dfrac{1}{2} + \dfrac{1}{2}i$

Powers of i

The successive powers of i ($i^1, i^2, i^3, i^4, i^5, i^6, i^7 \ldots$) cycle counterclockwise around the unit circle in the complex plane.

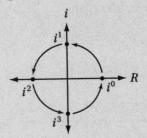

We can verify this by expanding any positive integer power of i.

Expression to be evaluated:	i^{13}
Expand:	$(i)(i)(i)(i)(i)(i)(i)(i)(i)(i)(i)(i)(i)$
Group in pairs:	$(i \times i)(i \times i)(i \times i)(i \times i)(i \times i)(i \times i)(i)$
Substitute $i^2 = -1$:	$(-1)(-1)(-1)(-1)(-1)(-1)(i)$
Simplify:	i

This implies that $i^n = 1$ if n is a multiple of 4. (That is, $i^4 = 1$, $i^8 = 1$, $i^{12} = 1$, etc.) This gives us a convenient way to simplify large powers of i: **just replace the exponent with the remainder when it is divided by 4.** For instance, $i^{39} = i^3 = -i$, because 3 is the remainder when 39 is divided by 4.

If $1 - i = \dfrac{K}{1+i}$, where $i = \sqrt{-1}$, which of the following

is equal to K^2?

A) $2i$

B) $4i$

C) $4 + i$

D) 4

(*Medium*)

Given equation:	$1 - i = \dfrac{K}{1+i}$
Multiply by $1 + i$:	$(1 - i)(1 + i) = K$
FOIL:	$1 + i - i - i^2 = K$
Simplify:	$1 - (-1) = 2 = K$
Square:	$4 = K^2$

Therefore, the correct answer is (D).

Which of the following is NOT equal to $i^6 - i^2$?

A) $i^5 - i$

B) i^4

C) $2i^3 + 2i$

D) $1 + i^6$

(*Medium*) Here, we have to use our knowledge about powers of i. Since $i^6 = (i \times i)(i \times i)(i \times i) = (-1)(-1)(-1) = -1$, and $i^2 = -1$, the given expression, $i^6 - i^2$, is equal to $(-1) - (-1) = 0$. Simplifying each choice gives us

A) $i^5 - i = i - i = 0$

B) $i^4 = 1$

C) $2i^3 + 2i = -2i + 2i = 0$

D) $1 + i^6 = 1 + (-1) = 0$

Therefore, the correct answer is (B).

Exercise Set 4: Complex Numbers (No Calculator)

1

If $a + bi = (1 + 2i)(3 - 4i)$, where a and b are constants and $i = \sqrt{-1}$, what is the value of $a + b$?

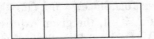

2

If $a + bi = \dfrac{4 + i}{2 - i}$, where a and b are constants and $i = \sqrt{-1}$, what is the value of a?

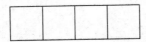

3

For what value of b does $(b + i)^2 = 80 + 18i$?

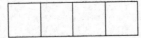

4

The solutions of the equation $x^2 - 2x + 15 = 0$ are $x = a + i\sqrt{b}$ and $x = a - i\sqrt{b}$, where a and b are positive numbers. What is the value of $a + b$?

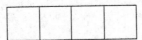

5

Given that $i = \sqrt{-1}$, which of the following is equal to $\dfrac{1}{(1 + i)^2}$?

A) $\dfrac{1}{2} - \dfrac{1}{2}i$

B) $-\dfrac{1}{2}i$

C) $\dfrac{1}{2}i$

D) $\dfrac{1}{2} + \dfrac{1}{2}i$

6

Which of the following expressions is equal to $(2 + 2i)^2$?

A) 0

B) $4i$

C) $8i$

D) $4 - 4i$

7

If $B(3 + i) = 3 - i$, what is the value of B?

A) $\dfrac{3}{5} + \dfrac{4}{5}i$

B) $\dfrac{4}{5} + \dfrac{3}{5}i$

C) $\dfrac{3}{5} - \dfrac{4}{5}i$

D) $\dfrac{4}{5} - \dfrac{3}{5}i$

8

$$x^2 + kx = -6$$

If one of the solutions to the equation above is $x = 1 - i\sqrt{5}$, what is the value of k?

A) -4

B) -2

C) 2

D) 4

9

If $i^m = -i$, which of the following CANNOT be the value of m?

A) 15

B) 18

C) 19

D) 27

EXERCISE SET 4: COMPLEX NUMBERS ANSWER KEY

No Calculator

1. 13

$$(1 + 2i)(3 - 4i)$$

FOIL: $(1)(3) + (1)(-4i) + (2i)(3) + (2i)(-4i)$

Simplify: $3 - 4i + 6i - 8i^2$

Substitute $i^2 = -1$: $3 - 4i + 6i - 8(-1)$

Combine like terms: $11 + 2i$

Therefore, $a = 11$ and $b = 2$, so $a + b = 13$.

---

2. 7/5 or 1.4

$$\frac{4 + i}{2 - i}$$

Multiply conjugate: $\dfrac{(4 + i)(2 + i)}{(2 - i)(2 + i)}$

FOIL: $\dfrac{8 + 4i + 2i + i^2}{4 + 2i - 2i - i^2}$

Substitute $i^2 = -1$: $\dfrac{8 + 4i + 2i - 1}{4 + 2i - 2i + 1}$

Combine like terms: $\dfrac{7 + 6i}{5}$

Distribute division: $\dfrac{7}{5} + \dfrac{6}{5}i$

---

3. 9

$$(b + i)^2$$

FOIL: $(b + i)(b + i) = b^2 + bi + bi + i^2$

Substitute $i^2 = -1$: $b^2 + bi + bi - 1$

Combine like terms: $(b^2 - 1) + 2bi$

Since this must equal $80 + 18i$, we can find b by solving either $b^2 - 1 = 80$ or $2b = 18$. The solution to both equations is $b = 9$.

---

4. 15 The equation we are given is a quadratic equation in which $a = 1$, $b = -2$, and $c = 15$. Therefore, we can use the quadratic formula:

Quadratic Formula: $\dfrac{-b \pm \sqrt{b^2 - 4ac}}{2a}$

Substitute: $\dfrac{2 \pm \sqrt{(-2)^2 - 4(1)(15)}}{2(1)}$

Simplify: $\dfrac{2 \pm \sqrt{-56}}{2}$

Simplify: $\dfrac{2 \pm 2i\sqrt{14}}{2}$

Distribute division: $1 \pm i\sqrt{14}$

Therefore, $a = 1$ and $b = 14$, so $a + b = 15$.

---

5. B

$$\frac{1}{(1 + i)^2}$$

FOIL: $\dfrac{1}{(1 + i)(1 + i)} = \dfrac{1}{1 + i + i + i^2}$

Substitute $i^2 = -1$: $\dfrac{1}{1 + i + i + (-1)}$

Simplify: $\dfrac{1}{2i}$

Multiply by i/i: $\dfrac{i}{2i^2}$

Substitute $i^2 = -1$: $\dfrac{i}{-2} = -\dfrac{1}{2}i$

---

6. C

$$(2 + 2i)^2$$

FOIL: $(2 + 2i)(2 + 2i) = 4 + 4i + 4i + 4i^2$

Substitute $i^2 = -1$: $4 + 8i - 4 = 8i$

---

7. D

$$B(3 + i) = 3 - i$$

Divide by $3 + i$: $B = \dfrac{3 - i}{3 + i}$

FOIL: $B = \dfrac{9 - 3i - 3i + i^2}{9 - 3i + 3i - i^2}$

Substitute $i^2 = -1$: $B = \dfrac{9 - 3i - 3i + (-1)}{9 - 3i + 3i - (-1)}$

Simplify: $B = \dfrac{8 - 6i}{10} = \dfrac{4 - 3i}{5}$

Distribute division: $B = \dfrac{4}{5} - \dfrac{3}{5}i$

---

8. B

$$x^2 + kx = -6$$

Add 6: $x^2 + kx + 6 = 0$

Substitute $x = 1 - i\sqrt{5}$: $\left(1 - i\sqrt{5}\right)^2 + k\left(1 - i\sqrt{5}\right) + 6 = 0$

FOIL: $\left(1 - 2i\sqrt{5} + 5i^2\right) + k\left(1 - i\sqrt{5}\right) + 6 = 0$

Simplify: $\left(-4 - 2i\sqrt{5}\right) + k\left(1 - i\sqrt{5}\right) + 6 = 0$

Distribute: $-4 - 2i\sqrt{5} + k - ik\sqrt{5} + 6 = 0$

Collect terms: $(2 + k) - \left(2\sqrt{5} + k\sqrt{5}\right)i = 0$

Therefore, both $2 + k = 0$ and $2\sqrt{5} + k\sqrt{5} = 0$. Solving either equation gives $k = -2$.

---

9. B As we discussed in Lesson 10, the powers of i are "cyclical," and $i^m = -i$ if and only if m is 3 more than a multiple of 4. The only number among the choices that is not 3 more than a multiple of 4 is (B) 18.

CHAPTER 11

PRACTICE TEST 1

ANSWER SHEET

Start with number 1 for each new section. If a section has fewer questions than answer spaces, leave the extra answer spaces blank. Be sure to erase any errors or stray marks completely.

SECTION 1

1 Ⓐ Ⓑ Ⓒ Ⓓ   13 Ⓐ Ⓑ Ⓒ Ⓓ   25 Ⓐ Ⓑ Ⓒ Ⓓ   37 Ⓐ Ⓑ Ⓒ Ⓓ   49 Ⓐ Ⓑ Ⓒ Ⓓ
2 Ⓐ Ⓑ Ⓒ Ⓓ   14 Ⓐ Ⓑ Ⓒ Ⓓ   26 Ⓐ Ⓑ Ⓒ Ⓓ   38 Ⓐ Ⓑ Ⓒ Ⓓ   50 Ⓐ Ⓑ Ⓒ Ⓓ
3 Ⓐ Ⓑ Ⓒ Ⓓ   15 Ⓐ Ⓑ Ⓒ Ⓓ   27 Ⓐ Ⓑ Ⓒ Ⓓ   39 Ⓐ Ⓑ Ⓒ Ⓓ   51 Ⓐ Ⓑ Ⓒ Ⓓ
4 Ⓐ Ⓑ Ⓒ Ⓓ   16 Ⓐ Ⓑ Ⓒ Ⓓ   28 Ⓐ Ⓑ Ⓒ Ⓓ   40 Ⓐ Ⓑ Ⓒ Ⓓ   52 Ⓐ Ⓑ Ⓒ Ⓓ
5 Ⓐ Ⓑ Ⓒ Ⓓ   17 Ⓐ Ⓑ Ⓒ Ⓓ   29 Ⓐ Ⓑ Ⓒ Ⓓ   41 Ⓐ Ⓑ Ⓒ Ⓓ
6 Ⓐ Ⓑ Ⓒ Ⓓ   18 Ⓐ Ⓑ Ⓒ Ⓓ   30 Ⓐ Ⓑ Ⓒ Ⓓ   42 Ⓐ Ⓑ Ⓒ Ⓓ
7 Ⓐ Ⓑ Ⓒ Ⓓ   19 Ⓐ Ⓑ Ⓒ Ⓓ   31 Ⓐ Ⓑ Ⓒ Ⓓ   43 Ⓐ Ⓑ Ⓒ Ⓓ
8 Ⓐ Ⓑ Ⓒ Ⓓ   20 Ⓐ Ⓑ Ⓒ Ⓓ   32 Ⓐ Ⓑ Ⓒ Ⓓ   44 Ⓐ Ⓑ Ⓒ Ⓓ
9 Ⓐ Ⓑ Ⓒ Ⓓ   21 Ⓐ Ⓑ Ⓒ Ⓓ   33 Ⓐ Ⓑ Ⓒ Ⓓ   45 Ⓐ Ⓑ Ⓒ Ⓓ
10 Ⓐ Ⓑ Ⓒ Ⓓ   22 Ⓐ Ⓑ Ⓒ Ⓓ   34 Ⓐ Ⓑ Ⓒ Ⓓ   46 Ⓐ Ⓑ Ⓒ Ⓓ
11 Ⓐ Ⓑ Ⓒ Ⓓ   23 Ⓐ Ⓑ Ⓒ Ⓓ   35 Ⓐ Ⓑ Ⓒ Ⓓ   47 Ⓐ Ⓑ Ⓒ Ⓓ
12 Ⓐ Ⓑ Ⓒ Ⓓ   24 Ⓐ Ⓑ Ⓒ Ⓓ   36 Ⓐ Ⓑ Ⓒ Ⓓ   48 Ⓐ Ⓑ Ⓒ Ⓓ

SECTION 2

1 Ⓐ Ⓑ Ⓒ Ⓓ   11 Ⓐ Ⓑ Ⓒ Ⓓ   21 Ⓐ Ⓑ Ⓒ Ⓓ   31 Ⓐ Ⓑ Ⓒ Ⓓ   41 Ⓐ Ⓑ Ⓒ Ⓓ
2 Ⓐ Ⓑ Ⓒ Ⓓ   12 Ⓐ Ⓑ Ⓒ Ⓓ   22 Ⓐ Ⓑ Ⓒ Ⓓ   32 Ⓐ Ⓑ Ⓒ Ⓓ   42 Ⓐ Ⓑ Ⓒ Ⓓ
3 Ⓐ Ⓑ Ⓒ Ⓓ   13 Ⓐ Ⓑ Ⓒ Ⓓ   23 Ⓐ Ⓑ Ⓒ Ⓓ   33 Ⓐ Ⓑ Ⓒ Ⓓ   43 Ⓐ Ⓑ Ⓒ Ⓓ
4 Ⓐ Ⓑ Ⓒ Ⓓ   14 Ⓐ Ⓑ Ⓒ Ⓓ   24 Ⓐ Ⓑ Ⓒ Ⓓ   34 Ⓐ Ⓑ Ⓒ Ⓓ   44 Ⓐ Ⓑ Ⓒ Ⓓ
5 Ⓐ Ⓑ Ⓒ Ⓓ   15 Ⓐ Ⓑ Ⓒ Ⓓ   25 Ⓐ Ⓑ Ⓒ Ⓓ   35 Ⓐ Ⓑ Ⓒ Ⓓ
6 Ⓐ Ⓑ Ⓒ Ⓓ   16 Ⓐ Ⓑ Ⓒ Ⓓ   26 Ⓐ Ⓑ Ⓒ Ⓓ   36 Ⓐ Ⓑ Ⓒ Ⓓ
7 Ⓐ Ⓑ Ⓒ Ⓓ   17 Ⓐ Ⓑ Ⓒ Ⓓ   27 Ⓐ Ⓑ Ⓒ Ⓓ   37 Ⓐ Ⓑ Ⓒ Ⓓ
8 Ⓐ Ⓑ Ⓒ Ⓓ   18 Ⓐ Ⓑ Ⓒ Ⓓ   28 Ⓐ Ⓑ Ⓒ Ⓓ   38 Ⓐ Ⓑ Ⓒ Ⓓ
9 Ⓐ Ⓑ Ⓒ Ⓓ   19 Ⓐ Ⓑ Ⓒ Ⓓ   29 Ⓐ Ⓑ Ⓒ Ⓓ   39 Ⓐ Ⓑ Ⓒ Ⓓ
10 Ⓐ Ⓑ Ⓒ Ⓓ   20 Ⓐ Ⓑ Ⓒ Ⓓ   30 Ⓐ Ⓑ Ⓒ Ⓓ   40 Ⓐ Ⓑ Ⓒ Ⓓ

Start with number 1 for each new section. If a section has fewer questions than answer spaces, leave the extra answer spaces blank. Be sure to erase any errors or stray marks completely.

SECTION 3

1. Ⓐ Ⓑ Ⓒ Ⓓ
2. Ⓐ Ⓑ Ⓒ Ⓓ
3. Ⓐ Ⓑ Ⓒ Ⓓ
4. Ⓐ Ⓑ Ⓒ Ⓓ
5. Ⓐ Ⓑ Ⓒ Ⓓ
6. Ⓐ Ⓑ Ⓒ Ⓓ
7. Ⓐ Ⓑ Ⓒ Ⓓ
8. Ⓐ Ⓑ Ⓒ Ⓓ
9. Ⓐ Ⓑ Ⓒ Ⓓ
10. Ⓐ Ⓑ Ⓒ Ⓓ

11. Ⓐ Ⓑ Ⓒ Ⓓ
12. Ⓐ Ⓑ Ⓒ Ⓓ
13. Ⓐ Ⓑ Ⓒ Ⓓ
14. Ⓐ Ⓑ Ⓒ Ⓓ
15. Ⓐ Ⓑ Ⓒ Ⓓ

CAUTION Use the answer spaces in the grids below for Section 3 only if you are told to do so in your test book.

Student-Produced Responses ONLY ANSWERS ENTERED IN THE CIRCLES IN EACH GRID WILL BE SCORED. YOU WILL NOT RECEIVE CREDIT FOR ANYTHING WRITTEN IN THE BOXES ABOVE THE CIRCLES.

16.

17.

18.

19.

20.

Start with number 1 for each new section. If a section has fewer questions than answer spaces, leave the extra answer spaces blank. Be sure to erase any errors or stray marks completely.

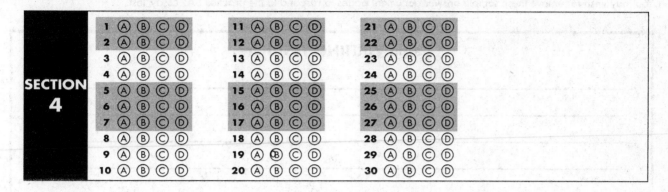

CAUTION   Use the answer spaces in the grids below for Section 4 only if you are told to do so in your test book.

Student-Produced Responses   ONLY ANSWERS ENTERED IN THE CIRCLES IN EACH GRID WILL BE SCORED. YOU WILL NOT RECEIVE CREDIT FOR ANYTHING WRITTEN IN THE BOXES ABOVE THE CIRCLES.

SECTION 5: ESSAY

You may wish to remove these sample answer document pages to respond to the practice SAT Essay Test.

Begin WRITING TEST here.

_____

_____

_____

_____

_____

_____

_____

_____

_____

_____

_____

_____

_____

_____

_____

_____

_____

_____

_____

_____

_____

_____

_____

_____

If you need more space, please continue on the next page.

1

SECTION 5: ESSAY

You may wish to remove these sample answer document pages to respond to the practice SAT Essay Test.

WRITING TEST

_____
_____
_____
_____
_____
_____
_____
_____
_____
_____
_____
_____
_____
_____
_____
_____
_____
_____
_____
_____
_____
_____
_____
_____
_____
_____

If you need more space, please continue on the next page.

SECTION 5: ESSAY

You may wish to remove these sample answer document pages to respond to the practice SAT Essay Test.

WRITING TEST

_____

_____

_____

_____

_____

_____

_____

_____

_____

_____

_____

_____

_____

_____

_____

_____

_____

_____

_____

_____

_____

_____

_____

_____

_____

_____

If you need more space, please continue on the next page.

3

Cut Here

SECTION 5: ESSAY

You may wish to remove these sample answer document pages to respond to the practice SAT Essay Test.

WRITING TEST

_____

_____

_____

_____

_____

_____

_____

_____

_____

_____

_____

_____

_____

_____

_____

_____

_____

_____

_____

_____

_____

_____

_____

_____

_____

_____

_____

_____

_____

_____

_____

STOP here with the Writing Test.

4

1   1

Reading Test

65 MINUTES, 52 QUESTIONS

Turn to Section 1 of your answer sheet to answer the questions in this section.

DIRECTIONS

Each passage or pair of passages below is followed by a number of questions. After reading each passage or pair, choose the best answer to each question based on what is stated or implied in the passage or passages and in any accompanying graphics.

Questions 1–12 are based on the following passage.

Passage 1 is adapted from Nicholas Heidorn, *"The Enduring Political Illusion of Farm Subsidies."* ©2004 The Independent Institute. Originally Published August 18, 2004 in the San Francisco Chronicle. Passage 2 is ©2015 by Mark Anestis. Since 1922, the U.S. government has subsidized the agricultural industry by supporting the price of crops (commodity subsidies), paying farmers let their fields go fallow (conservation subsidies), helping farmers purchase crop insurance (crop insurance subsidies), and compensating farmers for uninsured losses due to disasters (disaster subsidies). The following passages discuss these programs.

Passage 1

Something is rotten down on the farm. A recent General Accounting Office study found that the
Line U.S. farm subsidy program, a multibillion-dollar system of direct payments to American farm-
5   ers, uses administrators who are ill-trained and poorly monitored, and who give away millions of taxpayer dollars to farmers who are actually ineligible for the program. This report should horrify lawmakers, but it probably won't.

10   From 1995 to 2002, the United States Congress doled out more than $114 billion to farmers. Why?

One misconception is that subsidies are a boon to consumers because they lower food prices. This ignores the fact that consumers are
15   also paying for these subsidies through taxes. Because of inefficiencies in the program, we tax-payers will pay more in taxes than we will ever get back in lower corn or wheat prices.

In fact, farm subsidies are not even intended to
20   reduce food prices significantly. When prices are too low, farmers lose money. To prevent this situation, Congress also pays farmers additional "conservation subsidies" to leave their land fallow, thereby lower-ing supply and boosting prices again. We're taxed to
25   lower prices, and then taxed to raise them again.

Another myth is that subsidies increase exports, and thereby benefit the American econ-omy, by lowering the price of farm products and so making them more attractive to foreign consum-
30   ers. This ignores two realities. First, farm subsidies transfer wealth from taxpayers to foreign con-sumers just as efficiently as they transfer wealth to domestic consumers. Second, farm subsidies are actually harming American exporters. In
35   March 2005, the World Trade Organization ruled that American cotton subsidies violated global

free-trade rules, which could lead to billions of dollars in retaliatory tariffs or penalties.

40 The worst misconception is that we need these subsidies to save the small family farmer. Indeed, according to a 2009 poll, about 77 percent of Americans support giving subsidies to small family farms. But according to the Environmental Working Group, 71 percent of farm subsidies go to the top
45 10 percent of beneficiaries, almost all of which are large corporate farms. By subsidizing these rich farmers, we actually make it much harder for the small family farmers to compete, not to mention the millions of impoverished third world farmers
50 who rely on farming for their livelihood.

Rich corporate farmers are an enormously powerful lobby in American politics. Agribusiness and farm insurance lobbies pump nearly $100 million into political campaigns every
55 year, and the floodgates show no sign of closing. So don't be surprised if the GAO's reports of mismanagement and waste go unheeded. Politicians like their payouts almost as much as the big farmers and their insurance companies do.

Passage 2

60 The critics of the U.S. farm subsidy program fail to recognize just how vital these subsidies really are. They are not as burdensome to American taxpayers as the critics claim, and indeed provide important benefits. By protecting farmers from
65 damaging fluctuations in commodity prices due to weather disasters or market disruptions, these subsidies help sustain a vital American industry. At the same time, they protect consumers from price spikes that can accompany steep drops in
70 crop inventories. Before price supports became common in the 20th century, crop failures devastated the lives of farmers and consumers with horrifying frequency.

Opponents say that subsidies distort the free
75 market and create surpluses in supply. But halting subsidies would allow regular shortfalls, which are far more damaging. The year-to-year carryover of these surpluses protects farmers from low prices and consumers from high prices.

80 Another misconception is that subsidies only benefit the producers. In fact, they help many related industries as well, including food processing, distribution, and marketing, chiefly by helping to lower the cost of production. And, of course,
85 the consumers receive the benefit of lower prices.

When assessing the costs and benefits of farm payments, it is important to compare these subsidies to those of other industrialized nations. American farmers receive an average of just 20% of
90 their incomes from subsidies, compared to 70% for farmers from some other countries. The European Union spends about five times what the United States spends on farm subsidies, amounting to 45% of the EU budget, compared to less than 1%
95 of the U.S. federal budget. Although the U.S. farm subsidies programs are not perfect, they provide enormous benefits not only to farms but also to associated industries employing millions of people and to nearly every American consumer.

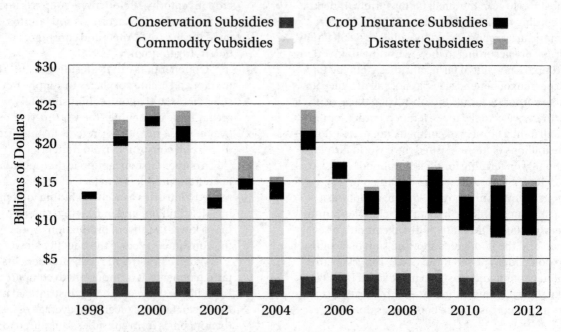

FEDERAL AGRICULTURAL SUBSIDIES IN THE UNITED STATES

Conservation Subsidies ■   Crop Insurance Subsidies ■
Commodity Subsidies ▨   Disaster Subsidies ▨

Source: From Environmental Working Group (farm.ewg.org)

1   1

1

Both passages acknowledge the effectiveness of U.S. farm subsidies in

A) stabilizing commodity prices.

B) expanding American exports.

C) assisting smaller farms.

D) increasing agricultural productivity.

2

The first sentence of Passage 1 refers primarily to the author's belief that

A) the American government is not doing enough to help small farmers.

B) some American farmers are violating the law.

C) a federal agricultural program is unfair and ineffective.

D) American farmers are struggling to compete in international markets.

3

The author of Passage 2 would most likely regard the "taxes" mentioned in line 15 as

A) a worthwhile expenditure.

B) a misplaced priority.

C) a political delusion.

D) a technical misnomer.

4

The author of Passage 1 believes that the GAO report "probably won't" (line 9) horrify lawmakers because

A) the report indicates that farm subsidies are not as harmful as many suggest.

B) most members of congress do not live in districts that receive farm subsidies.

C) the legislature is too divided along ideological party lines.

D) many members of congress receive benefits from pro-subsidy farm lobbies.

5

Which of the following provides the strongest evidence for the answer to the previous question?

A) Lines 16–18 ("Because of . . . wheat prices")

B) Lines 21–24 ("To prevent this . . . prices again")

C) Lines 40–43 ("Indeed . . . family farms")

D) Lines 53–55 ("Agribusiness . . . sign of closing")

6

Unlike Passage 1, Passage 2 emphasizes the danger of

A) corrupt political officials.

B) sudden changes in commodity prices.

C) competition in international markets.

D) onerous public tax burdens.

7

Passage 1 mentions the results of the 2009 poll (lines 40–43) primarily to

A) confirm a general sentiment.

B) refute a misconception.

C) change the focus of the discussion.

D) reveal a surprising finding.

8

If the author of Passage 1 were to use the data in the graph to support his main thesis, he would most likely mention

A) the general decline in total farm subsidies from 2005 to 2012.

B) the overall rate of change in commodity subsidies from 1998 to 2012.

C) the expansion of crop insurance subsidies from the late 1990s to the late 2000s.

D) the sudden spike in disaster subsidies from 2004 to 2005.

CONTINUE ➤

9

If the author of Passage 2 were to use the data in the graph to support his main thesis, he would most likely mention

A) the general decline in total farm subsidies from 2005 to 2012.

B) the overall rate of change in commodity subsidies from 1998 to 2012.

C) the expansion of crop insurance subsidies from the late 1990s to the late 2000s.

D) the sudden spike in disaster subsidies from 2004 to 2005.

10

The author of Passage 1 would most likely say that the "benefit" in line 85 is

A) offset by its costs.

B) an exception to a rule.

C) enjoyed only by the wealthy.

D) misrepresented by legislators.

11

Unlike Passage 2, Passage 1 makes a direct appeal to the reader's

A) sense of humor.

B) distaste for ineptitude.

C) environmental responsibility.

D) fiscal prudence.

12

In line 55, the "floodgates" are controls against

A) environmental destruction.

B) unscrupulous funding.

C) emotional outbursts.

D) necessary capital.

1   **1**

Questions 13–22 are based on the following passage.

This passage is adapted from Marie Myung-Ok Lee, *Somebody's Daughter.* ©2006 Beacon Press. The story is about a Korean-American girl adopted by an American family and raised in the Midwest.

When I was eight, they told me that my mother's death was preordained. She had been murdered.

Line   One Sunday after service, our minister, Reverend Jansen of the Lutheran Church of the
5   Good Shepherd, bent down in a cloud of Aqua Velva to explain. We had been learning in Sunday school about Heaven and Hell, and in the middle of class I had fallen into a panic, wondering how I would recognize my Korean mother when I saw
10 her in Heaven—or in Hell, if perhaps she and I both sinned too much.

Not to worry, I was told.

"God called your Korean parents home so that you could become the daughter of your
15 mother and father," he said, his eyes sliding sidewise, for just a second. His breath smelled vaguely of toast.

"It was all part of His plan—you see how much your mommy and daddy love you? When the time
20 comes, if you're a very good girl, you, your mommy, daddy, and your sister, Amanda—the whole Thorson family—will be in heaven together, thanks to the Lord's wonderful and mysterious ways."

"That's why we named you Sarah," Christine
25 and Ken added. "Because it means 'God's precious treasure.'"

God kills, I thought then. The same God who brought us Christmas and the Easter Bunny—he murdered my mother.

30 Shortly after that Sunday, I brought up my Korean mother again, asking about the car accident, how it happened, exactly—was it like Phil Haag's father, who fell asleep at the wheel? Or like our plumber's teenage son who drove into a semi
35 head-on?

"Sarah," Christine said patiently, looking up from the chopping board, where she was slicing carrot discs for pot roast. "We really knew nothing about her. *I'm* your mommy. Let's not talk

40 about this any more, it makes me sad." She made little crying motions, pretending to wipe away tears, the same thing she did when I was bad, to show how I had disappointed her.

I grew up in a house in which *Korea* had
45 always been the oddly charged word, never to be mentioned in connection to me, the same way we never said "Uncle Henry" and "alcoholic" in the same sentence. It was almost as if Ken and Christine thought I needed to be protected from
50 it, the way small children need to be protected from boors itching to tell them that Santa Claus is not real. The ban on Korea extended even to the aforementioned Uncle Henry, who was then deprived of his war stories at our Memorial Day
55 cookouts. Although he proudly wore his felt VFW hat with its flurry of pins, including ones from his tour "overseas," Christine or Ken would quietly slip him some of his favorite Pabst or Schlitz, and in return he'd set up residence in the lawn chair
60 at the far corner of our yard, away from everyone.

Somewhere back in the fuzzy clot of my teens (now, I'm at the worldly-wise age of almost-twenty), the '88 Summer Olympics were held in Seoul. We couldn't buck the Thorson family
65 tradition of watching absolutely everything (that winter we'd raptly watched curling, for God's sakes!). But I was aware that pains were taken to modulate voices, vocal cords twisted to an excru-ciating, studied casualness until *Korea* came out
70 "Korea," exactly the same way we'd say "Russia" or "Carl Lewis" or "Flo-Jo."

Then Bryant Gumbel invaded our living room with his special segment on how *Korea*, one of the four "Little Tiger" economic miracle countries, was
75 so enterprising that it had even made an export product out of its babies. Since the Korean War, more than a *hundred thousand children*, Made-in-Korea stamped on their foreheads, had left the country, their adoption fees fattening the govern-
80 ment coffers.

Top that, Singapore! Gumbel's cheery smirk seemed to say.

"Well, Sarah's really American, not Kor—" Amanda began, until the look on Christine's
85 face—despairing, fierce—stopped her.

We invent what becomes us.

CONTINUE ▶

13

The narrator characterizes Reverend Jansen primarily as

A) an aloof scholar.

B) a fierce taskmaster.

C) a sympathetic caregiver.

D) a patronizing figure.

14

The narrator's statement that her mother "had been murdered" (line 2) is best taken to mean that

A) her mother was killed by a negligent driver.

B) the reputation of her mother had been severely impugned.

C) the death of her mother was deliberate.

D) her adoptive family was trying to obliterate all memory of her biological mother.

15

The narrator's description of the reverend's "eyes" and "breath" in lines 15–16 primarily convey a sense of

A) empathy.

B) detachment.

C) geniality.

D) severity.

16

Christine believes that Sarah's ethnicity is

A) a source of pride.

B) an exotic mystery.

C) a sacred blessing.

D) an unfortunate fact.

17

Which choice provides the best evidence for the answer to the previous question?

A) Lines 13–16 ("God called . . . second")

B) Lines 24–26 ("That's why . . . treasure")

C) Lines 48–52 ("It was almost . . . is not real")

D) Lines 76–80 ("Since the Korean . . . government coffers")

18

Lines 26–28 ("God kills . . . my mother") are striking for their use of

A) juxtaposition.

B) metaphor.

C) personification.

D) understatement.

19

Lines 36–49 chiefly describe Christine's

A) cunning deceitfulness.

B) sense of superiority.

C) motherly sympathy.

D) emotional immaturity.

20

In line 45, "charged" most nearly means

A) loaded.

B) entrusted.

C) attacked.

D) demanded.

CONTINUE ▶

1   **1**

21

The passage suggests that Uncle Henry's role in the Thorson family is that of

A) a stern patriarch.

B) a bigoted lout.

C) a pitiable embarrassment.

D) a noble hero.

22

The "cheery smirk" (line 81) is taken by the narrator to indicate Gumbel's

A) satisfaction with the publicity the Olympics were receiving.

B) admiration for Korea's economic competitiveness.

C) pleasure that Korean children would be well cared for.

D) happiness that Singapore had finally been defeated.

Questions 23–32 are based on the following passage and any accompanying material.

This passage is adapted from Christopher F. Black, *"Baby Pictures of the Universe."* ©2015 by Christopher F. Black and College Hill Coaching.

At the breathtaking Gettysburg Cyclorama, a 377-foot-long, 42-foot-high painting of the bloody 1863 Battle of Gettysburg, visitors can turn in every direction and feel as if they have
5 been thrust into the midst of perhaps the most important battle in American history, a snapshot of a chaotic chapter in the early life of a nation. Yet right now you sit in the midst of an even more spectacular cyclorama of an even more cata-
10 clysmic historical event that took place *billions* of years ago. Unfortunately, to appreciate its full splendor, you would have to be able to see microwaves, which are invisible to our human eyes.

This real-life cyclorama is the cosmic micro-
15 wave background (CMB) radiation, a 13-billion-year-old panoramic snapshot of the universe as it appeared the moment it first released its primordial photons. Although it is an astonishingly detailed confirmation of the Big Bang theory,
20 it is not actually a picture of the Big Bang. On a human scale, it corresponds not to the instant of childbirth, but rather the moment a swaddled one-day-old opens its eyes and keeps them open.

For the first 380,000 years of its life (a mere
25 blink of an eye in cosmic history), the universe was "invisible" because its photons—the particles that are emitted from an object or event and that must reach a detector in order for us to "see" it—were trapped in a hot, opaque fog of hydrogen plasma.
30 Only when this super-heated plasma cooled to the point where protons and electrons could combine to form hydrogen atoms—a period called the "epoch of recombination"—did these photons begin to travel unimpeded through the universe.

35 Some of those photons, having traveled for half a billion generations, are just now reaching us.

One of the most striking aspects of the CMB radiation is its near-uniformity, or "isotropism." No matter where we look in the sky, the temperature of
40 the CMB radiation varies by no more than one part in 100,000. It's almost impossible to find another real-life example of such thermal homogeneity.

This uniformity is somewhat counterintuitive: the remnants of most explosions seem to spread
45 out in a spherical but non-uniform "debris field." For instance, the embers of a firework explosion are confined to a region around the explosion, but nowhere else. So why is the CMB radiation still found everywhere in the universe, and not just on
50 its "edges?" The first reason is that the universe *has* no edges: it is "boundless," just as the surface of a sphere is boundless. The second reason is that the CMB radiation did not originate from just one point in space, but from virtually *every* point in
55 space. Thus, every point in the modern universe is not only equally likely to be the source of the CMB radiation, it is also equally likely to be the current location of the CMB radiation.

This uniformity was predicted in a theory
60 published by George Gamow in 1948. His theory also made two other predictions that have been confirmed to astonishing precision by our current data. First, Gamow predicted that the CMB radiation should have a distinctive spectrum known as
65 a "blackbody" curve. Second, he predicted that the expanding universe would have cooled this radiation to below 5 degrees Kelvin today.

The CMB radiation went undetected until 1964, when Arno Penzias and Robert Wilson
70 at Bell Laboratories in Murray Hill, New Jersey became troubled by persistent background noise in a radio telescope that they had just built. Their initial explanation was that it was due to a "white dielectric substance," more commonly known as
75 pigeon droppings. Remarkably, less than 40 miles away, Princeton researchers Robert Dicke and

CONTINUE ▶

1

1

Dave Wilkinson had been searching for evidence supporting Gamow's predictions, and instantly knew of a much better explanation for the noise.
80 Penzias and Wilson shared the 1978 Nobel Prize in physics for their discovery of the CMB radiation.

Since then, much more careful observations, made by the NASA Cosmic Background Explorer (COBE) and the Wilkinson Microwave Anisotropy
85 Probe (WMAP) have confirmed that the CMB radiation indeed has a nearly perfect blackbody

spectrum corresponding to a temperature of 2.725° Kelvin, barely more than 2 degrees from Gamow's guess. In addition to confirming many
90 aspects of the Big Bang theory, these data have also helped scientists calibrate the age of the universe (13.772 ± 0.059 billion years), gauge the speed at which the universe is expanding, and even verify the existence of "dark energy," the
95 mysterious energy that propelled the rapid expansion of the early universe.

COSMIC BACKGROUND RADIATION SPECTRUM FROM COBE
AND BLACKBODY RADIATION CURVES FOR VARIOUS TEMPERATURES

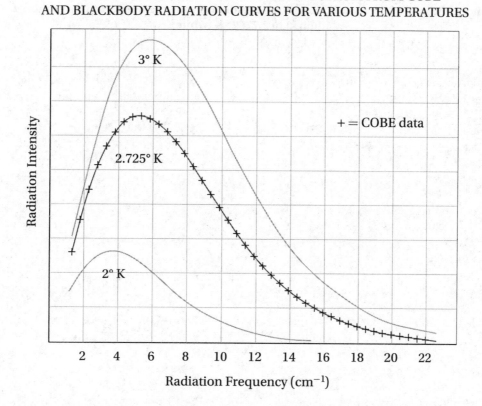

Figure 1.   Comparison of COBE radiation data to blackbody curves for 2° K and 3° K

CONTINUE ▶

Figure 2.   Panoramic map of the cosmic background radiation showing temperatures ranging from 2.7248° K (dark) to 2.7252° K (white)

23

This passage is primarily concerned with

A) chronicling the discoveries yielded by recent satellite telescopes.

B) examining the controversies surrounding a physical theory.

C) discussing the analysis and significance of a cosmological phenomenon.

D) describing similarities between the study of human history and the study of astronomy.

24

The author presents the "Gettysburg Cyclorama" (line 1) primarily as

A) an illustrative analogy.

B) a historical precedent.

C) a quaint anachronism.

D) an accidental success.

25

Lines 11–13 ("Unfortunately . . . human eyes") convey the author's disappointment in

A) the appropriateness of a comparison.

B) an audience's level of interest.

C) the magnitude of an event.

D) the accessibility of a phenomenon.

26

The quotation marks around the words "invisible" (line 26) and "see" (line 28) serve primarily to

A) draw attention to two relatively recent coinages.

B) imply that the author is speaking speculatively.

C) suggest an irony implicit in conventional terms.

D) indicate a technical usage of common words.

27

The "moment a swaddled one-day-old opens its eyes" (lines 22-23) corresponds to the instant that

A) scientists first discovered the cosmic microwave background radiation.

B) all of the particles and energy in the universe were created in the Big Bang.

C) the cosmic microwave background radiation was first released from the hydrogen plasma.

D) George Gamow first published his theory about the cosmic microwave background radiation.

28

In line 64, "distinctive" most nearly means

A) bizarre.

B) distinguishing.

C) elite.

D) irreconcilable.

29

Which of the following can be inferred about the work that earned Penzias and Wilson the Nobel Prize?

A) It was the product of decades of research.

B) It was the result of an accidental discovery.

C) It depended greatly on the data from the COBE satellite.

D) It provided a more plausible alternative to Gamow's theory.

30

Which choice provides the best evidence for the answer to the previous question?

A) Lines 60–63 ("His theory . . . current data")

B) Lines 72–75 ("Their initial . . . droppings")

C) Lines 82–89 ("Since then . . . Gamow's guess")

D) Lines 89–96 ("In addition . . . early universe")

CONTINUE

31

Figure 1 best confirms which claim made in the passage?

A) "For the first 380,000 years of its life . . . the universe was 'invisible'" (lines 24–26)

B) "the CMB radiation did not originate from just one point in space" (lines 53–54)

C) "the expanding universe would have cooled this radiation to below 5 degrees Kelvin today" (lines 66–67)

D) "CMB radiation . . . has a nearly perfect blackbody spectrum" (lines 85–87)

32

Figure 2 best confirms which claim made in the passage?

A) "For the first 380,000 years of its life . . . the universe was 'invisible'" (lines 24–26)

B) "the CMB radiation did not originate from just one point in space" (lines 53–54)

C) "the expanding universe would have cooled this radiation to about 5 degrees Kelvin" (lines 66–67)

D) "CMB radiation . . . has a nearly perfect blackbody spectrum" (lines 85–87)

Questions 33–42 are based on the following passage.

This passage is from John Adams, *"A Dissertation on Canon and Feudal law."* Originally published in 1765.

Liberty cannot be preserved without a general
knowledge among the people, who have a right,
Line from the frame of their nature, to knowledge,
and who have been given understandings,
5 and a desire to know. But besides this, they have a
right, an indisputable, unalienable, indefeasible,
divine right to that most dreaded and envied
kind of knowledge of the characters and conduct
of their rulers. Rulers are no more than attor-
10 neys, agents, and trustees, for the people. And
if the cause, the interest and trust, is insidiously
betrayed, or wantonly trifled away, the people
have a right to revoke the authority that they
themselves have deputed, and to constitute abler
15 and better agents, attorneys and trustees. And the
preservation of the means of knowledge among
the lowest ranks is of more importance to the
public than all the property of all the rich men in
the country. It is even of more consequence to the
20 rich themselves, and to their posterity. The only
question is whether it is a public emolument;[1]
and if it is, the rich ought undoubtedly to contribute, in the same proportion as to all other public
burdens—that is, in proportion to their wealth,
25 which is secured by public expenses. But none
of the means of information are more sacred, or
have been cherished with more tenderness and
care by the settlers of America, than the press.
Care has been taken that the art of printing
30 should be encouraged, and that it should be easy
and cheap and safe for any person to communicate his thoughts to the public.
Let us dare to read, think, speak and write.
Let every order and degree among the people

35 rouse their attention and animate their resolution. Let them all become attentive to the grounds
and principles of government, ecclesiastical[2] and
civil. Let us study the law of nature; search into
the spirit of the British Constitution; read the
40 histories of ancient ages; contemplate the great
examples of Greece and Rome; set before us the
conduct of our own British ancestors, who have
defended for us the inherent rights of mankind
against foreign and domestic tyrants and usurp-
45 ers, against arbitrary kings and cruel priests, in
short, against the gates of earth and hell. Let us
read and recollect and impress upon our souls
the views and ends of our own more immediate
forefathers in exchanging their native country for
50 a dreary, inhospitable wilderness. Let us examine
the nature of that power, and the cruelty of that
oppression, which drove them from their homes.
Recollect their amazing fortitude, their bitter
sufferings—the hunger, the nakedness, the cold,
55 which they patiently endured—the severe labors
of clearing their grounds, building their houses,
raising their provisions, amidst dangers from
wild beasts and savage men, before they had time
or money or materials for commerce. Recollect
60 the civil and religious principles and hopes and
expectations which constantly supported and
carried them through all hardships with patience
and resignation. Let us recollect it was liberty,
the hope of liberty for themselves and us and
65 ours, which conquered all the discouragements,
dangers and trials. In such researches as these
let us all in our several departments cheerfully
engage—but especially the proper patrons and
supporters of law, learning, and religion!

[1] benefit
[2] related to church matters

33

The first paragraph is primarily concerned with the right of citizens to

A) pursue academic interests.

B) learn more about their leaders.

C) become proficient in the art of printing.

D) propose helpful legislation.

34

In line 14, "constitute" most nearly means

A) place in power.

B) account for.

C) amount to.

D) be regarded as.

35

The passage indicates that our "forefathers" (line 49) endured all of the following EXCEPT

A) physical deprivation.

B) political oppression.

C) arduous physical labor.

D) a sense of despair.

36

The passage indicates that all people are born with

A) a curious nature.

B) a desire for power.

C) a dread of tyranny.

D) a sense of thrift.

37

Which sentence provides the best evidence for the answer to the previous question?

A) Lines 1–5 ("Liberty . . . to know")

B) Lines 10–15 ("And if the cause . . . trustees")

C) Lines 20–25 ("The only question . . . public expenses")

D) Lines 38–46 ("Let us study . . . earth and hell")

38

In line 34, the phrase "every order and degree" refers to

A) an anthology of official declarations.

B) a set of civic responsibilities.

C) the diverse groups within a society.

D) the highest standards of academic achievement.

39

Compared to the first paragraph, the second paragraph is more

A) prescriptive.

B) despondent.

C) critical.

D) ironic.

40

In line 51, "power" refers to

A) a personal ability.

B) a social virtue.

C) a despotic agent.

D) a mysterious spirit.

1   **1**

41

In line 46, "the gates of earth and hell" refer primarily to

A) the privations endured by our forefathers.

B) the superstitions of ancient cultures.

C) the dangers posed by an ignorant populace.

D) the brutality of oppressive leaders.

42

In the second paragraph, the discussion of the "views and ends" (line 48) of our forefathers primarily serves to

A) remind the reader of the importance of liberty.

B) establish a contrast between the past and the present.

C) emphasize the significance of hard work.

D) draw attention to an unfortunate tradition.

CONTINUE →

Questions 43–52 are based on the following passage and supplementary material.

This passage is from David Biello, *"Can Tiny Plankton Help Reverse Climate Change?"* ©2015 by David Biello. Originally published in Aeon (http://aeon.co/) on July 1, 2014.

Line
5

The forbidding sea known as the Southern Ocean surrounds Antarctica with a chilly current, locking it in a deep freeze like a moat reaching to the ocean floor. Dangerous icebergs hide in its gloom. Its churning swells sometimes serve up freak waves that can easily flip ships. In this violent place Victor Smetacek hopes to transform Earth's atmosphere.

10

Since the 1980s, Smetacek has studied the plankton—tiny animals, protists, algae, and bacteria—that fill the Southern Ocean. Plankton is our planet's most prolific life form, providing the base layer of the global food chain.

15

Much of the oxygen we breathe comes from just one species of cyanobacteria, *Prochlorococcus*, which has dominated Earth's oxygen production for the last 2.4 billion years. These minuscule marine plants produce more oxygen than all of the planet's forests combined.

20

Their steady breathing is limited only by a lack of key nutritional elements. If enough of these nutrients are supplied by dust off a continent or fertilizer run-off from farm fields, the oceans can produce blooms that can be seen from space.

25

Many of these plankton pastures are held back by iron shortages, especially in places that are largely cut off from continental dust and dirt. With access to more iron, the plankton would proliferate and siphon more and more planet-heating

30

CO_2 from the atmosphere. Back in 1988, the late John Martin, then an oceanographer at the Moss Landing Marine Observatory, said: "Give me a half tanker of iron, and I will give you an ice age."

35

Iron fertilization could potentially sequester as much as one billion metric tons of carbon dioxide annually, and keep it deep in the ocean for centuries. That is slightly more than the CO_2 output of the German economy, and roughly one-eighth of humanity's entire greenhouse gas output.

40

Using an iron sulphate waste sold as a lawn treatment in Germany, Smetacek and his colleagues set out in 2004 to supply the plankton with the nutrient they needed. Fertilizing the waters, they hoped, would promote blooms to

45

help sea life thrive all the way up the food chain, even to whale populations, which were still recovering from overhunting. And, more importantly, the uneaten plankton could suck out CO_2 from the air until they died and sank to the sea floor,

50

thereby providing natural carbon sequestration.

Smetacek's ship dumped enough of the iron sulfate to raise the iron concentration by 0.01 gram per square meter in a 167-square-kilometer self-contained swirl of water that could maintain

55

its shape for weeks or even months. Smetacek and his crew waited, as he described in his log, "with the fatalistic patience of the farmer, watching the crop develop in the painstakingly selected field." Over the course of two weeks, thirteen spe-

60

cies of diatoms bloomed down to depths of 100 meters. Then the bloom began to die in large enough numbers to overwhelm natural systems of decay, falling like snow to depths of 500 meters. About half of them continued on even further,

65

sinking more than 3,000 meters to the sea floor.

For two weeks, Smetacek induced carbon to fall to the sea floor at the highest rate ever observed—34 times faster than normal. This marine tinkering could help buffer the ever-

70

increasing concentrations of CO_2 in the atmosphere, concentrations that have touched 400 parts-per-million, levels never before experienced in the history of our species.

Yet environmentalists were outraged by

75

Smetacek's project. Activists stoked fears that the iron could lead to a toxic algal bloom or a "dead zone" like the one created each summer in the Gulf of Mexico, where the fertilizers from Midwestern cornfields gush out of the Mississippi

80

river, stoking algal blooms that then die and are consumed by other microbes, which consume all the available oxygen in the surrounding waters, causing fish to flee and suffocating crabs and worms. As a result of these objections, there

85

have been no scientific research cruises since 2009, and none are planned for the immediate future.

CONTINUE ▶

1

1

Smetacek suggests that commerce might be the only way to motivate further research into iron fertilization. Replenishing missing krill, and the whales it supports, could be the best route to broader acceptance of the practice.

90

The ocean is no longer a vast, unknowable wilderness. Instead, it's a viable arena

95 for large-scale manipulation of the planetary environment. We have tamed the heaving, alien world of the sea and, though doing so can make us uncomfortable, in the end it might undo a great deal of the damage we have already done.

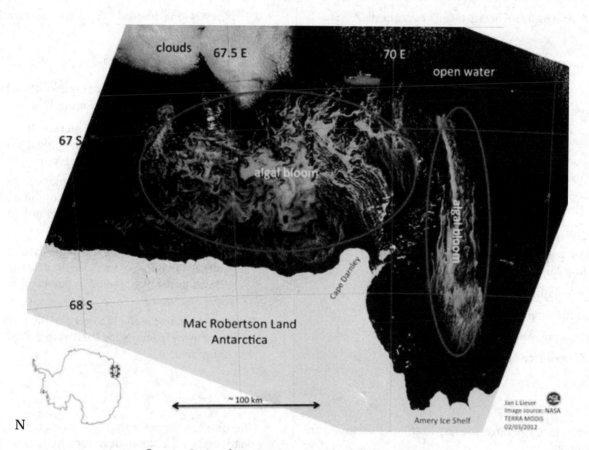

Source: Image from Jan Lieser and NASA Terra Modis

NASA satellite image of the largest recorded natural phytoplankton bloom in February 2012, believed to have been caused by the addition of iron dust blown into the sea around Antarctica by strong offshore winds.

CONTINUE

43

The characterization of the Southern Ocean in the first paragraph (lines 1–8) primarily serves to emphasize

A) the improbability of Smetacek's success.

B) the pessimism of Smetacek's detractors.

C) the boldness of Smetacek's experiment.

D) the promise of Smetacek's hypothesis.

44

In line 13, the word "base" most nearly means

A) sordid.

B) precarious.

C) stark.

D) foundational.

45

The passage indicates that the "fertilizer run-off" (line 23) is

A) an unfortunate by-product.

B) an environmental hazard.

C) a potential sustenance.

D) a source of oxygen.

46

The author regards the fertilization of oceans with iron as

A) a well-intentioned but environmentally dangerous activity.

B) a brave but needlessly expensive endeavor.

C) a promising and feasible solution to a global problem.

D) an established and valuable component of the worldwide economy.

47

Which sentence provides the best evidence for the answer to the previous question?

A) Lines 5–6 ("Its churning . . . ships")

B) Lines 75–84 ("Activists stoked . . . crabs and worms")

C) Lines 90–92 ("Replenishing . . . the practice")

D) Lines 94–96 ("Instead, it's . . . environment")

48

Which of the following statements about Smetacek's research is best supported by Figure 1?

A) The iron fertilization from Smetacek's experiment created a secondary algal bloom nearly as large as the primary bloom.

B) Smetacek's experiment would likely have been more successful if it were conducted in February, which is the warmest month in the southern hemisphere.

C) Naturally occurring algal blooms in the Southern Ocean can be more than 30 times as large as the one created in Smetacek's experiments.

D) Algal blooms are likely to get smaller as they move away from the ice shelves that surround Antarctica.

49

The passage suggests that Smetacek regarded the death of the alga bloom described in lines 61–65 as

A) vindication of his theory that iron fertilization can lead to carbon sequestration.

B) an indication of the potential dangers of "dead zones" such as those in the Gulf of Mexico.

C) evidence that there was insufficient oxygen in the Southern Ocean to support large blooms.

D) a disappointment because the diatoms were being removed from the food chain.

CONTINUE

1   1

50

The passage suggests that iron fertilization could potentially help the whale population primarily by

A) increasing the concentration of oxygen in the ecosphere.

B) decreasing the concentration of carbon dioxide in the atmosphere.

C) supporting an important food source for the whales.

D) reducing the demand for hunting in areas where the whales are endangered.

51

The "route" mentioned in line 91 refers to

A) an experimental procedure.

B) an economic difficulty.

C) an idealistic approach.

D) a mode of persuasion.

52

The tone of the final paragraph is best described as

A) sanguine.

B) awestruck.

C) apprehensive.

D) fatalistic.

STOP

**If you finish before time is called, you may check your work on this section only.
Do not turn to any other section of the test.**

2   2

Writing and Language Test

35 MINUTES, 44 QUESTIONS

Turn to Section 2 of your answer sheet to answer the questions in this section.

Each passage below is accompanied by a number of questions. For some questions, you will consider how the passage might be revised to improve the expression of ideas. For other questions, you will consider how the passage might be edited to correct errors in sentence structure, usage, or punctuation. A passage or a question may be accompanied by one or more graphics (such as a table or graph) that you will consider as you make revising and editing decisions.

Some questions will direct you to an underlined portion of a passage. Other questions will direct you to a location in a passage or ask you to think about the passage as a whole.

After reading each passage, choose the answer to each question that most effectively improves the quality of writing in the passage or that makes the passage conform to the conventions of Standard Written English. Many questions include a "NO CHANGE" option. Choose that option if you think the best choice is to leave the relevant portion of the passage as it is.

Questions 1–11 are based on the following passage.

The Carrot or the Stick?

Good teachers want their students to do well, but getting students **1** responding is not always easy. Simple suggestion works occasionally, but not often enough. Reasoning sometimes works, too, but explaining the logical nuances of behavioral standards **2** is often time-consuming and too often falls on deaf ears.

1

A) NO CHANGE
B) to become responsive
C) to respond
D) becoming more responsive

2

A) NO CHANGE
B) are often time-consuming
C) is consuming time
D) consume time

CONTINUE ▶

2   2

So the practical question becomes: the carrot or the stick? It's not always easy to choose **3** the potential motivator to consider: by punishment or incentive.

Most educators and psychologists agree that, as a teaching tool, **4** to reward is generally better than punishment, but a growing group of psychologists suggest that rewards can often be as **5** harmful, if not more so, than punishment. The introduction of a reward system, like gold stars on an attendance sheet or extra recess time for good behavior, can change the nature not only of the desired behavior, **6** but also of the student-teacher relationship.

Psychologist Edward Deci conducted a study in which people were given a challenging puzzle to solve. Some subjects were offered money as a reward for solving the puzzle, and others were not.

Afterward, both groups were observed secretly after the researcher left the room. Many of those who had not been paid as a reward for their work continued to play with the puzzle, presumably because they found

3

A) NO CHANGE

B) between punishment and incentive when considering potential motivators

C) the potential motivator to consider: either punishment or incentive

D) between punishment and incentive as potential motivators to be considered

4

A) NO CHANGE

B) reward

C) rewarding

D) a reward

5

A) NO CHANGE

B) harmful as, if not more harmful than,

C) harmful, if not more harmful, than

D) equally harmful, if not more harmful than,

6

A) NO CHANGE

B) but also the nature of the student-teacher relationship

C) but the student-teacher relationship as well

D) but the nature of the student-teacher relationship is changed as well

CONTINUE ➡

it interesting for its own sake. **7** <u>Those who had received the cash rewards, however, showed significantly less interest in returning to the puzzle.</u>

8 <u>Interpreting these results,</u> the subjects who were paid probably construed the task as being manipulative: the experimenter was trying to get them to do something through bribery. The unpaid subjects, however, could engage the puzzle on their own terms simply because it was fun.

This study and others like it have profound **9** <u>implications</u> for the classroom. Several experiments have demonstrated that "pay-to-read" programs, where students are given money or gift credits to read books, have surprisingly negative effects on literacy. Such programs do get students to "read" more books, but the kind of reading they do is not ideal. Students tend to read superficially and only to get the reward. In follow-up studies, these students show not only lower reading skills but also less desire to read. **10** <u>Nevertheless,</u> the reward system turns reading from a fun activity into drudgery. Students think, if reading is such a rewarding experience, why do they need to pay us to do it?

It would be a mistake to conclude from a few experiments that all rewards are bad. Certainly, honest praise from a respectful teacher can do a great deal to encourage not only good behavior but also intellectual curiosity. Teachers must be aware of their students' need to feel independent and in control. **11**

7

The author is considering deleting the final sentence to make the paragraph more concise. Should the author make this change?

A) Yes, because it conveys information that is already implied elsewhere in the paragraph.

B) Yes, because it conveys information that distracts from the discussion of student motivation.

C) No, because it explains why the experiment was so difficult to conduct.

D) No, because it provides information that is essential to this discussion of student motivation.

8

A) NO CHANGE

B) While interpreting these results

C) One interpretation of these results is that

D) In interpreting these results,

9

A) NO CHANGE

B) indications

C) improvisations

D) instigations

10

A) NO CHANGE

B) Evidently

C) However

D) Lastly

11

The final paragraph is notable primarily for its use of which two rhetorical devices?

A) prescription and qualification

B) illustration and quantification

C) anecdote and metaphor

D) irony and humor

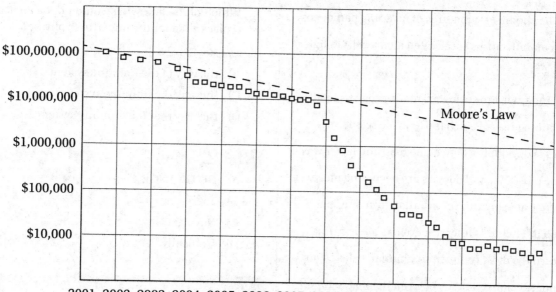

COST PER GENOME DECODED

Source: National Human Genome Research Institute: genome.gov/sequencingcosts

Questions 12–22 are based on the following passage.

The Promise of Bio-Informatics

Although scientists have always been interested in data, modern biologists are increasingly becoming "information scientists." Biological information science is the study of how chemical signals govern life processes. The most familiar biomolecular code is of course DNA, **12** serving as the chemical compound for the blueprint of life. Another biochemical code tells a fertilized egg how to differentiate into scores of unique cell types—heart, muscle, bone, nerve, gland, **13** blood—that assemble themselves into organs, which in turn assemble themselves into a complex organism.

12

A) NO CHANGE

B) this is the chemical compound serving as

C) the chemical compound that serves as

D) which is the chemical compound that is serving as

13

A) NO CHANGE

B) blood, that assemble themselves

C) blood; assembling themselves

D) blood—assembling itself

CONTINUE ▶

2　　　　　　　　　　　　　　　　　　　**2**

Yet another code governs [14] how the immune system "reads" the chemical signatures of invading pathogens and then manufactures specialized attack cells to fight infections.

　[15] Today we are seeing dramatic progress in all three of these areas of biochemistry. The science of genomics is developing better, cheaper, and faster ways to decode our DNA, and doctors are becoming more [16] apropos at using this information to create "personalized medicine." Other researchers are learning how to turn the most rudimentary human cells, "stem cells," into specialized tissues [17] for helping to repair damaged human organs. And oncologists—cancer specialists—are now coming to understand how the human immune system can be decoded to provide a crucial weapon against the most dangerous tumors.

[14]

Which of the following would <u>not</u> be an acceptable replacement for the underlined phrase?

A) NO CHANGE

B) the way of the immune system

C) the way the immune system

D) the way that the immune system

[15]

A) NO CHANGE

B) Therefore,

C) Nevertheless,

D) Ironically,

[16]

A) NO CHANGE

B) adept

C) liable

D) essential

[17]

A) NO CHANGE

B) in helping repair of

C) in order to help repairing

D) to help repair

2 ... **2**

18 In particular, the success of these new biological technologies **19** depends on our ability in translating vast quantities of chemical information into digital form. Specialized software and hardware **20** is needed to be developed to turn biochemical data into information that doctors and researchers can use to streamline research and make patients' lives better. Fortunately, the progress has so far been good. Since the Human Genome Project was completed in 2003, the National Human Genome Research Institute has monitored the cost of decoding a single human-sized genome. A famous law in computer science, known as "Moore's Law," says that the cost of processing a given quantity of information should decline by 50% every two years or so. In fact, with "second generation" techniques developed in 2008, the cost of decoding human genomes has plummeted even faster than Moore's Law predicted. **21**

18

Which choice most effectively establishes the main topic of the paragraph?

A) Some scientists are skeptical about the viability of such radical new therapies.

B) Researchers from all over the world are collaborating in these new discoveries.

C) These new therapies and cures depend heavily on progress in the computer sciences.

D) Many forms of alternative medicine are being combined with traditional therapies to treat a wide range of diseases.

19

A) NO CHANGE

B) depend on our ability to translate

C) depends on the ability of our translating

D) depends on our ability to translate

20

A) NO CHANGE

B) must be developed

C) must develop

D) needs developing

21

Which of the following statements is best supported by the data in Figure 1?

A) Since 2003, more people have been taking advantage of genome sequencing technologies, thereby reducing costs.

B) By the start of 2014, the cost per genome was less than 1% what Moore's Law had predicted.

C) Nevertheless, it still costs more than $10,000 to decode a single genome.

D) The cost of genome sequencing is declining more rapidly than that of any other information-based technology.

CONTINUE ➔

2

2

This integration of medicine and information technology is perhaps today's most promising scientific development. Using these new resources, perhaps **22** treatments and even cures for the most intractable diseases can be discovered by researchers.

CONTINUE

22

A) NO CHANGE

B) researchers will discover treatments and even cures for the most intractable diseases

C) treatments and even cures will be discovered by researchers for the most intractable diseases

D) researchers have discovered treatments and even cures for the most intractable diseases

2   **2**

Questions 23–33 are based on the following passage.

What is Art?

Look around you. Do you see art in your immediate surroundings? What qualities 23 decide that certain things are art? Definitions of art vary widely, but most tend to fall within general notions 24 that have developed over the centuries. The technical ability of an ancient Egyptian potter to produce a well-made clay vessel defined his "art." In Europe 600 years ago, trade and professional organizations from shoemaking to banking 25 would hold to this broad definition of art as skill in a particular field. The currently popular notion of the artist as the creator and definer of art—put simply, "Art is what artists create"—is a relatively recent one.

Some items and activities in our environment 26 stand out in a conspicuous way as somehow more "art" than others. The way that the visual elements of particular buildings, chairs, album covers, or athletic performances—their line, color, shape, texture, and other visual elements—combine to please the senses, is so satisfying that we call them beautiful. 27

Prior to the twentieth century, most philosophers of art believed that beauty was the defining feature of art. By the turn of the twentieth century, however, some aestheticians had begun to find this definition insufficient. Some said that the defining

---

23

A) NO CHANGE
B) arrange
C) regulate
D) determine

24

A) NO CHANGE
B) developing
C) which are developed
D) as developed

25

A) NO CHANGE
B) hold
C) had held
D) held

26

A) NO CHANGE
B) are conspicuous for how they stand out
C) stand out
D) stand out conspicuously

27

The end of the second paragraph could be best enhanced with a sentence about

A) an alternate theory of beauty
B) why a particular chair is beautiful
C) how to design more beautiful buildings
D) the benefits of art therapy

CONTINUE ➡

characteristic of art was the effective expression of [28] emotion; but others said the effective communication of ideas. One influential group, the formalists, argued that an object or activity qualifies as art [29] when its form is sufficiently compelling or inspiring or beautiful to provoke an intense sensory response. This echoed the ancient Greek definition of aesthetic: "of or pertaining to the senses" or "sensuous perception."

Aesthetic experiences are not as rare as you might think. If you have ever felt yourself swept away in the sensuous experience of a sports event, a musical performance, a film, a sunset, or a [30] painting: you have had an aesthetic experience. Look around again. Do any objects in your field of vision provoke an aesthetic experience? [31] Is it skill, beauty, expression, communication, compelling form, or all of the above that make these art for you? Or is it some other quality, such as originality or creativity, [32] that makes these objects or activities stand out as art?

[28]

A) NO CHANGE

B) emotion; others said it was

C) emotion, others said it was

D) emotion; while others said it was

[29]

A) NO CHANGE

B) if its form sufficiently compels

C) if its form is sufficiently compelling

D) if it's form is sufficiently compelling

[30]

A) NO CHANGE

B) painting; you

C) painting—you

D) painting, you

[31]

A) NO CHANGE

B) Are they

C) Do

D) Are

[32]

A) NO CHANGE

B) making these objects that stand out

C) that make these objects stand out

D) that stands out in these objects to make them

2   2

Does setting matter? Would a sports photo become more "artistic" if it were placed in an art museum? According to George Dickie's "institutional theory of art," major art institutions, such as museums, determine what is art in a given culture. **33**

Perhaps art is a concept that cannot have a fixed definition. Perhaps, like a living organism, it must evolve.

33

Which of the following sentences serves as the most effective concluding sentence for this paragraph?

A) Dickie, a professor emeritus of philosophy at the University of Illinois, has championed the work of philosopher David Hume.

B) Nearly every major city has museums dedicated to the display of works of fine art such as paintings, sculptures, and performance art.

C) Other institutions, such as schools and governments, also provide definitions for concepts like education and public value.

D) This theory forces us to ask: is art truly in the eye of the beholder, or is it in the eye of the artist, the curator, or some critical mass of the consuming public?

CONTINUE ▶

2   **2**

Questions 34–44 are based on the following passage.

The Little Tramp

Few people have had as strong an impact on an industry **34** as the impact that Charlie Chaplin had on the world of film. **35** Born in 1889 into an impoverished London family, Chaplin crossed the Atlantic and became a pioneer in silent comedic movies. **36** Early in his film career, Chaplin developed his signature character, the "Little Tramp," who amused audiences repeatedly with his clever physical comedy and endearing sensitivity. Modest yet clearly intelligent, shy yet always at the center of action, the **37** Tramp's embodiment was the genius of Chaplin's artistry.

34

A) NO CHANGE
B) as what Charlie Chaplin
C) than Charlie Chaplin
D) as Charlie Chaplin

35

A) NO CHANGE
B) He was born in 1889 into
C) Being born in 1889 into
D) He was born in 1889 of

36

The author is considering inserting the following sentence at this point in the paragraph.

> Charlie's mother suffered from severe mental illness and was institutionalized for a significant part of Charlie's young life.

Do you think this is appropriate?

A) Yes, because it helps to explain how Chaplin became a pioneer in film.
B) Yes, because it provides an important detail about health care in 19th-century London.
C) No, because it detracts from the discussion of Chaplin's impact on the film industry.
D) No, because it diminishes the humorous tone of the paragraph.

37

A) NO CHANGE
B) genius of Chaplin's artistry was embodied by the Tramp
C) Tramp embodied the genius of Chaplin's artistry
D) Tramp's embodiment was of the genius of Chaplin's artistry

2

2

38 Being writer, director, and editing his own work, Chaplin faced a daunting challenge with the rise of "talkie" films, which drew audiences away from silent stars like the Tramp. Chaplin responded by taking on the additional role of composer, writing beautiful scores to accompany his films and **39** thus allowing the Tramp to remain speechless. Chaplin managed to defy the odds and maintain a remarkable level of popularity and success in the face of technological advancement. **40** Not just a master of the craft of acting and filmmaking, but also the face of a character that resonated deeply with those suffering through the Depression.

A vocal liberal in a time of conservative domination, **41** he became a target for Senator Joseph McCarthy and his House Un-American Activities Committee. While he managed to avoid being named to McCarthy's Hollywood Ten, a list of black listed entertainment industry figures suspected of Communist connections, he drew the ire of J. Edgar Hoover **42** in the messages imbedded within his films.

Chaplin saw the dangers in Hitler's rise to power before most of the world had heard of the dictator. He

38

A) NO CHANGE
B) Writing, directing, and being editor of his own work,
C) Writing his own work, as well as directing and editing it too,
D) As the writer, director, and editor of his own work,

39

A) NO CHANGE
B) therefore he allowed the Tramp to remain
C) allowing the Tramp thus remaining
D) he allowed the Tramp thus to remain

40

A) NO CHANGE
B) Besides being
C) He was not only
D) In addition to being

41

A) NO CHANGE
B) Senator Joseph McCarthy and his house Un-American Activities Committee targeted him
C) the House Un-American Activities Committee of Senator Joseph McCarthy targeted him
D) he became targeted for Senator Joseph McCarthy's House Un-American Activities Committee.

42

A) NO CHANGE
B) by
C) because of
D) from

CONTINUE ➡

also believed that the development of the atomic bomb was a crime. Outraged at what **43** they viewed as subversive propaganda created by an immoral man, the United States government **44** eradicated Chaplin's reentry visa during a trip to London in 1952. Sixty-three years old and tired of fighting against a force unwilling to hear his message, Chaplin agreed to exile rather than going back to America and facing interrogation and lived the rest of his years in Europe. He returned twenty years later to receive an Academy Award for lifetime achievement.

43

A) NO CHANGE
B) it
C) would have been
D) were

44

A) NO CHANGE
B) revoked
C) excluded
D) abolished

STOP

**If you finish before time is called, you may check your work on this section only.
Do not turn to any other section of the test.**

3 **3**

Math Test – No Calculator

25 MINUTES, 20 QUESTIONS

Turn to Section 3 of your answer sheet to answer the questions in this section.

DIRECTIONS

For questions 1–15, solve each problem, choose the best answer from the choices provided, and fill in the corresponding circle on your answer sheet. **For questions 16–20,** solve the problem and enter your answer in the grid on the answer sheet. Please refer to the directions before question 16 on how to enter your answers in the grid. You may use any available space in your test booklet for scratch work.

NOTES

1. The use of a calculator is NOT permitted.
2. All variables and expressions used represent real numbers unless otherwise indicated.
3. Figures provided in this test are drawn to scale unless otherwise indicated.
4. All figures lie in a plane unless otherwise indicated.
5. Unless otherwise indicated, the domain of a given function f is the set of all real numbers for which $f(x)$ is a real number.

REFERENCE

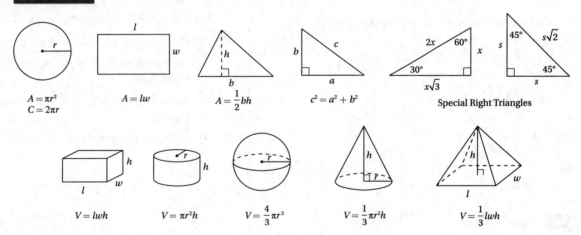

The number of degrees of arc in a circle is 360.
The number of radians of arc in a circle is 2π.
The sum of the measures in degrees of the angles of a triangle is 180.

CONTINUE ▶

3 **3**

1

If $8x + 6 = 6m$, what is the value of $4x + 3$ in terms of m?

A) $2m - 3$

B) $2m$

C) $3m - 3$

D) $3m$

2

$$3x + 4y = 18$$
$$y = \frac{3}{2}x$$

Which of the following ordered pairs (x, y) is a solution of the system of equations above?

A) $(2, 3)$

B) $(3, 2.25)$

C) $(4, 1.5)$

D) $(4, 6)$

3

Which of the following is equivalent to $\dfrac{3x + 4}{12}$?

A) $\dfrac{x + 4}{4}$

B) $\dfrac{3x + 1}{3}$

C) $\dfrac{x}{4} + \dfrac{1}{3}$

D) $\dfrac{x}{3} + \dfrac{1}{4}$

4

If $x - 3$ is a factor of the expression $x^2 + kx + 12$, what is the value of k?

A) -7

B) -5

C) 5

D) 7

5

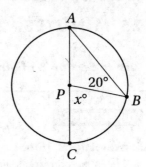

Note: Figure not drawn to scale.

In the figure above, P is the center of a circle and AC is its diameter. What is the value of x?

A) 60

B) 50

C) 40

D) 30

6

The nth term of a sequence is given by the expression $bn + 4$, where b is a positive constant. Which of the following is necessarily equal to b?

A) the value of the first term

B) the difference between the fourth term and the third term

C) the average (arithmetic mean) of the first three terms

D) the ratio of the second term to the first term

CONTINUE

3 **3**

7

If $m^3 = \sqrt{\sqrt{n}}$, where $n > 0$, what is the value of m in terms of n?

A) $n^{\frac{1}{12}}$

B) $n^{\frac{1}{7}}$

C) $n^{\frac{7}{12}}$

D) $n^{\frac{3}{4}}$

8

One bag of grass seed can cover 5,000 square feet of new lawn. If each bag costs p dollars, which of the following expressions gives the cost, in dollars, to cover a new rectangular lawn that measures a feet by b feet?

A) $\dfrac{5,000p}{ab}$

B) $\dfrac{abp}{5,000}$

C) $\dfrac{5,000ab}{p}$

D) $5,000abp$

9

If $\dfrac{5}{m} \le \dfrac{2}{3}$, where $m > 0$, what is the least possible value of m?

A) 6.5

B) 7

C) 7.5

D) 8

10

If $f(x) = 3x + n$, where n is a constant, and $f(2) = 0$, then $f(n) =$

A) −24

B) −18

C) −12

D) 12

11

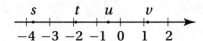

If s, t, u, and v are the coordinates of the indicated points on the number line above, which of the following is greatest?

A) $|s - v|$

B) $|s - t|$

C) $|s + v|$

D) $|u + v|$

12

How many solutions to the equation $4 \cos x = 1$ lie between $x = 0$ and $x = 3\pi$?

A) Two

B) Three

C) Four

D) Six

13

If $i = \sqrt{-1}$, which of the following is NOT equal to $i^3 + i$?

A) $(2i)^2 + 4$

B) $2 - 2i^4$

C) $2i^2 - 2$

D) $i^4 - 1$

CONTINUE ➤

3   **3**

14

If $m > 1$, which of the following could be the graph of $y = -(x + m)^2 + m$ in the xy-plane?

A)

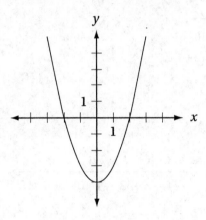

B)

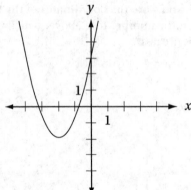

C)

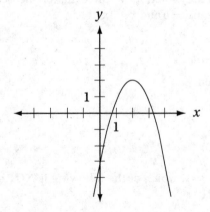

D)

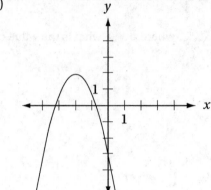

15

$$x - 3y = -2$$
$$y = \frac{5}{x}$$

The values of x that satisfy the system of equations above also satisfy which of the following equations?

A) $(x - 5)(x + 3) = 0$

B) $(x - 3)(x + 5) = 0$

C) $(x - 2)(x - 5) = 0$

D) $(x + 2)(x + 5) = 0$

3 3

DIRECTIONS

For questions 16–20, solve the problem and enter your answer in the grid, as described below, on the answer sheet.

1. Although not required, it is suggested that you write your answer in the boxes at the top of the columns to help you fill in the circles accurately. You will receive credit only if the circles are filled in correctly.

2. Mark no more than one circle in any column.

3. No question has a negative answer.

4. Some problems may have more than one correct answer. In such cases, grid only one answer.

5. **Mixed numbers** such as $3\frac{1}{2}$ must be gridded as 3.5 or $\frac{7}{2}$.

   (If $3\frac{1}{2}$ is entered into the grid as [3 1 / 2], it will be interpreted as $\frac{31}{2}$, not $3\frac{1}{2}$).

6. **Decimal answers:** If you obtain a decimal answer with more digits than the grid can accommodate, it may be either rounded or truncated, but it must fill the entire grid.

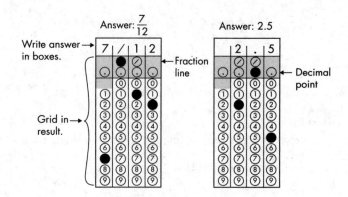

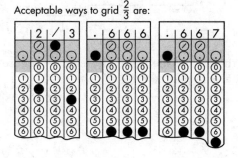

Acceptable ways to grid $\frac{2}{3}$ are:

CONTINUE

3   **3**

16

If $\frac{2}{3}a + \frac{1}{2}b = 5$, and $b = 4$, what is the value of a?

17

What is the smallest integer value of x such that $\frac{6}{x} + \frac{1}{2x}$ is less than 1?

18

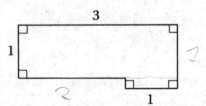

If the area of the figure above is $\frac{16}{5}$ square units, what is its perimeter?

19

What is one possible solution to the equation $\frac{6}{x+1} - \frac{3}{x-1} = \frac{1}{4}?$

20

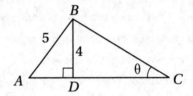

In the figure above, triangle ABC has an area of 19. What is the value of $\tan \theta$?

STOP

If you finish before time is called, you may check your work on this section only.
Do not turn to any other section of the test.

4   **4**

Math Test – Calculator

55 MINUTES, 38 QUESTIONS

Turn to Section 4 of your answer sheet to answer the questions in this section.

DIRECTIONS

For questions 1–30, solve each problem, choose the best answer from the choices provided, and fill in the corresponding circle on your answer sheet. **For questions 31–38,** solve the problem and enter your answer in the grid on the answer sheet. Please refer to the directions before question 31 on how to enter your answers in the grid. You may use any available space in your test booklet for scratch work.

NOTES

1. The use of a calculator is permitted.

2. All variables and expressions used represent real numbers unless otherwise indicated.

3. Figures provided in this test are drawn to scale unless otherwise indicated.

4. All figures lie in a plane unless otherwise indicated.

5. Unless otherwise indicated, the domain of a given function f is the set of all real numbers for which $f(x)$ is a real number.

REFERENCE

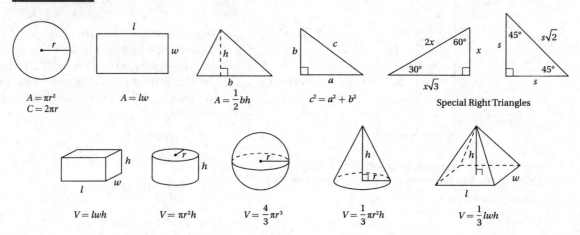

$A = \pi r^2$
$C = 2\pi r$

$A = lw$

$A = \frac{1}{2}bh$

$c^2 = a^2 + b^2$

Special Right Triangles

$V = lwh$

$V = \pi r^2 h$

$V = \frac{4}{3}\pi r^3$

$V = \frac{1}{3}\pi r^2 h$

$V = \frac{1}{3}lwh$

The number of degrees of arc in a circle is 360.
The number of radians of arc in a circle is 2π.
The sum of the measures in degrees of the angles of a triangle is 180.

CONTINUE ➡

1

The fraction $\dfrac{n}{20}$ is equal to 0.8. What is the value of n?

A) 4

B) 8

C) 12

D) 16

2

The median of the numbers x, 10, and 12 is 12. Which of the following CANNOT be the value of x?

A) 8

B) 12

C) 16

D) 20

3

x	y
0	2
1	4
2	6
4	8

Based on the ordered pairs in the table above, which of the following could express a relationship between x and y?

A) $y = x + 4$

B) $y = 2x$

C) $y = 2x + 2$

D) $y = 2x + 4$

4

The average (arithmetic mean) of a set of 3 positive integers is m. If the number 24 is added to this set, what is the average (arithmetic mean) of the new set of numbers?

A) $\dfrac{3m + 24}{24}$

B) $\dfrac{3m + 24}{4}$

C) $m + 8$

D) $\dfrac{m + 24}{4}$

5

If $\dfrac{6}{x} + 3 = -1$, what is the value of x?

A) -3

B) -2

C) $-\dfrac{3}{2}$

D) $-\dfrac{2}{3}$

6

The Municipal Electric Company charges each household $0.15 per kilowatt-hour of electricity plus a flat monthly service fee of $16. If a household uses 30 kilowatt-hours of electricity and is charged P in a given month, which of the following equations is true?

A) $0.15(30) + 16 = P$

B) $0.15P + 16 = 30$

C) $\dfrac{30}{0.15} + 16 = P$

D) $\dfrac{0.15}{P} + 16 = 30$

4   **4**

7

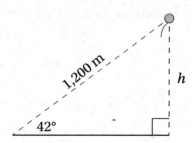

1,200 m

h

42°

Alyssa determines that a floating balloon is 1,200 meters away from her at an angle of 42° from the ground, as in the figure above. What is the height, h, of the balloon from the ground? (sin 42° = 0.669, cos 42° = 0.743, tan 42° = 0.900)

A) 802.8 meters

B) 891.6 meters

C) 1,080 meters

D) 1,793 meters

8

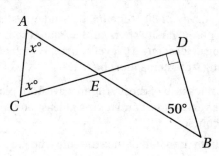

In the figure above, line segments $\overline{AB}$ and $\overline{CD}$ intersect at point E. What is the value of x?

A) 60°

B) 65°

C) 70°

D) 75°

Questions 9 and 10 are based on the graph below.

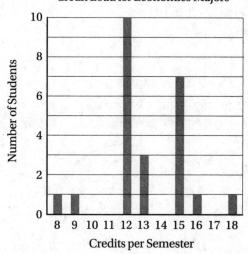

Credit Load for Economics Majors

9

A university surveyed 24 economics majors and asked them how many credits they received the previous semester. The results are represented in the graph above. What percentage of these students received 15 or more credits that semester?

A) 29%

B) $33\frac{1}{3}\%$

C) $37\frac{1}{2}\%$

D) 54%

10

What is the median number of credits these students received the previous semester?

A) 10.5

B) 11.5

C) 12

D) 12.5

CONTINUE ▶

4 **4**

11

If a and b are the coordinates of two points on the number line, then which of the following is equivalent to the statement that the absolute distance from a to b is greater than the absolute distance from -2 to 6?

A) $|a| > -2$ and $|b| > 6$

B) $|a - b| > -8$

C) $|a + 2| > |b - 6|$

D) $|a - b| > 8$

12

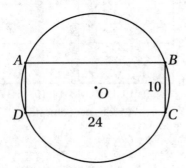

Note: Figure not drawn to scale.

In the figure above, rectangle $ABCD$ is inscribed in the circle with center O. What is the area of the circle?

A) 26π

B) 121π

C) 144π

D) 169π

13

Everyone in Niko's class has a different birth date. If Niko is both the 8th oldest person and the 12th youngest person in his class, how many students are in Niko's class?

A) 18

B) 19

C) 20

D) 21

14

If $i = \sqrt{-1}$, which of the following is equivalent to $(2 - i)(3 - 2i)$?

A) $8 - 7i$

B) $6 + 2i$

C) $6 - 6i$

D) $4 - 7i$

15

If $f(x) = (x^2)^{-2b}$ and $f(3) = 3$, what is the value of b?

A) $-\dfrac{1}{2}$

B) $-\dfrac{1}{4}$

C) $\dfrac{1}{4}$

D) $\dfrac{1}{2}$

16

In a survey of 80 students, 55 students stated that they play a varsity sport, and 35 stated that they are taking at least one AP level course. Which of the following statements must be true?

A) At least 10 of these students are both playing a varsity sport and taking at least one AP level course.

B) Less than half of the students who play a varsity sport are also taking at least one AP level course.

C) The number of students who do not play a varsity sport is greater than the number of students who do not take at least one AP level course.

D) At least one student who takes an AP level course does NOT play a varsity sport.

CONTINUE ➡

4 **4**

17

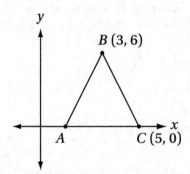

Note: Figure not drawn to scale.

In the figure above, $AB = BC$. If $\overline{AB}$ has a slope of m and $\overline{BC}$ has a slope of n, what is the value of mn?

A) -9

B) $-\dfrac{1}{9}$

C) $\dfrac{1}{9}$

D) 9

18

The functions f, g, and h are defined by the equations $f(x) = x^2$, $g(x) = x$, and $h(x) = \sqrt{x}$. Which of the following must be true?

A) $h\left(\dfrac{1}{2}\right) < f\left(\dfrac{1}{2}\right) < g\left(\dfrac{1}{2}\right)$

B) $h\left(\dfrac{1}{2}\right) < g\left(\dfrac{1}{2}\right) < f\left(\dfrac{1}{2}\right)$

C) $g\left(\dfrac{1}{2}\right) < h\left(\dfrac{1}{2}\right) < f\left(\dfrac{1}{2}\right)$

D) $f\left(\dfrac{1}{2}\right) < g\left(\dfrac{1}{2}\right) < h\left(\dfrac{1}{2}\right)$

19

Which of the following scatterplots provides the strongest evidence in support of the hypothesis that y varies inversely as the square of x?

A)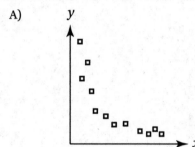

B)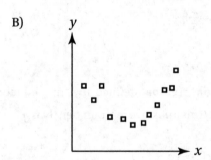

C)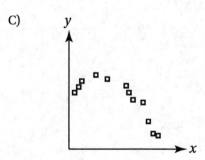

D)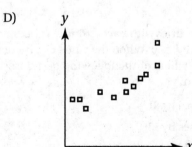

CONTINUE

4   **4**

20

The bird department of a pet store has 12 canaries, 30 finches, and 18 parrots. If the pet store purchased n more finches, then 80% of its birds would be finches. Which of the following equations must be true?

A) $\dfrac{1}{2} + n = \dfrac{4}{5}$

B) $\dfrac{30 + n}{60} = \dfrac{4}{5}$

C) $\dfrac{30 + n}{60 + n} = \dfrac{4}{5}$

D) $\dfrac{n}{60 + n} = \dfrac{4}{5}$

21

Let function $f(x)$ be defined by the equation $f(x) = x^2 - 1$. If b is a positive real number, then $f\left(\dfrac{1}{b}\right) =$

A) $\dfrac{(b-1)(b+1)}{b^2}$

B) $\dfrac{(1-b)(1+b)}{b^2}$

C) $\dfrac{b^2 - 1}{b}$

D) $\dfrac{b - 1}{b^2}$

22

The value of y varies with x according to the equation $y = kx^2$, where $k > 0$. When the value of x increases from 3 to 12, which of the following best describes the behavior of y?

A) It increases by 81.

B) It increases by 135.

C) It is multiplied by 4.

D) It is multiplied by 16.

23

If the function f is defined by the equation $f(x) = k(x + 6)(x - 1)$, where $k > 5$, then which of the following is equivalent to $f(7)$?

A) $f(-78)$

B) $f(-12)$

C) $f(-2)$

D) $f(78)$

24

After its initial offering, the price of a stock increased by 20% in the first year, decreased by 25% in the second year, then increased by 10% in the third year. What was the net change in the stock price over the entire three-year period?

A) It increased by 5%.

B) It increased by 1%.

C) It decreased by 1%.

D) It decreased by 5%.

25

If $y = x^2$, where $x \neq 0$, and $w = y^6$, which of the following expresses the value of $\dfrac{w}{y^3}$ in terms of x?

A) x^2

B) x^4

C) x^5

D) x^6

---

4   **4**

26

0	1	2	3	4	5
1	2	4	7		
2					
3					
4				x	
5					

With the exception of the shaded squares in the first row and first column, every square in the table above is to be filled in with a number equal to the sum of the number directly above it and the number directly to its left. For instance, the number 7 in the second row is the sum of 3 in the square above it and 4 in the square directly to its left. What is the value of x?

A) 16

B) 84

C) 96

D) 112

27

$$3x^2 = 4x + c$$

In the equation above, c is a constant. If $x = -1$ is a solution of this equation, what other value of x satisfies the equation?

A) $\dfrac{1}{7}$

B) $\dfrac{4}{3}$

C) $\dfrac{7}{3}$

D) 7

28

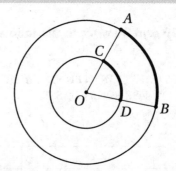

Note: Figure not drawn to scale.

The figure above shows two concentric circles with center O. If $OD = 3$, $DB = 5$, and the length of arc AB is 5π, what is the length of arc CD?

A) $\dfrac{7}{4}\pi$

B) $\dfrac{15}{8}\pi$

C) 3π

D) $\dfrac{25}{8}\pi$

CONTINUE

4 **4**

Questions 29 and 30 refer to the following graph.

PARTICIPATION IN FUND-RAISERS
FOR FOUR CLASSES

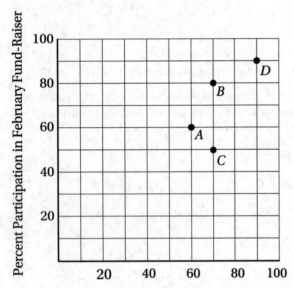

Percent Participation in May Fund-Raiser

29

Four different classes at Corbett Elementary School participated in two fund-raisers last year, one in February and another in May. The rates of participation for each class are recorded in the graph above. Which class had the greatest change in percent participation from the February fund-raiser to the May fund-raiser?

A) Class A

B) Class B

C) Class C

D) Class D

30

If there were 20 students each in Class A and Class C, and 30 students each in Class B and Class D, how many students participated in the May fund-raiser?

A) 71

B) 72

C) 74

D) 76

CONTINUE ▶

4   **4**

DIRECTIONS

For questions 31–38, solve the problem and enter your answer in the grid, as described below, on the answer sheet.

1. Although not required, it is suggested that you write your answer in the boxes at the top of the columns to help you fill in the circles accurately. You will receive credit only if the circles are filled in correctly.

2. Mark no more than one circle in any column.

3. No question has a negative answer.

4. Some problems may have more than one correct answer. In such cases, grid only one answer.

5. **Mixed numbers** such as $3\frac{1}{2}$ must be gridded as 3.5 or $\frac{7}{2}$.

   (If $3\frac{1}{2}$ is entered into the grid as 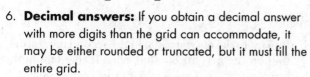, it will be interpreted as $\frac{31}{2}$, not $3\frac{1}{2}$.)

6. **Decimal answers:** If you obtain a decimal answer with more digits than the grid can accommodate, it may be either rounded or truncated, but it must fill the entire grid.

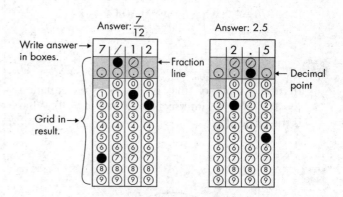

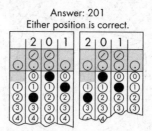

4 **4**

31

If $4 + \sqrt{b} = 7.2$, what is the value of $4 - \sqrt{b}$?

32

In the xy-plane, the graph of the equation $y = 3x^2 - kx - 35$ intersects the x-axis at $(5, 0)$. What is the value of k?

33

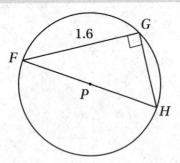

In the figure above, triangle FGH is inscribed in the circle with center P. If the area of the circle is π, what is the area of triangle FGH?

34

If $-\dfrac{3}{5} < -2t + 1 < -\dfrac{3}{7}$, what is one possible value of $6t$?

35

If $\cos(x - \pi) = 0.4$, what is the value of $\sin^2 x$?

36

If one pound of grain can feed either 5 chickens or 2 pigs, then ten pounds of grain can feed 20 chickens and how many pigs?

Questions 37 and 38 are based on the following information

Section	Price per Ticket	Number Sold
Front Orchestra	$60	50
Rear Orchestra	$50	60
First Mezzanine	$40	x
Second Mezzanine	$35	y
Third Mezzanine	$30	100

The table above shows information about the tickets sold for a recent performance by a theater troupe. The total revenue in ticket sales for this performance was $15,000.

37

If 15 more tickets were sold in the second mezzanine than in the first mezzanine, what is the total number of tickets that were sold for this performance?

38

Before the tickets for this performance went on sale, a consultant for the theater had predicted that n, the number of tickets sold per section, would vary with p, the price in dollars for a ticket in that section, according to the formula $n = \dfrac{2{,}800}{p}$. By how many tickets did this model underestimate the actual total number of tickets sold?

STOP

If you finish before time is called, you may check your work on this section only.
Do not turn to any other section of the test.

Essay

50 MINUTES, 1 QUESTION

DIRECTIONS

As you read the passage below, consider how Ellis Parker Butler uses

- evidence, such as facts or examples, to support his claims
- reasoning to develop ideas and connect claims and evidence
- stylistic or persuasive elements, such as word choice or appeals to emotion, to add power to the ideas expressed

Adapted from Ellis Parker Butler, "On Spelling." Originally published in 1906.

1   My own opinion of the spelling profession is that it has nothing to do with genius, except to kill it. I know that Shakespeare was a promiscuous sort of speller, even as to his own name, and no one can deny that he was a greater genius than Noah Webster. The reason America so long lagged behind Europe in the production of genius is that America, for many decades, was the slave of the spelling-book. No man who devotes the fiery days of his youth to learning to spell has time to be a genius.

2   My wife, Serena, says, and I agree with her, that it is the jealousy of a few college professors who are trying to undermine the younger writers. They know that it is excusable to spell incorrectly now, but they want this new phonetic spelling brought into use so that there shall be no excuse for bad spelling, and that then, Serena says, self-made authors like me, who never can spell but who simply blaze with genius, will be hooted out of the magazines to make room for a stupid sort of literature that is spelled correctly. Serena looks upon the whole thing as a direct, personal stab at me. I look at it more philosophically.

3   To me it seems that the spelling reformers are entirely on the wrong track. Their proposed changes are almost a revolution, and we Americans do not like sudden changes. We like our revolutions to come about gradually. Think how gradually automobiles have come to pass. If, in our horse age, the streets had suddenly been covered with sixty horsepower snorters going thirty miles an hour and smelling like an eighteenth-century literary debate, and killing people right and left, we Americans would have arisen and destroyed every vestige of the automobile. But the automobile came gradually—first the bicycle, then the motorcycle, and so, by stages, to the present monsters. So slowly and progressively did the automobile increase in size and number that it seemed a matter of course. We take to being killed by the automobile quite naturally now.

4   Of course, the silent letters in our words are objectionable. They are lazy letters. We want no idle class in America, whether tramp, aristocrat, or silent letter, but we do not kill the tramp and the aristocrat. We set them to work, or we would like to. My theory of spelling reform is to set the idle letters to work.

5   Take that prime offender, *although*. *Altho* does all the work, and *ugh* sits on the fence and whittles. I would put *ugh* to work. *Ugh* is a syllable in itself. I would have the *ugh* follow the pronounced *altho* as a third syllable. Doubtless the asthmatic islanders who concocted our English language actually pronounced it so.

6   I propose to have some millionaire endow my plan, and Serena and I will then form a society for the reforming of English pronunciation. I will not punch out the *i* of any chief, nor shall any one drag *me* from any programme, however dull. I will pronounce *programme* as it should be pronounced—*programmy*—and, as for *chief*, he shall be pronounced *chy-ef*.

7   The advantage of this plan is manifest. It is so manifest that I am afraid it will never be adopted.

8   Serena's plan is, perhaps, less intellectual, but more American. Serena's plan is to ignore all words that contain super-fluous letters. She would simply boycott them. Serena would have people get along with such words as are already phonetically spelled. Why should people write *although*, when they can write *notwithstanding that*, and not have a silent letter in it? I have myself often written a phrase twelve words long to stand instead of a single word I did not know how to spell. In fact, I abandoned my Platonic friendship for Serena, and replaced it with ardent love, because I did know how to spell *sweetheart*, but could not remember whether she was my *friend* or *freind*.

Write an essay in which you explain how Ellis Parker Butler builds an argument to persuade his audience that American English spelling conventions of 1906 need to be reformed. In your essay, analyze how Butler uses one or more of the features listed in the box above (or features of your own choice) to strengthen the logic and persuasiveness of his argument. Be sure that your analysis focuses on the most relevant features of the passage.

Your essay should NOT explain whether you agree with Butler's claims, but rather explain how Butler builds an argument to persuade his audience.

SAT PRACTICE TEST 1 ANSWER KEY

Section 1: Reading	Section 2: Writing and Language	Section 3: Math (No Calculator)	Section 4: Math (Calculator)
1. A	1. C	1. D	1. D
2. C	2. A	2. A	2. A
3. A	3. B	3. C	3. C
4. D	4. B	4. A	4. B
5. D	5. B	5. C	5. C
6. B	6. A	6. B	6. A
7. A	7. D	7. A	7. A
8. C	8. C	8. B	8. C
9. A	9. A	9. C	9. C
10. A	10. B	10. A	10. D
11. B	11. A	11. A	11. D
12. B	12. C	12. B	12. D
13. D	13. A	13. C	13. B
14. C	14. B	14. D	14. D
15. B	15. A	15. B	15. B
16. D	16. B	16. 4.5 or 9/2	16. A
17. C	17. D	17. 7	17. A
18. A	18. C	18. 8.4 or 42/5	18. D
19. D	19. D	19. 5 or 7	19. A
20. A	20. B	20. 8/13 or .615	20. C
21. C	21. B		21. B
22. B	22. B		22. D
23. C	23. D		23. B
24. A	24. A		24. C
25. D	25. D		25. D
26. D	26. C		26. D
27. C	27. B		27. C
28. B	28. B		28. B
29. B	29. C		29. C
30. B	30. D		30. C
31. D	31. A		31. 0.8 or 4/5
32. B	32. A		32. 8
33. B	33. D		33. .96
34. A	34. D		34. $4.29 \leq x \leq 4.79$
35. D	35. A		35. .84
36. A	36. C		36. 12
37. A	37. C		37. 371
38. C	38. D		38. 25
39. A	39. A		
40. C	40. C		
41. D	41. A		
42. A	42. C		
43. C	43. B		
44. D	44. B		
45. C			
46. C			
47. D			
48. C			
49. A			
50. C			
51. D			
52. A			

Total Reading Points (Section 1)	Total Writing and Language Points (Section 2)	Total Math Points (Section 3)	Total Math Points (Section 4)

SCORE CONVERSION TABLE

Scoring Your Test

1. Use the answer key to mark your responses on each section.

2. Total the number of correct responses for each section:

   1. Reading Test   Number correct: _____ **(Reading Raw Score)**

   2. Writing and Language Test   Number correct: _____ **(Writing and Language Raw Score)**

   3. Mathematics Test – No Calculator   Number correct: _____

   4. Mathematics Test – Calculator   Number correct: _____

3. Add the raw scores for sections 3 and 4. This is your **Math Raw Score:** _____

4. Use the Table 1 to calculate your **Scaled Test and Section Scores (10–40).**

   Math Section Score (200–800):   _____

   Reading Test Score (10–40):   _____

   Writing and Language Test Score (10–40):   _____

5. Add the **Reading Test Scaled Score** and the **Writing and Language Test Scaled Score** and multiply this sum by 10 to get your **Reading and Writing Test Section Score (20–80).**

   Sum of Reading + Writing and Language Scores: _____ $\times$ 10 =

   Reading and Writing Section Score: _____

Table 1: Scaled Section and Test Scores (10–40)

Raw Score	Math Section Score	Reading Test Score	Writing/ Language Test Score	Raw Score	Math Section Score	Reading Test Score	Writing/ Language Test Score
58	800			29	520	27	28
57	790			28	520	26	28
56	780			27	510	26	27
55	760			26	500	25	26
54	750			25	490	25	26
53	740			24	480	24	25
52	730	40		23	480	24	25
51	710	40		22	470	23	24
50	700	39		21	460	23	23
49	690	38		20	450	22	23
48	680	38		19	440	22	22
47	670	37		18	430	21	21
46	670	37		17	420	21	21
45	660	36		16	410	20	20
44	650	35	40	15	390	20	19
43	640	35	39	14	380	19	19
42	630	34	38	13	370	19	18
41	620	33	37	12	360	18	17
40	610	33	36	11	340	17	16
39	600	32	35	10	330	17	16
38	600	32	34	9	320	16	15
37	590	31	34	8	310	15	14
36	580	31	33	7	290	15	13
35	570	30	32	6	280	14	13
34	560	30	32	5	260	13	12
33	560	29	31	4	240	12	11
32	550	29	30	3	230	11	10
31	540	28	30	2	210	10	10
30	530	28	29	1	200	10	10

SAT PRACTICE TEST 1 DETAILED ANSWER KEY

Section 1: Reading

1. A   Detail

In lines 10–25, the author of Passage 1 discusses how farm subsidies are used both to lower food prices (by subsidizing farmers) when prices get too high, and to raise them (by paying farmers to leave their land fallow) when prices get too low. Although he disputes that these efforts to stabilize prices are worth the cost, he does indicate that they work. In the first paragraph of Passage 2 (lines 60–73), the author indicates that farm subsidies *protect consumers from price spikes* (lines 69–70).

2. C   Interpretation

In the first paragraph of Passage 1, the statement that *something is rotten down on the farm* (line 1) introduces the author's discussion of the U.S. farm subsidies program, which he claims gives away *millions of taxpayer dollars to farmers who are actually ineligible for the program* (lines 6–8) and is rife with *inefficiencies* (line 16).

3. A   Cross-Textual Inference

The thesis of Passage 2 is that U.S. farm subsidies are *vital* (line 61) to both farmers and American consumers. Therefore, he regards the *taxes* (line 15) we pay for these subsidies to be a *worthwhile expenditure.*

4. D   Inference

In lines 8–9, the author of Passage 1 states that the report about corruption and incompetence in the U.S. farm subsidies program *should horrify lawmakers, but it probably won't.* He explains why in the last paragraph (lines 51–59): *Rich corporate farmers are an enormously powerful lobby in American politics,* contributing *nearly $100 million into political campaigns every year.*

5. D   Textual Evidence

As the explanation to question 4 explains, the evidence for this answer is found in the last paragraph, particularly lines 53–55.

6. B   Passage Comparison

Although the author of Passage 1 does not think that the stabilization of commodity prices is worth the cost of higher taxes (lines 19–25), the author of Passage 2 indicates that *price spikes* (line 69) can be devastating to both farmers and consumers.

7. A   Specific Purpose

The 2009 poll cited in lines 40–43 indicates that most Americans support farm subsidies for small family farms,

confirming the author's statement that Americans feel that *we need these subsidies to save the small family farmer.* Choice (B) is incorrect because, although the author himself goes on to refute this misconception, the results of the poll do not. Rather, they *confirm a general sentiment.* Choice (C) is incorrect because the poll does not indicate any shift away from the discussion about the ineffectiveness of the U.S. farm subsidies program. Choice (D) is incorrect because the word *Indeed* (line 40) indicates that this result is unsurprising to him.

8. C   Data Analysis

The thesis of Passage 1 is that *something is rotten down on the farm* (line 1), namely, the fact that, in a recent seven-year period, *the U.S. Congress has doled out more than $114 billion to farmers* (lines 10–11) through a program that *uses administrators who are ill-trained and poorly monitored* (lines 5–6) and that implements programs that are not worthwhile to taxpayers, that *are actually harming American exporters* (lines 33–34) and that *make it much harder for the small family farmers to compete* (lines 47–48). The graph in Figure 1, however, shows about a 40% decline in these subsidies from 2000 to 2012, perhaps undercutting the author's claim that these subsidies are an overall burden on the American taxpayer.

He would most likely, then, choose to focus on the component of these subsidies that has grown significantly in the 15 years indicated on this graph, namely, crop insurance subsidies, which have expanded at a fairly steady rate and grew by about 500% from 1998 to 2012. As the introduction to the passage indicates, this program takes money from taxpayers to help farmers to buy crop insurance, thereby providing direct entitlements not only to farmers but also to insurance companies.

Choice (A), *the general decline in total farm subsidies from 2005 to 2012,* does not help the author make the point that these subsidies are a burden to American taxpayers. Similarly, choice (B), *the overall rate of change in commodity subsidies from 1998 to 2012* does not help his thesis, because after the first several years, the trend is generally downward. Choice (D), *the sudden spike in disaster subsidies from 2004 to 2005,* also does not support his thesis, because he does not make any particular claims about the benefit of disaster subsidies.

9. A   Data Analysis

The thesis of Passage 2 is that farm subsidies in the United States are *vital* (line 61) and *not as burdensome to American taxpayers as the critics claim* (lines 62–63). Therefore, the author of Passage 2 would most likely cite evidence that the total cost of the subsidies program is declining.

10. **A** — Cross-Textual Inference

The author of Passage 1 indicates that *we taxpayers will pay more in taxes than we will ever get back in lower corn or wheat prices* (lines 16–18), thereby indicating that the *benefit of lower prices* (line 85) is *offset by its costs*.

11. **B** — Cross-Textual Comparison

The author of Passage 1 mentions that the U.S. farm subsidy programs use administrators *who give away millions of taxpayer dollars to farmers who are actually ineligible for the program* (lines 6–8) and are rife with *inefficiencies* (line 16) to make the argument that they are not worthwhile to taxpayers. This is an appeal to the reader's *distaste for ineptitude* (incompetence).

Although this could also be seen as an appeal to the reader's *fiscal prudence* (sense of responsibility), the author of Passage 2 makes the same kind of appeal when he indicates that these subsidies are *vital* (line 61) to preventing *price spikes* (line 69) and *are not as burdensome to American taxpayers as the critics claim* (lines 62–63). Since the question asks us to find an appeal that is NOT also found in Passage 2, choice (D) is incorrect.

12. **B** — Interpretation

When the author of Passage 1 states that *Agribusiness and farm insurance lobbies pump nearly $100 million into political campaigns every year, and the floodgates show no sign of closing* (lines 53–55), he suggests that there seem to be no controls against this *unscrupulous* (unethical) *funding* of political campaigns by those who benefit from the decisions of those politicians.

13. **D** — Tone and Characterization

The narrator says that Reverend Jansen *bent down in a cloud of Aqua Velva* (lines 5–6) and told her *not to worry* (line 12). He then describes to the narrator why God *called [her] Korean parents home* (line 13). All of these descriptions work together to portray someone who is acting in a condescending and *patronizing* manner to a young child.

14. **C** — Interpretation

The statement that the narrator's mother *had been murdered* (line 2) is later explained to refer to the narrator's interpretation of the fact that she was told that *"God called [her] Korean parents home"* (line 13) and that *"It was all part of His plan"* (line 18), in other words, her death *was deliberate*. At first, choice (D) may seem plausible, because in lines 36–43, Sarah's mother does not want to talk about Sarah's biological mother. However, the passage makes it clear that the narrator attributed the "murder" to a divine plan (*God kills, I thought then*, line 27) rather than to any intention of her adoptive family.

15. **B** — Tone and Diction

The description of Reverend Jansen's eyes and breath in lines 13–17 indicates that he is somewhat emotionally detached (*his eyes sliding sideways*, lines 15–16) and that Sarah is likewise emotionally detached from him and his profound claims, instead distracted by his breath that *smelled vaguely of toast* (lines 16–17). These descriptions surprise us, because they are so incongruent with the expectation of respect for and contemplation of the reverend's deep spiritual pronouncements.

16. **D** — Interpretation

The narrator has Korean heritage, yet she *grew up in a house in which Korea had always been the oddly charged word, never to be mentioned in connection with [Sarah], the same way [they] never said "Uncle Henry" and "alcoholic" in the same sentence* (lines 44–47). The narrator's mother, Christine, *thought [Sarah] needed to protected from* (line 49) her ethnicity. In other words, she regarded Sarah's ethnicity as an *unfortunate fact*.

17. **C** — Textual Evidence

As the explanation to question 16 makes clear, the best evidence for the previous answer is in lines 48–52.

18. **A** — Literary Device

The contrast between *murder* and *Christmas and the Easter Bunny* (line 28) is a classic example of *juxtaposition*, the act of placing together two images with highly contrasting effects.

19. **D** — Interpretation

The paragraph states that Christine begins her reply *patiently* (line 36), which might suggest that she is demonstrating *motherly sympathy*. However, *sympathy* means "a feeling of common understanding," and the rest of Christine's reply suggests that she is *disappointed* (line 43) with Sarah rather than sympathetic with her. The point of the paragraph is that Christine is not emotionally ready (*it makes me sad*, line 40) to discuss something that her eight-year-old adopted daughter clearly wants to discuss, that is, she is *emotionally immature*.

20. **A** — Word in Context

When the narrator states that *Korea was the oddly charged word* (lines 44–45), she means that it was a word that was *never to be mentioned* (lines 45–46), because it was associated with potentially negative feelings. That is, it was an emotionally *loaded* word.

21. **C** — Interpretation

In lines 44–60, the narrator describes her Uncle Henry as an *"alcoholic"* (line 47) who sat drinking at family cookouts *at the far corner of our yard, away from everyone* (line 60). This is treatment appropriate to a *pitiable embarrassment* rather than a *stern patriarch* or *noble hero*. There is also no indication, despite Sarah's parents' discomfort with discussing her heritage, that Uncle Henry is a *bigoted lout*.

---

22. B   **Tone and Inference**

The reference to Bryant Gumbel's *cheery smirk* (line 81) follows the description of his television segment during the Olympic games about how Korea had become one of the *economic miracle countries* (line 74). According to the narrator, the cheery smirk seemed to say *Top that, Singapore!* thereby indicating that he admired Korea's ability to compete economically with other strong countries.

---

23. C   **General Purpose**

The passage as a whole describes the *spectacular cyclorama* (line 9) that is known as the *cosmic microwave background (CMB) radiation, a 13 billion year-old panoramic snapshot of the universe as it appeared the moment it first released its primordial photons* (lines 14–18). It then goes on to discuss the precise measurements that scientists have taken of this radiation and what they tell us about the early universe. In other words, the passage as a whole is *discussing the analysis and significance of a cosmological phenomenon*.

---

24. A   **Specific Purpose**

The description of the Gettysburg Cyclorama in the first paragraph is used to draw an analogy between two *cataclysmic historical event[s]* (lines 9–10), one of which we can see with our own eyes and one of which we can only detect with special tools. The answer is not (B), because although this Cyclorama depicts a historic battle, it is not itself *a historical precedent* (an event that serves as a model for future similar events). Choice (C) is incorrect because the painting is depicted neither as *quaint* nor *anachronistic* (out of historical order). Choice (D) is incorrect because although the passage later indicates that the discovery of the CMB was somewhat *accidental*, the Cyclorama was not.

---

25. D   **Interpretation**

The author indicates that *to appreciate [the] full splendor[of the Cosmic Background Radiation], you would have to be able to see microwaves* (lines 11–13). In other words, the disappointment is in the fact that we can't see the *spectacular cyclorama* (line 8) that is the cosmic microwave background; it is an *inaccessible phenomenon*, at least to our naked eyes.

---

26. D   **Specific Purpose**

The discussion in lines 23–28 concerns the emergence of the first photons (light particles) in the early universe. In saying that the *universe was "invisible"* (lines 25–26), the author means that photons—the particles that are required for us to be able to detect something visually—did not yet exist. Calling the early universe "invisible" is somewhat inappropriate, since there were no eyes to see it anyway during that stage in its development, so the quotes are drawing attention to the fact that these terms are being used to make a technical point a bit clearer by using common words that correspond with our everyday experience.

---

27. C   **Interpretation**

The *moment a swaddled one-day-old opens its eyes* (lines 22–23) refers to *the moment [the early universe] first released its primordial photons* (lines 17–18) which we now refer to as the cosmic microwave background radiation. The discussion in the next paragraph (lines 24–36) explains that these early photons were previously trapped in *an opaque fog of hydrogen plasma* (line 29). Choices (A) and (D) are incorrect because this moment describes when the photons were released, not when they were first discovered by humans. Choice (B) is incorrect because these particles, as it is explained in the third paragraph, were released 380,000 years *after* the Big Bang.

---

28. B   **Word in Context**

The *distinctive spectrum* (line 64) refers to the precise "blackbody" curve for 2.75° Kelvin as shown in Figure 1. It is the particular set of wavelength intensities that *distinguish* blackbody radiation from ordinary radiation, and confirm Gamow's theory about the origin of the signals detected at Murray Hill.

---

29. B   **Inference**

The passage states that Penzias and Wilson were initially *troubled* (line 71) by the signals that turned out to be from the CMB radiation, and in fact mistakenly attributed them to *pigeon droppings* (lines 74–75). This indicates that they were not looking for these signals, nor did they know how to interpret them. The work they did to receive the Nobel prize, therefore, was *the result of an accidental discovery*.

---

30. B   **General Structure**

As the explanation of question 29 indicates, lines 72–75 indicate that Penzias and Wilson did not understand the nature of the signals they were receiving, atttributing them erroneously to *pigeon droppings*.

---

31. D   **Data Analysis**

Figure 1 shows the blackbody spectrum for various temperatures, and compares these to the measurements taken of the cosmic microwave background, showing that the CMB radiation *has a nearly perfect blackbody spectrum*.

32. B   **Word in Context**

Figure 2 shows a panoramic map of the cosmic background radiation, showing that it *did not originate from just one point in space*, but rather from every direction.

33. B   **General Purpose**

The first paragraph states that the people *have a right . . . to that most dreaded and envied kind of knowledge of the characters and conduct of their rulers* (lines 5–9). In other words, they have the right to learn about who their leaders are and what they do. Choice (A) is incorrect because the right to *pursue academic interests* is discussed somewhat in the second paragraph (*Let us dare to read, think, speak, and write*, line 33) but not in the first. Choice (C) is incorrect, because although Adams says that *the art of printing should be encouraged* (line 28), this is not the primary point of the paragraph. Rather, it is secondary to the point that citizens should be well informed. Choice (D) is incorrect because although the first passage mentions the right of citizens to *revoke the authority* (line 13) of their leaders, it does not discuss the right of citizens to propose legislation themselves.

34. A   **Word in Context**

The statement *that the people have a right to revoke the authority that they themselves have deputed, and to **constitute** abler and better agents, attorneys and trustees* (lines 12–15) means that the people have the right to **place in power** better leaders to replace those whose authority has been revoked.

35. D   **Interpretation**

The passage indicates that our forefathers endured *physical deprivation* in the form of *the hunger, the nakedness, [and] the cold* (line 54), *political oppression* in the form of *domestic tyrants and usurpers* (lines 44–45), and *arduous physical labor* in the form of *the severe labors of clearing their grounds, building their houses, [and] raising their provisions* (lines 55–57). It does not mention, however, that they endured any feelings of *despair*. In fact, it says that they endured these with the *hopes and expectations which constantly supported and carried them through all hardships with patience and resignation* (lines 60–63).

36. A   **Interpretation**

The very first sentence states that all people have *a desire to know* (line 5), that is, a *curious nature*. Choice (B) is incorrect, because although the passage discusses at length the people's right to revoke the authority of those in power, it does not claim that people themselves have a desire for power. Choice (C) is incorrect, because although the passage discusses the right of the people

to revoke the authority of bad rulers, and mentions the *inherent rights of mankind against foreign and domestic tyrants and usurpers* (lines 43–45), it does not state specifically that the people have any *dread* of tyranny. Choice (D) is incorrect because the passage does not discuss thrift (resourcefulness with money).

37. A   **Textual Evidence**

As the explanation to question 36 explains, the best evidence for the previous answer is found in the very first sentence of the passage.

38. C   **Interpretation**

The phrase *every order and degree among the people* (line 34) refers to the entire society that Adams is addressing throughout the second paragraph.

39. A   **Structural Comparison**

The second paragraph is characterized primarily by its use of the imperative mood: *Let us dare . . . Let every order . . . Let them . . . Let us study . . . Let us read . . . Let us examine . . .* These sentences therefore have a much more urgent and suggestive diction than do the sentences in the first paragraph. While the first paragraph is primarily *descriptive* of the rights of free citizens, the second is *prescriptive* of their corresponding duties.

40. C   **Interpretation**

When Adams says *Let us examine the nature of that power* (lines 50–51) he is referring to the cruel power that *drove [our forefathers] from their homes* (line 52), that is, the *domestic tyrants* (line 44) that made it difficult for them to remain in their native countries. Clearly, then *power* refers to a *despotic* (tyrannical) *agent*.

41. D   **Interpretation**

Although this paragraph does discuss *the privations endured by our forefathers* in the form of *the hunger, the nakedness, [and]the cold* (line 54) and does implicitly warn against *the dangerous posed by an ignorant populace* because it strongly encourages us to *read, think, speak, and write* (line 33), this particular sentence is referring specifically to *arbitrary kings and cruel priests* (line 45). So the phrase *the gates of earth and hell* (line 46) is referring to the *brutality of oppressive leaders* who persecute us in our worldly existence and about an otherworldly existence.

42. A   **Purpose**

The sentence *Let us read and recollect and impress upon our souls the views and ends of our own more immediate forefathers in exchanging their native country for a dreary, inhospitable wilderness* (lines 46–50) invites us to learn about the beliefs and motivations of our forefathers who came to America to escape oppression. In other words, Adams wants to *remind the reader of the importance of liberty.*

---

43. C   **Specific Purpose**

The first paragraph characterizes the Southern Ocean as a foreboding place by evoking images of its *chilly current* (lines 2–3), the *dangerous icebergs [that] hide in its gloom* (lines 4–5), and the *churning swells [that] sometimes serve up freak waves that can easily flip ships* (lines 5–6). Such images might be used to make a case for *the improbability of Smetacek's success* or the *pessimism of Smetacek's detractors*, but his portion of the passage contains no such pessimism. Rather goes on directly to explain the promise of Smetacek's work. This description, therefore, must be regarded as emphasizing *the boldness of Smetacek's experiment.*

---

44. D   **Word in Context**

The phrase *the **base** layer of the food chain* refers to plankton's role in the global ecosystem, specifically how it serves as the *foundation* of the food chain.

---

45. C   **Interpretation**

Although many environmentalists may well regard *fertilizer run-off from farm fields* (line 23) as *an unfortunate by-product* of farming, or *an environmental hazard*, the author here presents it as supplying some of the *key nutritional elements* (line 21) for cyanobacteria. Therefore, it is a *potential sustenance* (nourishment).

---

46. C   **Characterization and Tone**

The passage as a whole characterizes Smetacek's experiments in iron fertilization to promote oceanic cyanobacterial blooms as a demonstration of the potential for *large-scale manipulation of the planetary environment* (lines 94–96) to *remove planet-heating CO_2 from the atmosphere* (lines 29–30). Therefore, according to the author, this fertilization is *a promising and feasible solution to a global problem.*

---

47. D   **Textual Evidence**

As the explanation to question 46 explains, the best evidence for this answer is found in lines 94–96.

---

48. C   **Data Analysis**

Figure 1 depicts a *satellite image of the largest recorded natural phytoplankton bloom in February 2012, believed to have been caused by the addition of iron dust blown into the sea around Antarctica by strong offshore winds* (from the caption beneath Figure 1). Choice (A) cannot be correct, because Smetacek's experiment took place in

2004, not 2012. Choice (B) cannot be correct, because the figure does not indicate anything about the relationship between algal bloom size and time of year. Choice (D) cannot be correct, because the figure does not contain any information about the relationship between bloom size and distance from the Antarctic ice shelves. The correct answer is (C) because the figure clearly shows a bloom that is well over 5,000 square kilometers (over 100 km long and over 50 km wide) in area, which is more than 30 times larger than Smetacek's *167 square kilometer* (line 53) bloom.

---

49. A   **Inference**

According to the passage, Smetacek's theory was that iron fertilization of plankton could *siphon more and more planet-heating CO_2 from the atmosphere* (lines 29–30) and then *sequester as much as one billion metric tons of carbon dioxide annually, keeping it deep in the ocean for centuries* (lines 34–37) by *[dying] and [sinking] to the sea floor, thereby providing natural carbon sequestration* (lines 49–50). Therefore, the death of the algal bloom described in lines 61–65 is *vindication of his theory that iron fertilization can lead to carbon sequestration.*

---

50. C   **Inference**

The passage states that plankton serves as *the base layer of the global food chain* (line 13) and therefore fertilizing phytoplankton with iron *would promote blooms to help sea life thrive all the way up the food chain, even to whale populations* (lines 44–46). Therefore, iron fertilization helps the whale population by *supporting an important food source for the whales.*

---

51. D   **Interpretation**

The second to last paragraph (lines 88–92) discusses a *way to motivate further research into iron fertilization* (lines 89–90) therefore the *route to broader acceptance of the practice* (lines 91–92) is a *mode of persuasion.* Choice (A) is incorrect because, although the research itself probably involves *an experimental procedure*, the *route* is not part of the research itself, but rather a means to gain support for that research. Choice (B) is incorrect because, although an appeal to the needs of *commerce* (line 88) shows an appreciation for economic concerns, the *route* is not itself an *economic difficulty.* Choice (C) is incorrect because appealing to the needs of commerce is not an *idealistic* approach, but rather a pragmatic one.

---

52. A   **Tone**

The last paragraph is *sanguine* (hopeful) about the potential for iron fertilization of the oceans to *undo a great deal of the damage we have already done* (lines 98–99).

Section 2: Writing and Language

1. **C** — Idiom

Although gerunds like *hiking* are often interchangeable with infinitives like *to hike* (for instance, saying *I like hiking* is essentially the same as saying *I like to hike*), often the conventions of idiom dictate a preference for one form over the other in a particular context. In this case, the phrase *getting students to respond* is proper idiom, whereas *getting students responding* is not proper idiom. Choice (B) uses an infinitive form, but the phrase *to become responsive* inappropriately changes the meaning of the sentence.

2. **A** — Subject-Verb Agreement

The subject-verb core of this clause is *explaining . . . is*. Notice that this subject and verb agree in number, whereas choices (B) and (D) would introduce subject-verb disagreement. Choice (C) is not idiomatic, so the original phrasing is best.

3. **B** — Coordination

The original phrasing misuses the colon, which should be used only to precede an explanatory clause or an explanatory list. Choice (C) is incorrect for the same reason. Choice (D) is incorrect because it commits a number shift: choosing *between punishment and incentive* is choosing a single motivator, not *motivators*. Choice (B) avoids these errors and conveys the idea clearly and concisely.

4. **B** — Parallelism/Logical Comparison

The phrase *better than* signals that this sentence is making a comparison, which must be both parallel and logical. In the original phrasing, *to reward* (infinitive) is being compared with *punishment* (abstract class noun), and since these are different parts of speech, it violates the law of parallelism. The only choice that provides another abstract class noun is (B) *reward*. Choice (C) is incorrect because *rewarding* is a gerund, not a class noun, and choice (D) is incorrect because *a reward* represents an event-instance, not a class of actions.

5. **B** — Modifier error/Idiom

Remember that any sentence must retain its grammatical integrity even when its modifying phrases are "trimmed" away. The phrase *if not more so* is an interrupting modifier, but when it is removed, the sentence reads . . . *as harmful . . . than punishment*, which is of course not idiomatic. The only choice that avoids this problem is choice (B).

6. **A** — Parallelism

This sentence contains the comparative idiom *not only A but also B*. When we use such idioms, we must make sure that we use the precise phrasing and that the words or phrases that replace *A* and *B* are parallel. The original phrasing is both idiomatic and parallel, because both phrases that replace *A* and *B* are prepositional phrases. Choice (B) is not parallel, and choices (C) and (D) are neither parallel nor idiomatic.

7. **D** — Coherence

The passage as a whole is discussing the use of rewards as a teaching tool, so the underlined sentence is important because it indicates their ineffectiveness in that role.

8. **C** — Dangling Participles

In the original phrasing, as well as in choices (B) and (D), the participle *interpreting* dangles: its subject does not match the subject of the main clause, *subjects*. Choice (C) does not have this problem, and conveys the idea clearly and concisely.

9. **A** — Diction

The original word choice is best. Choice (B) is incorrect because although the results of the study may *indicate* that changes be made in the classroom, the phrase *have profound indications for the classroom* is not idiomatic, because *indicate* is a transitive verb and so requires a direct object. Choice (D) has a similar problem, since the verb *instigate* is also a transitive verb. Choice (C) is incorrect because *improvisations* are performances without preparation, which studies cannot do.

10. **B** — Transitions

This paragraph is discussing the evidence regarding the ability of rewards to incentivize learning. This particular sentence mentions a possible interpretation of that evidence; therefore, the adverb *evidently* is the most logical sentence modifier. Choices (A) and (C) are incorrect because they inappropriately indicate a contrast. Choice (D) is incorrect because this point is not the last of a sequence of points.

11. **A** — Rhetorical Devices

The final paragraph contains a *prescription* (strong suggestion) in the last sentence: *Teachers must be aware of their students' need to feel independent and in control*. It also contains a *qualification* (a statement that moderates a previous claim) in the statement *it would be a mistake to conclude that all rewards are bad*. Choice (B) is incorrect because the paragraph contains no *quantification* (numerical measurement). Choice (C) is incorrect because it provides neither *anecdote* (illustrative story) nor *metaphor* (comparison that equates to things that are not literally equivalent). Choice (D) is incorrect because the paragraph contains no *irony* (reversal of reader expectations) or attempts at *humor*.

12. C   **Coordination**

The original phrasing is illogical because DNA does not *serve as a chemical compound*, it *is* a chemical compound. (Although someone can both *serve as* a nurse and *be* a nurse, this is because nursing is a service. Molecules do not perform services in the way that human professionals do.) Choice (B) is incorrect because it produces a comma splice, and choice (D) is incorrect because it is needlessly wordy, and because the present progressive form *is serving* incorrectly implies a current action rather than a general function. Choice (C) avoids these errors and conveys the idea clearly and effectively in the form of an appositive phrase.

13. A   **Punctuation/Pronoun Agreement**

Since the sentence uses the em-dash (—) to introduce the list of examples, it must likewise use the em-dash to close this list. Any interrupting phrase must start and end with the same punctuation marks: either commas or em-dashes. Although choice (D) uses the em-dash, it is incorrect because the pronoun *itself* does not agree in number with the antecedent *cell types*.

14. B   **Diction**

Choice (B) includes an illogical use of the preposition *of*.

15. A   **Transitions**

The original phrasing is best. Choice (B) is incorrect because the sentence does not indicate any logical consequence. Choice (C) is incorrect because the sentence does not indicate any contrast. Choice (D) is incorrect because the sentence does not indicate any irony.

16. B   **Diction**

This sentence describes the ability of doctors to use biological information to create *"personalized medicine."* One who is particularly skilled is *adept*. Choice (A) is incorrect because *apropos* means *appropriate to a given situation*. Choice (B) is incorrect because *liable* means *likely* or *legally responsible*. Choice (D) is incorrect because the phrase *essential at* is neither logical nor idiomatic.

17. D   **Idiom**

This sentence discusses using stem cells to repair damaged organs. The most concise and idiomatic way to express this functional relationship is with the infinitive *to help*. Choices (A), (B), and (C) all use nonidiomatic phrases.

18. C   **Logical Cohesiveness/Transitions**

This paragraph discusses the task of *translating vast quantities of chemical information into digital form*, and indicates that good progress has been made, thanks to

progress in *specialized hardware and software*. Therefore, the best introductory sentence is (C), which focuses on *progress in the computer sciences*.

19. D   **Subject-Verb Agreement/Idiom**

The original phrasing is incorrect because the phrase *our ability in translating* is not idiomatic. Choice (B) is incorrect because the verb *depend* does not agree in number with the subject *success*. Choice (C) is incorrect because the phrase *the ability of our translating* is illogical. Choice (D) avoids these errors and expresses the idea clearly and concisely.

20. B   **Idiom/Voice/Mood**

The original phrasing is not idiomatic. Choice (C) is incorrect because its use of the active voice is illogical. Choice (D) is also not idiomatic. Only choice (B) conveys the proper mood (necessity) idiomatically and concisely.

21. B   **Data Analysis**

Choice (A) is incorrect because the graph does not indicate anything about the reason for the declining costs in gene sequencing. Choice (B) is correct because in 2014 the actual cost per genome decoded was approximately \$8,000, whereas Moore's Law predicted a cost of over \$1,000,000 in 2014. This actual cost is less than 1% of the predicted cost. Choice (C) is incorrect because the cost to decode a single genome has been under \$10,000 ever since 2012. Choice (D) is incorrect because the graph makes no direct comparison of the cost of genome sequencing to that of other information-based technologies.

22. B   **Dangling Participles/Verb Tense**

The original phrasing is incorrect because the participle *using* dangles: it does not share its subject with the main clause. Choice (C) is incorrect for the same reason. Choice (D) is incorrect because, although it corrects the dangling participle, the present perfect form of the verb, *have discovered*, is illogical.

23. D   **Diction**

The original word choice is illogical since *qualities* are incapable of deciding anything. Choice (B) and (C) are incorrect for similar reasons: anything that *arranges* or *regulates* must have a mind and intention, which *qualities* lack. Choice (D) is the only reasonable choice, since qualities can *determine* (that is, *play a deciding role in an outcome*) whether or not something is art.

24. A   **Verb Aspect**

The original phrasing is best. The present perfect form *have developed* is appropriate because the status of the *notions* is the consequence of how they developed *over the centuries.* Recall that the **perfect** (or **consequential**) **aspect** is used to indicate a status-as-consequence (see Chapter 4, Lesson 23).

---

25. D   **Verb Tense**

This sentence indicates a historical fact, so the simple present tense is best.

---

26. C   **Redundancy**

The original phrasing is redundant, since being *conspicuous* is the same thing as *standing out.* Choice (C) is the only one that avoids the redundancy.

---

27. B   **Logical Cohesiveness**

The paragraph is about the fact that some things in our environment stand out obviously as "art." It would be reasonable, then, to follow this point with an explanation of why a particular object, such as a chair, qualifies as art.

---

28. B   **Coordination**

The original phrasing is incorrect because the clause that follows the semicolon is not independent, and the transitive verb *said* lacks a logical direct object. Choice (C) is incorrect because it creates a comma splice. Choice (D) is incorrect because the clause that follows the semicolon is not independent. Choice (B) avoids these problems.

---

29. C   **Punctuation/Coordination/Parallelism**

The original phrasing is illogical because the adverb *when* incorrectly implies that whether or not an object qualifies for art is a time-specific event, rather than a general criterion. Choice (B) is incorrect because it creates a non-parallel list: *compels . . . inspiring . . . beautiful.* Choice (D) is incorrect because *it's = it is.*

---

30. D   **Coordination/Punctuation**

The sentence is a compound sentence joining a dependent clause *If you have . . .* and an independent clause *you have had. . . .* The original phrasing is incorrect because a colon should be used only to join two independent clauses in which the second explains the first. Choice (B) is incorrect because a semicolon should only be used to join independent clauses. Choice (C) is incorrect because an em dash should only be used to separate an independent clause from an interrupting modifier. Choice (D) is best because a simple comma is most effective at joining a dependent clause and an independent one.

---

31. A   **Verb Form**

The original phrasing is best. Choice (B) is incorrect because the pronoun *they* disagrees in number with its antecedent *skill, beauty, or expression.* (The conjunction *or* implies that only one of these serves as the subject;

---

therefore, it is singular.) Choice (C) is incorrect because it does not coordinate with the phrase *that gives.* Choice (D) is incorrect because it has the disagreement problem of (B) as well as the coordination problem of (C).

---

32. A   **Coordination**

The original phrasing is best. Choice (B) is illogical. Choice (C) creates subject-verb disagreement. Choice (D) is awkward and creates an unidiomatic phrase: *to make them as art.*

---

33. D   **Logical Cohesiveness**

This paragraph introduces and defines the *"institutional theory of art,"* presumably because the author regards it as an interesting theory of aesthetics. Choice (D) is best because it poses an intriguing question that follows directly from that definition. Choices (A), (B), and (C), while true statements, are irrelevant to a discussion of this theory.

---

34. D   **Comparative Idiom/Logical Comparison**

This sentence uses the comparative idiom *as strong as*, so we must check that the comparison is idiomatic, parallel, and logical. The original phrasing and the phrasing in choice (B) are incorrect because they create illogical comparisons: they compare *people* to an *impact.* Choice (C) is incorrect because it is not idiomatic. Choice (D) provides an idiomatic, parallel, and logical comparison.

---

35. A   **Coordination/Idiom**

The original phrasing of the participial phrase is best: notice that the subject of the past participle *born* is also the subject of the main clause: *Chaplin.* Choices (B) and (D) are incorrect because they form comma splices. Choice (C) is incorrect because the present participle *being* implies that Chaplin was born at the same time that he crossed the Atlantic, which is illogical.

---

36. C   **Logical Cohesiveness**

Although this sentence introduces a true and interesting fact, it is inappropriate to this paragraph, which is about Chaplin's impact on the film industry.

---

37. C   **Coordination**

The sentence begins with two adjectival phrases that modify *the Tramp.* Therefore, these modifiers will dangle unless the subject of the main clause is *the Tramp.* The only choice that avoids this dangling is (C).

---

38. D   **Parallelism**

The original phrasing includes a list that is not parallel: *writer, director, and editing.* The only choice that does not violate the Law of Parallelism is (D).

39. A   **Parallelism**

The original phrasing is best because it creates the parallel phrasing *taking on . . . writing . . . and thus allowing.*

---

40. C   **Sentence Fragments/Comparative Idiom**

The original phrasing is incorrect because it creates a sentence fragment. Choices (B) and (D) commit the same error. Only choice (D) forms a sentence with an independent clause. Note also that is correctly applies the comparative idiom *not only A but also B.*

---

41. A   **Dangling Modifiers**

The original phrasing is best because it coordinates with the appositive phrase that begins the sentence. Choices (B) and (C) allow this appositive to dangle. Choice (D) is incorrect because the phrase *became targeted for* is not idiomatic.

---

42. C   **Logical Coordination/Idiom**

This sentence describes the reason that Chaplin *drew the ire of J. Edgar Hoover.* Choice (C) provides the most logical phrase to coordinate this state of being and its cause: *because of.* The prepositional phrases in the original phrasing and in choices (B) and (D) do not convey this logical relationship.

---

43. B   **Pronoun Agreement**

The original phrasing is incorrect because the definite pronoun *they* disagrees in number with the antecedent *government.* Choice (C) is incorrect because the subjunctive form *would have been* incorrectly implies that this clause in counterfactual. Choice (D) is incorrect because *propaganda*, although it sounds plural, is singular.

---

44. B   **Diction**

In this context, *eradicated* does not work because it means *destroy completely, as a scourge*, which does not accurately modify a visa. Choice (B), *revoked* (officially invalidated) works nicely. Choice (C) is illogical because the visa is not disallowed entry into a group, as *excluded* would imply. Choice (D) is illogical because *abolish* more properly describes the formal termination of an institution, practice, or system.

Section 3: Math (No Calculator)

1. D   **Algebra (solving equations) EASY**

$$8x + 6 = 6m$$

To solve in one step, just divide both sides by 2:

$$4x + 3 = 3m$$

2. A   **Algebra (linear systems) EASY**

To determine which ordered pair is a solution to the system, just "plug in" the values for x and y and choose the one that satisfies both equations. Notice that $x = 2$ and $y = 3$ is a solution because $3(2) + 4(3) = 18$, and $3 = \left(\dfrac{3}{2}\right)(2)$.

3. C   **Algebra (algebraic expressions) EASY**

$$\frac{3x + 4}{12}$$

Distribute:

$$\frac{3x}{12} + \frac{4}{12}$$

Simplify:

$$\frac{x}{4} + \frac{1}{3}$$

4. A   **Advanced Mathematics (polynomials) EASY**

There are several ways to approach this question. Perhaps the simplest is to use the Factor Theorem: If $x - c$ is a factor of a polynomial, then $x = c$ is a zero of that polynomial. Therefore, if $x - 3$ is a factor of our polynomial, $x = 3$ must be a zero:

$$x^2 + kx + 12 = (3)^2 + 3k + 12 = 0$$

Simplify: $9 + 3k + 12 = 0$

Subtract 21: $3k = -21$

Divide by 3: $k = -7$

Alternately, you might try to find the other factor of the quadratic. Since the constant term in the quadratic is 12, the constant term in the other binomial factor must be $12 \div -3 = -4$.

$$(x - 3)(x - 4) = x^2 + kx + 12$$
$$x^2 - 7x + 12 = x^2 + kx + 12$$

Subtract x and 12: $-7x = kx$

Divide by x: $-7 = k$

5. C   **Additional Topics (circles and triangles) MEDIUM**

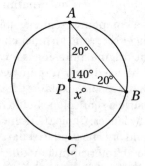

Since *PA* and *PB* are both radii of the circle, they are congruent, and so triangle *APB* is isosceles. By the Isosceles Triangle Theorem, then, angle *A* must also be 20°. From here, you might simply notice that the angle we're looking for, *CPB*, is the external angle to this triangle, and so it has a measure equal to the sum of the two remote interior angles: 20° + 20° = 40°. Alternately, you could notice that angle *APB* must have a measure of 140° (since all angles in a triangle have a sum of 180°), and since AC is a straight line, angle $CPB = 180° - 140° = 40°$.

---

6. B Advanced Mathematics (sequences) MEDIUM

Let's choose a value, like $b = 2$, for our positive constant. This gives us an expression of $2n + 4$ for the nth term of the sequence. Substituting $n = 1$, $n = 2$, $n = 3$, etc. gives us a sequence of 6, 8, 10, 12, 14, and so on. Choice (A) is clearly incorrect, because the first term of this sequence is not 2. Choice (C) is also incorrect because the average of the first three terms is $(6 + 8 + 10)/3 = 8$, not 2. Choice (D) is also incorrect because the ratio of the second term to the first is $8/6 = 4/3$. Only choice (B), the difference between the fourth term and the third term, $12 - 10$, gives us a value of 2.

---

7. A Advanced Mathematics (radical and exponential equations) MEDIUM

For this question, we need to know two Laws of Exponentials from Chapter 9: Law #8 and Law #9. First, we use Law #9 to translate the radicals into exponents.

Given equation: $m^3 = \sqrt{\sqrt{n}}$

Apply Law of Exponentials #9: $m^3 = \sqrt{n^{\frac{1}{2}}}$

Apply Law of Exponentials #9 again: $m^3 = \left(n^{\frac{1}{2}}\right)^{\frac{1}{2}}$

Apply Law of Exponentials #8: $m^3 = n^{\frac{1}{4}}$

Raise to the $\frac{1}{3}$ power: $(m^3)^{\frac{1}{3}} = \left(n^{\frac{1}{4}}\right)^{\frac{1}{3}}$

Apply Law of Exponentials #8 again: $m = n^{\frac{1}{12}}$

---

8. B Algebra (word problems) MEDIUM

Perhaps the most straightforward way to approach this question is to regard it as a conversion from a given *area of lawn* (in square feet) to *cost* (in dollars).

Area of rectangular lawn: $A = bh = ab$ square feet

Convert using given conversion factors:

$$ab \text{ square feet} \times \frac{1 \text{ bag}}{5{,}000 \text{ square feet}} \times \frac{\$p}{1 \text{ bag}} = \$\frac{abp}{5{,}000}$$

Make sure to check this calculation by noticing that all units "cancel" as common factors, except for the unit we want, dollars, which remains in the numerator.

---

9. C Advanced Mathematics (rational inequalities) MEDIUM

Original inequality: $\dfrac{5}{m} \le \dfrac{2}{3}$

Multiply by $3m$ (since $m > 0$, we don't "flip" the inequality): $15 \le 2m$

Divide by 2: $7.5 \le m$

Therefore, the least possible value of m is 7.5.

---

10. A Algebra (linear functions) MEDIUM-HARD

Given function: $f(x) = 3x + n$

Substitute $f(2) = 0$: $f(2) = 3(2) + n = 0$

Simplify: $6 + n = 0$

Subtract 6: $n = -6$

Therefore, the function is $f(x) = 3x - 6$.

Evaluate $f(n)$: $f(n) = f(-6) = 3(-6) - 6 = -18 - 6 = -24$

---

11. A Algebra (absolute values) MEDIUM-HARD

First, we should notice that each choice can be interpreted as a distance between two points on the number line.

A) $|s - v| =$ the distance between s and v

B) $|s - t| =$ the distance between s and t

C) $|s + v| = |s - (-v)| =$ the distance between s and $-v$

D) $|u + v| = |u - (-v)| =$ the distance between u and $-v$

Thinking this way gives us a very straightforward way to solve the problem without doing any calculation. First we need to locate $-v$ on the number line by just reflecting v over the origin at 0. (Recall that multiplication by -1 is equivalent to reflecting a point on the number line over the origin at 0.) This makes it easy to see the distances the problem is asking us to compare:

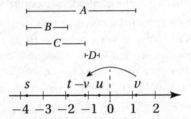

Clearly, the greatest of these distances is (A).

---

12. B Special Topics (trigonometry) MEDIUM-HARD

In order to solve this without a calculator, we need to know how to analyze this problem in terms of the unit circle. First, let's solve for $\cos x$: $4 \cos x = 1$

Divide by 4: $\cos x = \dfrac{1}{4}$

What does the mean in terms of the unit circle? Recall from Chapter 10, Lesson 9, that the cosine of any angle corresponds to the x-coordinate of the corresponding point for that angle on the unit circle:

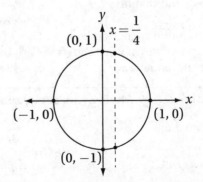

Notice that there are exactly two points on the unit circle that have an x-coordinate of 1/4. Now let's think about the angle. We are told that x goes from 0 to 3π. Remember that a full trip around the circle is 2π radians; therefore, a journey from $x = 0$ to $x = 3\pi$ is 1.5 trips around the circle counterclockwise starting from the positive x-axis. If you trace with your finger 1.5 times around the circle starting from the point (1, 0), you'll hit our "points of interest" exactly three times.

---

13. C   Additional Topics (complex numbers) HARD

To solve this without a calculator, you must be able to evaluate a few low powers of i. Recall from Chapter 10, Lesson 10, that $i^0 = 1$, $i^1 = i$, $i^2 = -1$, $i^3 = -i$, and $i^4 = 1$. Therefore $i^3 + i = -i + i = 0$. Now, it's just a matter of finding the choice that does NOT equal 0.

   A) $(2i)^2 + 4 = -4 + 4 = 0$

   B) $2 - 2i^4 = 2 - 2 = 0$

   C) $2i^2 - 2 = -2 - 2 = -4$

   D) $i^4 - 1 = 1 - 1 = 0$

Therefore, the correct answer is (C).

---

14. D Algebra (graphs of quadratic equations) HARD

Recall from Chapter 9, Lesson 6, that any equation in the form $y = a(x - h)^2 + k$ has a vertex at (h, k) and is open up if $a > 0$ and down if $a < 0$. In the equation $y = -(x + m)^2 + m$; therefore, the vertex is $(-m, m)$, and $a = -1$. Since $m > 1$, this means that the vertex of the parabola has a negative x-coordinate and a positive y-coordinate, which means the vertex is in quadrant II. And since $a < 0$, the parabola is open down. The only graph among the choices that is an open down parabola with a vertex in the second quadrant is the graph in choice (D).

---

15. B   Advanced Mathematics (linear and nonlinear systems) HARD

First, notice that the question is only asking us to find values of x, so it's a good idea to substitute in order to eliminate y from the system.

$$x - 3y = -2$$

Substitute $y = \dfrac{5}{x}$: $x - 3\left(\dfrac{5}{x}\right) = -2$

Multiply by x and simplify: $x^2 - 15 = -2x$

Add $2x$: $x^2 + 2x - 15 = 0$

Factor using Sum-Product Method: $(x - 3)(x + 5) = 0$

Therefore, the values of x that satisfy the original system also satisfy the equation $(x - 3)(x + 5) = 0$.

---

16. 4.5 or 9/2   Algebra (linear equations) EASY

Original equation: $\dfrac{2}{3}a + \dfrac{1}{2}b = 5$

Substitute $b = 4$: $\dfrac{2}{3}a + \dfrac{1}{2}(4) = 5$

Simplify: $\dfrac{2}{3}a + 2 = 5$

Subtract 2: $\dfrac{2}{3}a = 3$

Multiply by $\dfrac{3}{2}$: $a = \dfrac{9}{2}$

---

17. 7   Advanced Mathematics (rational equations) EASY

Given inequality: $\dfrac{6}{x} + \dfrac{1}{2x} < 1$

Multiply by $2x$: $12 + 1 < 2x$

Simplify: $13 < 2x$

Divide by 2: $6.5 < x$

The smallest integer that is greater than 6.5 is 7.

---

18. 8.4 or 42/5   Additional Topics (perimeters and area) MEDIUM-HARD

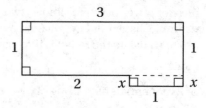

First, drawing a line as shown in the diagram shows that the figure is composed of two rectangles, but the height of the smaller one is unknown. Let's call it x. The area of the larger rectangle is $(3)(1) = 3$, and the area of the smaller rectangle is $(1)(x) = x$. Clearly, the area of the figure must be the sum of these two areas

$$\text{Area} = \frac{16}{5} = 3 + x$$

Subtract 3: $\dfrac{16}{5} - 3 = \dfrac{16}{5} - \dfrac{15}{5} = \dfrac{1}{5} = x$

Therefore, the perimeter of the figure is just the sum of the lengths of its sides. If we travel around the figure clockwise from the leftmost side, we get a perimeter of

$$1 + 3 + 1 + \frac{1}{5} + 1 + \frac{1}{5} + 2 = 8 + \frac{2}{5} = 8.4.$$

---

19. 5 or 7   Algebra (rational equations) MEDIUM-HARD

Original equation: $\dfrac{6}{x+1} - \dfrac{3}{x-1} = \dfrac{1}{4}$

Multiply by $4(x + 1)(x - 1)$:

$$\frac{24(x+1)(x-1)}{x+1} - \frac{12(x+1)(x-1)}{x-1} = \frac{4(x+1)(x-1)}{4}$$

We do this because $4(x + 1)(x - 1)$ is the least common multiple of the denominators, so multiplying both sides by this will eliminate the denominators and simplify the equation.

Cancel common factors:

$$24(x - 1) - 12(x + 1) = (x + 1)(x - 1)$$

Distribute and FOIL: $(24x - 24) - (12x + 12) = x^2 - 1$
Collect like terms: $12x - 36 = x^2 - 1$
Subtract 12x and add 36: $0 = x^2 - 12x + 35$
Factor: $0 = (x - 5)(x - 7)$
Solve using Zero Product Property: $x = 5$ or 7

---

20. **8/13 or .615**   Special Topics (trigonometry)
                                                    HARD

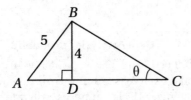

Find AD with Pythagorean Theorem: $(AD)^2 + 4^2 = 5^2$
Simplify: $(AD)^2 + 16 = 25$
Subtract 16: $(AD)^2 = 9$
Take square root: $AD = 3$
Or, even better, just notice that triangle ADB is a 3-4-5 right triangle.
Use triangle area formula to find AC:
$$\text{Area} = \frac{1}{2}bh = \frac{1}{2}(AC)(4) = 19$$
Simplify: $2(AC) = 19$
Divide by 2: $AC = \frac{19}{2}$
Find DC: $DC = AC - AD = \frac{19}{2} - 3 = \frac{19}{2} - \frac{6}{2} = \frac{13}{2}$
Find $\tan \theta$: $\tan \theta = \frac{\text{opp}}{\text{hyp}} = \frac{BD}{DC} = \frac{4}{\frac{13}{2}} = 4 \times \frac{2}{13} = \frac{8}{13}$

Section 4: Math (Calculator)

1. **D**   Algebra (solving equations) EASY
$$\frac{n}{20} = 0.8$$
Multiply by 20: $n = 0.8(20) = 16$

---

2. **A**   Data Analysis (central tendency) EASY

The median of three numbers is the one in the middle when they are listed in order. If two of the numbers are 10 and 12, with 12 as the median, then the third number must be greater than or equal to 12, otherwise 12 would not be in the middle. Of the choices, only (A) 8 is not greater than or equal to 12.

---

3. **C**   Algebra/Data Analysis (expressing
                                        relationships) EASY

The first ordered pair, $x = 0$ and $y = 2$, does not satisfy the equations in (A), (B), or (D), so those choices can be eliminated. You should also confirm that the equation in (C), $y = 2x + 2$, is satisfied by all four ordered pairs.

---

4. **B**   Data Analysis (central tendency) EASY

Let's call the 3 positive integers a, b, and c. If the average of these numbers is m, then
$$\frac{a+b+c}{3} = m$$
Multiply by 3: $a + b + c = 3m$
New average when 24 is included
in the set: $\frac{a+b+c+24}{4}$
Substitute $a + b + c = 3m$: $\frac{3m+24}{4}$

---

5. **C**   Algebra (rational equations) EASY
$$\frac{6}{x} + 3 = -1$$
Multiply by x: $6 + 3x = -x$
Subtract 3x: $6 = -4x$
Divide by -4: $x = \frac{6}{-4} = -\frac{3}{2}$

---

6. **A**   Algebra (representing quantities) EASY

The cost for a month's worth of energy is the cost per kilowatt-hour times the total number of kilowatt-hours used: ($0.15/kWh)(30 kWh). The total monthly charge, P, must also include the service fee: $P = 0.15(30) + 16$.

---

7. **A**   Advanced Mathematics (triangle
                                        trigonometry) EASY

Remember the definitions of the basic trigonometric functions: SOH CAH TOA. Since the "side of interest" (h) is the opposite side to the given angle (42°), and since we know the length of the hypotenuse (1,200), we should use SOH.
$$\sin x = \frac{\text{opp}}{\text{hyp}}$$
Plug in the values: $\sin 42° = \frac{h}{1,200}$
Substitute $\sin 42° = 0.669$: $0.669 = \frac{h}{1,200}$
Multiply by 1,002: $(1,200)(0.669) = 802.8 = h$

---

8. **C**   Special Topics (polygons) EASY

The sum of the measures if the interior angles of a triangle is 180°, therefore $m \angle BED + 90° + 50° = 180°$, and so $m \angle BED = 40°$. Since $\angle AEC$ is vertical to $\angle BED$, it must also have a measure of 40°, and so $40 + x + x = 180$
Simplify: $40 + 2x = 180$
Subtract 40: $2x = 140$
Divide by 2: $x = 70$

---

9. **C**   Data Analysis (histogram) MEDIUM

According to the histogram, 7 students received 15 credits, 1 student received 16 credits, and 1 student received 18 credits, for a total of 9 students who received 15 or more credits. This is 9/24 of the total, or 37.5%

10. D   Data Analysis (histogram/central tendency)
                                                    MEDIUM

Data set: 8, 9, 12, 12, 12, 12, 12, 12, 12, 12, 12, 12, 13, 13, 13,
15, 15, 15, 15, 15, 15, 15, 16, 18

The median of a set of numbers is the "middle" number of the set when the numbers are listed in order. If the
set contains an odd number of numbers, the median is
the middle number, but if the set contains an even number of numbers, it is the average of the two middle numbers. Since this set contains 24 numbers, the median is
the average or the 12th and the 13th numbers. The 12th
number in the set is 12, and the 13th number in the set is
13, the median is 12.5.

---

11. D   **Algebra (absolute values) EASY**

The absolute distance from a to b is $|a - b|$ and the absolute
distance from -2 to 6 is $|-2 - 6| = 8$. Therefore, $|a - b| > 8$.

---

12. D   **Special Topics (circles)**
                                                    MEDIUM

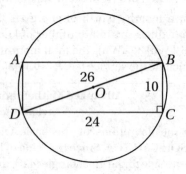

Since $ABCD$ is a rectangle, we can find the length of its
diagonal using the Pythagorean Theorem: $10^2 + 24^2 = d^2$.
Even better, we can notice that the two legs are in a
5:12 ratio, and therefore triangle BCD is a 5-12-13 triangle. In either case, we find that $DB = 26$. Since DB is
also a diameter of the circle, the radius of the circle is
$26/2 = 13$, and therefore, the area of the circle is $\pi r^2 =
\pi(13)^2 = 169\pi$.

---

13. B   **Problem Solving/Data Analysis**
                                    (enumeration of data) MEDIUM

If Niko is the 8th oldest person in the class, then there
are 7 students older than he is. If he is the 12th youngest person, then there are 11 students younger than he is.
Therefore, there are 18 students in addition to him, for a
total of 19 students.

---

14. D   **Additional Topics**
                                    (complex numbers) MEDIUM

$$(2 - i)(3 - 2i)$$

FOIL: $6 - 4i - 3i + 2i^2$
Substitute $i^2 = -1$: $6 - 4i - 3i + 2(-1)$
Combine like terms: $4 - 7i$

---

15. B   **Advanced Mathematics (exponentials)**
                                                    MEDIUM

$$f(3) = (3^2)^{-2b} = 3$$

Exponential Law #8
(from Chapter 9, Lesson 9): $3^{-4b} = 3^1$
Exponential Law #10
(from Chapter 9, Lesson 9) $-4b = 1$

Divide by -4: $b = -\dfrac{1}{4}$

---

16. A   **Data Analysis (probability) MEDIUM**

Since the sum of 55 and 35 is 90, which is 10 greater than
80, there must be at least 10 in the overlap between the
two sets. Statement (B) is not necessarily true, because it
is possible that all 35 students taking AP courses are also
varsity athletes, which is more than half of 55. Statement
(C) is not true because $80 - 55 = 25$ students do not play
varsity sports, and $80 - 35 = 45$ students do not take at
least one AP course. Statement (D) is not necessarily true,
because 35 students take at least one AP course and 25
students do not play a varsity sport, and this sum, $35 +
25 = 60$, is less than the total number of students, so it is
possible that there is no overlap between these two sets.

---

17. A   **Algebra (slopes) MEDIUM**

If $AB = BC$, then triangle ABC is isosceles and therefore the two base angles are congruent and the triangle has a vertical axis of symmetry at the line $x =
3$. This implies that the slopes of lines $\overline{AB}$ and $\overline{BC}$ are
opposites. We can calculate the slope of $\overline{BC}$ from its
endpoints:

$$\text{slope} = \frac{y_2 - y_1}{x_2 - x_1} = \frac{0 - 6}{5 - 3} = -\frac{6}{2} = -3$$

Therefore, the slope of $\overline{AB}$ is 3, and so $mn = (3)(-3) = -9$.

---

18. D   **Advanced Mathematics (functions)**
                                                    MEDIUM-HARD

To answer this question, we must evaluate each of the
three functions for an input of ½:

$$f\left(\frac{1}{2}\right) = \left(\frac{1}{2}\right)^2 = \frac{1}{4} = 0.25$$

$$g\left(\frac{1}{2}\right) = \frac{1}{2} = 0.50$$

$$h\left(\frac{1}{2}\right) = \sqrt{\frac{1}{2}} = \frac{1}{\sqrt{2}} = \frac{\sqrt{2}}{2} \approx 0.71$$

Therefore, $f\left(\dfrac{1}{2}\right) < g\left(\dfrac{1}{2}\right) < h\left(\dfrac{1}{2}\right)$.

---

19. A **Data Analysis (graphing data) MEDIUM-HARD**

If y varies inversely as the square of x, then the variables
are related by the equation $f = \dfrac{k}{x^2}$, where k is a positive

constant. The graph of such an equation in the xy-plane looks like this:

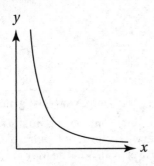

This most closely resembles the scatterplot in choice (A).

---

20. C   **Algebra (expressing relationships) MEDIUM-HARD**

The portion of the birds that are finches is just the number of finches divided by the total number of birds. Since there are already 30 finches, adding n finches makes $30 + n$ finches. Since there are already $12 + 30 + 18 = 60$ total birds, adding n finches makes $60 + n$ total birds.

Since $80\% = 4/5$, $\dfrac{30+n}{60+n} = \dfrac{4}{5}$.

---

21. B   **Advanced Mathematics (functions) MEDIUM-HARD**

$$f(x) = x^2 - 1$$

Substitute $x = \dfrac{1}{b}$: $f\left(\dfrac{1}{b}\right) = \left(\dfrac{1}{b}\right)^2 - 1$

Simplify: $f\left(\dfrac{1}{b}\right) = \dfrac{1}{b^2} - 1$

Get common denominator: $f\left(\dfrac{1}{b}\right) = \dfrac{1}{b^2} - \dfrac{b^2}{b^2}$

Subtract fractions: $f\left(\dfrac{1}{b}\right) = \dfrac{1 - b^2}{b^2}$

Factor numerator: $f\left(\dfrac{1}{b}\right) = \dfrac{(1-b)(1+b)}{b^2}$

---

22. D   **Advanced Mathematics (quadratics) MEDIUM-HARD**

Since k can be any number greater than 0, let's pick $k = 1$ for convenience. If $x = 3$, then $y = (1)(3)^2 = 9$, and if $x = 12$, then $y = (1)(12)^2 = 144$. In this case, both statement (B) and statement (D) are true, since $9 + 135 = 144$ and $9(16) = 144$; therefore, we can eliminate choices (A) and (C). Now let's choose $k = 2$. If $x = 3$, then $y = (2)(3)^2 = 18$, and if $x = 12$, then $y = 2(12)^2 = 288$. Since $18 + 135 \neq 288$, but $18(16) = 288$, the correct answer is (D).

    Notice, also, that since y varies directly as the square of x, then when x is multiplied by n, y is multiplied by n^2. Since x is being multiplied by 4 (to go from 3 to 12), then y must be multiplied by $4^2 = 16$.

---

23. B   **Advanced Mathematics (analyzing quadratics) HARD**

One way to tackle this question is simply to simplify the expression for $f(7)$, and then see which choice gives the same expression.

$$f(7) = k(7 + 6)(7 - 1) = k(13)(6) = 78k$$

Evaluate (A):
$$f(-78) = k(-78 + 6)(-78 - 1) = k(-72)(-79) = 5{,}688k$$
Evaluate (B):
$$f(-12) = k(-12 + 6)(-12 - 1) = k(-6)(-13) = 78k$$
Evaluate (C):
$$f(-2) = k(-2 + 6)(-2 - 1) = k(4)(-3) = -12k$$
Evaluate (D):
$$f(78) = k(78 + 6)(78 - 1) = k(84)(77) = 6{,}468k$$

This shows that $f(-12)$ is equal to $f(7)$. Alternately, you might just make a quick sketch of the parabola and take advantage of the symmetry:

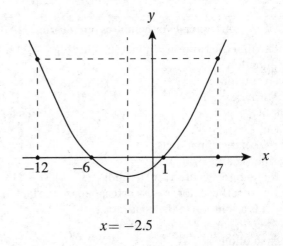

$$x = -2.5$$

---

24. C   **Problem Solving (percentages) MEDIUM-HARD**

Let p = the initial price per share of the stock. After the first year, its price increased by 20%, so its price was $(1.20)p$. After the second year, this price declined 25%, so its price was $(0.75)(1.20)p$. After the second year, this price increased by 10% so its price was $(1.10)(0.75)(1.20)p = 0.99p$, which means that overall the price decreased by 1%.

---

25. D   **Algebra (exponentials) MEDIUM-HARD**

Expression to be evaluated: $\dfrac{w}{y^3}$

Substitute $w = y^6$: $\dfrac{y^6}{y^3}$

Simplify with Exponential Law #6 (from Chapter 9, Lesson 9): y^3

Substitute $y = x^2$: $(x^2)^3$

Simplify with Exponential Law #8 (from Chapter 9, Lesson 9): x^6

26. D   **Data Analysis (tables) MEDIUM-HARD**

Although we don't need to fill in the entire table, it's interesting to note that it has a "diagonal symmetry" when it is completed. Just following the rule and moving systematically toward x reveals that it is $56 + 56 = 112$.

0	1	2	3	4	5
1	2	4	7	11	16
2	4	8	15	26	42
3	7	15	30	56	98
4	11	26	56	**112**	210
5	16	42	98	210	420

27. C   **Advanced Mathematics (quadratics) HARD**

We can find the value of c by just substituting $x = -1$ into the equation.

Given equation:	$3x^2 = 4x + c$
Substitute $x = -1$:	$3(-1)^2 = 4(-1) + c$
Simplify:	$3 = -4 + c$
Add 4:	$7 = c$
Therefore, the equation is:	$3x^2 = 4x + 7$
Subtract $4x$ and 7:	$3x^2 - 4x - 7 = 0$
Factor using Sum-Product Method:	$(x + 1)(3x - 7) = 0$

(Notice that the factor $(x + 1)$ corresponds to the fact that $x = -1$ is a solution to the quadratic.)

Use Zero Product Property to find
other solution:	$3x - 7 = 0$
Add 7:	$3x = 7$
Divide by 3:	$x = 7/3$

28. B   **Special Topics (arcs) HARD**

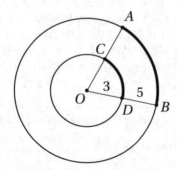

First, we should make sure we mark up the diagram with the measurements we know: $OD = 3$ and $DB = 5$. This means that the radius of the small circle is 3 and the radius of the large circle is 8. Notice that sectors AOB and COD share a central angle, and therefore are similar. So the measures of arc CD and arc AB are

in a ratio of 3:8.

$$\frac{m\widehat{CD}}{m\widehat{AB}} = \frac{m\widehat{CD}}{5\pi} = \frac{3}{8}$$

Cross multiply: $8\left(m\widehat{CD}\right) = 15\pi$

Divide by 8: $m\widehat{CD} = \dfrac{15\pi}{8}$

29. C   **Data Analysis (graphs) MEDIUM**

Since there are only four data points, it's not hard to list the February-May ordered pairs. Notice that the February axis is vertical, and the May axis is horizontal, so the typical x-y relationship is reversed:
Class A: February: 60, May: 60
Class B: February: 80, May: 70
Class C: February: 50, May: 70
Class D: February: 90, May: 90
Notice that the only class that saw an increase in percent participation is Class C.

30. C   **Data Analysis (graphs) HARD**

We just need to tally the number of students who participated from each class.
Class A: 60% of 20 students = 12 students
Class B: 70% of 30 students = 21 students
Class C: 70% of 20 students = 14 students
Class D: 90% of 30 students = 27 students
$12 + 21 + 14 + 27 = 74$ students

31. 0.8 or 4/5   **Algebra
(radical equations) EASY**

| Given equation: | $4 + \sqrt{b} = 7.2$ |
| Subtract 4: | $\sqrt{b} = 3.2$ |

Therefore, $4 - \sqrt{b} = 4 - 3.2 = 0.8$.

32. 8   **Advance Mathematics (quadratics) EASY**

Given equation:	$y = 3x^2 - kx - 35$
Substitute $x = 5$ and $y = 0$:	$0 = 3(5)^2 - k(5) - 35$
Simplify:	$0 = 75 - 5k - 35$
Simplify:	$0 = 40 - 5k$
Add $5k$:	$5k = 40$
Divide by 5:	$k = 8$

33. .96   **Additional Topics (circles/triangles)
MEDIUM-HARD**

When looking for the area of the triangle, remember that there are two basic methods: the direct method and the indirect method. With the direct method, we simply plug the base and height measurements into the formula $A = \dfrac{bh}{2}$, and with the indirect method, we find the area as the sum or difference of other areas. In this case, since we know the lengths of one of the sides, the direct method is probably best. But we will need to find the height as well.

Area of the circle is π:	$\pi r^2 = \pi$
Divide by π:	$r^2 = 1$
Take square root:	$r = 1$

Now let's mark up the diagram with this information. Since the radius of the circle is 1, the diameter FH has a length of 2. Now we can use the Pythagorean Theorem to find the length of GH, which is the height of the triangle if FG is taken as the base. $(1.6)^2 + (GH)^2 = 2^2$

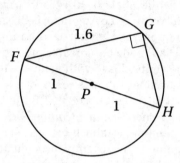

Simplify:	$2.56 + (GH)^2 = 4$
Subtract 2.56:	$(GH)^2 = 1.44$
Take square root:	$GH = 1.2$

(Notice that this is in fact a 3-4-5 triangle: if we multiply 3-4-5 by 0.4, we get 1.2-1.6-2.)

Plug into area formula: $A = \dfrac{bh}{2} = \dfrac{(1.2)(1.6)}{2} = 0.96$

---

34. $4.29 \leq x \leq 4.79$ Algebra (solving inequalities) HARD

$$-\frac{3}{5} < -2t + 1 < -\frac{3}{7}$$

Multiply by -3 and "flip" inequalities: $\dfrac{9}{5} > 6t - 3 > \dfrac{9}{7}$

Add 3: $\dfrac{24}{5} > 6t > \dfrac{30}{7}$

Divide to get decimal form: $4.80 > 6t > 4.2857$

Therefore any decimal value between 4.29 and 4.79, inclusive, is acceptable.

---

35. .84   Advanced Mathematics (trigonometry) MEDIUM-HARD

You may find it helpful to make a quick sketch of the unit circle on the xy-plane, as we discussed in Chapter 10. Subtracting π radians (or 180°) from an angle just means rotating the terminal ray of that angle 180° clockwise. It should be clear, then, that in the xy-plane, the angle with measure $x - \pi$ points in the opposite direction of the angle with measure x. Recall that the cosine of an angle is just the x-coordinate of the point where its terminal ray intersects the unit circle. Since $\cos(x - \pi) = 0.4$ (that

is, its cosine is positive), its terminal ray must be in a quadrant where the x-coordinates are positive: either quadrant I or quadrant IV. Let's just put it in quadrant I. This means that the angle with measure x is in quadrant III, and so it has the opposite cosine:

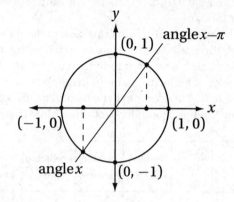

$$\cos x = -0.4$$

Recall Pythagorean Identity from Chapter 10:	$\sin^2 x + \cos^2 x = 1$
Substitute $\cos x = 0.4$:	$\sin^2 x + (-0.4)^2 = 1$
Simplify:	$\sin^2 x + 0.16 = 1$
Subtract 0.16:	$\sin^2 x = 0.84$

---

36. 12   Problem Solving/Data Analysis (word problem) MEDIUM-HARD

This one is a bit trickier than it looks. We have 10 pounds of grain and have used it to feed 20 chickens. Since one pound of grain feeds 5 chickens, proportionally we need 4 pounds of grain to feed 20 chickens. This leaves us $10 - 4 = 6$ pounds of grain to feed the pigs. Since 1 pound of grain can feed 2 pigs, proportionally 6 pounds of grain can feed 12 pigs.

---

37. 371   Problem Solving (extended thinking) HARD

The total revenue from the tickets sold is $\$60(50) + \$50(60) + \$40x + \$35y + \$30(100)$. If the total revenue was \$15,000, then $3,000 + 3,000 + 40x + 35x + 3,000 = 15,000$

Subtract 9,000:	$40x + 35y = 6,000$
Divide by 5:	$8x + 7y = 1,200$
If 15 more tickets were sold in the second mezzanine than the first mezzanine:	$y = x + 15$
Substitute $y = x + 15$ in previous equation:	$8x + 7(x + 15) = 1,200$
Distribute:	$8x + 7x + 105 = 1,200$
Subtract 105:	$15x = 1,095$
Divide by 15:	$x = 73$
Substitute to find y:	$y = x + 15 = 73 + 15 = 88$

Therefore, the total number of tickets sold is $50 + 60 + 73 + 88 + 100 = 371$.

38. **25**   **Problem Solving (extended thinking) HARD**

The mathematical model $n = \dfrac{2{,}800}{p}$ has embedded in it the predicted revenue per section: np = revenue per section = $2,800. Notice that this prediction is $200 less than the actual average revenue per section of $3,000, so clearly the model underestimated the number of tickets sold per section.

If we want to analyze this situation in detail, we can compare the predicted tickets sold to the actual tickets sold by adding a new column to the table entitled "predicted sold," which we can fill in using the calculations from our model. Also, it might be helpful to also add columns for "total revenue" for each situation.

Section	Price Per Ticket	Number Sold	Section Revenue	Predicted Sold	Predicted Revenue
Front Orchestra	$60	50	$3,000	46.667	$2,800
Rear Orchestra	$50	60	$3,000	56	$2,800
First Mezzanine	$40	73	$2,920	70	$2,800
Second Mezzanine	$35	88	$3,080	80	$2,800
Third Mezzanine	$30	100	$3,000	93.333	$2,800
Total		371	$15,000	346	$14,000

You might notice that the predicted number of tickets sold in the Front Orchestra and the Third Mezzanine are fractions, which seems strange. (Of course we can't sell a fraction of a ticket!) But even if we round these predictions to the nearest whole numbers, 47 and 93, the total number of tickets is the same: 346, which underestimates the number of tickets sold by 25.

Section 5: Essay

Sample Response

Reading Score: 8 out of 8
Analysis Score: 8 out of 8
Writing Score: 8 out of 8

As Ellis Parker Butler sees it, American English spelling at the turn of the 20th century is a disaster. It defies logic and common sense, and it even destroys reason itself. Or so it seems. In fact, Butler's essay is not so much about American English spelling rules as it is about American intellectual culture at the turn of the 20th century: it is inclined toward the petty and the self-important. In his essay, Butler builds his argument with humor and charm, and proposes tongue-in-cheek alternatives to traditional standards of, and more recent revisions to, American English spelling. In so doing he pokes ample fun at how Americans think and behave, delving into commentary on politics, technology, and cultural expectations. He uses metaphor, personification, anecdote, and sharp irony to skewer not only the American elite but also himself.

Butler begins his essay with mock-anger at "the spelling profession." He claims it is "the reason America so long lagged behind Europe in the production of genius," noting that, while Shakespeare (a Brit) was clearly a genius, Noah Webster (the American lexicographer) was less so. He mounts his high horse with indignant braggadocio: ". . . self-made authors like me, who never can spell but who simply blaze with genius, will be hooted out of the magazines to make room for a stupid sort of literature that is spelled correctly." Butler's juxtaposition of overconfidence and incompetence (at least in the arena of spelling) establish his wry and ironic tone, which he maintains consistently throughout the essay.

Butler then lashes the "spelling reformers" who want "this new phonetic spelling brought into use" for doing what "we Americans do not like," namely, advocating for sudden change. He illustrates this cultural foible with the example of automobiles, "sixty horsepower snorters" that smell "like an eighteenth-century literary debate" that became acceptable because they were introduced gradually. In fact, Butler says, "we take to being killed by the automobile quite naturally now." At this point, the reader is probably wondering if this essay is really about spelling after all.

Then he turns his gaze to the problem at hand: silent letters. But to Butler, unlike the "spelling reformers," the problem is not practical but moral: we despise silent letters in our words because "we want no idle class in America, whether tramp, aristocrat, or silent letter." His solution? To "set the idle letters to work." Butler then announces that he, perhaps as a lone insurgent, will commence pronouncing them: "although" will now be a three-syllable word with an audible "ugh" at the end.

At this point, the reader probably recognizes Butler's shift in topic to be a feint: in fact, the object of his satire is not spelling at all, but those who are obsessed with the idea of reform. The preposterousness of his theory is intended to reflect the preposterousness of those who spend so much time and mental energy on silly rules. His satire even extends to the peculiarly American obsession with committee meetings and reform projects: "I propose to have some millionaire endow my plan, and Serena (Butler's wife) and I will then form a society for the reforming of English pronunciation."

The greatest disadvantage of Butler's plan, he admits, is that it is too commonsensical: it's advantage is "so manifest that I am afraid it will never be adopted." Here, we readers can't help but wonder if Butler is making a wry commentary on bureaucratic incompetence in government and business.

Butler concludes by considering a "Plan B" offered by his wife, Serena: boycott words with silent letters. To Butler, this plan is less intellectual, but "more American": "Why should people write 'although' when they can write 'notwithstanding that,' and not have a silent letter in it?" By calling Serena's plan "more American," he seems to be criticizing the fickleness of the American consumer, who will change habits sometimes for nonsensical reasons.

Butler uses ironic humor to skewer the American habit of arguing over silly things. By using himself as a foil, together with skillful use of metaphor, anecdote, and personification ("'Although' does all the work, and 'ugh' sits on the fence and whittles"), Butler encourages us to laugh at ourselves, and perhaps then move on to more serious matters.

Scoring

Reading—8 (both readers gave it a score of 4)

This response demonstrates thorough comprehension of Butler's essay through skillful use of summary, paraphrases, and direct quotations. The author summarizes Butler's central purpose and main idea (*Butler's essay is not so much about American English spelling rules as it is about American intellectual culture at the turn of the 20th century: it is inclined toward the petty and the self-important*) and presents many details from the text, including abundant direct quotations. Each quotation is accompanied by insightful commentary that demonstrates that this author has thoroughly comprehended Butler's central idea, as well as his skillful use of devices like irony, metaphor, and personification to support that claim.

Analysis—8 (both readers gave it a score of 4)

This response presents an insightful analysis of Butler's essay and demonstrates a sophisticated understanding of the analytical task. This author has identified Butler's primary modes of expression (*metaphor, personification, anecdote, and sharp irony*) and has uncovered the core message of the essay by exploring Butler's use of these devices (*he pokes ample fun at how Americans think and behave, delving into commentary on politics, technology, and cultural expectations*). For example, the author identifies the devices that establish the essay's overall tone (*Butler's juxtaposition of overconfidence and incompetence (at least in the arena of spelling) establish his wry and ironic tone, which he maintains consistently throughout the essay*) as well as elements that establish layers of meaning (*we readers can't help but wonder if Butler is making a wry commentary on bureaucratic incompetence in government and business*) and shift focus to more subtle ideas (*the reader probably recognizes Butler's shift in topic to be a feint: in fact, the object of his satire is not spelling at all, but those who are obsessed with the idea of reform*). This response explores Butler's essay systematically, from introduction to conclusion, with thoughtful commentary throughout.

Writing—8 (both readers gave it a score of 4)

This response shows a masterful use of language and sentence structure to establish a clear and insightful central claim (*Butler's essay is not so much about American English spelling rules as it is about American intellectual culture at the turn of the 20th century: it is inclined toward the petty and the self-important. . . . He uses metaphor, personification, anecdote, and sharp irony to skewer not only the American elite but also himself*). The response maintains a consistent focus on this central claim, and supports it with a clear and deliberate analysis of Butler's essay. The author shows particular skill in verb choice (*defies logic . . . builds his argument . . . delving into commentary . . . establish his wry and ironic tone . . . lashes the "spelling reformers"*), strength in using parallel structures (*not only the American elite but also himself . . . while Shakespeare (a Brit) was clearly a genius, Noah Webster (the American lexicographer) was less so . . . the problem is not practical but moral*), and thoughtfulness in diction and phrasing (*[h]e mounts his high horse with indignant braggadocio . . . perhaps as a lone insurgent . . . perhaps as a lone insurgent . . . [h]is satire even extends to the peculiarly American obsession with committee meetings and reform projects*). Largely free of grammatical error, this response demonstrates strong command of language and advanced proficiency in writing.

PRACTICE TEST 2

SECTION 5: ESSAY

You may wish to remove these sample answer document pages to respond to the practice SAT Essay Test.

WRITING TEST

_____

_____

_____

_____

_____

_____

_____

_____

_____

_____

_____

_____

_____

_____

_____

_____

_____

_____

_____

_____

_____

_____

_____

_____

_____

If you need more space, please continue on the next page.

Cut Here

SECTION 5: ESSAY

You may wish to remove these sample answer document pages to respond to the practice SAT Essay Test.

WRITING TEST

_____
_____
_____
_____
_____
_____
_____
_____
_____
_____
_____
_____
_____
_____
_____
_____
_____
_____
_____
_____
_____
_____
_____
_____
_____

If you need more space, please continue on the next page.

Cut Here

SECTION 5: ESSAY

You may wish to remove these sample answer document pages to respond to the practice SAT Essay Test.

WRITING TEST

Cut Here

STOP here with the Writing Test.

4

1

1

Reading Test

65 MINUTES, 52 QUESTIONS

Turn to Section 1 of your answer sheet to answer the questions in this section.

Questions 1–10 are based on the following passage.

This passage is from Ralph Waldo Emerson, *"Prudence."* Public domain. First published in 1841.

What right have I to write on prudence, of which I have little, and that of the negative sort?
Line My prudence consists in avoiding and going without, not in the inventing of means and
5 methods, not in adroit steering, not in gentle repairing. I have no skill to make money spend well, no genius in my economy, and whoever sees my garden discovers that I must have some other garden. Yet I love facts, and hate shiftiness and
10 people without perception.

Then I have the same title to write on prudence that I have to write on poetry or holiness. We write from aspiration as well as from experience.

15 We paint those qualities that we do not possess. The poet admires the man of energy and tactics; the merchant breeds his son for the church or the bar; and where a man is not vain and egotistic you shall find what he lacks, by his praise.

20 Yet it would be hardly honest for me not to balance these fine lyric words with words of coarser sound. Prudence is the virtue of the senses. It is the science of appearances. It is the outmost action of the inward life. It is God taking
25 thought for oxen. It moves matter after the laws of matter. It is content to seek health of body by

complying with physical conditions, and health of mind by the laws of the intellect.

The world of the senses is a world of shows; it
30 does not exist for itself, but has a symbolic character; and a true prudence or law of shows recognizes the co-presence of other laws and knows that its own office is secondary; knows that it is surface and not center where it works. Prudence
35 is false when detached. It is legitimate when it is the natural history of the soul incarnate, when it unfolds the beauty of laws within the narrow scope of the senses.

There are all degrees of proficiency in knowl-
40 edge of the world. It is sufficient to our present purpose to indicate three. One class lives to the utility of the symbol, esteeming health and wealth a final good. Another class lives above this mark, to the beauty of the symbol, as the poet and
45 artist and the naturalist and man of science. A third class lives above the beauty of the symbol to the beauty of the thing signified; these are wise men. The first class has common sense; the second, taste; and the third, spiritual perception.
50 Once in a long time, a man traverses the whole scale, and sees and enjoys the symbol solidly, then also has a clear eye for its beauty, and lastly, while he pitches his tent on this sacred volcanic isle of nature, does not offer to build houses and barns
55 thereon, reverencing the splendor of the God which he sees bursting through each chink and cranny.

CONTINUE

1

The world is filled with the proverbs and acts of a base prudence, which is a devotion to
60 matter, as if we possessed no other faculties than the palate, the nose, the touch, the eye and ear; a prudence that never subscribes, that never gives, that seldom lends, and asks but one question of any project: will it bake bread? This is a disease
65 like a thickening of the skin until the vital organs are destroyed. But culture, revealing the high origin of the apparent world and aiming at the perfection of the man as the end, degrades every thing else, as health and bodily life, into means.

70 It sees prudence not to be a separate faculty, but a name for wisdom and virtue conversing with the body and its wants. Cultivated men always feel and speak so, as if a great fortune, the achievement of a civil or social measure, great personal
75 influence, a graceful and commanding address, had their value as proofs of the energy of the spirit. If a man loses his balance and immerses himself in any trades or pleasures for their own sake, he may be a good wheel or pin, but he is not
80 a cultivated man.

1

The tone of the first paragraph is best described as

A) self-effacing.

B) pontifical.

C) aspirational.

D) sardonic.

2

The author's reference to "some other garden" (lines 8–9) primarily suggests that he

A) finds solace in the art of planting.

B) seeks new challenges and experiences.

C) considers arable land to be a valuable resource.

D) lacks the particular skills associated with farming.

3

In line 11, "title" most nearly means

A) ownership.

B) office.

C) authority.

D) publication.

4

The author believes that he is justified in acting as an authority on prudence primarily because of his

A) experience in making decisions.

B) regret for his past mistakes.

C) studies in classical philosophy.

D) yearning for wisdom.

5

Which choice provides the strongest evidence for the answer to the previous question?

A) Lines 6–9 ("I have no skill . . . some other garden")

B) Lines 13–14 ("We write from . . . as well as from experience")

C) Lines 20–22 ("Yet it would . . . coarser sound")

D) Lines 26–28 ("It is content . . . laws of the intellect")

CONTINUE ▶

6

The passage suggests that members of the "third class" (line 46) are superior for their ability to

A) solve important problems.

B) discern sublime qualities.

C) create works of beauty.

D) reason logically.

7

The "houses and barns" (line 54) represent

A) an unwise allegiance to worldly things.

B) the rejection of mere symbols.

C) the nobility of living with nature.

D) the importance of strong belief.

8

In line 58, "base" most nearly means

A) supportive.

B) ignoble.

C) necessary.

D) straightforward.

9

The "disease" mentioned in line 64 is best described as

A) apathy.

B) gluttony.

C) sensuousness.

D) egotism.

10

The passage as a whole characterizes prudence primarily as.

A) the aspiration to wisdom and righteousness.

B) a commitment to aesthetic principles.

C) the pursuit of practical skills and sensory experience.

D) the noble pursuit of spiritual goals.

CONTINUE ➔

1   **1**

Questions 11–21 are based on the following passage.

This passage is from Joseph Conrad, *The Secret Sharer*. It was originally published in 1912. The narrator of this story is the captain of a ship about to begin a voyage.

She floated at the starting point of a long journey, very still in an immense stillness, the shad-
Line ows of her spars flung far to the eastward by the
setting sun. At that moment I was alone on her
5 decks. There was not a sound in her—and around
us nothing moved, nothing lived, not a canoe on
the water, not a bird in the air, not a cloud in the
sky. In this breathless pause at the threshold of
a long passage we seemed to be measuring our
10 fitness for a long and arduous enterprise, the
appointed task of both our existences to be carried out, far from all human eyes, with only sky
and sea for spectators and for judges.

There must have been some glare in the
15 air to interfere with one's sight, because it was
only just before the sun left us that my roaming eyes made out beyond the highest ridges of
the principal islet of the group something that
did away with the solemnity of perfect solitude.
20 The tide of darkness flowed on swiftly; and with
tropical suddenness a swarm of stars came out
above the shadowy earth, while I lingered yet,
my hand resting lightly on my ship's rail as if on
the shoulder of a trusted friend. But, with all that
25 multitude of celestial bodies staring down at one,
the comfort of quiet communion with her was
gone for good. And there were also disturbing
sounds by this time—voices, footsteps forward;
the steward flitted along the main-deck, a busily
30 ministering spirit; a hand bell tinkled urgently
under the poop deck.

I found my two officers waiting for me near
the supper table, in the lighted cuddy. We sat
down at once, and as I helped the chief mate, I
35 said: "Are you aware that there is a ship anchored
inside the islands? I saw her mastheads above the
ridge as the sun went down."

He raised sharply his simple face, over-
charged by a terrible growth of whisker, and emit-
40 ted his usual ejaculations:

"Bless my soul, sir! You don't say so!"

My second mate was a round-cheeked, silent
young man, grave beyond his years, I thought; but
as our eyes happened to meet I detected a slight
45 quiver on his lips. I looked down at once. It was
not my part to encourage sneering on board my
ship. It must be said, too, that I knew very little of
my officers. In consequence of certain events of
no particular significance, except to myself, I had
50 been appointed to the command only a fortnight
before. Neither did I know much of the hands
forward. All these people had been together for
eighteen months or so, and my position was that
of the only stranger on board. I mention this
55 because it has some bearing on what is to follow.
But what I felt most was my being a stranger to
the ship; and if all the truth must be told, I was
somewhat of a stranger to myself. The youngest
man on board (barring the second mate), and
60 untried as yet by a position of the fullest responsibility, I was willing to take the adequacy of the
others for granted. They had simply to be equal to
their tasks. But I wondered how far I should turn
out faithful to that ideal conception of one's own
65 personality every man sets up for himself secretly.

Meantime the chief mate, with an almost
visible effect of collaboration on the part of his
round eyes and frightful whiskers, was trying to
evolve a theory of the anchored ship. His domi-
70 nant trait was to take all things into earnest consideration. He was of a painstaking turn of mind.
As he used to say, he "liked to account to himself"
for practically everything that came in his way,
down to a miserable scorpion he had found in his
75 cabin a week before. The why and the wherefore
of that scorpion—how it got on board and came
to select his room rather than the pantry (which
was a dark place and more what a scorpion would
be partial to), and how on earth it managed to
80 drown itself in the inkwell of his writing desk—
had exercised him infinitely.

The ship within the islands was much more
easily accounted for.

CONTINUE ▶

11

The tone of the first paragraph (lines 1–13) is primarily one of

A) reflective anticipation.

B) anxious dread.

C) unrestrained excitement.

D) objective analysis.

12

The reference to "some glare" (line 14) serves primarily to make the point that

A) the mastheads of another ship were not immediately visible.

B) the weather was about to change.

C) the ocean around the ship was choppy.

D) the crew was eager to get into the open sea.

13

In lines 20–24 ("The tide . . . friend") the narrator describes

A) signs of impending danger.

B) reflections of his deep inner turmoil.

C) objects of wistful contemplation.

D) the recollection of a tragic experience.

14

The captain is portrayed primarily as

A) self-conscious and diffident.

B) rugged and adventurous.

C) anxious and short-tempered.

D) scholarly yet intimidating.

15

Which choice provides the strongest evidence for the answer to the previous question?

A) Lines 4–5 ("At that moment . . . her decks")

B) Lines 24–27 (But, with . . . for good")

C) Lines 48–51 ("In consequence . . . fortnight before")

D) Lines 63–65 ("But I . . . himself secretly")

16

In line 55, "bearing" most nearly means

A) direction.

B) demeanor.

C) relevance.

D) endurance.

17

In line 69, "evolve" most nearly means

A) change slowly.

B) ponder strenuously.

C) persuade earnestly.

D) advance randomly.

18

The "truth" to which the narrator refers in lines 57 is his

A) skepticism about his crew's ability.

B) apprehension about a dangerous voyage.

C) lack of self-confidence.

D) sense that he may be going insane.

1   **1**

19

In line 81, "exercised" most nearly means

A) practiced.

B) strengthened.

C) utilized.

D) disquieted.

20

The "collaboration" (line 67) refers to an act of

A) selfless assistance.

B) deliberate menace.

C) contrived deceit.

D) strained contemplation.

21

The chief mate believed that, compared to the recently discovered ship, the "scorpion" (line 74) was

A) less explicable.

B) more frightening.

C) more ominous.

D) less miserable.

CONTINUE ➤

Therapeutic Cloning Strategies

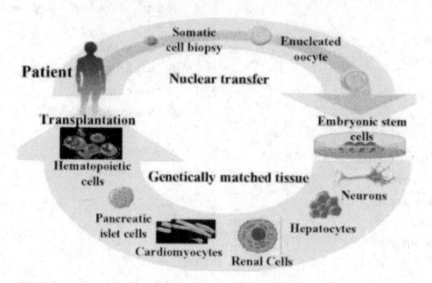

Source: National Institutes of Health

Questions 22–32 are based on the following passages.

Passage 1 is from Lindsay Smith-Doyle, *"Thoughts on the Value of Life."* ©2015 by College Hill Coaching. Passage 2 is from Christopher F. Black, "Who's Afraid of Cloning?" ©2015 by Christopher F. Black. Since 1996, when scientists at the Roslin Institute in England cloned a sheep from the cells of another adult sheep, many have debated the ethics of cloning human cells. These passages are excerpts from arguments on this issue.

Passage 1

How should human life be bestowed? With human cloning looming as a real scientific pos-
Line sibility, we must question the provenance of this ultimate gift. Our intimate participation in the
5 creation of life must never be misconstrued as control. Rather, our attitude toward the creation of life must be one of humility.

The idea of "outsourcing" the creation of
35 human life, of relegating it to a laboratory, of reducing the anticipation of childbirth to a trip to the mall or a selection from a catalog, mocks the profundity of life. The mystery is replaced by

design and control. Should we turn our noses up at the most precious gift in the universe, only to
15 say: "Sorry, but I think I can do better?"

Cloning is the engineering of human life. We have for the first time the ability to determine the exact genetic makeup of a human being. Whether you believe in evolution or creationism, cloning
20 thwarts an essential step of the conception process: randomness in the case of natural selection, and guided purpose in the case of creationism. A child can be created that is no longer uniquely human but the end product of an assembly line,
25 with carefully designed and tested features. Are the astonishing processes of nature somehow deficient?

If human cloning becomes acceptable, we will have created a new society in which the value
30 of human life is marginalized. Industries will arise that turn human procreation into a profitable free-market enterprise. The executive boards of these companies will decide the course of human evolution, with more concern for quarterly profit reports than for the fate of humanity.
10 These are not idle concerns. Even as we ponder the ethical implications of human cloning, companies are forging ahead with procedures

CONTINUE ▶

1   **1**

to clone human cells for seemingly beneficial
40   purposes, marching steadily toward a Brave New
World in which humanity will be forever less
human.

Passage 2

The breathless fears about human cloning
should not surprise anyone who knows the his-
45   tory of science. Every step in human progress is
met with close-mindedness that often verges on
paranoia. Not even medicine is spared. As doctors
toil to save, prolong, and improve lives, the unin-
formed rage at the arrogance of science. Before
50   the merits of surgery and vaccination became
commonplace and obvious, many refused to
believe that cutting flesh or introducing degraded
germs could do more good than harm. Perhaps
we should turn from science and return to super-
55   stition and magic spells?

At first glance, it might seem that cloning is
a whole new ballgame. After all, cloning is "the
engineering of human life," isn't it? It is the mass
production of designer babies. It is the end of
60   evolution, or at least the beginning of its corporate
management. It is certainly a slap in the face of
God. Or is it?

Cloning foe Jeremy Rifkin is afraid of nothing
so much as duplication: "It's a horrendous crime
65   to make a Xerox of someone. You're putting a
human into a genetic straitjacket." The horror! I
wonder how Mr. Rifkin would feel at the annual
Twins Days Festival in Twinsburg, Ohio. Genetic
Xeroxes everywhere!

70   Identical twins are not monsters. Rifkin's
fear is vacuous. Each identical twin has his or her
own unique thoughts, talents, experiences, and
beliefs. Mr. Rifkin must learn that human beings
are more than just their DNA; they are the prod-
75   ucts of the continual and inscrutably complex
interactions of environment and biology. Human
clones would be no different.

"But you are playing God!" we hear. It is the
cry of all whose power is threatened by the march
80   of human progress. It is the reasoning of the Dark
Ages, used to keep the subservient masses in their
place. Every great step humanity has ever taken
has disrupted the "natural order." Should we be
shivering in caves, eating uncooked bugs, and
85   dying of parasites, as nature intended?

But perhaps procreation is different—more
sacred. Then why have the technologies of fertil-
ity enhancement, in vitro fertilization, embryo
transfer, and birth control become so widely
90   accepted? Each of these technologies was met at
first with legions of strident opponents. But over
time, reality and compassion overcame unreason
and paranoia. Familiarity dissipates fear.

These supposedly "moral" objections are in
95   fact impeding moral progress. With genetic engineering, cloning, and stem cell research, scientists finally have within their grasp technologies
that can provide ample food for a starving world,
cure devastating illnesses, and replace diseased
100 organs. Only ignorant superstition stands in
their way.

CONTINUE →

22

In line 13, "control" refers specifically to control over

A) the effects of cloning.

B) the development of genetic technologies.

C) the process of conception.

D) the ethical debate about cloning.

23

In Passage 1, the author's attitude toward "outsourcing" (line 8) is one of

A) grudging approval.

B) blunt disdain.

C) firm support.

D) ironic detachment.

24

The quotations in line 15 and line 78 are similar in that both

A) represent the opinions of cloning opponents.

B) indicate cautious advocacy for genetic engineering.

C) are presented as being insincere.

D) contradict the viewpoints of the respective authors.

25

Jeremy Rifkin (line 63) would most likely advocate

A) the "humility" mentioned in line 7.

B) the "design and control" mentioned in line 13.

C) the "engineering" mentioned in line 16.

D) the "industries" mentioned in line 30.

26

The accompanying diagram best illustrates

A) the "guided purpose" mentioned in line 22.

B) the "assembly line" mentioned in line 24.

C) the "course of human evolution" mentioned in lines 33–34.

D) the "procedures" mentioned in line 38.

27

In line 52, "introducing" refers to an act of

A) explanation.

B) proposition.

C) announcement.

D) injection.

28

The author of Passage 1 would most likely regard the "management" (line 61) as

A) a necessary measure to avoid the abuse of procreative technologies.

B) an acceptable means by which the medical community can find alternatives to cloning.

C) a regrettable invasion of commercial interests into human reproduction.

D) a dangerous impediment to the development of effective cloning techniques.

29

Passage 2 quotes Jeremy Rifkin in line 64 primarily to

A) exemplify an untenable position.

B) illustrate the potential dangers of cloning.

C) reveal the interests of the corporate community.

D) cite a corroborating opinion from an expert.

CONTINUE ▶

30

Passage 2 refers to the Twin's Day Festival in line 68 as an example of

A) a movement that promotes beneficial cloning.

B) a seemingly harmless event that harbors hidden dangers.

C) the innocuousness of genetic duplication.

D) the logical consequences of procreative technologies.

31

The author of Passage 2 would most likely argue that the "procedures" to which the author of Passage 1 objects in line 38 are in fact

A) inconsequential aspects of the cloning debate.

B) necessary contributions to medical progress.

C) not representative of the methods used by real genetic researchers.

D) ways of manipulating public opinion.

32

Which choice provides the strongest evidence for the answer to the previous question?

A) Lines 59–61 ("It is the end . . . management")

B) Lines 71–73 ("Each identical . . . beliefs")

C) Lines 80–82 ("It is the reasoning . . . place")

D) Lines 95–100 ("With genetic . . . organs")

CONTINUE

1   1

Questions 33–42 are based on the following passage.

This passage is from Steven Pinker, *An Invitation to Cognitive Science* (Gleitman, Liberman, and Osherson, eds.) ©1995 by Bradford Book.

Language is the main vehicle by which we know about other people's thoughts, and the two
Line must be intimately related. Every time we speak we are revealing something about language, so
5 the facts of language structure are easy to come by; these data hint at a system of extraordinary complexity. Nonetheless, learning a first language is something every child does successfully, in a matter of a few years and without the need for
10 formal lessons. With language so close to the core of what it means to be human, it is not surprising that children's acquisition of language has received so much attention.

Is language simply grafted on top of cogni-
15 tion as a way of sticking communicable labels on thoughts? Or does learning a language some-how mean learning to think in that language? A famous hypothesis, outlined by Benjamin Whorf, asserts that the categories and relations that we
20 use to understand the world come from our par-ticular language, so that speakers of different lan-guages conceptualize the world in different ways. Language acquisition, then, would be learning to think, not just learning to talk.

25 This is an intriguing hypothesis, but virtually all modern cognitive scientists believe it is false. Babies can think before they can talk. Cognitive psychology has shown that people think not just in words but also in images and abstract
30 logical propositions. And linguistics has shown that human languages are too ambiguous and schematic to use as a medium of internal compu-tation: when people think about "spring," surely they are not confused as to whether they are
35 thinking about a season or something that goes "boing"—and if one word can correspond to two thoughts, thoughts can't be words.

But language acquisition has a unique contribution to make to this issue. It is virtu-
40 ally impossible to show how children could learn a language unless you assume they have a considerable amount of nonlinguistic cognitive machinery in place before they start.

All humans talk but no house pets do, no
45 matter how pampered, so heredity must be involved. But a child growing up in Japan speaks Japanese whereas the same child brought up in California would speak English, so environment is also crucial. Thus there is no question about
50 whether heredity or environment is involved in language, or even whether one or the other is "more important." Instead, language acquisi-tion might be our best hope of finding out how heredity and environment interact. We know
55 that adult language is intricately complex, and we know that children become adults. Therefore something in the child's mind must be capable of attaining that complexity. Any theory that posits too little innate structure, so that its hypothetical
60 child ends up speaking something less than a real language, must be false. The same is true for any theory that posits too much innate structure, so that the hypothetical child can acquire English but not, say, Bantu or Vietnamese.

65 And not only do we know about the output of language acquisition, we know a fair amount about the input to it, namely, parents' speech to their children. So even if language acquisi-tion, like all cognitive processes, is essentially a
70 "black box," we know enough about its input and output to be able to make precise guesses about its contents.

The study of language acquisition began around the same time as the birth of cognitive
75 science, in the late 1950s. We can see now why that is not a coincidence. The historical catalyst was Noam Chomsky's review of Skinner's *Verbal Behavior* in 1959. At that time, Anglo-American natural science, social science, and philoso-
80 phy had come to a virtual consensus about the answers to the questions listed above. The mind consisted of sensorimotor abilities plus a few simple laws of learning governing gradual changes in an organism's behavioral repertoire.
85 Therefore, language must be learned; it cannot be a module; and thinking must be a form of verbal behavior, since verbal behavior is the prime manifestation of "thought" that can be observed externally. Chomsky argued that language

CONTINUE

90 acquisition falsified these beliefs in a single stroke: children learn languages that are governed by highly subtle and abstract principles, and they do so without explicit instruction or any other environmental clues to the nature of such prin-

95 ciples. Hence language acquisition depends on an innate, species-specific module that is distinct from general intelligence. Much of the debate in language acquisition has attempted to test this once-revolutionary, and still controversial, collec-

100 tion of ideas. The implications extend to the rest of human cognition.

CONTINUE

33

This passage as a whole is primarily concerned with

A) delineating the general principles of linguistics.

B) comparing the structural qualities of various languages.

C) exploring academic questions about how we learn language.

D) examining the claims of one influential linguist.

34

The "data" mentioned in line 6 most likely include information regarding

A) the literacy levels of various countries.

B) methods for teaching infants to speak.

C) the syntax rules of different languages.

D) the structures of the human cerebral cortex.

35

In line 2, "the two" refers to

A) self and other.

B) thinking and expressing.

C) grammar and syntax.

D) learning and teaching.

36

In line 15, "sticking" most nearly means

A) applying.

B) upholding.

C) piercing.

D) maintaining.

37

The author's attitude toward Whorf's "hypothesis" (line 18) is best described as

A) dismissive.

B) supportive.

C) ambivalent.

D) antagonistic.

38

The statement "Babies can think before they can talk" (line 27) is intended to indicate that

A) learning to talk is much more cognitively challenging than most people believe.

B) skills associated with basic reasoning are not dependent on verbal communication.

C) both physical and cognitive skills tend to develop according to rigid timelines.

D) researchers sometimes do not take into account the particular needs of infants.

39

Which if the following best summarizes the author's view on human language acquisition?

A) Learning a language is a crucial step in learning to think, because thinking is verbal behavior.

B) The structures for learning language seem to be much simpler than what scientists previously thought.

C) Humans are born with very intricate cognitive structures for learning language.

D) Environmental input is more important than heredity in language acquisition.

CONTINUE ➤

1 **1**

40

Which choice provides the strongest evidence for the answer to the previous question?

A) Lines 1–3 ("Language is . . . intimately related")

B) Lines 23–24 ("Language acquisition . . . to talk")

C) Lines 61–64 ("The same . . . Vietnamese")

D) Lines 95–97 ("Hence language . . . general intelligence")

41

In line 62, "structure" refers to

A) the grammatical rules of a language.

B) the functional organization of the mind.

C) the environment in which infants learn.

D) the systems for investigating linguistic claims.

42

The subjects listed in lines 78–80 are given as examples of disciplines that, in 1959,

A) accepted the hypothesis that cognition depends on verbal skills.

B) considered the scientific method inadequate to the study of language acquisition.

C) regarded most of the processes in involved in language acquisitions to be innate.

D) questioned the conventional theories regarding how humans learn language.

CONTINUE

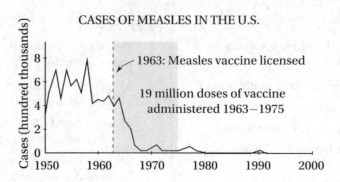

CASES OF MEASLES IN THE U.S.

1963: Measles vaccine licensed

19 million doses of vaccine
administered 1963–1975

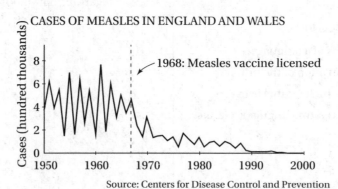

CASES OF MEASLES IN ENGLAND AND WALES

1968: Measles vaccine licensed

Source: Centers for Disease Control and Prevention

Questions 43–52 are based on the following passage and supplementary material.

This passage is adapted from Rick Smolan and Phillip Moffitt, *"Medicine's Great Journey."* ©1992 by Schering Laboratories, Calloway Editions.

Vaccination is one of medicine's cleverest tricks: making the body believe it is sick and thus
Line causing it to marshal just the right forces to ward off that particular sickness. The development
5 of this practice stands as a twentieth-century accomplishment, but its roots reach far back into the past. Centuries ago, the Chinese and the Turks knew enough to produce a medicine against smallpox by grinding up the scabs of
10 people with mild cases of the disease. In 1796, Dr. Edward Jenner found he could induce resistance to smallpox by using the vaccinia virus (*vacca* is Latin for cow) to infect people with the relatively mild cowpox. But it was Louis Pasteur, working
15 a century later, who did the research that finally gave the field of immunology the creative boost that would propel it to the forefront of modern medicine. In 1895, Pasteur produced a rabies vaccine without actually realizing that he was
20 enhancing the body's own immune system; he knew only that the vaccine worked.

But what was the infectious agent that vaccines fought? Could it have been a bacterium? In Germany, in 1882, Robert Koch had shown
25 that just such a germ caused tuberculosis. Microscopic parasites with similarities both to plants and animals, bacteria were certainly the cause of much human misery. But they were not to play the starring role in the vaccine story.
30 The first tantalizing awareness of a virus—a microorganism even stranger than the invisible bacteria and like nothing else ever known before—came in 1898 when Martinus Willem Beijerinick discovered a minuscule living thing he described

35 with a name, "virus," derived from the Latin for poisonous slime. A virus is really no more than a protein bag carrying its own set of genetic instructions. A virus cannot reproduce on its own. It must attach itself to a cell, impregnate the cell with the

40 viral genes, and then, parasite that it is, turn that cell into a reproductive machine for the virus's benefit. The body, for the most part, is able to recognize these viruses as foreign invaders by the signature proteins on their surface. It then attacks

45 them with antibodies and sends killer cells to destroy the cells that have already been infected. If the immune system is overwhelmed by the invasion, the body becomes sick and may die. If the body wins, then its immune system keeps a record

50 of this particular enemy and is better prepared to resist the next time. Sometimes the immunity is lifelong. Vaccines work by introducing the viral proteins without the dangerous genes, thereby stimulating the immune response without creat-

55 ing the disease.

Thanks to advances in modern vaccines, measles are nearly gone, and chicken pox, whooping cough, typhoid, and cholera are under control. From a purely psychological point of

60 view, perhaps the biggest vaccine success of the century was the almost total victory over polio, an effort that called upon everything scientists had learned in the new fields of immunology and virology. Polio was thought to be a true childhood

65 plague, a crippler and a destroyer of young lives. It seemed to come from nowhere in 1916 and was virtually eradicated fifty years later.

The advances against viruses continue. There is now a vaccine for the vicious hepatitis B virus,

70 and vaccines for the potentially deadly influenza viruses. But herpes, another viral affliction, still flourishes, and the most ubiquitous of all the viral maladies—the common cold, caused by well over a hundred different viruses—may never be

75 thwarted by a vaccine because the viruses are too numerous. Scientists have come a long way in the fight against viruses, but further advances are necessary as it seems new viruses appear as old viral foes are eradicated. The fight will probably

80 never be completely won.

CONTINUE

43

The passage as a whole serves primarily to

A) outline the various means by which the human immune system fights infection.

B) describe the history and scientific underpinnings of a medical technique.

C) compare the medical practices of different cultures throughout history.

D) identify particular controversies surrounding a therapeutic method.

44

The passage mentions the "Chinese and Turks" (lines 7–8) as examples of cultures that

A) identified the cause of viral infections.

B) employed early forms of vaccination.

C) were misguided in their use of medical remedies.

D) were decimated by deadly infectious diseases.

45

The passage indicates that viruses cause all of the following EXCEPT

A) tuberculosis.

B) cowpox.

C) polio.

D) hepatitis.

46

Which of the following statements about vaccines is best supported by the passage?

A) Some effective remedies for infectious disease were used before their mechanisms were understood.

B) The discovery of bacteria was key to the development of the first successful vaccine.

C) Vaccines consist of antibodies that are introduced into the bloodstream to ward off infections.

D) Vaccines work by thwarting the process that allows viruses to reproduce themselves.

47

Which sentence provides the best evidence for the answer to the previous question?

A) Lines 1–4 ("Vaccination is . . . sickness")

B) Lines 18–21 ("In 1895 . . . worked")

C) Lines 24–25 ("In Germany . . . tuberculosis")

D) Lines 38–42 ("It must . . . benefit")

48

The discussion in the third paragraph (lines 30–55) suggests that relationship between the virus and the cell is most similar to the relationship between

A) a cowbird and the Eastern phoebe, in which the cowbird lays its eggs in the nest of the phoebe, which raises the young as its own.

B) a grizzly bear and a salmon, in which the bear captures and eats the salmon before it can spawn, thereby reducing the population of the next generation.

C) a tickbird and a rhinoceros, in which the tickbird cleans the parasites that live on the rhinoceros, thereby providing benefit to both animals.

D) a bumblebee and a flower, in which the bumblebee gathers nectar from the flower, while also distributing the pollen of the flower to distant plants.

49

The passage suggests that bacteria are similar to viruses in that they

A) can provide benefit as well as inflict harm.

B) can reproduce even in very harsh environments.

C) have played a major role in the development of vaccines.

D) can be parasitic to their hosts.

CONTINUE ▶

1 | **1**

50

In line 44, "signature" most nearly means

A) proprietary.

B) deleterious.

C) distinctive.

D) advantageous.

51

Which of the following best describes the function of the final paragraph?

A) It presents a generalization to explain the examples mentioned in the previous paragraph.

B) It answers a question suggested in the previous paragraph.

C) It gives an example illustrating a concept introduced in the previous paragraph.

D) It qualifies the tone of the previous paragraph.

52

The two graphs (Figure 1 and Figure 2) are presented together most likely to illustrate

A) the fact that measles cases were already beginning to decline before the vaccines were licensed.

B) the wide range of variables that can affect the communicability of an infectious disease.

C) the merits of administering a vaccine in a single dose as opposed to over an extended period.

D) the effects of the measles vaccine administered to comparable populations but at different times.

STOP

If you finish before time is called, you may check your work on this section only.
Do not turn to any other section of the test.

2

2

Writing and Language Test

35 MINUTES, 44 QUESTIONS

Turn to Section 2 of your answer sheet to answer the questions in this section.

Each passage below is accompanied by a number of questions. For some questions, you will consider how the passage might be revised to improve the expression of ideas. For other questions, you will consider how the passage might be edited to correct errors in sentence structure, usage, or punctuation. A passage or a question may be accompanied by one or more graphics (such as a table or graph) that you will consider as you make revising and editing decisions.

Some questions will direct you to an underlined portion of a passage. Other questions will direct you to a location in a passage or ask you to think about the passage as a whole.

After reading each passage, choose the answer to each question that most effectively improves the quality of writing in the passage or that makes the passage conform to the conventions of Standard Written English. Many questions include a "NO CHANGE" option. Choose that option if you think the best choice is to leave the relevant portion of the passage as it is.

CONTINUE

2   2

Questions 1–11 are based on the following passage and supplementary material.

Who Really Owns American Media?

In this era of blogging, news websites, and personalized Twitter feeds, most of us believe that we have more choice than ever **1** <u>in how we get</u> our news. But unless you're particularly **2** <u>apt</u> about the world of journalism, you might be surprised to learn how few choices we really have.

Thirty years ago, 50 different corporations owned 90% of the American broadcast and news media. Today, just 6 large conglomerates **3** <u>have the same control over that media, which is still 90%.</u> These huge corporations have successfully lobbied the U.S. Congress to loosen or dismantle federal antitrust regulations. These regulations were designed to prevent any one corporation from driving out **4** <u>their competition</u> and controlling public discourse. The debate on this issue centers on the balance between liberties and governmental interference. Some argue that a corporation's freedom to acquire media and voice its opinion trumps any right the public may have to diverse points of view. **5** <u>The other argument would be</u> that our constitutional freedom of the press requires regulation in order to maintain a free market of ideas and an informed citizenry.

1

A) NO CHANGE
B) with getting
C) of the way we get
D) of getting

2

A) NO CHANGE
B) acute
C) savvy
D) comprehensive

3

A) NO CHANGE
B) control that same 90% of all media
C) control the same media, all 90% of it
D) are in the same 90% control of all media

4

A) NO CHANGE
B) the competition they have
C) its competition
D) it's competition

5

A) NO CHANGE
B) Others argue
C) Others would argue
D) Another being

CONTINUE ➡

According to data from 2007, the American media does not quite look like America. Although fully 33% of the American population was minority, **6** only 3.2% of American broadcast television outlets were controlled by minorities.

One potent antidote **7** regarding media consolidation is the Internet. **8** With some research, it reveals many resources for the curious and intelligent media consumer to hear informed voices from a wide variety of perspectives.

6

Which of the following best represents the information from Figure 1?

A) NO CHANGE

B) only 3.2% of the minority population controlled American broadcast television outlets

C) only 3.2% of the American population included minorities in control of broadcast television outlets

D) only 3.2% of American broadcast television stations were watched by minorities

7

A) NO CHANGE

B) about

C) against

D) to

8

A) NO CHANGE

B) It will reveal with some research

C) Some research will reveal

D) With some research, it will reveal

MINORITY REPRESENTATION IN BROADCAST TELEVISION

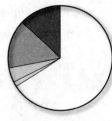

U.S. Population
2007

U.S. Media Ownership
2007

	Population	Media Ownership
African American ■	13.0%	0.6%
Hispanic American ▩	15.0%	1.3%
Asian American ▨	4.5%	0.9%
Other Minority ▢	1.5%	0.4%
White Non-Minority □	66.0%	96.8%

Source: Freepress

CONTINUE ➡

2   **2**

9 Although the Web abounds with gossip, partisanship, and fear-mongering from many major outlets, and conspiracy theorists on the fringe, the careful viewer can also find thoughtful analysis and civilized debate of the issues. Sites like ProPublica, FactCheck.org, and NPR provide in-depth, nonprofit, public-supported journalism that is less influenced by any corporate or political agenda.

10 Therefore, sensationalism sells, and the media conglomerates have mastered the art. As the first great American media mogul, William Randolph Hearst, said, "If you want the public in sufficient numbers, construct a highway. Advertising is that highway." Without large advertising and lobbying budgets, these nonpartisan **11** instances of journalism will have a difficult time competing with the big boys.

9

The author wants to introduce this sentence with a representation of modern media that contrasts with the ideal of "civilized debate." Does this introduction accomplish this task?

A) Yes, because it suggests that controversial matters are ignored in modern media.

B) Yes, because it refers to relatively unsophisticated modes of conversation.

C) No, because it focuses on entertainment rather than any examination of issues.

D) No, because it refers to hypothetical situations rather than real ones.

10

A) NO CHANGE
B) Still
C) Lastly
D) In summary

11

A) NO CHANGE
B) patterns
C) receptacles
D) repositories

CONTINUE ➤

2

2

Questions 12–22 are based on the following passage.

The Dangers of Superstition

Have you ever knocked on wood to dodge a jinx? Do you avoid stepping on cracks in the sidewalk? Do you feel uneasy about the number 13? Most of us realize that these **12** rituals, which are based on ancient and discredited beliefs, but we can't so easily rid our minds of superstitious thinking. Every culture has its own superstitious beliefs, **13** and now anthropologists and psychologists are beginning to understand why.

Our brains constantly work to find cause-and-effect patterns in the world. When something strange happens that we can't explain, or seems to **14** collid against what we already believe, we get an uncomfortable feeling known as "cognitive dissonance." We reflexively fill this gap in knowledge with the explanations that are most easily available to us. **15** Since we are willful beings surrounded by other willful beings, and every conscious moment of our lives is filled with a sense of "agency," **16** that is: intentional action. Therefore, we imagine tiny beings living in wood, or vaporous spirits roaming the clouds that do strange or harmful things when we displease them. Willful agency is our "default" explanation.

12

A) NO CHANGE
B) rituals, that are based on
C) rituals have been based on
D) rituals are based on

13

A) NO CHANGE
B) for
C) so
D) while

14

A) NO CHANGE
B) contradict
C) disengage
D) go away from

15

A) NO CHANGE
B) Because we
C) We
D) So we

16

A) NO CHANGE
B) that is, intentional action
C) which is what intentional action is
D) which is: intentional action

CONTINUE ▶

2   **2**

[1] Our brains are creative. [2] They can design buildings, compose music, and **17** can formulate scientific theories. [3] But this creativity is sometimes hard to discipline, and so we are susceptible to strange thoughts and superstitions. [4] Many of these, like blessing people when they sneeze, are harmless if not quaint. [5] In 2014, villagers in Nigeria brought a goat into a police station, accusing it of being a witch that had attempted to steal a car and then changed into a goat. **18**

17

A) NO CHANGE
B) also can formulate
C) have formulated
D) formulate

18

The author is considering adding the following sentence to this paragraph.

> *Others are sad and bizarre, such as the belief in shape-shifting.*

Where should it be placed?

A) before sentence 2
B) before sentence 3
C) before sentence 4
D) before sentence 5

Although superstitious explanations relieve our cognitive dissonance, **19** it might also lead to tragedy. In 2014, people in Paraguay and Tanzania were killed because locals accused them of witchcraft. **20** Some superstitious parents have even beaten or disowned their own children because their strange behavior is attributed to demonic possession. Superstitions are also not harmless when they impede the pursuit of science, placing obstacles in the way of medical and technological breakthroughs that can improve the human condition.

Rituals intended to help your favorite football team score, like dancing or wearing your hat backward, are fun and innocuous. They **21** substitute a craving in our brains for control over situations that otherwise mystify us. **22**

19

A) NO CHANGE
B) it can
C) they can
D) they would

20

A) NO CHANGE
B) Some superstitious parents, believing that any strange behavior is a sign of demonic possession, have even beaten or disowned their own children.
C) Even beating or disowning their own children, many superstitious parents attribute their strange behavior to demonic possession.
D) Some superstitious parents, believing that their strange behavior is a sign of demonic possession, have even beaten or disowned their own children.

21

A) NO CHANGE
B) discharge
C) exempt
D) satisfy

22

Which concluding sentence would be most in keeping with the content and tone of the passage as a whole?

A) However, feeling like we have control over a situation is not always the same as understanding it.
B) They represent some of humanity's greatest accomplishments, and have inspired some of our greatest works of art.
C) Centuries from now, our rituals may become so elaborate that we would scarcely recognize them as such today.
D) Without such rituals, we would not feel as connected to the people or the natural world around us.

2   2

Questions 23–33 are based on the following passage.

Skepticism and the Scientific Method

Even scientists sometimes forget how essential skepticism, particularly self-skepticism, is to the scientific process. But scientific skepticism is driven by evidence, not agenda. Today, the field of climatology seems to have more than its share of skeptics, debating **23** a warming planet and the things that should be done by us about it, if anything.

24 They are coming from outside of the scientific community, many of these skeptics couch their arguments in political terms. Some claim that global warming is part of a partisan "left-wing" plot or a ploy by the scientific community to ensure funding for yet another "Chicken Little" scare. Others suggest that attempts to reduce greenhouse gas emissions by changing energy or land use policies **25** would provide a needless cost of the American taxpayer of tens to hundreds of billions of dollars annually. Some even suggest that they are really part of an international conspiracy to undermine America's competitiveness in the global marketplace.

23

A) NO CHANGE

B) what should be done about a warming planet, if we should

C) what, if anything, we should do about a warming planet

D) the things we should do about a warming planet, if we should

24

A) NO CHANGE

B) While coming

C) Their coming

D) Coming

25

A) NO CHANGE

B) would be needless in costing the American taxpayer

C) would needlessly cost the American taxpayer

D) is a needless cost to the American taxpayer of

At the same time, others who legitimately question the data or theories related to climate change are too quickly labeled right-wing "deniers," even if their concerns are not motivated by any partisan convictions.

In fact, science has, or should have, nothing to do with ideology. Rather, it **26** is a process of identifying significant natural phenomena, gathering evidence about those phenomena, and **27** then we must find the most reliable explanation for that evidence. The preponderance of the evidence suggests that the earth is getting warmer, that the effects of that warming will be problematic, that there are things we can do to prevent or at least mitigate the worst outcomes, and **28** perhaps that many of these things are well worth doing. There is still plenty of uncertainty about the complex systems that make up our planetary climate, but we know enough to be concerned, **29** and to discuss the issue without politicizing it.

26

A) NO CHANGE
B) accounts for
C) represents
D) symbolizes

27

A) NO CHANGE
B) finding the most reliable explanation for
C) then explaining in the most reliable way
D) finding the most reliable way for explaining

28

A) NO CHANGE
B) also that many of these things perhaps may be
C) many of these things perhaps may be
D) that many of these things may be

29

In the context of the passage as a whole, which of the following completes the sentence most appropriately?

A) NO CHANGE
B) and to expose the agendas of those who stand in the way of saving our planet
C) but not enough to risk sacrificing our political or economic security
D) and to create a strong incentive program to transform our national energy policy

2

2

The skeptics point out, rightly, that science isn't about consensus. The fact that 98% of climatologists regard something as true **30** isn't the same as it being true. After all, only centuries ago the majority of physicians worldwide believed that illnesses were caused not by germs or genetics, **31** but by demons or imbalances in "humors."

[1] Having an honest and productive conversation about global warming **32** requires an educated public. [2] When we, as public citizens, become more informed about the science of climatology, we become less susceptible to political sniping and to "consensus" as an argument. [3] Most important, perhaps, we become better able to make good decisions about the future of our nation and our planet. **33**

30

A) NO CHANGE
B) won't make that true
C) would not mean it's that way
D) doesn't make it so

31

A) NO CHANGE
B) but instead from
C) but from
D) they thought it was by

32

A) NO CHANGE
B) requires the need for
C) requires our being
D) require having

33

The author is considering inserting the following sentence into this paragraph.

Furthermore, we become more adept at evaluating the facts and theories at the heart of the matter.

Where should it be placed?

A) before sentence 1
B) before sentence 2
C) before sentence 3
D) after sentence 3

CONTINUE

2   2

Questions 34–44 are based on the following passage.

The Magic of Bohemia

Bohemia is a landlocked country in central **34** Europe, and until 1918 they were ruled from Vienna by the Austrian Hapsburgs. Today it **35** regards a major part of the modern Czech Republic, and its largest city, Prague, serves as the nation's capital. Bohemia is also another, less clearly defined country, a country of the mind. This Bohemia in fact derives from misconceptions about the true Bohemia that go back as far as Shakespeare, **36** designating Bohemia as the land of gypsies and the spiritual habitation of artists.

By 1843, when Michael William Balfe's opera *The Bohemian Girl* premiered in London, the term *Bohemian* **37** would come to mean any wandering or vagabond soul, who need not have been associated with the arts. The Parisian poet Henry Murger clinched the term's special association with the life of artists.

In November 1849, a dramatized version of Murger's *Latin Quarter* tales was staged in Paris with the title *La Vie de Bohème*. So extraordinarily successful **38** did this prove that the stories themselves were published as *Scènes de la Vie de Bohème*. The public's appetite was whetted and a popular cult of the gypsy-artist was underway. Murger's volume of stories became the textbook for the artistic life throughout the late nineteenth and early twentieth centuries.

34

- A) NO CHANGE
- B) Europe, until 1918 it was ruled
- C) Europe, which, until 1918, was ruled
- D) Europe, having been, until 1918, ruled

35

- A) NO CHANGE
- B) amounts to
- C) establishes
- D) comprises

36

- A) NO CHANGE
- B) who designated Bohemia
- C) he had designated Bohemia
- D) being designated by him

37

- A) NO CHANGE
- B) had come to mean
- C) came to have meant
- D) had meant

38

- A) NO CHANGE
- B) was this proven
- C) this was proved
- D) this proved

CONTINUE

2   2

39 What was it that were the basic elements of this Bohemia as it evolved under Murger? To start with, Bohemia belonged to the romantic movements that preached the power of the individual imagination and came to adopt a secular religion of art. Like early Christianity, it had its true believers and its heathens. The believers in this case were the artists themselves, the elect of the spirit, touched with the divine power of imagination, while the heathen were the commercial middle classes who had **40** propagated as a result of increased commodity production in the wake of the Industrial Revolution.

[1] To the artists, these were people of no imagination who were only concerned with material things. [2] As Philistines, they seemed inhabit a different country from that of the **41** Bohemians; Murger's achievement was to define, quite persuasively, the boundaries of Bohemia in terms of a particular lifestyle. [3] In his Bohemia, the production of art was in fact less important than **42** whether one had the capacity for art. [4] Murger was also responsible for the term *Bohemian* becoming inseparably linked with the supposedly unconventional, outlandish behavior of artists, yet it is evident that he did not invent Bohemianism. [5]

39

A) NO CHANGE
B) What were they that were the basic elements
C) What basic elements were there
D) What were the basic elements

40

A) NO CHANGE
B) propitiated
C) prospered
D) preempted

41

A) NO CHANGE
B) Bohemians, Murger had the achievement of defining
C) Bohemians, but Murger's achievement was in defining
D) Bohemians; but Murger achieved defining

42

A) NO CHANGE
B) the capacity for art
C) whether one has the capacity for art
D) one's capacity of art

CONTINUE ➡

2   2

Most of its ingredients had existed in Paris for at least two decades before he started writing. **43**

Bohemia had been a haven for the political rebel and, as the nineteenth century drew to a close, more than one French observer had seen it as the breeding-ground of cynicism, as the source of much potential danger. "It is quite clear," Jules Claretie wrote indignantly in 1888, "that every country has its Bohemians. But they do not have the influence over the rest of the nation which they do in France—thanks to that poisonous element in the French character which is known as *la blague*—or cynicism." **44**

43

The author is considering including the following sentence in this paragraph.

> *Murger can thus be described as a Bohemian of the second generation.*

Where should it be placed?

A) after sentence 1

B) after sentence 2

C) after sentence 3

D) after sentence 5

44

If the author were to delete the quotation from Jules Claretie at the conclusion of this paragraph, the passage would primarily lose

A) a sanguine view of the late nineteenth-century French culture

B) an scathing perspective on Murger's literary work

C) a dire assessment of France's national temperament

D) an urgent warning against a potential immigration problem

STOP

If you finish before time is called, you may check your work on this section only.
Do not turn to any other section of the test.

3   3

Math Test – No Calculator

25 MINUTES, 20 QUESTIONS

Turn to Section 3 of your answer sheet to answer the questions in this section.

DIRECTIONS

For questions 1–15, solve each problem, choose the best answer from the choices provided, and fill in the corresponding circle on your answer sheet. **For questions 16–20,** solve the problem and enter your answer in the grid on the answer sheet. Please refer to the directions before question 16 on how to enter you answers in the grid. You may use any available space in your test booklet for scratch work.

NOTES

1. The use of a calculator is NOT permitted.
2. All variables and expressions used represent real numbers unless otherwise indicated.
3. Figures provided in this test are drawn to scale unless otherwise indicated.
4. All figures lie in a plane unless otherwise indicated.
5. Unless otherwise indicated, the domain of a given function f is the set of all real numbers for which $f(x)$ is a real number.

REFERENCE

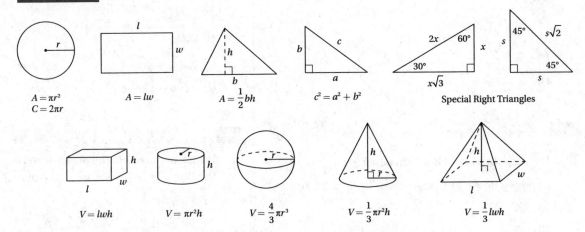

$A = \pi r^2$
$C = 2\pi r$

$A = lw$

$A = \frac{1}{2}bh$

$c^2 = a^2 + b^2$

Special Right Triangles

$V = lwh$

$V = \pi r^2 h$

$V = \frac{4}{3}\pi r^3$

$V = \frac{1}{3}\pi r^2 h$

$V = \frac{1}{3}lwh$

The number of degrees of arc in a circle is 360.
The number of radians of arc in a circle is 2π.
The sum of the measures in degrees of the angles of a triangle is 180.

CONTINUE

1

If $2b - 1 = 5$, what is the value of $2b^2 - 1$?

A) 15

B) 17

C) 24

D) 25

2

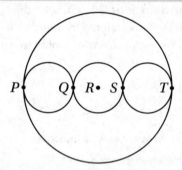

In the figure above, points P, Q, R, S, and T lie on the same line, and R is the center of the large circle. If the three smaller circles are congruent and the radius of the large circle is 6, what is the radius of one of the smaller circles?

A) 1

B) 2

C) 3

D) 4

3

Jeri has edited $\dfrac{1}{5}$ of her term paper. If she has edited 15 pages, how many pages does she have left to edit?

A) 45

B) 50

C) 60

D) 75

4

7, 12, 22, 42, 82

Which of the following gives a rule for finding each term in the sequence after the first?

A) Add 5 to the preceding number.

B) Add 5 to the sum of all of the preceding terms.

C) Double the preceding term and then subtract 2 from the result.

D) Add 14 to the preceding term and divide that result by 2.

5

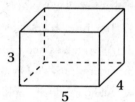

The figure above shows a rectangular box. What is the longest length of a diagonal of one of the faces of this box?

A) $\sqrt{24}$

B) $\sqrt{41}$

C) $\sqrt{50}$

D) $\sqrt{60}$

6

Which of the following points is NOT on the graph of the line $-2x - 3y = 36$ in the xy-plane?

A) $(-9, 6)$

B) $(-24, 4)$

C) $(6, -16)$

D) $(12, -20)$

CONTINUE ➤

7

During a coyote repopulation study, researchers determine that the equation $P = 250(1.32)^t$ describes the population P of coyotes t years after their introduction into a new region. Which of the following gives the values of I, the initial population of coyotes, and r, the annual percent increase in this population?

A) $I = 250, r = 32\%$

B) $I = 250, r = 132\%$

C) $I = 330, r = 32\%$

D) $I = 330, r = 132\%$

8

Which of the following is equal to $\dfrac{1}{\sqrt{3}+1}$?

A) $\dfrac{\sqrt{3}}{2} - \dfrac{1}{2}$

B) $\dfrac{\sqrt{3}}{2} + \dfrac{1}{2}$

C) $\dfrac{\sqrt{3}}{4} - \dfrac{1}{4}$

D) $\dfrac{\sqrt{3}}{4} + \dfrac{1}{4}$

9

Which of the following could be the x-intercept and y-intercept of a line that is perpendicular to the line $3x + 6y = 0$?

A) $(-6, 0)$ and $(0, 3)$

B) $(3, 0)$ and $(0, -6)$

C) $(3, 0)$ and $(0, 6)$

D) $(6, 0)$ and $(0, 3)$

10

The function f is defined by the equation $f(x) = x - x^2$. Which of the following represents a quadratic with no real zeros?

A) $f(x) + \dfrac{1}{2}$

B) $f(x) - \dfrac{1}{2}$

C) $f\left(\dfrac{x}{2}\right)$

D) $f\left(x - \dfrac{1}{2}\right)$

11

In the xy-plane, the graph of the line $y = \dfrac{15}{4}$ intersects the graph of the equation $y = x^2 + x$ at two points. What is the distance between these two points?

A) $\dfrac{3}{2}$

B) $\dfrac{5}{2}$

C) $\dfrac{15}{4}$

D) 4

12

If $i^{2k} = 1$, and $i = \sqrt{-1}$, which of the following must be true about k?

A) k is a multiple of 4.

B) k is a positive integer.

C) When $2k$ is divided by 4, the remainder is 1.

D) $\dfrac{k}{2}$ is an integer.

CONTINUE ▶

3 **3**

13

For all numbers x and y, let z be defined by the equation $z = |2^2 - x^2 - y^2| + 2^2$. What is the smallest possible value of z?

A) 0

B) 4

C) 8

D) 16

14

If the polynomial $P(x)$ has factors of 12, $(x - 5)$, and $(x + 4)$, which of the following must also be a factor of $P(x)$?

A) $2x^2 + 8$

B) $4x^2 - 20$

C) $6x^2 - 6x - 120$

D) $x^2 - 10x + 25$

15

If $f(x) = -x + 7$ and $g(f(x)) = 2x + 1$, what is the value of $g(2)$?

A) -11

B) -5

C) 5

D) 11

CONTINUE ➤

3   3

DIRECTIONS

For questions 16–20, solve the problem and enter your answer in the grid, as described below, on the answer sheet.

1. Although not required, it is suggested that you write your answer in the boxes at the top of the columns to help you fill in the circles accurately. You will receive credit only if the circles are filled in correctly.

2. Mark no more than one circle in any column.

3. No question has a negative answer.

4. Some problems may have more than one correct answer. In such cases, grid only one answer.

5. **Mixed numbers** such as $3\frac{1}{2}$ must be gridded as 3.5 or $\frac{7}{2}$.

    (If $3\frac{1}{2}$ is entered into the grid as [3 1 / 2], it will be interpreted as $\frac{31}{2}$, not $3\frac{1}{2}$.)

6. **Decimal answers:** If you obtain a decimal answer with more digits than the grid can accommodate, it may be either rounded or truncated, but it must fill the entire grid.

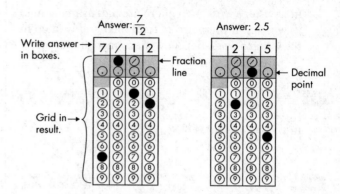

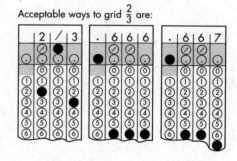

Acceptable ways to grid $\frac{2}{3}$ are:

CONTINUE ➡

16

In a writer's workshop, there are half as many men as women. If there are 24 total men and women in the writer's workshop, how many men are there?

17

If $3 - \dfrac{1}{b} = \dfrac{3}{2}$ what is the value of b?

18

The square of a positive number is 0.24 greater than the number itself. What is the number?

19

The function f is a quadratic function with zeros at $x = 1$ and $x = 5$. The graph of $y = f(x)$ in the xy-plane is a parabola with a vertex at $(3, -2)$. What is the y-intercept of this graph?

20

When graphed in the xy-plane, the line $y = mx - 4$ intersects the x-axis at an angle of θ. If $m > 0$, $0° < \theta < 90°$, and $\cos\theta = \dfrac{3}{\sqrt{58}}$, what is the value of m?

STOP

**If you finish before time is called, you may check your work on this section only.
Do not turn to any other section of the test.**

4 **4**

Math Test – Calculator

55 MINUTES, 38 QUESTIONS

Turn to Section 4 of your answer sheet to answer the questions in this section.

DIRECTIONS

For questions 1–30, solve each problem, choose the best answer from the choices provided, and fill in the corresponding circle on your answer sheet. **For questions 31–38,** solve the problem and enter your answer in the grid on the answer sheet. Please refer to the directions before question 31 on how to enter you answers in the grid. You may use any available space in your test booklet for scratch work.

NOTES

1. The use of a calculator is permitted.
2. All variables and expressions used represent real numbers unless otherwise indicated.
3. Figures provided in this test are drawn to scale unless otherwise indicated.
4. All figures lie in a plane unless otherwise indicated.
5. Unless otherwise indicated, the domain of a given function f is the set of all real numbers for which $f(x)$ is a real number.

REFERENCE

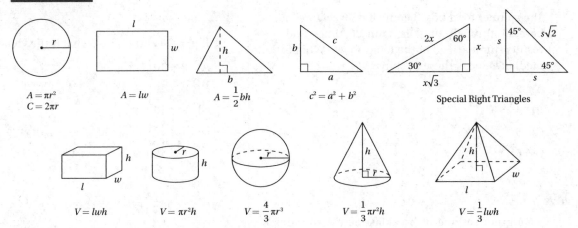

$A = \pi r^2$
$C = 2\pi r$

$A = lw$

$A = \frac{1}{2}bh$

$c^2 = a^2 + b^2$

Special Right Triangles

$V = lwh$

$V = \pi r^2 h$

$V = \frac{4}{3}\pi r^3$

$V = \frac{1}{3}\pi r^2 h$

$V = \frac{1}{3}lwh$

The number of degrees of arc in a circle is 360.
The number of radians of arc in a circle is 2π.
The sum of the measures in degrees of the angles of a triangle is 180.

CONTINUE

4 **4**

1

If $a = \frac{1}{2}b$ and $2a + 4b = 20$, what is the value of b?

A) 2.5

B) 4

C) 5

D) 15

2

Spin	Frequency
1	3
2	4
3	3
4	0
5	1
6	1
7	1
8	3
9	1
10	3

The spinner for a board game has 10 sectors, numbered 1 through 10. It is spun 20 times and the results summarized in the table above. What is the median value of these 20 spins?

A) 2

B) 4

C) 5

D) 6

3

A 48-gram serving of breakfast cereal contains 8 grams of sugar. How many grams of sugar are there in a 57-gram serving of the same cereal?

A) 9.5

B) 10.5

C) 11.5

D) 12.5

4

STATEWIDE COLLEGE SCHOLARSHIP
APPLICANTS AND FINALISTS

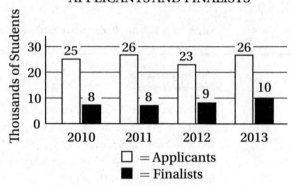

The graph above shows the number of applicants and finalists for a statewide college scholarship program over four consecutive years. For which year was the ratio of finalists to applicants the greatest?

A) 2010

B) 2011

C) 2012

D) 2013

5

If $y^3 = 20$ and $z^2 = 10$, what is the value of $(yz)^6$?

A) 2×10^5

B) 4×10^4

C) 2×10^5

D) 4×10^5

CONTINUE

4   **4**

6

If the sum of a, b, and c is three times the sum of a and b, which of the following expresses the value of a in terms of b and c?

A) $\dfrac{c - 2b}{2}$

B) $\dfrac{2b - c}{2}$

C) $\dfrac{c - 3b}{3}$

D) $\dfrac{3b - c}{3}$

7

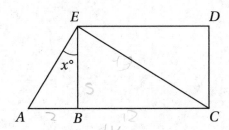

Note: Figure not drawn to scale.

In the figure above, $BCDE$ is a rectangle, $AC = 14$, $BC = 12$, and $EC = 13$. What is the value of $\tan x$?

A) 0.4

B) 0.6

C) 1.3

D) 2.5

8

Which of the following binomials is a factor of $x^2 - 6x + 8$?

A) $x - 4$

B) $x + 4$

C) $x + 2$

D) $x - 8$

Questions 9–11 are based on the graph below.

MONTHLY SALES

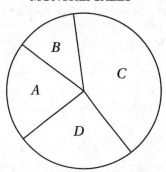

The pie graph above represents the monthly ad sales for four salespeople—Maria, Eli, Georgia, and Zoe—at a social media website. For the month, Maria's sales accounted for 25% of the total, Eli had $3,000 in sales, Georgia had $5,000 in sales, and Zoe had $10,000 in sales.

9

Which sector represents Georgia's sales for the month?

A) Sector A

B) Sector B

C) Sector C

D) Sector D

10

What is the sum of the monthly sales for all four salespeople?

A) $22,500

B) $24,000

C) $25,000

D) $27,000

CONTINUE ➤

11

If Eli and Georgia both earn 10% commission on their sales, and Maria and Zoe both earn 15% commission on their sales, how much more did Maria earn in monthly commissions than Georgia?

A) $300

B) $360

C) $375

D) $400

12

Let the function f be defined by $f(x) = 2 - |x - 4|$ for all real values of x. What is the greatest value of f?

A) -2

B) 2

C) 4

D) 6

13

If $\dfrac{3}{b} - \dfrac{2}{5} = 1$, what is the value of b?

A) $\dfrac{5}{7}$

B) $\dfrac{6}{5}$

C) $\dfrac{15}{7}$

D) 5

14

For the function f, $f(1) = 4$ and $f(2) = 13$. Which of the following equations could describe f?

A) $f(x) = x^2 + 3$

B) $f(x) = x^2 + 9$

C) $f(x) = 2x^2 + 2$

D) $f(x) = 3x^2 + 1$

15

Which of the following is NOT equivalent to $12b^2$?

A) $(6b)(6b)$

B) $12b(b)$

C) $\left(b\sqrt{12}\right)^2$

D) $6b^2 + 6b^2$

16

If m is a number chosen randomly from the set {2, 3, 4, 6} and n is a number chosen randomly from the set {1, 2, 3, 4}, what is the probability that mn is a multiple of 12?

A) $\dfrac{1}{16}$

B) $\dfrac{1}{8}$

C) $\dfrac{1}{4}$

D) $\dfrac{1}{2}$

17

If $y = 3x + 4$ and $x < 3$, which of the following represents all the possible values of y?

A) $y > 7$

B) $y < 13$

C) $7 < y < 13$

D) $y > 13$

18

If $g(x + 1) = x^2 + 2x + 4$ for all values of x, which of the following is equal to $g(x)$?

A) $x^2 + 4$

B) $x^2 + 3$

C) $(x - 1)^2 + 4$

D) $(x - 1)^2 + 3$

19

A: 2, 7, 12, 17, 22, . . .

B: 5, 15, 25, 35, 45, . . .

Two sequences, A and B, follow the patterns shown above. If the nth term of sequence A is 72, what is the nth term of sequence B?

A) 125

B) 135

C) 145

D) 155

20

A website received 2,100 visitors in July from both subscribers and nonsubscribers. If the ratio of subscribers to nonsubscribers among this group was 2:5, how many more nonsubscribers visited the site in July than subscribers?

A) 126

B) 630

C) 900

D) 1,260

21

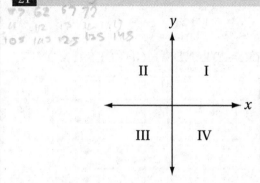

The figure above shows the locations of quadrants I–IV in the xy-plane. Which of the following represents a pair of linear equations that do NOT intersect in quadrant I?

A) $3x + 5y = 15$

   $y = 4$

B) $5x + 3y = 15$

   $y = 4$

C) $5x - 3y = 15$

   $y = 4$

D) $3x - 5y = 15$

   $y = 4$

22

During a 40-minute session at a 220 volt charging station, the charge on an electric car battery increases from an initial charge of 50 power units to a final charge of 106 power units. If this charge increases linearly with time, which of the following best describes the charge, q, in power units, on this same battery after charging for t hours from an initial charge of 20 power units? (1 hour = 60 minutes)

A) $q = 55t + 50$

B) $q = 84t + 50$

C) $q = 55t + 20$

D) $q = 84t + 20$

CONTINUE ▶

4 **4**

Questions 23 and 24 are based on the graph below.

LENGTH AND WEIGHT OF SALMON

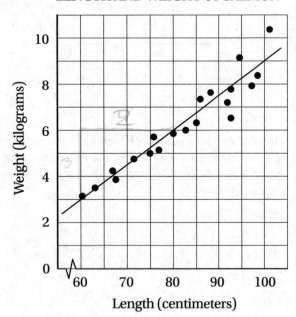

Length (centimeters)

23

The scatterplot above shows the length and weight of a group of 20 salmon and the line of best fit for the data. According to this line of best fit, which of the following best approximates the weight, in kilograms, of a salmon that is 95 centimeters long?

A) 7.6

B) 7.8

C) 8.3

D) 8.8

24

Which of the following equations best describes the relationship between w, the weight in kilograms of each salmon, and l, its length in centimeters?

A) $w = \dfrac{3}{20}l + 2$

B) $w = \dfrac{20}{3}l + 2$

C) $w = \dfrac{3}{40}l - 6$

D) $w = \dfrac{3}{20}l - 6$

25

The average size of a compressed image file is 750 kB. If Ronika's data plan allows her to send 2 GB of data each month before she pays any overage charges, but she plans to use 85% of that data for texting, approximately how many compressed images can she send each month before she incurs any overage charges? (1 GB = 1,000 MB; 1 MB = 1,000 kB)

A) 227

B) 400

C) 2,267

D) 4,000

CONTINUE ➡

26

Perfectioner's Chocolate Company makes two varieties of truffles: dark chocolate and milk chocolate. Each dark chocolate truffle requires 0.65 ounces of cocoa powder, and each milk chocolate truffle requires 0.45 ounces of cocoa powder. If cocoa powder costs c dollars per pound, and Perfectioner's Chocolate Company has budgeted $200 per week for cocoa powder, which of the following inequalities indicates the restrictions on the number of dark chocolate truffles, d, and the number of milk chocolate truffles, m, the company can make in one week? (1 pound = 16 ounces)

A) $\dfrac{200}{c} \geq 0.65d + 0.45m$

B) $\dfrac{200}{16c} \geq 0.65d + 0.45m$

C) $\dfrac{3,200}{c} \geq 0.65d + 0.45m$

D) $3,200c \geq \dfrac{0.65}{d} + \dfrac{0.45}{m}$

27

If n is a positive integer and $m = 2^{n+2} + 2^n$, what is 2^{n+3} in terms of m?

A) m

B) $\dfrac{2m}{5}$

C) $\dfrac{8m}{5}$

D) $3m^2$

28

For how many values of x between 0 and 2π does

$\sin 3x = \dfrac{1}{2}$?

A) Two

B) Three

C) Four

D) Six

29

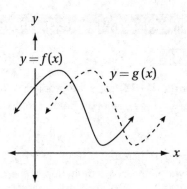

The figure above shows the graphs of functions f and g in the xy-plane. Which of the following equations could express the relationship between f and g?

A) $f(x) = g(x - 2)$

B) $f(x) = g(x + 2)$

C) $f(x) = g(x) + 2$

D) $f(x) = g(x) - 2$

30

A researcher is trying to estimate the daily amount of time undergraduate computer science majors spend on nonrecreational computer activities. She surveys 120 students from among the computer science majors at a large state university and asks them, "How much time do you spend in nonrecreational computer activities each day?" The mean of these responses is 210 minutes per day, with a standard deviation of 16.5 minutes. If another researcher wishes to present the same question to a new set of subjects at the same university, which of the following subject groups would most likely yield a data set with a smaller margin of error for the estimated daily amount of time undergraduate computer science majors spend on nonrecreational computer activities?

A) 240 randomly selected computer science majors

B) 240 randomly selected liberal arts majors

C) 80 randomly selected computer science majors

D) 80 randomly selected liberal art majors

CONTINUE

4   4

Student-Produced Response Questions

DIRECTIONS

For questions 31–38, solve the problem and enter your answer in the grid, as described below, on the answer sheet.

1. Although not required, it is suggested that you write your answer in the boxes at the top of the columns to help you fill in the circles accurately. You will receive credit only if the circles are filled in correctly.

2. Mark no more than one circle in any column.

3. No question has a negative answer.

4. Some problems may have more than one correct answer. In such cases, grid only one answer.

5. **Mixed numbers** such as $3\frac{1}{2}$ must be gridded as 3.5 or $\frac{7}{2}$.

   (If $3\frac{1}{2}$ is entered into the grid as $\boxed{3\,1\,/\,2}$, it will be interpreted as $\frac{31}{2}$, not $3\frac{1}{2}$.)

6. **Decimal answers:** If you obtain a decimal answer with more digits than the grid can accommodate, it may be either rounded or truncated, but it must fill the entire grid.

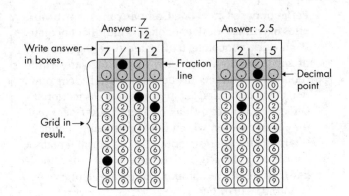

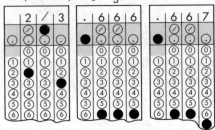

4 **4**

31

What number is 40% greater than the sum of 40 and 80?

32

x	h(x)
3	6
5	14

The table above shows a set of ordered pairs that correspond to the function $h(x) = \dfrac{x^2}{2} + k$. What is the value of k?

33

$$hx + 4y = -3$$

The equation above is the equation of a line in the xy-plane, and h is a constant. If the slope of this line is -13, what is the value of h?

34

The sum of two numbers is four times their difference. The smaller of these numbers is 15. What is the greater number?

35

If $0 < x < 2\pi$ and $5\cos x = \sqrt{5}$, what is the value of $\left(\dfrac{\sin x}{3}\right)^2$?

36

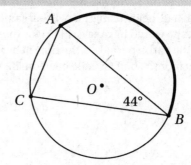

Note: Figure not drawn to scale.

In the figure above, the circle with center O has a circumference of 50, and $AB = BC$. What is the length of arc AB?

CONTINUE ▶

4   **4**

Questions 37 and 38 are based on the scenario described below.

An Internet service provider offers three different plans for residential users. Plan A charges users $500 for the first year of service, and $80 per month thereafter. Plan B charges users $68 per month. Plan C is a "high speed" plan that offers 200% higher speeds for $92 per month.

37

Isabelle has been using Plan A for over a year. She recently reviewed her plan and realized that if she had been using Plan B for same amount of time, she would have saved $104 for Internet service over the entire period. At the time of her review, how many months had Isabelle been on Plan A?

38

Isabelle is now considering switching to either Plan B or Plan C for her home business, but she calculates that having the "high speed" plan will save her only approximately 45 minutes of work each month. At what minimum hourly rate, in dollars per hour, would she have to value her work (that is, how much more would she have to value one hour of free time over one hour of work time) for Plan C to be worth the extra cost over Plan B?

STOP
**If you finish before time is called, you may check your work on this section only.
Do not turn to any other section of the test.**

5   **5**

Essay

50 MINUTES, 1 QUESTION

DIRECTIONS

As you read the passage below, consider how James Schlesinger uses

- evidence, such as facts or examples, to support his claims
- reasoning to develop ideas and connect claims and evidence
- stylistic or persuasive elements, such as word choice or appeals to emotion, to add power to the ideas expressed

---

Adapted from James Schlesinger, "Cold Facts on Global Warming." ©2004 by The Los Angeles Times. Originally published January 22, 2004.

1 We live in an age in which facts and logic have a hard time competing with rhetoric—especially when the rhetoric is political alarmism over global warming.

2 We continue to hear that "the science is settled" in the global warming debate, that we know enough to take significant action to counter it. Those who hold this view believe emissions of carbon dioxide are the primary cause of any change in global temperature and inevitably will lead to serious environmental harm in the decades ahead.

3 In 1997, for instance, Vice President Al Gore played a leading role in the negotiation of the Kyoto Protocol, the international agreement to deal with the fears about global warming. He was willing to embrace severe reductions in U.S. emissions, even though the Clinton administration's own Department of Energy estimated that Kyoto-like restrictions could cost $300 billion annually. Then, when it became clear that the Senate would not agree to a treaty that would harm the economy and exempt developing countries like China and India, the Clinton administration did not forward it for ratification. Since then, the treaty's flaws have become more evident, and too few countries have ratified it to allow it to "enter into force."

4 The Bush administration, as an alternative to such energy-suppressing measures, has focused on filling gaps in our state of knowledge, promoting the development of new technology, encouraging voluntary programs and working with other nations on controlling the growth of greenhouse gas emissions. Collectively, these actions involve spending more than $4 billion annually, and the U.S. is doing more than any other nation to address the climate-change issue.

5 Of these efforts, filling the gaps in our knowledge may be the most important. What we know for sure is quite limited. For example, we know that since the early 1900s, the Earth's surface temperature has risen about 1 degree Fahrenheit. We also know that carbon dioxide, a greenhouse gas, has been increasing in the atmosphere. And we know that the theory that increasing concentrations of greenhouse gases like carbon dioxide will lead to further warming is at least an oversimplification. It is inconsistent with the fact that satellite measurements over 35 years show no significant warming in the lower atmosphere, which is an essential part of the global-warming theory.

CONTINUE →

6   Much of the warming in the 20th century happened from 1900 to 1940. That warming was followed by atmospheric cooling from 1940 to around 1975. During that period, frost damaged crops in the Midwest during summer months, and glaciers in Europe advanced. This happened despite the rise in greenhouse gases. These facts, too, are not in dispute.

7   And that's just our recent past. Taking a longer view of climate history deepens our perspective. For example, during what's known as the Climatic Optimum of the early Middle Ages, the Earth's temperatures were 1 to 2 degrees warmer than they are today. That period was succeeded by the Little Ice Age, which lasted until the early 19th century. Neither of these climate periods had anything to do with man-made greenhouse gases.

8   The lessons of our recent history and of this longer history are clear: It is not possible to know now how much of the warming over the last 100 or so years was caused by human activities and how much was because of natural forces. Acknowledging that we know too little about a system as complicated as the planet's climate is not a sign of neglect by policymakers or the scientific community. Indeed, admitting that there is much we do not know is the first step to greater understanding.

9   Meanwhile, it is important that we not be unduly influenced by political rhetoric and scare tactics. Wise policy involves a continued emphasis on science, technology, engagement of the business community on voluntary programs and balancing actions with knowledge and economic priorities. As a nation, by focusing on these priorities, we show leadership and concern about the well-being of this generation and the ones to follow.

Write an essay in which you explain how James Schlesinger builds an argument to persuade his audience that the debate on global warming is unduly influenced by political alarmism. In your essay, analyze how Schlesinger uses one or more of the features listed in the box above (or features of your own choice) to strengthen the logic and persuasiveness of his argument. Be sure that your analysis focuses on the most relevant features of the passage.

Your essay should NOT explain whether you agree with Schlesinger's claims, but rather explain how Schlesinger builds an argument to persuade his audience.

SAT PRACTICE TEST 2 ANSWER KEY

Section 1: Reading	Section 2: Writing and Language	Section 3: Math (No Calculator)	Section 4: Math (Calculator)
1. A	**1.** A	**1.** B	**1.** B
2. D	**2.** C	**2.** B	**2.** B
3. C	**3.** B	**3.** C	**3.** A
4. D	**4.** C	**4.** C	**4.** C
5. B	**5.** B	**5.** B	**5.** D
6. B	**6.** A	**6.** A	**6.** A
7. A	**7.** D	**7.** A	**7.** A
8. B	**8.** C	**8.** A	**8.** A
9. C	**9.** B	**9.** B	**9.** A
10. C	**10.** B	**10.** B	**10.** B
11. A	**11.** D	**11.** D	**11.** D
12. A	**12.** D	**12.** D	**12.** B
13. C	**13.** A	**13.** B	**13.** C
14. A	**14.** B	**14.** C	**14.** D
15. D	**15.** C	**15.** D	**15.** A
16. C	**16.** B	-------	**16.** C
17. B	**17.** D	**16.** 8	**17.** B
18. C	**18.** D	**17.** 2/3 or .666 or .667	**18.** B
19. D	**19.** C	**18.** 1.2 or 6/5	**19.** C
20. D	**20.** B	**19.** 2.5 or 5/2	**20.** C
21. A	**21.** D	**20.** 7/3 or 2.33	**21.** A
22. C	**22.** A		**22.** D
23. B	**23.** C		**23.** C
24. D	**24.** D		**24.** D
25. A	**25.** C		**25.** B
26. D	**26.** A		**26.** C
27. D	**27.** B		**27.** C
28. C	**28.** D		**28.** D
29. A	**29.** A		**29.** B
30. C	**30.** D		**30.** A
31. B	**31.** A		----------------
32. D	**32.** A		**31** 168
33. C	**33.** C		**32.** 3/2 or 1.5
34. C	**34.** C		**33.** 52
35. B	**35.** D		**34.** 25
36. A	**36.** B		**35.** 4/45 or .088 or .089
37. D	**37.** B		**36.** 75/4 or 18.75
38. B	**38.** A		**37.** 47
39. C	**39.** D		**38.** 32
40. D	**40.** C		
41. B	**41.** A		
42. A	**42.** B		
43. B	**43.** D		
44. B	**44.** C		
45. A			
46. A			
47. B			
48. A			
49. D			
50. C			
51. D			
52. D			

Total Reading Points (Section 1)	Total Writing and Language Points (Section 2)	Total Math Points (Section 3)	Total Math Points (Section 4)

SCORE CONVERSION TABLE

Scoring Your Test

1. Use the answer key to mark your responses on each section.

2. Total the number of correct responses for each section:

   1. Reading Test   Number correct: _____ **(Reading Raw Score)**

   2. Writing and Language Test   Number correct: _____ **(Writing and Language Raw Score)**

   3. Mathematics Test – No Calculator   Number correct: _____

   4. Mathematics Test – Calculator   Number correct: _____

3. Add the raw scores for sections 3 and 4. This is your **Math Raw Score**: _____

4. Use the Table 1 to calculate your **Scaled Test and Section Scores (10–40)**.

   Math Section Score (200–800):   _____

   Reading Test Score (10–40):   _____

   Writing and Language Test Score (10–40):   _____

5. Add the **Reading Test Scaled Score** and the **Writing and Language Test Scaled Score** and multiply this sum by 10 to get your **Reading and Writing Test Section Score (20–80)**.

   Sum of Reading + Writing and Language Scores: _____ × 10 =

   Reading and Writing Section Score: _____

Table 1: Scaled Section and Test Scores (10–40)

Raw Score	Math Section Score	Reading Test Score	Writing/ Language Test Score	Raw Score	Math Section Score	Reading Test Score	Writing/ Language Test Score
58	800			29	520	27	28
57	790			28	520	26	28
56	780			27	510	26	27
55	760			26	500	25	26
54	750			25	490	25	26
53	740			24	480	24	25
52	730	40		23	480	24	25
51	710	40		22	470	23	24
50	700	39		21	460	23	23
49	690	38		20	450	22	23
48	680	38		19	440	22	22
47	670	37		18	430	21	21
46	670	37		17	420	21	21
45	660	36		16	410	20	20
44	650	35	40	15	390	20	19
43	640	35	39	14	380	19	19
42	630	34	38	13	370	19	18
41	620	33	37	12	360	18	17
40	610	33	36	11	340	17	16
39	600	32	35	10	330	17	16
38	600	32	34	9	320	16	15
37	590	31	34	8	310	15	14
36	580	31	33	7	290	15	13
35	570	30	32	6	280	14	13
34	560	30	32	5	260	13	12
33	560	29	31	4	240	12	11
32	550	29	30	3	230	11	10
31	540	28	30	2	210	10	10
30	530	28	29	1	200	10	10

SAT PRACTICE TEST 2 DETAILED ANSWER KEY

Section 1: Reading

1. **A**   Tone

In the first paragraph, the author tells us that he has little prudence and no skill in *inventing of means and methods . . . in adroit steering . . .* nor in *gentle repairing*. He also has *no skill to make money spend well*. These are *self-effacing* descriptions. They are certainly not *pontifical* (speaking as a high priest), *aspirational* (expressing high hopes and goals), or *sardonic* (grimly cynical).

2. **D**   Inference

The statement that *whoever sees my garden discovers that I must have some other garden* is the last statement in the author's list of his personal inadequacies. Therefore, this statement must be taken to be *self-effacing* as the other statements are, and specifically to mean that he lacks gardening skill.

3. **C**   Word in Context

Recall that the first paragraph begins with the question *What right have I to write on prudence . . . ?* The second provides a response to this question about his *right*: in saying *I have the same title to write on prudence as I have to write on poetry or holiness*, then, he is clearly saying that he has the *standing* or *authority* to write on prudence.

4. **D**   Inference

In following his declaration that he has the right to write on prudence (lines 11-12), Emerson states that *[w]e write from aspiration as well as from experience*. In other words, we gain the standing to write on prudence not only from expertise in prudent behavior, but also from a focused *yearning*.

5. **B**   Textual Evidence

As the explanation to the previous question indicates, the best support for this answer is in lines 13-14.

6. **B**   Specific Purpose

The sixth paragraph (lines 39-57) discusses three classes of people according to their *proficiency of knowledge of the world* (lines 39-40). The first class values *health and wealth [as] a final good* (lines 42-43). The second class values the *beauty of the symbol* (line 46-47). The third class *lives above the beauty of the symbol to the beauty of the thing signified* (lines 46-47). This last group has *spiritual perception* (line 49). Therefore, its members are superior for their ability to *discern sublime qualities*.

7. **A**   Interpretation

This phrase appears in a discussion of the individual who *traverses the whole scale* (line 50-51), that is, who has the skills of all three classes: practicality, taste, and spiritual perception. In saying that such a person *does not offer to build houses and barns* (lines 54) on the *sacred volcanic isle of nature* (lines 53-54), Emerson is saying that nature is merely a *symbol* that points to the *splendor of God* (55), and therefore not what a truly wise person chooses to fix his or her gaze upon. In other words, the building of *houses and barns* is an *unwise allegiance to worldly things*.

8. **B**   Word in Context

In saying that *the world is filled with the proverbs and acts of a base prudence* (lines 58-59), Emerson means that most of our actions and words are devoted to practical things, like the question *will it bake bread* (lines 64)? As Emerson made clear in his previous paragraph, these considerations are those of the lowest and least noble class, so theirs is an *ignoble* prudence.

9. **C**   Interpretation

As a whole, this paragraph discusses the problem that *the world is filled with the proverbs and acts of a base prudence* (lines 58-59), in other words, that our words and actions are too focused on *a devotion to matter* (lines 59-60) and its effect on our senses, *as if we possessed no other faculties than the palate, the nose, the eye and ear* (lines 60-61). Emerson describes this problem with a simile: *this is a disease like a thickening of the skin until the vital organs are destroyed* (lines 64-66). To Emerson, then, the *disease* is the problem of *sensuousness* (devotion to the senses rather than the intellect).

10. **C**   Characterization

In line 20, Emerson defines prudence as *the virtue of the senses*, but he regards the *world of the senses [as] a world of shows* (lines 22-23), that *is false when detached* (line 35) from *the thing signified* (line 47) by the natural, sensory, intellectual world, that is, from *the splendor of God* (lines 55). Furthermore, he says that prudence is *a devotion to matter, as if we possessed no other faculties than the palate, the nose, the touch, the eye and ear* (lines 59-61). Therefore, as a whole, the passage characterizes prudence as a *pursuit of practical skills and sensory experience*.

11. A Tone

The opening paragraph describes *this breathless pause at the threshold of a long passage* (lines 8–9) in which the narrator and his crew *seemed to be measuring our fitness for a long and arduous enterprise* (lines 9–10). This describes the *reflective anticipation* of a journey. Notice that this description provides no evidence of *anxiety* or *excitement*. In fact, the scene is described in peaceful terms, with the ship *very still in an immense stillness* (line 2).

12. A Specific Purpose

The narrator states that *some glare in the air* (lines 14–15) prevented him from seeing sooner *something that did away with the solemnity of perfect solitude* (lines 18–19). That is, he saw something that led him to believe they were not alone. In the next paragraph, this *something* is revealed to be the mastheads of *a ship anchored inside the islands* (lines 35–36).

13. C Specific Detail

This sentence describes the scene as the narrator surveys the *tide of darkness* and *a swarm of stars* (lines 20–21) while resting his hand on the rail of the ship as if it were *the shoulder of a trusted friend* (line 24). In the next sentence, he describes this as a moment of *quiet communion* (line 26) with the ship, now interrupted by the sight of a strange ship beyond and the *disturbing sounds* (lines 27–28) being made by the crew. In other words, this sentence describes a moment of *wistful (expressing vague longing) contemplation*. Choice (A) is incorrect because, although the *disturbing sounds* and the omen of a distant ship may seem to be *signs of impending danger*, the sentence in lines 20–24 makes no mention of these things. Choice (B) is incorrect, because this moment is described as a moment of *quiet communion*, not *deep inner turmoil*. Choice (D) is incorrect, because there is no mention of any *tragic experience*.

14. A Characterization

Since this story is being told from the perspective of the captain, we can infer his character from the nature of his narration. In the opening paragraph, the captain states that *we seemed to be measuring our fitness for a long arduous enterprise, the point of our existences to be carried out* (lines 9–12), demonstrating that he is more *reflective* than *reactive* as a leader. Much later he says, *what I felt most was my being a stranger to the ship; and if all the truth must be told, I was somewhat of a stranger to myself . . . I wondered how far I should turn out faithful to that ideal conception of one's own personality every man sets up for himself secretly* (lines 56–65). These descriptions of reflection and self-doubt reveal the captain as being *self-conscious and diffident*.

15. D Textual Evidence

As the explanation to question 14 shows, the best evidence for this answer can be found in lines 63–65.

16. C Word in Context

In saying *I mention this because it has some bearing on what is to follow* (lines 54–55), the narrator means that the fact that he was *the only stranger on board* (line 54) is *relevant* to what he is about to say.

17. B Word in Context

This sentence describes how the chief mate, described as *earnest* (line 70) *and painstaking* (71), is trying strenuously to figure out why there is another ship anchored nearby. In saying that he *was trying to evolve a theory*, the narrator means he *is pondering* (thinking) *strenuously*.

18. C Specific Detail

The *truth* that the narrator mentions in line 57 is the fact that *I am a stranger to myself*. He later goes on to explain what he means by this: *I wondered how far I should turn out faithful to that ideal conception of one's own personality every man sets up for himself secretly* (lines 63–65). In other words, this truth is the fact that he lacks *self-confidence*.

19. D Word in Context

In saying that *the why and the wherefore of that scorpion . . . had exercised him infinitely* (lines 75–81), the narrator means that the chief mate was using his *dominant trait . . . [of] earnest consideration* (lines 69–71) to figure out how a scorpion had made its way into his cabin. That is, the questions about the scorpion had *disquieted* (unsettled) *him infinitely*.

20. D Textual Evidence

The *collaboration on the part of [the chief mate's] round eyes and frightful whiskers* (lines 67–68) describes his facial contortions as he deliberates about the anchored ship. In other words, it is an act of *strained contemplation*.

21. A Interpretation

In the final line, the narrator says that *the ship within the islands was much more easily accounted for*. In other words, the scorpion was *less* easily accounted for, or *less explicable*.

22. C Inference

The second paragraph discusses the *"outsourcing" [of] the creation of human life* (lines 8–9), so the *design and control* mentioned in line 13 refer specifically to the design and control of the *process of conception*.

23. B   **Tone**

The author of Passage 1 states that the *"outsourcing" [of] the creation of human life . . . mocks the profundity of life* (lines 8–12) and he provides no indication in the passage that he otherwise approves of it. Clearly, then, he regards it with *blunt disdain*.

24. D   **Cross-Textual Analysis**

Both of these quotations represent viewpoints with which the authors of the respective passages disagree. In Passage 1, the quotation *"Sorry, but I think I can do better"* (line 15) is from those who *turn [their] noses up at the most precious gift in the universe* (lines 13–14) much to the chagrin of the author. In Passage 2, the quotation *"But you are playing God"* (line 78) is described as *the cry of all whose power is threatened by the march of human progress*, and with whom the author clearly disagrees.

25. A   **Cross-Textual Analysis**

Jeremy Rifkin is described in Passage 2 as a *cloning foe* (line 63) who is quoted as saying *"It's a horrendous crime to make a Xerox of someone. You're putting a human into a genetic straitjacket."* Presumably, then, he would agree that *our attitude toward the creation of life must be one of humility* (line 7).

26. D   **Graphical Analysis**

The illustration shows a schematic overview of some *Therapeutic Cloning Strategies* that involve removing a somatic cell from a patient and transferring its nucleus to stem cells that can then be cultured into genetically matched tissue that can then replace diseased cells and tissues in the patient. This is an example of one of the *procedures to clone human cells for seemingly beneficial purposes* (lines 38–40) described in Passage 1. Choice (A) is incorrect because the *guided purpose* refers to a principle of creationism, which is not indicated at all in the diagram. Choice (B) is incorrect because, although the process in the diagram might resemble an assembly line, it is not the *assembly line* that could be used to create a child *that is no longer uniquely human* (lines 23–24), but *with carefully designed and tested features* (line 25). Choice (C) is incorrect because the diagram does not describe the *course of human evolution*, which would need to show how humans evolved from more primitive species.

27. D   **Specific Meaning**

The process *of introducing degraded germs* (lines 52–53) describes the basic process of vaccination, which, like *cutting flesh* (line 52) (that is, surgery), must have seemed dangerous at first, but in fact can be a life-saving technology. This process is the *injection* of vaccines.

28. C   **Inference**

In this paragraph, the author of Passage 2 describes the position of cloning foes who believe that cloning *is the end of evolution, or at least the beginning of its corporate management* (lines 59–61). The author of Passage 1 is deeply concerned that *the executive boards of these [cloning] companies will decide the course of human evolution, with more concern for quarterly profit reports than for the sake of humanity* (lines 32–35). Clearly, then, the author of Passage 1 regards this management as *a regrettable invasion of commercial interests into human reproduction*.

29. A   **Specific Purpose**

Jeremy Rifkin's belief that cloning is *a horrendous crime* (line 64) directly contradicts the thesis of Passage 2, which is that cloning and similar technologies can *provide ample food for a starving world, cure devastating illnesses, and replace diseased organs* (lines 98–100). Therefore, to the author of Passage 2, Rifkin's opinion *exemplifies an untenable* (indefensible) *position*. Choice (B) may seem plausible, since Rifkin is warning of *the potential dangers of cloning*, but notice that this cannot be the reason that the author of Passage 2 quotes Rifkin, because the passage clearly disagrees with his sentiments.

30. C   **Specific Purpose**

The author of Passage 2 mentions the *Twins Days Festival* (line 68) in order to demonstrate the absurdity of Jeremy Rifkin's statement that creating a genetic *Xerox* of a person is a *horrendous crime* (line 64). To the author of Passage 2, then, the Twins Days Festival represents *the innocuousness* (harmlessness) *of genetic duplication*, since twins are genetic duplicates, and nothing to be feared.

31. B   **Cross-Textual Inference**

The author of Passage 2 does not object to the *procedures to clone human cells for seemingly beneficial purposes* (lines 38–40), and in fact believes they are *necessary contributions to medical progress* since they potentially provide technologies to *provide ample food for a starving world, cure devastating illnesses, and replace diseased organs* (lines 98–100).

32. D   **Textual Evidence**

As the explanation to question 31 indicates, the best evidence for this answer is found in lines 95–100.

33. C   **General Purpose**

The first paragraph establishes that this passage is focused on the specific processes involved in *children's acquisition of language* (line 12). Therefore, the passage is primarily concerned with *exploring academic questions about how we learn language.* Choice (A) is incorrect because the passage does not begin to *delineate the general principles of linguistics,* which is a far greater subject than simply language acquisition. Choice (B) is incorrect, because although the passage does refer to children's ability to acquire diverse languages like *English . . . Bantu or Vietnamese* (lines 63–64), it does not compare their structural qualities. Choice (D) is incorrect because, although the passage does discuss the ideas of the influential linguists Benjamin Whorf (in the second paragraph) and Noam Chomsky (in the last paragraph), these references only serve the larger purpose of exploring the questions of language acquisition, and do not serve as the overall focus of the passage.

---

34. C   **Inference**

In the first paragraph, the author indicates that *[e]very time we speak we are revealing something about language, so the facts of language structure are easy to come by* (lines 3–6). Therefore, the *data* mentioned in line 6 are *the facts of language structure,* which would likely include *the syntax* (rules governing word order) *of different languages.* Choice (A) is incorrect because information about *literacy levels* is not information about *language structure.* Choice (B) is incorrect because methods of teaching are not *facts of language structure.* Choice (D) is incorrect because, although the passage does mention the innate *structure* (line 59) of the brain a few paragraphs later, this is clearly not what line 6 is referring to.

---

35. B   **Inference**

The phrase *the two* (line 2) refers to two nouns in the previous clause: *language* and *thoughts,* in other words, *thinking and expressing.*

---

36. A   **Word in Context**

The author uses the phrase *sticking communicable labels on thoughts* (lines 15–16) to describe one particularly simplistic theory about the language acquisition. The author is using the metaphor of *applying* name tags or labels to describe one way of describing how words are used. Choice (B) is incorrect because *upholding* refers to a process of confirming an official claim or pronouncement. Choice (C) is incorrect because, although *sticking* (as with a needle) can mean *piercing,* this reference clearly does not imply any act of puncturing. Choice (D) is incorrect because this phrase describes an act of *acquisition,* that is, learning something new, rather than *maintaining* something old.

---

37. D   **Tone/Attitude**

After describing Benjamin Whorf's theory, the author then states that *virtually all modern cognitive scientists believe it is false* (lines 25–26). The author's ensuing

discussion makes it clear that he agrees with these cognitive scientists. That is, he is *antagonistic* toward Whorf's hypothesis. Choice (A) is wrong because the author does not *dismiss* Whorf's hypothesis, but rather regards it as *an intriguing hypothesis* which just happens to be incorrect. (To *dismiss* an idea is to believe it is not even worthy of consideration, not merely to reject it after consideration.) Choice (B) is clearly wrong because the author does not *support* Whorf's hypothesis. Choice (C) is wrong because the author does not have any conflicting feelings about the hypothesis.

---

38. B   **Interpretation**

The author states that *babies can think before they can talk* (line 27) in order to refute Whorf's hypothesis that we can't think in terms of *categories and relations* (line 19) until our language gives us the words to do so. Whorf believes that language precedes thought. The author of this passage is saying the opposite: that *skills associated with basic reasoning are not dependent on verbal communication.*

---

39. C   **Thesis**

The author's view on human language acquisition can be found in lines 95–97: *language acquisition depends on an innate, species-specific module that is distinct from general intelligence.* This module must have an intricate *innate structure* (line 59) in order to acquire a language that is itself *intricately complex* (line 55). Choice (A) is incorrect because it represents the Whorf hypothesis, which the author explicitly rejects. Choice (B) is incorrect because the author does not state that the structures for learning language are simple. Choice (D) is incorrect because the author places more emphasis on the innate structure in the brain that enables language acquisition than he does on environmental input.

---

40. D   **Textual Evidence**

As the explanation to question 39 indicates, the best evidence for this answer is found in lines 95–97.

---

41. B   **Interpretation**

Lines 58–64 discuss the author's belief that the *innate structure* in the brain dedicated to language acquisition cannot be either too simple or too complex. This kind of *structure* refers to the *functional organization of the mind.* Notice that the *structure* being discussed here is not the same as the *structure* mentioned in line 5, which refers to the structure of language itself.

---

42. A   **Inference**

The author states that, in 1959, *Anglo-American natural science, social science, and philosophy had come to a virtual consensus about the answers to the questions listed above* (lines 78–81), that is, the questions listed in lines 14–17: *Is language simply grafted on top of cognition as a way of sticking communicable labels on thoughts? Or does learning a language somehow mean learning to think in that language?* The *consensus* on these topics was that *language must be learned; it cannot be a module; and thinking must be a form of verbal behavior* (lines 85–87) Therefore, the disciplines *accepted the hypothesis that cognition depends on verbal skills.*

---

43. B　　　　　　　　　　　　　　　　**General Purpose**

The passage as a whole describes *the history and scientific underpinnings* of the *medical technique* of vaccination. Choice (A) is incorrect, because the passage does not discuss the *various means* by which the human immune system works, but only the particular method in which vaccination "tricks" our immune system into fighting particularly virulent infections that it could not fight on its own. Choice (C) is incorrect because, although the passage does discuss some medical practices of cultures like the *Chinese and the Turks* (lines 7–8), as well as techniques develop by German, British, and French scientists, the passage as a whole is not concerned with cross-cultural comparisons of medical practices. Choice (D) is incorrect because the passage does not focus on the *controversies* surrounding vaccination, but rather the science behind and history of the technique.

---

44. B　　　　　　　　　　　　　　　　　**Interpretation**

The *Chinese and the Turks* (lines 7–8) are mentioned as civilizations that produced *a medicine against smallpox by grinding up the scabs of people with mild cases of the disease* (lines 8–10). This process closely resembles the same process currently used in vaccinations, that is, infecting patients with mild forms of the disease agent.

---

45. A　　　　　　　　　　　　　　　　　　　　**Detail**

From lines 23–25: *Could it have been a bacterium? In Germany, in 1882, Robert Koch had shown that just such a germ caused tuberculosis.* In other words, tuberculosis is cause by a bacterium, not a virus.

---

46. A　　　　　　　　　　　　　　　　　　**Inference**

In the first paragraph, the passage states that *Pasteur produced a rabies vaccine without actually realizing that he was enhancing the body's own immune system; he knew only that the vaccine worked* (lines 18–21). Therefore, *some effective remedies for infectious disease were used before their mechanisms were understood.*

---

47. B　　　　　　　　　　　　　　　**Textual Evidence**

As the explanation to the previous question indicates, the evidence for this answer is in lines 18–21.

---

48. A　　　　　　　　　　　　　　　　　　**Inference**

The third paragraph states that a virus *must attach itself to a cell, impregnate the cell with the viral genes, and then, parasite that it is, turn that cell into a reproductive machine for the virus's benefit* (lines 38–42). That is, it invades another organism and exploits its reproductive process. The cowbird-phoebe relationship as described in (A) is the closest to this relationship.

---

49. D　　　　　　　　　　　　　　　　　　**Inference**

The passage indicates that both viruses and bacteria can *be parasitic* (that is, harmful to their hosts without providing any compensatory benefit). Viruses can cause measles, chicken pox, polio, herpes, and whooping cough, and bacteria can cause *tuberculosis* (line 25) as well as *much human misery* (line 28). Choice (A) is incorrect because the passage does not discuss any potential benefit of bacteria. Choice (B) is incorrect because the passage does not discuss the harshness of the conditions under which bacteria can live. Choice (C) is incorrect because bacteria *were not to play the starring role in the vaccine story* (lines 28–29).

---

50. C　　　　　　　　　　　　　　　**Word in Context**

This sentence says that *the body, for the most part, is able to recognize these viruses as foreign invaders by the signature proteins on their surface* (lines 42–46), in other words, the viruses have unique proteins that enable the body's immune system to identify and attack them. That is, these are *distinctive* proteins that enable the immune systems to distinguish them from other proteins.

---

51. D　　　　　　　　　　　　　**Structure and Purpose**

The final paragraph begins by saying that although *advances against viruses continue* (line 68) . . . *herpes, another viral affliction, still flourishes, and the most ubiquitous of all the viral maladies—the common cold . . . may never be thwarted* (lines 71–75). This contrasts sharply with the triumphant tone of the previous paragraph, which said that *thanks to advances in modern vaccines, measles are nearly gone, and chicken pox, whooping cough, typhoid, and cholera are under control* (lines 56–58). Therefore, the final paragraph *qualifies* (makes less absolute) *the tone of the previous paragraph.*

---

52. D　　　　　　　　　　　　　**Graphical Inference**

The two graphs in Figure 1 and Figure 2 show the incidence of measles infections in the United States as well as in England and Wales from 1950 to 2000. The measles vaccine was introduced five years later in England and Wales than it was in the United States, but in both cases the decline in incidence occurred almost immediately. Therefore, the two graphs are presented together in order to *illustrate the effects of the measles vaccine administered to comparable populations but at different times.*

Section 2: Writing and Language

1. A   **Idiom**

The original phrasing is best. Choice (B) is incorrect because *choice with getting* is not idiomatic. Choice (C) is incorrect because *choice of the way* is not idiomatic. Choice (D) is incorrect *choice of getting*, although idiomatic conveys an illogical idea in this context.

2. C   **Diction**

Here we are asked to choose the best word to convey the appropriate idea in this sentence. The sentence indicates that we *might be surprised to learn* something about the world of journalism, and hence that most of us are not as informed about the world of journalism as we could be. In other words, we are not particularly *savvy* (knowledgeable) about the world of journalism. *Apt* = suitable to the circumstances; *acute* = sharp; *comprehensive* = complete.

3. B   **Diction/Logic**

In the original phrasing, the pronoun *which* is illogical, since it refers to *the media*: that is, saying *the media is 90%* does not make sense. Choice (C) is incorrect because the phrase *all 90% of it* is illogical: *all of it* means 100% of it. Choice (D) is incorrect because it is both unidiomatic and illogical.

4. C   **Possessive Form/Pronoun Agreement**

In the original phrasing, the pronoun *their* disagrees with its antecedent *corporation*, which is singular. Recall that the possessive form of the pronoun *it* is *its* (*it's* = *it is*). The only choice that avoids both the agreement error and the diction error is (C).

5. B   **Parallelism**

This phrase should be parallel to the subject-verb pair in the previous sentence, *Some argue*. The only choice with a parallel verb form is (B).

6. A   **Data Analysis**

The original phrasing is the only option that represents the data in Figure 1 accurately. Since the second circle graph represents all broadcast television media and its ownership, it indicates that 3.2% (0.6% + 1.3% + 0.9% + 0.4%) of American broadcast television outlets were controlled by minorities.

7. D   **Idiom**

The idiomatic form of this phrase is *antidote to*.

8. C   **Clear Expression/Pronoun Antecedents**

In choices (A), (B), and (D), the pronoun *it* lacks any clear referent. The only choice that avoids this problem is (C).

9. B   **Cohesiveness/Purpose**

Examples that contrast *civilized debate* would have to be examples of *uncivilized* debate. *Gossip* and *fear-mongering* certainly qualify as relatively *uncivilized* and *unsophisticated* forms of discourse.

10. B   **Idiom, Pronoun-Antecedent Agreement**

Here, we are looking for the most appropriate logical transition from the previous paragraph to the new one. The last sentence of the previous paragraph gave examples of *in-depth, nonprofit, public-supported journalism that is less influenced by any corporate or political agenda*. The new paragraph, however, begins with a discussion of *sensationalism* and how it *sells*, which provides a stark contrast to the previous paragraph. This requires a contrasting coordinator, such as *nevertheless* or *still*.

11. D   **Diction/Clear Expression of Ideas**

We want a word to represent the websites like ProPublica and NPR, as mentioned in the previous paragraph, that engage in relatively noncorporate and apolitical journalism. The phrase *instances of journalism* indicates specific articles or broadcasts, rather than the organizations themselves. The phrase *patterns of journalism* indicates trends in those articles or broadcasts, rather than the organizations themselves. The phrase *receptacles of journalism* indicates containers that receive journalism rather than organizations that produce it. Only (D) *repositories of journalism* provides a phrase that refers to the organizations themselves.

12. D   **Coordination/Verb Tense**

The original phrasing creates a sentence fragment rather than an independent clause. Choice (B) is incorrect because it commits the same error. Choices (C) and (D) both form independent and idiomatic clauses, but choice (C) is incorrect because the sentence is clearly making a claim about the *current state of being* of these rituals, rather than the *current status-as-consequence* of these rituals, so the present perfect (or "present consequential") form is not appropriate. (For more on using the "perfect" or "consequential" aspect, see Chapter 4, Lesson 23.)

13. A   **Coordination/Conjunctions**

The original phrasing is best. Choice (B) is incorrect because the second clause does not explain the first. Choice (C) is incorrect because the second clause does not follow as a consequence of the first. Choice (D) is incorrect because there is no tonal or semantic contrast between the clauses.

---

14. B — Diction/Clear Expression of Ideas

The phrase *collide against* is not idiomatic: *collide with* is the correct idiom, although this phrase would imply more of a physical relationship than the sentence intends. Since the sentence indicates a conflict between an *event* and a *belief* so the verb should express a relationship between *ideas*, rather than *objects*. Of the choices, only (B) *contradict* serves this purpose effectively.

---

15. C — Coordination

In this sentence, the conjunction *and* establishes the relationship between the coordinate independent clauses, so any subordinating conjunction like *since, so,* or *because* is inappropriate.

---

16. B — Diction, Agreement

Colons must always follow independent clauses, so choices (A) and (D) are incorrect. This phrase must provide a definition of the term "agency," which is precisely what choice (B) *that is, intentional action* does. Choice (C) is incorrect because it categorizes rather than defines.

---

17. D — Parallelism

This sentence presents a list of present tense verbs: *design . . . compose . . . and formulate.* The original phrasing is incorrect because it reinserts the auxiliary *can*, which breaks the parallel structure of the list. Only choice (D) maintains this parallel form.

---

18. D — Cohesiveness

This sentence belongs before sentence 5, because it provides a parallel idea to the one presented in sentence 4. Sentence 4 states that *Many of these [superstitions] are harmless if not quaint*, so the next sentence should provide a transition to some of the less pleasant aspects of superstitious thinking.

---

19. C — Pronoun-Antecedent Agreement/Verb Mood

In the original phrasing, the pronoun *it* does not agree with its plural antecedent *explanations*; therefore, choices (A) and (B) are incorrect. Choice (D) is incorrect because the auxiliary *would* implies necessity, rather than ability, which is illogical in this context.

---

20. B — Clear Expression/Pronoun Antecedents

The original phrasing is incorrect because the two instances of the pronoun *their* have conflicting antecedents, and the second clause is needlessly in the passive voice. Choices (C) and (D) have similar pronoun referent problems. Only choice (B) is phrased without ambiguous pronouns.

---

21. D — Diction

The previous sentence, as well as the passage as a whole, indicates that superstitious rituals are used to *satisfy a craving in our brains for control*.

---

22. A — Cohesiveness

Only choice (A) maintains the skeptical and analytical tone toward superstitious rituals that is established in the rest of the passage.

---

23. C — Clear Expression

The original phrasing is incorrect because the phrase *debating a warming planet* is illogical: only *theories, claims*, or *ideas* can be topics of debate. Choices (B) and (D) are incorrect because the clause *if we should* lacks a logical object.

---

24. D — Comma Splices/Coordination

The original phrasing is incorrect because it creates a comma splice. Two independent clauses may not be joined by only a comma. Choice (B) is incorrect because the conjunction *while* is illogical. Choice (C) is incorrect because it forms a noun phrase, which does not coordinate with any part of the main clause. Choice (D) creates a participial phrase that appropriately modifies the subject of the main clause.

---

25. C — Clear Expression/Idiom

In the original phrasing, the verb *provide* is used illogically and the phrase *cost of the American taxpayer* is unidiomatic. Choice (B) is incorrect because *needless in costing* is unidiomatic. Choice (D) is incorrect because the verb *is* disagrees in number with its subject *attempts*.

---

26. A — Diction

The original phrasing is best. The verb *is* serves most effectively in the role of defining *science*.

---

27. B — Parallelism

The underlined phrase is the third item in a parallel list: *identifying . . . gathering . . . and finding*. Choice (B) best maintains this parallel structure without introducing any other error. Choice (D) provides a parallel form, but the phrase *way for explaining* is unidiomatic.

---

28. D — Parallelism

The underlined phrase is part of a parallel list: *that the earth . . . that the effects . . . that there are things . . . and that many of these things . . .* Only choice (D) maintains this parallel structure.

---

29. A — Logical Cohesiveness

The original phrasing best, since the passage is about eliminating politics and ideology from discussions about climate change. The other choices insert points of advocacy that conflict with the tone and purpose of the passage as a whole.

---

30. D   **Clear Expression of Ideas/Verb Mood/ Verb Tense**

The original phrasing includes an illogical core: *the fact . . . isn't the same as it being true.* Choice (B) is incorrect because a statement of general fact should not be in the future tense. Choice (C) is incorrect because a statement of general fact should not be in the subjunctive mood. Choice (D) uses the idiom *make it so* logically and grammatically.

---

31. A   **Parallelism**

The original phrasing is the only option that completes the parallel construction *caused not by germs . . . but by demons.*

---

32. A   **Verb Form/Clear Expression**

The original phrasing is the most logical and concise.

---

33. C   **Logical Coherence**

The adverb *furthermore* indicates that this sentence is extending a line of reasoning. Since it clearly follows the parallel clauses of sentence 2, *When we . . . become . . . we become . . .* and therefore it most logically follows sentence 2 but precedes sentence 3.

---

34. C   **Pronoun Agreement/Verb Aspect**

The original phrasing is incorrect because the pronoun *they* disagrees in number with the antecedent *Bohemia.* Choice (B) is incorrect because it produces a comma splice. Choice (D) is illogical because the use of the present perfect participle *having been* improperly implies a consequence.

---

35. D   **Diction**

The original phrasing is illogical because a country cannot *regard* (consider in a particular way; concern) anything. This verb must show a relationship between a particular country and a particular geographical region. Only choice (D) *comprises* (makes up) expresses this relationship in a logical way.

---

36. B   **Coordination**

The original phrasing is incorrect because it creates a dangling participle: the participle *designating* does not share its subject with the main clause. Choice (C) is incorrect because it creates a comma splice. Choice (D) is incorrect because it also creates a dangling participle. Choice (B) is best because it avoids both the comma splice and dangling participle.

---

37. B   **Verb Tense/Verb Aspect**

The phrase *by 1843* indicates that the status of the term *Bohemian* had become established prior to that point in time. Therefore, the verb requires the *past perfect* or *past consequential* form: *had come to mean.* Although choice (D) is a verb in the past consequential form, it incorrectly implies that the term no longer had that particular meaning in 1843.

---

38. A   **Coordinating Modifiers**

This sentence is trying to convey the fact that *[La Vie de Bohème] proved [to be so] extraordinarily successful that the stories themselves were published.* This requires the active voice, so choices (B) and (C) are incorrect. Choice (D) is incorrect because it is unidiomatic.

---

39. D   **Number Shift**

The original phrasing is incorrect because of the number shift between *it* and *elements.* Choices (B) and (C) are needlessly wordy. Choice (D) is clear and concise.

---

40. C   **Diction/Logical Coherence**

This sentence indicates the effect that *increased commodity production* had on the *commercial middle class.* It is illogical to say that the middle class *propagated* (was transmitted), *propitiated* (won the favor of someone), or *preempted* (took action to prevent something) as a result of this increased production. It is, however, logical to say that the middle class *prospered* (flourished) as a result of it.

---

41. A   **Coordination of Clauses**

The original phrasing best coordinates the two related, but independent, clauses. Choice (B) produces a run-on sentence with a comma splice. Choice (C) is illogical and unidiomatic. Choice (D) is illogical and misuses the semicolon.

---

42. B   **Clarity of Expression/Parallelism**

Choice (B) provides the most parallel comparison: *the production of art was in fact less important than the capacity for art.*

---

43. D   **Coordination of Ideas**

The use of the adverb *thus* indicates that this sentence represents a logical consequence of some particular state of affairs. That state of affairs is best indicated by sentence 5: *Most of its ingredients had existed in Paris for at least two decades before he started writing.* This explains why Murger can be described as a *Bohemian of the second generation.*

---

44. C   **Coherence/Meaning**

This question is essentially asking us to describe the function of Claretie's quotation. Since it refers to a *poisonous element in the French character,* it is clearly indicating a *dire assessment of France's national temperament.*

Section 3: Math (No Calculator)

1. B   **Algebra (solving equations) EASY**

Original equation:	$2b - 1 = 5$
Add 1:	$2b = 6$
Divide by 2:	$b = 3$
Substitute $b = 3$ into $2b^2 - 1$:	$2b^2 - 1 = 2(3)^2 - 1$
	$= 18 - 1 = 17$

---

2. B   **Special Topics (circles) EASY**

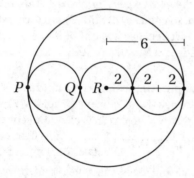

Marking up the diagram with the given information, as shown, shows that three of the smaller radii make up one larger radius. Therefore, the radius of each small circle is 6/3 = 2.

---

3. C   **Algebra (word problems/fractions) EASY**

If 1/5 of her term paper is 15 pages, then the entire paper must be $15 \times 5 = 75$ pages long. This means she has $75 - 15 = 60$ more pages to edit.

---

4. C   **Advanced Mathematics (functions and sequences) EASY**

Notice that the rule in choice (C) generates the entire sequence: 7 (times 2 minus 2 equals) 12 (times 2 minus 2 equals) 22 (times 2 minus 2 equals) 42 (times 2 minus 2 equals) 82.

---

5. B   **Special Topics (three dimensional geometry) MEDIUM**

Notice that the question asks us for the longest length of a diagonal on one of the *faces* of the box, and that there are three different rectangles as faces: a 3×4 rectangle, a 3×5 rectangle, and a 4×5 rectangle. Clearly the one with the two greatest dimensions will have the longest diagonal, which we can find using the Pythagorean Theorem.

	$4^2 + 5^2 = d^2$
Simplify:	$16 + 25 = d^2$
Simplify:	$41 = d^2$
Take the square root:	$\sqrt{41} = d$

6. A   **Algebra (linear equations) MEDIUM**

We can test each point to find the one that does NOT satisfy the equation.

(A) $-2(-9) - 3(6) = 18 - 18 = 0 \neq 36$
(B) $-2(-24) - 3(4) = 48 - 12 = 36$
(C) $-2(6) - 3(-16) = -12 + 48 = 36$
(D) $-2(12) - 3(-20) = -24 + 60 = 36$

Therefore, the correct answer is (A).

---

7. A   **Advanced Mathematics (parabolas) MEDIUM**

The initial population, I, is the population when the time is 0. Therefore, $I = 250(1.32)^0 = 250(1) = 250$. The annual percent increase in the population, r, can be calculated by finding the population at $t = 1$ and then calculating the percent change from the initial population. If $t = 1$, $P = 250(1.32)^1$. As we discussed in Chapter 8, Lesson 7, multiplying a quantity by 1.32 is equivalent to increasing a number by 32% (that is, $1.32 = 100\% + 32\%$), so $r = 32\%$.

---

8. A   **Advanced Mathematics (rational expressions) MEDIUM**

$$\frac{1}{\sqrt{3}+1}$$

$$3 + 1$$

Multiply the numerator and denominator by the conjugate $\left(\sqrt{3}-1\right)$:

$$\frac{1}{\sqrt{3}+1} \times \frac{\sqrt{3}-1}{\sqrt{3}-1}$$

Simplify:

$$\frac{\sqrt{3}-1}{3-1}$$

Simplify:

$$\frac{\sqrt{3}-1}{2}$$

Distribute:

$$\frac{\sqrt{3}}{2} - \frac{1}{2}$$

---

9. B   **Algebra (linear relationships) MEDIUM**

As we discussed in Chapter 7, Lesson 5, a line in the form $ax + by = c$ has a slope of $-a/b$. Therefore, the line $3x + 6y = 0$ has a slope of $-3/6 = -1/2$. Recall, also, from Chapter 7, Lesson 7, that perpendicular lines have slopes that are opposite reciprocals. Therefore, the line we are looking for must have a slope of 2. You might draw a quick sketch of the xy-plane and plot the points given in each choice to find the line that has a slope of 2, or you could use the slope formula from Chapter 7, Lesson 5: slope = $(y_2 - y_1)/(x_2 - x_1)$.

(A) slope = $(3 - 0)/(0 - (-6)) = 3/6 = 1/2$
(B) slope = $(-6 - 0)/(0 - 3) = -6/-3 = 2$
(C) slope = $(6 - 0)/(0 - 3) = 6/-3 = -2$
(D) slope = $(3 - 0)/(0 - 6) = 3/-6 = -1/2$

The only choice that gives a slope of 2 is (B).

10. **B**   Advanced Mathematics (quadratics) HARD

Perhaps the simplest way to begin this problem is to draw a quick sketch of the function in the xy-plane, and then compare this graph to the transformations of the original function given in the choices. Notice that the original function $f(x) = x - x^2$ is easily factored *as* $f(x) = x(1 - x)$. The Zero Product Property (Chapter 9, Lesson 5) tells us that this function must have zeros at $x = 0$ and $x = 1$. Notice, also, that since the coefficient of the x^2 term in the original function is negative (-1), the graph of this quadratic is an "open-down" parabola. Also, the axis of symmetry is halfway between the zeros, at $x = \frac{1}{2}$. Plugging $x = \frac{1}{2}$ back into the function gives us $f\left(\dfrac{1}{2}\right) = \dfrac{1}{2} - \left(\dfrac{1}{2}\right)^2 = \dfrac{1}{2} - \dfrac{1}{4} = \dfrac{1}{4}$, and therefore, the vertex of the parabola is $\left(\dfrac{1}{2}, \dfrac{1}{4}\right)$.

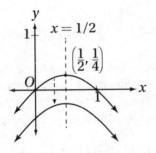

The question asks us to find the function that has no real zeros. This means that the graph of this function must not intersect the x-axis at all. Each answer choice indicates a different transformation of the function f. Recall from Chapter 9, Lesson 3, that choice (A) $f(x) + \frac{1}{2}$ is the graph of f shifted *up* $\frac{1}{2}$ unit, choice (B) $f(x) - \frac{1}{2}$ is the graph of f shifted *down* $\frac{1}{2}$ unit, choice (C) $f(x/2)$ is the graph of f *stretched* by a factor of 2 in the horizontal direction, and choice (D) $f(x - \frac{1}{2})$ is the graph of f shifted *right* $\frac{1}{2}$ unit. As the sketch above shows, only (B) yields a graph that does not intersect the x-axis.

11. **D**   Advanced Mathematics (polynomials) MEDIUM-HARD

Given equation:	$y = x^2 + x$
Substitute $y = \dfrac{15}{4}$:	$\dfrac{15}{4} = x^2 + x$
Multiply by 4:	$15 = 4x^2 + 4x$
Subtract 15:	$0 = 4x^2 + 4x - 15$
Factor using the Product-Sum Method (Chapter 9, Lesson 4):	$0 = (2x + 5)(2x - 3)$
Use Zero Product Property (Chapter 9, Lesson 5):	$2x + 5 = 0;\ 2x - 3 = 0$

Solve each equation for x: $x = -5/2;\ x = 3/2$

Therefore, the two points of intersection are $\left(-\dfrac{5}{2}, \dfrac{15}{4}\right)$ and $\left(\dfrac{3}{2}, \dfrac{15}{4}\right)$, and the distance between these points is

$$\frac{3}{2} - \left(-\frac{5}{2}\right) = \frac{3}{2} + \frac{5}{2} = \frac{8}{2} = 4$$

12. **D**   Special Topics (complex numbers) MEDIUM-HARD

Recall from Chapter 10, Lesson 10, that $i^n = 1$ if and only if n is a multiple of 4. (If you need refreshing, just confirm that $i^4 = 1$, $i^8 = 1$, $i^{12} = 1$, etc.) Therefore, if $i^{2k} = 1$, then $2k$ must be a multiple of 4, and therefore, k must be a multiple of 2. If k is a multiple of 2, then $k/2$ must be an integer. Choice (A) is incorrect, because $k = 2$ is a solution, but 2 is not a multiple of 4. Choice (B) is incorrect because $k = -2$ is a solution, and -2 is not a positive integer. Choice (C) is incorrect because $k = 2$ is a solution, but when $2(2) = 4$ is divided by 4, the remainder is 0, not 1.

13. **B**   Algebra (absolute values) MEDIUM-HARD

In order to minimize the value of $|2^2 - x^2 - y^2| + 2^2$, we must minimize the absolute value. But the least possible value *of any* absolute value expression is 0, so we must ask: is it possible for the expression inside the absolute value operator to equal 0? A little trial and error should reveal that it can if, for instance, $x = 2$ and $y = 0$. Notice that this gives us $|2 - 2^2 - 0^2| + 2 = |0| + 2^2 = 4$. Since the absolute value cannot be less than 0, this must be the minimum possible value.

14. **C**   Advanced Mathematics (analyzing polynomial functions) HARD

The simplest polynomial with factors of 12, $(x - 5)$, and $(x + 4)$ is $P(x) = 12(x - 5)(x + 4)$. The completely factored form (including the prime factorization of the coefficient) of this polynomial is $P(x) = (2)^2(3)(x - 5)(x + 4)$.

Now, using the methods we discussed in Chapter 9, Lesson 4, we can look at the factored form of each choice:

(A) $2x^2 + 8 = 2(x^2 + 8)$ ($x^2 + 8$ is not factorable over the reals, but it does equal $(x - \sqrt{8i})(x + \sqrt{8i})$

(B) $4x^2 - 20 = 4(x^2 - 5) = (2)^2(x - \sqrt{5})(x - \sqrt{5})$

(C) $6x^2 - 6x - 120 = 6(x^2 - x - 20) = (2)(3)(x - 5)(x + 4)$

(D) $x^2 - 10x + 25 = (x - 5)(x - 5)$

Notice that every polynomial in (A), (B), and (D) contains at least one factor that is NOT in the factored form of $P(x)$. (In (D), the factor $(x - 5)$ appears twice, but it appears only once in $P(x)$.) Only choice (C) contains ONLY factors that appear in $P(x)$, so it is the only choice that must be a factor of $P(x)$.

15. D   **Advanced Mathematics (functions) HARD**

Given function: $g(f(x)) = 2x + 1$
Substitute $f(x) = -x + 7$: $g(-x + 7) = 2x + 1$
To evaluate $g(2)$, we must
let $-x + 7 = 2$: $-x + 7 = 2$
Subtract 7: $-x = -5$
Multiply by -1: $x = 5$
Substitute $x = 5$: $g(-5 + 7) = 2(5) + 1$
Simplify: $g(2) = 11$

---

16. 8   **Algebra (ratios/word problems) EASY**

Let x equal the number of men in the workshop. If there are half as many men as women, there must be $2x$ women in the workshop, or a total of $x + 2x = 3x$ men and women in the workshop. Since this total equals 24: $3x = 24$
Divide by 3: $x = 8$

As with all algebra problems, make sure you confirm that the value you've solved for is the value the question is asking for. Since x is in fact the number of men, it is the final answer.

---

17. 2/3 or .666 or .667   **Advanced Mathematics (rational equations) EASY**

$$3 - \frac{1}{b} = \frac{3}{2}$$

Multiply by the common
denominator, $2b$: $6b - 2 = 3b$
Add 2: $6b = 3b + 2$
Subtract $3b$: $3b = 2$
Divide by 3: $b = \dfrac{2}{3}$

---

18. 1.2 or 6/5   **Algebra (word problems) HARD**

First, translate the given fact into an equation.
The square of a positive number is
0.24 greater than the number itself: $x^2 = x + 0.24$
Subtract x and 0.24: $x^2 - x - 0.24 = 0$
Multiply by 100 to eliminate
the decimal: $100x^2 - 100x - 24 = 0$

Now we factor using Product-Sum Method. Remember that the product number is $ac = (100)(-24) = -2{,}400$, and the sum number is $b = -100$. The two numbers with a sum of -100 and a product of $-2{,}400$ are 20 and -120.
Expand middle term using
$-100 = 20 - 120$: $100x^2 + 20x - 120x - 24 = 0$
Factor by grouping in
pairs: $20x(5x + 1) - 24(5x + 1) = 0$
Take out common factor: $(5x + 1)(20x - 24) = 0$

Using the Zero Product Property, we see that $x = -1/5$ or $x = 24/20 = 6/5$. Since we are told that x is a positive number, $x = 6/5$ or 1.2.

---

19. 5/2 or 2.5   **Advanced Mathematics (quadratics) MEDIUM-HARD**

Using the Factor Theorem from Chapter 9, Lesson 7, we know that if a quadratic has zeroes at $x = 1$ and $x = 5$, it must have factors of $(x - 1)$ and $(x - 5)$. Since a quadratic can only have two linear factors, f must be of the form $f(x) = k(x - 1)(x - 5)$.
Substitute $x = 3$ and $y = -2$ for the
coordinates of vertex: $-2 = k(3 - 1)(3 - 5)$
Simplify: $-2 = k(2)(-2)$
Simplify: $-2 = -4k$
Divide by -4: $\dfrac{1}{2} = k$

Therefore the equation of the function is $f(x) = \dfrac{1}{2}(x - 1)(x - 5)$, and we can find its y-intercept by substituting $x = 0$: $f(0) = \dfrac{1}{2}(0 - 1)(0 - 5)$
Simplify: $f(0) = \dfrac{5}{2}$

---

20. 7/3 or 2.33   **Special Topics (trigonometry) HARD**

The graph of the line $y = mx - 4$ has a slope of m and a y-intercept of -4. Since $m > 0$, this slope is positive. We are told that this line intersects the x-axis at an angle of θ, where $\cos \theta = \dfrac{3}{\sqrt{58}}$. This gives us enough information to sketch a fairly detailed graph:

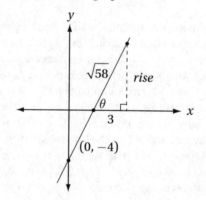

Notice that this information lets us construct a right triangle that includes θ, in which the adjacent side has length 3 and the hypotenuse has length $\sqrt{58}$ (remember $\cos \theta = $ adjacent/hypotenuse). This triangle is particularly handy because it depicts the *rise* and the *run* for a portion of the line, which will enable us to find the slope. We simply have to find the rise with the Pythagorean Theorem: $3^2 + rise^2 = \left(\sqrt{58}\right)^2$
Simplify: $9 + rise^2 = 58$
Subtract 9: $rise^2 = 49$
Take square root: $rise = 7$
Therefore, the slope of the line is $m = rise/run = 7/3$.

Section 4: Math (Calculator)

1. **B**   Algebra (systems) EASY

Since the question asks for the value of b, it makes sense to substitute for a so that we get a single equation in terms of b.

Second equation:	$2a + 4b = 20$
Substitute $a = \frac{1}{2}b$	$2\left(\frac{1}{2}b\right) + 4b = 20$
Simplify and combine:	$b + 4b = 5b = 20$
Divide by 5:	$b = 4$

2. **B**   Data Analysis (central tendency) EASY

The table summarizes the following list of 20 numbers: 1, 1, 1, 2, 2, 2, 2, 3, 3, 3, 5, 6, 7, 8, 8, 8, 9, 10, 10, 10. If a set of numbers is listed in increasing order, the median is the middle number (if the set contains an odd number of elements) or the average of the *two* middle terms (if the set contains an even number of elements). The median of a set of 20 numbers, therefore, is the average of the 10th and 11th terms. Since the 10th number is 3 and the 11th number is 5, the median is $(3 + 5)/2 = 4$.

3. **A**   Problem Solving/Data Analysis (proportions) EASY

Set up a proportion:	$\dfrac{48}{8} = \dfrac{57}{x}$
Cross multiply:	$456 = 48x$
Divide by 48:	$9.5 = x$

4. **C**   Data Analysis (tables) EASY

The ratio of applicants to finalists is simply the quotient of those two values, which we can calculate for each year.
(A) $8/25 = 0.32$,
(B) $8/26 \approx 0.31$,
(C) $9/23 \approx 0.39$,
(D) $10/26 \approx 0.38$.

5. **D**   Algebra (exponentials) EASY

Although solving for y and z isn't hard, it is even simpler to just express $(yz)^6$ in terms of y^3 and z^2, using the Laws of Exponentials from Chapter 9, Lesson 9.

Original expression:	$(yz)^6$
Law of Exponentials #5:	$y^6 z^6$
Law of Exponentials #8:	$(y^3)^2(z^2)^3$
Substitute $y^3 = 20$ and $z^2 = 10$:	$(20)^2(10)^3$
Substitute $20 = (2)(10)$:	$(2)^2(10)^2(10)^3$
Combine terms with like bases with	
Law of Exponents #4:	$2^2(10)^5$
Simplify:	4×10^5

6. **A**   Algebra (word problems) EASY

The sum of a, b, and c is three times the sum of a and b:	$a + b + c = 3(a + b)$
Distribute:	$a + b + c = 3a + 3b$
Subtract a:	$b + c = 2a + 3b$
Subtract $3b$:	$-2b + c = 2a$
Divide by 2:	$\dfrac{c - 2b}{2} = a$

7. **A**   Advanced Mathematics (triangle trigonometry) EASY

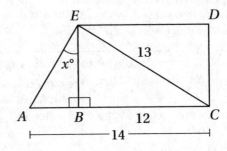

First, let's mark up the diagram with the given lengths, as above. Remember from SOH CAH TOA that the tangent of an angle is equal to the opposite side over the adjacent side, so $\tan x = AB/EB$. $AB = AC - BC = 14 - 12 = 2$, and we can find EB with the Pythagorean Theorem:

	$EB^2 + 12^2 = 13^2$
Simplify:	$EB^2 + 144 = 169$
Subtract 144:	$EB^2 = 25$
Take the square root:	$EB = 5$

Or, even better, just notice that triangle EBC is a 5-12-13 triangle.
So, $\tan x = AB/EB = 2/5 = 0.4$

8. **A**   Advanced Math (quadratics) EASY

We can factor this quadratic easily with the Product-Sum Method from Chapter 9, Lesson 4.
$x^2 - 6x + 8 = (x - 4)(x - 2)$

9. **A**   Data Analysis (pie graph) MEDIUM

Since Maria's sales accounted for 25% of the total, her sector must be $0.25(360°) = 90°$, which is sector D. This means that Eli ($3,000), Georgia ($5,000), and Zoe ($10,000) account for sectors A, B, and C. Since Georgia's total is between Eli's and Zoe's, her sector is the neither the largest nor the smallest of the remaining sectors. Therefore, it must be sector A, which is in the middle.

10. **B**   Data Analysis (pie graph) MEDIUM

Perhaps the simplest way to approach this is to notice that, since Maria's sales account for 25% of the total, the other salespeople must account for $100\% - 25\% = 75\%$ of the total. Since this total is $3,000 + $5,000 + $10,000 = $18,000, we can find the total with a proportion.

$$\frac{\$18,000}{75} = \frac{x}{100}$$

Cross multiply: $1,800,000 = 75x$

Divide by 75: $24,000 = x$

---

11. D   **Data Analysis (pie graph) MEDIUM**

Since Maria accounted for 25% of the total sales, she accounted for $(0.25)(\$24,000) = \$6,000$ in sales. If she earned 15% commission for all sales, she earned $(0.15)(\$6,000) = \$900$ in commissions. If Georgia earns 10% in commissions, she earned $(0.10)(\$5,000) = \$500$. Therefore, Maria earned $\$900 - \$500 = \$400$ more in commissions that Georgia did.

---

12. B   **Algebra (absolute value) MEDIUM**

The function $f(x) = 2 - |x - 4|$ reaches its greatest value when the absolute value is minimized. Since absolute values cannot be negative, the least value $|x - 4|$ can have is 0, which it has when $x = 4$:

$f(4) = 2 - |4 - 4| = 2 - 0 = 2$

---

13. C Advanced Math (rational equations) MEDIUM

Original equation: $\dfrac{3}{b} - \dfrac{2}{5} = 1$

Multiply both sides by common
denominator $5b$: $15 - 2b = 5b$

Add $2b$: $15 = 7b$

Divide by 7: $\dfrac{15}{7} = b$

---

14. D Advanced Mathematics (functions) MEDIUM

(A) $f(1) = 1^2 + 3 = 4; f(2) = 2^2 + 3 = 7$
(B) $f(1) = 1^2 + 9 = 10; f(2) = 2^2 + 9 = 13$
(C) $f(1) = 2(1)^2 + 2 = 4; f(2) = 2(2)^2 + 2 = 10$
(D) $f(1) = 3(1)^2 + 1 = 4; f(2) = 3(2)^2 + 1 = 13$
The only function that satisfies the two given equations is (D).

**15. A   Advanced Mathematics (exponentials)
MEDIUM**

(A) $(6b)(6b) = 36b^2$
(B) $12b(b) = 12b^2$
(C) $\left(b\sqrt{12}\right)^2 = \left(b\sqrt{12}\right)\left(b\sqrt{12}\right) = 12b^2$
(D) $6b^2 + 6b^2 = b^2(6 + 6) = 12b^2$

---

16. C   Data Analysis (probability) MEDIUM

One way to represent this problem clearly is to construct a table that shows all of the possible products mn. A representation of all the equally likely possible outcomes of an event is called the **sample space** for that event. We can label the columns with the possible values of m and

the rows with the possible values of n. As we write in the products, let's shade in those that are multiples of 12.

×	2	3	4	6
1	2	3	4	6
2	4	6	8	12
3	6	9	12	18
4	8	12	16	24

This shows that 4 out of the possible 16 products are multiples of 12, and therefore, the probability is 4/16 or $\dfrac{1}{4}$.

---

17. B   Algebra (inequalities) MEDIUM

Original inequality: $x < 3$

Multiply by 3: $3x < 9$

Add 4: $3x + 4 < 13$

Substitute $y = 3x + 4$: $y < 13$

**18. B   Advanced Mathematics (functions)
MEDIUM-HARD**

Since the function takes "all values of x," one way to solve this problem is to choose a value of x to work with, like $x = 1$.

Original function: $g(x + 1) = x^2 + 2x + 4$

Substitute $x = 1$: $g(2) = (1)^2 + 2(1) + 4 = 1 + 2 + 4 = 7$

Therefore, the function $g(x)$ will give an output of 7 for an input of 2. We can now test our choices for an input of $x = 2$. (Notice $g(x)$ and $g(x + 1)$ have different inputs.)

(A) $(2)^2 + 4 = 8$
(B) $(2)^2 + 3 = 7$
(C) $(2 - 1)^2 + 4 = 5$
(D) $(2 - 1)^2 + 3 = 4$

Notice that only the expression in (B) gives the correct output.

**19. C   Advanced Mathematics (sequences)
MEDIUM-HARD**

The "brute force" method is to write out sequence A until you reach 72, and see which element in sequence B "matches up" to it. But first we must determine the rule for each sequence. A little guessing and checking should confirm that sequence A follows the "add 5" rule, and sequence B follows the "add 10" rule.

A	2	7	12	17	22	27	32	37
B	5	15	25	35	45	55	65	75
A	42	47	52	57	62	67	72	
B	85	95	105	115	125	135	145	

A more elegant method, however, is to find the formulas for the nth term of A and the nth term of B. This would be a much more efficient method, also, if it takes a while for 72 to appear in set A. If you recall the general formula for the nth term of an arithmetic sequence $(a_n = a_1 + (n - 1)d)$, then it's straightforward to see that the formula for A is $a_n = 2 + (n - 1)5 = 5n - 3$ and the formula for B is $b_n = 5 + (n - 1)10 = 10n - 5$. Since we're looking for where the number 72 appears in set A, we can solve $5n - 3 = 72$ to find $n = 15$, then insert this value for n into the formula for B: $b_{15} = 10(15) - 5 = 145$.

---

20. **C**   Problem Solving and Data Analysis (ratios) MEDIUM

If the ratio of subscribers to nonsubscribers is 2:5, then we can say there are $2n$ subscribers and $5n$ non-subscribers, where n is some integer. This means there were a total of $2n + 5n = 7n$ July visitors to the website. Since we know that there were 2,100 visitors in July, we can solve for n: $2,100 = 7n$
Divide by 7: $300 = n$
Therefore, there were $2(300) = 600$ subscriber visits and $5(300) = 1,500$ nonsubscriber visits, and so there were $1,500 - 600 = 900$ more nonsubscribing visitors than subscribing visitors.

---

21. **A**   Algebra (graphing lines) MEDIUM-HARD

In quadrant I, both the x- and y-coordinates are positive. Since $y = 4$ in all four systems, we simply need to find the system for which the x-coordinate of the solution is *not* positive. We can find the corresponding x-coordinate for each system by just substituting $y = 4$ and solving for x.
Substitute $y = 4$ into first equation in (A): $3x + 5(4) = 15$
Simplify: $3x + 20 = 15$
Subtract 20: $3x = -5$
Divide by 3: $x = -5/3$
In this case, we don't need to go any further, because the solution to the system in (A) is $(-5/3, 4)$, which is in quadrant II, not quadrant I.

---

22. **D**   Advanced Mathematics (quadratics) MEDIUM-HARD

Read the question carefully, and note particularly what it is asking for and what information can help you find it. We are asked to find an equation to relate two variables, q, the number of power units, and t, the number of hours the battery has been charging. We are told that the *initial* charge is 20 power units, so $q = 20$ when $t = 0$. We are also told that the charge increases from 50 power units to 106 power units in 40 minutes. But since our time unit t is in *hours*, we should convert 40 minutes to $40/60 = 2/3$ hours. Therefore, the charging station charges at a rate of $(106 - 50)/(2/3) = (56)/(2/3) = 84$ charging units per hour. This unit rate is the slope of the line, as we discussed in Chapter 8, Lesson 5. Therefore, the equation should represent a line with slope of 84 that contains the point $t = 0$ and $q = 20$, which is the equation in (D) $q = 84t + 20$.

---

23. **C**   Data Analysis (scatterplots) EASY

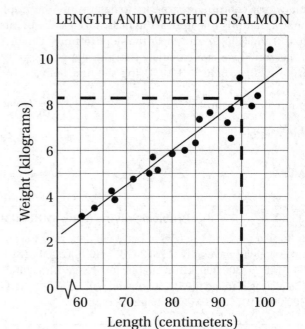

LENGTH AND WEIGHT OF SALMON

This question simply asks us to find the point on the line of best fit that corresponds to a length of 95 centimeters. As the dotted lines show below, this corresponds to a weight less than halfway between 8 and 9 kilograms, so (C) 8.3 is the best approximation among the choices.

---

24. **D**   Data Analysis (scatterplots) HARD

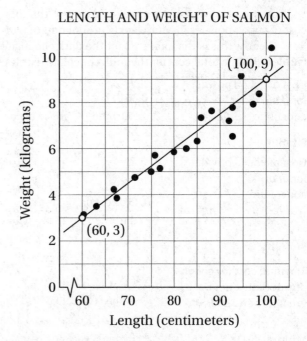

LENGTH AND WEIGHT OF SALMON

To find the equation of the line of best fit, we can take two points on the line and then use the point-slope formula (Chapter 7, Lesson 5) to find the equation of the line. To get the most accurate representation of the line, we should choose two points that are fairly far apart, but whose coordinates are easy to determine. The graph shows that this line appears to pass through the points (60, 3) and (100, 9), and so, by the slope formula (Chapter 7, Lesson 5) we can calculate that the slope is $(9 - 3)/(100 - 60) = 6/40 = 3/20$. Using the first point in the

point-slope formula gives $\qquad w - 3 = \dfrac{3}{20}(l - 60)$

Distribute: $\qquad\qquad\qquad\qquad w - 3 = \dfrac{3}{20}l - 9$

Add 3: $\qquad\qquad\qquad\qquad\quad w = \dfrac{3}{20}l - 6$

---

25. B   **Problem Solving (rates) MEDIUM**

If Ronika plans to use 85% of her 2 GB data plan for texting, she will have only (15%)(2 GB) = (0.15)(2,000 MB) = 300 MB = 300,000 kB available for image files. Since the average image file is 750 kB, she will be able to send 300,000 kB/750 kB = 400 images per month.

---

26. C   **Problem Solving (rates) HARD**

This question asks us to write a mathematical statement that "indicates the restrictions" in this situation. So, what keeps us from making as many truffles as we want? Simple: we are only allowed to spend $200 per week on cocoa powder. Therefore, we can state the restriction on truffles as "the total cost of cocoa powder for our weekly production of truffles must be less than or equal to $200."

Now we must figure out a way to express "the total cost of cocoa powder for our weekly production of truffles." Clearly, this is the total cost for the dark chocolate truffles *plus* the total cost for the milk chocolate truffles:

Cost of cocoa powder for d dark chocolate truffles: $\quad d \text{ truffles} \times \dfrac{0.65 \text{ oz cocoa}}{1 \text{ truffle}} \times \dfrac{\$c}{16 \text{ oz cocoa}}$

Simplify: $\qquad\qquad\qquad\qquad \$\dfrac{0.65cd}{16}$

Cost of cocoa powder for m milk chocolate truffles: $\quad m \text{ truffles} \times \dfrac{0.45 \text{ oz cocoa}}{1 \text{ truffle}} \times \dfrac{\$c}{16 \text{ oz cocoa}}$

Simplify: $\qquad\qquad\qquad\qquad \$\dfrac{0.45cm}{16}$

The total cost for cocoa powder must not be greater than $200: $\quad 200 \geq \dfrac{0.65cd}{16} + \dfrac{0.45cm}{16}$

Multiply by 16: $\qquad 3{,}200 \geq 0.65cd + 0.45cm$

Divide by c: $\qquad\qquad \dfrac{3{,}200}{c} \geq 0.65d + 0.45m$

---

27. C   **Advanced Mathematics (exponentials) HARD**

Notice that this question asks us to find the value of 2^{n+3}, so we should try to solve the given equation for 2^{n+3}.

Original equation: $\qquad\qquad\qquad m = 2^{n+2} + 2^n$

Factor $2n$ from the terms on the right side: $\qquad\qquad m = 2^n(2^2 + 1)$

Simplify: $\qquad\qquad\qquad\qquad\qquad m = 2^n(5)$

Divide by 5: $\qquad\qquad\qquad\qquad \dfrac{m}{5} = 2^n$

Multiply by 2^3: $\qquad\qquad 2^3\left(\dfrac{m}{5}\right) = 2^n \times 2^3$

Simplify: $\qquad\qquad\qquad\qquad \dfrac{8m}{5} = 2^{n+3}$

---

28. D   **Special Topics (trigonometry) HARD**

Although this question can be solved by graphing, it is simpler and more efficient to imagine the unit circle, as we discussed in Chapter 10, Lesson 9.

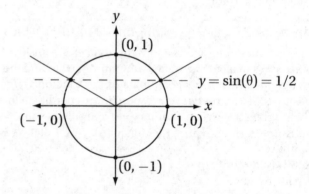

We are asked to consider those angles that have a sine of ½. As you recall from Chapter 10, Lesson 9, the angles whose sine is ½ correspond to those angles that intersect the unit circle at any point where $y = \frac{1}{2}$, as shown in the diagram above. Notice that the line $y = \frac{1}{2}$ intersects the unit circle in two points. We are asked to consider $\sin 3x$, where x takes values from 0 to 2π. This means that $3x$ takes values from 0 to 6π. In other words, we are taking three complete trips around the unit circle (since each trip around is 2π radians). How many times will we visit those two points if we take three trips around the circle? Clearly $(3)(2) = 6$ times.

---

29. B   **Advanced Mathematics (function transformations) HARD**

The figure clearly shows that the function $y = f(x)$ is similar in shape to the function $y = g(x)$, but is shifted to the left by some positive distance. Recall from Chapter 9, Lesson 3, that when the graph of $y = g(x)$ is shifted to the left by k units, the equation of the new function is $y = g(x + k)$. The only equation that has this form is (B) $f(x) = g(x + 2)$.

30. A   Data Analysis (data spread) HARD

One important rule in data gathering is, **the more data we can gather on a population, the more reliable our statistics about that population will be**. More specifically, the greater fraction of the population we can sample, the smaller our margin of error from the true value of the population statistic. Another important rule in data gathering is **the more similar our sample is to the population of interest, the smaller our statistical error will be**. Since the sample size is highest and the group is most like the population (of undergraduate computer science majors) in choice (A), that group should produce the smallest margin of error in the data.

31. 168   Algebra (percents) EASY

The sum of 40 and 80 is 120, and 40% of 120 is (0.40)(120) = 48, so the number that is 40% greater than 120 is 120 + 48 = 168. Also remember that increasing a number by 40% is equivalent to multiplying it by 1.4.

32. 3/2 or 1.5   Advance Mathematics (quadratics) MEDIUM

Original function: $h(x) = \dfrac{x^2}{2} + k$

Substitute $h(3) = 6$ (from table): $6 = \dfrac{3^2}{2} + k$

Simplify: $6 = 4.5 + k$
Subtract 4.5: $1.5 = k$

To check your answer, you can plug in the second row of the table to verify that $\dfrac{5^2}{2} + 1.5 = 14$

33. 52   Algebra (linear equations) MEDIUM

In Chapter 7, Lesson 5 we discussed the fact that the slope of a linear equation in "standard form," $ax + by = c$ is equal to $-a/b$. Therefore, the linear equation $hx + 4y = -3$ has a slope of $-h/4$. If this slope equals -3, then

$$\frac{-h}{4} = -13$$

Multiply by -4: $h = 52$

34. 25   Algebra (word problems) EASY

Let's let x be the larger number. 15 is the smaller number. The sum of the numbers is four times their difference:

$x + 15 = 4(x - 15)$

Distribute: $x + 15 = 4x - 60$
Add 60: $x + 75 = 4x$
Subtract x: $75 = 3x$
Divide by 3: $25 = x$

35. 4/45 or .088 or .089   Special Topics (trigonometry) MEDIUM-HARD

Given equation: $5\cos x = \sqrt{5}$

Divide by 5: $\cos x = \dfrac{\sqrt{5}}{5}$

This gives us the value of cos x, but we are asked to evaluate $\left(\dfrac{\sin x}{3}\right)^2$, which of course is in terms of sin x.

This should remind you of the Pythagorean Identity we discussed in Chapter 10, Lesson 9: for all real numbers x, $\sin^2 x + \cos^2 x = 1$.

Pythagorean Identity: $\sin^2 x + \cos^2 x = 1$
Subtract $\cos^2 x$: $\sin^2 x = 1 - \cos^2 x$

Expression to be evaluated: $\left(\dfrac{\sin x}{3}\right)^2$

Simplify: $\dfrac{\sin^2 x}{9}$

Substitute $\sin^2 x = 1 - \cos^2 x$: $\dfrac{1 - \cos^2 x}{9}$

Substitute $\cos x = \dfrac{\sqrt{5}}{5}$: $\dfrac{1 - \left(\dfrac{\sqrt{5}}{5}\right)^2}{9}$

Simplify: $\dfrac{1 - \dfrac{5}{25}}{9}$

Simplify: $\dfrac{\dfrac{4}{5}}{9}$

Simplify by multiplying $\dfrac{5}{5}$: $\dfrac{4}{45}$

36. 75/4 or 18.75   Special Topics (arcs and triangles) MEDIUM-HARD

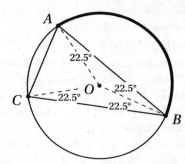

Let's start by drawing the three radii OA, OB, and OC. Since these radii are all congruent, and because $AB = BC$, the triangles AOB and COB are congruent (by the SSS Theorem). This implies that OB bisects angle ABC, so the base angles of both isosceles triangles must have measure $45°/2 = 22.5°$. Therefore, angle AOB, which is the central angle for arc AB, must have measure $180° - 22.5° - 22.5° = 135°$. Now we can use the fact that the circumference of the circle is 50 to find the length or arc AB.

$$\frac{m\overset{\frown}{AB}}{135°} = \frac{50}{360°}$$

Let $x = m\widehat{AB}$ and cross multiply: $360x = 6{,}750$
Divide by 360: $x = 75/4 = 18.75$

---

37. **47**   Problem Solving (extended thinking) HARD

Let n equal the number of months that Isabelle has been on Plan A. If she has been on Plan A for over a year, then $n > 12$. This means that she has been on Plan A for $n - 12$ months beyond the first year. Since Plan A costs $500 for the first year and $80 per month thereafter, the total cost for her n months of service is $500 + \$80(n - 12)$. If she had been on Plan B, the cost would have been $68 per month, or a total of $68n$. If Plan B would have saved her $104 over this period, $500 + 80(n - 12) - 104 = 68n$
Distribute and simplify: $396 + 80n - 960 = 68n$
Simplify: $80n - 564 = 68n$
Add 564: $80n = 68n + 564$
Subtract 68n: $12n = 564$
Divide by 12: $n = 47$

---

38. **32**   Problem Solving (extended thinking) HARD

Since Plan C costs $92 per month and Plan B costs $68 per month, Plan C costs $92 − \$68 = \$24$ more dollars per month than plan B. Since shifting plans would save her only 45 minutes of work, or 3/4 hour, each month, she would have to value one hour of free time over one hour of work time at $24/(\%$ hour$) = \$32$.

Section 5: Essay

Sample Response

Reading Score: 8 out of 8
Analysis Score: 8 out of 8
Writing Score: 8 out of 8

James Schlesinger's essay, "Cold Facts on Global Warming," is a counterargument to the "political alarmism" (to use Schlesinger's words) over global warming. His tone is critical but sober, and he makes frequent use of carefully selected scientific and historical data, juxtaposed with hints at the dangers of political posturing, to make the case for caution in addressing the issue of climate change. He appeals frequently to the ethics of economic prudence and global stewardship, as well as the value of scientific judiciousness. Unfortunately, because Schlesinger's essay was written over a decade ago, it lacks the evidence from the current golden age of climate science. More substantially, however, Schlesinger undermines his own purpose by making political criticisms while calling for nonpartisan objectivity, by mongering fearsome scenarios while arguing against "scare tactics," and by ignoring the scientific evidence against his claims while advocating an "emphasis on science."

Schlesinger begins his discussion with a call for "facts and logic" over "rhetoric." This is classic polemical posturing: we all believe that our positions are "factual and logical" and that our opponents' are merely "rhetoric." In Schlesinger's view, the "rhetoric" includes the claims that "emissions of carbon dioxide are the primary cause of any change in global temperature and inevitably will lead to serious environmental harm in the decades ahead." By inserting the modifiers "any" and "inevitably," he creates a straw man. Most who argue about the seriousness of climate change generally avoid such absolute assertions and instead present evidence from satellites, ice cores, atmospheric analysis, and comprehensive long-term climatic studies to build a case for action. Schlesinger does not address this evidence.

In his argument, Schlesinger appears to value small government and the protection of American industry over the stewardship of the planet. His concern about the Kyoto Protocol of 1997 is not that it eschews the "facts and logic" of climate science, but rather that it "could cost $300 billion annually." He presents no scientific critique of the Kyoto Protocol of 1997 beyond the assertion that Democrat Al Gore was "willing to embrace" a "treaty that would harm the economy," and the vague claim that "the treaty's flaws have become more evident." His method of argumentation here appears to contradict his call for "facts and logic" over "rhetoric."

In contrast to the irresponsibility of Al Gore and the Clinton administration, Schlesinger offers the soberly scientific Bush administration, which "focused on filling in gaps in our state of knowledge, promoting the development of new technology, encouraging volunteer programs, and working with other nations on controlling the growth of greenhouse gas emissions." Schlesinger does not offer a specific benefit our planet has gained from these efforts, which even Schlesinger himself admits involved "spending more than $4 billion annually." Someone pleading for fiscal responsibility might try to account for such a huge expenditure.

Schlesinger believes that our inaction on climate change is a virtue: that scientific prudence requires "filling the gaps in our state of knowledge" above everything else, including industrial restraint. He states that "what we know for sure is quite limited," yet is confident enough in his limited knowledge to assert that "the theory that increasing concentrations of greenhouse gases like carbon dioxide will lead to further warming is at least an oversimplification," directly contradicting the simple middle school experiment showing that a soda bottle filled with carbon dioxide warms far more quickly than one filled only with air.

Schlesinger then selects data trends that seem to support his call for caution, rather than action: he asserts that "satellite measurements over 35 years show no significant warming in the lower atmosphere" and that there was "atmospheric cooling from 1940 to around

1975." Schlesinger does not explain why climate scientists, who are certainly aware of these data, nevertheless believe in anthropogenic global warming.

Not to be accused of cherry-picking data, Schlesinger next offers "a longer view of climate history." He asserts that temperatures "were 1 to 2 degrees warmer than they are today" during the Climatic Optimum of the early Middle Ages, and this warming did not have "anything to do with man-made greenhouse gases." Evidently, we should think that because it was warmer a very long time ago, burning coal today must not be changing the climate.

In the last two paragraphs, Schlesinger essentially retracts his concern about "filling the gaps in our state of knowledge" after all, because he believes it is impossible to fill the most important gaps: "It is not possible to know now how much of the warming over the last 100 years or so was caused by human activities and how much was because of natural forces." So if it is impossible to know, we might ask, why should we expend "more than $4 billion annually" to study it? He does not say. We get Schlesinger's most sonorous call to action in the last paragraph, where he suggests "engagement of the business community on voluntary programs." That is, get big government off the backs of corporations and let them do as they please.

Scoring

Reading—8 (both readers gave it a score of 4)

This response demonstrates a very strong and thorough comprehension of Schlesinger's essay through skillful use of summary, paraphrase, and direct quotations. The author summarizes Schlesinger's central tone, thesis, and modes of persuasion (*His tone is critical but sober, and he makes frequent use of carefully selected scientific and historical data, juxtaposed with hints at the dangers of political posturing, to make the case for caution in addressing the issue of climate change.*) and shows a clear understanding of how Schlesinger's supporting ideas string together and serve his overall thesis (*Schlesinger begins his discussion with a call . . . He appears to value small government . . . Schlesinger offers the soberly scientific Bush administration . . . Schlesinger believes that our inaction on global warming is a virtue . . . Schlesinger next offers . . . In the last two paragraph, Schlesinger essentially*

retracts his concern). Importantly, this response also offers abundant supporting quotations to illustrate each paraphrase. Taken together, these elements demonstrate outstanding comprehension of Schlesinger's essay.

Analysis—8 (both readers gave it a score of 4)

Although this response occasionally veers toward advocacy, it never turns away from careful analysis. Indeed, its thoughtful and thorough critique of Schlesinger's essay demonstrates a sophisticated understanding of the analytical task. The author has identified Schlesinger's primary modes of argument (*He appeals frequently to the ethics of economic prudence and global stewardship, as well as the value of scientific judiciousness*) and even uses those standards to analyze Schlesinger's essay itself, and indicates points at which Schlesinger's argument seems self-defeating (*Schlesinger undermines his own purpose by making political criticisms while calling for nonpartisan objectivity, by mongering fearsome scenarios while arguing against "scare tactics," and by ignoring the scientific evidence against his claims while advocating an "emphasis on science"*). Overall, this analysis of Schlesinger's essays demonstrates a thorough understanding not only of the rhetorical task that Schlesinger has set for himself, but also of the degree to which it upholds its own standards.

Writing—8 (both readers gave it a score of 4)

This response demonstrates an articulate and effective use of language and sentence structure to establish and develop a clear and insightful central claim that *Schlesinger's essay is a counterargument to the "political alarmism" . . . over global warming . . . but that it undermines [its] own purpose.* The response maintains a consistent focus on this central claim, and supports it with a well-developed and cohesive analysis of Schlesinger's essay. The author demonstrates effective choice of words and phrasing (*undermines his own purpose . . . mongering fearsome scenarios . . . Schlesinger believes that our inaction on climate change is a virtue*), strong grasp of relevant analytical and rhetorical terms, like *economic prudence, nonpartisan objectivity,* and *polemical posturing.* The response is well-developed, progressing from general claim to specific analysis to considered evaluation. Largely free from grammatical error, this response demonstrates strong command of language and proficiency in writing.